Procedural Justice?
Victim Participation in International Criminal Proceedings

SCHOOL OF HUMAN RIGHTS RESEARCH SERIES, Volume 42.

The titles published in this series are listed at the end of this volume.

Procedural Justice?
Victim Participation in International Criminal Proceedings

Brianne McGonigle Leyh

intersentia

Cambridge – Antwerp – Portland

Brianne McGonigle Leyh
Procedural Justice?
Victim Participation in International Criminal Proceedings

Cover image © Giovanni van Heusden

Typesetting: G.J. Wiarda Institute for Legal Research, Utrecht

ISBN 978-1-78068-020-0
NUR 828

www.intersentia.com

British Library Cataloguing in Publication Data. A catalogue record for this book is available from the British Library.

One must not forget, [...] that international criminal law does not provide all the answers. It is only one component of the highly complicated reactions to humanitarian emergencies.[1]

THEODOR MERON

---

1 Meron, T., Reflections on the Prosecution of War Crimes by International Tribunals, 100 *American Journal of International Law* 551, 578 (2006).

ACKNOWLEDGMENTS

When I first began researching and writing this book in the fall of 2006, victim participation in international criminal proceedings was a novel concept. No one really knew how the inclusion of victims would impact proceedings and very little had been written on the subject. In fact, a number of individuals openly questioned my choice to write a book on a subject that they argued could be covered in a medium-sized academic article. In the years that followed, however, the topic of victim participation became increasingly important. Significant developments were underfoot and interest in this aspect of the law grew substantially. I have been very fortunate to have been able to research this issue at such a dynamic time. Nonetheless it has also been challenging to write about such a divisive subject and one which remains in a state of unrest. Thankfully, I have been fortunate enough to have received an enormous amount of valuable support from colleagues, friends and family. I am truly grateful. Unfortunately, I am unable to name everyone who has assisted and encouraged me throughout the past five years, but there are a number of individuals who I would very much like to mention.

I would first like to recognize and thank my supervisors, Prof. Jenny Goldschmidt and Prof. Geert-Jan Alexander Knoops. They gave me the freedom to explore the topic and shape my research. Moreover, they were always there for me in times of need. For instance, when funding was initially not available for my research visit to Cambodia both of my supervisors found ways to make it possible. For this, and many other things, I am truly grateful. I would also like to thank my reading committee members, including Prof. Marc Groenhuijsen, Prof. François Kristen, Prof. Hector Olásolo, Prof. Michael Scharf, and Prof. Elies van Sliedregt. Their academic writings have greatly influenced my work and the final version of my manuscript has benefited from their comments.

In addition to my supervisors and my reading committee members, there is one individual, in particular, who has been a constant source of support and motivation. I am indebted, both professionally and personally, to Prof. Tom Zwart. Over the past five years it has been a pleasure working with him on a variety of projects. There is no one else I would rather co-teach American law with. Every class, every debate (and there have been many) was enjoyable.

It is often said that doctoral research is a lonely endeavor. Luckily, I never experienced moments of loneliness. I have been fortunate to work in a fantastic academic environment led by Prof. Jenny Goldschmidt. The Netherlands Institute of Human Rights (SIM) is truly a home away from home. Many thanks to all of my colleagues at SIM—I value being part of the SIM family. Specifically, I would like to thank

Leo Zwaak and Antoine Buyse for their professional mentorship as well as for their friendship. I would also like to express my gratitude to Hanneke van Denderen, Marcella Kiel, Esther Heldenbergh-Bode, Maeyken Hoeneveld and Remko Zwerver for all of their assistance on matters big and small. Further, a special thank you to Saskia Bal. She has very often guided me through the maze of academia and never gave up hope that I would someday speak Dutch.

Each day as I walked into my office I was greeted by a framed poster hanging on my wall with Rosie the Riveter exclaiming 'We Can Do It!" This poster (a gift from my sister), together with photos of my family and other images, were a constant source of motivation. However, it has been my fellow PhD candidates, and not the objects or images I surround myself with, who provided the greatest source of inspiration. Our lunch time chats and out-of-office get-togethers have made working on a PhD seem like a collaborative effort. Thank you especially to Diana Contreras Guadano and Marthe Lot Vermeulen for reading over draft sections of my work, to Marie Elske Gispen who brought order to my bibliography, and to my roommates, past and present: Gentian Zyberi, Sarah Haverkort and Masha Fedorova, all of whom read over draft sections of my book. Masha, in particular, deserves special thanks. Simply put, I could not have completed this book without her. Throughout the years she offered wonderful advice and suggestions and constantly forced me to question my assumptions. I owe her a great professional debt and I value her friendship above anything. I would also like to thank her partner and graphic designer, Giovanni van Heusden, for the cover photo. In addition to those at SIM, I am grateful to Titia Kloos and Peter Morris from the Wiarda Institute for their assistance in editing the book. I am also grateful to Jill Coster van Voorhout, Enrique Carnaro Rojo, Anand Shah, Joeri Maas and Helen Hamzei for their detailed comments upon draft chapters. My final book certainly profited from their feedback and suggestions. A special thanks is also in order for Tom Scheirs from Intersentia.

Throughout the period of my doctoral research I have had the honor to work with and learn from a number of amazing practitioners. In this regard, I would like to thank Paolina Massidda with the Office of Public Counsel for Victims at the International Criminal Court. I felt very welcome there during my time as a Visiting Professional and genuinely appreciate all of the support she has offered me over the years. I continue to be impressed by the incredibly dedicated staff of that office. I am also sincerely grateful to Karim A.A. Khan. It was a privilege working under his leadership and having the opportunity to help represent victims before the Extraordinary Chambers in the Courts of Cambodia together with Alain Werner, Srinna Ty, Daniella Ku, and Kate Gibson. I would also like to thank Terith Chy and Sokvisal Kimsroy from the Documentation Center of Cambodia. Our representation would not have been possible without the work of this NGO. Furthermore, I am grateful to everyone at both of these Courts who took the time to sit down with me for formal and informal interviews. The interviews gave me great insight into the complexities of participation at the international level and allowed me to view the topic from a broader mindset.

My growth as an academic and practitioner in the field of international criminal law was largely assisted through my work with an amazing NGO, the Public International Law & Policy Group (PILPG). Paul Williams, its Executive Director, has been instrumental in showing me the importance of bridging in the gap between theory and practice. I would also like to thank Marieke de Hoon. Together we co-direct PILPG's Netherlands Office, and I do not know what I would have done without her friendship and assistance during my maternity leave and the final stages of my PhD.

Unquestionably, the love and support of my friends and family has meant the most to me during this adventure. It is difficult to express how grateful I am to friends who offered to babysit during my maternity leave so that I could finalize a chapter or who encouraged me to enjoy life away from my computer screen. Whether in the US or the Netherlands, I am surrounded by remarkable people who never fail to amaze me with their ability to give of themselves.

Finally, I cannot even begin to convey my gratitude to my family. Since the day that I started my doctoral research the parents and brother of my husband have always been there for me, asking about my progress, cutting out related articles from the newspapers, and babysitting for Evelien so that I can meet deadlines. It was so comforting to know that I could rely on them for support. Likewise, my parents and sister have been incredible. Despite her demanding work schedule, my sister read through all of my chapters. Where others may have been afraid to give their honest feedback, my sister never held back, and I thank her for that. I am grateful to my Dad, who might not have always known what I was working on, but who cheered me on nonetheless. I would also like to thank my Mom. More than any other person throughout my life she has offered me unwavering love and support. Lastly, I would like to acknowledge my husband, Theo, and our daughter, Evelien, who remind me everyday what is truly important in life. Without Theo's patience, jokes, cooking, feedback, encouragement and love I could never have produced this book. I am truly blessed. Any errors or omissions are entirely my own.

Utrecht, June 2011

TABLE OF CONTENTS

Part II Experimenting Laboratories

CONCLUSION

List of Abbreviations

Art.	Article(s)
ACHR	American Convention on Human Rights
ACmHPR	African Commission on Human and Peoples' Rights
ACtHPR	African Court on Human and Peoples' Rights
AfCHPR	African Charter on Human and Peoples' Rights
ASP	Assembly of States Parties
CAVR	Commission for Reception, Truth and Reconciliation in East Timor
CHR	UN Commission on Human Rights
DRC	Democratic Republic of Congo
DSS	Defense Support Section
ECHR	European Convention on Human Rights and Fundamental Freedoms
ECOSOC	United Nations Economic and Social Council
ECtHR	European Court of Human Rights
e.g.	exempli gratia (for example)
EU	European Union
EULEX	European Union Rule of Law Mission in Kosovo
GA	General Assembly
HRC	Human Rights Committee
IACHR	Inter-American Commission on Human Rights
IACtHR	Inter-American Court of Human Rights
Ibid.	Ibidem
ICC	International Criminal Court
ICCPR	International Covenant on Civil and Political Rights
ICESCR	International Covenant on Economic, Social and Cultural Rights
ICJ	International Court of Justice
ICTR	International Criminal Tribunal for Rwanda
ICTY	International Criminal Tribunal for the former Yugoslavia
i.e.	id est (namely)
IGO	Inter-Governmental Organization
ILC	International Law Commission
IMT	International Military Tribunal (Nuremberg)
IMTFE	International Military Tribunal for the Far East
NGO	Non-Governmental Organization

OAS	Organization of American States
OAU	Organization for African Unity
OTP	Office of the Prosecutor
OPCD	Office of Public Counsel for Defense
OPCV	Office of Public Counsel for Victims
par.	paragraph
para.	paragraphs
p.	page
pp.	pages
RPE	Rules of Procedure and Evidence
SC	Security Council
SCSL	Special Court for Sierra Leone
SCU	Special Crimes Unit of the SPSC
SPSC	Special Panel for Serious Crimes in East Timor
TRCs	Truth and reconciliation commissions
UDHR	Universal Declaration of Human Rights
UN	United Nations
UNCHR	United Nations Commission on Human Rights
UNIIIC	United Nations International Independent Investigation Commission
UNSubCHR	United Nations Sub-Commission on Human Rights
UNPO	Unrepresented Nations and Peoples Organization
UNMIK	United Nations Interim Administration Mission in Kosovo
VPRS	Victim Participation and Reparation Section
VSS	Victim Support Section
VWU	Victims and Witnesses Unit
WSV	World Society of Victimology
WWII	World War II

INTRODUCTION

Chapter 1
Introduction

1.1 Victims and Criminal Justice

On 28 June 1944 a group of men working with the French Resistance arrived at the home of Philippe Henrio, Vichy State Secretary for Information. When he opened the door they shot him on the spot. In response to this act, the Lyons Milice, an auxiliary of the Gestapo under the leadership of Paul Touvier, went looking for Jewish hostages to execute in reprisal. Seven men, six of whom can positively be identified as Jewish, Siefried Prock, Leon Glaeser, Claude Ben Zimra, Emile Zeizig, Maurice Schiusselman, Louis Krzyzkowski, and an unknown individual, were later lined up and shot, receiving multiple bullet wounds to their heads and chests. Paul Touvier would later face criminal charges for these murders and other acts, becoming the first French citizen to be convicted of crimes against humanity in France. His trial raised many issues about confronting the past and the role played by the Vichy government and its treatment of Jews during World War II (WWII).[1] Importantly for this study, his trial also served as a vehicle for victims of crimes against humanity to participate directly in the judicial process.

Following the war, Touvier was tried in absentia and sentenced to death twice for the crimes of treason and conspiring with the enemy. He successfully escaped capture and had hopes of hiding from the authorities (who were not seriously looking for him) until the 20-year statute of limitations for the crimes ran out.[2] To complicate matters, under the misguided notion of national unity, the French President Georges Pompidou pardoned Touvier in 1971.[3] Soon thereafter suits were filed in 1973 and 1974 in French courts by the families of Touvier's victims under the then newly-enacted charge of crimes against humanity which does not carry a statute of limitations and for which he had not received a pardon.[4] The legal battle would continue for another 20 years.

---

1 For an overview of the trial, see Merchant (1995).

2 For a detailed account of how Touvier was found and arrested by French authorities, see Morgan, T., L'Affaire Touvier: Opening Old Wounds, *New York Times Magazine*, 1 October 1989.

3 Merchant (1995) at 428.

4 Sadat (1995) at 200; Morgan, T., L'Affaire Touvier: Opening Old Wounds, *New York Times Magazine*, 1 October 1989.

In 1989 French authorities found and arrested Touvier. After legal wrangling over the specific charges he would face,[5] trial finally began on 17 March 1994 in the Court of Assizes before three judges and nine jurors. He faced charges of crimes against humanity for ordering and assisting in the murder of the seven men in 1944 – to which he admitted taking part.[6] No less than 30 attorneys representing victims' families and Jewish and resistance organizations participated as *parties civiles*, attaching their claim or damages to the criminal process.[7] In five weeks of trial, more than 50 witnesses, experts, and civil parties were heard, as well as Touvier himself.[8]

The trial is revealing for a number of reasons. On the one hand, it suggests that a trial, incorporating the participation of a multitude of victim perspectives, each with their own legal representation, is feasible. Although it certainly helped that all parties were familiar with the French legal system, which clearly delimits the roles and rights of all participants, the trial also shows that victims and victim organizations have an interest in participating. On the other hand, the trial highlights the complexities of such an undertaking. For instance, while it had been relatively easy to enlarge the courtroom in order to accommodate all of the lawyers and spectators, it proved less straightforward to have all of the civil party lawyers cooperate on strategy,[9] to have all civil party lawyers support the case brought by the prosecution, and to strengthen the protection of the rights of the accused.

Arno Klarsfeld, the then 27-year-old son of the famed Nazi-hunting team of Serge and Beate Klarsfeld and one of the civil party lawyers, was intent on bringing to light a view of events that stood in contrast with the prosecution's strategy of presenting and proving the case as well as with the position adopted by the other civil party legal teams.[10] When Touvier was originally indicted he claimed that he had acted under orders from the Gestapo, believing that this could help exonerate him. However, the High Court reversed the Paris Court of Appeals decision, finding that French collaborators could be prosecuted under the newly-enacted crimes against humanity law only if they were working "in the interests of the European Axis countries."[11] Therefore his earlier defense of 'following orders' was now a vital element in proving the case

5 The investigating magistrate indicted Touvier on 5 of the 11 charges lodged against him; however, the appellate chamber, which had been responsible for reviewing the indictment, reversed the magistrate's opinion and threw out the indictment, finding 10 of the 11 charges insufficient and finding no legal basis for the one crime in which his participation was undeniable. Civil parties appealed this decision and on 28 November 1992 the French Court of Cassation reversed the lower (appellate) chamber's decision. The case was remanded to the Indicting Chamber of the Court of Appeals of Versailles, which indicted him on 2 June 1993. He subsequently lost another appeal. See Sadat (1995) at 202-203.

6 *Ibid.* at 214.

7 Chayes (1995) at 343; Sadat (1995) at 205.

8 Sadat (1995) at 204.

9 Chayes (1995) at 343, noting that Arno Klarsfeld referred to the other civil party lawyers as "vulgar old fish."

10 Sadat (1995) at 208 and Merchant (1995) 430, footnote 11, writing that civil party lawyer Alain Jakubowicz opined that Klarsfeld was pleading more as a historian than an attorney.

11 Sadat (1995) at 208, citing Judgment of 28 November 1992, cass. crim.

against him. Indeed, Touvier could be prosecuted for the murders *because* the Gestapo had given the orders. In spite of this, Klarsveld was intent on proving the Vichy government's responsibility by attempting to show that Touvier was not acting under Gestapo orders but in fact was acting on his own initiative. He was attempting to help establish what he viewed as the truth (i.e. the culpability of the Vichy government), but at the same time, many felt that this position compromised the case against the accused because his arguments could have helped destroy the necessary link between Touvier and the Gestapo, which the High Court seemed to require.

Although the accused in this case largely admitted his involvement, the defense was made to face multiple accusers arguing various theories of a case. Despite the fact that having to do so may not elicit much sympathy, it is alarming from a fair trial perspective. The sheer magnitude of the number of lawyers facing the accused raises cause for concern in terms of a distribution of time and resources. Ultimately, after decades of legal wrangling, Touvier was convicted of aiding and abetting a crime against humanity and sentenced to life imprisonment where he died in 1996. A symbolic one franc requested by the civil parties was awarded in damages.[12]

In many ways, at the domestic level, the *Touvier* trial exemplifies the complexities encountered when a large number of victims play a greater role in the criminal process. Undoubtedly, the victims in this case were the driving force behind bringing Touvier to trial and seeking justice. Additionally, during trial, the civil parties not only played a symbolic role (such as requesting one franc in compensation), but one civil party in particular sought to provide substantive information to the court that was not being provided by the prosecution. However, despite the fact that all those participating were familiar with the French legal system, challenges surrounding the participation of the victims in the proceedings certainly arose, begging a number of questions: Is it desirable to have so many civil party legal teams represented at trial? Should civil party legal teams be able to present a different theory of the case, separate from the prosecution? Could the defense be unfairly disadvantaged by having to defend against multiple theories of a case, let alone face over 30 lawyers seeking conviction?

As with the *Touvier* trial, victims in domestic criminal justice systems have often played prominent roles in a number of high-profile cases related to international crimes, including the initiation of cases against Augusto Pinochet and Hissène Habre and joining as auxiliary prosecutors in the case against John Demjanjuk.[13] However, a prominent role for victims in criminal law and criminal policy has not always enjoyed full support. Modern criminal justice has tended to focus on crimes and offenders, with only minor appreciation for the role of victims. This focus on the accused is largely attributable to the fact that the primary purpose of criminal trials is to investigate and prosecute individuals believed to be responsible for committing

12 *Ibid.* at 209.
13 See Langer (2011).

crimes and if found guilty to then punish those individuals.[14] As a result, the criminal paradigm places greater emphasis on the wrong that has been committed and on whether an individual should be found accountable for that wrong and punished.

In spite of this, over the past half-century the largely exclusive focus on the accused has begun to change. The notion that victims should have greater rights within national criminal justice systems surfaced. Throughout much of the world, researchers, policy-makers, those working with victims and victims themselves all voiced their concern over the apparent disregard of the victim in the criminal justice process.[15] Social movements centered on victims of crime began to mobilize at local, national and international levels and the belief that there should be a greater focus on victims gradually developed into what became known as the victims' rights movement.[16] The victims' rights movement stresses that victims are directly affected by criminal processes and therefore criminal justice systems must reform in order to better meet their needs and concerns.

The victims' rights movement has been one of the most successful political and social movements in recent history.[17] It generally advocates for improved *service-related* and *procedural* rights through greater protection, participation and reparation for victims. Service-related rights include increased victim support in the form of protective measures, medical and psychological services and information services. Procedural rights entail victims having a greater say in the decision-making processes and being able to file reparation claims. Service-related and procedural rights are closely connected concepts that enhance the overall position of the victim within the criminal justice framework. Without a doubt, the victims' rights movement has been particularly successful in influencing criminal justice policy,[18] and increasingly,

---

14 Dembour and Haslam (2004) at 152; Gallant (2000) at 21; Doak (2005) at 295; Jackson, J., Transnational Faces of Justice, 239, in Jackson, et al. (2008); see also, Boas (2001).

15 A number of surveys revealed displeasure with the criminal justice system, see Shapland, et al. (1985) at 3, citing, amongst others, Knudten, R.D., et al., *Victims and Witnesses: Their Experiences with Crime and the Criminal Justice System*, National Institute of Law Enforcement and Criminal Justice (1977).

16 Tobolowsky (1999) at 21, referencing Carrington, F. and Nicholson, G., The Victims' Movement: An Idea Whose Time Has Come, 11 *Pepperdine Law Review* 1, 1-5 (1984).

17 See, e.g., Davis (2007) at 64. In the United States, between 1982 and 2004 Congress adopted at least seven pieces of victims' rights legislation, see O'Hear (2006a) at 1, citing the Victims and Witness Protection Act of 1982, the Victims of Crime Act of 1984, the Victims' Rights and Restitution Act of 1990, the Violent Crime Control and Law Enforcement Act of 1994, the Antiterrorism and Effective Death Penalty Act of 1996, the Victim Rights Clarification Act of 1997, and the Crime Victims' Rights Act of 2004. In Europe, as part of a campaign to improve the position of victims in criminal justice systems, in 1985 the Committee of Ministers of the Council of Europe adopted Recommendation (85)11 on the Position of the Victim in the Framework of Criminal Law and Procedure. Other measures include Resolution (77)27 on compensation of victims of crime, the European Convention on the compensation of victims of violent crime, and Recommendation (87)21 on assistance to victims and the prevention of victimization. In addition, in 2001 the European Union Council Framework Decision on the standing of victims in criminal proceedings was passed, requiring all European Union Member States to adopt certain procedures aimed at improving the position of victims.

18 Robinson (2002) at 749; O'Hear (2006b) at 83; Pizzi and Perron (1996) at 37.

victims' rights have been construed in terms of human rights.[19] The success of the movement is due, in part, to the wide range of supporters of victims' rights, and, in part, to the readily acceptable image of "good" victims versus "bad" defendants, leading to increased calls for defendants and victims to have equal procedural rights.[20] Certainly, the rhetoric at the national level has called for a "balancing" of rights between victims and accused in the criminal justice process.[21]

However, just as with the *Touvier* trial, the success of the victims' rights movement raises a number of questions. Is a balancing of procedural rights appropriate? What should the extent of procedural rights be? With regard to substantive criminal law, should victims have influence over its adjudication? National jurisdictions have been grappling with these questions and each jurisdiction has developed its own ideas on the appropriate role of victims in proceedings based upon their unique judicial contexts. Some states allow victims to act as private prosecutors or civil parties whereas other states allow the submission of victim impact statements following the conviction of the accused. Notwithstanding the wide range of domestic practices, in 1985 states reached a broad consensus on the general rights of victims in criminal proceedings through the adoption of the United Nations Declaration of Basic Principles of Justice for Victims of Crime and Abuse of Power (Victims' Declaration).[22]

The Victims' Declaration recognizes the right to respect and recognition; the right to receive information; the right to provide information; the right to legal advice or representation; the right to protection of privacy and physical safety; the right to financial compensation from the offender and from the state; and the right to receive victim support.[23] The rights acknowledged in this non-binding declaration represent both the service-related and procedural rights sought by the victims' rights movement and relate to their goals of acquiring greater rights of protection, participation and reparation for victims. With regard to victims' procedural rights, Article 6(b) provides:

> The responsiveness of judicial and administrative processes to the needs of victims should be facilitated by: Allowing the views and concerns of victims to be presented and considered at appropriate stages of the proceedings where their personal interests are affected, without prejudice to the accused and consistent with the relevant national criminal justice system.

Worded broadly, Article 6(b) serves as a reminder to states that they have an obligation to be receptive to the needs and concerns of victims in judicial processes.

---

19 Doak (2005) at 302; see also Doak (2003) and Klug, F., Human Rights and Victims, in Cape (2004).

20 O'Hear (2006b) at 83; Dubber (1999) at 8-9; Edwards (2004) at 968-969.

21 Edwards (2004) at 968; Butler (2006) at 21; Trumbull (2008) at 822.

22 The Declaration of Basic Principles of Justice for Victims of Crime and Abuse of Power, UN Doc. A/Res/40/34/Annex (1985) [hereinafter Victims' Declaration].

23 Victims' Declaration; See also, De Brouwer, A.M. and Groenhuijsen, M., The Role of Victims in International Criminal Proceedings, 153-154, in Sluiter and Vasiliev (2009).

Despite the gains made by the victims' rights movement and the key role often played by victims in domestic jurisdictions, victims have not always featured prominently in criminal trials at the international level. At the Nuremberg and Tokyo international military tribunals, the International Criminal Tribunal for the former Yugoslavia (ICTY) and Rwanda (ICTR) as well as at the Special Court for Sierra Leone (SCSL) victims could generally only participate in the criminal process as witnesses.[24] For the most part, they were only called to testify in court if their testimony could corroborate arguments made by one of the parties, usually on behalf of the prosecution. Although what can be referred to as victim impact statements were submitted in some cases, victims themselves were never called before the courts to express their views and concerns. Protection measures were only provided for victim-witnesses and victims were unable to claim reparations directly through these courts, and instead, had to pursue redress through national systems (which often was not a feasible option).

When preparing the Statute for the ICTY, drafters rejected proposals for greater victim rights, such as allowing the appointment of separate counsel for victims or the ability to seek reparations directly through the court.[25] The rejection was out of fear that third-party participation would lead to conflicts with the prosecution's case, delays in the proceedings and infringements of the rights of the accused.[26] Whether or not these fears were valid, victims' rights groups, together with a handful of states, called for reform. More specifically, victims' rights advocates stressed a need for greater rights of protection, participation and reparation in international criminal justice.

In answering this call, international criminal courts are increasingly broadening their mandates in an attempt to better address the needs and concerns of victims. As such, courts created after the *Ad Hoc* Tribunals and SCSL, including the Special Panels for Serious Crimes in East Timor (SPSC), the UNMIK/EULEX war crimes panels in Kosovo, the International Criminal Court (ICC), the Extraordinary Chambers in the Courts of Cambodia (ECCC) and the Special Tribunal for Lebanon (STL), provide for increased recognition of and rights for victims.[27] Thus, in addition to their primary function of investigating, prosecuting and punishing those found to be responsible for war crimes, crimes against humanity and genocide these courts have taken on additional tasks pertaining to victims' service-related and procedural rights.

24 See Van Boven, T., The Position of the Victim in Statute of the International Criminal Court, 77-89, in Von Hebel, et al. (1999).

25 See Morris and Scharf (1995).

26 *Ibid.* at 167; Tochilovsky, V.N., Victims' Procedural Rights at Trial: Approach of Continental Europe and the International Tribunal for the Former Yugoslavia, 287-89 in Van Dijk, et al. (1999).

27 See Article 80 of the Provisional Criminal Procedural Code of Kosovo, *available at*: http://www.unmikonline.org/regulations/2003/RE2003-26.pdf; UNTAET Regulation 2000/30 on Transitional Rules of Criminal Procedure, as amended by UNTAET Regulation 2001/25, Section 12(3); and ECCC, Internal Rules, as revised 9 February 2010, Rule 23. See also McGonigle, B., Apples and Oranges? Comparing the Victim Participation Approaches at the ICC and ECCC, 91, in Ryngeart (2009).

With regard to their procedural rights, victims have been afforded both general and specific rights to participate in the criminal process. These courts are allowing victims to be represented by legal counsel and to play an active role in proceedings. Moreover, some courts have allowed victims to claim reparations through the criminal process for their harm suffered.

Much can be and has been written on the rights of victims at both the domestic and international levels. The subject of victims' rights in international criminal law is too broad to be exhaustively examined in this study. Instead, this study will focus on victims' participatory rights while only touching upon the closely related rights of protection and reparation. A relatively new phenomenon, victim participation at the international level has posed many of the same questions that domestic jurisdictions face but it has also presented new questions unique to the international criminal law context.

1.2 International Criminal Trials

It is commonly asserted that "to respond to mass atrocity with legal prosecutions is to embrace the rule of law."[28] The rule of law embodies a number of notions.[29] First, the rule of law recognizes society's condemnation of criminal behavior for acts that the society finds morally objectionable. Second, the rule of law condones the sanctioned (and proportional) punishment of those individuals found responsible for violations of the law. Third, the rule of law supports the call for a formal system committed to hearing both accusations of criminal charges as well as defenses. Accordingly, it implies a sense of fairness of process. The focus on condemnation, punishment and fairness is particularly relevant in trials for serious crimes, and helps explain why the establishment and proliferation of international criminal institutions has been welcomed by many.[30]

A branch of international law, international criminal law is said to be "the criminal law of the international community."[31] It can generally be defined as the field of law that assigns individual criminal responsibility for serious violations of public international law. This field of law is largely developed and enforced through the creation of international criminal courts. In the wake of egregious human rights and humanitarian law violations, international criminal courts have been established through a variety of ways in an attempt to address impunity and hold individuals accountable for violations of international criminal law. Since the Nuremberg and Tokyo military tribunals an increasing number of international or hybrid criminal tribunals have been

28 Minow (1998) at 25.
29 On the concept of the Rule of Law see Raitio (2003) at 134-146.
30 See Goldstone (1997) at 2; Akhavan (1997) at 327; Cf. Drumbl (2007) at 10.
31 Zahar and Sluiter (2008) at vii. In addition to affirming the rule of law, international criminal justice is said to assist in post-conflict democracy building, foster reconciliation, and create an historical record; see Cassese (1998) at 9-10.

created.[32] According to Drumbl, the establishment of these courts amounts to "one of the more extensive waves of institution-building in modern international relations."[33]

Although they vary in their structure, there are a number of special characteristics unique to international criminal proceedings, distinguishing them in many ways from domestic criminal proceedings. To begin with, international criminal law and international criminal proceedings only deal with specific types of cases, namely with the most serious crimes of concern to the international community, including war crimes, crimes against humanity, and genocide.[34] These crimes are all, in some way, closely associated with the idea of mass or collective victimization.[35] War crimes must occur within the context of an armed conflict, crimes against humanity require a widespread or systematic violation against a civilian population, and genocide is generally connected to the notion of targeting individuals belonging to a protected group or collectivity, as such. To a large extent, it is the mass victimization aspect of these crimes that propels them to the level of international crimes.

In addition to subject-matter constraints, other factors, such as the make-up and structure of international criminal courts, also make these systems of justice unique from domestic jurisdictions. The make-up of international criminal institutions is diverse, with court staff hailing from all around the world and bringing with them particular experiences and deeply ingrained beliefs about law and procedure. As such, the differences in legal culture amongst the lawyers and professional judges selected to serve the courts are readily apparent.[36] For instance, while some judges view an active judicial role as improper, other judges view passivity as "an abdication of the proper judicial role."[37] It is virtually impossible to disassociate oneself from the legal traditions in which one is familiar. For this reason, both lawyers and "Judges associated with particular traditions have been known to, consciously or unconsciously,

32 Including, *inter alia*, International Criminal Tribunal for the former Yugoslavia [hereinafter ICTY]; International Criminal Tribunal for Rwanda [hereinafter ICTR]; International Criminal Court [hereinafter ICC]; Special Court for Sierra Leone [hereinafter SCSL]; UNMIK/EULEX panels in Kosovo; Special Panels in East Timor [hereinafter SPSC]; Extraordinary Chambers in the Courts of Cambodia [hereinafter ECCC], Special Tribunal for Lebanon [hereinafter STL], and the Bangladesh War Crimes Tribunal.

33 Drumbl (2007) at 10.

34 The ICC also has jurisdiction over the crime of aggression. In the summer of 2010 the Assembly of States Parties (ASP) adopted the definition for the crime of aggression falling under the ICC's jurisdiction (Article 8*bis* of the Rome Statute). However, the provision will not come into effect until 2017 (at the earliest). Additionally, hybrid international courts often have jurisdiction over serious national crimes. For instance, the STL has jurisdiction over the domestic crime of terrorism, which in itself implies a multiplicity of victims. Moreover, though using the domestic definition of the crime, the act of terrorism is of fundamental concern to the international community.

35 Bassiouni, M.C., The Protection of 'Collective Victims' in International Law, 183, in Bassiouni (1998).

36 Tochilovsky, V., Legal Systems and Cultures in the International Criminal Court: The Experience from the International Criminal Tribunal in Yugoslavia, 627, in Fischer, et al. (2001).

37 Langer (2005) at 849.

promote certain features of criminal procedure with which they are familiar,"[38] and "[d]omestic criminal lawyers newly involved in international trials have tended to view problems in light of the tradition in which they have been trained."[39] Unsurprisingly, lawyers and judges hold deep-rooted beliefs about the nature of justice that are largely inseparable from their own system's dogma.[40] Thus, all of the participants of the international criminal justice system will have distinctive understandings of criminal processes, procedures and respective roles for judges, prosecutors, defense and victims – which is generally not the case at the domestic level.

The structural differences of an organization's authority, the perceptions of the goals of justice and the perceived role of the authority all influence and shape what procedural approach a court adopts. Nevertheless, the emergence of international criminal institutions has demanded the development of procedural rules that are acceptable to the two legal traditions predominating at the international level, namely the common law tradition and the civil law tradition.[41] The merging of legal cultures in international criminal law is also reflected in the statutes and rules adopted by the courts as well as in the decisions handed down by judicial benches. The result of this transplanting of rules from different legal traditions is that the procedures of the international courts are often a hodge-podge of features from the two dominant legal traditions, which employ a mixture of adversarial and inquisitorial approaches in their proceedings.[42] While some international courts adopt a more adversarial approach and others adopt a more inquisitorial approach, all have grappled with the difficulties of "melding civil law and common law rules and international human rights standards into a truly 'international' body of procedural and substantive criminal law."[43] Obvious tensions exist between the two dominant legal systems. One of the most notable tensions to arise concerns how the various chambers view the proper role of victims in the criminal process, which in turn has affected the procedural rules adopted by the courts.[44]

Although speaking abstractly, an individual familiar with the accusatorial approach may adopt the belief that judicial truth best emerges from a contest between two subjective parties whereas an individual familiar with the inquisitorial approach may adopt the belief that judicial truth is best discovered through the objective assessment of all available facts. These two beliefs are based on fundamentally different assumptions, making it more challenging to bring the two approaches together coherently.[45] In addition to notions about judicial truth, the two legal traditions and their procedural

38 Mégret (2009) at 44; see also, Mundis (2001) at 369.
39 Mégret (2009) at 45.
40 See generally Anderson and Otto (2003); Groenhuijsen, M., Victims' Rights and the International Criminal Court: The Model of the Rome Statute and Its Operation, 309, in Van Genugten, et al. (2009).
41 See Findlay (2001).
42 Mégret (2009) at 38.
43 Patel King and La Rosa (1997) at 125.
44 Zappalá (2003) at 15.
45 Mégret (2009) at 46.

approaches view the role and rights of the individual facing prosecution, the judge, the prosecuting authority, and the victim differently. Added to this dilemma is the fact that procedural traditions are highly complex and rarely static.

In addition to the mass victimization aspect to international trials and the unique make-up and structure of international criminal courts, the costs of international trials are also significantly higher than those associated with domestic trials. Although the purpose of this study is not to carry out a detailed cost-benefit analysis of victim participation, it is, nevertheless, an important factor to consider when assessing international criminal institutions. Trials for war crimes, crimes against humanity and genocide are expensive. The very nature of these crimes makes investigation of the facts surrounding them more difficult to prove and more expensive to process. In addition to expensive investigations, the costs of staffing, translation, protection services, court management, detention, and the provision of defense services for indigent defendants through legal aid makes the operational budgets of international criminal institutions skyrocket.

To be sure, financial and other practical constraints, such as the ability to collect evidence, dictate that the courts (usually through the prosecutor) must focus on issues of judicial economy and, in turn, selectively decide which cases to prosecute.[46] Although domestic criminal systems are also familiar with operating under resource constraints, these limitations are particularly alarming when dealing with a large number of victims and crimes on a massive scale. Moreover, when deciding on what cases to pursue, some international courts have further criteria to meet, including the gravity of an offense or the leadership role of an accused. The result is that only a small number of cases can be taken up. Indeed, international criminal courts are not set up to try a large number of individuals. Instead, they are meant to selectively prosecute those believed to be most responsible for serious crimes. Accordingly, the selective prosecution of only a limited number of cases means that not all complaints of crimes can be the subject of prosecution, which in turn means that not all victims of serious crimes will have their voices heard.

1.3 Core Themes: The Link between Human Rights, International Criminal Justice, and Victims' Rights

In law the term 'human rights' dates back to the UN Charter and the concept of the inherent human dignity of every individual as a fundamental and universal right, requiring respect and protection on the part of states towards individuals.[47] The proclamation of human rights at the international level, however, did not immediately bring with it clarification as to the meaning, content and scope of human rights protections. Unquestionably, these remain controversial. Nevertheless, over the past

46 Knoops (2005) at 1573.

47 Francioni (2007) at 27.

65 years, since the adoption of the UN Charter and the 1948 Universal Declaration of Human Rights (UDHR), an international system for the promotion and protection of human rights has emerged.[48] And in the realm of criminal proceedings, where individuals (both accused and victims) have rights vis-à-vis the state, human rights protections are of particular importance. Moreover, with the development of international criminal law, human rights protections in criminal proceedings have been extended beyond the state-individual construct.[49]

1.3.1 Fair Trial Standards

Dating back to the Magna Carta (1215),[50] the most widely acknowledged human rights norm in criminal proceedings is the right to a fair trial.[51] Although there is no single international agreement dedicated solely to international standards of due process and fair trial principles for criminal proceedings, there is a collection of international and regional agreements that provide for fair trial and due process guarantees. The leading international human rights agreements, both binding and non-binding, which explicitly provide for fair trial protections include,[52] *inter alia*, the: UDHR (Art. 10, 11);[53] International Covenant on Civil and Political Rights (ICCPR) (Art. 9, 14, 15);[54] European Convention on the Protection of Human Rights and Fundamental Freedoms (ECHR) (Art. 5, 6, 7);[55] American Convention on Human Rights (ACHR) (Art. 7, 8, 9);[56] and African Charter on Human and People's Rights (AfCHR) (Art. 3, 6, 7).[57]

These international human rights instruments are based on liberal theories and values. In the liberal model the state is viewed as substantially more powerful than any of its citizens. In order to protect the rights of citizens vis-à-vis thc state limits need to be placed on state authority. The need for limits is particularly important in the field of criminal law, where states exert the most power over an individual. Because the

48 Universal Declaration of Human Rights (1948) [hereinafter UDHR].

49 It was considered self-evident that certain human rights, most notably those related to fair trial rights, were to be fully respected by the newly created International Criminal Tribunal for the former Yugoslavia, see Report of the Secretary-General pursuant to par. 2 of Security Council Resolution 808, UN Doc. S/25704 (1993), par. 106.

50 See Van Dijk (1983).

51 See Harris (1967); Stapleton (1998-1999) at 535; Van Dijk, P., Universal Legal Principles of Fair Trial in Criminal Proceedings, 89-90, in Rosas and Helgesen (1990).

52 These documents have been highlighted because they have often been used as models for national and international standards and some are the governing documents for the European Court of Human Rights, the Inter-American Court of Human Rights and the Human Rights Committee. Moreover, these documents enumerate rights guaranteed in both common law and civil law legal traditions.

53 UDHR.

54 International Covenant on Civil and Political Rights (1966) [hereinafter ICCPR].

55 European Convention for the Protection of Human Rights and Fundamental Freedoms (1950) [hereinafter ECHR].

56 American Convention on Human Rights (1969) [hereinafter ACHR].

57 African Charter on Human and Peoples' Rights (1981) [hereinafter AfCHPR].

individual may be marginalized and unpopular, criminal procedures adhering to strict standards of fair trial and due process rights will lessen the inherent imbalance of power. Liberal values therefore specifically provide for and promote defendants' rights in the criminal process.

The rights enumerated in the above listed documents and recognized by human rights bodies established to enforce the rights found therein include, but are not limited to:

- The right to be judged by an independent and impartial tribunal
- The prohibition on arbitrary arrest and detention
- The right to be informed of the nature and cause of the criminal charges
- The right to humane conditions during detention
- The right to a fair and public hearing
- The right not to incriminate oneself
- Presumption of innocence
- The right not to be subjected to any form of coercion
- The right to an interpreter
- The right not to be subject to arbitrary arrest or detention
- The right to remain silent
- The right to legal assistance
- The right to disclosure
- The right to a fair and expeditious trial
- The right to have adequate time and facilities to prepare a defense
- The right to be present at trial
- The right to confront witnesses and obtain their attendance
- The right to a reasoned judgment
- The right to appeal
- Limitations on double jeopardy
- The prohibition on retroactive application of criminal laws[58]

All of the above mentioned human rights documents recognize that the fair trial rights provided for in their respective provisions provide minimum guarantees. In fact, a trial may meet all of the enumerated rights and nevertheless not meet fair trial standards.[59] This is because courts must look at proceedings as a whole and not to their component parts.

In addition to the rights listed above the principle of equality of arms is often invoked when speaking of fair trial rights. Indeed, "the observance of the principle of equality of arms between the defense and the prosecution," is arguably seen as "the

58 See Bassiouni (1992-1993) at Appendix II.

59 Lawyers Committee for Human Rights, What is a Fair Trial? A Basic Guide to Legal Standards and Practice, March 2000 at 12.

single most important criterion in evaluating the fairness of a trial."[60] Therefore, although there is no specific reference to equality of arms in international or regional agreements, it is nevertheless recognized as an essential aspect of a fair trial.[61] In this respect, Article 14 of the ICCPR conveys a general guarantee of equality before the courts and tribunals, Article 6 of the ECHR provides that "everyone is entitled to a fair and public hearing," and the rights of defense, found in Article 8(2) of the ACHR, are introduced by the phrase "with full equality."

Yet, despite the fact that the principle of equality of arms is widely accepted and relied upon by accused in criminal proceedings, there is debate over what exactly the principle covers. The European Court of Human Rights (ECtHR) has found that:

> In criminal trials, where the prosecution has all the machinery of the state behind it, the principle of equality of arms is an essential guarantee of the right to defend oneself. The principle of equality of arms ensures that the defence has a reasonable opportunity to prepare and present its case on a footing equal to that of the prosecution. Its requirements include the right to adequate time and facilities to prepare a defence, including disclosure by the prosecution of material information. Its requirements also include the right to legal counsel, the right to call and examine witnesses and the right to be present at the trial. This principle would be violated, for example, if the accused was not given access to information necessary for the preparation of the defence, if the accused was denied access to expert witnesses, or if the accused was excluded from an appeal hearing where the prosecutor was present.[62]

The ECtHR generally defines the principle of equality of arms as requiring that "each party must be afforded a reasonable opportunity to present his case in conditions that do not place him at a disadvantage vis-à-vis his opponent."[63] Similarly, in its case law and general commentaries the Human Rights Committee has found that equality of arms requires "that the same procedural rights are to be provided to all the parties unless distinctions are based on law and can be justified on objective and reasonable grounds, not entailing actual disadvantage or other unfairness to the defendant."[64]

---

60 *Ibid.*

61 Trechsel (2005) at 94.

62 See ECtHR, *Foucher v France*, App. No. 22209/93, 18 March 1997.

63 ECtHR, *Kaufman v. Belgium*, App. No. 10938/84, 9 December 1986, p. 115; *Bulut v. Austria,* App. No. 17358/90, 22 February 1996, par. 47. The same definition is also applied in administrative cases, see e.g., *Gorraiz Lizarraga and Others v. Spain,* App. No. 62543/00, 27 April 2004, par. 56; *Foucher v France*, App. No. 22209/93, 18 March 1997, par. 34.

64 HRC, General Comment No. 32, Article 14: Right to equality before courts and tribunals and to a fair trial, UN Doc. CCPR/C/GC/32 (2007), par. 13; HRC, *Dudko v. Australia*, Comm. No. 1347/2005, 29 August 2007, par. 7.4; The right to equality before the courts, expressly guaranteed in Art. 14(1) of the ICCPR, is a specific provision related to the general right to equality (Art. 26), which should also be read together with the general prohibition of discrimination under Art. 2 (1). The provision generally refers to a right of equal access to a court by all persons, without distinction as to race, religion, sex, property, etc. There is a difference between equality before courts and the principle of equality of arms.

Closely linked with the principle of adversarial proceedings,[65] the principle is an essential aspect of fair trial standards.[66] However, there is still disagreement over who can claim a violation of the principle. Can civil parties or victim participants in the criminal process claim a violation? Or is the principle for the benefit of the defense only? For the purpose of this study, the principle of equality of arms will refer mainly to claims made by the defense vis-à-vis either the prosecuting authorities or the victims, whom the defense argue are acting as subsidiary prosecutors. Nevertheless, reference will be made to claims made by other parties and participants, seeking to protect their procedural rights in the criminal process.

Together with the principle of equality of arms, the multi-faceted principle of legal certainty is also closely related to the right to a fair trial.[67] The principal of legal certainty has not been defined with any degree of precision in law or legal literature,[68] and whether it can be defined with any precision at all is open to debate. Nevertheless, it is recognized as a general principle of law in that it is common to almost all legal systems.[69] It is not the intention of this study to examine the various definitions of legal certainty found in national and international case law. Rather, this study will adopt the general concept of the principle embraced by the European Court of Justice (ECJ) and leading academics. In accordance with Schermers' and Waelbroeck's approach as well as the view adopted by Hartley, the principle of legal certainty underpins any legal system and is related to the notion of predictability.[70] In addition, Barling, Davies and Stratford find the principle of legal certainty and the related principle of legitimate expectation to "provide useful tools with which to challenge measures which are uncertain or unexpected in their introduction and effects."[71] Thus, closely related to the notion of predictability, the principle of legitimate expectation and the rule of law,[72] the principle of legal certainty for the purposes of this study will refer to the requirement that legal rules be sufficiently clear and precise, and that situations and legal relationships remain foreseeable.[73]

Only the HRC derives both from the more general right to equality before the law. See also Nowak (2005).

65 ECtHR, *Brandstetter v. Austria,* App. No. 11170/84; 12876/87; 13468/87, 28 August 1991, par. 66; *Ruiz-Mateos v. Spain*, App. No. 12952/87, 23 June 1993, par. 63; *Belziuk v. Poland,* App. No. 23103/93, 25 March 1998, par. 37; *Rowe and Davis v. United Kingdom,* App. No. 28901/95, 16 February 2000, par. 60.

66 Knoops (2005) at 1566.

67 See Zappalá (2010); Emmerson, et al. (2007) at 401.

68 Raitio (2003) at 125.

69 *Ibid.*

70 *Ibid.* at 128-129; citing Hartley, T.C., *The Foundations of European Community Law*, 4th Ed., 142-143, Oxford University Press (1998).

71 *Ibid.* at 125, citing Barling, J., Davies, G. and Stratford, H., Fundamental and General Principles of Community Law, 89, in, Barling, G. and Brealey, M., eds., *Practitioners' Handbook of EC Law*, Trenton Publishing (1998).

72 *Ibid.* at 127.

73 *Ibid.* at 126; See also ECJ, *Jokela and Pitkäranta*, C-9/97 and C-118/97, 22 October 1998, para. 48-50.

Today there is little doubt about the importance of human rights in domestic criminal proceedings. And as with national systems, human rights have played an equally important role in international criminal proceedings. Despite the theoretical differences between human rights law and international criminal law, "human rights have provided the bedrock for achieving a common procedure for the international criminal tribunals."[74] Nevertheless, within international criminal proceedings, the interconnected notions, discussed above, pose challenges for the courts.[75]

Although the human rights instruments and rights and principles found therein generally do not have a direct legal consequence for international criminal court practice because they provide for rights in domestic situations, they have had an important influence on the drafting of statutes and rules of procedure and evidence at the international level. Fair trial rights are acknowledged as fundamental human rights norms in both domestic and international criminal justice processes. From the drafting of the London Charter of the Nuremberg Tribunal to today, international criminal courts recognize the specific fair trial rights detailed above.[76] Thus, at each of the international criminal courts the fundamental right to a fair trial is recognized – even if the contours of these rights are not always clear. In addition to the explicit references to the rights of the accused, the Rome Statute of the ICC requires the application and interpretation of law be consistent with recognized human rights standards.[77] Moreover, jurisprudence from the various courts recognizes the principle of equality of arms and the need to ensure legal certainty. Therefore, although human rights standards were originally drafted and meant to apply in a national context, international criminal courts have embraced the liberal model, finding that the minimum fair trial standards apply equally in an international criminal procedural context.

In addition, where previously international criminal courts struggled with ensuring human rights standards in relation to the accused, they now must also take into account

---

74 Jackson, J., Transitional Faces of Justice: Two Attempts to Build Common Standards beyond National Boundaries, 236, in Jackson, et al. (2008).

75 See generally Fedorova and Sluiter (2009).

76 See, e.g., the London Charter of the International Military Tribunal at Nuremberg (IMT) and its Rules of Procedure; Charter of the International Military Tribunal for the Far East (IMTFE) and its Rules of Procedure; ICTY Statute and its Rules of Procedure and Evidence (ICTY RPE); ICTR Statute and its Rules of Procedure and Evidence (ICTR RPE); SCSL Statute and its Rules of Procedure and Evidence (SCSL RPE); UNTAET Regulation 2000/30 on Transitional Rules of Criminal Procedure (as amended by UNTAET Regulation 2001/25); Code of Criminal Procedure of Timor-Leste, Law No. 15/2005, replacing UNTAET Regulation 2000/30; UNMIK/EULEX Courts in Kosovo, UNMIK Reg. 1999/24, the Constitutional Framework, and the Provisional Criminal Procedural Code; Agreement between the United Nations and the Royal Government of Cambodia concerning the prosecution under Cambodian law of crimes committed during the period of democratic Kampuchea (Framework Agreement); Law on the Establishment of Extraordinary Chambers in the Courts of Cambodia for the Prosecution of Crimes Committed during the Period of Democratic Kampuchea (ECCC Law); ECCC Internal Rules; Rome Statute of the ICC and its Rules of Procedure and Evidence (ICC RPE); and the Resolution, Agreement and Statute for the STL and its Rules of Procedure and Evidence (STL RPE).

77 ICC Rome Statute, Art. 21(3); see also Sheppard (2010).

human rights standards in relation to victims. How the various international courts approach these new challenges is a matter of great interest, not only for scholars, but foremost for those involved in international criminal justice processes.

1.3.2 Victims' Procedural Rights

As with the rights of the accused and fair trial standards in criminal proceedings human rights instruments also focus on the relationship between victims and the state.[78] States have obligations towards victims and victims increasingly have enforceable rights in the domestic criminal process. To this end, a number of international and regional texts, both explicitly and implicitly, call for greater recognition of victims' rights in the criminal process and even go so far as to call for victims' procedural rights in criminal proceedings. The non-binding texts include:

- UN Declaration of Basic Principles of Justice for Victims of Crime and Abuse of Power;[79]
- UN Basic Principles and Guidelines on the Right to a Remedy and Reparation for Victims of Gross Violations of International Human Rights Law and Serious Violations of International Humanitarian Law;[80]
- Council of Europe, Committee of Ministers, Recommendation (85)11 on the Position of the Victim in the Framework of Criminal Law and Procedure;
- African Commission on Human and Peoples' Rights, Principles and Guidelines on the Right to a Fair Trial and Legal Assistance in Africa.

The binding texts include:

- UN Convention against Transnational Organized Crime and its Protocol to Prevent, Suppress and Punish Trafficking in Persons, Especially Women and Children;
- European Convention on Human Rights;
- American Convention on Human Rights;
- European Union-Council Framework Decision on the standing of victims in criminal proceedings of 15 March 2001.

The non-binding UN instruments listed above have sought to clarify, in broad terms, the various rights belonging to victims. These UN documents are generally advanced as a reflection of accepted standards rather than as creating international norms that

78 Aldana-Pindell (2004) at 610.

79 See Victims' Declaration.

80 Basic Principles and Guidelines on the Right to a Remedy and Reparation for Victims of Gross Violations of International Human Rights Law and Serious Violations of International Humanitarian Law, UN Doc. A/RES/60/147 (2005) [hereinafter Basic Principles].

have immediate application in domestic practice.[81] Nevertheless, these documents are important because they stress the fact that victims have rights. The Victims' Declaration, in particular, was the first UN instrument dedicated solely to the rights of victims and the first to encourage victim participation in domestic criminal proceedings. Worded broadly, the provision on victim participation is applicable in a wide range of legal systems and as will be discussed in later chapters has greatly influenced participation at the international criminal law level. Likewise, the UN Basic Principles and Guidelines on the Right to a Remedy and Reparation for Victims of Gross Violations of International Human Rights Law and Serious Violations of International Humanitarian Law (Basic Principles), while not specifically calling for participation, imply the importance of participation through its emphasis on equal and effective access to justice, adequate, effective and prompt reparation and the right to truth.

Drawing upon the language found in Article 6(b) of the Victims' Declaration, one international treaty specifically requires ratifying states to provide for victim participation in the criminal process, subject to their domestic laws. The Convention against Transnational Organized Crime and its Protocol to Prevent, Suppress and Punish Trafficking in Persons provide that victims *shall* be permitted to present their views and concerns at appropriate stages of proceedings. It is still rare, however, to find international treaties including such specific reference to victim participation in criminal proceedings. States are nevertheless free to interpret these provisions on participation within their own legal contexts. Therefore, some states will allow victims the right to challenge decisions not to prosecute whereas other states will only allow victims to submit written victim impact statements for the purposes of sentencing.

Regional initiatives within the European and African systems have also drawn upon Article 6(b) of the Victims' Declaration in support of allowing victims the opportunity to share their views and concerns at appropriate stages of proceedings. The Council of Europe and the European Union have both sought to provide greater clarity to the need to provide victims a means through which they can participate in the criminal process. The European Union's Framework Decision is binding on Member States, requiring them to change their criminal procedural laws to be in compliance with the victim reforms. Similarly, the African Commission has sought to promote the rights of victims in criminal proceedings. Again, however, these developments respect the divergent approaches taken in domestic criminal justice systems. None of the documents favor one procedural approach or call for a total overhaul of domestic procedures. Instead, they acknowledge that different systems can meet the needs of victims in different ways.

In addition to the texts listed above, the ECtHR and the IACtHR have interpreted their respective conventions as providing for the procedural rights of victims in criminal proceedings. Beginning in the 1980s these courts have been finding that in addition to a state's obligations to investigate, prosecute and repair, victims and their

81 Joutsen (1987) at 62.

families should have standing in their respective criminal justice systems to (i) ensure that the state complies with its duty to investigate and prosecute and (ii) have a means by which they can seek reparation through the criminal process (if permitted in the domestic context). Moreover, the ECtHR has even interpreted the right to a fair trial, which traditionally was only constructed to protect the rights of the accused, as encompassing both accused and victims. Thus, the ECtHR concluded that a civil party complaint is within the scope of Article 6(1) and the right to a fair trial under the Convention so long as the civil component is closely related to the criminal one.[82]

These developments have come to mean that human rights courts recognize victims' participatory rights, through human rights provisions, in criminal proceedings. However, the human rights courts have only interpreted the human rights provisions as supporting victim participation within the procedural context of the domestic law. Consequently, while stipulating that a general right for victim participation exists in some legal systems, these courts acknowledge that states differ with regard to their victim participation models and their decisions take account of and respect these differences. Overall, international human rights law and the bodies interpreting the law have "sought to slightly expand victims' rights to access, disclosure, compensation, reparations, and above all, symbolic recognition in the context of criminal proceedings."[83] And although a "significant gap exists between international human rights law and international criminal law" the norms which developed between the state-victim relationship at the domestic, regional and international level have had a profound impact on the way in which victims' rights are interpreted and applied within international criminal justice.[84]

Despite this profound impact, in many ways the interpretation of victims' rights in international criminal law is decidedly different than in relation to victims' rights in domestic criminal proceedings. Victims' participatory rights have been limited when it comes to ensuring compliance with a 'duty' to investigate and prosecute as well as seeking reparation through the criminal process when permitted to do so. In addition to differences with domestic systems, the content and scope of participation is decidedly different in every international criminal court. While some courts allow victims to address issues of sentencing, others strictly forbid such a practice. As a result, a study of victim participation provides an excellent medium through which to learn more about the interconnected notions of international criminal justice and human rights, encompassing fair trial standards and victims' rights. Reconciling the fair trial rights of the accused and victims' procedural rights will certainly be one of the goals of international criminal justice institutions as they wade their way through the murky waters encountered when victims are afforded greater participatory rights in the criminal process.

82 ECtHR, *Perez v. France*, App. No. 47287/99, 12 February 2004, par. 64.
83 Bassiouni (2006) at 205.
84 *Ibid.* See also Bassiouni (1982).

1.4 Central Research Question

In early 2006, the Office of the High Commissioner for Human Rights called for more detailed research into the relevant international standards and national and international practices concerning the role of victims in criminal proceedings.[85] In response to this call, this study will explore victim participation in international criminal proceedings. There are a number of approaches a study of victim participation in international criminal proceedings can take. As noted by Bassiouni:

> The literature on victims is as disparate as are the disciplines concerned with the subject. This includes victimology, criminology, penology, criminal law and procedure, comparative criminal law and procedure, international criminal law and human rights. Each of these disciplines pursues different goals, relies on different methodologies, employs different terminology and provides for different roles and rights for the victims. More importantly, there is a lack of commonly-shared understanding between these disciplines as to the role and rights of victims.[86]

In contrast with the bulk of the research dedicated to the subject of victims in the criminal process this study does not discuss victim participation from the standpoint of victims, except to the extent that their participatory rights can be recognized as a form of human rights. Approaches from the victim's perspective are valuable and there are many significant contributions to this subject.[87] However, this study seeks to examine victim participation in international criminal proceedings through the lens of human rights and criminal justice generally, rather than a victims' perspective specifically. A human rights and criminal justice approach within the narrower field of international criminal justice provides a useful method with which to examine the participatory rights of victims in international criminal proceedings. Such an approach takes into account the role and rights of all individuals involved in the criminal process and readily identifiable and applicable norms are discernable. Thus, the central research question is:

---

85 Implementation of General Assembly Resolution 60/251 of 15 March 2006 entitled "Human Rights Council," Right to the truth, Report of the Office of the High Commissioner for Human Rights, UN Doc. A/HRC/5/7 (2007), para. 89-90.

86 Bassiouni (2006) at 204.

87 See, e.g., Heikkilä (2004) at 4, stating that her study "aims both at elucidating the role granted to victims and at identifying factors influencing what the role is" and assessing "whether the role is satisfactory from the perspective of the victims." See also Findlay and Henham (2005) at ix, arguing for the harmonization of restorative and retributive processes "through wider access, greater inclusion and a more protected victim voice in the process and outcomes of ICJ." Stanley (2009) at 11, stating that her research "resolutely stands 'on the side' of those who have suffered violations."

In light of the specific characteristics of international criminal law and human rights standards, what is the proper scope and content of victim participation in international criminal proceedings?

It is hoped that by answering this question, the findings of this study may contribute to a better understanding of competing rights within international criminal justice and provide those involved in the shaping of international criminal justice with a means through which to view the participatory rights of victims. To structure the analysis, the framework will focus on two central concepts: (i) the unique characteristics of international criminal proceedings and (ii) human rights standards. In order to fully clarify the parameters of this study it is useful to break apart the research question into its component parts.

In light of the specific characteristics of international criminal law

When looking at human rights within a criminal procedural context it is necessary to delimit the context: the specific characteristics of international criminal law will be used to this effect. The specific characteristics focused on in this study will be the mass victimization aspect to the trials, the make-up and structure of the courts and the financial and practical constraints faced by the courts (see Section 1.2). The choice to highlight these specific characteristics was made because in combination they are the dominant characteristics that distinguish international criminal justice from most domestic prosecutions.

Human rights standards

The body of human rights law offers an excellent interpretive tool for the examination and analysis of the procedural rights of individuals in international criminal proceedings.[88] Jackson notes that courts have been able to use a common human rights standard to develop procedural models that reach across the dominant common law and civil law traditions without necessarily preferring the norms of one system over another.[89] Using the ECtHR's interpretation of Article 6, which is applicable across the varied criminal justice systems of the Member States of the Council of Europe, he argues that international criminal justice institutions can do the same, although admitting that the latter is more difficult.[90] Adopting his approach, this study will examine what common human rights standards related to victim participation should be applied by international criminal institutions and how to shape participation when participatory standards conflict with other human rights standards such as fair trial

88 See Zappalá (2003); Andrews (1982); Emmerson, et al. (2007).

89 Jackson, J., Transitional Faces of Justice: Two Attempts to Build Common Standards beyond National Boundaries, 226, in Jackson, et al. (2008).

90 *Ibid.* at 224-225.

standards. In doing so, the analysis will also build upon Porat's theory in the field of constitutional law, which asks whether the balancing of individual rights and interests should take place.[91] He terms the widespread acceptance of the rhetoric of 'balancing' rights as the 'balancing consciousness' or the view that every problem can and should be solved through balancing conflicting considerations. This view, which he argues is shared by legal and non-legal thinkers, is misleading. It distorts the weight that should be afforded to various interests in law, at times unnecessarily *elevating* certain rights, and at other times, unnecessarily *lowering* them, depending on the case and the type of right.

For the purpose of this study, human rights standards will refer first and foremost to fair trial rights found both in human rights instruments as well as in international criminal court documents. This study will focus on those fair trial standards that most conflict with a victim's right to participate in proceedings, including the principles of equality of arms and legal certainty. Although other principles of law are affected through the inclusion of the victim in the criminal process, these two principles of law are closely related to human rights standards of fairness in the proceedings and they play an increasingly prominent role in the case law and academic literature related to victim participation. In addition, human rights standards will also refer to victims' participatory rights in the criminal process in as much as these rights can be viewed as rising to the level of a protected human right (see Section 1.3).

What is the proper scope and content of victim participation

The research carried out for this study is meant to be normative legal research. Normative research seeks to understand not only what criminal law is but also what shape it should take. 'Scope' refers to the range of factors that a subject, in this case, victim participation, deals with, and 'content' refers to specific aspects of participation within the criminal process. It is important to note that throughout this study the term 'victim' will be used to refer to individuals who have suffered direct and indirect physical, material, mental or emotional harm as the result of a crime. And within the context of criminal proceedings, a victim may participate as a complainant, civil party, private, subsidiary or auxiliary prosecutor, witness, or as a victim submitting a victim impact statement. This study may also refer to victims as injured parties as this term is also prevalent in many legal systems. Reference to victims as survivors will not be done due to the fact that the term 'survivors' has not been commonly used in legal texts either domestically or internationally although it is used in sociological and historical studies.[92] In its most basic sense, the term 'participation' refers to the "act of sharing or taking part."[93] Because participation is difficult to delineate, various conceptualiza-

91 See Porat (2005-2006).

92 Cf. Thomas, S. and Chy, T., Including the Survivors in the Tribunal Process, 214-293, in Ciorciari and Heindel (2009).

93 Edwards (2004) at 973.

tion will be explored and the most familiar groupings or models will be drawn upon in order to best describe the various forms of participation. Importantly, although this study will mainly focus on the procedural role for victims, attention will also be paid to service-related rights because these rights are very often interconnected with the notion of participation. Moreover, like procedural rights, they are increasingly being provided by criminal institutions to victims.

In international criminal proceedings

The choice to focus on international criminal proceedings stems from the fact that the inclusion of the victim within the international criminal law paradigm is relatively new and potentially affects millions of individuals affected by the crimes falling under the jurisdiction of the courts. In addition, similar to the domestic level, the various international criminal courts incorporating victim participation into their proceedings provide different levels of participatory rights. Even the various chambers within the same international criminal court interpret victim participatory provisions differently, affording dissimilar rights within the same court. These differences will be explored.

In addition to the primary research question discussed above, three sub-questions that this study will inevitably need to address include:

1. *To what extent can the right of victims to participate in criminal proceedings be classified as an existing or emerging human rights standard?*

Before examining victims' participatory rights at the international criminal law level it will first be necessary to clarify the scope of human rights protection related to participation within a traditional human rights context, i.e. between states and individuals. In determining whether and to what extent victims' participatory rights can be classified as an existing or emerging human rights standard, this study will rely on references to treaties, general principles of law and jurisprudence from human rights bodies and regional courts.

2. *What are the current models of victim participation and their practical application in international criminal proceedings?*

In order to determine the proper scope and content of victim participation in international criminal proceedings, it is first necessary to examine the existing participation models and their function in international criminal proceedings. Rather than being truly representative of any existing system, the models are meant to embody general categories of participation familiar to criminal justice systems.

3. *In light of the specific characteristics of international criminal proceedings, is the current scope and content of victim participation consistent with human rights standards?*

Before the study can answer the main research question it will also be necessary to address whether, in light of the specific characteristics of international criminal proceedings, the current scope and content of victim participation is consistent with human rights standards and general principles of law.

1.5 STRUCTURE

The structure of this study is broken up into two main parts. Part I, comprising Chapters 2-4, covers the origins and current role afforded to victims in domestic jurisdictions and the development of their procedural rights both domestically and internationally. Part II, comprising Chapters 5-7, deals exclusively with international criminal justice institutions and the participatory rights afforded to victims therein. Finally, conclusions and recommendations are provided for in Chapter 8.

The underlining subject of the research is the field of criminal justice generally and international criminal justice specifically. Thus, theories of criminal justice provide an important backdrop for understanding the current (and future) role of victims in criminal proceedings. Theories of criminal justice help to both *explain* criminal justice systems and their purpose in societies and *shape* criminal justice systems and how they operate in societies. Chapter 2 examines the three main theoretical frameworks for criminal justice, which all shed light on the roles provided to the accused and victims. These include the retributive framework, the utilitarian framework and the restorative framework. These three theoretical frameworks represent the major theories of criminal justice that have impacted those judicial systems that have been most influential on international criminal institutions and the procedures they apply. Moreover, as noted by Groenhuijsen, the issue of victims' rights in international criminal procedures cannot be fruitfully studied or understood without taking into account "the broader framework of the emancipation of crime victims in general."[94] For this reason, the chapter will also examine the important contribution made by the victims' rights movement and explore what it is that victims want from criminal justice systems.

The theoretical underpinnings of criminal justice must be understood against the backdrop of what actually occurs in regards to criminal law, the courts and the societies in which they operate. Therefore, Chapter 3 addresses the dominant legal traditions and criminal procedural approaches which have most influenced international criminal procedures. The chapter will bring attention to the various approaches scholars have adopted concerning the study of different legal traditions, including the influential

94 Groenhuijsen, M., Victims' Rights and the International Criminal Court: The Model of the Rome Statute and Its Operation, 300, in Van Genugten, et al. (2009).

scholarship of Packer, Damaška and Vogler. Rather than examine particular domestic legal systems and the role they afford to victims,[95] this study, instead, focuses on the various models of participation that exist amongst many legal systems. Therefore, after exploring conceptualizations of participation developed by Arnstein and Edwards, the main models through which victims can participate in domestic criminal proceedings will be explored. The models of participation include (i) complainant; (ii) witness; (iii) civil party; (iv) private or auxiliary prosecutor; and (v) impact statement provider. Linked to the dominant procedural approaches, these models are not mutually exclusive and can be complementary. Moreover, these conceptualizations and simplified models highlight the wide range of participatory rights afforded to victims in domestic criminal proceedings and are useful as a means through which to view the participatory rights afforded to victims at the international level.

Chapter 4 focuses on the growing attention paid to victim participation at the international level with regard to participation in domestic criminal proceedings. This chapter will show that at the international level, calls for greater victim-oriented measures have not necessarily provided for a more active role for victims in criminal proceedings than that already provided for under domestic jurisdictions. However, the emphasis on victim participation at the international level has provided for a broad standard to which states and international criminal courts should aspire to meet. The broad international standards on victim participation are usually couched in terms of human rights, applying to victims in criminal proceedings. It is therefore necessary to determine the parameters of these rights as deduced from international and regional bodies. With regard to regional bodies, although touching upon the African system, this study will focus on the European and Inter-American regional systems. This focus is largely due to the fact that human rights law emanating from these regional systems has significantly impacted domestic legal systems and the international criminal law legal system.

Part II of this study will focus exclusively on international criminal justice institutions. Before delving into the two main case studies, Chapter 5 touches upon the participatory roles afforded to victims at many of the international criminal courts. The Nuremberg and Tokyo military tribunals, the *Ad Hoc* Tribunals, the SCSL, the SPSC, the UNMIK/EULEX panels in Kosovo and the STL will all be examined. Chapter 5 will show that there has been a wide range of participatory roles afforded to victims at the international criminal law level, utilized to varying degrees by victims.

Building upon Chapter 5, Chapters 6 and 7 provide the bulk of the research of this study. Taking into account case law until 1 February 2011,[96] Chapter 6 is a case study of the ECCC and its approach to victim participation in its proceedings and Chapter 7

95 See, e.g., Heikkilä (2004) at 43-56, which focuses on the national jurisdictions of the United States of America, France and Finland.

96 Although these institutions continue to produce jurisprudence on victims' participation issues, the practices examined in this study shed light on common themes that all international criminal institutions adopting victim participation in their proceedings would encounter.

is a case study of the ICC and its approach to victim participation in its proceedings. The choice to focus on these two case studies is because in addition to the procedural rights afforded in their governing documents, unlike the other courts, they have produced a significant amount of jurisprudence on a breadth of issues related to victim participation. Moreover, there is an increasing amount of academic literature on these courts and their treatment of victims in the criminal process, which aids in understanding the different participatory roles provided to victims at the international level. The case studies shed light on the complex challenges of affording victims greater procedural rights in the international criminal process.

Chapter 8 provides conclusions and recommendations. It addresses the specific characteristics of international criminal proceedings which make participation in such proceedings decidedly different from participation in the domestic context and address concerns arising from the impact of participation on human rights standards in international criminal proceedings. It further address the central research question and seek to delimit in a broad sense what the proper scope and content of victim participation should be in international criminal proceedings. Chapter 8 concludes with some recommendations, which endeavor to promote respect for human rights standards within the field of international criminal law while taking into account other considerations relevant to courts.

1.6 Aim and Methodology

The aim of this study is threefold: (i) to describe, explain and clarify the procedural role afforded to victims in international criminal proceedings; (ii) to evaluate whether the current approaches to victim participation in international criminal proceedings are consistent with human rights standards; and (iii) to determine the proper scope and content of victim participation in international criminal proceedings.

With the exceptions of Chapter 2 and parts of Chapter 3, which adopt a more philosophical and theoretical approach, Chapters 4-7 look to existing legal systems, as sources of empirical material for determining how various systems interpret the rights of victims in the criminal process, and how these legal systems reconcile these rights with conflicting legal positions. This empirical material is used to the extent that it can show how one system addresses an issue versus how another system addresses the same issue but comes to a different conclusion. In relation to international criminal courts, this study strives to understand why solutions adopted in one system seem to function (or not) in another and what rationale the courts rely upon when deciding what works. However, although some comparisons will be made it is important to acknowledge that a true comparative method is not used given the difficulty (if not the impossibility) of such a study due to the differences amongst national legal systems and international criminal courts. Moreover, this study neither aims to test the conceptualization models presented in Chapter 3 nor has as its goal the development of a new conceptualization model for participation. Rather, this study seeks to test the practical application of victims' rights in international criminal proceedings and uses existing conceptualization models as a constructive reference and background framework.

Although most of the international criminal courts will be examined with regard to their victim participation schemes, two in particular are analyzed in detail: the ICC and the ECCC. These case studies allow for greater examination into the specific issues arising out of victim participation throughout all stages of the criminal process. As mentioned above, these case studies were selected because of all the international criminal courts allowing for victim participation these have produced the most jurisprudence on the subject, making it possible to research participation issues in more detail.

In addition to examining the proceedings of these courts in detail, this study explores victim participation in international criminal proceedings through a human rights framework (discussed above). The human rights paradigm within international criminal justice will provide for a specific normative setting through which victim participation at the international level can be evaluated. If opinions differ with regard to the procedural role of victims in proceedings, and they do, the normative human rights framework, within the unique context of international criminal proceedings, should help evaluate the importance of one argument over another, at times dispelling what Porat refers to as the *balancing consciousness*.

Owing to the breadth of sources on human rights and international criminal procedure, a variety of data sources have been used in the research for this study. First, since this study focuses on the procedures of international criminal courts, the statutes and rules of procedure and evidence of the various courts have been examined in detail. This examination included plain readings of the various texts and use of preparatory works, when available. Second, treaties, conventions, international custom, general principles, judicial decisions, and academic writings have also been explored.[97] Sources of law other than the hierarchy of sources mentioned in Article 38(1) of the Statute of the International Court of Justice have also been drawn upon, including, for example, UN Security Council resolutions, UN General Assembly resolutions and principles, resolutions and reports from inter-governmental organizations (IGO) and non-governmental organizations (NGO), reports and findings from human rights monitoring bodies, and judicial filings. As such, sources considered both 'hard law' and 'soft law' have been employed, with emphasis placed on the source's influence

97 As international criminal law is often said to be a part of public international law, the relevant sources of law outlined in Article 38(1) of the Statute of the International Court of Justice (ICJ) have been used. See also decisions of the Appeals Chambers from the ICTY and ICTR, embracing the classical sources of international law, ICTY, *Prosecutor v. Furundžija*, Case No. IT-95-17/1-A, Declaration of Judge Patrick Robinson, Appeals Chamber, 21 July 2000, footnote 10; *Prosecutor v. Aleksovski*, Case No. IT-95-14/1-A, Declaration of Judge David Hunt, Appeals Chamber, 24 March 2000, footnote 1; and *Prosecutor v. Erdemović*, Case No. IT-96-22-A, Joint and Separate Opinion of Judge McDonald and Judge Vorah, Trial Chamber I, 7 October 1997, par. 40.

in a particular field. Finally, observation and interviews have further aided the research.

With regard to observation, the bulk of the observation research can be categorized as participant-observation. Field research was carried out at the International Criminal Court where the author worked as a Visiting Professional for three months with the Office of Public Counsel for Victims and at the Extraordinary Chambers in the Courts of Cambodia. Here the author worked as a junior co-counsel on a legal team representing civil parties in the *Duch* trial.[98] Participant-observation is a qualitative method whose objective is to help researchers learn the perspectives held by study populations,[99] in this case, the international criminal courts. Informal conversations and interaction with staff and victims at the courts were important components of the method, which greatly added to the study. It was also useful as a means through which to gain a nuanced understanding of the contexts in which victims participate. A disadvantage of participant-observation, however, is that it is inherently a subjective exercise, which may jeopardize the requisite objectivity in carrying out academic research. It was therefore important to guard against personal biases when carrying out the observations.

Interviews, another qualitative method, were also employed. The interviews carried out were with court personnel at the ICC, the ECCC, and the STL, and they were done both formally and informally. Almost all interviews were conducted face-to-face. The interviewees were guaranteed anonymity with the hope that this would make them feel more comfortable about discussing challenges associated with victim participation. The interviews were meant to both elicit individual experiences as well as to identify group norms. For the purposes of this study the interviews are only meant to color the research findings and help shed light on the complexity of the issues under review.

The methodology of this study is undoubtedly a legal one, which carries with it aspects of interpretation, systematization and argumentation techniques.[100] Although the study will certainly attempt to describe and explain the current procedural role afforded to victims it will, as with most legal scholarship, also seek to establish what ought to be rather than just explaining the *status quo*. Hence, the foundation of the research is an examination into conflicting normative positions and arguments.

At the core of the arguments presented in this study, and ultimately at the core of all normative research, is that there is no one objective truth.[101] The conflict of norms is central both to the research and to the findings. If law is about conflicting normative positions then certainly there will be conflicting opinions about what the law should say since law basically boils down to competing ideas and arguments. Accordingly,

98 See ECCC, *Case of Kaing Guek Eav (Case 001)*, Judgment, Trial Chamber, 26 July 2010.

99 Mack, N., et al., Qualitative Research Methods: A Data Collector's Field Guide, Participant Observation, p. 13, *available at*: http://www.fhi.org/nr/rdonlyres/ed2ruznpftevg34lxuftzjiho65asz7betpqigb byorggs6tetjic367v44baysyomnbdjkdtbsium/participantobservation1.pdf.

100 Smits, J.M., Redefining Normative Legal Science: Towards an Argumentative Discipline, 45, in Coomans, et al. (2009).

101 *Ibid.* at 50.

this study holds the belief that legal research is an argumentative discipline and it becomes necessary to carefully consider which arguments are being put forward at any given time.

1.7 CONCLUSION

If it is accepted that fair procedures generally lead to equitable outcomes and if the notion of procedural justice is taken to mean both fairness of process and having a voice then it becomes essential to address the inclusion of the victim in international criminal justice processes in order to determine whether procedural justice is attainable or whether it is illusionary both for victims and accused.[102] Undoubtedly, the increased inclusion of the victim has changed the landscape of international criminal proceedings. Presently, the international courts are essentially acting as 'experimenting laboratories' in the sense that the are struggling to find the most appropriate way in which to incorporate victim participation without jeopardizing core functions and infringing upon the rights of the accused. It is still unknown exactly what impact these changes will have but already areas of concern have arisen, particularly with regard to reconciling competing rights and ensuring the effective and efficient operation of the court. Nevertheless, the importance of delimiting the appropriate scope of participation cannot be understated. International criminal courts were created to address issues of impunity for the gravest of crimes, and victims, together with their communities, are meant to be the direct beneficiaries of these justice processes. At the same time, however, international criminal courts are meant to be examples of institutions observing the right to a fair trial where human rights norms are upheld.

102 See generally, Rawls (1971); with regard to procedural justice and victims, see Wemmers (1996) at 148; see also Tyler and Lind (1992).

PART I

ORIGINS AND INFLUENCE

CHAPTER 2
VICTIMS AND THEORIES OF CRIMINAL JUSTICE

2.1 INTRODUCTION

Why is it important to examine the influence of criminal law theories and their approach towards victims? One response to this question is the fact that the adopted attitude on the purpose (or goal) of a criminal justice system or institution reflects the mind-set of the community in which the system or institution serves. The primary and auxiliary goals of a criminal justice system in turn affect the procedures that system or institution will implement in order to meet the purported aims. Therefore only once the proper aims and limits of criminal law within a specific system are understood can decisions about its internal structure be addressed and assessed.

Theories of criminal law seek to obtain, among other things, a better appreciation of the nature of law, legal systems and legal institutions. Theories help both to *explain* criminal justice systems and their purpose in societies and to *shape* criminal justice systems and how they actually operate in societies. In other words, theories attempt to clarify the philosophical motivations behind criminal justice practices and often inform the criminal procedures utilized by different justice systems. Generally the procedures applied by criminal justice systems are meant to further the overarching goals of that system.

Analytical theorists seek to identify and *explain* the central features of a system of criminal law and to develop a paradigm of criminal law from which others can recognize and compare. Normative theorists, on the other hand, seek to understand not only what criminal law is but also what *shape* it should take. Normative theorists wonder what goals criminal law should serve, what values it should have and what structure it should adopt. This chapter looks at both the analytical and normative approaches to criminal law theories. First, the two predominant traditional legal theories of retributivism and utilitarianism and the role of the victim within these theories will be examined. Given the fact that the traditional theories tend to marginalize the role afforded to victims, this chapter will then explore what it is that victims want from criminal justice systems and look at alternative theories that have been developed which seek to emphasize the needs and concerns of victims at the domestic level.

This chapter concludes by considering how the domestic theories of criminal justice apply at the international level. However, it is important to bear in mind that one of the major challenges in examining criminal theories as they pertain to international criminal law is that existing theories almost exclusively focus on the domestic criminal law of nation states. Although an entire book could be written on criminal law theory at the international level, this chapter merely hopes to highlight how the domestic theories aid in both *explaining* international criminal justice systems and their purpose in societies and *shaping* international criminal justice systems and how they operate in society. Said differently, this chapter aims to show how the various theories contribute to the current motivations and scope of international criminal law and procedure, with emphasis on the role of the victim in these processes.

2.2 Distinctions between Civil Litigation and Criminal Law

Before assessing the prominent criminal justice theories and their influence on the role of victims in criminal justice, it is first useful to distinguish civil law (or the law of tort) from criminal law and to recognize the substantive and procedural differences between the two types of law. This distinction is important for two reasons. First, there are fundamental differences between the two types of law and how they approach a wrong. Second, almost all modern legal systems, both national and international, differentiate civil wrongs from criminal violations. To better understand the problems arising from the existing overlap between civil and criminal law, conceptualizing the differences between these types of law is crucial.

Domestic jurisdictions usually treat civil wrongs as 'private' matters in that they are initiated directly by the victim against an alleged wrongdoer. Although the state may provide for the institutions through which the victim can bring a case, the laws and standards by which it will be adjudicated or settled, establish the remedies available and often help in the collection of damages from the persons determined to be responsible for the harm, it is, nonetheless, the responsibility of the injured party to pursue a case. It is considered part of the private realm because if the individual chooses not to pursue a case the state will not interfere. Accordingly, the civil paradigm places greater emphasis on the harm suffered by the victim and on how to repair that harm.

In contrast, modern criminal law is situated in the public realm and is based on a public investigation, public prosecution and publicly administered punishment.[1] The state must first identify the crimes which, if committed, will be publically sanctioned. In doing so, the state must explain, with specificity, the requirements of the mental state of the offender, and the justifications for punishment, or in certain circumstances, the reasons why punishment is not appropriate.[2] The state institution acts not only in the name of the individual victim harmed by the crime but also on behalf of the entire community. The prosecuting authority will not always have the same interests as the individual victim because the state will always represent interests which are broader than those of the individual.[3] Regardless of whether the victim wants to pursue a

1 However, it was only in the eighteenth century when the state took over the role of prosecutor, see Strang (2002) at 4-5.
2 Ripstein (1999) at 133.
3 Davis (2007) at 66.

prosecution, once a crime is reported, it is the public authority, acting on behalf of the victim and the larger community, which seeks to hold someone criminally responsible. As a result, the criminal paradigm places greater emphasis on the wrong that has been committed and on whether an individual should be found accountable for that wrong and punished.

Additionally, the punishments that follow a finding of guilt differ significantly from the damages that are awarded following a verdict in a civil case. Private law does not result in any penal sanctions on the part of the wrongdoer. Instead, if the alleged wrongdoer is found responsible he is usually made to "make the victim whole again" through monetary or non-monetary compensation. Moreover, because there is no threat of the loss of liberty, the standards of proof are generally lower in civil wrongs as compared with criminal cases.[4] Criminal cases differ from civil cases in that they result in either a conviction or an acquittal of the accused. If the defendant is convicted then he will likely face some sort of punishment in the penal system or a punitive fine. Even when criminal trials and civil trials result in the same fine, the reasons behind imposing the fines differ. Civil damages are almost always meant to be proportional to the harm suffered whereas criminal fines are meant to be punitive and proportional to the seriousness of the crime and culpability of the defendant.[5]

Despite these differences, as mentioned above, there is a substantive and procedural overlap between the two types of law. For example acts such as murder and rape (and their counterparts in international criminal law) can substantively fall under both civil and criminal law. These acts both harm an individual and violate a society's norms by offending the moral values of a community; therefore, having both an individual and public dimension. Examples of procedural overlap include the possibility of private prosecutions for certain crimes,[6] allowing victims of crime to join their civil case for damages in a criminal trial,[7] and handing down punitive damages in civil courts.[8] As noted by Doak:

> Whatever the historical explanations for the de facto distinctions between public and private realms of law, the distinction has been artificial since its inception in the Middle Ages. Indeed, a closer look at the actual nature of individual crimes and torts suggests that it is not so easy to separate neatly the public from the private interests. [...] Civil

4 In the United States for example, the standard of proof in criminal cases is proof 'beyond a reasonable doubt' whereas in civil cases the standard of proof is based on a 'preponderance of the evidence'.

5 Punishment in criminal matters is meant to be proportional both to the seriousness of the wrong and the intention of the wrongdoer; see Ripstein (1999) at 140.

6 For examples of European criminal law systems which allow private prosecutions, see Brienen and Hoegen (2000).

7 For examples of European criminal law systems which allow the *partie civile* system, see Brienen and Hoegen (2000).

8 Punitive damages in civil cases have a long history dating back to the Code of Hammurabi, see Belli (1980-1981) at 2.

> and criminal liability are each based on overlapping concepts of fault, recklessness and strict liability [...].[9]

However, the differences that exist between the public aspect of criminal trials and the private character of civil trials are reflective of the processes and outcomes of justice institutions. Therefore, despite the overlap, distinctions between the two areas of law are important because it is these differences that inform the procedures applied by justice systems. What is clear is that the entirety of a criminal case is focused on the wrong committed, standing in contrast to civil cases which often place a greater focus on the harm suffered. In proceedings that incorporate these two divergent focal points, finding an acceptable balance between the goals of criminal justice and the goals of civil liability remains a challenge both at the domestic and international level.

Now that the two paradigms have been distinguished and the inherent overlap acknowledged it is necessary to examine the various theories of criminal law and how these theories have contributed to the current role afforded to victims at the national and international level.

2.3 Traditional Theories of Criminal Justice: Where Do Victims Fit In?

Although criminology has for centuries focused on theories of punishment, most modern theories of criminal law have transcended this narrow view and expanded with comprehensive theories of criminal justice generally.[10] This section, therefore, examines comprehensive theories of criminal justice and not merely theories of punishment – although the two are closely related. The shift from punishment to broader justice theories better reflects the current conception of criminal law and judicial systems. As a result, criminal law theory, as Lacey aptly points out:

> [...] stretches from relatively technical discussion of the fundamental tenets of and issues within criminal law doctrine, through more abstract attempts to conceptualize the general framework within which that doctrine operates, to historical analyses of the development of criminal justice ideologies and practices and normative arguments about the proper or ideal shape of that conceptual framework in a liberal, socialist, or other form of political society.[11]

The theories of criminal justice discussed below all deal with different approaches of conceptualizing criminal law and criminal justice institutions. That is, should criminal law be utilized as a means to achieve some broader aims or is criminal law an end in

9 Doak (2005) at 300.

10 For the purpose of this study, justice responses at the national level range from family conferencing and mediation to criminal trials, and justice responses at the international level range from truth and reconciliation commissions to criminal trials.

11 Lacey, N., Contingency, Coherence, Conceptualism, 12, in Duff (1998).

itself? How should crime be conceived and, most importantly for this study, what structures should be adopted in order to achieve a purported goal?

Traditional criminal law theories can be categorized into two philosophical groupings, consequentialist theories and non-consequentialist theories.[12] The difference between the groupings is significant because the differences are based on their focus and goals. The consequentialist grouping is forward-looking in that the theories that fall within this grouping focus on the future consequences of the punishment following a finding of guilt. The non-consequentialist grouping is backward-looking in that these theories are solely interested in the past acts and mental states of the perpetrator.[13] The following sections will first examine the two traditional theories of retributivism and utilitarianism, which have dominated criminal justice dialogue, and how they conceptualize the role of the various actors in the criminal process.

2.3.1 Retributivism

Retributivism is the primary theory falling within the non-consequentialist grouping. Retributive justice emphasizes the imposition of punishment for offenders because it is deserved due to the commission of a crime. The retributive school of justice asserts the traditional justification for punishment in criminal trials which is that punishment is justified as an end in itself, emphasizing the link between punishment and moral wrongdoing.[14] Essentially, an individual deserves punishment if he commits a wrongful act, encapsulating the notion of punishment for "just deserts."[15] A Kantian imperative is implicitly found in the word 'deserts' in that certain things are wrong and ought to be punished.[16] In contrast to consequentialist theories, retributivists argue that criminal institutions, which pronounce upon the wrongful act, should "produce morally correct decisions regardless of ultimate effects on society."[17] In this sense, retribution conveys a society's condemnation of the criminal act in question and of the perpetrator found guilty.[18] The theory is backward-looking in that it looks back at the

12 See Duff (2001).

13 Cf. Cottingham (1979) at 240: "A retrospective or backward-looking element in a theory is never normally characterized as 'retributive'; it is only in the literature on punishment that these two notions are muddled [...];" See also, Fatić (1995) at 9.

14 Heikkilä (2004) at 23; Fatić (1995) at 9, noting that the theory is often linked to morality.

15 Cf. Dubber (2005) at 697, citing Binding, K., Das Problem der Strafe in der heutigen Wissenschaft, 1 *Strafrechtliche und Strafprozessuale Abhandlungen* 61, 84 (1915) (Binding argued that crime is a violation of a positive law rather than of a wrongful act generally and that the purpose of punishment is to maintain the authority of the laws violated; in other words punishment is justified when a state norm is violated).

16 Braithwaite and Pettit (1990) at 6, citing Gaylin, W. and Rothman, D., Introduction, xxxix, in Von Hirsch, A., *Doing Justice*, Northeastern University Press (1976).

17 Luna (2003) at 216.

18 ICTY, *Prosecutor v. Aleksovski*, Case No. IT-95-14/1-A, Appeal Judgment, Appeals Chamber, 24 March 2000, par. 185.

wrong action in order to explain why an individual deserves punishment.[19] Retributive criminal justice systems assess punishment based on the seriousness of the crime and the mental state of the offender.[20] Therefore, disproportionate punishment based on the likelihood of recidivism is frowned upon,[21] as is disproportionate punishment based on forgiveness or revenge.

It is noteworthy to mention that retributive theories vary in scope and justification.[22] Moore, for example, argues a rather pure form of retributivism, submitting that criminal law should be understood functionally in that its purpose is to achieve retributive justice through punishing "only those who are morally culpable in the doing of some morally wrongful action."[23] Thus, he argues that criminal law has no use beyond the punishment of individuals for immoral conduct. Others view punishment as an emotional response to crime that is both natural and acceptable,[24] as a form of sanctioned revenge,[25] or as a form of communication to the offender, victim and larger society.[26] With regard to communication, where the offender once dominated the victim, the criminal justice system can now pronounce upon the guilt of the accused and acknowledge the suffering of the victim, thereby restoring the victim's moral worth.[27]

However, in systems based on the rule of law, the state cannot simply punish individuals without some formal process. Therefore, judicial retributivism, the most commonly accepted form of state retribution, requires publicly promulgated procedures and due process guarantees.[28] This focus on due process rights is at the heart of a retributive system which emphasizes punishing only those individuals who have committed a wrong.[29] The practical consequences of implementing the goals of retributive justice theories are that retributive systems "often strictly adhere to the ideas of state punishment and fair procedures for the accused."[30] Therefore, during criminal proceedings the rights of the accused and the notion of impartiality of the decision-maker are emphasized.

---

19 Whiteley (1998) at 42.

20 Heikkilä (2004) at 26; Fatić (1995) at 17.

21 See Cottingham (1979).

22 Ten (1987) at 38; Braithwaite and Pettit (1990) at 156-181; see also Luna (2003) at 217; Moore (1999-2000) at 67, comparing standard-issue retributivism with victim-oriented retributivism.

23 Moore (1997) at 35.

24 Luna (2003) at 217.

25 Moore, M., The Moral Worth of Retributivism, 216, in Schoeman (1987); on punishment as sanctioned revenge, see Murphy, J.G., Retributive hatred: an essay on criminal liability and the emotions, 353, in Frey and Morris (1991).

26 Fletcher (1994) at 109-110.

27 *Ibid.* at 110.

28 Oldenquist (1988) at 474.

29 Barnett (1977) at 284: "The slow, ponderous nature of our system of justice is largely due to a fear of an unjust infliction of punishment on the innocent (or even on the guilty)."

30 Heikkilä (2004) at 26.

Despite the widespread acceptance of retributive practices, there are many critics of the non-consequentialist approach. Some critics argue that because the theories are based largely on moral grounds (legal violations arguably are linked with a society's moral values) it is almost impossible to come to any widespread acceptance of morality since moral values change over time.[31] Furthermore, critics argue that retributive justice theories simply constitute sanctioned revenge and that they fail to take into consideration traditional values important in human relationships, such as reconciliation, mercy, compassion and forgiveness.[32] Cragg, a critic of retributive theories, notes:

> Retributive justice stresses impartiality. This is one of its strengths [...]. The effect, however, is to depersonalize the process. Justice on this account is concerned with wrongs and not with persons, except in so far as they are the perpetrators of wrongs. However, the inability to focus on the individuals involved blinds justice to the crime's victim as well as to the personal characteristics of the offender. [...] It distances justice from those intense emotions that can distort an objective assessment of guilt and the nature of the offence. This means [...] that the victim loses his central role in the drama whose focus is the wrong committed and not the person wronged.[33]

Therefore, although the entire process begins once an individual (the perpetrator) commits a wrong against another individual (the victim), as a whole, retributive theories are not victim-centered. Retributive theories view punishment as a response to a wrong and not a response to the harm experienced by the victim.[34] Rather than focusing on the subjective suffering of the victim, the punishment focuses on the objective element of the act itself so as to avoid disparate sentencing of similarly situated defendants. This is also due, in part, because the victim's suffering is difficult to measure and can be disproportionate to the crime.

As a defender of the traditional, retributive approach, Hall supports the view that a victim's suffering should have little influence on trial procedures and sentencing. He provides a useful example of how the active participation of victims in a domestic system may lead to disparate sentencing practices by presenting a hypothetical situation in which a defendant, a 22-year-old educated white female with no criminal record, drives while intoxicated and kills a 10-year-old boy riding his bicycle.[35] The case is heard in a court which allows the parents of the deceased victims an opportunity to actively participate during the sentencing phase of the criminal process. He then adumbrates varying hypothetical situations.

In the first situation the parents are well-educated and active in the process, refusing to allow a negotiated plea, asking that the maximum penalty be imposed, and demonstrating a profound grief to the judge deciding the case. The defendant is

31 *Ibid.*
32 Cragg (1992) at 18-19.
33 *Ibid.* at 19.
34 Heikkilä (2004) at 26-27.
35 See Hall (1990-1991).

sentenced to five years – the maximum. In the second scenario, the parents have only a mediocre education, they are unable to express their grief in an articulate or organized way, and they cannot appear at the sentencing hearing because they will lose their jobs if they leave work. The defendant is sentenced to two years. In the third situation, the parent of the victim is a single mom who has a history of mental instability. She was distraught by the loss of her only child but relocated from the city in which the accident occurred. The prosecutor could not locate her, the case ended on a plea agreement and the defendant received a sentence of one year. Finally, in the fourth scenario, the parents of the victim are very religious and decide not to seek punishment of the accused. Instead they request probation, which is granted. In all of the illustrated cases, the actual harm to the victim and the defendant's culpability are identical; only the "victim's voice" varies, leading to a range of sentences for the defendant.[36]

According to Hall, the various outcomes are unacceptable, both from a policy perspective and because it introduces an element of arbitrariness into the process. He asserts that neither revenge nor forgiveness of the victim should play a role.[37] Instead, Hall advances the argument that a criminal offender should "be held accountable for those harms intended, or those within the realm of reasonable foreseeable consequences to the victim."[38] Therefore, in his view, the criminal process, while allowing for participation on some matters, should carefully evaluate participation measures that affect the disparity of treatment of the accused.[39]

The above example highlights one argument for excluding the victim's voice from actively influencing procedures, such as sentencing. This exclusion is one of the most important reasons why retributive justice theories are not considered victim-centered. Retributive theorists hardly ever enter into a dialogue about the role of the victim in the criminal process. For these theorists, the wrongfulness of the deed depends on the act itself and the offender's state of mind, or put in legal terms, the *actus reus* and *mens rea*. The degree of guilt and punishment should not vary with the identity of the victim.[40] It is the accused individual's actions, and not the suffering of the victim, that are on trial. If the accused person has intentionally committed the wrong then that person should be proportionately punished.

Nothing in the retributive theories suggests that victims need to be given a central, procedural role in proceedings; rather it is quite the opposite. Moore, for instance, contends that retributivists require a norm violation in order to justify punishment and this is the point at which victims play a role. According to Moore, "[h]ow much wrong

---

36 The example by Hall is notably an American criminal law example but the situation could equally occur in civil law jurisdictions where the court allows the victim to comment upon the impact of the crime in order to properly determine the sentence.

37 Moore (1999-2000) at 77.

38 Hall (1990-1991) at 256.

39 *Ibid.* at 258.

40 Cragg (1992) at 16-17.

was done depends on how many times the norm was violated, and this depends in part on how many victims are involved."[41] The victims are therefore at the center of the norm violation – which is the core of the criminal law. In this sense, victims are important to the process as information providers about the norm violation. Moore argues that the substantive role of victims in retributive theory does not, however, justify any procedural role for them in the criminal trial process, aside from providing testimony as a witness.[42] In other words, "[a] procedural conclusion does not follow from the substantive premise."[43] Too great a procedural role for victims could be seen as an infringement on the rights of the accused and the fairness of proceedings either because it introduces arbitrariness into the proceedings or because it can influence the impartiality of the decision maker.

Nevertheless, not all retributivists agree. Fletcher argues that "doing justice to victims should be part of the theory of retributive punishment."[44] More specifically, he argues that the *suffering* of victims should be a more central part of the process and accordingly that a procedural role for victims should flow from their substantive role (as information providers for example) so that they can share their suffering with the court. Fletcher, however, does not address concerns about arbitrariness or impartiality that may flow from a greater victim's voice in the process. Therefore, despite his calls for a greater role for victims within retributive theories, retributive justice systems generally do not provide for a central role for victims in proceedings. In fact, a central role could undermine the rights of an accused individual because the focus would be on the harm experienced by the victim rather than on the alleged wrong that took place, leading to disparate sentencing or fair trial violations.

2.3.2 Utilitarianism

Utilitarianism is the primary consequentialist theory. The utilitarian school regards criminal justice as an appropriate means to a justifiable end and views deterrence, prevention, reform and/or imprisonment as the main objectives of criminal justice.[45] Unlike retributive justice theories, which are backward-looking, utilitarian theories are forward-looking because they focus on the benefits of criminal justice, such as the predictability of punishment as a consequence of a wrongful act.[46] Moreover, utilitarian theories are forward-looking because they seek to reduce the occurrence and gravity of crime in society. For example, society should punish offenders in order to

41 Moore (1999-2000) at 71.
42 *Ibid.* at 72.
43 *Ibid.* at 73.
44 Fletcher (1999-2000) at 55.
45 Heikkilä (2004) at 23.
46 Fatić (1995) at 1.

prevent future crimes, thereby serving the common good.[47] Utilitarian theories assert that the imposition of criminal sanctions may serve a number of goals, including:

1) specific deterrence (deterring the specific defender from committing future crimes)
2) general deterrence (deterring others from committing future crimes)
3) rehabilitation (rehabilitating the specific offender from committing future crimes)
4) incapacitation (disabling the specific offender from committing future crimes).[48]

Specific deterrence assumes that the specific offender is sufficiently rational to carry out a cost-benefit analysis of committing a crime and the punishment that may ensue. General deterrence assumes the rationality of individuals in a community in that the punishment of one individual will serve as an example to others in the community not to commit the same crime. Rehabilitation serves to treat the offender in the hope that the offender can re-enter society as a law-abiding citizen, and finally, incapacitation prevents an offender from committing another crime by keeping the offender (temporarily) locked away from society.[49] The various utilitarian theories depart from one another when having to decide what good consequences criminal justice in fact produces. However, reduction of crime, often through deterrence, is almost always an important consequence of punishment in utilitarian justice theory models.[50] Consequently, measures targeting both specific deterrence, targeted at individual offenders, and general deterrence, targeted at the public, are central to utilitarian theories.[51]

Within this consequentialist theory, often referred to as instrumental theory, there are differences between pure instrumentalists and non-pure instrumentalists. The pure instrumentalists seek to explain aspects of a justified criminal justice system in pure consequentialist terms. They only ask which doctrines, practices and rules will efficiently serve the articulated goals. In contrast, non-pure instrumentalists take into account non-consequentialist values and argue that requirements of justice may preclude some practices even if those practices would efficiently serve the system's goals. The "proper structure" of a criminal justice system, for pure instrumentalists, depends on studies into how the goals can be most efficiently met, whereas for non-pure instrumentalists issues outside of the system must also be taken into consideration, such as the gravity of the crimes or fair trial rights.

A purely instrumentalist approach to criminal law faces criticism in that it fails to properly take into account individuals and their rights. Such critics argue that the pure instrumentalist approach too easily sacrifices the individual to the needs/concerns of

47 Dubber (2005) at 699-703, explaining the German theory of punishment: "positive general prevention" or positive Generalprävention, which seeks to prevent crime by bolstering the law abidingness of the population.
48 Luna (2003) at 209.
49 *Ibid.*
50 Ten (1987) at 7.
51 *Ibid.*

the greater community. Non-pure instrumentalists would argue that justice requires the acknowledgment of individual rights in the criminal process but that the emphasis should still be on the broader goals of deterrence or rehabilitation. Regardless of these differences, both the pure instrumentalists and the non-pure instrumentalists believe that the justification for criminal law and criminal justice institutions lies in their beneficial effects for society.

Critics of utilitarian theories argue: (1) that empirical studies do not support the argument that the deterrent effect actually works to curb crime; (2) that punishment often reflects the broader goals of criminal law rather than reflecting the seriousness of the crime, leading to un-proportionate penalties, i.e., harsh punishments for petty crimes to encourage deterrence, for example; (3) that the theories fail to answer why an innocent person should not be punished if the punishment has a positive result on society or that individual; and (4) the theories rest on the premise that individuals are rational thinkers, which often is not the case.[52] Opponents of utilitarian theories also question whether incapacitation and deterrence achieve their stated goals.[53] Arguably, there are too many assumptions surrounding the notion that increased incapacitation will decrease crime and increase social utility, such as the assumptions that others will not commit the crimes in the absence of the offender, that the offender will in fact reoffend if not incarcerated or that crime does not occur within incarceration facilities.[54] As with incapacitation, the deterrence theory is problematic for the mere fact that offenders often do not carry out risk-benefit analysis or if they do they simply decide that a short-term gain outweighs the chance of long-term detention. Moreover, some offenders commit crimes not for tangible rewards but instead for intangible ends such as respect or attention.[55]

Another criticism leveled against utilitarianism is the fact that practices may not be in accordance with the principles of fairness and justice.[56] Utilitarian theories reject the idea that individual rights should "trump" certain security interests of a community.[57] Instead, under pure utilitarianism individual rights may be sacrificed or marginalized so as to promote the "common good" (however defined). As a result, the procedural safeguards, such as due process and fair trial rights, may not take precedence. Along the same lines, there is no emphasis on the pursuit of truth or protection of innocence – legal principles which arguably should be central to any criminal legal theory.[58]

Problematic from the position of the accused, classical utilitarian theories are also problematic from the victim's perspective. This has to do with the fact that, like

52 Luna (2003) at 210-215; Fatić (1995) at 87.

53 Luna (2003) at 211.

54 *Ibid.*

55 *Ibid.* at 212, citing Katz, J., *Seductions of Crime: Moral and Sensual Attractions in Doing Evil*, 80-110, Basic Books (1988).

56 *Ibid.* at 213.

57 Cf., Dworkin (1977) at 190-191.

58 Luna (2003) at 215.

retributive theories, utilitarian theories do not directly allow for a central role for the victim. Heikkilä notes that "the goals of deterrence, prevention, reformation, incapacitation and education are all society-oriented and/or offender-oriented."[59] Therefore, under classical utilitarian theories the interests of society or of the offender will always take precedence over those of the victim. Importantly, utilitarian theories view society as the victim of crime in addition to the victimized individual.[60] This classical form of criminal justice therefore focuses on the accused and on society in criminal proceedings, rather than on the victim's suffering. As a result, many criminal justice systems, which incorporate utilitarian beliefs and structures, often fail to focus on victims in criminal proceedings.[61]

2.4 Reforming Criminal Justice Institutions

The two traditional criminal justice theories discussed above, and the retributive theory in particular, have found wide support around the world. The focus is on the crime and society, with less emphasis on the individual victim. However, in the late 1960s and early 1970s the idea that victims, like accused, should have greater rights within national criminal justice systems began to surface. Throughout much of the world, researchers, policy-makers, those working with victims and victims themselves all voiced their concern over the disregard of the victim in the criminal process.[62] Social movements centered on victims of crime began to mobilize at local and national levels and the notion that there should be a greater focus on victims gradually developed into what became known collectively as the victims' rights movement.[63] Parallel with the growth of national victims' rights movements, academics around the world began studying victims and crime. This field of study soon became known as victimology. The growth of victimology as a distinct discipline, which began in earnest in the 1970s,[64] has played a profound role in the achievements related to victims and criminal justice reform at the domestic level.

One of the first objectives of national victims' movements was the creation of state compensation schemes but soon these movements articulated broader goals.[65] Depend

59 Heikkilä (2004) at 31.

60 *Ibid.* at 32.

61 *Ibid.* at 33, noting that these theories of criminal justice are not the only reasons why justice systems marginalize victims because historical and societal developments also play a role.

62 A number of surveys revealed displeasure with the criminal justice system, see, e.g., Shapland, et al. (1985) at 3, citing, amongst others, Knudten, R.D., et al., *Victims and Witnesses: Their Experiences with Crime and the Criminal Justice System*, National Institute of Law Enforcement and Criminal Justice (1977).

63 Tobolowsky (1999) at 21, referencing Carrington, F. and Nicholson, G., The Victims' Movement: An Idea Whose Time Has Come, 11 *Pepperdine Law Review* 1, 1-5 (1984).

64 Aldana-Pindell (2004) at 614-615.

65 Shapland, et al. (1985) at 1-2, noting that state compensation schemes were set up in New Zealand in 1963 and England, Scotland and Wales in 1964, followed by victim support schemes offering practical and emotional support to victims in the 1970s. Importantly, most state compensation schemes operate

ing upon the domestic context, the various national movements were closely aligned with the social welfare reform movements, the conservative "law and order" response to the social welfare reform movements and importantly the women's movement.[66] These seemingly contradictory interest groups,[67] from which the various victims' movements were largely born out of, provide insight into why the victims' rights movement (collectively speaking) is so varied and successful across the world.[68]

Victims' rights campaigners assert that victims are re-victimized by the very judicial systems that are designed to protect and support them, and argue that government institutions must do more to address their needs and concerns. At its most basic level, the victims' rights movement advocates for improved *service-related* and *procedural* rights through greater protection, participation and reparation.[69] Increased victim support in the form of protective measures, medical and psychological services and information services are all considered service-related rights whereas victims

---

based on an "ideal victim" image, which generally means that state funds only go to victims who are completely free of any wrongdoing, see Joutsen (1987) at 32.

66 Heikkilä (2004) at 35; Dignan (2005) at 14-16.

67 Dubber comments on the "absence of a coherent theory underlying the victims' rights movement" and refers to it as a "manifestation of a communal self-protective reflect or impulse," see Dubber (1999) at 7.

68 Davis (2007) at 64; in the United States, between 1982 and 2004 Congress adopted at least seven pieces of victims' rights legislation, see O'Hear (2006a) at 1, citing the Victims and Witness Protection Act of 1982, the Victims of Crime Act of 1984, the Victims' Rights and Restitution Act of 1990, the Violent Crime Control and Law Enforcement Act of 1994, the Antiterrorism and Effective Death Penalty Act of 1996, the Victim Rights Clarification Act of 1997, and the Crime Victims' Rights Act of 2004. In Europe, as part of a campaign to improve the position of victims in criminal justice systems, in 1985 the Committee of Ministers of the Council of Europe adopted Recommendation (85)11 on the Position of the Victim in the Framework of Criminal Law and Procedure. Other measures include Resolution (77)27 on compensation of victims of crime, the European Convention on the compensation of victims of violent crime, and Recommendation (87)21 on assistance to victims and the prevention of victimization. In addition, in 2001 the European Union's Council Framework Decision on the standing of victims in criminal proceedings was passed, requiring all European Union Member States to adopt certain procedures aimed at improving the position of victims. Interestingly, the vast majority of those who campaign for victims rights do not necessarily represent the average victims of crime. In the United States, for example, one survey found that the overwhelming majority of victim advocates are white, female, middle-aged with over half having a college education, see Weed (1995) at 117. Moreover, these victims tend to be more in favor of retributive responses to crime than the average victim, see Beckett and Sasson (2004) at 145-146.

69 Van Dijk breaks the victims' movement into four ideologies: care ideology (believes that the community should assist the victim with trauma, stress and financial needs); rehabilitation ideology (focuses on restitution, restoration, and mediation between the victim and offender); retribution ideology (calls for proportional punishment of the wrongdoer); and the abolitionist ideology (calls for a smaller role for traditional criminal justice institutions and a larger role for victims in the process), see Joutsen (1987) at 51-52, citing Van Dijk, J.J.M., Introductory Report at the Council of Europe's 16th Criminological Research Conference, Research on Victimization (1986), p. 9-12; Groenhuijsen argues that it is necessary to transcend the rights model and service model and embrace a holistic approach based on participation, protection and reparation, see Groenhuijsen, M., Victims' Rights and the International Criminal Court: The Model of the Rome Statute and Its Operation, 304, in Van Genugten, et al. (2009).

having a greater say in the decision-making processes related to their case or some type of standing/acknowledgment before the court to share their views and concerns are considered procedural rights. Regardless of whether victims' concerns are grouped into service and procedural models or whether they are grouped under the headings of protection, participation and reparation, the various tactics adopted by the movement can be broken down into three general approaches: (1) one which aims at ameliorating the situation for victims without hampering the existing functioning of criminal courts; (2) one which works on elevating the status of victims before criminal courts by granting them certain procedural rights which would affect the functioning of criminal courts; and (3) one which advocates for non-criminal proceedings with victim-centered approaches.[70]

The first approach focuses on support mechanisms such as rape crisis centers and mental health services, and pushes for legislative reform like privacy laws for victims of crime. The second approach is generally considered the most controversial. It can be broken further down into two methodologies. The first methodology is a non-punitive tactic in that it attempts to change existing criminal systems by making them more victim-friendly without making them less defendant-friendly. This tactic suggests that victims and accused should have minimum guarantees of justice and participatory rights in criminal proceedings. It argues that victims should be protected from the accused, they should be notified of proceedings, have the right to be heard during proceedings,[71] the right to restitution and the right to be treated fairly and to have respect for their privacy. The second methodology is a punitive tactic, in that it attempts to make the criminal system less defendant-friendly.[72] This tactic questions why accused individuals are afforded more rights than victims.[73] Finally, the third approach reflects the theory of restorative justice, which will be discussed below. It stresses victim and offender participation outside of the typical criminal justice process and its emphasis is on addressing the harm suffered by the victim rather than the crime committed. Importantly, the victims' rights movement's arguments, which can be found in all three approaches, and which generally argue that justice should not only punish the offender but should also provide to the offended, resonated with many policy makers. But what is it, exactly, that victims want from criminal justice systems?

70 Heikkilä (2004) at 35.

71 In common law jurisdictions this generally means proceedings related to release, plea agreements, and sentencing and in civil law jurisdictions this generally means throughout the pre-trial, trial and appeals relating mainly to reparation requests.

72 Heikkilä (2004) at 35, citing Karmen, A., Crime Victims: An Introduction to Victimology, 20, Brooks/Cole Publishing (1984); For commentators who argue that defendants have too many rights, see the colloquium "Do Criminal Defendants have too many rights?" 33 *American Criminal Law Review* 1193 (1996).

73 This branch spearheaded a number of conservative campaigns resulting, for example, in mandatory sentencing guidelines in the United States.

2.5 VICTIMS' INTERESTS: WHAT DO VICTIMS WANT?

The scholarship of social psychology sheds light on answering the question, *what do victims want from criminal justice systems?* Building upon Thibaut and Walker's influential study from the mid-1970s on procedural justice,[74] research indicates that individuals affected by criminal justice processes determine fairness (of a legal system for example) by how fair and satisfactory they consider the outcomes they receive (distributive justice) *and* how fair and satisfactory they consider the procedures used to reach those outcomes (procedural justice).[75] In fact, studies suggest that procedural justice may even be more important than distributive justice because in general individuals value process control irrespective of the outcomes they receive.[76] Thus, in addition to the outcome of a judicial matter, individuals, including victims, are concerned with the procedural justice they receive, and research on procedural fairness indicates that having a 'voice' in the process is associated with an increased perception of fairness.

The benefits of procedural justice include increased satisfaction with the process and greater acceptance of the outcomes.[77] In addition, O'Hear argues that when individuals (or consumers) of the justice process are treated fairly the legitimacy of the judicial institutions and the role of the authority are enhanced.[78] For a victim, procedural justice may refer to a broad range of available support services as well as procedural rights in proceedings.[79] Thus, the research on victims within the criminal justice process generally shows that in order to view proceedings as fair and satisfactory they want: (i) to be treated with dignity and respect; (ii) to be notified about important developments and informed about their rights; (iii) to receive victim support; (iv) to receive protection from the accused; (v) to attend and participate in proceedings

---

74 See Thibaut and Walker (1975); their work set up two criteria of justice: decision control and process control. Decision control refers to the amount of influence an individual has on the outcome. Process control refers to the amount of influence an individual has on the process by which the outcome is derived. Their research showed that individuals were willing to forgo decision control so long as they maintained process control.

75 See Lind and Tyler (1988); building upon Thibaut and Walker's work, Lind and Tyler assert that if individuals view procedures as fair, they are less resistant to unfavorable outcomes; and having a "voice" is one of the main components of procedural justice; Van den Bos et al. (1997a), their findings indicated that what people judge to be fair is strongly affected by initial information received than by subsequently received information; Van den Bos, et al. (1997b), this study highlighted the fact that in many situations individuals find it difficult to assess whether their outcome was fair or unfair because they do not know the outcomes of others and therefore cannot make a comparison. In such situations, individuals use the fairness of the procedure as a way in which to measure their own outcomes.

76 See Lind and Tyler (1988).

77 See Greenberg (1987); Tyler and Lind (1992); Lind and Tyler (1988); Tyler (1989); see also Koper, G., et al. (1993).

78 See O'Hear (2008).

79 For an accused, procedural justice may refer to his due process and fair trial rights or his ability to negotiate a plea agreement.

in order to have their voices heard; (vi) to receive reparation; and (vii) to receive legal assistance.[80]

To be treated with dignity and respect

Numerous studies from a variety of legal systems demonstrate that victims often feel they are being treated unfairly and without respect.[81] The terms "secondary victimization" and "re-victimization" refer to the trauma victims experience when they feel that they are being disrespected or unfairly treated in the criminal process after having already suffered as a result of the crime.[82] In an attempt to address secondary victimization, one of the central themes of the victims' movement has been the need for greater dignity, respect and recognition for victims in the criminal justice process.[83] In a European study, Joutsen concluded that "the major factor in victim satisfaction with the operation of the criminal justice system is probably not the formal role of the victim, but the extent to which the victim is accorded dignity and respect."[84] Similarly, Bies and Moag introduced the notion of interactional justice, which is the idea that individuals want to be treated with respect and sensitivity and want to have explained to them the rationale behind decision making.[85] Along the same lines, interpersonal justice has been defined as "the degree to which people are treated with politeness, dignity and respect by the authority in question."[86] Undoubtedly, these studies suggest that without the state treating victims with dignity and respect, their overall interests cannot be met.

To be notified and informed

In their study of victims of crime in 22 European legal systems Hoegen and Brienen found that:

---

80 De Brouwer, A.M. and Groenhuijsen, M., The Role of Victims in International Criminal Proceedings, 153-154, in Sluiter and Vasiliev (2009).

81 Christie (1977) at 3.

82 Stanley (2009) at 65; Doak (2008) at 51-52; United Nations Office for Drug Control and Crime Prevention: Center for International Crime Prevention, Handbook on Justice for Victims: On the Use and Application of the Declaration of Basic Principles of Justice for Victims of Crime and Abuse of Power (1999) [hereinafter Handbook on Justice for Victims] at 43, defining "secondary victimization" as the harm that may be caused to a victim by the investigation and prosecution of the case or by publicizing the details of the case in the media.

83 Shapland, et al. (1985) at 176-178.

84 Strang (2002) at 14, citing Joutsen, M., *International co-operation: The development of crime prevention and criminal justice in Central and Eastern Europe*, 65, European Institute for Crime Prevention and Control (1994).

85 See Colquitt (2001) at 389-390, citing Bies, R.J. and Moag, J.F., Interactional Justice: Communication criteria of fairness, in Lewicki, R.J., Sheppard, B.H. and Bazerman, M.H., eds., *Research on negotiations in organizations*, Vol. 1, JAI Press (1986).

86 Klaming and Giesen (2008) at 17.

> Information is the lifeblood of the criminal justice system. Only if the victim knows his rights and opportunities within the legal system, can he exercise them. Few victims are knowledgeable of the workings of the criminal justice system, or know their way around it. It is therefore essential that they are informed at an early stage of what to expect, whom they can turn to for assistance, and what they themselves can do to secure their legal rights. In sum, the provision of information to the victim is crucial to the effective use of his rights.[87]

Moreover, studies have confirmed that perceptions of justice are influenced by the amount and content of information individuals receive concerning the procedures and outcomes.[88] It appears that, when authorities provide information to and explanations about procedures and outcomes, perceptions of fairness increase together with levels of cooperation.[89] Thus, victims want to be notified about important developments in a case and informed about rights and services.

To receive victim support

Victims experience intense emotional and psychological harm as the result of crimes. There are feelings of insecurity, mistrust and an overall sense of a loss of control.[90] Often they are in great need of support and have little knowledge of what is available to them. Therefore, victims' rights advocates, including Braithwaite and Pettit, argue that criminal justice systems must try to provide aid and comfort to victims in addition to procedural justice, reparation and respect.[91] Accordingly, receiving either direct support or information about support services is important to victims coping with the stress of a criminal process.

To be protected

Given the fact that most criminal trials would not occur without the participation of the victim as a participating witness, protective and special measures for victims of crime are critical in order to ensure their safety and security, to protect their privacy, and to minimize trauma that may occur as a consequence of their participation. Protective and special measures include, *inter alia*, (1) the non-disclosure of identity until necessary for the adequate preparation of the defense; (2) protection from the public and media; (3) protection from confrontation with the accused; and (4) special measures for victims of sexual violence such as counseling. Unquestionably, concerns about protection are a major factor in determining whether or not a victim will become involved with the criminal justice system in the first place.

---

87 Brienen and Hoegen (2000) at 995.
88 See Van den Bos, Vermunt and Wilke (1996).
89 See *Ibid.* See also Klaming and Giesen (2008) at 11.
90 Strang (2002) at 19.
91 Braithwaite and Pettit (1990) at 209.

To attend and be 'heard' in the criminal process

Although gaining greater acknowledgement, respect, support and rights to notification have been important objectives of the victims' rights movement; one of the ultimate objectives, but also the most controversial,[92] has always "been to achieve greater victim input into the central decisions affecting the outcome of the prosecution."[93] Victim attendance at proceedings and participation in proceedings, whether broad or limited, serves as formal acknowledgement that victims of crime have a stake in the criminal process that is different from the judicial authorities and prosecution. Even when they share similar views as those held by the prosecution victims look at the case from a different perspective and they want their interests to be taken into account. Moreover, studies have shown that individuals perceive a judicial process as fair when procedures allow them a voice.[94] As such, in order for authorities to take into account victims' interests victims must be given an opportunity to provide information and share their views and concerns.

To receive reparations

The victims' rights movement grew, in part, out of the call for restitution for victims of crime. This call for direct restitution of victims soon developed into the call for reparations generally. The key aspects of a reparations program are usually restitution, compensation, rehabilitation, satisfaction and guarantees of non-repetition.[95] Restitution is meant to restore victims to their original situation before the violation occurred. Where restitution is not possible, compensation is appropriate for economically assessable damage, including for physical or mental harm, lost opportunities such as employment, material damages and loss of earnings, moral damages, and the costs of medical, legal and social services. Rehabilitation includes medical and psychological care, and legal and social services. Satisfaction usually refers to a wide range of measures including those aimed at the cessation of violations, public disclosure of the truth, a public apology, sanctions against persons liable for the violations, and commemorations and tributes to the victims. Finally, guarantees of non-repetition refer to a wide range of measures aimed at preventing the recurrence of violations, including measures to strengthen the rule of law and the adherence to legal and ethical norms by domestic institutions. Of the studies conducted throughout common and civil law

---

92 Edwards (2004) at 967.

93 Tobolowsky (1999) at 58, citing Kelly, D.P. and Erez, E., Victim Participation in the Criminal Justice System, 231-242, in Davis, R.C., et al., eds., *Victims of Crime*, Sage Publications (1997) (referring to the 'right to be heard').

94 See, e.g., Lind and Tyler (1988); Klaming and Giesen (2008) at 9-10.

95 Ramji, J., A Collective Response to Mass Violence: Reparations and Healing in Cambodia, 360, in Ramji and Van Schaack (2005).

jurisdictions, it is clear that victims want reparation of some kind.[96] More than just providing satisfaction to the victim, reparation takes on a kind of symbolic gesture. It formally acknowledges the offense and the victim. Indeed, it appears that receiving any form of reparation, whether from the state or from the offender, lends itself to greater victim satisfaction with the process.[97]

To have access to legal assistance

Finally, while some countries provide for legal aid to cover the costs of legal counsel for those victims who do not have the means to pay themselves, other jurisdictions do not cover such expenses due to the high costs. To be sure, because of the costs of legal assistance, almost all national jurisdictions limit the right to legal aid. Nevertheless, in practice, many of the statutory rights afforded to victims would amount to nothing without access to competent and effective legal assistance. Therefore, victims' rights advocates have argued for greater access to legal counsel as well as better training for victims' legal counsel.

2.6 Restorativism

In an attempt to meet the needs and concerns of victims of crime mentioned above a new theory of criminal justice emerged. In contrast to traditional criminal law theories, this modern theory, based on restorative justice principles, has begun to focus attention on the role of the victim within criminal justice. Although the exact role and status of victims varies widely within retributive and utilitarian theories, advocates of restorative justice argue that classical criminal justice models ignore victims by placing too much focus on the offender or on the interests of society.[98] Though some commentators view restorativism as a social movement it is in fact distinct from the victims' rights movement and is itself a theory of criminal justice.[99] The theory focuses on shared values between the offender and victim and seeks to repair the harm suffered, through an inclusive process.

Restorative justice principles have existed for centuries, in some form or another, throughout the world, and have greatly influenced conflict resolution practices. Greek, Roman and Arab systems have all recognized the benefits of restorative justice even for the crime of murder.[100] Early codes formally acknowledged the right to reparation,

96 Strang (2002) at 18.

97 *Ibid.* at 17-18. Nonetheless, there are numerous challenges criminal courts face with regard to reparation. Judges in criminal courts are often reluctant to get entangled in financial assessments based on harm and the ability to pay, challenges arise when having to determine who qualifies as a victim and compliance and enforcement of reparation orders is problematic

98 Garvey (2003) at 303.

99 Luna (2003) at 227.

100 Garvey (2003) at 304; see also Weitekamp (1992) at 74-75. In general early codes called for pecuniary sanctions to be paid to the victims.

which is an important aspect of restorativism.[101] However, almost all systems of criminal prosecutions depended upon individual victims.[102] Victims and their families would be responsible for apprehending those believed to be responsible and facilitating the reparation. The benefit of such practices was the fact that the harm suffered by the victim could be emphasized. The drawback, however, was that victims with little financial means or family support would often have little redress if harmed.

As communities grew and power became centralized, the state became increasingly more prominent in the resolution of disputes so as to preserve order.[103] Joutsen opines that "the increased community interest in preventing and punishing undesirable behavior corresponds to a new public conception of crime as an act that directly affects the entire community" rather than simply one individual.[104] Often the religious power or the local ruling party would play a dominant role in the private settlement of cases in order to ensure compensation and avoid blood feuds.[105] While the shift from private apprehension and prosecution to public apprehension and prosecution (or a mixture thereof) was slow, the central authority had better resources and specialization. The result of this shift is that the centralized power gradually took the emphasis away from the harm suffered by the victim and placed it on the criminal act of the accused.[106]

Gillin has found that the major shift to a centralized power and a more retributive form of justice allowed tribunals to publically pronounce upon offenses. Moreover, fines would be paid to the state rather than to the victim, thereby further entrenching the state's monopoly on the criminal process and punishment.[107] For example, in England, by the late twelfth century, the private settlement of serious criminal cases was no longer permitted and adjudication of the crime became matters for the Crown.[108] However, it was not until the nineteenth century when victims themselves could no longer bring prosecutions in the name of the Crown.[109] Similarly, in Continental Europe the state began playing a greater role in the administration of justice which coincides with the revival of Roman law and the emphasis on state authority. The philosophical justifications for the shift from private or local community dispute resolution to state control is that the wrong done to an individual extends to the wider community.[110] One of the most influential reasons for this shift can be traced back to ideas from the Enlightenment, asserting that criminal prosecutions should serve the

101 *Ibid.* at 71-73.
102 Shapland, et al. (1985) at 174.
103 Laster (1970) at 71-80.
104 Joutsen (1987) at 39.
105 Gillin (1927) at 294-308.
106 Laster (1970) at 71-80.
107 Gillin (1927) at 308; Tobolowsky (1999) at 23-24; Joutsen (1987) at 44, noting that stolen goods were forfeited to the Crown unless the victim had been responsible for the apprehension and conviction of the offender.
108 Wright (1991) at 5-6.
109 Strang (2002) at 5.
110 Wright (1991) at 5.

societal interests of retribution and deterrence as opposed to private redress.[111] The growth of public prosecution offices facilitated this shift.[112] The justification for the shift reflects a major development in the way civil society began to operate. Although a benefit of state control over criminal matters is that victims do not carry the financial burden and responsibility for investigating and prosecuting crimes,[113] over time this development has led to the marginalization of the victim in criminal proceedings, particularly in common law jurisdictions.[114] The victim became "just another witness" for the state.[115]

The 'rediscovery' of reparation, restoration and a central role for victims would proceed slowly, beginning in the early twentieth century and taking concrete shape in the decades following the Second World War.[116] One of the first modern advocates for reparation and victims in criminal proceedings was the British prison reformer, Margery Fry. She argued that offenders should make direct reparation to their victims, thereby recognizing the harm to the individual.[117] Around the same time, the study of victimology slowly emerged.[118] Victimology studies the impact of crimes on victims as well as their omission from the criminal justice process,[119] and like Fry, those working in the field of victimology questioned why victims were being marginalized. However, it was not until the 1970s when the modern restorative justice theories developed, calling for "mediated as opposed to adjudicated justice."[120] Dr. Albert Eglash is usually credited with developing the foundations of 'restorative justice'.[121] However, the term has since been extended well beyond the original application Eglash envisioned, which was mainly within the context of restitution.

At present, the precise definition of restorative justice is unclear.[122] However, it is generally used to describe a process after guilt has been established whereby the offender, victim and potentially the wider community begin to attempt to repair the

---

111 Tobolowsky (1999) at 26; Beccaria [1764] (1971).

112 Tobolowsky (1999) at 26.

113 Shapland, et al. (1985) at 174.

114 Strang (2002) at 5; however, Jousten warns that the increase in state participation in criminal matters corresponds directly with decreased victim participation; even before the emergence of state criminal models it was the larger group or clan to which the victim belonged who handled disputes rather than the individual victim, see Joutsen (1987) at 49.

115 Strang (2002) at 5.

116 Joutsen (1987) at 48-49, noting that in the late 1800s and early 1900s attempts were made to incorporate restitution payments into punishment but these ideas were never turned into concrete results.

117 Fry (1951) at 121-126.

118 Joutsen (1987) at 50-51.

119 Tobolowsky (1999) at 26-27.

120 Van Ness, D.W., Restorative Justice and International Human Rights, 23, in Galaway and Hudson (1996).

121 See Eglash, A., Beyond Restitution: Creative Restitution, 91-129, in Hudson and Galaway (1977).

122 Wenzel, et al. (2008) at 377; Harris, M.K., Transformative Justice: the transformation of restorative justice, 555, in Sullivan and Tifft (2006); Garvey (2003) at 304.

harm suffered by the victim.[123] Wenzel, for example, defines restorative justice as "the repair of justice through reaffirming a shared value-consensus in a bilateral process."[124] Barnett, another early advocate of restorative justice ideas, argues that the traditional criminal justice paradigm, which focuses on punishment of an accused and conceives of a crime as an offense against the state (or society) rather than against an individual, should instead be seen as an offense of one individual against the rights of another individual and that the restitution of the victim should be the main objective of the criminal justice system rather than punishment.[125] Bazemore and Walgrave prefer the 'maximalist' approach, whereby the term restorative justice covers "every action that is primarily oriented towards doing justice by repairing the harm that has been caused by crime."[126] And finally, Marshall, who formulated the most widely accepted definition to date, submits that "[r]estorative justice is a process whereby parties with a stake in a specific offence collectively resolve how to deal with the aftermath of that offence and its implications for the future."[127]

In addition to the underlying definitional difficulties, Dignan notes that there has been a "degree of conceptual confusion with regard to the term 'restorative justice'"[128] due, in part, to the fact that the term covers a range of practices including: victim-offender mediation; forms of conferencing; services by victim support organizations; victim compensation schemes; procedural reforms like victim impact statements or participatory rights; and sentencing reforms like community service initiatives.[129] As a result of this conceptual uncertainty, he argues that it is practically impossible to find a universally accepted definition. Dignan's critic of 'restorative justice' definitions is that these definitions usually restrict themselves to the criminal justice arena but that restorative justice has been applied outside of this context.[130] He also criticizes the fact that although definitions deal with the *process* of restorative justice they do not reference the possible *outcomes* of restorative justice.[131]

Like Dignan, Braithwaite and Pettit also sought to better conceptualize the theory of restorative justice, constructing a 'republican theory of criminal justice' based on

123 See Rauschenbach and Scalia (2008) at 441-459; ECOSOC's Basic Principles on the use of Restorative Justice Programs in Criminal Matters do not require an admission of guilt but rather find that agreements on basic facts are sufficient, see ECOSOC's Basic Principles on the use of Restorative Justice Programs in Criminal Matters 2002/12, UN Doc. E/CN.15/2002/5/Add.1 (2002).
124 Wenzel, et al. (2008) at 375.
125 Barnett (1977) at 287-291.
126 Bazemore and Walgrave (1999) at 48.
127 Marshall (1999) at 5.
128 Dignan (2005) at 2.
129 Heikkilä (2004) at 37-38; Weitekamp (1992) at 81-84; see also Christie (1977) at 1-15, stressing that criminal conflicts have been hijacked by lawyers at the expense of the parties directly involved.
130 The South African Truth and Reconciliation Commission is an example of how restorative justice practices are used largely outside of a criminal context.
131 Therefore, he created an analytical framework in order to provide conceptual clarification, see Dignan (2005) at 5-10.

restorative justice principles.[132] They argue for less government intrusion (i.e. through the criminal justice system) into the lives or dominion of individual citizens.[133] The greater the role of the state the fewer benefits for the individual. There is a great focus on shaming and community disapproval of wrongful behavior. The emphasis is on denouncing the act and not the offender, while at the same time reasserting the rights and dignity of the victim. The right to restitution as well as symbolic reparation is also important. Victims, offenders and the community, rather than state institutions play a greater role in the outcome processes. More recently, Braithwaite and Strang made a distinction between restorative justice as a "process conception" and as a "values conception".[134] While the process conception emphasizes the bringing together of stakeholders to resolve a conflict, the value conception emphasizes the healing value of restorative justice.[135]

Drawing on the breath of restorative justice theories, it is clear that restorative justice is far ranging and it is not the intention of this chapter to formulate a concrete definition of restorative justice within criminal law. Nevertheless, it is safe to argue that restorative justice emphasizes shared values and consensus building among all stakeholders with a focus on the direct participation of those involved.[136] And that the key features of 'restorative justice' are: (1) restoring the victim by way of reparation, compensation or apology; (2) restoring the offender; (3) restoring the wider community by way of reparation, compensation or apology; and (4) participation of the victim and the offender in the process (whether legal or non-legal).[137] Indeed, all parties are expected to be involved in addressing an offense. Crime is not simply the violation of a law or norm. Instead, the focus is on the injury to the victim and community. Restorative justice views an offense primarily as a breach of social relationships and secondly as a violation of a law.[138] Furthermore, the distinction between criminal law and civil law is blurred in the theory of restorative justice.[139] Accordingly, the distinction is contrary to the traditional notion of conflict-resolution and in many instances civil suits have a public character which undermines the main reason for the distinction between the two types of adjudication.[140]

In practice, restorative justice models often bring victims and offenders together to discuss the harm and to learn about each other's backgrounds. After meeting with the victim and/or community, offenders are meant to gain an understanding of the

---

132 See Braithwaite and Pettit (1990).

133 For the definition of dominion, see Braithwaite and Pettit (1990) at 9.

134 Braithwaite, J. and Strang, H., Introduction: restorative justice and civil society, 1-2, in Braithwaite and Strang (2001).

135 *Ibid.* at 1.

136 See Wenzel (2008).

137 Ashworth, A., Victims' Rights, Defendants' Rights and Criminal Procedure, 185, 193, in Crawford, and Goodey (2000); Luna (2003) at 228; Gromet and Darley (2006) at 396.

138 Luna (2003) at 229.

139 Fatić (1995) at 178.

140 *Ibid.* at 178-179.

effect their behavior has had on others and to develop feelings of remorse.[141] The idea is to come to an agreement on either a 'penalty' or 'sanction.'[142] Theoretically both the victim and offender are empowered by taking part in and having control over the process. Most importantly, within restorative justice crimes are not committed against states but against individuals and their local communities. The offense is first and foremost a breach of a social relationship and secondly a violation of the law.[143] The objective therefore is to redress the harm experienced by the victim rather than inflict pain or punishment upon the offender. While offenders are encouraged to fully accept responsibility and offer meaningful apologies, victims are implicitly encouraged to offer forgiveness.[144]

Gromet and Darley offer an example of a typical restorative justice procedure known as conferencing:

> Restorative justice procedures usually involve a face-to-face meeting of the victim, the offender, and supporters for both sides. Community members are frequently present as representatives of the community interests. Before a restorative justice procedure can be initiated, offenders must admit their guilt. Once they do, a "conference" is scheduled, to be led by a trained facilitator. During the conference, offenders explain what they did and why they did it. Victims then have a chance to explain how the crime harmed them, and the offenders have an opportunity to apologize for the harm they caused. Together, the conference participants work out an agreement for what the offenders must do to repair the harm that followed from the offense. These agreements usually involve an apology, monetary compensation, some services that the offender does for the victim, community service, and the like.

Like the other theories of criminal justice, restorative justice has also faced criticism. One of the criticisms is the fact that models which focus on shaming and reintegration fail to acknowledge the cultural contexts in which shaming may or may not work.[145] For example, shaming in Asian cultures may have a greater impact upon the wrong-doer than in American culture where the emphasis tends to be more on the individual. Along the same lines, restorative justice models, which focus on shared values be-

---

141 Luna (2003) at 228.

142 *Ibid.* There is debate as to whether the restorative justice process should include punitive measures. Garvey argues for example that restorative justice "cannot achieve the restoration of the victim it seeks without the punishment it rejects." In other words, punishment is an essential part of repairing the wrong. However, Garvey argues that it is only when the wrongdoer assumes the burden as a sort of atonement, in contrast to being made to carry out the punishment, can repair begin. Nonetheless, on the whole, while punishment may be part of a restorative justice model it is not central to it. See Gromet and Darley (2006) at 397; Garvey (2003) at 303, 312; Wenzel (2008) at 376.

143 Luna (2003) at 228.

144 See Strang, H., Is Restorative Justice Imposing Its Agenda on Victims? 95-106, in Zehr and Towes (2004); Jennifer Gerarda Brown argues that victim offender mediation can actually harm victims by stressing forgiveness while at the same time denying them a public pronouncement on the guilt of the offender, see Brown (1994) at 1250-51.

145 Braithwaite (1989) at 8.

tween the primary actors, do not always take into account situations in which those involved do not perceive to share an identity with one another.[146] Other critics argue that restorative justice practices can, at times, place too much power in the hands of victims.[147] This power can lead to further marginalization of the offender or encourage vengeful behavior on the part of victims.

Finally, restorative theories are plagued by limitations in practice. While there are some empirical studies that suggest that domestic restorative justice procedures have increased satisfaction with the overall criminal justice process because the needs and concerns of victims are being met,[148] for a variety of reasons, restorative justice programs are not fully successful and are not viewed as alternatives to incarceration and traditional criminal justice institutions.[149] The seriousness of the offense plays a major role in whether individuals at the domestic level accept a restorative justice approach.[150] For instance, when the gravity of a crime increases so too does an individual's and the community's desire for punitive punishment. At the domestic level it appears that there is little support for restorative justice sanctions for serious offenses. There appears to be a 'symbolic moral significance' attributed to punishment for serious crimes and the desire to have public authorities express condemnation of the offense.[151]

2.7 Mixed Theories of Criminal Justice

As the above sections show, every criminal justice theory faces some form of criticism and does not wholly reflect actual practice. Therefore, scholars have looked to mixed theories of criminal justice to address the criticisms leveled against so-called pure theories. These mixed approaches reject pure theories and usually aim to combine the two traditional criminal law theories so as to produce a 'best of both worlds' theory. More recently, however, mixed theories also include the combination of traditional theories with restorative justice alternatives.

The usual hybrid theories are either primarily retributive with elements of utility present or primarily utilitarian with elements of retribution present.[152] For example, Hart argues that pure theories fail to provide enough satisfactory answers when examining the goals of criminal justice, law and punishment.[153] Instead, he maintains that a mixed system based primarily on utilitarian theories but with notable elements of retributive theories is necessary. Deterrence theories, he argues, must also work

146 See Wenzel (2008).
147 Delgado (2000) at 760.
148 Gromet and Darley (2006) at 396-397.
149 Weitekamp (1992) at 74.
150 Gromet and Darley (2006) at 399.
151 *Ibid.* See also Vidmar and Miller (1980).
152 Luna (2003) at 225.
153 See Hart (1968).

together with prohibitions against sanctioning innocent individuals or disproportionate punishment amongst other things.[154] In contrast with Hart, Robinson argues that a mixed system based primarily on retributive theories but limited by utilitarian concerns should determine punishment.[155]

Theorists have also argued for the adoption of a criminal justice system primarily based on traditional criminal law theories but infused with restorative justice practices or values. Many restorative justice advocates argue that in order to achieve a broader meaning of justice both restorative and retributive elements should be combined.[156] One combined approach may include the approval of a restorative justice process within an otherwise retributive system. For example, even if the victim and offender were to agree on a purely restorative approach the state would still need to sanction the agreement and ultimately decide whether additional punitive measures are necessary in order to also reflect the society's disapproval of the wrong committed. Other examples may include the incorporation of mediation and conferencing, which can either complement or replace traditional criminal processes. Alternatively, Luna asserts that "a procedural conception of an otherwise substantive theory – commonly known as 'restorative justice' – allows distinct voices to contribute to an appropriate outcome without necessarily assenting to the same theory."[157] In other words, the procedural conception of restorative justice is better suited to serve the various purposes of criminal law theory than any one substantive theory of criminal justice.[158] Therefore, the inclusion of restorative justice procedures within the dominant traditional system attempts to acknowledge and incorporate the needs and concerns of those individuals directly injured by crime.

Despite the appeal of mixed models, critics have still found these mixed theories problematic for one reason or another. With traditional hybrid models, usually proponents of utilitarian theories argue against the inclusion of too many retributive elements and proponents of retributive theories argue against the inclusion of too many utilitarian elements.[159] The same is true for mixed theories incorporating restorative justice practices. Critics argue that restorative justice models, when paired with traditional systems, are almost always only successful for minor crimes. Moreover, although it may be acceptable to many to have restorative processes and retributive processes compliment one another, incorporating restorative values in the retributive process (and visa versa) may contradict the premise of the process as a whole.

154 Luna (2003) at 225; Hart (1968) at 8-13.
155 Robinson (1987) at 38.
156 Gromet and Darley (2006) at 19; Duff, A., Restoration and Restribution, 50, in Von Hirsch, et al. (2003).
157 Luna (2003) at 205.
158 *Ibid.*
159 *Ibid.* at 226; see also, e.g., Goldman (1979) at 49; Robinson (1987).

2.8 Criminal Justice Theories, Victims and International Criminal Justice

This chapter has thus far attempted to show the philosophical debates surrounding the competing theories of criminal justice and their approaches towards victims of crime at the domestic level. Traditional theories have undoubtedly focused on crime, society and the accused with only minor acknowledgement of the individual victim within the criminal justice system. As a result of this marginalization, victims of crimes grew dissatisfied with criminal justice institutions because their needs and concerns were not being met and began to demand more. Out of this frustration, restorative justice theories (re-)emerged, which seek to emphasize the harms suffered by victims and to bring together all stakeholders of an offense. However, whether retributive, utilitarian or restorative, no one domestic criminal justice theory has been whole-heartedly embraced. There are merits and demerits of any individual theory. Instead, national systems tend to support a variety of approaches – at times preferring one approach to another depending upon the political climate at any specific time.

Although the theories discussed above are not entirely applicable to international criminal justice processes, given that they were developed with the notion of the state construct in mind, their principles are nevertheless pertinent to the international level. Just as with domestic criminal justice systems, at the international level those individuals creating and shaping post-conflict responses have competing conceptions of what the primary objectives of these responses should be. These competing conceptions, in turn, affect how the responses are ultimately shaped.

There are a number of international post-conflict responses, ranging from setting up or aiding truth and reconciliation commissions, historical commissions, claims commissions or establishing criminal tribunals. Favoring one response over another, as evidenced by financial backing and commitment, largely comes down to what values the international community seeks to emphasize.[160] And, due in large part to the domination of traditional notions of justice, the creation of international criminal courts has become a favored response to mass crimes.

Aptly, these international criminal institutions have integrated many procedures which reflect a retributive and utilitarian approach often found in domestic systems. At the same time, however, there have been calls from civil society and the victims' rights movement for greater inclusion of restorative justice principles and practices in post-conflict responses. These calls have led to the increase of truth and reconciliation commissions or claims commissions, which can broadly be seen as restorative responses to mass crimes due to their focus on the victims by either repairing the harm suffered through reparation or bringing torn communities together through dialogue

160 In this study, "international community" refers to those powers that create and shape post-conflict justice institutions including the UN (Security Council and General Assembly) or international funders of courts and commissions.

and education. In addition to these separate post-conflict responses, advocates of restorative justice have also called for restorative justice practices to be incorporated into the traditional criminal law paradigm. However, just as at the national level, tensions exist between international criminal responses employing retributive practices and non-criminal responses employing restorative practices.[161] The following section will briefly highlight the theories of criminal justice and how in a general sense they are germane to the international level.

2.8.1 Traditional Theories at the International Level

The retributive approach at the international level holds that the crimes falling under the jurisdiction of international courts are crimes that shock the conscience of mankind and therefore individuals who commit these crimes deserve to be punished if for no other reason than for the fact that they have committed these crimes. In fact, one of the main goals for establishing these courts is to address problems with impunity for these crimes. Retributivists support the establishment of international criminal courts because they help ensure that individuals who commit these morally reprehensible crimes, and only those individuals, are given their 'just deserts' through proportional punishment. Even if courts and punishment were to provide a proper deterrent effect for international crimes, which is highly debatable, the court's main role is to publically pronounce upon the moral wrongdoing of the accused. Thus, punishment at this level may be useful for reasons of deterrence or social utility, but these are only beneficial side-effects and not the purpose of the punishment itself. Most would agree that the crimes of genocide, war crimes and crimes against humanity warrant punishment regardless of whether deterrence is achieved. Therefore, retributivists assert that the central purpose of international criminal justice is to define and declare certain kinds of behavior and actions criminal because intrinsically they violate society's moral values and are deserving of punishment.

The crimes under the jurisdictions of the international criminal courts can certainly be considered public harms because they affront the fundamental values which are held to define the international community. Prosecuting former Khmer Rouge leaders who for decades lived peaceful lives and contributed to Cambodian society would not be justified under the utilitarian paradigm because there is no likely chance of recidivism and their punishment would generally not deter others from committing the same crimes because of the context in which many the crimes were committed are not likely to return. Nevertheless, retributive notions hold that such prosecutions are necessary. Any violation of these norms or values needs to be publicly condemned and the wrongdoers publicly punished because "[s]erious crimes, when they go unpunished,

161 Findlay and Henham (2005) at xxi.

diminish the value we place on our social identities, and hence our valuation of ourselves."[162]

All of the international criminal courts established to date affirm the retributive goal of pronouncing upon crime and punishing individuals for committing egregious wrongs regardless of whether the punishment has a deterrent effect. The structures of international criminal institutions also adhere to the philosophical foundations of retributivism. Accordingly, impartiality is stressed – both for the prosecutor and for the judges as are fair trial rights of the accused. Punishment at the courts also follows a retributive mindset in that it is meant to be proportional to the crime committed and the culpability of the wrongdoer. Punishment is not meant to fluctuate – depending upon either the vengefulness or forgiveness of the victims.

In addition to these retributive attributes found within international criminal law, very often international criminal justice is viewed as a "technique or instrument" that can be used by the international community to achieve intended goals. Thus international criminal law is also conceptualized in instrumental or consequential terms. Specifically, international criminal courts have added value because they are efficient ways of achieving worthwhile ends such as the prevention of future crimes or the securing of peace and stability in a conflict region. In this sense, the establishment of international courts under the UN Security Council's Chapter VII powers can arguably be considered a utilitarian response in that the courts are seen as a means through which peace and security can be facilitated.

To the extent that international criminal institutions are utilitarian in nature, the non-pure instrumentalist approach dominates at the international level. Procedures are adopted to achieve certain goals but the requirements of justice may preclude some practices regardless of whether or not those practices help meet the intended goals. For example, it may be more cost effective and efficient to have all witnesses testify anonymously but the fair trial rights of the accused would preclude such practices. The criticisms faced by utilitarianism, that it too easily sacrifices the rights of the individual, are therefore lessoned.

Thus, it is the retributive paradigm that has most influenced international criminal justice responses to mass crimes with some influence from utilitarianism. The focus is generally on the crimes committed and the rights of the accused – with marginal emphasis on the harms suffered by individual victims.

2.8.2 Restorativism at the International Level

Like retributivism and utilitarianism, the restorative justice approach has also influenced post-conflict responses at the international level. Restorative justice at the international level is a philosophy that aims to emphasize certain values such as the need for parties with a stake in a specific offense to collectively resolve how to deal

162 Oldenquist (1988) at 467.

with both the aftermath of that offense as well as its implications for the future. Restorative justice embraces an inclusive process where the victim and the harm suffered rather than the wrongdoer and the crime are central. At the international level, the restorative justice approach most widely employed is the creation of truth and reconciliation commissions (TRCs).[163]

Beginning in the mid-1970s through to the present, TRCs have emerged as viable, strategic tools that can address human rights and humanitarian law violations and promote reconciliation.[164] TRCs are usually established to research and report on abuses that occurred over a specific period of time, under a specific regime or in relation to a specific conflict. At the international level, international organizations like the UN or non-governmental organizations typically sponsor or financially support these institutions. In many cases, TRCs have been a favored response because they have the capability of collecting a broader range of 'truth' due to the fact that they are able to look at wider patterns of crimes rather than simply the individual criminal responsibility of a handful of accused.

A distinguishing characteristic of TRCs, which reflects a restorative justice approach, is their emphasis on the inclusion of all stakeholders in the process (offenders, victims and the wider community) in order to help address the harms suffered by victims. It is noteworthy that most commissions seek to facilitate national reconciliation and address impunity collectively rather than individually.[165] Due to this broad focus, Hayner credits truth commissions with the ability to advance "national" reconciliation rather than "individual" reconciliation.[166] Essential to this collective reconciliation process is the inclusion of testimony from both victims and perpetrators. Victims especially are encouraged to tell their stories in narrative form, which stands in contrast to most criminal trial procedures. In addition to the taking of testimony, truth and reconciliation commissions can often aid in the reparation process. Through reports and recommendations they can either directly or indirectly contribute to the redress of victims.

Despite the widespread acceptance of TRCs, they have usually been created as justice-supportive processes, "designed to compliment rather than replace national or international prosecution."[167] The simultaneous and complementary operation reflects the argument put forward by mixed theorists at the national level. Indeed, there are situations in which the parallel operation of a TRC and the courts complements one

---

163 International claims commissions may also be seen to be restorative. Gacaca courts in Rwanda are also hailed as a restorative justice response but this response, while it may be considered restorative, is a national response to mass victimization and not an international one.

164 El Salvador, Guatemala, Somalia, the former Yugoslavia, Rwanda, South Africa, and Sierra Leone have all created some form of a truth and reconciliation commission; see Scharf (1997) at 377-379.

165 For example, the South African Truth and Reconciliation Commission's mandate was to facilitate national reconciliation (1995-1998); see South African Promotion of National Unity and Reconciliation Act (1995).

166 Hayner (2001) at 155.

167 Stahn (2001) at 954.

another's functions. For example, the SCSL and that country's truth and reconciliation commission illustrate a successful combination of two independent institutions performing complementary roles.[168]

However, as mentioned in previous sections, restorative justice processes are almost always only effectively employed after the finding of guilt, acceptance of guilt or the acceptance of basic underlying facts of the crime by the accused. As a result, numerous authors on restorative justice have reminded scholars and policy-makers that "before a restorative justice procedure can be initiated, offenders must admit their guilt."[169] Due to this underlying premise, autonomous participation by victims in proceedings (a practice supported by Fletcher and others) may offer a tangible avenue for expressing emotional suffering but it does not necessarily make a process restorative. Therefore, it is important to distinguish between victims' procedural rights within criminal trials and restorative justice processes.[170]

In some cases, procedural rights and restorative processes may overlap but it is equally probable that they may not. In other words, extensive procedural rights for victims within the framework of a traditional criminal justice system may be granted without necessarily transforming that system into a restorative one.[171] Chapter 3 will look at how criminal trials in both common law and civil law jurisdictions have incorporated greater victim participation into their proceedings without changing the proceedings into restorative ones. These domestic proceedings, while not adopting a restorative justice approach, most certainly adopt a victim-oriented approach (in an attempt to meet the needs and concerns of victims) and it is this approach which most closely resembles the victim schemes at the international courts. Thus, the application of the phrase 'restorative justice' to the international criminal law construct is misleading.

2.9 Conclusion

Theoretical disputes may seem at first glance to have little practical relevance for criminal justice policy-makers, but in fact, that is not the case. At the national level, criminal justice theories have directly or indirectly informed mediation schemes, charging policies, procedural norms, sentencing schemes,[172] and most importantly for this study, the role of the victim in the criminal justice system. Although traditional theories of criminal justice continue to dominate domestic criminal justice systems, more recently, restorative justice theories at the national level have also impacted

168 See Schabas (2004); McGonigle (2009).

169 Gromet and Darley (2006) at 396; Garvey (2003) at 312, stating that restorative justice comes into play only after the guilt of a defendant has been established.

170 Ashworth, A., Victims' Rights, Defendants' Rights and Criminal Procedure, 192, in Crawford and Goodey (2000).

171 *Ibid.*

172 Luna (2003) at 250.

domestic criminal processes and dispute resolution.[173] Certainly, there has been greater emphasis on including the victim in various justice processes by focusing on their harms suffered. Nonetheless, there is still reluctance to provide too great a role for victims within traditional criminal justice systems.

For the purpose of this chapter it was most helpful to first look at the various theories in their purest forms so as to examine their influence on national criminal justice and procedure. In turn, this influence on the national level carried over to the international level in many respects. At both levels, no pure theory is whole-heartedly accepted. This lack of acceptance of pure theories simply reflects the complex nature of crime and criminal justice. To be sure, international criminal justice systems pursue a plurality of goals, including deterrence, retribution, and restoration. While clearly international criminal justice is not based on one clear philosophical justification, the various criminal law theories (both traditional and modern) have helped shape the structures employed by the system and the procedures adopted therein. This influence, as previously noted, is apparent because the procedures of the criminal process should arguably be determined by asking how best to serve the goals of the criminal system most efficiently.

However useful these theories are, the competing conceptions of criminal justice must, nevertheless, be appreciated within real world practices. Therefore, the following chapter examines domestic criminal justice systems with specific emphasis on the victim in criminal proceedings (i.e. victim-oriented procedures) and will explore how the diverse approaches adopted at the domestic level have contributed to the current role afforded to victims in international criminal proceedings.

---

173 To some extent utilitarian theories are also evident, such as in the goal of deterrence, but these theories are far overshadowed by retributive theories. But like retributive theories, utilitarian theories focus on the accused and on society rather than on the interests of victims. See Heikkilä (2004) at 29-32.

CHAPTER 3
DOMESTIC CRIMINAL JUSTICE AND VICTIM PARTICIPATION MODELS

3.1 INTRODUCTION

Legal systems throughout the world have distinct approaches to how victims may participate in their criminal justice processes. No one system is the same as another although some similarities exist. These similarities are largely dependent on the historical legal tradition of that system and the procedural approach it adopts. In order to understand these differences and similarities it is necessary to examine the distinctions between legal systems, legal traditions and the procedural approaches they implement.

First, a legal system can be defined as "an operating set of legal institutions, procedures and rules."[1] There are, for instance, multiple legal systems or jurisdictions in the United States. Likewise, there are many distinct legal systems within the European Union. Lawyers authorized to practice law in the state of New York are not permitted to practice law in the state of California before acquiring the necessary knowledge of California's legal system. The same is true for an Italian lawyer wishing to lead a case in the Netherlands. Restrictions to practicing law are in place because although legal systems or jurisdictions may share many characteristics they often have very different rules, procedures and institutions.

Second, a legal tradition can be viewed as "a set of deeply rooted, historically conditioned attitudes about the nature of law, about the role of law in society and the polity, about the proper organization and operation of a legal system, and about the way law is or should be made, applied, studied, perfected, and taught."[2] National legal systems are habitually grouped into legal traditions or legal families in order to make comparative research easier.[3] Indeed, comparative legal scholars have long embraced the idea of grouping, disagreeing, however, on how best to group.[4] The groupings are usually based on a jurisdiction's history, characteristics, institutions, use of legal sources and, importantly, a jurisdiction's ideology.[5] Various legal traditions include:

---

1 Merryman (1969) at 1.

2 *Ibid.* at 2.

3 Vogler (2005) at 3.

4 *Ibid.*, noting Esmein's proposed grouping into Romanic, Germanic, Anglo-Saxon, Slav and Islamic Families; Nolde and Wolfe's proposed grouping into French, German, Scandinavian, English, Russian, Islamic and Hindu; David and Brierley's grouping into three major legal traditions (Romano-Germanic, Socialist and Common Law) with residual traditions including Muslim, Indian, Far Eastern, African and Malagasy.

5 Heikkilä (2004) at 43.

the common law, civil law, Islamic law, Chinese law and the socialist legal tradition.[6] This study focuses solely on the groupings of the common law and civil law traditions due to the fact that international criminal law and procedure draws almost exclusively from these two legal traditions.

Finally, those legal systems, which can generally be said to fall into either the civil law or common law tradition, employ a wide variety of procedural approaches in order to meet their purported goals. The two most widely referenced procedural approaches are the inquisitorial approach and the adversarial approach. While some authors refer to these procedural approaches as traditions, due to their long-standing use and relationship with the common law and civil traditions, this study maintains they are better classified as procedural approaches. It is believed that this distinction is necessary to better understand legal systems because legal systems, regardless of what tradition they belong to, employ elements from both types of procedural approaches, albeit with a tendency to lean more towards one than the other.[7]

This chapter examines the participatory roles afforded to victims in domestic systems, but before doing so, it will touch upon three prominent theoretical models developed to help compare traditions, systems and approaches. It then explores, in a general sense, the various structures of national systems, including their legal traditions and procedural approaches to criminal justice. Thereafter, this chapter examines the participatory models in place within national jurisdictions. Restorative practices will also be examined. The conclusion will highlight the fact that the fundamental differences in how legal systems conceptualize the trial process and the models they have adopted have had significant consequences for victim participation both at the national and international level.

---

6 The so-called Socialist Law is often considered to be a particular case of the Romano-Germanic civil law, though in the past it was sometimes classified as a separate legal system, see, e.g., Merryman (1969) at 1.

7 As an introductory note, by using the term "Anglo-American" or "common law" this study does not mean to imply that the criminal procedures found in Great Britain and the United States, for example, are the same. Clearly, there is a great deal of variation between the two countries and within their respective jurisdictions. Likewise, European civil law jurisdictions, or Continental systems, differ remarkably from one another. Instead, the terms common law and civil law are used in a general manner to help emphasize the philosophical divides between these two traditions and the dominant approaches they adopt. In other words, along the lines of a party-driven approach found in adversarial systems (prosecution and defense) versus a judge-dominated approach generally associated with inquisitorial systems (state agency responsible for finding the truth), see McGonigle (2009b); see also Ambos (2003) at 1-5, explaining that the terms 'adversarial' and 'inquisitorial' are only used in a general sense to reflect the still existing common law-civil law divide; and Damaška (1986) at 16-17, constructing a theory which reflects the notion that Continental legal systems employ the traditional judicial apparatus while the British system employs a more coordinate apparatus.

3.2 Comparing Traditions, Systems and Approaches

Despite the benefits of comparative studies and groupings of national systems into legal families, one of the biggest problems with groupings is that often they are based primarily upon statutory or textual law rather than on practices or procedures employed within the various systems.[8] Another problem is that approaches taken within the legal systems are sometimes forced to square with legal traditions even when that may not be the case. For example, legal systems that historically employed inquisitorial procedures are forced into the civil law tradition regardless of present-day practice or reform. To be sure, the blurring of the objectives and values of a system with a system's preferred procedural method has been problematic for comparativists.[9] In an attempt to take into account wider social and political factors and to make comparisons easier, comparativists have sought to redefine existing comparative models. Most, however, meet with the same problems of confusion. Nonetheless, there are a handful of models that have greatly influenced the way modern scholars look at national judicial systems and the procedural choices they make.[10]

The first theoretical model to really impact how modern national criminal justice systems are viewed was Packer's model. Packer identified two value systems that compete with one another in the criminal process found in common law systems: the Crime Control Model and the Due Process Model.[11] The Crime Control Model values the efficient suppression of crime while the Due Process Model values the primacy of the defendant and the concept of limited governmental power.[12] The role of the victim is largely forgotten in his model. Therefore, his work has subsequently been modified and amended by a number of theorists aiming to better reflect a position for victims.[13] For example, Roach attempts to build upon Packer's theories in order to take the independent role of the victim into account.[14] Similarly, Beloof has developed a third model of the criminal process, referred to as the Victim Participation Model, which also builds on Packer's theories.[15] Beloof argues that laws recognizing the rights of victim participation "represent a shift in a dominant paradigm of criminal procedure."[16]

---

8 Vogler (2005) at 4.

9 Amongst others, Vogler points out that Packer's long accepted legal grouping, the crime control model and the due process model, confuses *objective* with *method* and therefore does not aid in comparing traditions or systems of law, see Vogler (2005) at 6-7. Cf. Roberts (2008) at 378, pointing out that Vogler's criticisms are misplaced since Packer was "trying to model competing values within the same procedural system, rather than two opposed models of procedure."

10 In addition, some scholars have attempted to use these models based on state authority and judicial systems as a way of conceptualizing international criminal structures, see, e.g., Swart (2008) at 87.

11 Some authors have mistakenly attributed Packer's work to both common law and civil law systems.

12 Packer (1968) at 149-153.

13 Beloof (1999) at 291, footnote 8.

14 See Roach (1999).

15 See Beloof (1999); Vogler (2005) at 4.

16 Beloof (1999) at 292.

Like Packer's model, these newer models, however, are most applicable to the common law justice structures as they reflect the underlying values of this tradition.

In addition to Packer's conceptualization, two scholars, Damaška and Vogler, have attempted to address the shortcomings of earlier groupings and models by developing their own paradigms for comparison. In *The Faces of Justice and State Authority* Damaška developed ideal theoretical models for the structure and function of government. The structure of government refers to the "character of procedural authority" and the function of government refers to "views on the purpose to be served by the administration of justice."[17] The ideal types for structure are hierarchial and coordinate. The ideal types for function of government are the purely reactive state and the activist state. In reactive states, conflicts between citizens and criminal proceedings resemble a contest between two parties. In the activist state, law is an expression of state policy. Criminal proceedings, therefore, are a means of implementing state policies. Damaška creates a theory which examines the *structures* of judicial authority, arguing that the nature of proceedings is determined by the character of the institution which operates it. He proposes that hierarchical authorities operate in a type of pyramid structure where officials are carefully ranked, usually based on professionalism. In contrast, coordinate authority models are horizontally structured and include amateur participants working alongside professional officials. Damaška views these two types of judicial authority in terms of state values which are either conflict-solving or policy-implementing. By linking different procedural systems to larger concepts such as state structure and authority, Damaška broadens the conceptualization of criminal procedure beyond the usual categorizations. Ultimately, in his view, the different procedural approaches adopted by judicial systems can be traced to how those systems view the criminal trial process: as a contest between sides or as an official inquiry. His work sheds light on the deeper, philosophical differences between legal traditions and systems.

In contrast with Damaška, Vogler proposes a comparative approach that reflects the fundamental concepts of community, state and individual which takes into account social and political factors.[18] To this end, in his book *A World View of Criminal Justice* Volger, through a historical examination, compares three paradigms, including one based on Gemeinschaft (community), one on Gesellschaft (society) and one on bureaucratic organization, together with three types of procedure, including inquisitorial, adversarial and popular justice. He attempts to take into account a wider variety of actors including independent defense counsel, individual participants such as victims and civil society. Adopting Thibaut and Walker's approach,[19] he argues that "an understanding of the balance of interests between participants within the criminal process is essential [...]."[20] Ultimately he argues that inquisitorial, adversarial and

17 Damaška (1986) at 9.
18 Vogler (2005) at 11.
19 See Thibaut and Walker (1975).
20 Vogler (2005) at 15.

popular justice procedures should be balanced within a justice system, without allowing one of them to dominate.[21]

Packer, Damaška and Vogler all concede that criminal justice traditions and systems will not wholly fit within their various models or paradigms and it is not the objective of this chapter to discuss the relative merits of each of these theories. Instead they are offered to better conceptualize criminal law and procedure as they provide important tools for understanding the similarities and differences between various legal systems throughout the world. Interestingly, all of their theories hold that it is misleading to think solely in terms of adversarial and inquisitorial systems.[22] In fact, it appears to be *in vogue* at the moment to reject established descriptive systems of the criminal process, most notably in terms of the dichotomy between inquisitorial and adversarial approaches.[23] However, this division may in fact be useful in order to gain a better understanding of why certain procedural approaches are selected over others. Contrary to the position that conventional classifications are meaningless because legal jurisdictions combine features associated with both approaches thereby making them hard to classify, conventional classifications shed light on how the divergent legal approaches to trial and procedure have shaped both national and international proceedings. Field notes that although authors have used the terms 'inquisitorial' and 'adversarial' in diverse ways, differing based upon which procedural practices to associate with them, this does not mean that one cannot identify central concepts related to the terms.[24] Specifically he mentions that one can readily recognize one approach's vision of the criminal trial as a contest between parties where oratory and public presentation take precedence while identifying another approach's vision as an active state investigation where written evidence is collected in an official dossier and evaluated.[25]

In fact, almost all scholars have taken note of these key concepts. Nevertheless, there is great disagreement over which particular procedural features square with which approach.[26] This disagreement, however, does not mean that the conventional distinctions are at all times misplaced. Field correctly notes that if legal classifications are understood in a "sociologically complex way," recognizing that they are fluid concepts, then the legal distinctions between inquisitorial and adversarial approaches can be used to show how different systems are shaped.[27] Due to the fact that present rhetoric and scholarship on criminal procedures and criminal justice systems use both the traditional groupings as well as newer models it is important to understand them

21 *Ibid.* at 286; although praising Vogler's historical contribution, Roberts has criticized his work for being largely descriptive despite his calls for a normative approach. In addition, Roberts argues that Vogler muddles theories and offers little conceptual clarifications, see generally Roberts (2008).
22 Jackson, J., Transnational Faces of Justice: Two Attempts to Build Common Standards beyond National Boundaries, 222, in Jackson, et al. (2008); Pizzi (1999) at 257.
23 See, e.g., Summers (2007).
24 Field (2009) at 368.
25 *Ibid.*
26 Jackson (2005) at 744.
27 Field (2009) at 370.

as well as the underlying value in each of them. This will further aid in the conceptualization of the trial process. For this reason, this study will largely discuss the traditions and legal approaches in accordance with the traditional groupings, but with the caveat that such groupings are useful for broader comparative purposes and do not necessarily reflect specific practices. Reference will also be made to the various models proposed by Packer, Damaška and Vogler.

3.3 Civil Law and Common Law Traditions

Differences between civil law and common law are based in large part on their underlying beliefs and values regarding criminal law and the procedures applied by their judicial institutions. Unlike common law systems, civil law systems generally do not view "the law primarily as a means of settling disputes or of restoring the peace" or of remedying for specific cases, but rather they adopt a "more conceptual and abstract approach to the law, preferring to see it in terms of fundamental principles."[28] Reasons for the divergent perspectives between common law systems and civil law systems largely have to do with their historical legal developments.[29]

Civil law, also referred to as Romano-Germanic law or European Continental law,[30] is the oldest, most widely influential and predominant legal tradition in the world.[31] It characterizes many legal systems in Europe, Africa, Asia, South America and North America.[32] Although civil law legal systems have adopted local variations on the law which glorify their own indigenous practices, it is the commonality between these systems which forms the substance of the civil law tradition. Two of the main characteristics often associated with the civil law tradition are a perception of the trial process as one seeking to obtain truth through the application of legal principles and the adoption of a largely inquisitorial approach in proceedings.

Common law, also referred to as Anglo-American law, arguably began in England following the Norman Conquest in 1066.[33] It is the dominant tradition in the United Kingdom, Ireland, the United States (with the exception of Louisiana), Canada (with the exception of Quebec), Australia, New Zealand, the Caribbean, and the former British colonies, including countries such as Uganda. Two of the defining characteris-

---

28 Dadomo and Ferran (1993) at 12, citing Nicholas, B. in his preface to Harris, D. and Tallon D., *Contract Law Today: Anglo-French Comparisons*, Oxford University Press (1989); David (1980) at 4.

29 Dadomo and Ferran (1993) at 12; see also Merryman (1969); Vogler (2005).

30 The term 'civil law' originates in English-speaking countries where it is used to refer collectively to all non-English legal traditions so as to make comparisons easier with the English common law. However, Continental European traditions vary considerably and many scholars of comparative law, particularly those promoting the legal origins theory, regularly refer to the various civil law jurisdictions as Romano-Germanic law.

31 Merryman (1969) at 1-2, noting that civil law dates back to 450 BC, which is the date most often quoted for the publication of the XII Tables in Rome.

32 *Ibid.* at 2-3.

33 Vogler and Huber (2008) at 46; Merryman (1969) at 4.

tics of the common law tradition include a belief that the best way to uncover the truth of a matter is to allow opposing sides the opportunity to present their case in a subjective manner and the adoption of the adversarial approach to proceedings which stresses orality and public trial.

3.4 The Inquisitorial Procedural Approach

Those unfamiliar with civil law systems often associate the inquisitorial approach with images of ecclesiastical investigations from times past, which involved the goal of obtaining a confession to a crime through torture or other dubious means. Contemporary inquisitorial procedures could not be further removed, however, from these practices. Simply put, legal systems adopting an inquisitorial approach generally place a larger duty on the state authorities, i.e. judges, rather than the parties, to investigate facts and seek the truth.[34] In other words, the inquisitorial approach represents a process whereby judicial authorities predominantly control the investigation, appraisal of evidence and general shape of trial. It is important to note that at the various stages of a criminal process different authorities will play a role and, as a result, one can make a clear distinction between the authority responsible for the criminal inquiry and the judicial authority responsible for trial. In this sense, the rights of accused are safeguarded by the various levels of judicial control. Moreoever, at all stages, the judicial or central authority is meant to be objective, investigating inculpatory as well as exculpatory evidence in the pursuit of truth.[35]

At the heart of the inquisitorial process is the pre-trial phase. In many countries, such as France, this phase is not public with unlimited inquiry rights of the investigating judge assisted by (and largely conducted by) the police.[36] Indeed, police investigations are largely supervised by an investigating and/or prosecuting magistrate.[37] In Spain, for example, the *Juez Instructor* has broad powers and conducts proceedings, which, like in France, are usually held in secret.[38] This early stage centers on the official *dossier*.[39] All parties have access to the case file. The preparation of a comprehensive case file of written evidence is the responsibility of the judicial authority, often with the assistance of the police. Witness statements are then placed in the official dossier. It is not necessarily the function of the lawyers to seek out witnesses or interview such witnesses prior to trial. If the victim or defendant would like someone to be interviewed their attorney usually brings the name of that potential witness to the

34 Pizzi and Perron (1996) at 51.
35 Dadomo and Ferran (1993) at 160.
36 Vogler, R., France, 177, in Vogler and Huber (2008).
37 Field (2009) at 367.
38 Merino-Blanco (1996) at 174.
39 The official dossier becomes formally immaterial at trial, Vogler, R., France, 177, in Vogler and Huber (2008).

attention of the investigation authority whether that be the prosecutors' office or the investigating judge.

The pre-trial phase in inquisitorial systems usually includes the successive questioning of the accused by the judicial police, prosecutor, magistrate and others.[40] If there are discrepancies between the defendant's statements and those of other witnesses the judge may set up a confrontation.[41] Whereas an accusatorial system might view the interrogations as a possible infringement of the right to remain silent, the opposite is true in many inquisitorial systems. Often, it can be viewed as an opportunity for the accused to establish his innocence.[42] The role of counsel during the pre-trial phase is to ensure that procedures and fair trial rights are adhered to and that all enquiries are investigated.[43] In this respect, parties may request the investigating judge to carry out further investigations.[44] The pre-trial phase is meant to be so thorough that the trial phase assumes much less importance. However, "there has [...] been a tendency in domestic civil law systems to move away from the concept of the investigating judge as an ideal model."[45] Delmas-Marty notes that "[m]ost countries on the Continent have progressively abolished the position of investigating magistrate and have given a more active role to the defense" in an attempt to better safeguard fair trial rights.[46] Undoubtedly, present-day civil law systems adopting an inquisitorial approach provide the accused with opportunities to defend themselves against the crimes charged, to request witnesses for their defense and offer counter arguments against those asserted by the state and victim.[47]

In contrast with the pre-trial phase, the trial is conducted in public and takes on an adversarial character.[48] In France, for example, where its pre-trial phase is not public and largely dominated by judicial or investigating authorities, its trial phase is public and incorporates many adversarial elements.[49] The trial judges, however, do not need to rehear all of the evidence collected during the pre-trial phase. Instead, they can usually rely on depositions previously carried out before judicial authorities so long as defense counsel were present and had the opportunity to submit questions. Despite the adversarial nature of trials, when questioning witnesses at trial, procedures for

40 *Ibid.* at 239.
41 Merino-Blanco (1996) at 176.
42 Vogler, R., France, 239, in Vogler and Huber (2008).
43 *Ibid.* at 179.
44 Merino-Blanco (1996) at 174.
45 Jackson, J., Transnational Faces of Justice: Two Attempts to Build Common Standards beyond National Boundaries, 245, in Jackson, et al. (2008).
46 Delmas-Marty, M., Reflections on the 'Hybridisation' of Criminal Procedure, 253, in Jackson, et al. (2008); see also, Vogler, R., France, 177, in Vogler and Huber (2008).
47 Jackson, J., Transnational Faces of Justice: Two Attempts to Build Common Standards beyond National Boundaries, 231, in Jackson, et al. (2008).
48 Dadomo and Ferran (1993) at 161.
49 Vogler, R., France, 179, in Vogler and Huber (2008).

doing so differ from questioning associated with adversarial proceedings. Pizzi and Perron summarize the German procedure as follows:

> After the presiding judge has informed the witness of her obligation to testify truthfully and completely about the matter at hand, and has obtained a few pieces of background information from the witness, such as her name and address, the presiding judge will always ask the witness to explain fully and completely what happened. In short, the witness is invited to tell all she knows about the crime and its surrounding circumstances in a narrative fashion.[50]

The emphasis on narrative testimony in inquisitorial proceedings reflects the idea that testimony should be presented in an unrehearsed and un-manipulated fashion,[51] believing this to be the best way in which the court can make a reasoned decision on the facts. Witnesses, victims and the accused all generally have the opportunity of speaking in narrative form. Often this narrative testimony results in hearsay, opinion or irrelevant testimony that may be prejudicial to the defense but it is believed that the professional judges are capable of filtering out these evidentiary concerns.[52] Usually, once the witness has finished telling his story the judge will then begin to ask questions, followed by the parties. While the various parties to the proceedings, including victims, may comment upon evidence, it is the judges who shape court proceedings by deciding on which witnesses they wish to call and how they would like to initially question them.[53] As such, generally, the judges carry out the bulk of the witness examinations, requiring the lawyers for the prosecution, defense and victims to only play a subordinate role.

Another defining feature of the inquisitorial approach is that generally the guilt and sentencing phases are combined, meaning that there is no separate sentencing hearing. The consequence of having a combined process is that the court will always ask the victims about the impact of the crime on them during the guilt phase.

The structural framework of inquisitorial proceedings arguably provides a far easier process for victim inclusion.[54] The ability to participate as a party in the proceedings, to request certain investigations and not be responsible for investigating facts, to gain access to the case file, to have the opportunity to tell their story in narrative form, and to attach a reparations claim are only a few examples of how civil law systems

---

50 Pizzi and Perron (1996) at 42.

51 See, e.g, the German Code of Criminal Procedure, Section 69, stating that the witness shall be directed to state coherently all he knows about the subject of his examination, after which the witness will be asked clarifying questions.

52 Pizzi and Perron (1996) at 43.

53 Hodgson, J., Conceptions of the trial in Inquisitorial and Adversarial Procedure, 223-226, in Duff, Farmer, Marshall, and Tadros (2006).

54 Hogen and Brienen at 1169: "The adhesion procedure should be maintained for participatory purposes. It has the major advantage of allowing the victim to have a voice in the criminal process and of granting him several participatory rights in the pre-trial stages." Damaška (1986) at 200-204.

adopting an inquisitorial approach allow for greater victim-oriented provisions. Therefore, civil law systems are generally viewed as providing for broader victim participatory rights.

3.5 The Adversarial Procedural Approach

Although there are aspects of adversariality that are present in legal systems that have adopted largely inquisitorial procedures, the inquisitorial procedural approach differs from the adversarial approach adopted by common law systems.[55] The adversarial procedural approach is a method of adjudication characterized by three important factors (1) an impartial tribunal; (2) formal procedural rules; and (3) party control over the proceedings, meaning that the parties are responsible for presenting their own case and challenging their opponent's case.[56] The last of which is the most important for the purpose of this study. The duty of the advocate is to represent his side's interests zealously; therefore, partisan advocacy is crucial.

Damaška writes that "the adversarial mode of proceedings takes its shape from a contest or a dispute: it unfolds as an engagement of two adversaries before a relatively passive decision maker whose principal duty is to reach a verdict," whereas the "non-adversarial mode is structured as an official inquiry."[57] Similarly, Freedman defines the adversarial system as a system that "resolves disputes by presenting conflicting views of fact and law to an impartial and relatively passive arbiter."[58] Therefore, in adversarial systems the two competing parties bear the burden of evidence collection,[59] and the court plays an inactive role. The entire trial depends primarily upon the parties and the decisions they make.[60] The defense in adversarial proceedings engages in "combat" against the prosecutor and therefore retains the right to carry out its own investigations, gather evidence, and call witness. Thus, at pre-trial the court takes no part in the preparation or investigation of the case and at trial the court does not initiate the lines of inquiry. It is the prosecution and the defense who define the issues and present evidence supporting their respective positions. The judge is meant to be impartial and any interference or influence may result in the perception that the trial was not conducted fairly. In fact, the judges, while often able to play an active role, usually refrain from doing so, preferring to play the role of a neutral decision maker and rule enforcer.

The structure of the adversarial criminal trial therefore is seen as a clash between two sides – one accusing and the other defending. The long-standing belief behind this

---

55 See generally Jackson, J., Transnational Faces of Justice: Two Attempts to Build Common Standards beyond National Boundaries, 233, in Jackson, et al. (2008).

56 Luban (1998) at 57.

57 Damaška (1986) at 3.

58 Freedman (1998) at 57.

59 Kutnjak Ivkovic (2001) at 275.

60 *Ibid.*

structure is that zealous advocacy for those accused of a criminal offense "is the greatest safeguard of individual liberty against the encroachment of the state."[61] The frequently quoted adage, 'better that a hundred criminals go free than that one person be wrongly convicted' was borne out of the common law system and reflects the emphasis on protecting the defendant from miscarriages of justice. The distrust of the 'powers that be' is reflected in the procedures applied in many common law jurisdictions where the procedural rights of the accused are emphasized.[62] There is a strong emphasis on the protection of the individual from tyranny in the extreme and abuse of process in the least. Although the primary goal of adversarial systems is legal justice, some commentators argue that the adversarial approach makes protection from the state a higher priority than obtaining justice.[63] Nevertheless, obtaining justice and protection from abuse of state power are not mutually exclusive.

The consequentialist justifications for the adversarial system are that it is the best way at uncovering the facts of a case and getting at the 'truth'. Proponents of the adversarial system argue that "the truth is best served by self-interested rather than disinterested investigation."[64] One of the main non-consequentialist justifications is that the adversarial approach is intrinsic with the notion of upholding the human dignity of the accused. Respect for human dignity demands that only after a formal process, like a criminal trial, can the state formally condemn an individual's actions. The notion of the presumption of innocence and the burden of proof placed on the state reinforce this liberal model of justice. As such, the legal system must provide a forum in which an accuser (the State) and the accused get to present their case.

Over time, the victim, who at one point led the accusation, became marginalized in adversarial proceedings. As independent prosecution associations emerged and the state gained control of criminal prosecutions, the victim's role was relegated to a complainant and/or witness for the state.[65] Recently, some adversarial jurisdictions have adopted procedures whereby victims, through their legal representatives, may participate in relation to specific issues at trial. For example some jurisdictions allow criminal courts to provide for civil damages while others allow victims to participate with regard to very narrowly tailored issues such as sexual history.[66] Generally speaking, however, the increased participation of victims would "potentially cause immense structural and normative problems within any adversarial system" due to its construction as a battle of two sides.[67]

61 Luban (1988) at 58.
62 However, as Luban aptly points out, in the real world persons accused of crimes enjoy very few real advantages no matter how many rights they have because most of their trial rights can never be exercised due to the use of plea bargains, see *Ibid.* at 60.
63 *Ibid.* at 63.
64 *Ibid.* at 73.
65 On the evolution of the independent prosecution associations, see Vogler (2005) at 140.
66 For examples see Doak (2005) at 296.
67 *Ibid.* at 297.

3.6 Conceptualizing Participation

In its simplest form, participation means the "act of sharing or taking part."[68] However, the term 'participation' is diverse and incorporates any number of things.[69] In the late 1960s, Arnstein developed a conceptualization of participation for the specific context of town planning and development, which created an eight-rung 'ladder of participation'.[70] Though, by her own admission, her typology is meant to be provocative, it serves as a useful illustration of different forms of participation even outside of the town-planning construct. Her classifications range from having real power or decision-making control in the outcome to 'empty ritual' participation that is only meant to maintain the *status quo* and serve the interests of decision-making institutions. Thus, the two lowest rungs on the ladder are 'manipulation' and 'therapy', which she views as forms of non-participation "contrived by some to substitute for genuine participation."[71] The next three rungs are what Arnstein describes as forms of token participation. These include participation in the form of receiving 'information', participation in the form of 'consultation', or participation in the form of 'placation'. Placation allows greater input and influence than 'information' or 'consultation' but those in power are not required to consider the participant's views. Finally, the top of the ladder represents true citizen power and includes 'partnership', 'delegated power' and 'citizen control'. In these forms of participation, the participant has some decision-making control.

Building upon Arnstein's work, Edwards has proposed his own typology of victim participation specifically for the criminal process.[72] His conceptualization consists of four different participatory roles for victims that are either dispositive or non-dispositive. The first and most extreme type of participation identified by Edwards is 'control'. Under this form of participation, victims have decision-making power. Criminal justice institutions and authorities are required to hear from the victim and follow a course of action based upon the victim's preference. He gives the example of Sharia law as an example where victims often have the final say in what form of punishment is administered on a wrongdoer. The second type of participation is 'consultation'. Consultation obliges the authorities to seek out information from victims but they would not be required to follow the victims' preferences. He notes that consultation takes place in a number of domestic systems and could include situations where a prosecutor seeks the views of victims with regard to a plea agreement. Importantly, the victim is not required to participate but does so at his or her own discretion. The third type of participation identified by Edwards includes participation limited to the 'provision of information'. Criminal justice decision-makers

68 Edwards (2004) at 973.
69 *Ibid.*
70 Arnstein (1969).
71 Arnstein (1969) at 217.
72 Edwards (2004).

would be required to seek out and consider information provided by victims. Under this form of participation, victims would actually be obliged to supply the information to the authorities. Resembling the role of complainant and witness, victims act as information-providers and play a crucial role in the determination of a case. The final type of participation is that of 'expression'. According to Edwards, expression obliges authorities to provide victims with an opportunity to share their feelings and emotions. Victims are not required to do so but if they participate they are able to communicate their feelings and express their views and concerns. Edwards notes that victim impact statements are a way in which victims can be emotive. Edwards excludes the act of receiving information from his typology since he views this as non-participation.[73] However, Wemmers would consider it a form of passive participation as it "sends a message to victims that they are not forgotten and that their interest in the case is recognized by authorities."[74]

These conceptualizations of participation are useful as a way in which to view different modalities of participation available to victims in the criminal process. Together with basic models of participation, discussed below in Section 3.7, they indicate that participation incorporates a range of acts from full decision-making control to receiving information and support.

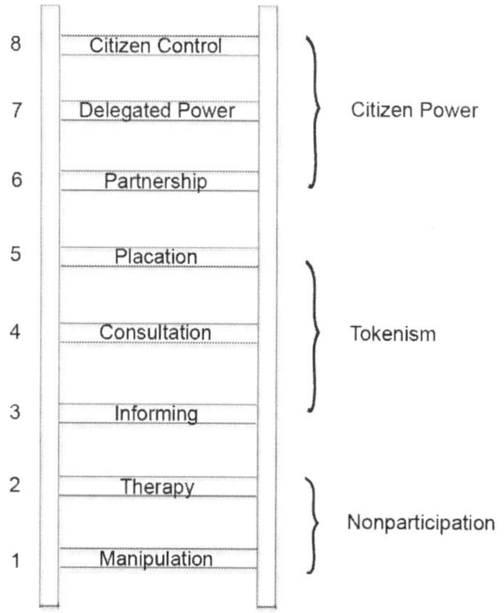

Table 1. Arnstein's Ladder of Citizen Participation

73 *Ibid.* at 976-977.
74 Wemmers (2010) at 635.

	Participation Type	Obligation on Criminal Justice Decision-Maker	Obligation on Victim
Dispositive	**CONTROL**	To seek and apply victim preferences	Non-optional ; victim is the decision-maker
Non-Dispositive	**CONSULTATION**	To seek and consider victim preferences	Optional supply of preferences
Non-Dispositive	**INFORMATION-PROVIDER**	To seek and consider victim information	Non-optional supply of information
Non-Dispositive	**EXPRESSION**	To allow victim expression	Optional supply of information/emotion

Table 2. Edwards' Typologies of Participation in the Criminal Justice System

3.7 Models of Victim Participation at the Domestic Level

Assuming that in fact systems adopting a more inquisitorial approach have an easier time incorporating victims into proceedings as compared to systems adopting a more adversarial approach, how have the various national systems, falling within one of the two dominant traditions, interpreted, adapted and applied procedures with regard to victims in criminal proceedings? The following section outlines the five most common models or archetypes of victim participation that dominate at the domestic level. These models include victims participating as: (i) complainants; (ii) victim-witnesses; (iii) civil parties; (iv) private, subsidiary, or auxiliary prosecutors; and (v) impact statement providers. Because participation varies from jurisdiction to jurisdiction, these models are not meant to reflect any one system. Instead, they are general categories of participation that are useful as a means for understanding the wide range of participation practices utilized at the domestic level. Moreover, they will be useful when examining the participation of victims at international criminal institutions, not only because they are familiar categories, but also because they can make it easier to understand the multiple participatory options. In addition to these forms of participation, many national systems have also adopted restorative justice approaches. These approaches will also be discussed as they offer victims another form of participation connected to the criminal process but falling largely outside of traditional criminal justice structures.

3.7.1 Complainant

In all judicial systems a victim may report a crime by submitting a complaint to the police or other appropriate authority. In most common law jurisdictions there are few, if any, legal rights that attach to an individual who files a complaint. In contrast, in civil law jurisdictions many offenses cannot be prosecuted without a victim first filing a complaint with that victim retaining the power to withdraw the complaint and end the prosecution.[75] Generally, the complaint procedure kicks off an investigation by the police and may lead to a decision by the state on whether or not to prosecute an individual for a crime. If the state chooses to prosecute then the victim-complainant may then be asked or summoned to act as a victim-witness. If the state chooses not to prosecute an alleged offense, some jurisdictions allow the victim to force a prosecution.[76] Therefore, depending on the specific jurisdiction the rights of the complainant vary considerably. The importance of the role of the complainant cannot be underscored enough because without it many crimes would go unacknowledged and unpunished.

3.7.2 Victim-Witness

Another fundamental role played by victims in criminal adjudication is that of victim-witness due to the fact that the testimony of a victim can be one of the most crucial aspects in a trial against an accused perpetrator.[77] As a witness, the victim swears under oath that what they testify to at trial is a correct version of events; though some jurisdictions allow the victim-witness to forgo testifying at trial and instead submit their pre-trial testimony as evidence.[78] Very often, victims acting as witnesses are not entitled to the same rights as they have when acting as civil parties or private/subsidiary/auxiliary prosecutors. For example, the victim-witness may be excluded from attending trial before testifying so that he cannot be influenced by those testifying before him. In addition, victim-witnesses are generally not entitled to legal counsel.

3.7.3 Civil Party / Civil Complainant

In almost every civil law jurisdiction victims have the opportunity of joining their civil claims to the criminal prosecution or triggering criminal proceedings themselves, making the victims civil parties in the case (*partie civile* in France, *actor civil* in Argentina, *burgerlijke partij* in the Netherlands).[79] This adhesion model, however, is generally unknown in common law jurisdictions. In theory, this process recognizes the

75 Brienen and Hoegen (2000) at 26.

76 Dadomo and Ferran (1993) at 200.

77 Handbook on Justice for Victims, Chapter II, D-8-(d).

78 The victim-witness' role is not easy. The victim-witness must often recount their story to police/investigating authorities, prosecuting authorities and then again at trial. The effects of having to re-tell their story multiple times to various audiences are often emotionally burdensome if not traumatic and studies suggest that many cross-examination techniques familiar in common law jurisdictions exacerbate the trauma and may cause feelings of re-victimization. See Brienen and Hoegen (2000) at 29.

79 *Ibid.* at 1069.

fact that a wrongdoer is answerable both to the individual he harmed as well as to the state. Many advocates of the process argue that being a party to the proceedings "assist[s] victims to take back control of their lives and to ensure that their voices are heard, respected, and understood."[80] Advocates also argue that it saves time and money both for victims and the state.[81] Critics argue the opposite, arguing that depending on the complexity of the case it can delay and complicate proceedings.[82]

Although somewhat similar to the role of auxiliary prosecutor, discussed below, the adhesion procedure acknowledges the victim and his legal counsel as a separate party to the proceedings. Victims who become civil parties are often able to initiate a prosecution, actively participate in proceedings and claim reparations for harms suffered.[83] The adhesion model has the major advantage of allowing the victim to have a voice in the criminal process and of granting him several important participatory rights.[84]

At the pre-trial stage, he has the right to examine the dossier and to make requests to the examining magistrate for investigations. In fact, throughout the pre-trial phase, the civil party has much the same rights as the accused, including the right to appeal all decisions of the examining magistrate (except for bail and custody). He also has the right to counsel and in many jurisdictions the court will appoint counsel for those unable to afford their own. At trial, civil parties generally have the right to attend hearings, put questions to witnesses and the accused, and lead and challenge evidence. However, although theoretically victims may examine witnesses and make submissions regarding the guilt of the accused, in practice, participation at trial is usually limited to their civil claim for damages.[85] When addressing the court, unlike a victim-witness, the civil party may be heard without taking an oath.[86] Civil parties may also make closing arguments. In France, for example, the victims make their closing remarks before the prosecution and defense.[87]

Importantly, the participatory rights for civil parties are generally only available insofar as they pertain to a victim's claim for damages against the accused.[88] The civil claim is always viewed as subordinate to the objectives of the criminal proceedings. If for example a court determines that the criminal trial is too complex or the civil trial

80 Danieli, Y., Victims: Essential Voices at the Court, Victims Rights Working Group Bulletin, September 2004, p. 6.
81 In fact, in Argentina, "the victim's decision to become a party to the criminal proceedings is aimed at forcing a deal with the defendant." If the defendant reaches a settlement with the victim there is a greater chance that the criminal prosecution will be dismissed. Bradley (1999) at 46.
82 Joutsen (1987-1988) at 116-117.
83 Doak (2005) at 311.
84 Brienen and Hoegen (2000) at 1169.
85 Bacik, et al. (1998) at 59.
86 Sheehan (1975) at 22.
87 Vogler, R., France, 241, in Vogler and Huber (2008).
88 Doak (2005) at 311; Van Dijk, J.J.M., Victim Rights: A Right to Better Services or a Right to Active Participation? 354, in Van Dijk, et al. (1986).

would require too many court resources then the victims can be made to bring their civil claim separately in a civil court. In addition, if a criminal case does not proceed the victim may still bring a civil case in the civil court.[89]

Despite the usefulness of this model construct, it must be mentioned that the rights generally associated with civil party status vary considerably across jurisdictions. For instance, in contrast with broad rights of civil parties in Spain, France and Belgium, in Italy, civil parties have only a limited capacity to participate as it relates to their claim for damages and play a "very modest role."[90] They do not have the right to appeal an acquittal and are excluded from the sentencing process.[91] Henham and Mannozzi attribute the modest role to two main factors (1) the focus of the proceedings on the public interest of justice and punishment in sharp contrast to a focus on private compensation and (2) the court's 'hostility' or distrust towards overly active victims, equating active victims with the notion of revenge.[92] Despite the differences that exist between jurisdictions on the extent of civil party rights, all civil law jurisdictions recognize that civil parties have certain procedural rights in order to ensure compensation by the wrongdoer (or state) for harms suffered.

3.7.4 Private / Subsidiary / Auxiliary Prosecutor

In some civil law and common law jurisdictions victims may participate by contributing to or substituting for the prosecution.[93] In this form of participation the victim is usually referred to as the private prosecutor, subsidiary prosecutor or auxiliary prosecutor.[94]

The private prosecution model (*querellante particular* in Argentina, *Privatkläger* in Germany) generally allows victims to have full prosecutorial rights. Participation starts from the beginning of the investigation where the victim's counsel may suggest that the judicial magistrate or police carry out specific investigations,[95] and they have the right to bring charges and conduct the prosecution at trial. Unlike civil parties their interventions are not confined to their claim for damages. However, one major difference between acting as a private prosecutor and a civil party is that victims acting as private prosecutors are usually obliged to cover the costs of trial if the case is dis-

89 Brienen and Hoegen (2000) at 1069.
90 Henham and Mannozzi (2003) at 288.
91 *Ibid.*
92 *Ibid.* at 290.
93 See Brienen and Hoegen (2000): civil law jurisdictions include, for instance, France, Spain and Germany; common law jurisdictions include England and Wales. As a private, subsidiary or auxiliary prosecutor victims may also attach their civil claim for damages.
94 Doak (2005) at 311, largely considering these roles to be beneficial to both victims and the criminal justice systems in general.
95 Bradley (1999) at 45.

missed or an acquittal ensues.[96] They may also have to pay damages to the accused if a case is found to be brought as an abuse of process.

Though this model is appealing due to its broad participatory role for victims, it also has its drawbacks, especially when there is a poor legal aid system for victims and when the victim-prosecutor lacks legal knowledge.[97] Moreover, in most countries private prosecutions are limited to a certain category of crimes such as misdemeanors.[98] Joutsen agrees with these limitations and argues that private prosecutions should occur only (i) if [the alleged crime] is of a low degree so that public order is not implicated; (ii) if the victim's attitude is critical in establishing facts such as in cases of libel and defamation; (iii) if social or family relations are involved; or (iv) if a victim's right to privacy or other interests that take precedence over public interests are present.[99] Brienen and Hoegen argue that the private prosecution model is "an antiquated institution that should be supplemented with, or even replaced by, the right to judicial review of a decision to discontinue a prosecution."[100] This is because the private prosecution model places too much responsibility on the victim and, in their view, can be seen as a victim's attempt at revenge.

The subsidiary or auxiliary prosecution model refers to a situation where the prosecuting authority has chosen not to prosecute an offense falling within the public domain and the victim forces a prosecution. In many jurisdictions this requires permission from the court and usually the public prosecutor is then required to take over the prosecution.[101] The subsidiary/auxiliary prosecution model (*Nebenkläger* in Germany and Austria) allows victims, through their own legal counsel, to work alongside public prosecutors.[102] Although the public prosecutor retains the responsibility of presenting the case, the victim, acting as a subsidiary/auxiliary prosecutor, and represented by legal counsel, has the right to be present at all proceedings, to question the witnesses, to submit evidence, to make statements on law and fact, and to claim reparations.[103] As with the private prosecutor, the subsidiary/auxiliary prosecutor's participation is not limited to his or her claim for reparation.[104] Moreover, an additional benefit of this model is that the subsidiary/auxiliary prosecutor is not usually under an obligation to pay costs should the accused be acquitted. Doak finds that these proceedings recognize "the special status of the complainant as the alleged victim of the

96 Brienen and Hoegen (2000) at 78; See also Juy-Birmann, R., The German System, 302, in Delmas-Marty and Spencer (2002).
97 Joutsen (1987-1988) at 102 and 113.
98 Brienen and Hoegen (2000) at 28.
99 Joutsen (1987-1988) at 98-99.
100 Brienen and Hoegen (2000) at 4.
101 *Ibid.* at 28.
102 *Ibid.*
103 Doak (2005) at 308; Brienen and Hoegen (2000) at 29.
104 *Ibid.*

criminal offense, whilst acknowledging at the same time the normative role of the state in prosecuting crime."[105]

Germany has had some form of subsidiary/auxiliary prosecution since 1924 although it was largely unused until the victims' rights movement gained momentum in the 1980s.[106] However, even since this time subsidiary prosecutions are only utilized limitedly,[107] and when in use victims and their legal counsel tend to play a passive role – intervening only occasionally.[108]

Although most common law jurisdictions do not formally allow for private, subsidiary or auxiliary prosecutions, the English common law did recognize that a crime was primarily an offense against an individual rather than the state. This philosophical attitude can be found in modern common law jurisdictions allowing private individuals to either assist or lead prosecutions. For example, numerous state courts in the United States allow victims and their families the 'right' to act as prosecutor or to heavily assist the prosecution.[109] Particularly in jurisdictions where there are limited resources, states have allowed victims to privately prosecute minor offenses, including assault and battery.[110] Usually, a trial court's decision to allow private prosecutors to lead or assist public prosecutions will only be reversed if there is an abuse of discretion or abuse of process.[111] In the jurisdictions which have not statutorily prohibited private or auxiliary prosecutions, usually the court treats the private prosecutors as if they are a temporary public prosecutor representing the interests of the state rather than the

105 Doak (2005) at 308.

106 Sanders (1999) at 12. In Germany, auxiliary prosecutors are provided for only in cases of serious crimes and crimes that have a personal impact on the victim or the victim's family, including libel or defamation, murder, assault, sexual assault, and kidnapping, see Pizzi (1996) at 55.

107 One reason for its limited use can be traced back to providing victims proper information about their rights within the criminal justice system, see Doak (2005) at 309-310; see also Pizzi (1996) at 58.

108 Kaiser, M., The Status of the Victim in the Criminal Justice System According to the Victim Protection Act, 604, in Kaiser, et al. (1991).

109 See *People ex rel. Luceno v. Cuozzo*, 412 N.Y.S.2d 748, 751 (1978), holding that a private individual may act as a prosecutor subject to the discretion of the trial judge; *State of West Virginia v. Calvin O. Atkins*, 261 S.E.2d 55, 58 (W. Va. 1979), allowing a private prosecution and finding that "it is not inappropriate to consider that in certain cases, the victim's family may wish to satisfy itself that the case is being vigorously prosecuted." See also, Cardenas (1986) at 376-378.

110 See, e.g., *New Jersey v Kinder*, 701 F. Supp. 486, 491-492 (D.N.J. 1988), holding that a private prosecutor can both prosecute in the criminal court and represent the interests of the victim in civil proceedings and noting that the state allows citizens to enforce the laws in instances where the prosecutor routinely does not prosecute because of a lack of resources, Cf., *United States ex rel v. Vuitton*, 481 U.S. 787 (1987), holding that the a private attorney should be as disinterested as a public prosecutor and that the appointment of an interested prosecutor is a fundamental error which means that it undermines confidence in the integrity of the criminal proceedings.

111 *People v. Blevins*, 96 N.E. 214 (1911), holding that the court abused its discretion in allowing two private prosecutors and another assisting prosecutor to work against an inexperienced, court-appointed defense counsel.

interests of the victim who hired them.[112] Nonetheless, the opportunity to act as private or auxiliary prosecutor is limited to specific jurisdictions and the private prosecutor does not act as a prosecutor for the victim but rather as a prosecutor for the state authority. Moreover, state courts which have invalidated private criminal prosecutions have done so in cases involving serious crimes as well as in cases where the public prosecutor expressly refused to prosecute.[113]

3.7.5 Impact Statement Provider

In common law countries like the United States, the United Kingdom, Canada, and Australia, victims' participatory rights before findings of guilt or acquittal are limited in that victims usually are not represented by legal counsel, they may not request investigations, they are not allowed to question witnesses, submit evidence, or attach a claim for civil damages. In fact, in most cases victims can only participate as a witness for one of the parties. However, once the accused is found or pleads guilty victims in most common law jurisdictions do generally have the limited right to submit and/or read victim impact statements or victim impact testimony to the court.[114] These statements (whether written or oral) reflect the physical, emotional and economic harm they and their families have suffered as a result of the crime committed. They are a way for victims to express their views as well as to influence the severity of a sentence, the appropriateness of parole and sometimes the terms of plea bargaining agreements.[115] Most commonly the written statements are included as attachments to the pre-sentence investigation report submitted to the court.[116]

In Australia, victims have the right to give information about their safety concerns at bail hearings, and they may provide victim impact statements and make submissions at parole hearings.[117] Similarly, in 2001 the United Kingdom introduced the Victim

---

112 Cardenas (1986) at 381; one court in the state of North Carolina found that "[t]he prosecuting attorney, whether the solicitor or privately employed counsel, represents the State." See *State v. Westbrook*, 181 S.E.2d 572, 583 (1972).

113 See, e.g., *State v. Harton*, 296 S.E.2d 112 (1982), barring private prosecution for vehicular homicide without the consent and oversight of the district attorney; *State ex rel. Wild v. Otis*, 257 N.W.2d 361 (Minn. 1977), appeal dismissed, 434 U.S. 1003 (1978), prohibiting private prosecution where the county attorney refused to prosecute and the grand jury refused to indict on charges of perjury, conspiracy and corruptly influencing a legislator; *Commonwealth v. Eisemann*, 453 A.2d 1045 (1982), nothing in the Pennsylvania Rules of Civil Procedure requires that a person who is not a police officer must get the district attorney's approval to file felony or misdemeanor charges which do not involve a clear and present danger to the community; *People ex rel. Luceno v. Cuozzo*, 412 N.Y.S.2d 748 (1978), disallowing private prosecution against a police officer when complainant was charged with a criminal offense arising out of the same incident.

114 See Kool and Moerings (2004) at 46, noting that there is a crucial difference between written and oral statements.

115 Tobolowsky (1999) at 70.

116 *Ibid.*

117 Refshauge (2006) at 4.

Personal Statement Scheme, which allows victims to express how the crime has impacted them in a statement made to the police. The statement is then attached to the prosecution's sentencing report. The Australian Consolidated Criminal Practice Direction provides that victims may make a personal statement to the police during the investigation; it may then be updated throughout the process and should be taken into account during the sentencing phase (along with supporting evidence).[118] The Practice Direction from the Lord Chief Justice makes clear, however, that the "opinion of the victim or the victim's close relatives as to what the sentence should be are [...] not relevant, unlike the consequence of the offence on them."[119] This stands in contrast to other procedures adopted in the United States and Canada where victim impact statements can (although they rarely do) affect sentence determinations. Certainly, there are mixed responses to victim impact statements in the United Kingdom.[120] Studies warn against raising victims' expectations, particularly with regard to their capacity to influence punishment.[121] A study conducted by Hoyle and others suggests that victim statement programs in the United Kingdom have unrealistically raised victims' expectations because they believe their submissions may impact upon sentencing.[122]

Importantly, victim impact statements are not confined to common law jurisdictions. The Netherlands, for example, also employs victim statements for specific categories of crimes.[123] However, unlike in many common law countries, judges in the Netherlands provide defendants the opportunity of responding, through the presiding Judge, to victim statements presented in court.[124] Because of the combined guilt and

---

118 See, Australian Consolidated Criminal Practice Direction, Part III, section 28 (2004).

119 Doak (2005) at 296, footnote 6; citing Practice Direction issued by the Lord Chief Justice as set out at Part III.28 of the Consolidated Criminal Practice Direction, Victim Personal Statement, 1 Cr. App. R. (S) 482 (2002); see also Henham and Mannozzi (2003) at 285.

120 *Ibid.* at 280, comparing Ashworth, A., Victims' Rights, Defendants' Rights and Criminal Procedure, in Crawford and Goodey (2000), Erez, E. and Tontodonato, P., The Effect of Victim Participation in Sentencing on Sentence Outcome, 28 *Criminology* 451 (1990) and Erez, E., Victim Participation in Sentencing: And the Debate Goes On, 3 *International Review of Victimology* 17 (1994), amongst others.

121 Strang (2002) at 13.

122 Henham and Mannozzi (2003) at 280, citing Hoyle et al., Evaluation of the 'One Stop Shop' and Victim Statement Pilot Projects, Home Office Research, Development and Statistics Directorate Report (London 1998).

123 See Kool and Moerings (2004); see also, Artikel 302, Wetboek van Strafvordering and Wet van 17 december 2009 tot wijziging van het Wetboek van Strafvordering, het Wetboek van Strafrecht en de Wet schadefonds geweldsmisdrijven ter versterking van de positie van het slachtoffer in het strafproces, Stb. 2010 1 [Article 302, Code of Criminal Procedure and Law of 17 December 2009 amending the Code of Criminal Procedure, the Criminal Code and the Law on Criminal Injuries and Compensation Fund in order to strengthen the position of the victim in the criminal process, Stb. 2010 1]

124 Kool and Moerings (2004) at 54; see also, Artikel 302, Wetboek van Strafvordering and Wet van 17 december 2009 tot wijziging van het Wetboek van Strafvordering, het Wetboek van Strafrecht en de Wet schadefonds geweldsmisdrijven ter versterking van de positie van het slachtoffer in het

sentencing phases, traditionally the Dutch system has been weary of oral victim statements. In their study on victim statements in the Dutch criminal process, Kool and Moerings note that in response to oral participation legal officials responded that "[i]f victims and their next-of-kin were to speak in court before a decision is reached on the evidence and the issue of guilt, this would detract, [...], from the presumption of innocence and perhaps give the impression the judge is being influenced, which is contrary to the required unprejudiced stance" of the judiciary.[125] The legal officiers' distrust of oral participation was not based on a fear of bringing emotion into the courtroom but rather on the fear that certain fair trial principles could be seen to be encroached. Despite this general distrust, the Netherlands, like many other European countries have pushed forward with reforms to strengthen the position of victims in the criminal justice system.[126] Nevertheless, there is little push to have victim impact statements affect sentencing. In many civil law systems, it is an "unwritten rule" that victims' attorneys do not request or recommend a specific length of sentence in their closing argument, believing that this is the responsibility of the state's attorney.[127]

There is debate as to whether victim impact statements influence outcomes of proceedings (whether trial or sentencing) and also whether they *should* influence proceedings.[128] Ashworth has concluded that "[i]n the context of a sentencing system whose primary aim is not restorative [...] there must be grave doubts about allowing a victim to voice an opinion as to sentence."[129] Ultimately, it appears that despite its wide adoption in common law countries and some civil law jurisdictions, there is still a great deal of controversy and confusion surrounding victim impact statements and the real impact they should have.

3.7.6 Restorative Practices

In addition to the five models of victim-oriented participation discussed above, domestic jurisdictions have also adopted a wide range of restorative practices aimed at refocusing criminal justice on the needs and concerns of victims. Restorative justice

strafproces, Stb. 2010 1 [Article 302, Code of Criminal Procedure and Law of 17 December 2009 amending the Code of Criminal Procedure, the Criminal Code and the Law on Criminal Injuries and Compensation Fund in order to strengthen the position of the victim in the criminal process, Stb. 2010 1]

125 Kool and Moerings (2004) at 56.

126 See Wet van 17 december 2009 tot wijziging van het Wetboek van Strafvordering, het Wetboek van Strafrecht en de Wet schadefonds geweldsmisdrijven ter versterking van de positie van het slachtoffer in het strafproces, Stb. 2010 1 [Law of 17 December 2009 amending the Code of Criminal Procedure, the Criminal Code and the Law on Criminal Injuries and Compensation Fund in order to strengthen the position of the victim in the criminal process, Stb. 2010 1]

127 Pizzi and Perron (1996) at 62-63.

128 See Erez and Laster (1999), suggesting that the influence tends to be marginal; see also Erez (1999); Kool and Moerings (2004) at 1.

129 Ashworth (2005) at 356.

practices are viewed as a new way in which to view criminal justice,[130] and although it has never been clearly defined Van Ness has found that the three foundations of restorative justice are:

1) Crime is primarily conflict between individuals resulting in injuries to victims, communities and the offenders themselves; only secondarily is it lawbreaking;
2) The overarching aim of the criminal justice process should be to reconcile parties while repairing the injuries caused by the crime;
3) The criminal justice process should facilitate active participation by victims, offenders and their communities. It should not be dominated by the government at the exclusion of others.[131]

Various types of restorative justice approaches include victim-offender reconciliation programs and family conferencing. The programs are similar in that they all involve direct participation of the victim and offender in the process and are generally utilized after a finding of fault. They differ in many ways, including on whether they focus more on reparation or more on reconciliation, whether the community is also represented, or whether it is attached to a punitive measure.

In the Netherlands, a program modeled on New Zealand's model of the Family Group Conference has been established. The so-called *Echt-Recht* conference allows defendants, victims and their families the opportunity to discuss the crime, how it has affected them, and to provide reasons for why it occurred. While conditioned upon the premise that the offender has taken responsibility for the crime, the conferencing has met with positive feedback.[132] In Germany, various victim-offender mediation (*Täter-Opfer-Ausgleich*) programs have also been successful. They focus on the participation of both victims and offenders and stress reconciliation and conflict resolution.[133] These victim-offender mediation programs emphasize the "peacemaking aspect of the law" and demand that reconciliation be taken into account during the criminal process.[134] Originally developed for juvenile offenders and their victims, the successful programs now apply to adult criminal processes. However, there continue to be problems with training mediation staff and acceptance of these programs by traditional criminal justice players. Nonetheless, the WAAGE program (*Verein für Konfliktschlichtung und Wiedergutmachung*) in Hannover was one specific mediation attempt by the German authorities to test a restorative approach.[135] In this program, victims and offenders are given the opportunity to discuss the offense and how to redress the harm

130 See Zehr (1990).
131 Van Ness (1993) at 259.
132 Malsh (2003) at 6.
133 Netzig, L. and Trenczek, T., Restorative Justice as Participation: Theory, Law, Experience and Research, 245, in Galaway and Hudson (1996).
134 *Ibid.* at 247.
135 *Ibid.* at 249.

suffered. While not contingent upon the seriousness of a crime it does depend upon the acceptance of the process by those involved. In other words, both sides of the conflict must want to participate and the offender must have already accepted responsibility for the wrongdoing. Early studies suggest that the program is successful although possibly underutilized.[136]

Research suggests that restorative practices, which are now commonly used in many common law and civil law jurisdictions, are widely accepted for minor crimes, whereas conventional punishment is considered necessary for more serious offenses.[137] Research also suggests that the public prefers a combination of retributive and restorative responses.[138] Therefore, although national systems have adopted some restorative models to complement existing criminal justice institutions, it has been the victim-oriented procedures that have really impacted the role of the victim in criminal cases.

In short, all of the forms of participation in the criminal process are associated with providing information either to authorities, or, in a general sense, through the notion of 'truth-telling', which has been held out as being highly beneficial in validating the victim's experiences and helping the victim heal.[139] Doak notes that the elevated role of the victim in national systems "can be said to emanate primarily from the victims' emerging status as consumers of the criminal justice services."[140] Many of the reforms concerning victims, including victim impact statements, notification rights and protection rights, have been largely accepted because they have not been viewed as infringing the due process rights of an accused and generally do not overburden national systems. These victim-oriented procedures, championed by the victims' movement, have sought to include victims, to varying degrees, in the criminal process, depending on the structure and tradition of the system. However, despite the fact that the above mentioned means of participation may exist on paper, this does not mean that they are actively pursued in practice,[141] or that concerns do not exist about the extent of participation in domestic jurisdictions.

---

136 *Ibid.* at 255-258.

137 Frehsee (1999) at 237, citing Sessar, K., Wiedergutmachen oder Strafen: Einstellungen in der Bevölkerung und der Justiz, 107, Centaurus (1992).

138 *Ibid.*, citing Baurmann, M. and Schädler, W., Das Opfer nach der Straftat: seine Erwartungen und Perspektiven, 95, Bundeskriminalamt [BKA Research Series] (1991).

139 Mahon (2009) at 737; see also Danieli, Y., Victims: Essential Voices at the Court, Victims Rights Working Group Bulletin, September 2004.

140 Doak (2005) at 295.

141 Joutsen (1987) at 183.

3.8 Reflections on Victim Participation: A Fundamental Divide Concerning the Role and Rights of Parties, Participants and Courts

There are deep-seated differences between Anglo-American, or common law, systems employing predominantly 'adversarial' procedures and Romano-Germanic, or civil law, systems employing predominantly 'inquisitorial' procedures. One of the fundamental differences concerns the roles and rights of parties and participants in the criminal process.[142] The divide between these two legal traditions is due, in part, to the differences in the perception of the trial process and the methods adopted in reaching their primary and ancillary goals. An example of a primary goal would include the search for truth or holding an individual accountable for committing a crime. An example of an important ancillary goal includes greater participation of victims in proceedings.

Using Damaška's models it is possible to categorize the above mentioned goals as either goals of a conflict-solving nature or goals of a policy-implementing nature.[143] On the one hand, a trial process structured as a contest between two parties best serves reactive states having criminal justice systems with goals of a conflict-solving nature. These systems predominantly employ adversarial approaches.[144] On the other hand, a trial process structured as an official inquiry best serves activist states having criminal justice systems with goals related to the implementation of policies. These systems predominantly adopt inquisitorial elements.[145] Despite both civil and common law systems sharing the similar primary goals such as pursuing the truth and establishing the guilt of an accused,[146] it is the method by which the systems arrive at these goals which differ. These differing methods highlight whether the goals are conflict-solving or policy implementing.[147] Damaška therefore contends that "it is thus precisely because Continental criminal procedure is *not* a bipolar contest, […], that the voice of the victim can easily be accommodated."[148] Similarly, Vogler finds that "[i]n a party-driven, adversarial process, […], it must be questioned whether [the] radical empowerment of the victim contributes to the orderly and fair administration of justice. It disturbs the symmetry of the adversarial conflict, as well as potentially compromising the strategic approach to prosecution of the state prosecutor."[149]

Doak also argues that a trial environment set up as a contest between two parties is ill-equipped to address the emotional trauma that comes into play when victims

142 See generally, Ambos (2003); Damaška (1986).
143 *Ibid.* at 88-96.
144 *Ibid.* at 97-146.
145 *Ibid.* at 147-180.
146 There is a widely held misconception that inquisitorial systems seek truth while adversarial systems seek to protect the rights of an accused. In fact both systems share these aims, see Ambos (2003).
147 Ambos (2003) at 21.
148 Damaška (1986) at 201.
149 Vogler (2008) at 23.

actively participate.[150] In predominately adversarial systems, witnesses, whether they are victims or not, are not given the opportunity to tell their stories in narrative form. In general, legal counsel in adversarial proceedings seek to control witness testimony by asking only those questions which aid in their case, reflecting partial truth – rather than questions that will elicit the whole truth of an incident. For Doak, the "contest culture of the courtroom is not at all conducive to *listening* to the accounts of individual witnesses, let along healing conflicts."[151] In addition, the presence of the victim as a party may inject too high a degree of emotion into the proceedings, detracting from the calm and rational resolution of the case.[152]

Another obstacle to victim participation in the trial phase in systems adopting adversarial proceedings stems from the bifurcated structure of the adversarial approach. A proceeding structured as a contest between parties, where the prosecutor has the burden of proving the guilt of the accused, makes adding a third party difficult if not infeasible. To be sure, "without radical reform, existing trial structures could not easily be adapted to accommodate the meaningful participation of any third party. Proceedings would undoubtedly become lengthy, awkward affairs – particularly if victim's counsel were to call their own witnesses and spend a considerable amount of time cross-examining others called by either the prosecution or defense."[153] Thus, many commentators and theorists view the adversarial system as a barrier to effective victim participation on par with that commonly found in civil law systems.[154]

Nevertheless, despite all of the obstacles to active victim participation during the pre-trial and trial phase, common law systems very often provide for victims' rights in other ways. For example, English law has created one of the strongest state compensation schemes and victim support services in all of Europe.[155] In fact, one clear conclusion drawn by Brienen and Hoegen in their comparative study of 22 European criminal justice systems is that "the compensation order is significantly more successful than the adhesion procedure in as far as the awarding and actual receiving of compensation from the offender is concerned."[156] Additionally, as noted above many jurisdictions have begun to use victim impact statements following a determination of guilt, allowing victims the opportunity to convey the harm they have suffered to the court once a finding of guilt has been determined.[157]

---

150 Doak (2005) at 297.

151 *Ibid.* at 298.

152 Vogler and Huber (2008) at 23.

153 Doak (2005) at 297.

154 *Ibid.* See also, Jorda, C. and De Hemptinne, J., The Status and Role of the Victim, 1387-1388, in Cassese, et al. (2002).

155 Brienen and Hoegen (2000) at 285. It is important to note that state compensation schemes usually operate with an 'ideal victim' in mind, meaning that they only pay out when it is determined that the victim was in no way connected with the offense, see Joutsen (1987) at 32.

156 Brienen and Hoegen (2000) at 4.

157 See Erez, E., Integrating a Victim Perspective in Criminal Justice Through Victim Impact Statements, 165-184, in Crawford and Goodey (2000).

Victims in all systems clearly have a legitimate interest in participating in the criminal justice process. There are numerous precedents at the national level as well as policy considerations supporting victim participation. The rights vary from jurisdiction to jurisdiction but almost every legal system from the two dominant legal traditions has adopted at least some form victim participatory rights. The issue for domestic systems has really been: to what extent should victims be able to participate given the normative and structural constraints of the operating system?

3.9 Conclusion

Judge Pikis from the ICC once stated that the main victim participation provision from the Rome Statute "has no immediate parallel or association with the participation of victims in criminal proceedings in either common law system of justice…or the Romano-Germanic system of justice."[158] However, this statement is certainly not that clear-cut. Inevitably, international criminal courts are created and designed by those individuals who hold deeply engrained beliefs from their own domestic systems and the methods those systems employ to meet their purported goals. As a result, "[j]udges and other protagonists steeped in their own domestic culture still tend to view processes through adversarial and non-adversarial lenses."[159] Therefore, the international criminal law landscape has undoubtedly been shaped by approaches employed at the national level.

For this reason, this chapter has attempted to show the dichotomy between the various national traditions and procedural approaches concerning trial proceedings generally and victim participation specifically. For the most part, the two legal traditions that the various international criminal courts have grown out of are the common law tradition, largely associated with the adversarial procedural approach, and the civil law tradition, largely associated with the inquisitorial procedural approach. These two judicial traditions differ in a number of respects – most notably in their focus on the roles and rights provided for the judges, prosecutors, defense and victims.

Indeed, the roles and rights of victims differ greatly between the civil and common law systems.[160] Although crude simplifications are generally superfluous, in this case, they are justified because, to a large extent, it appears that legal traditions have a direct correlation with the roles provided to victims in proceedings.[161] In this sense, all civil law legal systems provide victims with participatory rights under the civil party

---

158 ICC, *The Prosecutor v. Thomas Lubanga Dyilo*, No. ICC-01/04-01/06-925 (separate opinion of Judge Pikis), 13 June 2007, par. 11.

159 Jackson, J., Transnational Faces of Justice: Two Attempts to Build Common Standards beyond National Boundaries, 238, in Jackson, et al. (2008).

160 Bassiouni (2006) at 206-211, examining the evolution of victims' rights in international law.

161 Heikkilä (2004) at 43.

model.[162] Hence, a victim may often appear both as a source of information for the court (as a witness) and then subsequently as an individual who has suffered harm (as a victim).[163] In addition, in many civil law systems victims may either appeal decisions by the prosecutor to not go through with a prosecution or may initiate criminal proceedings themselves, thereby acting as private or auxiliary prosecutors.[164] Despite these broad participatory rights, however, victims in civil law systems rarely have an opportunity to voice their views and concerns in regard to sentencing issues, believing instead that this is best left to the public prosecutor. In contrast, common law legal systems typically do not afford victims the broad right to participate in the criminal process but they are often given broader rights to participate in specific hearings related to release, plea agreements, sentencing, or parole. At trial, victims may generally only participate as witnesses for either the prosecution or defense because they are not formal parties to the case. Their main role, therefore, is to provide accurate information to the court.[165]

Essentially, almost all domestic jurisdictions from the common law and civil law traditions now recognize victims should have *some* form of participatory rights in the criminal process, ranging from forms of tokenism or expression to decision-maker. A system's legal tradition is in many ways determinant of the manner and scope of permissible participation. In this regard, the procedural approach largely adopted by civil law countries allows for a greater participatory role for the victim, whereas the procedural approach largely adopted by common law countries provides for a more limited right of participation. Although there is general agreement among states on the right of victims to have some form of participatory rights it is evident that there is very little agreement on how far participation should extend.

Given the vast divergence amongst domestic practices it was somewhat surprising that states unanimously adopted the Victims' Declaration in 1985. This document calls upon states to allow victims the opportunity to share their views and concerns in domestic justice systems and has reinforced international developments related to the expanding rights of victims in criminal proceedings. The next chapter will examine international developments concerning the participatory rights of victims and how they influence (or not) the current procedural frameworks and practices of international criminal courts and the role of the victim in international criminal proceedings.

---

162 Jouet (2007) at 253-254.

163 Tochilovsky (2000) at 7.

164 Brienen and Hoegen at 28, 857-58, explaining that Spain has one of the most far-reaching laws concerning private prosecutions due to the fact that Spain allows virtually any person (including non-victims or non-citizens) to pursue a prosecution so long as the government has declined to prosecute the case. The most prominent case brought by victims in Spain being against General Augusto Pinochet in 1996. See also, Langer (2011).

165 Tochilovsky, V., Victims' Procedural Rights at Trial: Approach of Continental Europe and the International Tribunal for the Former Yugoslavia, 287-291, in Van Dijk, et al. (1999).

CHAPTER 4
INTERNATIONAL DEVELOPMENTS AND VICTIMS OF CRIME

4.1 INTRODUCTION

As touched upon in the previous chapters, the marginalization of the victim in the criminal process occurred with the growth of the modern state.[1] As states consolidated their power they soon exercised a monopoly over criminal matters. State monopoly over criminal matters, which until recently almost exclusively reflected a retributive and utilitarian approach to crime control, punishment and the judicial process, became so great that victims played little to no role in either civil law or common law systems – certainly there was no systemic focus on victims of crime.[2] Moreover, the structural and historical barriers to victim participation in both civil law and common law systems have contributed greatly to the general dissatisfaction of victims and their advocates with criminal processes. Out of this dissatisfaction grew the victims' rights movement and a new found interest in studying the role of victims in legal systems. Both the victims' rights movement and the field of study known as victimology made important contributions to criminal justice reform. Both asserted the position and role of victims within domestic judicial processes, leading domestic systems to either strengthen existing victim-oriented provisions or to create new rights for victims. Parallel with the attention paid to victims at the domestic level a number of important developments have also occurred at the international level, calling upon states to strengthen their victim-oriented measures in judicial proceedings.

This chapter examines these developments at the international level. First, the UN General Assembly declarations pertaining to victims of crime will be reviewed. Next this chapter will look at developments within human rights bodies and their approaches to victims in criminal justice processes. Subsequently, other developments and initiatives focused on victims of crime will be explored both internationally and regionally. Specific attention will also be paid to calls for a convention focused exclusively on the rights of victims. This chapter will appraise whether, and to what extent, the developments at the international level have impacted the call for greater rights for victims in domestic criminal justice systems, and what this may mean for the rights of accused.

---

1 Tobolowsky (1999) at 21; Laster (1970) at 71-80.
2 Ashworth (1993) at 278.

4.2 UN General Assembly Declarations

As a consequence of the initiatives of the victims' rights movement, the growth of the field of victimology,[3] and the political environment at the UN at that time a change in focus began to occur at the international level.[4] Although victims of crime have been the implicit subject of many UN reports and initiatives, including those documents and conventions related to genocide, war crimes and crimes against humanity, prior to the mid-1970s the UN focused almost exclusively on crime and the treatment of suspects, accused and prisoners. The liberal model emphasizing the rights of accused vis-à-vis the state completely dominated discourse. After this time, however, the UN began to turn its attention towards victims. For example, the UN Crime Prevention and Criminal Justice Program, the Quinquennial UN Congresses for the Prevention of Crime and the Treatment of Offenders and the 1975 Fifth UN Congress for the Prevention of Crime all contributed to a greater emphasis on the rights of victims.[5] Similarly, during the 1980 Sixth UN Congress for the Prevention of Crime participants considered issues concerning victims of abuse of power.[6] Finally, at the 1985 Seventh UN Congress for the Prevention of Crime issues affecting victims were made a major agenda item.[7] By emphasizing a connection between victims and abuse of power and transnational crime, victims' rights advocates were able to bring the spotlight on victims at the international level.[8]

---

3 In particular, the international conferences and symposia, bringing together experts on victimology, facilitated much of the development of victims' rights at the macro-level. These victimology conferences have focused on various themes related to victims. They provided the meeting place for an international community of academics and practitioners to form and push for greater victim rights. The topics discussed at these conferences included topics ranging from offender-victim relationships and victims' perceptions about criminal justice systems to reparations and restorative responses. Fairly early on, topics began to focus on improving the position of victims in criminal justice systems. For instance, in 1976 at the Second International Symposium on Victimology, the question was raised whether victims should play an active role in the criminal process, and very soon, international associations were formed to study and promote the rights of victims. Following the Third International Symposium on Victimology the World Society of Victimology (WSV) was created. The WSV is a non-governmental, non-profit organization that brings together experts to promote research in victimology and to promote reforms in legislation and services that focus on victims' rights. The work of the WSV, and other prominent international victim-oriented organizations, includes lobbying at the UN for the rights of victims of crime. See Van Dijk, J., Ideological Trends within the Victims Movement: An International Perspective, 119-25, in Pointing and Maguire (1988); Joutsen, M., Changing Victim Policy: International Dimensions, 238, in Kirchhoff, et al. (1991), noting the concern for victims as expressed by the Association of Penal Law, the International Association of Judges, and the International Association of Chiefs of Police.

4 Joutsen (1987) at 64, believing the political environment had more to do with the inclusion.

5 Aldana-Pindell (2004) at 617.

6 Issues pertaining to victims of abuse of power generally deal with victims who suffer harm as the result of state action or inaction that may or may not be criminalized.

7 Joutsen (1987) at 63.

8 *Ibid.* at 64.

On the recommendation of the Seventh UN Congress for the Prevention of Crime, the UN General Assembly adopted, by consensus, the Declaration of the Basic Principles of Justice for Victims of Crime and Abuse of Power (Victims' Declaration).[9] The Victims' Declaration provides for two sets of standards for victims' rights: one pertaining to victims of traditional crimes and another related to victims of abuse of power.[10] It includes provisions focusing on victim acknowledgement, reparation, access to justice and fair treatment. The document would be the first of a long line of documents that would continue to assert the individual rights of victims and the right to participation in particular.

4.2.1 Victims' Declaration

Described as "a reflection of the collective will of the international community to restore the balance between the fundamental rights of suspects and offenders, and the rights and interests of victims,"[11] it has been referred to as the Magna Carta for victims.[12] Based on Article 8 of the Universal Declaration of Human Rights, which deals with the right to an effective remedy,[13] the Victims' Declaration was the first instrument to explicitly state that victims have a right of access to justice and to obtain

9 The Declaration of Basic Principles of Justice for Victims of Crime and Abuse of Power, UN Doc. A/Res/40/34/Annex (1985) [hereinafter Victims' Declaration]. In addition to the Victims' Declaration, the UNGA adopted other publications relating to its implementation, including the United Nations Office for Drug Control and Crime Prevention: Center for International Crime Prevention, Guide for Policy Makers on the Implementation of the United Nations Declaration of Basic Principles for Justice for Victims of Crime and Abuse of Power (1999) [hereinafter Guide for Policy Makers], and the United Nations Office for Drug Control and Crime Prevention: Center for International Crime Prevention, Handbook on Justice for Victims: On the Use and Application of the Declaration of Basic Principles of Justice for Victims of Crime and Abuse of Power (1999) [hereinafter Handbook on Justice for Victims]. These documents were prepared by over 40 experts from around the world, also in cooperation with the UN Office of Vienna, Center for International Crime Prevention, Office for Drug Control and Crime Prevention, and with funding from the Office of Victims of Crime, US Department of Justice.

10 These two focal points created a tension within the international victimology and human rights movement. The evidence of this tension was later evident in the drafts of the Victims' Declaration because part of the work on the drafting of what was to later become the Victims' Declaration began outside of the UN. A Committee of Conduct for the Protection and Assistance of Victims at the 1982 International Symposium on Victimology prepared a 'Draft Declaration on the Protection and Assistance of Crime Victims.' This draft declaration was later endorsed in 1983 by the World Federation of Mental Health. At the same time, within the UN, a draft 'Declaration on Crime, Abuses of Power and the Rights of Victims' was drafted. The two drafts were later merged by a working group at the *ad hoc* UN Interregional Meeting of Experts in 1984, with the view to creating a document that would be approved by the UN General Assembly.

11 Handbook on Justice for Victims at iv.

12 *Ibid.* at 105.

13 Universal Declaration of Human Rights (1948), Article 8: "Everyone has the right to an effective remedy by the competent national tribunals for acts violating the fundamental rights granted him by the constitution or by law."

reparations for their harm suffered. Although it is considered soft law, meaning that it is only binding on states to the extent that it reflects customary law norms or general principles of law, it has been cited in many court decisions including regional human rights courts and international criminal courts.

The Victims' Declaration is divided into two parts. Part A of the Declaration prescribes specific provisions for the rights of victims of crime and certain abuses of power. It recommends that states adopt measures that will improve victims' access to justice and fair treatment, allow for restitution from the offender and state compensation, treat victims with dignity and respect, inform victims of their respective rights, and provide overall general assistance.[14] Part B calls on states to criminalize abuse of power violations, provide remedies for harm suffered and provide for social services and support.[15]

The definition of victims of crime under Part A includes victims of conventional crimes committed by state or private actors. The definition also refers to victims of non-enforcement abuse of power. The definition is not limited to direct victims. It also includes, where appropriate, immediate family members, dependents and those individuals who intervened in order to assist victims or prevent victimization.[16] Moreover, victims may be identified regardless of whether a perpetrator is identified, apprehended, prosecuted or convicted.[17] The Victims' Declaration, therefore, provides that (1) victims can be both *direct* (victims proper) and *indirect* victims (family members, for example) and (2) victims are victims regardless of whether or not the perpetrator is identified.

Although there was general agreement on the contents of the draft declaration, there was little agreement on the scope of the document. This disagreement is particularly relevant to the issue of victim participation in the domestic criminal process. Joutsen notes that "the question of to what extent the complainant should be allowed to express his views and concerns in the criminal justice process caused considerable debate in the drafting of the United Nations Declaration."[18] After much discussion the provision on victim participation, Article 6(b), found under the heading 'Access to Justice and Fair Treatment', reads:

> The responsiveness of judicial and administrative processes to the needs of victims should be facilitated by: Allowing the views and concerns of victims to be presented and considered at appropriate stages of the proceedings where their personal interests are affected, without prejudice to the accused and consistent with the relevant national criminal justice system.[19]

---

14 Victims' Declaration, Art. 1-17.
15 *Ibid.*, Art. 19.
16 *Ibid.*, Art. 1.
17 *Ibid.*, Art. 2.
18 Joutsen (1987) at 179.
19 Victims' Declaration, Art. 6(b).

The original provision in earlier drafts was copied from the United States Presidential Task Force on Victims of Crime, which called for victims "to be present and to be heard at all critical stages of the proceedings,"[20] which in the United States usually pertains to proceedings related to arrest, sentencing and parole. However, some states, including the United Kingdom and the Netherlands, feared, among other things, that this language expressed a stance towards the right of victims to participate in proceedings related to the punishment of the offender. At that time, these states argued that the punishment of the offender was solely the prerogative of the state. Therefore the language was altered to what it now provides. In addition, it was the Netherlands that requested the phrase "without prejudice to the accused" be added for fear that too great an involvement in critical stages could undermine fair trial rights for the defense.[21]

Importantly, no rights of specific involvement in the trial process were included, such as the right to present evidence at trial. Instead, it was worded broadly enough so that states could shape their own systems to interpret the best way to adhere to the general aim of the provision.[22] One state could find participation in proceedings on the guilt of the accused contrary to its criminal justice system whereas others could find it perfectly appropriate. Along the same lines, one state could find participation at sentencing hearings perfectly acceptable and another state would never allow such a form of participation. Due in part to its broad language, on 11 November 1985 the Third Committee of the General Assembly adopted the draft declaration by consensus and on 29 November 1985 the declaration was formally approved.[23]

Subsequent publications elaborating on best practices for how states can implement the Victims' Declaration have interpreted it as providing for participation early in the criminal process. For example, the Handbook on Justice for Victims interprets the Declaration as requiring states to provide for some sort of review mechanism for challenging decisions not to prosecute.[24] It notes that "[i]mplicit in access to justice is the provision of a means for obtaining a review of a decision taken."[25] Accordingly, many states have implemented mechanisms whereby victims can seek a review of decisions that adversely affect their interests concerning investigation, identification and prosecution. Again, however, because of the broad wording of the Declaration

---

20 Aldana-Pindell (2004) at 655, citing van Dijk, J.J.M, Towards a Research-Based Victim Policy: Report of the General Rapporteurs, Part III, 23, in Ben David, S. and Kirchhoff, G.F., et al., eds., *International Faces of Victimology*, Mönchengladbach: WSV Publishing (1988).

21 *Ibid.* at 657, citing Soetenhorst, J., Victim Support Programs: Between Doing Good and Doing Justice, 113, in Viano, E.C., ed., *Crime and Its Victims: International Research and Public Policy Issues*, Hemisphere Publishing Corporation (1989).

22 This broad wording is in line with Article 2 of the UN Charter which explicitly provides that the UN is not authorized to intervene in matters which essentially fall within the domestic jurisdiction of any state – and generally speaking, criminal policy and the role of victims therein are usually matters falling under the authority of domestic jurisdictions.

23 Joutsen (1987) at 66, footnote 1.

24 Handbook on Justice for Victims, at 39.

25 *Ibid.*

states are able to adopt a wide range of review procedures. For instance, some states allow for private prosecutions by victims when prosecutors decide not to prosecute;[26] other states allow victims the right to directly contest decisions not to prosecute by bringing complaints to a judge;[27] and still other states have established ombudsman or other administrative offices to hear complaints outside of the criminal process.[28]

Although not providing for specific participatory rights in the criminal process the Victims' Declaration is hugely significant because it was the first international document to explicitly mention the right of victims to present their views and concerns at appropriate stages of proceedings. While leaving it to domestic jurisdictions to work out the details, it certainly reflects a general consensus among national jurisdictions, including civil law and common law jurisdictions, of the right of victims to have some role in the criminal process.

4.2.2 Basic Principles

Following the adoption of the Victims' Declaration in 1985, in 1989 the main subsidiary body of the UN Commission on Human Rights (CHR), the Sub-Commission on the Prevention of Discrimination and Protection of Minorities, appointed Professor Theo van Boven as Special Rapporteur to prepare a study on the status of the right to reparation for victims of human rights violations. Over the ensuing years, a consultation process, which included the insight of experts, states, IGOs and NGOs, took shape. In 1993 van Boven presented the first text, and upon the request of the CHR, presented a revised draft in 1996. The final version of the Draft Basic Principles and Guidelines on the Right to Restitution, Compensation and Rehabilitation for Victims of Gross Violations of Human Rights and Fundamental Freedoms was submitted in 1997.[29]

This draft was once again circulated among states and other interested parties. They, in turn, returned with a number of substantive comments. In 1998 the CHR appointed Professor M. Cherif Bassiouni as an independent expert to finalize the document with a view towards adoption by the General Assembly. The subsequent drafting process produced the Draft Basic Principles and Guidelines on the Right to a Remedy and Reparation for Victims of Gross Violations of International Human Rights Law and Serious Violations of International Humanitarian Law, which was

26 See Guide for Policy Makers at 19, citing Austria and Finland as examples.
27 For example, the Dutch Code of Criminal Procedure, Art. 12, allows an appellate court (on request from victims for instance) to reverse the prosecutor's decision not to prosecute.
28 Aldana-Pindell (2004) at 656.
29 Draft Basic Principles and Guidelines on the Right to Restitution, Compensation, and Rehabilitation for Victims of Gross Violations of Human Rights and Fundamental Freedoms, UN Doc. E/CN.4/1997/104 (1997) [hereinafter 1997 Draft Basic Principles].

presented to the CHR in April 2000.[30] The High Commissioner for Human Rights then circulated this latest draft to states, IGOs and NGOs.[31]

The adoption of the text, however, was delayed due to concerns raised by states at the 2001 World Conference on Racism that opposed victim compensation out of fear that they would be required to pay victim compensation for past racist policies.[32] Nevertheless, based on CHR resolutions and decisions from 2000, 2001 and 2002,[33] the Office of the High Commissioner for Human Rights, together with the Chilean Government, pushed ahead, organizing the first of three consultative meetings in September of 2002.[34] These meetings were meant to finalize the principles. With the participation of the independent experts, van Boven and Bassiouni, states, IGOs and NGOs a revised version of the text was formed. Finally in 2005, Member States of the CHR approved the Basic Principles and Guidelines on the Right to a Remedy and Reparation for Victims of Gross Violations of International Human Rights Law and Serious Violations of International Humanitarian Law (Basic Principles).[35] The approved document received wide support from the Group of Latin-American and Caribbean countries, almost unanimous support from European countries and impor-

30 Draft Basic Principles and Guidelines on the Right to a Remedy and Reparation for Victims of Violations of International Human Rights and Humanitarian Law, UN Doc. E/CN.4/2000/62 (2000) [hereinafter 2000 Draft Basic Principles].

31 UN Commission on Human Rights, The right to restitution, compensation and rehabilitation for victims of grave violations of human rights and fundamental freedoms, UN Doc. E/CN.4/RES/2000/41 (2000).

32 Bassiouni (2006) at 249.

33 See UN Commission on Human Rights, The right to restitution, compensation and rehabilitation for victims of grave violations of human rights and fundamental freedoms, UN Doc. E/CN.4/RES/2000/41 (2000) and UN Commission on Human Rights, Question of enforced or involuntary disappearances, UN Doc. E/CN.4/RES/2002/41 (2002).

34 Reports of the consultative meetings are available in the following documents: UN Commission on Human Rights, Draft basic principles on the right to a remedy and reparation for victims of violations of international human rights and humanitarian law, UN Doc. E/CN.4/2003/63 (2003), UN Commission on Human Rights, Draft basic principles the right to a remedy and reparation for victims of violations of international human rights and humanitarian law, UN Doc. E/CN.4/2004/57 (2004), and UN Commission on Human Rights, Draft basic principles on the right to a remedy and reparation for victims of violations of international human rights and humanitarian law - Note by the High Commissioner for Human Rights, UN Doc. E/CN.4/2005/59 (2005) (final version).

35 After the United States requested a roll-call vote, 41 countries voted in favour, none against and 12 abstained. Those in favor included Argentina, Armenia, Bhutan, Brazil, Burkina Faso, Canada, China, Congo, Costa Rica, Cuba, Dominican Republic, Ecuador, Finland, France, Gabon, Guatemala, Guinea, Honduras, Hungary, Indonesia, Ireland, Italy, Japan, Kenya, Malaysia, Mexico, the Netherlands, Nigeria, Pakistan, Paraguay, Peru, the Republic of Korea, Romania, the Russian Federation, South Africa, Sri Lanka, Swaziland, Ukraine, the United Kingdom, and Zimbabwe. The states which abstained were Australia, Egypt, Eritrea, Ethiopia, Germany, India, Mauritania, Nepal, Qatar, Saudi Arabia, Togo and the United States.

tantly no member state voted against it. On 16 December 2005 the General Assembly adopted by consensus the Basic Principles.[36]

The Basic Principles are meant as a Bill of Rights for victims of serious international crimes. Like the Victims' Declaration, it does not create any substantive international or domestic legal obligations but is meant as a reflection of international norms. Deliberately drafted from a "victim-based perspective," the Basic Principles provide "mechanisms, modalities, procedures and methods for the implementation of existing legal obligations under international human rights law and international humanitarian law."[37] The goal was to minimize the diversity of approaches found in domestic systems by providing a standard to follow. Put simply, the document says that violations require remedies, whether for human rights violations or humanitarian law violations. It also elaborates on the protection of victims and their families and witnesses participating in judicial proceedings.[38]

In the document victims are defined as "persons who individually or collectively suffered harm, including physical or mental injury, emotional suffering, economic loss or substantial impairment of their fundamental rights, through acts or omissions that constitute gross violations of international human rights law or serious violations of international humanitarian law."[39] Victims may also include immediate family members of the direct victim and persons who have suffered harm in intervening to assist victims in distress or to prevent victimization.[40] Although not specifically calling for victim participation, the Basic Principles focus on three overarching rights: (1) equal and effective access to justice; (2) adequate, effective and prompt reparation for harm suffered; and (3) the right to truth.[41] All of these rights, however, can be interpreted to imply a right to participation.

Access to Justice

The notion of a right of access to justice evolved from the right to a remedy. The right to a remedy, which is found in many human rights documents, is a general term comprising various elements that seek to redress wrongs. It can be seen as "the range of measures that may be taken in response to an actual or threatened violation of human rights."[42] Human rights bodies, which will be discussed below, have interpreted

36 Basic Principles and Guidelines on the Right to a Remedy and Reparation for Victims of Gross Violations of International Human Rights Law and Serious Violations of International Humanitarian Law, UN Doc. A/RES/60/147 (2005) [hereinafter Basic Principles].

37 UN Commission on Human Rights, Draft basic principles and guidelines on the right to a remedy and reparation for victims of violations of international human rights and humanitarian law, UN Doc. E/CN.4/2004/57 (2004) at 26 (Explanatory Comments).

38 Bassiouni (2006) at 258.

39 Basic Principles, Section V, Principle 8.

40 *Ibid.*

41 Bassiouni (2006) at 260; Aldana-Pindell (2004) at 647.

42 Shelton (1999) at 4.

the right to a remedy as placing an obligation on the state to investigate, prosecute and punish, as well as an individual victim's right to seek redress, which includes access to justice, ascertainment of the truth and the right to seek reparation. Thus, the right of access to justice has been interpreted to involve the state's duty to investigate, prosecute and punish those responsible for gross violations of human rights and humanitarian law and the victim's individual right to enforce this duty.[43] Bassiouni notes that "[t]he framing of prosecutions as a victim's right has emerged primarily from international human rights tribunals' interpretation of provisions in human rights treaties that establish a right to access to justice or to be heard and the right to an effective remedy."[44] Indeed, the notion of access to justice was first included in the Victims' Declaration and has come to refer to the quality of procedures available to victims as well as the quality of outcomes.

Right to Reparation

Adequate, effective and prompt reparation involves providing a means through which victims, or their families and dependants, who suffer harm as the result of an international human rights or humanitarian law violation, have access to an effective remedy. The five main types of reparation include: restitution, compensation, rehabilitation, satisfaction, and guarantees of non-repetition. Restitution entails that the victims should be restored, as best as possible, to the position they held before the violation occurred. Restitution can mean anything from restoration of liberty to the return of one's residence, employment or property.[45] Compensation entails financial payment for damages, including for physical damages or mental/emotional damages. Compensation also includes payment for lost opportunities such as the loss of employment, education or social benefits.[46] Rehabilitation includes medical care, psychological care, legal services and social services.[47] Finally, satisfaction and guarantees of non-repetition can include anything from policy measures aimed at acknowledging the harm, public disclosure about the truth of the harm suffered (unless this would be harmful to the victims), a public apology, memorials and commemorations for victims, and

43 UN Commission on Human Rights, Draft basic principles and guidelines on the right to a remedy and reparation for victims of violations of international human rights and humanitarian law, UN Doc. E/CN.4/2004/57 (2004) at 27 (Explanatory Comment 3), noting that the duty to prosecute was not meant to influence the issue of complementarity or theories of criminal jurisdictions that states and international jurisdictions rely on.

44 Bassiouni (2006) at 263.

45 *Ibid.* at 268.

46 UN Commission on Human Rights, Draft basic principles and guidelines on the right to a remedy and reparation for victims of violations of international human rights and humanitarian law, UN Doc. E/CN.4/2004/57 (2004) at 27; concerns were expressed about compensation for lost opportunities, arguing they are too difficult to assess.

47 Bassiouni (2006) at 270.

education initiatives.[48] Ideally the reparation should be proportional to the harm suffered and states should strive to establish assistance programs for victims in the event where the party responsible is unable to meet their obligations. Moreover, collective reparations are viewed as entirely appropriate; therefore, there should be a means by which victims can collectively present their claims, in either criminal or non-criminal forums.[49] Accordingly, the right to be heard, such as through participation in criminal proceedings, is often associated with the right to claim reparations.

Right to Truth

With the rise of enforced disappearances that took place in Central and South America in the 1970s an increasing amount of attention was given to the concept of the right to truth. It encompasses a victim's right to factual information concerning his or her family members. Although this right was initially only referenced in the context of enforced disappearances, it has gradually extended to cover other serious violations of human rights and humanitarian law.[50] The right to truth "implies knowing the full and complete truth as to the events that transpired, their specific circumstances, and who participated in them, including knowing the circumstances in which the violations took place, as well as the reasons for them."[51] As such, Principle 24 of the Basic Principles states that "victims and their representatives should be entitled to seek and obtain information on the causes leading to their victimization and to learn the truth in regard to these functions." Paragraph 22(b) further states that by way of the reparation of satisfaction, where applicable, states should strive for the "[v]erification of the facts and full and public disclosure of the truth [...]." The right to truth has both an individual and collective (or societal) dimension.[52] It is closely linked to several state

48 For information on the right to an apology see UNSubCHR, Recognition of responsibility and reparation for massive and flagrant violations of human rights which constitute crimes against humanity and which took place during the period of slavery, colonialism and wars of conquest, UN Doc. E/CN.4/SUB.2/RES/2002/5 (2002), par. 3.

49 Bassiouni (2006) at 261.

50 Study on the right to the truth, Report of the Office of the United Nations High Commissioner for Human Rights, UN Doc. E/CN.4/2006/91 (2006), par. 3, 8. Pursuant to Resolution 2005/66 of the Commission on Human Rights, the Office of the High Commissioner for Human Rights (OHCHR) was requested to "prepare a study on the right to the truth, including information on the basis, scope, and content of the right under international law, as well as best practices and recommendations for effective implementation of this right, in particular, legislative, administrative or any other measures that may be adopted in this respect, taking into account the views of States and relevant intergovernmental and non-governmental organizations, for consideration at its sixty-second session." See Right to the truth, Commission on Human Rights Resolution 2005/66, UN Doc. E/CN.4/RES/2005/66 (2005), par 6.

51 Study on the right to the truth, Report of the Office of the United Nations High Commissioner for Human Rights, UN Doc. E/CN.4/2006/91 (2006), par. 59

52 *Ibid.*, para. 58, 60; Implementation of General Assembly Resolution 60/251 of 15 March 2006 entitled "Human Rights Council," Right to the truth, Report of the Office of the High Commissioner for Human Rights, UN Doc. A/HRC/5/7 (2007), par. 83; See also Updated set of principles for the protection and promotion of human rights through action to combat impunity, UN Doc. E/CN.4/2005/102/Add.1

obligations, including obligations of states to protect and guarantee human rights, to effectively investigate gross human rights violations and serious violations of humanitarian law, to combat impunity, and to provide adequate remedies and reparation for victims.[53] It is also closely linked to individual rights, including the right to an effective remedy, the right to protection by the law, the right to a family life, the right an effective investigation, the right to a hearing by a competent, independent and impartial tribunal, the right to obtain reparation, the right not to be subjected to torture or ill-treatment, and the right to seek and impart information.[54] Its connection to state obligations and fundamental individual rights means that the right to truth is an inalienable and non-derogable right.[55] The Office of the High Commissioner for Human Rights has been appraised of a diverse range of modalities of guaranteeing, safeguarding and implementing the right to truth.[56] The range of modalities includes international criminal courts, truth commissions, investigation commissions, national criminal courts, national human rights institutions and other administrative procedures.[57] In particular, the role played by criminal proceedings in upholding the right to truth has been stressed,[58] as has the role played by victims in criminal proceed-

(2005), Principle 2: Every people has the inalienable right to know the truth about past events concerning the perpetration of heinous crimes and about the circumstances and reasons that led, through massive or systematic violations, to the perpetration of those crimes. Full and effective exercise of the right to the truth provides a vital safeguard against the recurrence of violations. Principle 3: A people's knowledge of the history of its oppression is part of its heritage and, as such, must be ensured by appropriate measures in fulfillment of the State's duty to preserve archives and other evidence concerning violations of human rights and humanitarian law and to facilitate knowledge of those violations.

53 Study on the right to the truth, Report of the Office of the United Nations High Commissioner for Human Rights, UN Doc. E/CN.4/2006/91 (2006), par. 56; Implementation of General Assembly Resolution 60/251 of 15 March 2006 entitled "Human Rights Council," Right to the truth, Report of the Office of the High Commissioner for Human Rights, UN Doc. A/HRC/5/7 (2007), para. 84, 86.

54 Study on the right to the truth, Report of the Office of the United Nations High Commissioner for Human Rights, UN Doc. E/CN.4/2006/91 (2006), par. 57; Implementation of General Assembly Resolution 60/251 of 15 March 2006 entitled "Human Rights Council," Right to the truth, Report of the Office of the High Commissioner for Human Rights, UN Doc. A/HRC/5/7 (2007), par. 85.

55 Study on the right to the truth, Report of the Office of the United Nations High Commissioner for Human Rights, UN Doc. E/CN.4/2006/91 (2006), para. 55, 60; Implementation of General Assembly Resolution 60/251 of 15 March 2006 entitled "Human Rights Council," Right to the truth, Report of the Office of the High Commissioner for Human Rights, UN Doc. A/HRC/5/7 (2007), par. 86.

56 Implementation of General Assembly Resolution 60/251 of 15 March 2006 entitled "Human Rights Council," Right to the truth, Report of the Office of the High Commissioner for Human Rights, UN Doc. A/HRC/5/7 (2007), par. 90

57 Study on the right to the truth, Report of the Office of the United Nations High Commissioner for Human Rights, UN Doc. E/CN.4/2006/91 (2006), par. 61; Implementation of General Assembly Resolution 60/251 of 15 March 2006 entitled "Human Rights Council," Right to the truth, Report of the Office of the High Commissioner for Human Rights, UN Doc. A/HRC/5/7 (2007), par. 90

58 *Ibid.*, par. 89; Right to the truth, Commission on Human Rights Resolution 2005/66, UN Doc. E/CN.4/RES/2005/66 (2005); Aldana-Pindell (2002) at 1442.

ings.[59] Thus, the right to truth "has emerged as a legal concept at the national, regional and international levels,"[60] and "is fundamental to the inherent dignity of the human person."[61]

Equal and effective access to justice, adequate, effective and prompt reparation for harm suffered, and the right to truth are therefore interconnected obligations that encompass not only obligations for states but also various rights for victims, including the right to be heard in the criminal process. Accordingly, although the Basic Principles do not explicitly call for victim participatory rights in judicial processes, as does the Victims' Declaration, these principles implicitly support the notion of victims having some form of participatory rights in criminal justice processes. The victim must be heard in order to ensure a state's duty to investigate, prosecute and punish. The victim must be heard when claiming reparations in a criminal proceeding. And, finally, if the right to truth contributes to ending impunity, the victim should be heard in the criminal process so as to contribute to the uncovering of the truth.

4.3 Human Rights Bodies and Victims' Rights

In addition to the UN declarations mentioned above, human rights bodies have long elaborated on a number of rights for victims. Though rights explicitly targeting victims are not generally found in human rights treaties, human rights bodies have interpreted violations of the right to life and the prohibition against torture and ill-treatment in conjunction with other rights such as the right of access to justice, the right to reparation, the right to truth, the right to a fair trial, the right to be heard and, most importantly, the right to an effective remedy as a way in which to ensure human rights protections for victims of crime. Although the decisions of these human rights bodies very often pronounce upon the rights of victims in a broad sense, that is, beyond the construct of the criminal process, increasingly, they emphasize state obligations to criminally prosecute and call upon states to provide victims with rights within the criminal process, in part through a greater participatory role.

---

59 Updated set of principles for the protection and promotion of human rights through action to combat impunity, UN Doc. E/CN.4/2005/102/Add.1 (2005), Principle 19: [...]Although the decision to prosecute lies primarily within the competence of the State, victims, their families and heirs should be able to institute proceedings, on either an individual or collective basis, particularly as *parties civiles* or as persons conducting private prosecutions in States whose law of criminal procedure recognizes these procedures. States should guarantee broad legal standing in the judicial process to any wronged party and to any person or non-governmental organization having a legitimate interest therein. See also, Study on the right to the truth, Report of the Office of the United Nations High Commissioner for Human Rights, UN Doc. E/CN.4/2006/91 (2006), par. 61

60 Naqvi (2006) at 245.

61 Study on the right to the truth, Report of the Office of the United Nations High Commissioner for Human Rights, UN Doc. E/CN.4/2006/91 (2006), par. 57.

4.3.1 Human Rights Committee

The rights found in the International Covenant on Civil and Political Rights (ICCPR) include, amongst others, the right to an effective remedy.[62] The Covenant is monitored by the Human Rights Committee (HRC), which, in addition to considering periodic reports submitted by Member States on their compliance with the treaty, also reviews individual complaints in accordance with the First Optional Protocol.[63] With regard to individual complaints, the HRC has routinely interpreted the right to an effective remedy as requiring states to carry out prosecutions for serious violations as well as to provide compensation to victims in appropriate situations.[64] An effective prosecution includes a criminal investigation that brings to justice those determined to be most responsible. In addition, the HRC has acknowledged the right of victims to know the truth as a way to end or prevent the psychological torture of families of victims of enforced disappearances or secret executions,[65] and as such, it has found that as a means of providing an effective remedy states should provide information to the victim about the violation.[66] The HRC, while finding that the right to an effective remedy requires states to investigate and prosecute human rights violations, has not interpreted the Covenant as providing for a private right to demand criminal prosecutions and thereby participate (in some form) in the criminal process.[67] Thus, the ICCPR neither provides for a private right to prosecutions nor a right to participation. Moreover, the HRC has never derived such private rights as stemming from other rights either found explicitly in the ICCPR or arising from such rights.

---

62 International Covenant on Civil and Political Rights (1966), Art. 2(3)(a) (effective remedy). See also, Nowak (2005).

63 Optional Protocol to the International Covenant on Civil and Political Rights (1966).

64 See, e.g., HRC, *Vicente et al. v. Colombia*, Comm. No. 612/1995 (1997), par. 10; *Vaca v. Colombia*, Comm. No. 859/1999, 25 March 2002, par. 9; *Chonwe v. Zambia*, Comm. No. 821/1998, 25 October 2000, par. 7; *Laureano Atachahua v. Peru*, Comm. No. 540/1993, 25 March 1996, par. 10; *Bleier Lewenhoff and Valiño de Bleier v. Uruguay*, Comm. No. 30/1978, 29 March 1982, par. 15, *Grille Motta v. Uruguay*, Comm. No. 11/1977, 29 July 1980, par. 14; *Dante Santullo Valcada v. Uruguay*, Comm. No. 9/1977, 26 October 1979, par. 11; *Torres Ramirez v. Uruguay*, Comm. No. 4/1977, 26 January 1978, par. 16.

65 See HRC, *R.A.V.N. et al. v. Argentina*, Comm. No. 343, 344 and 345/1988, 5 April 1990 (with the individual opinion of Mr. Bertil Wennergren); *Staselovich and Lyashkevich v. Belarus*, Comm. No. 887/1999, 3 April 2003; *Sarma v. Sri Lanka*, Comm No. 950/2000, 31 July 2003.

66 HRC, *Staselovich and Lyashkevich v. Belarus*, Comm. No. 887/1999, 3 April 2003, par. 11; *Khalilov v. Tajikistan,* Comm. No. 973/2001, 30 March 2005, par. 9; and *Aliboev v. Tajikistan*, Comm. No. 985/2001, 18 October 2005, par. 6.7.

67 See, e.g., HRC, *Vicente et al. v. Colombia*, Comm. No. 612/1995, 14 June 1994; see also Aldana-Pindell (2004) at 645-646.

4.3.2 European Court of Human Rights

Following WWII a number of regional human rights systems began to operate. The European human rights system is one of the most prominent of these developments. After the exhaustion of domestic remedies, the European human rights system allows individuals to bring claims before the European Court of Human Rights (ECtHR or European Court) for violations of the European Convention on the Protection of Human Rights and Fundamental Freedoms (ECHR).[68] Much in line with liberal theories and values, the system focuses on the obligations of states and the rights of individuals.

The ECtHR has examined Articles 1 (duty to secure rights), together with 2 (right to life), 3 (prohibition against torture and inhuman and degrading treatment), 6 (fair trial rights) and 13 (right to a remedy) to find that a state's violation of its duties may also violate the private rights of victims. The right to a remedy for violations of the right to life and the prohibition against torture, inhuman and degrading treatment entails obligations on states to carry out effective official investigations that can lead to the identification and possible punishment of those found to be responsible.[69] Thus, the duty to prosecute is part of the right to an effective remedy for violations of the Convention.[70] The duty of the state to carry out effective investigations and prosecutions has, in turn, been found to impact the private rights of victims to participate in judicial proceedings when national proceedings allow for participation. These rights generally include the right to obtain information and to provide information. Thus, in addition to state obligations the Court also emphasizes the private rights of victims when participating in the criminal process. As such, the ECtHR has also expanded the notion of fair trial under the Convention, which originally was exclusively used to protect the rights of the accused, to extend to victims.

Cases shedding light on how the Court has approached the rights of victims under the ECHR have arisen largely out of complaints against Turkey and the United Kingdom. The rights conferred upon victims have been found to apply to direct

---

68 Originally the ECHR established both a Court and a Commission. See ECHR, Art. 19, 38 and 56. However, these institutions were abolished and new Court was created in 1998. See European Convention Protocol 11, 11 May 1994.

69 See ECtHR, *McCann and Others v. The United Kingdom*, App. No. 18984/91, 5 September 1995, par. 161 (relating to Article 2); *Assenov and Others v. Bulgaria*, App. No. 24760/94, 28 October 1998, par. 102 (relating to Article 3). See also, *Hugh Jordan v. United Kingdom*, App. No. 24746/94, 4 August 2001; *McKerr v. United Kingdom*, App. No. 28883/95, 4 August 2001; *Kelly and Others v. United Kingdom*, App. No. 30054/96, 4 August 2001; *Shanaghan v. United Kingdom*, App. No. 37715/97, 4 August 2001.

70 See ECtHR, *Aksoy v. Turkey*, App. No. 21987/93, 18 December 1996; *Aydin v. Turkey*, App. No. 23178/94, 25 September 1997.

victims as well as their next-of-kin, which can be determined by the closeness of the relationship rather than strictly by familial bonds.[71]

In cases involving a violation of Article 2 (right to life) or Article 3 (prohibition against torture, inhuman and degrading treatment) the Court has interpreted Article 13 (right to remedy) as placing a duty on states to investigate and prosecute alleged perpetrators.[72] Thus when states fail to conduct investigations and prosecutions, or when they are ineffectual, the Court has consistently found violations of Articles 1 and 13.[73] The duty of the state to carry out effective investigations and prosecutions directly relates to the rights of victims to participate in the criminal process. In this regard, the Court has read Articles 1, 2, 3 and 13 as conferring upon victims certain participatory rights.[74]

For instance, the Court has interpreted Article 2 as requiring states to provide for elements of public scrutiny over investigations related to an alleged right to life violation. To this end, it has held that although public scrutiny may vary from case to case, in all cases "the next-of-kin [...] must be involved in the procedure to the extent necessary to safeguard his or her legitimate interests."[75] In the cases emanating out of the United Kingdom the Court found violations of Article 2 of the Convention for denying victims certain participatory rights in inquest proceedings. Inquests in England, Wales and Northern Ireland are independent judicial investigations, usually sitting with juries, meant to determine the facts surrounding a suspicious death. These inquests are meant to be public and the juries may reach a verdict identifying the cause of death, which often leads to criminal prosecution. Inquests, therefore, are a critical stage of an investigation into a suspicious death and victims and their families are permitted to participate in the proceedings through their legal counsel. The Court criticized the lack of reasoning provided to victims for decisions not to prosecute and

71 ECtHR, *Timurtas v. Turkey*, App. No. 23531/94, 13 June 2000, par. 95; *Çakici v. Turkey*, App. No. 23657/94, 8 July 1999, par. 98.

72 See ECtHR, *Salman v. Turkey*, App. No. 21986/93, 27 June 2000; *Timurtas v. Turkey*, App. No. 23531/94, 13 June 2000; *Çakici v. Turkey*, App. No. 23657/94, 8 July 1999; *Oğur v. Turkey*, App. No. 21594/93, 20 May 1999; *Güleç v. Turkey*, App. No. 21593/93, 27 July 1998; *Kaya v. Turkey*, App. No. 22729/93, 19 February 1998.

73 See ECtHR, *Kaya v. Turkey*, App. No. 22729/93, 19 February 1998; *McCann and Others v. The United Kingdom*, App. No. 18984/91, 5 September 1995.

74 See ECtHR, *Hugh Jordan v. United Kingdom*, App. No. 24746/94, 4 August 2001; *McKerr v. United Kingdom*, App. No. 28883/95, 4 August 2001; *Kelly and Others v. United Kingdom*, App. No. 30054/96, 4 August 2001; *Shanaghan v. United Kingdom*, App. No. 37715/97, 4 August 2001.

75 ECtHR, *Hugh Jordan v. United Kingdom*, App. No. 24746/94, 4 August 2001, par. 109; *McKerr v. United Kingdom*, App. No. 28883/95, 4 August 2001, par. 115; *Kelly and Others v. United Kingdom*, App. No. 30054/96, 4 August 2001, par. 98; *Shanaghan v. United Kingdom*, App. No. 37715/97, 4 August 2001, par. 92; see also, *Güleç v. Turkey*, App. No. 21593/93, 27 July 1998, par. 82; *Oğur v. Turkey*, App. No. 21594/93, 20 May 1999, par. 92 and *Gül v. Turkey*, App. No. 22676/93, 14 December 2000, par. 93.

for not subjecting these decisions to judicial review.[76] The Court also criticized the fact that victims' families had difficulty obtaining copies of witness statements before that witness was called to testify.[77] The lack of access to documents and information placed the victims' families "at a disadvantage in terms of preparation and ability to participate in questioning."[78]

To be sure, the right to information is viewed as essential. In a number of cases against Turkey the ECtHR found a violation of Article 2 when the state failed to inform victims and their next-of-kin of decisions not to prosecute.[79] These omissions were particularly troublesome because they denied victims a right of access to justice. The victims were unable to appeal the decisions not to prosecute. The context of the majority of these cases against Turkey had to do with Turkish security forces and their treatment of individuals allegedly involved with the Kurdish Worker's Party. The crimes alleged included torture, murder, forced disappearance and other inhuman treatment. Almost always, the Turkish authorities refused to investigate or prosecute any allegations of criminal wrongdoing. Therefore, no individual was prosecuted or punished for the alleged violations. The Court also found Article 2 violations when victims and their families were not given access to the investigation and other court documents.[80] The Court required that victims be given access to documents in the investigation and also to be given the right to introduce evidence in order to add to the record of the case.[81] Indeed, the Court has found that a thorough investigation "must include the possibility of the complainant having effective access to the investigation procedure."[82]

Given the fundamental importance of the right to life, the Court has further found that the right to a remedy requires that states provide victims with the opportunity to

---

76 ECtHR, *Hugh Jordan v. United Kingdom*, App. No. 24746/94, 4 August 2001, par. 122; *McKerr v. United Kingdom*, App. No. 28883/95, 4 August 2001, par. 130; *Kelly and Others v. United Kingdom*, App. No. 30054/96, 4 August 2001, par. 116; *Shanaghan v. United Kingdom*, App. No. 37715/97, 4 August 2001, par. 106.

77 ECtHR, *Hugh Jordan v. United Kingdom*, App. No. 24746/94, 4 August 2001, par. 133; *McKerr v. United Kingdom*, App. No. 28883/95, 4 August 2001, par. 147; *Kelly and Others v. United Kingdom*, App. No. 30054/96, 4 August 2001, par. 128; *Shanaghan v. United Kingdom*, App. No. 37715/97, 4 August 2001, par. 116.

78 ECtHR, *Hugh Jordan v. United Kingdom*, App. No. 24746/94, 4 August 2001, par. 134; *McKerr v. United Kingdom*, App. No. 28883/95, 4 August 2001, par. 148; *Kelly and Others v. United Kingdom*, App. No. 30054/96, 4 August 2001, par. 128, *Shanaghan v. United Kingdom*, App. No. 37715/97, 4 August 2001, par. 117.

79 ECtHR, *Güleç v. Turkey*, App. No. 21593/93, 27 July 1998, par. 82; *Oğur v. Turkey*, App. No. 21594/93, 20 May 1999, par. 92.

80 ECtHR, *Oğur v. Turkey*, App. No. 21594/93, 20 May 1999, par. 92; *Gül v. Turkey*, App. No. 22676/93, 14 December 2000, par. 93.

81 ECtHR, *Oğur v. Turkey*, App. No. 21594/93, 20 May 1999, par. 92.

82 ECtHR, *Çakici v. Turkey*, App. No. 23657/94, 8 July 1999 and *Yasa v. Turkey*, App. No. 22495/93, 2 September 1998, par. 114; See also *Tanrikulu v. Turkey*, App. No. 23763/94, 8 July 1999 and *Salman v. Turkey*, App. No. 21986/93, 27 June 2000, par. 121.

claim compensation.[83] In the Turkish cases the Court granted victims (and their families) the right to allege violations arising out of procedural errors in the criminal process – including those pertaining to compensation. In other words, in the Turkish cases the Court has found that Article 13 guarantees victims a remedy to enforce rights, such as the right to reparation, in criminal proceedings protected under the Convention and it is a duty of the state to provide appropriate damages. Thus, victims must have access to justice in order to claim compensation where appropriate.[84]

Depending upon the domestic procedures in place, it makes no difference whether the reparation results from civil or criminal proceedings. Therefore, the opportunity to claim reparation in civil proceedings may satisfy Article 13 obligations for the right to a remedy so long as an effective criminal investigation has also taken place.[85] For instance, in the United Kingdom cases, although the Court found a violation of the duty to investigate, stemming from the procedural aspect of Article 2, it declined to find a violation of Article 13 since the victims could still seek compensation from civil proceedings. However, in legal systems that provide for the adhesion of civil claims to criminal proceedings, such as Turkey, the Court has required both a thorough and effective investigation and prosecution and the payment of reparations where appropriate. The Court found that because the right to damages hinges upon the outcome of the criminal proceeding there is a close procedural relationship between the criminal investigation and the remedies available to the victim.

This appears to mean that in jurisdictions where victims may attach their civil claims to the criminal process and the compensation award depends upon the criminal investigation the Court could find violations of Article 2, 3 and 13 when victims are precluded from participation in the investigation. In jurisdictions where civil compensation does not depend upon the criminal proceeding, the Court will be reluctant to find a violation of Article 13 and instead will find violations of Article 2 and 3 when victims are precluded from effective participation in the criminal process. In this way, the decisions recognize the two types of legal systems, one in which victims can adhere their civil claims to the criminal process and one in which they cannot.

Finally, in addition to the finding of the Court with relation to participation during investigations, the Court has relied upon Article 6 (fair trial) of the Convention to develop procedural human rights norms for victims.[86] Article 6(1) provides that "In the determination of his civil rights and obligations [...] everyone is entitled to a fair and public hearing within a reasonable time by an independent and impartial tribunal

83 ECtHR, *Kaya v. Turkey*, App. No. 22729/93, 19 February 1998, par. 107.

84 Aldana-Pindell (2004) at 637.

85 ECtHR, *Hugh Jordan v. United Kingdom*, App. No. 24746/94, 4 August 2001, para. 161-162; *McKerr v. United Kingdom*, App. No. 28883/95, 4 August 2001, para. 172-173; *Kelly and Others v. United Kingdom*, App. No. 30054/96, 4 August 2001, para. 154-156, *Shanaghan v. United Kingdom*, App. No. 37715/97, 4 August 2001, para. 136-137.

86 Jackson, J., Transitional Faces of Justice: Two Attempts to Build Common Standards beyond National Boundaries, 227, in Jackson, et al. (2008).

established by law [...]." Traditionally, Article 6(3) only provided for procedural guarantees in criminal proceedings to those individuals facing criminal charges. It specifically mentions "everyone charged with a criminal offence."[87] Article 6(3) lays out specific rights including the right to adequate time and facilities for the preparation of a defense, the right to legal counsel, and the right to examine witnesses against the defense. Hence, for a long period of time, victim applications based on Article 6(3) were rejected as being inadmissible *ratione personae*.[88]

However, the interpretation of Article 6 soon evolved. The Court began to recognize violations of Article 6(1) submitted by victims in cases where the victims had attached their civil reparation claim to the criminal trial.[89] Moreover, in *Perez v. France* the court recognized a violation of Article 6 asserted by a victim at the end of the criminal investigation. The Court unequivocally held that Article 6(1) does in fact apply with regard to civil party participation in criminal trials.[90] Although declining to find a violation, in contrast with the earlier cases, the Court found that a victim who has become a party to the criminal proceedings has a right to a fair trial even when the victim has not yet claimed a civil remedy.[91] When victims become a civil party to criminal proceedings they are demonstrating the importance of contributing to the criminal conviction of the offender and also to securing financial reparation.[92] The Court noted that "the right to a fair trial holds so prominent a place in a democratic society that there can be no justification for interpreting Article 6(1) restrictively [...]."[93] It determined that the right to a fair trial "includes the right of the parties to the trial to submit any observations that they consider relevant to their case. The purpose of the Convention being to guarantee not rights that are theoretical or illusory but rights that are practical and effective [...], this right can only be seen to be effective if the observations are actually heard."[94] It further stated that "the decisive factor for the applicability of Article 6(1) is whether, from the moment when the applicant is joined as a civil party until the conclusion of those criminal proceedings, the civil component remains closely connected with the criminal component."[95] Thus, the Court concluded that a civil party complaint is within the scope of the right to a fair trial

87 ECHR, Art. 6(2) and (3).

88 Trechsel (2005) at 37, citing Vogler, T., Artikel 6, note 240, in Golsong, H., et al., eds., Internationaler Kommentar zur Europäischen Menschenrechtskonvention, Carl Heymanns Verlag (1986).

89 See ECtHR, *Tomasi v. France*, App. No. 12850/87, 27 August 1992; *Acquaviva v. France*, App. No. 19248/91, 21 November 1995; see also, *Aksoy v. Turkey*, App. No. 21987/93, 18 December 1996, par. 92; See also *Hamer v. France*, App. No. 19953/92, 7 August 1996, where the Court found that, unlike in Acquaviva, Article 6(1) did not apply since the civil party did not claim for compensation.

90 ECtHR, *Perez v France*, App. No. 47287/99, 12 February 2004, para. 62-63.

91 *Ibid.*, par. 64; however, in paragraph 65 the Court used less strong language when it noted that "it is conceivable that Article 6 *may* be applicable even in the absence of a claim for financial reparation" (emphasis added).

92 *Ibid.*

93 *Ibid.*

94 *Ibid.*, par. 80.

95 *Ibid.*, par. 67, citing *Calvelli and Ciglio v. Italy*, App. No. 32967/96, 17 January 2002, par. 62.

under the Convention so long as the civil component is directly related to the criminal one.

This holding essentially means that the Court did put restrictions on the right of victims to claim a violation under Article 6(1). It found that the Convention does not confer any right to "private revenge" and therefore "the right to have a third party prosecuted or sentenced for a criminal charge cannot be asserted independently."[96] A victim can only claim an Article 6(1) violation if they have made clear that their civil component is closely related to the criminal component. In this regard, the Court found that attempts to secure symbolic reparation or attempts to protect a civil right such as "good reputation" will suffice to establish the connection.[97] Therefore, victims may claim Article 6 violations so long as their civil party complaints are attached to criminal proceedings and they may do so from the moment they join their claim. However, they may not claim an Article 6 violation if they have waived the right to reparation in an unequivocal manner.

The Court's jurisprudence displays an acknowledgement of the symbolic nature of victim participation.[98] Nevertheless, the ECtHR has never recognized that under the Convention a victim has an absolute right to participate in domestic criminal proceedings if the domestic law does not provide for such a right. However, the lack of standing in criminal proceedings cannot limit the rights of victims to seek redress in other proceedings with respect to reparations.

4.3.3 Inter-American Court of Human Rights

In the aftermath of WWII, twenty-one American states joined together to form the Organization of American States (OAS). This collective group of American states adopted the first ever regional human rights instrument, the American Declaration of the Rights and Duties of Man,[99] and later passed the American Convention on Human Rights (ACHR),[100] which created the Inter-American Commission on Human Rights (IACHR) and the Inter-American Court of Human Rights (IACtHR).

The IACtHR is mandated with enforcing and interpreting provisions of the ACHR. Its two main duties are to rule on specific cases alleging state violations under the Convention and issuing advisory opinions on matters brought to its attention by OAS bodies or Member States. Unlike in the European system where victims can, in their own capacity, bring a claim before the Court, in the Inter-American system victims wishing to pursue a claim or seek redress under the Convention must, after exhausting remedies at the domestic level, present their case to the Inter-American Commission.[101]

96 *Ibid.*, par. 70.
97 *Ibid.*
98 Bassiouni (2006) at 239.
99 American Declaration of the Rights and Duties of Man (1948).
100 American Convention on Human Rights (1969) [hereinafter ACHR].
101 ACHR, Art. 44.

The Commission then investigates the claim and tries to facilitate a settlement with the state in question.[102] If a settlement is not forthcoming and the claim has merit, the Commission (and not the individual victim) submits the claim to the IACtHR so long as the state in question has accepted the Court's jurisdiction.[103]

Both the IACHR and the IACtHR have often led the way in recognizing victims' rights, particularly with regard to rights in the criminal process through their interpretations of the right to life and rights relating to personal integrity together with Articles 1(1), 8(1), and 25 of the ACHR.[104] Article 1(1) imposes a general duty on states to ensure the full exercise of the rights enumerated in the Convention. Article 8(1) provides for the right to a fair trial and Article 25 provides the right to an effective remedy. In general, the Court has found that, when read together, the Convention obliges states to investigate, prosecute and punish allegations of serious human rights violations. These duties are, in turn, closely linked with a number of important individual rights in the criminal process such as the right of access to justice, the right to truth, the right to participate, and the right to reparations.[105] Undoubtedly, victims' access to criminal proceedings has been found to help ensure that states comply with their duty to prosecute gross human rights violations.[106] The Court has determined that laws which impede access to justice, interpreted to some extent as participation in the criminal process, amount to an obstacle to an effective prosecution. Accordingly, the Court has found a general principle of a victim's right to have full access to proceedings, meaning that victims should be given standing to participate in all phases before courts investigating human rights violations.[107]

Due to the fact that the history of the American states has often been turbulent with many instances of civil unrest, much of the case law from the Court deals with state commission of torture, murder, and forced disappearances. As such, early in its jurisprudence, in a case concerning the disappearance of Velásquez-Rodriguez in Honduras,[108] the Court had to determine the extent of obligations and rights for serious violations of human rights. The Court found that Article 1(1) has a criminal law

102 *Ibid.*, Art. 48.

103 *Ibid.*, Art. 60-61.

104 This study focuses on the decisions handed down by the IACtHR but in many cases it was the IACHR, on behalf of the victims, that first pushed for an expansion of the rights of victims. Rights relating to personal integrity include the right to humane treatment (Art. 5), freedom from slavery (Art. 6), and the right to personal liberty (Art. 7).

105 Although the right to truth began as a form of reparation relating to the right to know the whereabouts of family members who were victims of forced disappearance, it has been held that a victim's right to truth should be accorded through the criminal process, See IACtHR, *Bámaca-Velásquez v. Guatemala*, Judgment, 25 November 2000, par. 86.

106 Aldana-Pindell (2004) at 668.

107 *Ibid.* at 668.

108 In this case, the Court found a violation of Article 7 of the Convention. See IACtHR, *Velasquez Rodriguez v. Honduras*, Judgment, 29 July 1988.

component, obliging states to investigate grave violations of human rights.[109] It held that the duty to investigate is closely connected with the right of victims to know all the facts surrounding the disappearance of their loved ones. Thus, in this case and others, the Court implicitly linked the duty to investigate with the right to truth.[110]

However, it was still unclear whether the Court's decision in *Velásquez-Rodriguez* required the state to initiate criminal prosecutions or whether other non-criminal investigations would suffice given the fact that the Court declined to require criminal proceedings in this case as requested by the victims' families. As time passed the Court clarified its position as victims in subsequent cases attempted to ensure their respective state's compliance with the Convention. The Court began to recognize that impunity has a great impact on victims and therefore linked the right to truth with the state obligation to carry out effective prosecutions. Interpreting the general obligation of states to give effect to the Convention together with the right to be heard and the right to an effective remedy, the Court has found a duty to prosecute in cases concerning the right to life and personal integrity.[111]

Similarly the Court has found, together with the duty to investigate and prosecute, the duty to punish.[112] When the Court addressed the issue of amnesty laws precluding prosecution in the case of *Castillo Páez*, it reasoned that "only a criminal trial could guarantee [the victims] the appropriate remedy; namely, the punishment of the perpetrators."[113] The Court has therefore found that victims have the right to state investigation of crimes, state prosecution of those suspected of perpetrating the offense and state punishment of those found guilty of the criminal act.[114]

In addition to the duty to investigate, prosecute and punish, the Court has held that the state is also obliged to provide compensation for the resulting damages.[115] In the case of *Blake*, for example, the victims alleged a violation of their right to judicial protection under Article 25 and a violation of Article 8(1). The case concerned the death of Nicholas Blake who was an American journalist who disappeared in Guate-

109 *Ibid.*, par. 188. See also, IACtHR, *Godínez Cruz v. Honduras*, Judgment, 20 January 1989, par. 198; *Fairen Garbi and Solís Corrales v. Honduras*, Judgment, 15 March 1989, par. 159-160.

110 IACtHR, *Velasquez Rodriguez v. Honduras*, Judgment, 29 July 1988, par. 188. See also, *Bámaca-Velásquez v. Guatemala*, Judgment, 25 November 2000, par. 201; *Barrios Altos v. Peru*, Judgment, 14 March 2001, par. 48; *Castillo Páez v. Peru*, Judgment, 3 November 1997, par. 90, linking the right to truth with the state's duty to investigate.

111 IACtHR, *Paniagua-Morales et al. v. Guatemala*, Judgment, 8 March 1998, para. 173, 181; *Durand and Ugarte v. Peru*, Judgment, 16 August 2000, par. 140; *Blake v. Guatemala*, Judgment, 24 Jaunary 1998, par. 121; see also *Villagrán Morales et al. v. Guatemala*, Judgment, 19 November 1999; *Bámaca-Velásquez v. Guatemala*, Judgment, 25 November 2000.

112 IACtHR, *Velasquez Rodriguez v. Honduras*, Judgment, 29 July 1988, par. 174.

113 IACtHR, *Castillo Páez v. Peru*, Judgment (Reparations and Costs), 27 November 1998, para. 105-07.

114 IACtHR, *Paniagua-Morales et al. v. Guatemala*, Judgment, 8 March 1998, para 155-156; *Durand and Ugarte v. Peru*, Judgment, 16 August 2000, par. 130; *Genie Lacayo v. Nicaragua*, Judgment, 29 January 1997, par. 76; *Villagrán Morales et al. v. Guatemala*, Judgment, 19 November 1999, par. 226-227; *Bámaca-Velásquez v. Guatemala*, Judgment, 25 November 2000, para. 220-222, 230.

115 See IACtHR, *Velasquez Rodriguez v. Honduras*, Judgment, 29 July 1988.

mala. The Court held that Article 8(1) includes the right of victims' relatives to criminal investigation, prosecution and punishment, as well as compensation.[116] It found:

> [...] Article 8(1) of the American Convention recognizes the right of Mr. Nicholas Blake's relatives to have his disappearance and death effectively investigated by the Guatemalan authorities; to have those responsible prosecuted for committing said unlawful acts; to have the relevant punishment, where appropriate, meted out; and to be compensated for the damages and injuries they sustained.[117]

These duties and obligations of states to investigate, prosecute, punish, and provide reparation also entail the individual rights of victims to truth and justice in the criminal process. Accordingly, reading Article 25 and 8(1) together the Court has determined that a victim's right of access to justice, right to truth, and right to be heard entails their right to participation in criminal proceedings. In the *Street Children Case*, the Court found that "it is evident from article 8 of the Convention that the victims of human rights violations and their next-of-kin should have substantial possibilities of being heard and acting in the respective proceedings, both in order to clarify the facts and punish those responsible, and to seek due reparation."[118] The rationale behind the decision being that the role of victims in the investigations can prove to be essential in guaranteeing compliance under the Convention. It has consistently found that states are obliged to provide victims with access to a criminal process and that the process must be fair.[119] In this sense, victims are entitled to due process guarantees which are also applicable to the accused. Although the Court originally confined Article 8(1) to generally only refer to the rights of accused in criminal trials,[120] in 1998 the Court found that the right to a fair trial includes a victim's due process rights.[121] More specifically it recognized that "the right to a fair trial includes victims' relatives right to judicial guarantees, and specifically to a criminal investigation for the purpose of identifying and, when appropriate, prosecuting and punishing those responsible."[122] In this way, when read together with Article 25, the Court is able to provide for a broad array of victims' rights in criminal proceedings.

---

116 IACtHR, *Blake v. Guatemala*, Judgment, 24 Jaunary 1998, para. 96-97.

117 IACtHR, *Blake v. Guatemala*, Judgment, 24 Jaunary 1998, par. 97.

118 IACtHR, *Villagrán Morales et al. v. Guatemala*, Judgment, 19 November 1999, par. 227.

119 IACtHR, *Castillo Páez v. Peru*, Judgment, 3 November 1997, par. 90; *Durand and Ugarte v. Peru*, Judgment, 16 August 2000, para. 111-30; *Bámaca-Velásquez v. Guatemala*, Judgment, 25 November 2000, para. 182-196; *Villagrán Morales et al. v. Guatemala*, Judgment, 19 November 1999, para. 199-238; *Barrios Altos v. Peru*, Judgment, 14 March 2001, par. 51.

120 IACtHR, *Neira Alegría v. Peru*, Judgment, 19 January 1995, par. 86; *Cabellero-Delgado and Santana v. Colombia*, Judgment, 8 December 1995, par. 64.

121 See IACtHR, *Blake v. Guatemala*, Judgment, 24 Jaunary 1998.

122 *Ibid.* at para. 96-97.

Apart from holding that victims should play a role in the criminal process, with an emphasis on the investigation stage of proceedings, the Court has not prescribed the extent that participation should take. This holding back of sorts is likely due to the fact that the Court, like its European counterpart, must take into the account the specific procedure laws applicable in Member States. However, most of the cases dealing with victims' rights have arisen in jurisdictions which allow victims to participate as civil parties in criminal proceedings and therefore the decisions on victims reflect the broad role afforded in domestic proceedings.

4.3.4 Inter-American Commission on Human Rights

In addition to the IACtHR, the IACHR has also supported or pronounced upon the importance of victim participation in criminal proceedings. For example, in the Commission's Third Report on the human rights situation in Colombia, it explained that the inability of victims in Colombia to participate as civil parties in the criminal process before the naming or charging of a suspect precludes victims from exercising important participatory rights.[123] These rights include the requesting of specific investigations and gathering of evidence and the taking of testimony that could lead to the identification of the perpetrators.[124] More recently, the Commission, once again involving Colombia, pronounced upon the importance of victims. In 2007 the Commission issued a report on the peace process in Colombia,[125] which touches upon Colombia's judicial proceedings concerning the implementation of its demobilization process under its Justice and Peace Law. The fourth part of the report addresses the issues of victim protection, victim reparation and victim participation, including the question of the participation of victims in the initial stages of the judicial process.[126]

In accordance with domestic criminal procedures and the Justice and Peace Law, victims in Colombia have active participatory rights in criminal proceedings.[127] They may be recognized as full parties in the proceedings, attend hearings, lead and challenge evidence, have access to the case file and claim reparations. Decree 315 of 2007

123 See IACHR, Third Report on the Human Rights Situation in Colombia, OEA/ser. L./V./II.102, doc. 9 rev. 1, 26 February 1999.

124 *Ibid.*, Ch. V, par. 71.

125 Part of the objectives of the Organization of American States' Mission to Support the Peace Process in Colombia (MAPP/OEA Mission) was to establish the responsibility of demobilized personnel who committed crimes and to arrange for victim reparation pursuant to Law 975 of 2005 [hereinafter referred to as the Justice and Peace Law]. Since 2004 the IACHR has followed the human rights situation as part of its advisory role to OAS members and the MAPP/OAS Mission.

126 See IACHR, Third Report on the Human Rights Situation in Colombia, OEA/ser. L./V./II.102, doc. 9 rev. 1, 26 February 1999; Report on the Demobilization Process in Colombia, OEA/Ser.L/V/II.120, doc. 60, 13 December 2004; Statement of the Inter-American Commission on Human Rights on the Application and Scope of the Justice and Peace Law in Colombia, 2006, OEA/Ser/L/V/II. 125, doc. 15, 1 August 2006; see also, Chapter IV (Human Rights Development in the Region) of the IACHR Annual Reports for the years 1995, 1996, 1999, 2000, 2001, 2002, 2003, 2004, 2005 and 2006.

127 See Justice and Peace Law, Art. 4.

of the Ministry of Interior and Justice, which regulates the intervention of victims in the investigation stage of the Justice and Peace proceedings, provides that victims or their legal representatives may have direct access to the taking of statements, formulation of indictments and charges and other procedural steps in the criminal process.[128] However, despite these rights that exist on paper, the report indicates that victims often face challenges when trying to ensure their participatory rights. One problem the Commission identified had to do with the possibility of questioning individuals:

> [...] Questioning by victims is confined to the second phase of the hearing, but it takes place through an indirect mechanism, where the questions are incorporated into a form that is delivered to members of the [Technical Investigations Core], who in turn deliver it to the prosecutor. It must be noted that the prosecutor is in a different room from that where the victims are. The prosecutor transmits to the candidate only those questions from the victims that he deems pertinent. The victims and their representatives have no possibility to raise new questions, to seek clarifications for further details, or to cross-examine. This indirect mechanism severely restricts the possibility of the victim to use questioning as a suitable means of obtaining the truth of the facts. Moreover, the prosecution thereby loses a valuable strategy for comparing the voluntary depositions and verifying compliance with the legal requirements for access to benefits.[129]

Despite the problems identified in the report, the Commission positively noted that Colombia indicated in submissions that its Ombudsman Office provided advice to almost 10,000 victims of violence and provided legal representation to over 2,000 victims in criminal proceedings connected with the Justice and Peace Law.[130] Importantly, the Commission views the participation of victims in all stages of the criminal process as essential in seeking the truth.[131] The emphasis on the right to truth has prompted the Commission to require genuine and effective implementation of victims' rights in the criminal process. Importantly, the large number of victims involved in this process does make a difference with regard to the positive obligations of the state and the recognition of individual rights of victims.

4.3.5 African Court of Human and Peoples' Rights

Like the ECHR and ACHR, the African Charter on Human and Peoples' Rights (AfCHPR or Charter) is a regional human rights instrument which seeks to promote respect for human rights and basic freedoms in Africa. The African Commission on

---

128 IACHR, Report on the implementation of the Justice and Peace Law: Initial stages in the demobilization of the AUC and first judicial proceedings, OEA/Ser.L/V/II.129, Doc. 3, 2 October 2007, par. 81, citing Ministry of Interior and Justice, Decree 315 of 7 February 2007, regulating victim intervention in the investigation stage of justice and peace proceedings in accordance with Law 975 of 2005.

129 IACHR, Report on the implementation of the Justice and Peace Law: Initial stages in the demobilization of the AUC and first judicial proceedings, OEA/Ser.L/V/II.129, Doc. 3, 2 October 2007, par. 82.

130 *Ibid.* at par. 85.

131 *Ibid.* at par. 100.

Human and People's Rights (ACmHPR or African Commission), a quasi-judicial body with no binding powers, has the task of interpreting the Charter. However, in accordance with the 1998 protocol, the African Court on Human and Peoples' Rights (ACtHPR) was established and is also meant to play a role in interpreting the rights provided for under the Charter.[132]

The ACtHPR is the most recent of the now three regional human rights courts. At the time of writing the Court has heard only one case and its relationship with the African Commission is still to be elaborated.[133] Though it can be argued that the right to a remedy is implicit in human rights instruments, the African Charter makes no mention of the right to a remedy, redress or the right of access to justice. Therefore it is not likely that jurisprudence from the ACtHPR will develop along the same lines as that from the ECtHR or IACtHR. Nevertheless, the African Charter does contain provisions relating to the right to a fair trial, which includes a provision stating "Every individual shall have the right to have his cause heard."[134] Therefore, in theory, it is conceivable that the African Court could seek to strengthen a right of victims to participate in domestic criminal proceedings through the right to a fair trial if participation in the criminal process is provided for in the respective national jurisdiction.

4.3.6 African Commission on Human and Peoples' Rights

Due to the fact that the African Charter does not provide for the right to an effective remedy there is only limited jurisprudence by the ACmHPR on effective remedies for violations of the Charter and recognition of a victim's rights in criminal processes.[135] Even so, the ACmHPR has expounded upon the rights of individuals, including victims, in other ways. For instance, Article 45(c) of the AfCHPR provides that the ACmHPR is to formulate principles and rules aimed at solving legal problems relating to rights and fundamental freedoms upon which African states may base their legislation. To this end, in 2001 the Commission adopted Principles and Guidelines on the Right to a Fair Trial and Legal Assistance in Africa.[136]

The Principles and Guidelines on the Rights to a Fair Trial and Legal Assistance are remarkable because they clearly include victims' rights in criminal proceedings within the concept of fair trial rights. They provide that the right to an effective remedy is a fair trial right and further provide that the right to an effective remedy includes access to justice, reparation for the harm suffered and access to the factual

---

132 In July 2004 the Organization for African Unity (OAU) determined that the ACtHPR would merge with the African Court of Justice.

133 See ACtHPR, *Yogogombaye v. Republic of Senegal*, App. No. 001/2008, Judgment, 15 December 2009.

134 AfCHPR, Article 7(1); See also Articles 5, 6, 7 and 26.

135 See, e.g., ACmHPR, *Amnesty International v. Zambia*, Comm. No. 212/98, 5 May 1999, para. 47-48, 52, 57, 59, 61, finding violations of the Charter but providing little by way of effective remedies.

136 ACmHPR, Principles and Guidelines on the Right to a Fair Trial and Legal Assistance, UN Doc. DOC/05/(XXX)247 (2001) [hereinafter ACmHPR Principles and Guidelines on the Right to a Fair Trial], Section C(b)(1-3).

information concerning the violations.[137] Other rights of victims can be found in the duty of prosecutors to consider the views and concerns of victims when their personal interests are affected and to ensure that victims are informed of their rights. Under its section concerning victims of crime and abuse of power, it emphasizes that victims should be treated with compassion and respect for their dignity, that they are entitled to mechanisms of justice and prompt redress, and the right to be informed of their rights and the progress of proceedings. Importantly the Principles and Guidelines mirror the language found in Article 6(b) of the Victims' Declaration by stating that judicial officers, prosecutors and lawyers should facilitate the needs of victims by:

> Allowing their views and concerns to be presented and considered at appropriate stages of the proceedings where their personal interests are affected, without prejudice to the accused and consistent with the relevant national criminal justice system.[138]

The Principles and Guidelines further state that victims should be provided with proper assistance throughout the legal process and that any unnecessary delays should be avoided. Restitution is emphasized by stating that victims, their families or dependents are entitled to reparation and police, justice, health and social service personnel should receive special training to sensitize them to the needs of victims. Finally, informal mechanisms for the resolution of disputes, including traditional and customary practices, are encouraged where appropriate to facilitate conciliation and redress for victims. Importantly, the Principles and Guidelines define the term victim to mean:

> [P]ersons who individually or collectively have suffered harm, including physical or mental injury, emotional suffering, economic loss or substantial impairment of their fundamental rights, through acts or omissions that are in violation of criminal laws or that do not yet constitute violations of national criminal laws but of internationally recognized norms relating to human rights. The term "victim" also includes, where appropriate, the immediate family or dependants of the direct victim and persons who have suffered harm in intervening to assist victims in distress.[139]

It is striking that this provision limits the status of victims to immediate family members or dependents given the fact that in many African communities the notion or concept of family is broad. Perhaps, because of this broadness, drafters felt that the definition should be limited. Regardless, the Principles and Guidelines reproduce language found in other regional documents and builds upon the notion that victims are entitled to fair trial rights in criminal proceedings. They further suggest that despite a country's legal system victims are also entitled to basic minimum rights – phrased in terms of human rights.

---

137 *Ibid.*
138 *Ibid.*, Section P(f)(ii).
139 *Ibid.*, Section S(n).

4.4 Other International Developments and Initiatives

In addition to the developments taking place within human rights bodies there have been important advancements related to victims' rights in the criminal process occurring in other regional and international spheres.

4.4.1 International Treaties, Resolutions and Principles

Drawing upon the language found in Article 6(b) of the Victims' Declaration, two international conventions have specifically provided for the participatory rights of victims. These conventions are only binding on those states that have ratified them but they reflect agreement towards incorporating provisions specifically mentioning a victim's right to participation in the criminal process. Article 25(3) of the Convention against Transnational Organized Crime requires that "each State Party shall, subject to its domestic law, enable views and concerns of victims to be presented and considered at appropriate stages of criminal proceedings."[140] Similarly, Article 6 of its Protocol to Prevent, Suppress and Punish Trafficking in Persons, Especially Women and Children provides that trafficking victims shall be "assisted to express their views and concerns at appropriate stages of criminal proceedings in a manner not prejudicial to the rights of the defense."[141] Both documents have the wide support of states.[142] Notably, however, both documents are worded broadly so as to take into account a wide margin of appreciation for the domestic practice of states.

Unlike the Convention against Transnational Organized Crime and its Protocol on Human Trafficking most international treaties do not make explicit reference to the right of victims to have standing or even to be heard in criminal proceedings. Instead, human rights treaties usually only explicitly provide for the right to an effective remedy or fair trial rights. Additionally, as noted in the sections above, bodies interpreting human rights treaties infer additional state obligations and individual rights such as the legal obligations to investigate, prosecute and punish and the right of access to justice, the right to reparation, and the right to truth.

Recently, the International Convention for the Protection of All Persons from Enforced Disappearance (Convention on Enforced Disappearance) became the first human rights treaty to explicitly confer upon victims of enforced disappearances the right to truth.[143] The Convention on Enforced Disappearance recognizes important

140 UN Convention against Transnational Organized Crime (2000).

141 Protocol to Prevent, Suppress and Punish Trafficking in Persons, Especially Women and Children, Supplementing the United Nations Convention Against Transnational Organized Crime, UN Doc. A/45/49 (Vol. I) (2001) [hereinafter Protocol on Human Trafficking].

142 As of March 2011, 159 states have ratified the UN Convention against Transnational Organized Crime and 143 states have ratified the Protocol on Human Trafficking.

143 International Convention for the Protection of All Persons from Enforced Disappearance (2006), Art. 24(2).

obligations for states and broad individual rights for victims though it does not explicitly mention the right to participation in the criminal process. Article 3 recognizes a state's duty to investigate alleged violations by non-state actors. Article 6 holds that states must take necessary measures to hold perpetrators criminally responsible. Article 8(2) recognizes the right to a remedy during the term of the applicable statute of limitations for the crime of enforced disappearance. Article 11 further recognizes the obligation of states to criminally prosecute those suspected of being responsible for enforced disappearances. Article 12 recognizes an individual's right to file a complaint for alleged violations and the state's duty to carry out impartial and thorough investigations. Articles 18 and 24 recognize the right of victims to have access to information and the truth. Article 24 also recognizes the right of victims to obtain reparations for harms suffered.

In addition to international treaties a handful of UN resolutions explicitly call upon states to provide victims with greater rights in criminal processes. For instance, Paragraph 8 of the UN Resolution on children as victims and perpetrators of crime holds that states "in a manner consistent with the procedural rules of national law and the administration of justice, [...] should enable children to participate as appropriate, in criminal justice proceedings, including the investigative stage and throughout the trial and post-trial process period, to be heard and given information about their status and any proceedings that might subsequently take place."[144] Similarly, Principle 4 of the Principles on the Effective Investigation and Documentation of Torture and Other Cruel, Inhuman or Degrading Treatment or Punishment prescribes that victims and their legal representatives have rights to be informed of and to have access to any hearing and to any relevant information about the investigation, including the right to present other evidence.[145]

4.4.2 European Initiatives

It is clear that the changes to the role of victims in the criminal process have been one part of a larger, more profound transformation of criminal justice. With regard to the European system, Vogler argues that the three major influences on contemporary European criminal justice include the drive towards adversariality (touched upon in Chapter 3), the ECHR (discussed above), and Europe's desire to develop a common sense of justice throughout Member States.[146] In relation to the last of these major influences, the Council of Europe and the European Union have played an essential

144 Resolution on Children as victims and perpetrators, adopted by the Ninth UN Congress on the Prevention of Crime and the Treatment of Offenders, UN Doc. A/CONF.169/16 (1995), par. 8.

145 Principles on the Effective Investigation and Documentation of Torture and Other Cruel, Inhuman, or Degrading Treatment or Punishment, UN Doc. A/RES/55/89 (2000), Principle 4.

146 Vogler, R., Introduction, 11-24, in Vogler and Huber (2008).

role with regard to the criminal policy of their Member States. They have also played a principal role with regard to victim policies.[147]

Council of Europe

The Council of Europe, whose main objective is to strengthen democracy, human rights and the rule of law, strives to promote common values shared by Member States. The Council of Europe works on areas of common interest to Member States and often touches upon issues related to criminal law. As early as 1975 the Council of Europe began to address crime and victim policies,[148] though its focus on victims usually centered on state compensation to victims of violent crime.[149] For example, in 1977 the Council of Europe passed a resolution on state compensation and in 1983 the Committee of Ministers adopted the European Convention on the Compensation of Victims of Violent Crime which further developed state compensation initiatives. The focus of the Council of Europe soon turned, however, to the role of the victim in the criminal justice process. To this end, in the early 1980s the Council of Europe's European Committee on Crime Problems, with the approval of the Committee of Ministers, established a Select Committee of Experts on the Victim and Criminal and Social Policy.

The Select Committee was entrusted with developing recommendations for the protection of crime victims and of drafting human rights instruments that focus on the treatment of victims by the police, prosecutors and judges.[150] One such Recommendation entitled "On Participation of the Public in Crime Policy" emphasized the need to take into account victims' interests.[151] Among the recommendations, which were aimed at providing information and other assistance to victims, was the establishment of legal aid for victims to help ensure access to justice.[152]

In 1985 the Committee of Ministers adopted Recommendation (85)11 which concerned the Position of the Victim in the Framework of Criminal Law and Procedure. The Preamble to the Recommendation explicitly states that its purpose is to address the exclusion of the victim from the criminal process. The Recommendation was designed for immediate implementation by Member States. In many ways it mirrors the guidelines found in the Victims' Declaration, and was based upon earlier studies on victims within various national criminal jurisdictions employing a wide

147 See Joutsen (1987) at 69-70.

148 Mawby and Walklate (1994) at 89.

149 In 1983 the Council of Europe opened for signature the Convention on the Compensation of Victims and Violent Crime, which entered into force in early 1988. See European Convention on the Compensation of Victims of Violent Crime (1983).

150 In 1981 the European Committee on Crime Problems created a Select Committee of Experts to examine victims and policy, see Brienen and Hoegen (2000) at 9.

151 Recommendation of the Committee of Ministers on participation of the public in crime policy, 361st meeting of the Ministers' Deputies, Doc. No. R (83) 7 (1983).

152 *Ibid.*

range of procedures. Although the Recommendation greatly overlaps with the Victims' Declaration, the differences between Recommendation (85)11 and the Victims' Declaration are important.

The primary difference has to do with the fact that the guidelines as laid down in the Recommendation are more concrete than those found in the Victims' Declaration, the rationale being that they are easier for individual states to implement.[153] For instance, whereas the Victims' Declaration states that victims have the right to be informed of health and social services the Recommendation states unequivocally that the police should inform victims of these services.[154] Overall, the Recommendation contains 16 guidelines on the ways in which states should treat victims of crime within their criminal justice systems. It focuses on three main themes: information, compensation and treatment/protection.[155] The Council of Europe views the Recommendation as part of a long-term campaign to improve the position of victims within criminal justice systems.[156] Importantly, the underlying agreement is that criminal justice systems "should do justice to the interests of victims without undermining the other objectives of the system such as the upholding of social norms, the rights and rehabilitation of offenders, and the possible reconciliation between the victims and the offender."[157]

The research carried out by Brienen and Hoegen "demonstrates without a doubt that the body of thought of Recommendation (85)11 has had an impact on the vast majority of the criminal justice systems of the Council of Europe's Member States."[158] When examining the overriding issues of information, reparation and treatment and protection, their study found that the best overall practices were achieved in the Netherlands, England and Wales and Sweden, although no system implemented the Recommendation perfectly. Their findings suggest that the implementation of victim-oriented measures does not depend on a specific type of legal system. Similarly no one legal system, in itself, is an advantage for meeting victim-oriented goals. However, they found that if the Recommendation focused on the right of victims to participate throughout the proceedings the type of legal system would indeed make a difference, emphasizing that common law-based systems would struggle.[159]

---

153 Brienen and Hoegen (2000) at 11.

154 Joutsen (1987) at 70.

155 Brienen and Hoegen (2000) at 1; The Guidelines of Recommendation 85(11) stress the importance of criminal justice institutions providing information to victims about the criminal process (guidelines A.2. and D.9, A.3 and B.6). All of these guidelines provide that victims should be informed about the basic workings of the system, their rights within the system, and the outcomes of investigations and hearings. Guideline B.5 further stresses the importance of victim compensation by stating that a "decision of whether to prosecute the offender should not be taken without due consideration of the question of compensation of the victim, including any serious effort made to that end by the offender."

156 *Ibid.* at 5.

157 *Ibid.* at 10, citing Report of the European Committee on Crime Problems (1985), p. 16.

158 *Ibid.* at 1156.

159 *Ibid.* at 1158.

Following Recommendation 85(11) the Council of Europe would continue to highlight the need to support victims in criminal justice systems. In 1987, the Committee of Ministers adopted Recommendation (87)21 on assistance to victims and the prevention of victimization.[160] This document promotes greater awareness for the position of victims and the need to provide victims with information on their rights and assistance during the criminal process. It also calls for experiments in mediation practices between victims and offenders. The Committee of Ministers has also issued a recommendation calling for states to allow victims to challenge decisions not to prosecute or to alternatively allow private prosecutions.[161] In its Recommendation on the role of the public prosecutor, the Committee suggests that victims in particular "should be able to challenge decisions of public prosecutors not to prosecute; such a challenge may be made, where appropriate after an hierarchical review, either by way of judicial review, or by authorising parties to engage private prosecution."[162] This recommendation is line with the belief that victims should be afforded access to justice and should have the opportunity to ensure their right to a remedy. Finally, in 2006 the Committee of Ministers continued to support the position of victims through adoption of a recommendation on assistance to victims.[163] In this recommendation the Committee of Ministers reiterated many of the points found in Recommendation (87)21 but elaborated upon important matters. For instance, it calls for protection from secondary victimization, it states that victims should be provided with explanations of decisions made with regard to their case, and it asserts that victims should be able to both provide and receive information as well as legal advice when dealing with criminal justice agencies.

European Union

In addition to the Council of Europe, the European Union has also contributed to the current role afforded to victims in European criminal justice systems. The Council of the European Union, commonly referred to as the Council of Ministers, is the decision-making body which together with the European Parliament and the European Commission support and coordinate the activities of Member States of the European Union and adopt measures in the area of judicial cooperation and criminal matters. The European Union's Council Framework Decision on the standing of victims in criminal proceedings of 15 March 2001 provides certain rights to victims of crime.[164] The Framework

160 Recommendation of the Committee of Ministers on assistance to victims and the prevention of victimization, 410th meeting of the Ministers' Deputies, Doc. No. R (1987) 21 (1987).

161 Recommendation of the Committee of Ministers on the role of public prosecution in the criminal justice system, 724th meeting of the Ministers' Deputies, Doc. No. R (2000) 19 (2000).

162 *Ibid.* at par. 34.

163 Recommendation of the Committee of Ministers on assistance to crime victims, 967th meeting of the Ministers' Deputies, Doc. No. R (2006) 8 (2006).

164 Council Framework Decision 2001/220/JHA, 15 March 2001.

Decision was created on the initiative of Portugal and further develops principles found in the Victims' Declaration and Recommendation (85)11, as well as the European Convention on Human Rights. In contrast with Recommendation (85)11, the Framework Decision is binding on Member States as to the result to be achieved but leaves the choice of form and methods to domestic authorities. The Framework Decision is comprised of 19 articles dealing with reasons for establishing the decision and addressing national jurisdictions about victims of crime. It attempts to promote the acknowledgment of crime victims as legal subjects so that they can have "a real and appropriate role in the criminal legal system."[165] For the European Union's judicial systems, the European Union's Council Framework Decision provides the central reference point on the legal position of victims.

The Framework Decision defines a victim as a natural person who has suffered harm directly caused by acts or omission that violate the criminal law of a Member State.[166] The harm may be physical, mental, emotional or material. The victim shall be treated with due respect in proceedings, including special reference to criminal proceedings. It further calls on states to provide victims with information about the criminal process and to allow those victims who have the status of party to the proceedings or a witness in the proceedings to be reimbursed for the expense of participation.[167] National jurisdictions shall provide advice and legal aid free of charge and all other expenses incurred as a result of their participation in criminal proceedings. Moreover, victims and their families are entitled to protection and privacy. Furthermore, they are entitled to compensation in the course of criminal proceedings and penal mediation, sometimes referred to as victim-offender mediation, should be encouraged in all appropriate cases. NGO involvement is promoted as are infrastructural changes necessary to avoid secondary victimization.

As regards the right to be heard and to participate in the criminal process, the Framework Decision does not specifically provide victims with a formal right to this effect. However, it calls on Member States to safeguard the 'possibility' to be heard during criminal proceedings and to supply evidence.[168] Member States are therefore not obliged to afford victims of crime a legal right to speak orally in the courtroom, be represented by counsel in proceedings or to act as parties in criminal proceedings.[169] Thus, while not directly calling for Member States to allow victims to assume the role of civil parties in criminal proceedings,[170] it certainly suggests that such a role would facilitate the filing of reparation claims.

Ten years after adoption of the Framework Decision, the Council of the European Union has stated that it is necessary to revise and supplement the principles promoted

165 *Ibid.*, Art. 2(1).
166 *Ibid.*, Art. 1.
167 *Ibid.*, Art. 4, 7.
168 *Ibid.*, Art. 3.
169 Kool and Moerings (2004) at 46.
170 Council Framework Decision 2001/220/JHA, 15 March 2001, Art. 9.

therein. Accordingly, the Council has adopted a Resolution aimed at strengthening the rights of victims, particularly in criminal proceedings, and the Commission has proposed that the principles from the Framework Decision be turned into a Directive.[171] The benefit of such an action is that Directives provide uniform rules for Member States, requiring direct implementation into national law. Additionally, non-compliance may result in an infringement decision by the European Commission, which may eventually lead to a complaint before the European Court of Justice. The proposed Directive would help ensure that victims across Europe would have the same, non-discriminatory minimum level of rights, services and access to justice. More specifically, the proposed Directive provides that victims will have a right to review a decision not to prosecute (something that is not currently possible in all Member States) and emphasizes the use of restorative justice measures after the accused person has accepted responsibility for their act.

The developments in Europe with regard to the role of the victim in the criminal process are important. The European Union and the Council of Europe have time and again sought to promote the rights of victims in criminal proceedings while at the same time respecting the different procedural approaches of Member States. The result has been an increase in rights and services for victims within the criminal justice systems of Member States without an overhaul of criminal procedures.

4.4.3 A Victims' Convention?

In an attempt to reinforce and strengthen legal and financial support for victims the World Society of Victimology, the world's leading organization lobbying for victims' rights internationally, and its partners have sought to develop more ways in which the United Nations can aid victims of crime by ensuring compliance with the Victims' Declaration. Beginning in 2005 the idea for a convention aimed at supporting victims first materialized.[172] The draft UN Convention on Justice and Support for Victims of Crime and Abuse of Power was developed and it includes enhanced international standards and norms that go beyond those found in the Victims' Declaration.[173] For instance, the draft Convention calls on states to provide victims, "where appropriate, the right of appeal against decisions of the prosecutorial authority not to prosecute in cases where they were victimized"[174] and to reimburse victims for their reasonable expenses related to their participation in the criminal process.[175] The Convention also

171 European Commission, Proposal for a Directive of the European Parliament and of the Council Establishing Minimum Standards on the Rights, Support and Protection of Victims of Crime, Procedure No. COD(2011)0129, 18 May 2011; see also, Council Note, Proposal for a Resolution of the Council on a Roadmap for Strengthening the Rights and Protection of Victims, in Particular in Criminal Proceedings, Doc. No. 9359/11, 28 April 2011.

172 Van Genugten, et al. (2006) at 109.

173 See Van Genugten, et al. (2006).

174 Draft Convention on Justice and Support for Victims of Crime and Abuse of Power (2006), Art. 2(e).

175 *Ibid.*, Art. 3.

calls upon states to support restorative justice measures alongside the traditional criminal process.[176] In addition the Convention would create a Committee of Experts.[177] It is envisioned that States Parties to the Convention will regularly submit country reports to the Committee and it will evaluate whether and to what extent the states comply with the standards and norms found in the Convention. Though the Convention has not yet come to fruition, it is believed that a so-called hard law document will exert even greater pressure on states to implement and enforce the rights of victims.[178]

4.5 A Shift in Emphasis?

All major regional and international human rights conventions specifically stress the rights of the accused in criminal proceedings because they are based on liberal theories and values. In the liberal model, in order to protect the human rights of individuals limits need to be placed on state authority because the state is seen as being infinitely more powerful than any of its citizens.[179] The power of the state is exemplified in the field of criminal law where the state has the power to incarcerate individuals and in some jurisdictions to sentence individuals to death.[180] Procedural limitations are one way in which to curb (potential) abuse of power. Moreover, because individuals accused of crime are usually marginalized politically and socially within society, procedural limitations, due process rights, and adherence to strict standards of fair trial assist in lessening the imbalance of power between the state and the individual. Thus, liberal values recognize the imbalance of power between state authorities and individuals accused of crime and provide for defendants' rights in the criminal process. In fact, the drafters of the regional human rights conventions exclusively envisioned them for the protection of the rights of the accused because the underlying assumption was that the state wields great power over the defendant and therefore must abide by certain procedural standards in order to ensure the defendant's fair trial and fundamental human rights.[181] The interests of victims were seen to be the same as those of the state prosecuting crime. Victims did not have a prominent role in the liberal human rights model.

However, a shift from liberal values focused on the defendant to a more victim-oriented focus has occurred within the regional human rights systems.[182] State crimes committed in Latin America in the 1980s helped facilitate this shift due to the fact that the context of these crimes challenged the underlying assumption of the liberal model

176 *Ibid.*, Art. 9(1) and (2).
177 *Ibid.*, Art. 14.
178 Van Genugten, et al. (2006) at 109.
179 Packer (1968) at 16.
180 *Ibid.* at 165-166.
181 Trechsel (2005) at 36-38.
182 Aldana-Pindell (2002) at 1413-1414.

of human rights.[183] State authorities were protecting state agents accused of human rights abuses by failing to investigate, prosecute and punish violations. The imbalance of power was not between the accused and the state but rather between victims and the state. Therefore it fell to the IACtHR to address these failings by its Member States. As a result, the court began adopting a strong victims' rights jurisprudence despite there being no explicit mention of such rights in the ACHR. To some extent the ECtHR did the same.

The case law shows that out of the broad individual rights and state obligations, including the right of access to justice, the right to a remedy, and the right to a fair trial the courts (and the Inter-American Court in particular) implied the duty to investigate, prosecute and punish human rights violations.[184] Despite the fact that the duty to prosecute was originally interpreted as an obligation to the public generally and not to individuals specifically a change in thinking occurred. The courts were not only finding that individuals could privately enforce the duty to prosecute, investigate and in some cases seek punishment, but also found that in order to ensure the duty to prosecute, investigate and punish states must ensure that victims have the opportunity to participate in proceedings and have their interests and concerns heard. The procedural rights sanctioned by the courts include the right to information, the right to be heard (to express views and concerns), the right to legal advice or counsel and the right to reparation through the criminal process. The courts have found that victims should have greater access to the criminal process and greater participatory rights in order to ensure effective investigations and prosecutions. The recognition of these participatory rights, i.e. the right to have standing to enforce state obligations and the right to be heard in domestic criminal processes, is not limited to crimes committed by state agents or authorities. Increasingly, the courts have determined that victims have these rights in relation to crimes committed by those not affiliated with the state.[185]

Though the two regional systems have adopted two distinct styles they have nonetheless moved towards the same result: greater victim-oriented jurisprudence. The approach of the ECtHR appears to want to avoid overt conflicts with the liberal / due process model but nevertheless still recognizes victims' rights in the criminal process. The approach of the IACtHR takes a more direct approach, openly pushing for greater rights of victims, often at the expense of the rights of the accused and legal certainty.[186]

183 Sorochinsky (2009) at 186-187.

184 Aldana-Pindell (2002) at 1413.

185 See, e.g., IACtHR, *Albán-Cornejo v. Ecuador*, Judgment, 22 November 2007 and ECtHR, *Siliadin v. France*, App. No. 73316/01, 26 July 2005.

186 For example the IACtHR places such an emphasis on the duty to prosecute that it has found that the state may never apply amnesty laws, raise the statute of limitations, non-ex post facto nature of criminal laws or *res judicata* defenses, or rely upon the principle of double jeopardy, or resort to any other similar measure designed to eliminate responsibility in order to escape its duty to investigate and punish those responsible. Arguably the waiver of the statute of limitations and the principle of double jeopardy comprise the rights of accused and the principle of legal certainty. See IACtHR, *Barrios Altos v. Peru*, Judgment, 14 March 2001, par. 41; *Almonacid-Arellano, et al., v. Chile*, Preliminary Objections,

While the case law from the two major human rights courts may seem like isolated decisions, taken together they are, in fact, indicative of a less sympathetic stance against defendants.

To be clear, an increased recognition of the rights of victims is not always in conflict with the rights of the accused. However, it can be the case that greater emphasis on the rights of victims does in fact conflict with the traditional, liberal model of human rights that stress due process rights for the accused. The continued emphasis on the duty to prosecute and punish can result in states taking away procedural safeguards protecting the due process and fair trial rights of the accused. The shift in emphasis sends a mixed message to domestic systems where they are required on the one hand to ensure fair trial rights for the accused and on the other hand are increasingly encouraged to prosecute, punish and provide for (and even balance) victims' rights.[187] In so doing, victims' rights get elevated at the expense of defendants' rights.

It is also alarming that the courts fail to openly acknowledge the shift in emphasis.[188] The courts publically declare the fundamental importance of fair trial rights for accused while simultaneously bolstering the rights of victims and omitting any evaluation of whether doing so could potentially affect the rights of accused.[189] There is also little to no discussion about the difference between competing rights when one side can point to explicit provisions in the convention compared with implicit rights derived from the convention. Without detracting from the beneficial aspects of the recognition of victims' rights in human rights law, it is nevertheless important to acknowledge that departure from the liberal model and the failure to acknowledge reasons for doing so undermine perceptions of fairness generally and confuse domestic legal systems looking to human rights decisions for guidance on how to best address conflicting rights.

4.6 Conclusion

This chapter has appraised the developments at the international level with regard to the rights of victims in judicial processes, with particular emphasis on criminal justice processes. In the past few decades an increasing amount of attention at the international level has been paid to the rights and interests of victims in domestic criminal proceedings. Non-binding UN General Assembly declarations have sought to clarify, in broad terms, the various rights belonging to victims. These UN documents generally serve as a reflection of accepted standards rather than as creating international norms

---

Merits, Reparations and Costs, 26 September 2006, para. 151-154; *La Cantuta v. Peru*, Judgment, 29 November 2006, par. 226.

187 Sorochinsky (2009) at 209.

188 *Ibid.*

189 See, e.g., IACtHR, *Tibi v. Ecuador*, Judgment, 7 September 2004; *Gutiérrez Soler v. Colombia*, Judgment, 12 September 2005.

that have immediate application in domestic practice.[190] Nevertheless, these documents are important because they stress the fact that victims have interests that should be taken into account by states. In particular, the Victims' Declaration was the first UN instrument dedicated solely to the rights of victims. It was the first instrument to directly encourage greater victim participation in domestic justice processes. Worded broadly, the provision on victim participation is applicable in a wide range of legal systems. Likewise, the Basic Principles, while not specifically calling for participation in criminal proceedings, arguably imply the importance of participation through their emphasis on equal and effective access to justice, adequate, effective and prompt reparation and the right to truth.

In addition to the UN declarations, the human rights bodies have interpreted the broad categories of rights, such as those found in the Basic Principles, to infer greater procedural rights for victims of crime. Despite the fact that no explicit rights of victims are provided for in the regional human rights conventions or the ICCPR, international human rights bodies have developed an assortment of rights for victims of crime together with corresponding obligations for states. This inference of rights for victims has, in many ways, shifted the emphasis away from the liberal model of human rights focused on the rights of accused towards a more victim-focused paradigm.

Without a doubt, the most controversial inclusion of the victim in domestic criminal proceedings has to do with the right to be involved in decision-making.[191] Decision-making may include having input into decisions whether or not to prosecute, pre-trial detention matters, the charges to be brought, plea agreements, sentencing and parole. States disagree over all of these issues depending upon the degree to which victims may participate in their national systems. Legal instruments and regional court decisions rarely go so far as to dictate participation during specific proceedings, and given the widely divergent domestic legal systems and their diverse approaches to appropriate victim participation, it appears logical that victims' participatory rights at the international level are worded in broad, inspirational terms, providing for minimum standards that states should try to meet. Along the same lines, it is logical that regional human rights courts give wide deference to domestic law and practice. However, when a state provides for victim involvement, courts seem to place an emphasis on allowing effective participation early in the criminal process.[192] The rationale for allowing victim participation during the investigation stage is so that victims may ensure that governments are properly investigating and prosecuting alleged violations. The

190 Joutsen (1987) at 62.

191 Edwards (2004); Aldana-Pindell (2004) at 657.

192 The Tenth Congress for the Prevention of Crime and Treatment of Offenders noted that most states recognize a victim's right to initiate criminal proceedings when prosecutors decline to move forward with a prosecution or in the least to seek a review of such a decision, See Working Paper: Offenders and Victims: Accountability and Fairness in the Criminal Justice Process, Tenth United Nations Congress on the Prevention of Crime and the Treatment of Offenders, UN Doc. A/CONF.187/8, 10-17 April 2000, para. 24 and 27.

involvement of victims in the criminal process is viewed as a means for ensuring state compliance with human rights obligations. Nonetheless, in general, international standards concerning victim participation provide "little indication of the extent to which victims ought to be able to participate, or how far their views should hold sway."[193] This is particularly true with regard to what form participation should take in the criminal trial and at what stage of the proceedings participation is appropriate.

Just as domestic criminal justice systems have struggled with determining the proper scope and content of victim participation in their own criminal proceedings, international criminal justice systems face similar challenges. Moreover, it remains to be seen whether standards created for domestic criminal justice systems are wholly applicable to the international criminal justice system where there may not necessarily be a state-victim relationship but rather an institution-victim relationship. Even states, for which the standards were meant for, struggle with proper implementation – let alone newly created court systems in which those involved have little conceptual agreement or understanding of the procedural processes.[194] Part II of this study will therefore examine international criminal justice institutions and their approach towards victim participation. Chapter 5 explores a number of courts that have, to varying degrees, attempted to include the victim in their respective criminal processes. Next, Chapters 6 and 7 focus on the Extraordinary Chambers in the Courts of Cambodia and the International Criminal Court, respectively.

193 Doak (2008) at 157.
194 Groenhuijsen, M.S., Victims' Rights in the Criminal Justice System: A Call for More Comprehensive Implementation Theory, 88-89, in Van Dijk, Van Kaam and Wemmers (1999).

Part II

Experimenting Laboratories

CHAPTER 5
INTERNATIONAL CRIMINAL COURTS: A WIDE RANGE OF PRACTICES

5.1 INTRODUCTION

The origins of modern international criminal law date back to the military tribunals established after WWII. The Allied Powers had the option to summarily execute their enemies but instead opted to hold trials. Thus, in many ways, the Nuremberg and Tokyo trials "represent the possibility of legal responses, rather than responses grounded in sheer power politics or military aggression."[1] Although the trials have been largely criticized for the fact that they operated without precedent; there was no separation between lawmakers, prosecutors and judges; new norms were applied that previously did not exist; they failed to examine crimes committed by the Allies; and the defense rights were limited with regard to, amongst other things, their access to documents and investigations,[2] the trials' legacies have endured and their jurisprudence has aided in the further development of international criminal law. Indeed, the legal principles underlying the trials were developed into what became referred to as the Nuremberg Principles.

Following the military trials, the UN, through the International Law Commission (ILC), sought to codify the Nuremberg Principles, proposing the creation of a permanent international criminal court. However, the establishment of such a court would be postponed during the Cold War. It would not be until almost fifty years following WWII that pursuant to its Chapter VII powers, the UN Security Council established the International Criminal Tribunals for the former Yugoslavia (ICTY) and Rwanda (ICTR). The *Ad Hoc* Tribunals, as they became known, further developed the doctrines first expanded upon after WWII. Not long after the creation of these tribunals, in July 1998 states gathered in Rome, Italy and adopted the Rome Statute establishing the permanent International Criminal Court (ICC). The required number of state ratifications was met in April 2002 and the court began operation on 1 July 2002.

In addition to the *Ad Hoc* Tribunals and the permanent ICC, the world also witnessed the creation of a new type of international court: the hybrid court. As with the *Ad Hoc* Tribunals and the ICC, hybrid courts seek to sanction violations of international criminal law by holding individuals criminally responsible. However, unlike these courts, hybrid courts combine international and national features, making them an attractive option in the fight against impunity. Amongst other locations, hybrid

1 Minow (1998) at 27.

2 *Ibid.* at 30.

courts have been established for East Timor (Special Panels for Serious Crimes (SPSC)), Sierra Leone (Special Court for Sierra Leone (SCSL)), Cambodia (Extraordinary Chambers in the Courts of Cambodia (ECCC)), Kosovo (UNMIK / EULEX War Crimes Panels), and Lebanon (Special Tribunal for Lebanon (STL)).

All of these international criminal courts seek to hold individuals accountable for the commission of international crimes. As such, they play a crucial role in the development and enforcement of substantive international criminal law. The criminal proceedings at these courts not only underscore the importance of the rule of law but they also serve to remind states of their primary responsibility for the enforcement of such laws.[3] These international institutions operate and function pursuant to their own statutes and rules as well as international norms and general principles of law. In their governing documents and jurisprudence these courts have routinely acknowledged human rights norms in criminal proceedings, with particular emphasis on the right to a fair trial. Though the statutory guarantees have not always translated into practical guarantees, the recognition of the liberal model, detailing the rights of accused in criminal proceedings vis-à-vis a more powerful authority is significant. At the same time, however, the governing documents of many of the international criminal courts have paid little attention to the rights or interests of victims. This oversight has not gone unnoticed. In fact, it has led to greater calls for victims' rights in international criminal proceedings.

This chapter explores the development of the role of the victim beginning with the military tribunals following WWII. The chapter then examines the procedural role afforded to victims at the *Ad Hoc* Tribunals. Subsequently the procedural role of victims at a number of hybrid courts will be reviewed, including at the SCSL, the courts in East Timor and Kosovo, and finally at the STL. Given the fact that little case law from these courts directly related to the procedural role of victims exist emphasis will be placed on the statutory options available to victims. Moreover, when applicable, mention will be made of non-judicial, post-conflict mechanisms catering to the needs and concerns of victims. Neither the ECCC nor the ICC will be reviewed in this chapter because, as mentioned in Chapter 1, they form the two main case studies for this research and will be discussed in detail in Chapters 6 and 7, respectively. In its review of the various courts, this chapter seeks to assess whether a clear development with regard to the procedural role afforded to victims can be established and whether the approaches adopted by the various courts reflect not only advancements made in victims' rights but to what extent the unique characteristics of the courts and the contexts in which they operate were taken into account.

3 Zahar and Sluiter (2008) at 4.

5.2 Nuremberg and Tokyo Military Tribunals

During WWII the Allied Powers routinely called for the prosecution and punishment of alleged German and Japanese war criminals,[4] although no one knew whether such trials would in fact take place given the unsuccessful attempt at trials following World War I.[5] However, in August 1945 the Four Major Allied Powers, all with different domestic procedural models, created the International Military Tribunal (IMT or Nuremberg Tribunal).[6] The significance of this task cannot be understated. In a continent ravaged by war, the victorious powers sought to enforce the rule of law through a joint legal effort aimed at holding individuals criminally responsible for violations of international law. The procedural model of the IMT was largely mirrored on the adversarial approach with some key elements, such as relaxed rules of evidence, largely associated with the inquisitorial approach.[7] Despite the handful of inquisitorial elements, the IMT clearly favored the adversarial approach with a common law emphasis. As a result, there were no provisions for victim participation other than as witnesses and records do not indicate that such an idea to include victims as civil parties was even mentioned by those states that have civil party participation in their domestic systems. The IMT indicted 24 individuals of whom 22 were prosecuted. Twelve defendants were sentenced to death by hanging, three were sentenced to life imprisonment, four received sentences ranging from ten to 20 years and three were acquitted.[8]

Similarly in January 1946, General MacArthur of the United States issued a proclamation establishing the International Military Tribunal for the Far East (IMTFE or Tokyo Tribunal).[9] In contrast to the four powers running the IMT, the Judges and prosecution team were made up of individuals from 11 Allied nations.[10] With regard to procedural rules, the IMTFE adopted similar procedures to those adopted at Nuremberg, namely a largely adversarial approach, but with even more relaxed rules of evidence. Accordingly, no provisions for victim participation other than as witnesses were included. All Japanese Class A criminals were tried before the IMTFE,[11] which

---

4 Taylor (1992) at 32; Bassiouni (2003) at 403.

5 See Willis (1982).

6 Agreement for the Prosecution and Punishment of Major War Criminals of the European Axis (1945).

7 DeFrancia (2001) at 1397.

8 Bassiouni (2003) at 411. Following the international trial before the IMT, a number of other trials were carried out under Control Council Law No. 10 by the United States. These trials, however, were not international in character given the growing distrust between the four allied powers.

9 IMTFE Charter

10 The countries that participated included: Australia, Canada, Republic of China, Provisional Government of the French Republic, British India, the Netherlands, New Zealand, the Philippines, the United Kingdom, the United States and the Soviet Union.

11 Class A criminals were those individuals who were believed to have participated in a joint conspiracy to start and wage war, including those associated with the highest decision-making bodies; Class B criminals were those individuals believed to have committed other atrocities or crimes against humanity; Class C criminals were those individuals suspected of planning, ordering, authorizing, or failing to prevent such crimes within the higher levels of the command structure.

amounted to 28 individuals. Trials lasted two and half years (three times longer than the Nuremberg Tribunal) and of the 28 defendants two died of natural causes, one had a mental breakdown before trial and was eventually released, and the remaining 25 were found guilty and received sentences ranging from seven years to death. Thirteen of the individuals found guilty and sentenced to life imprisonment were paroled after serving less than eight years.

While the trials before the IMT and IMTFE represent a significant achievement in the field of international criminal law, they are also viewed critically, in part, because they did not provide an adequate forum for victims. At the IMT, victims of Nazi atrocities played only minor roles at trial. One reason for this is the fact that the IMT relied mainly on documentary evidence rather than on live testimony. The prosecution compiled over 200,000 affidavits, but only 94 witnesses testified and most of the affidavits and witnesses were former SS members, camp guards and Nazi party members.[12] Although the Judges did take into consideration reports of national state commissions which held oral hearings and collected oral testimony from some direct victims, these reports were used as a main source of evidence.

In contrast to the Nuremberg convictions, which were supported by large amounts of documentary evidence, the IMTFE had to rely on a greater amount of victim-witness testimony. The need to rely on victim-witness testimony is directly related to the fact that prosecuting authorities had less documentary evidence at their disposal given the fact that the Japanese destroyed most of their military records prior to surrender. Thus, the IMTFE heard 416 witnesses in court and accepted unsubstantiated affidavits and depositions from a further 779 individuals, many of which came from victims. Of the victims who were called to testify before either the IMT or IMTFE, they were only those direct victims who could contribute to establishing the guilt of the accused. Moreover, the selection of victims to testify as witnesses did not necessarily reflect the realities of the crimes committed. For instance, despite the wide occurrences of gender crimes in both Nazi and Japanese controlled areas no victims of rape were called before either court.[13]

Notwithstanding the limited role afforded to victims in court proceedings, both the IMT and to a lesser degree the IMTFE are viewed as success stories in international criminal law for shedding light on the crimes committed and holding individuals accountable for these crimes.[14] The successful prosecutions are principally the result of the large teams assembled to prosecute these cases and the large amount of financial resources (pledged mostly by the US) poured into both courts. To be sure, more than a thousand lawyers and support staff worked to sift through the evidence presented at the trials. The success associated with the Nuremberg and Tokyo Tribunals facilitated proposals for a permanent international criminal court, but little progress would be

12 See Bassiouni (2003) at 411. The large amount of Nazi documentation generally minimized the need for victim testimony.
13 Nicola (2009) at 115.
14 Griffen (2001) at 407.

made during the Cold War period. During the time between the Nuremberg and Tokyo military tribunals and the civilian tribunals for the former Yugoslavia and Rwanda it was national trials that took up the call for accountability.[15]

5.3 THE *AD HOC* TRIBUNALS

After condemning the violence in the former Yugoslavia, in July 1992 the UN Security Council affirmed that individuals would be held accountable for grave breaches of the Geneva Conventions of 1949.[16] Subsequently a Commission of Experts was created to study the notion of accountability further.[17] Shortly thereafter the UN Security Council announced in Resolution 808 of 22 February 1993 that under its Chapter VII powers "an international tribunal shall be established for the prosecution of persons responsible for serious violations of international humanitarian law committed in the territory of the former Yugoslavia since 1991."[18] The UN Secretary-General was then tasked with developing the Statute for the International Criminal Tribunal for the former Yugoslavia (ICTY). In a number of confidential meetings,[19] the Secretary-General, together with the assistance of the UN Office of Legal Advisor and legal officers of UN Member States, developed a draft statute and a commentary thereto.[20] The UN Security Council then adopted this report in Resolution 827 of 25 May 1993, officially establishing the Statute of the ICTY, which serves as the primary governing document of the Court.

In many ways the creation of the ICTY paved the way for the establishment of the International Criminal Tribunal for Rwanda (ICTR). In response to reports of atrocities in Rwanda, the UN Commission on Human Rights appointed a Special Rapporteur to investigate alleged violations of international law.[21] The Special Rapporteur issued its report on 25 May 1994,[22] and shortly thereafter the UN Security Council appointed a Commission of Experts to look at accountability issues.[23] In its report the Commission recommended the prosecution of alleged war criminals.[24] Subsequently in November 1994 the UN Security Council passed Resolution 955, establishing the International

15 Foremost among the national trials are the Eichmann trial in Israel and the trials of former Vichy Government agents in France.
16 UNSC Res. 764, UN Doc. S/RES/764 (1992).
17 UNSC Res. 780, UN Doc. S/RES/780 (1992).
18 UNSC Res. 808, UN Doc. S/RES/808 (1993).
19 DeFrancia (2001) at 1387.
20 Secretary-General's Report on Aspects of Establishing an International Tribunal for the Prosecution of Persons Responsible for Serious Violations of International Humanitarian Law Committed in the Territory of the former Yugoslavia, UN SCOR, UN Doc. s/25704 (1993).
21 Morris and Scharf (1998) at 61.
22 Report of the Commission on Human Rights on Its Third Special Session, UN Doc. E/1994/24/Add.2 (1994).
23 UNSC Res. 935, UN Doc. S/RES/935 (1994).
24 Preliminary Report of the Independent Commission of Experts established in accordance with SC Res. 935 (1994), UN Doc. S/1994/1125 (1994).

Criminal Tribunal for Rwanda (ICTR).[25] The ICTR Statute was mirrored on the Statute of the ICTY. The creation of these international tribunals, the first since Nuremberg and Tokyo,[26] has ushered in a new and modern era in international law and international criminal justice.

The Statutes of these Tribunals outline their jurisdiction over individuals accused of grave breaches of the Geneva Conventions, violations of the laws and customs of war, genocide and crimes against humanity.[27] They also provide basic protections for the rights of accused and the protection of victims.[28] With regard to the Rules of Procedure and Evidence, when the ICTY was created there was no existing code of international criminal procedure. Due to time constraints and the technical nature of rule drafting, the Judges of the newly established ICTY were entrusted with drafting the procedural rules.[29] Jackson notes that Judges "chose to adopt the pragmatic approach of working from what was available to them rather than start completely afresh to consider which rules would be best suited for the purposes of the tribunals within a human rights context."[30] Thus, the Judges worked off of proposals submitted by states, organizations and drafts submitted by Judges themselves.[31] The United States submitted "by far the most comprehensive set of proposed rules with commentary,"[32] suggesting why many of their proposals ultimately found their way into the final draft. However, reaching a consensus between individuals from a variety of legal systems was not easy. Nevertheless, between the Judges there was a common goal of drafting rules that would enable the tribunal to function effectively.[33] Ultimately, after having taken into account the two major legal systems of the world, the Judges adopted a largely adversarial approach, rather than an inquisitorial one.[34] Thus, the procedures employed by the ICTY and ICTR are predominantly adversarial, meaning they are party-driven, with a clear focus on identification, prosecution and punishment.

Neither the Statute nor the Rules of Procedure and Evidence for the ICTY and ICTR provide for active victim involvement in the criminal process other than as witnesses. However, when preparing the Statute for the ICTY (which, as mentioned above, later formed the basis for the ICTR Statute) a proposal for allowing the appoint-

---

25 Statute for the International Criminal Tribunal for Rwanda [hereinafter ICTR Statute], SC Res. 955, S/RES/955 Annex (1994).

26 The IMT and IMTFE were military tribunals whereas the ICTY and ICTR are civilian courts.

27 ICTY Statute, Art. 2-5; ICTR Statute, Art. 2-4.

28 ICTY and ICTR Statute, Art. 21 and 22.

29 ICTY Statute, Art. 15. The ICTR adopted the Rules of Procedure and Evidence of the ICTY and left it to the Judges to amend as necessary and appropriate, see ICTR Statute, Art. 14.

30 Jackson, J., Transnational Faces of Justice: Two Attempts to Build Common Standards beyond National Boundaries, 236, in Jackson, et al. (2008).

31 Morris and Scharf (1995) at 176-177. Submissions from countries and organizations were received from Argentina, Australia, Canada, France, Norway, Sweden and the United States as well as from the American Bar Association.

32 *Ibid.* at 177.

33 *Ibid.* at 179.

34 Fairlie (2004) at 245.

ment of separate counsel for victims was submitted and later rejected. The rejection, mainly by delegates from the US, was largely out of fear that third-party participation would lead to conflicts with the prosecution's case.[35] Morris and Scharf note that:

> In preparing the Statute, consideration was also given to authorizing the appointment of a separate counsel for the victims to protect their interests. This would be similar to the concept of *parties civil* employed in many civil law countries. However, the proposal was not accepted for several reasons. First, the Prosecutor is entrusted with the responsibility for protecting the interests of the international community in ensuring the prosecution and punishment of the perpetrators. In this respect, the victims' interests would be coextensive with those of the international community and would be adequately protected by the Prosecutor. The victims' interest in obtaining compensation is not within the jurisdiction of the International Tribunal which was established for the purpose of prosecuting and punishing the persons responsible for the atrocities. Furthermore, the participation of counsel for the victim as a third party to the criminal proceedings could lead to interference with the case presented by the Prosecutor or divert the attention of the court from the relevant issue in the criminal proceedings thereby prolonging the trial. To the extent that a victim's interests are not considered to be adequately represented by the Prosecutor, it may be possible to bring such interests to the attention of the Trial Chamber of the Appeals Chamber with respect to relevant issues by means of an *amicus curiae* brief, [...].[36]

The prosecutor's duty to protect the interests of the international community has later been reaffirmed in case law: "the Prosecution acts on behalf of and in the interests of the community, including the interests of the victims of the offence charged (in cases before the Tribunal the Prosecutor acts on behalf of the international community)."[37] Without a doubt, at the *Ad Hoc* Tribunals the primacy of the role of the prosecutor, both to shape the case and to represent the interests of victims and the international community, is clearly evident in the Statutes' language.

Unlike many domestic legal systems, the court systems of the ICTY and ICTR were bare-boned or basic, meaning that they simply did not have the structures in place to provide for broad services. Victims would therefore not be permitted to initiate proceedings, participate as civil parties or directly seek compensation for damages. The Court was reluctant to expand victim participatory rights beyond the existing framework of allowing a chosen few to testify as witnesses, request leave to submit

---

35 Tochilovsky, V., Victims' Procedural Rights at Trial: Approach of Continental Europe and the International Tribunal for the Former Yugoslavia, 287-89 in Van Dijk, Van Kaam and Wemmers (1999); Wierda (2002) at 20.

36 Morris and Scharf (1995) at 167.

37 ICTY, *Prosecutor v. Aleksovski*, Case No. IT-95-14/1-A, Decision on Prosecutor's Appeal on Admissibility of Evidence, Appeals Chamber, 16 February 1999, par. 25; *Prosecutor v. Kvocka et al.*, Case No. IT-98-30/1, Decision on Interlocutory Appeal by the Accused Zoran Zigic against the Decision of Trial Chamber I dated 5 December 2000, Appeals Chamber, 25 May 2001, par. 21.

observations as amicus curiae, and occasionally having the Prosecution submit victim impact statements on victims' behalf as a way to influence sentencing.

5.3.1 Participation as Witnesses

The testimony of witnesses before any court of law is very often crucial in the determination of the case and the ascertainment of the truth. At the *Ad Hoc* Tribunals, victim-witnesses play an important role.[38] Former Chief Prosecutor, Carla Del Ponte, poignantly explained the value of this role:

> The courtroom testimonies of eyewitnesses are fundamentally important – they tell us about the horrifying conditions of the detention camps, ethic cleansing campaigns, torture, rape and sexual slavery, mass executions, destruction of property and religious institutions, plunder and looting. Most importantly they tell us about human suffering. They must be told and listened to. [...] Their personalized stories make us feel how it was to be there – in that particular place at that particular time. [...] Those willing to listen will understand that the testimonies of the very modest, not sophisticated people, very ordinary people can bring to understanding the core issues.[39]

Not all victims, however, have been able to tell their stories before the Courts. Only those victims whose testimony would contribute to the determination of the case were called to testify. Rule 89, common to both the ICTY and ICTR, which contains the provisions on evidence, provides that a Chamber may admit any relevant evidence that it deems to have probative value. Rule 89 of the ICTY further provides that a Chamber may exclude evidence if its probative value is substantially outweighed by the need to ensure a fair trial, and that a Chamber may receive evidence through a witness either orally or in written form when in the interests of justice. At the Tribunals both parties may call witnesses to support their case and the Chamber may also call witnesses *proprio motu*. Therefore, in order for a victim to appear before the Court that victim must be called as a witness either by one of the parties or the Chamber acting under its *proprio motu* powers. Generally, most victims have appeared before the Tribunals as prosecution witnesses.

Because the structure of the Tribunals is based on the adversarial approach to trials, meaning that a clear distinction is made between the prosecution case and the defense case, the Judges, while not precluded from interfering, rarely try to change prosecution or defense strategies, and the examination of witnesses is tightly controlled by the questions asked. This approach usually means that witnesses are not provided an opportunity to tell their stories in narrative form. Not being able to tell a narrative story, coupled with repetitive questioning from the parties, has been viewed as a

38 See Stover (2005).

39 Del Ponte, C., Address by Chief Prosecutor Carla Del Ponte at the conference on "Establishing the truth about war crimes and conflicts," Zagreb, Croatia, 8-9 February 2007.

problem for victims as well as efficient court operation, prompting one expert group to criticize Judges for allowing such repetitive and irrelevant questioning.[40] Although Common Rule 75 requires the Chambers to, when necessary, control the manner of witness questioning so as to avoid harassment and intimidation, and Common Rule 46(A) allows a Chamber to sanction defense counsel for offensive and abusive behavior,[41] commentators found that at both Tribunals victim-witnesses often considered questioning aggressive and degrading.[42]

Studies by Hodžić and Stover demonstrate that although those victims who testified before the ICTY had a wide array of experiences, both positive and negative, a number of factors contribute to their overall perceptions of participation.[43] These factors include "their personal experience of testifying, the perceived preferential treatment of the accused compared to victims, their (lack of) knowledge and understanding of the procedural mechanisms relevant to these proceedings, and, most importantly, the length of sentences handed down to the accused and the early release of convicted persons."[44] Notwithstanding the importance of victim testimony and the instances of positive experiences related by victims after testifying, many victim-witnesses have been prohibited from recounting their stories in narrative form because of the procedural construct of the trial process. Moreover, other victim-witnesses have been interrupted by Judges when their stories deviate from the purpose of assessing guilt or innocence and have been asked by Judges to refrain from crying and to calm down while answering questions about traumatic events. It is due to these negative experiences that victims' groups began to campaign for greater victim acknowledgement, greater victim rights and better victim representation at subsequent international courts.

5.3.2 Participation as Amici Curiae

'Amicus curiae' is a legal Latin phrase literally translated as "friend of the court." It allows someone, who is not a party to the case, to provide information on a point of law or some other aspect of the case in order to aid the court in deciding a matter before it. The information may come in the form of a written brief, learned treatise or oral testimony. Rule 74 of both the ICTY and ICTR Rules of Procedure and Evidence prescribe that "[a] Chamber may, if it considers it desirable for the proper determina-

40 Letter dated 14 June 2000 from the Secretary-General addressed to the President of the Security Council, UN Doc. S/2000/597, para. 75-76.

41 The ICTY Rule only refers to defense counsel whereas the ICTR provision is *mutatis mutandis* applicable to counsel for the prosecution as well.

42 International Federation for Human Rights (FIDH), Victims in the Balance: Challenges ahead for the International Criminal Tribunal for Rwanda, 8-9, FIDH Report, No. 329/2 (2002); For example, in the *Butare* case at the ICTR the judges were laughing during the questioning of a rape victim, apparently in response to the questioning and behavior of counsel, see Heikkilä (2004) at 115, footnote 461.

43 See Hodžić (2010); Stover (2005).

44 Hodžić (2010) at 123.

tion of the case, invite or grant leave to a State, organization or person to appear before it and make submissions on any issue specified by the Chamber." The decision of whether or not to admit the information lies with the discretion of the court. On deciding whether to accept or reject a request to act as an amicus the Tribunals have emphasized the significance of information for the proper determination of the case. At the Tribunals, amici are generally invited by the Court and usually this is only with respect to a single issue.[45]

In theory the provision on amicus curiae could provide victims or victims' rights groups with a form of participation in the criminal process.[46] On at least two occasions, those acting on behalf of victims' interests sought to intervene in proceedings through the amicus provisions. For example, at the ICTR in *Bagosora*, the Belgian government sought to intervene as amicus, in part, on "The right of Belgians or their rightful claimants, [...], to appear before the Tribunal as plaintiffs and not as mere witnesses [...]."[47] The Rwandan government similarly sought to intervene as amicus in order to help prove the guilt of the accused and seek damages for the unlawful taking of property.[48] The Court rejected both requests. It rejected the Belgian request because it determined that the request was not yet ripe for their consideration because the discussion of penalties does not arise before a determination of guilt.[49] It rejected the Rwandan request because the indictments did not allege that any property had been unlawfully taken and that restitution claims were premature before a finding of guilt.[50] These decisions highlight the fact that the participation of victims as amici curiae is not *per se* barred but that the Judges were nevertheless reluctant to turn victims, or those acting on behalf of victims, into plaintiffs through the amicus provision. In

45 See generally, ICTY, *Prosecutor v. Furundžija*, Case No. IT-95-17/1, Order Granting Leave to File *Amicus Curiae* Brief, Trial Chamber II, 10 November 1998; *Prosecutor v. Furundžija*, Case No. IT-95-17/1, Order Granting Leave to File *Amicus Curiae* Brief, Trial Chamber II, 11 November 1998; *Prosecutor v. Blaškić*, Case. No. IT-95-14, Orders Granting Leave to Appear as Amicus Curiae, Trial Chamber I, 11 April 1997; *Prosecutor v. Tadić*, Case No. IT-94-1, Order Denying Leave to Appear as *Amicus Curiae*, Trial Chamber II, 25 November 1996 and *Prosecutor v. Tadić*, Case No. IT-94-1, Opinion and Judgement, Trial Chamber II, 7 May 1997, para. 11 and 35; see also ICTR, *Prosecutor v. Semanza*, Case No. ICTR-97-20-T, Decision on the Kingdom of Belgium's application to file an *amicus curiae* and on the defense application to strike out observations of the Kingdom of Belgium concerning the preliminary response by the Defense, Trial Chamber III, 9 February 2001; *Prosecutor v. Musema*, Case No. ICTR-96-13-T, Decision on an application by African Concern for leave to appear as amicus curiae, Trial Chamber I, 17 March 1999; *Prosecutor v. Akayesu*, Case No. ICTR-96-4-T, Order Granting Leave for Amicus Curiae to Appear, Trial Chamber I, 12 February 1998.

46 Morris and Scharf (1995) at 167 and 270.

47 ICTR, *Prosecutor v. Bagosora et al.*, Case No. ICTR-96-7-T, Decision on the amicus curiae application by the Government of the Kingdom of Belgium, Trial Chamber II, 6 June 1998, p. 2.

48 ICTR, *Prosecutor v. Bagosora et al.*, Case No. ICTR-98-41-T, Decision on Amicus Curiae Request by the Rwandan Government, Trial Chamber II, 13 October 2004.

49 ICTR, *Prosecutor v. Bagosora et al.*, Case No. ICTR-96-7-T, Decision on the amicus curiae application by the Government of the Kingdom of Belgium, Trial Chamber II, 6 June 1998, p. 2-3.

50 ICTR, *Prosecutor v. Bagosora et al.*, Case No. ICTR-98-41-T, Decision on Amicus Curiae Request by the Rwandan Government, Trial Chamber II, 13 October 2004.

another instance, a women's rights group representing the interests of victims at the ICTR sought to submit an amicus brief in order ask the Court to direct the prosecution to amend the charges against the accused so as to include charges of sexual violence.[51] The Court, however, declined, finding that it is the prosecutor's role to prosecute and not that of the Chamber or amici.[52] Again, it appears that the Judges have been reluctant to grant any form of broad amicus participation for victims even when it was in pursuit of civil redress but particularly when it relates to infringing upon the role assigned to the prosecutor.

5.3.3 Participation in the Form of Victim Impact Statements

As touched upon in Chapter 3, a victim impact statement is "an opportunity not only to relate what impact the offense has had on the victim, but also what, in the victim's view, should be done about the matter."[53] These statements can either be prepared and presented by the victims themselves or are collected and presented by victim assistance or prosecution personnel.[54] The statements, written or oral, are usually utilized during the sentencing stage of the proceedings, after the determination of guilt.[55]

Although the Statute and Rules of the *Ad Hoc* Tribunals did not originally foresee the use of active victim participation in the proceedings or the use of victim impact statements, the ICTY and ICTR have allowed, for the purposes of sentencing, the submission of victim impact statements provided by the prosecution.[56] Additionally, Rule 92 *bis* of both Tribunals provides:

> (a) that a Trial Chamber may admit, in whole or in part, the evidence of a witness in the form of a written statement in lieu of oral testimony which goes to proof of a matter other than the acts and conduct of the accused as charged in the indictment; and
> (b) that the fact that the evidence in question concerns the impact of crimes upon victims is a factor of admitting evidence in the form of a written statement.

---

51 ICTR, *Prosecutor v. Ntagerura et al.*, Case No. ICTR-99-46-T, Decision on the Application to File an *Amicus Curiae* Brief According to Rule 74 of the Rules of Procedure and Evidence Filed on Behalf of the NGO Coalition for Women's Human Rights in Conflict Situations, Trial Chamber III, 24 May 2001, pp. 6-7.

52 *Ibid.*

53 Handbook on Justice for Victims at 39.

54 Erez (1999) at 546 and 548.

55 Handbook on Justice for Victims at 36; Wemmers (1996) at 208-209; Cf. Kool and Moerings (2004).

56 See, e.g., ICTY, *Prosecutor v. Mucić et al.*, Case No. IT-96-21, Judgement, Trial Chamber II quater, 16 November 1998, par. 1263, where the Court cites a statement from the victim's impact statement submitted by the Prosecution concerning the harms suffered by that victim: "[t]he wounds that I carry from the rapes in Celebici will never go away." See also, ICTY, *Prosecutor v. Tadić*, Case No. IT-94-1, Sentencing Judgment, Trial Chamber II, 11 November 1999, par. 4 and *Prosecutor v. Todorović*, Case No. IT-95-9/1, Sentencing Judgment, Trial Chamber III, 31 July 2001, par. 53; ICTR, *Prosecutor v. Akayesu*, Case. No. ICTR-96-4-T, Sentencing Judgment, Trial Chamber I, 2 October 1998.

Accordingly, when Trial Chambers consider aggravating and mitigating factors at sentencing the victim impact statements help provide a picture of the defenselessness of the victims and the gravity of the crimes. Unquestionably, the degree of suffering by the victims is a relevant consideration.[57] In *Kristic*, the Trial Chamber found that it "must assess the seriousness of the crimes in the light of their individual circumstances and consequences. [...] [And] the number of victims and their suffering are relevant factors in determining the sentence."[58] The Court went on to state that "appropriate consideration of those circumstances gives 'a voice' to the suffering of the victims."[59] Trial Chambers have further found that the specific characteristics of individual victims can also be important. This importance is especially relevant when the victim is a child or woman or is particularly defenseless.[60] In *Bralo*, the Court specifically recognized the value of victim impact statements:

> In addition to examining the manner in which Bralo committed the crimes of which he has been convicted, the Trial Chamber takes into consideration the submissions of the Prosecution on the impact of these crimes on his victims. [...] The Defense has further agreed with the Prosecution that the victim impact statements provided to the Trial Chamber are both powerful and affecting.
> [...]
> These statements paint a picture of shattered lives and livelihoods, and of tremendous ongoing pain and trauma. The Trial Chamber is therefore mindful of the suffering of these victims, and of all the other Muslim residents of Ahmici and Nadioci who were persecuted or otherwise abused by Bralo in the course of the attacks on their villages. It observes that the consequences of the persecution, murders, rape, and other crimes committed by Bralo are profound and long-lasting and takes this into consideration in its determination of sentence.[61]

57 ICTY, *Prosecutor v. Blaškić*, Case No. IT-95-14, Judgment, Trial Chamber I, 3 March 2000, para. 784 and 786-787; *Prosecutor v. Mucić et al.*, Case No. IT-96-21, Judgement, Trial Chamber II, 16 November 1998, para. 1225-1226, 1260 and 1273; *Prosecutor v. Erdemović*, Case No. IT-96-22, Sentencing Judgment, Trial Chamber I, 5 March 1998, par. 15; *Prosecutor v. Kordić & Čerkez*, Case No. IT-95-14/2, Judgment, Trial Chamber III, 26 February 2001, par. 847, footnote 1793; *Prosecutor v. Tadić*, Case No. IT-94-1, Sentencing Judgment, Trial Chamber II, 14 July 1997, par. 56 and *Prosecutor v. Tadić*, Case No. IT-94-1, Sentencing Judgment (II), Trial Chamber II, 11 November 1999, par. 19; See also ICTR, *Prosecutor v. Kambanda*, Case no.: ICTR 97-23-S, Judgment and Sentence, Trial Chamber I, 4 September 1998, par. 42.

58 ICTY, *Prosecutor v. Krstić*, Case No. IT-98-33, Judgment, Trial Chamber I, 2 August 2001, para. 701-703.

59 *Ibid.* at par. 703.

60 ICTY, *Prosecutor v. Kunarac et al.*, Case. No. IT-96-23 & 23/1, Judgment, Trial Chamber II, 22 February 2001, para. 864, 874 and 879; *Prosecutor v. Kunarac et al.*, Case. No. IT-96-23 & 23/1, Appeal Judgment, Appeals Chamber, 12 June 2002, para. 352 and 354-355.

61 ICTY, *Prosecutor v. Bralo*, Case No. IT-95-17, Sentencing Judgment, Trial Chamber III, 7 December 2005, para. 36-40.

In addition to submitting written impact statements, the prosecutor at the ICTY has on occasion called victim-witnesses to testify about the impact of the crimes on their lives and the character of the accused during the period in which the crimes were committed.[62] It is clear that the prosecution at both the ICTY and ICTR often resorted to using victim impact statements as they are a way in which harm experienced by the victims was conveyed to the Judges in their own words.

5.3.4 Calls for Greater Participation in Relation to Reparations

Although the Statutes and Rules of Procedure and Evidence of the ICTY and ICTR fail to provide for active victim participatory rights other than as witnesses, Article 24(3) of the ICTY Statute and Article 23(3) of the ICTR Statute, dealing with penalties, provide that "[i]n addition to imprisonment, the Trial Chambers may order the return of any property and proceeds acquired by criminal conduct, including by means of duress, to their rightful owners." Likewise, Rules 105 and 106 of the Rules of Procedure and Evidence for both Tribunals prescribe further guidance on restitution of property and compensation to victims. Rule 105 states that the Trial Chamber shall, at the request of the prosecutor, or on its own initiative, "hold a special hearing to determine the matter of the restitution of the property or the proceeds thereof, and may in the meantime order such provisional measures for the preservation and protection of the property or proceeds as it considers appropriate." Rule 106 also provides that the Registrar shall transmit to relevant states concerned guilty verdicts which have caused injury to a victim. Thereafter, pursuant to national legislation, a victim may bring a legal claim in a national court or other competent body to obtain compensation. Because national courts are bound by the findings of the tribunals it was thought that victims could bring claims in domestic courts. However, national courts in the former Yugoslavia and in Rwanda have been "ill-prepared" to deal with these cases.[63] Moreover, neither the ICTY nor ICTR has ever put Rule 105 or 106 into effect.[64] Thus, the legal right to claim reparations at these Tribunals has been a hollow right since there is no proper mechanism in place that can both award and enforce reparation orders.

In response to this failure, in 2000 the then Chief Prosecutor Carla del Ponte raised the issue of incorporating victims' compensation and participation in proceedings. The Judges from the ICTY examined the issue at the July plenary and adopted a report on the issue. Although favoring the proposals in principle, the Judges envisioned too many problems that would stem from amending the Statute and Rules to include compensation and participation. The Judges noted in their report that the additional responsibility for the Registry would have resource implications, that the work of the prosecutor would clearly be affected by the presence of victims' legal counsel, and that

62 See, e.g., ICTY, *Prosecutor v. Nikolic*, Case No. IT-94-2-S, Sentencing Judgment, Trial Chamber II, 18 December 2003, para. 41-43.
63 Bassiouni (2006) at 242-243.
64 See Chifflet, P., The Role and Status of the Victim, 75, in Boas and Schabas (2003).

the length of the proceedings would be negatively affected.[65] More specifically, the report found that the length of the proceedings could impact upon the rights of the defense. The report concluded that "it would not be wise to implement a new system which would counter all the efforts of the last few years to minimize the length of preventive detention, which is a fundamental right of the accused, by shortening trials."[66] The report nevertheless recommended that an international compensation commission be set up, which would be a faster, fairer option for ensuring that the needs and concerns of victims would be met.[67]

In October 2000 the report was forwarded to the then Secretary-General Kofi Annan for transmission to the UN Security Council. When transmitting the report Annan noted that:

> [...] the judges have, [...], come to the conclusion that it is neither advisable nor appropriate that the Tribunal be possessed of such a power, in particular, for the reason that it would result in a significant increase in the workload of the Chambers and would further increase the length and complexity of trials. The judges doubt, moreover, whether it would be possible for the Tribunal to secure adequate resources to fund such awards as it might make. Furthermore, they consider that it would be inequitable that the victims of crimes which were committed by persons who are not prosecuted and convicted by the Tribunal would not benefit from any orders of compensation that the Tribunal might make.[68]

Arguably, once this event took place it ended any chance of the Tribunal holding independent hearings on compensation and no such commission has been created.[69] Likewise, Judges at the ICTR have turned down proposals to amend the ICTR Statute

65 Letter dated 2 November 2000 from the Secretary-General addressed to the President of the Security Council, UN Doc. S/2000/1063 (Annex) (2000), para 32, 35-36. Paragraphs 35-36 read as follows: "The length of trial proceedings would also be affected, as a number of new procedural steps would be introduced in the trials. These, which are outlined above, include determinations on certification of victims and their representatives and additional evidence to be adduced to prove financial and other losses to victims, including the testimony of victims. Furthermore, the Chambers, and perhaps the prosecution, would need to ensure that victims and their representatives are fully informed of their rights; additional court time would also be necessary to hear any interventions that the victims' representatives may have. Finally, additional time and work would be necessary to hear and adjudicate the actual claims for compensation, including determining the appropriate quantum of any award. While the above can only serve as an overview of the impact that a system of victims' compensation claims would have on the work of the Chambers and trial length, it is clear that there would be some increase in the Chambers' workload and in the length of trials. Thus, consideration must be given to the effect on the right of the accused to an expeditious trial."

66 Letter dated 2 November 2000 from the Secretary-General addressed to the President of the Security Council, UN Doc. S/2000/1063 (Annex) (2000), p. 3.

67 *Ibid.* at 4; Chifflet, P., The Role and Status of the Victim, 102, in Boas and Schabas (2003).

68 Letter dated 2 November 2000 from the Secretary-General addressed to the President of the Security Council, UN Doc. S/2000/1063 (Annex) (2000), p. 1.

69 Chifflet, P., The Role and Status of the Victim, 104, in Boas and Schabas.

that would allow victims the right to direct redress,[70] with the then Judge Pillay forewarning, "The Court is neither designed nor in a position to act as a public forum or claims commission for thousands of individual communications from victims of each situation."[71]

The budgetary limitations of the tribunals further restrict what the Court can do for victims. As of June 2010 the ICTY employed more than 1000 staff and operates under a budget for 2010-2011 of 301,895,900 USD (net) – down slightly from the years before due to the implementation of its completion strategy.[72] Similar to the ICTY, the ICTR employs approximately 600 staff and operates under a budget for 2010-2011 of 227,246,500 USD (net).[73] Both of these figures include costs for victim outreach and protection but they do not include costs associated with direct victim participation in the proceedings given that no such participatory rights exist, as such. Even without costs associated with participation Trumbull notes that "[t]he inability to prosecute serious offenders due to lack of resources was a constant frustration for prosecutors and victims at the ICTY and ICTR."[74] Had there been participation costs it is very likely that even fewer prosecutions would have taken place.

Victims before the *Ad Hoc* Tribunals therefore do not have the opportunity to participate in their own right during the proceedings. And attempts to change this framework have been rejected. The reality of the tribunals is that victim involvement is limited to those who can testify as witnesses and be instrumental in the determination of the case. As such, if they are not acting as a witness or if they have already testified as a witness then they can only view the hearings in the public gallery or on the internet like anyone else.[75] These limitations on victim participation seem to call into question the validity of the Tribunal's claim of "bringing justice to thousands of victims and giving them a voice," as a major achievement of the Tribunal. Whether or not and the extent to which this claim is valid can be debated, but the approach taken by the ICTY and ICTR towards victim participation certainly affected the later practice of other international criminal courts.

---

70 Letter of 14 December 2000 from the Secretary-General addressed to President of the Security Council, UN Doc. S/2000/1198 (2000), at Annex.

71 *Ibid.* at Annex; Stahn, et al. (2006) at 223.

72 See, ICTY, 2009 Report of the International Criminal Tribunal for the former Yugoslavia to the UN General Assembly, UN Doc. A/64/205-S/2009/394 (2009).

73 See ICTR website: http://www.unictr.org/tabid/101/default.aspx, *last visited* 28 March 2011.

74 See International Federation for Human Rights (FIDH), Victims in the Balance: Challenges ahead for the International Criminal Tribunal for Rwanda, FIDH Report, No. 329/2 (2002).

75 The 'rule on witnesses' precludes witnesses, who have not yet testified, from viewing the testimony of another witness, see ICTY RPE, Rule 90(c) and ICTR RPE, Rule 90(d). However, the RPE of both tribunals also provide that "a witness who has heard the testimony of another witness shall not for that reason alone be disqualified from testifying."

5.4. Hybrid Courts

Following the establishment of the *Ad Hoc* Tribunals, there was a proliferation of internationalized criminal jurisdictions that became precursors to the International Criminal Court. Established through a variety of ways such as through the UN Secretariat or through treaty provisions, these new jurisdictions are now commonly referred to as hybrid courts because they combine international and national elements, such as specific domestic laws and/or staff with international laws and staff. The taxonomy of a court as 'hybrid' may depend on a variety of criteria. The criteria range from the court's legal basis, its location within or outside of a domestic court system, its subject-matter jurisdiction and the composition of the court's personnel.[76] The allure of hybrid courts has even continued after the establishment of the ICC. The establishment of the STL suggests that hybrid courts will continue to be attractive accountability options in the fight against impunity for serious and international crimes. The hybrid tribunals discussed in this chapter include the SCSL, the Serious Panels in East Timor, the UNMIK-established war crimes courts in Kosovo, and finally the most recently created court, the STL.[77] All of these courts approached victim participation in unique ways taking into account their specific characteristics.

5.4.1 Special Court for Sierra Leone

Established in early 2002 to prosecute those believed to be the most responsible for crimes committed during the 10-year conflict in that country in the 1990s[78] the SCSL was the first hybrid court established after the creation of the *Ad Hoc* Tribunals. The conflict in Sierra Leone was exceptionally violent, leaving the country devastated and its domestic justice system ill-equipped to investigate and prosecute individuals accused of serious human rights and humanitarian law violations. However, recourse to a purely international court modeled on the ICTY and ICTR was not favored by the then President Ahmed Tejan Kabbah, who believed that domestic involvement was of critical importance. Therefore, in 2000 he sought assistance from the UN in establishing a new type of accountability model,[79] and in 2002, the UN and the government of

76 See Cerone, J. and Baldwin, C., Explaining and Evaluating the UNMIK Court System, 41, footnote 2, in Romano, et al. (2004).

77 The ECCC is a hybrid tribunal but will be discussed separately in Part II of this study. The State Court of Bosnia and Herzegovina will not be discussed.

78 For background on the establishment of the SCSL, see Mochochoko, P. and Tortora, G., The Management Committee for the Special Court for Sierra Leone, 141-156, in Romano, et al. (2004).

79 See Letter from the permanent Representative of Sierra Leone to the United Nations to the President of the Security Council, UN Doc S/2000/786 (2000).

Sierra Leone signed an agreement establishing the SCSL – marking the first time that a court had been established between the UN and a domestic government.[80]

The SCSL is a "treaty-based *sui generis* court of mixed jurisdiction and composition," operating, for the most part, in the country where the crimes occurred.[81] The national government retains the power to appoint individuals to staff positions with many of the positions at the court filled by Sierra Leoneans. Despite the fact that the SCSL operates outside of the local court system it has primacy over national courts and may give binding orders to the government.[82] The procedural framework of the court is mirrored on that of the ICTR as amended for the particular circumstances for the Special Court.[83]

The novelties of the SCSL include its location in Sierra Leone, its mix of domestic and international court personnel (including Judges), and its creation of a Defense Office. Designed to avoid some of the challenges encountered by predecessor courts and foreseen as more cost effective and efficient, the Court:

> has been rightfully hailed as having created a new model of international criminal justice. It has shown that it is possible to have an international court that is directly accessible to the population affected by the crimes committed, both by locating the Court in the country where the crimes took place and by developing a very effective outreach program. Likewise, the establishment of the Defence Office to provide an institutional counterbalance to the Prosecution has been widely viewed as a creative advance that should be considered in all future courts.[84]

As of early 2011, the SCSL had indicted 13 individuals. Three of these individuals died before their trials could be completed. Eight have been found guilty and sentenced. One individual is considered still-at-large and the judgment against Charles Taylor, the former President of Liberia, is expected in the summer of 2011. With the exception of the Charles Taylor trial, all of the trial proceedings took place in Sierra Leone.

The SCSL has a procedural framework similar to that of the *Ad Hoc* Tribunals and adopted the advanced provisions on the protection of victims and witnesses from the

80 Statute of the Special Court of Sierra Leone [hereinafter SCSL Statute], attached to the Agreement between the United Nations and the Government of Sierra Leone on the Establishment of the Special Court for Sierra Leone [hereinafter Special Court Agreement], UN Doc S/2002/246 (2002).

81 Report of the Secretary-General on the Establishment of a Special Court for Sierra Leone, U.N. SCOR, 55 th Sess., 915 th Mtg., U.N. Doc. S/2000/915 (2000), par. 9; the one exception to holding proceedings in Sierra Leone is the trial of Charles Taylor, which is carried out in The Hague due to security concerns.

82 SCSL Statute, Art. 8(2).

83 *Ibid.*, Art. 14; Special Court for Sierra Leone, The Rules of Procedure and Evidence, last amended 27 May 2008 [hereinafter SCSL RPE].

84 Cassese, A., Report on the Special Court for Sierra Leone [hereinafter Cassese Report], submitted by the Independent Expert, 12 December 2006, p. 1.

ICTR Rules.[85] Therefore, like the *Ad Hoc* Tribunals, victims do not have the right to participate as victims as such. Instead, they may only actively participate as witnesses called by the parties or the Judge or have impact statements submitted on their behalf by the prosecutor. Moreover, issues of victims' compensation and reparation have been left to domestic courts despite the fact that within domestic proceedings a criminal court can order compensation awards on applications by the prosecutor on behalf of victims.[86]

Praiseworthy in many respects (such as being the first international court to establish a Defense Office), the SCSL has nevertheless failed to live up to its expectations, particularly with regard to the expeditiousness of proceedings.[87] In his expert report on the court Cassese observes that (i) the financial insecurity resulting from funding based on voluntary contributions; (ii) the lack of strong judicial leadership; and (iii) the initial failure to draw fully upon the available experience in international criminal proceedings have contributed to the court's challenges.[88] Additionally, perceived prosecutorial insensitivity to local culture and victims has exacerbated negative reactions to the court.[89] Critics of the court argue that the prosecutorial narrative provided a politically skewed reading of the conflict,[90] alienating much of the population.[91]

While not having the opportunity to share their victim narratives at the court, victims did have the opportunity to do so through a non-judicial, post-conflict mechanism. At the same time the Court was created, so too was a national truth and reconciliation commission. The SCSL and that country's truth and reconciliation commission illustrate a successful combination of two independent institutions performing complementary roles. Despite some of their goals overlapping, such as examining the responsibility of groups, their primary goals were distinct. The criminal court was designed to prosecute individuals alleged to have committed serious crimes. In contrast, the Sierra Leone Truth and Reconciliation Commission (SLTRC) was established to create an impartial historical record of violations and abuses of human rights and international humanitarian law related to the armed conflict in Sierra Leone, from the beginning of the conflict in 1991 to the signing of the Lome Peace Agreement, to address

85 See SCSL RPE, Rules 69 and 75.
86 Friman, H., Procedural Law of Internationalized Criminal Courts, 351, in Romano, et al. (2004), citing Proposal by Glenna Thompson for the Sierra Leone Bar Association, proposing a similar situation to that provided for under domestic law.
87 Cassese Report, p. 1.
88 *Ibid.* at 2.
89 See Mibenge (2011).
90 International Crisis Group, The special court for Sierra Leone: promises and pitfalls of a new model, Africa Briefing, 4 August 2003, p. 14; Cockayne (2005) at 460.
91 For instance, the indictment of Hinga-Norman, who was seen by much of the population as the individual responsible for restoring the government to power, was particularly controversial due to the fact that the overwhelming amount of atrocities were committed by RUF and AFRC rebels.

impunity, to respond to the needs of victims, to promote healing and reconciliation and to prevent a repetition of the violations and abuses suffered.[92]

Operating parallel to one another,[93] the two institutions primarily functioned at the same time with a slight overlap in jurisdiction. Nevertheless, the SLTRC was able to investigate a number of issues that the SCSL could not, such as events that occurred prior to the conflict as well as the role of external actors. And although the two institutions showed the feasibility of simultaneous operations of a court and a TRC, tensions did exist. The major concerns centered on whether the two institutions should have an agreement detailing their relationship and whether they would share information. Essentially, the two institutions agreed not to share information or sign agreements with each other, creating a cordial, albeit ill-defined relationship.[94] Moreover, the two institutions suffered from competition for resources, in terms of both monetary contributions and trained personnel.[95] Nevertheless, victims, while unable to participate in their own right before the court, were encouraged to share their experiences (in narrative form) with the truth commission.

5.4.2 East Timor: Special Panels for Serious Crimes

In 1999 after East Timorese voted for their independence from Indonesia, the Indonesian National Army and a number of Timorese militias violently attacked the people of East Timor. The attacks destroyed most of East Timor's infrastructure, killing thousands and displacing an estimated 500,000 civilians.[96] Following the violence, the UN Security Council created the United Nations Transitional Administration in East Timor (UNTAET), which was responsible for stabilizing the region and the administration of justice.[97]

Despite the fact that the violence destroyed almost all of the courts and prisons located in East Timor and many of the qualified legal professionals fled, UNTAET established a court in Dili to try those suspected of committing crimes associated with the conflict. The new courts were referred to as the Special Panels for Serious Crimes (SPSC). UNTAET's decision to establish these courts was based, in part, on the fact that Indonesia opposed an international court.[98] Given the complete lack of domestic infrastructure, a hybrid court became a favorable alternative. The SPSC in Dili were "the first specially constructed internationalized courts which have tried serious crimes

92 Sierra Leone Truth and Reconciliation Commission Act 2000, Section 6(1).

93 Although they operated parallel for more than 18 months, the SLTRC essentially completed its work by the time the actual trials before the SCSL began in June 2004, see Schabas, W.A., Internationalized Courts and their Relationship with Alternative Accountability Mechanisms: The Case for Sierra Leone,157-180, in Romano, et al. (2004).

94 Schabas (2004) at 1084.

95 *Ibid.* at 1088.

96 Bassiouni (2003) at 559.

97 UNSC Res. 1272, UN Doc. S/Res/1272, 25 October 1999 (establishing UNTAET).

98 Kermani Mendez (2009) at 67; Stanley (2009) at 91.

within a local justice system."[99] Thus, the SPSC were created as part of the Dili District Court and were composed of both domestic and international Judges. The applicable procedural law for the SPSC came from UNTAET Regulation 2000/30,[100] and resembled civil law practice with recourse to an Investigating Judge. At the same time, however, many of the procedural provisions are similar to those found in the Rome Statute, reflecting both adversarial and inquisitorial elements.

Although commentators have taken exception to the court given its many institutional flaws,[101] with respect to victims, on paper the SPSC in East Timor employed a sophisticated approach echoing many international developments and domestic practice.[102] A 'victim' was defined as:

> a person who, individually or as a part of a collective, has suffered damage, including physical or mental injury, emotional suffering, economic loss or substantial impairment of his or her fundamental rights through acts or omissions in violation of criminal law. By way of illustration and not limitation, a victim may be the spouse, partner or immediate family member of a deceased person whose death was caused by criminal conduct; a shareholder of a corporation with respect to criminal fraud by the administrators or officers of the corporation; or an organization or institution directly affected by a criminal act.[103]

Moreover, Section 12.2 of UNTAET Regulation 2000/30 states that the status of a person, organization or institution as a victim is not related to whether the perpetrator is identified, apprehended, prosecuted or convicted. Nevertheless, the Regulation time and again refers to the victim as an "alleged victim."[104] In accordance with the Regulations, the Court must take appropriate measures to ensure victim safety, physical and psychological well-being, dignity, and privacy,[105] and the prosecutor is required to respect the interests and personal circumstances of victims and witnesses when ensuring the effective investigation and prosecution of crimes.[106]

---

99 De Bertodano, S., East Timor: Trials and Tribulations, 79, in Romano, et al. (2004); See UNTAET Reg. 2000/11, 6 March 2000 and UNTAET Reg. 2000/15, 6 June 2000.

100 See UNTAET Reg. 2000/30, 25 September 2000, on Transitional Rules of Criminal Procedure (as amended by UNTAET Reg. 2001/25, 14 September 2001). On 1 January 2006, a new Code of Criminal Procedure of Timor-Leste, Law No. 15/2005 of 16 September 2005, replaced UNTAET Regulation 2000/30.

101 See, De Bertodano, S., Mixed Tribunals: East Timor, 703-704, in Bohlander, et al. (2006); Stanley (2009) at 93-96.

102 UNTAET Reg. 2000/15, 6 June 2000, sections 24-25; Othman (2001) at 122; Friman, H., Procedural Law of Internationalized Criminal Courts, 351, in Romano, et al. (2004).

103 See UNTAET Reg. 2000/30, 25 September 2000 (as amended by UNTAET Regulation 2001/25 of 14 September 2001), x.

104 *Ibid.*, sections 9.1; 19.2; 19.8; 25.2; 44.5.

105 *Ibid.*, sections 36.8; 14.3 "In any interview of a victim of a crime under investigation: [...] (c) the proceedings shall be conducted by a female officer in cases of a female victim of a sexual assault, unless the victim does not object to a different procedure."

106 *Ibid.*, section 7.3.

Most importantly for this study is that victims were afforded active participatory rights in the criminal proceedings beyond the victim-witness model. During the pre-trial stages, victims were entitled to request the prosecutor to conduct specific investigations.[107] However, the prosecutors had full discretion to either act upon or reject such requests. Victims also had the right to be heard at a review hearing before the Investigating Judge and at any hearing on an application for conditional release. Victims could be represented in court by legal counsel (at its discretion the Court had the power to group victims under one common legal representative). They had the right to notification of hearings and progress of the case, and could request the court to be heard at stages of the criminal proceedings other than review hearings.[108] Furthermore, they were able to request a review of the prosecutor's decision not to go forward with a prosecution.[109] Again, however, the General Prosecutor maintained the discretion to confirm the dismissal or to continue with an investigation.[110]

Although the SPSC's code of criminal procedure did not afford victims an absolute right to participate at trial, UNTAET regulations permitted the Court to allow for participation when appropriate. In this regard, victims had the right to request the Court to be heard at any stage of the criminal process other than in review hearings.[111] In addition to acting as victim-participants victims could testify as witnesses if called by the parties or Judges. Victims did in fact testify at many trials. For example, in *Cardoso*, over a dozen victims testified about the war crimes and crimes against humanity they witnessed.[112] When appropriate, the Court would protect the identities of victims and took note of the fact that just because some witnesses were uneducated and could not fully understand questions posed to them, this would not invalidate their testimony.[113] Nevertheless, it does not appear that any lawyers representing victims took part in proceedings.[114] Therefore, victim participation was mainly in the form of acting as witnesses.

With regard to post-trial decisions, UNTAET explicitly provides that victims had the right to be heard at sentencing hearings and hearings for conditional release after the convicted individual served a portion of his sentence.[115] However, no court documents make reference to victims participating in these hearings. Finally, with regard to reparations, UNTAET resolutions provide for compensation claims by victims. Section 49.1 provides that "[i]ndependent from the commencement or completion of a criminal proceeding, an alleged victim may claim compensation for

107 *Ibid.*, section 12.
108 *Ibid.*, section 12.
109 *Ibid.*, section 25.
110 *Ibid.*, section 25.2.
111 *Ibid.*, section 12.5.
112 See SPSC, *Prosecutor v. Cardoso Ferreira*, Case No. 04c/2001, Judgment, (Dist. Ct. Dili) 4 May 2003.
113 *Ibid.* at par. 277.
114 Although some cases are available, a number of trial proceedings went largely unrecorded.
115 UNTAET Reg. 2000/30, 25 September 2000 (as amended by UNTAET Regulation 2001/25 of 14 September 2001), section 12.3.

damages or losses suffered or inflicted by a suspected crime by filing a civil action before a competent court." In addition, the court had the power to include reparation orders in its final judgments notwithstanding any separate civil action but would be credited towards satisfaction of any civil judgment rendered in the matter.[116] However, with regard to their ability to claim reparations attached to the criminal process, Bassiouni has stated that "the rights of victims were not truly taken into account or properly addressed in the decisions of the [SPSC] panels."[117]

Until its closure in 2005, the SPSC issued approximately 400 indictments and handled 55 trials involving 87 accused, with a total of 84 convictions.[118] In early 2005 the Secretary-General appointed a Commission of Experts to review the work of the SPSC and in May 2005 the Commission issued its Report.[119] The Report notes that the Special Crimes Unit (SCU) of the SPSC, in charge of investigations, interviewed approximately 6,000 witnesses, and that many victim-witnesses testified in proceedings.[120] However, practically speaking, victims had little role during the investigations or trials. Indeed, provisions providing for participation were simply not utilized. Most victims had little knowledge about their rights or even about the work of the panels.[121] The Report also states that victims' groups remain dissatisfied with the SCU for not locating missing persons, completing all investigations, or bringing those most responsible to justice.[122]

Many of the challenges encountered at the Court had to do with the lack of institutional capacity with regards to both lawyers and Judges, and the inadequate and irregular funding.[123] Stanley notes that both the SCU and the Defense Lawyers Unit were so poorly resourced that both were hindered in carrying out their duties.[124] For instance, in the first 14 trials no defense witnesses were called, due to the overall lack of experience of defense attorneys, some of whom had never tried a case.[125] The level of funding was simply not enough for the Court to fully meet its mandate, providing some reasons behind the fact that very few victims took advantage of their broad participatory rights.

Despite these failings, the Commission concludes that the process provided an effective forum for victims to relate their experiences and encouraged the community

116 *Ibid.*, section 49.2.
117 Bassiouni (2006) at 242, footnote 202.
118 Stanley (2009) at 92.
119 See Report to the Secretary-General of the Commission of Experts to Review the Prosecution of Serious Violations of Human Rights in Timor-Leste (then East Timor) in 1999, UN Doc. S/2005/458 (Annex) (2005).
120 *Ibid.* at par. 53.
121 Stanley (2009) at 91, 105.
122 Report to the Secretary-General of the Commission of Experts to Review the Prosecution of Serious Violations of Human Rights in Timor-Leste (then East Timor) in 1999, UN Doc. S/2005/458 (Annex) (2005), par. 54.
123 *Ibid.* at para. 93-104; 112-119; 127-138; Stanley (2009) at 93-96.
124 Stanley (2009) at 95.
125 *Ibid.*

to participate in the process of reconciliation and justice.[126] The realities are far removed, however, from their theoretical rights. The tempered-down victim participation reflects the need to budget precious judicial resources. To be sure, the experiences at the SPSC provide valuable lessons for future courts on the practical limitations that may exist in implementing well-intentioned provisions on victim participation. Although the resolutions establishing the Court clearly support the goals of victim participation, the Judges ultimately concluded that toning down participation at the discretion of the Court was better for a Court emerging from a history of conflict.[127]

In addition to the SPSC, in 2001 a Commission for Reception, Truth and Reconciliation (referred to as the CAVR after the Portuguese acronym Comissão de Acolhimento, Verdade e Reconciliação de Timor Leste) was established.[128] Designed to complement the criminal trials of the SPSC, which had exclusive jurisdiction over serious criminal offenses, the CAVR had three functions: (i) to seek the truth about human rights violations; (ii) to promote community reconciliation; and (iii) to produce a report which documents the human rights violations and recommends how to protect human rights, and to promote reconciliation.[129] As with Sierra Leone, this is another example of a hybrid court and a TRC acting complementarily to one another.

The mandate of the CAVR was wide-ranging. In addition to establishing the truth about past human rights violations by reporting on their nature, causes, and extent, it could make recommendations regarding reforms and initiatives to help to prevent such violations in the future.[130] The CAVR recommended that the government implement a program of reparations for the most vulnerable victims, including those living in extreme poverty, who were disabled, or who were shunned by their communities for any number of reasons.[131] It also had the ability to recommend prosecution to the Office of the General Prosecutor.[132] Like the SLTRC, the CAVR had a relatively good relationship with the UN-administered courts;[133] however, the CAVR also struggled

---

126 Report to the Secretary-General of the Commission of Experts to Review the Prosecution of Serious Violations of Human Rights in Timor-Leste (then East Timor) in 1999, UN Doc. S/2005/458 (Annex) (2005), para. 125-126.

127 Linton (2001) at 175.

128 UNTAET Reg. 2001/10, 13 July 2001, On the Establishment of a Commission for Reception, Truth and Reconciliation in East Timor. Although the UN actively supported the establishment of truth and reconciliation processes in a number of situations, including in El Salvador, Haiti, Guatemala, and Sierra Leone, the CRTR marked the first time that it had acted as the formal founding authority. Stahn (2001) at 956.

129 See Lyons, B.S., Getting Untrapped, Struggling for Truths: The Commission for Reception, Truth and Reconciliation (CAVR) in East Timor, 99-124, in Romano, et al. (2004).

130 UNTAET Reg. 2001/10, 13 July 2001, sections 2(2), 3(1)(c), and 13(1).

131 See Commission for Reception, Truth and Reconciliation in East Timor, Final Report, 30 January 2006.

132 UNTAET Reg. 2001/10, 13 July 2001, sections 3(1)(e) and 38.

133 Stanley (2009) at 122.

to find adequate funding and often clashed with the court over its jurisdiction.[134] Nevertheless, the added benefit of the TRC in this situation is that it was able to better acknowledge the broader concerns of victims, which the criminal court could not. In all, the CAVR took 7,669 victim statements, 1,541 perpetrator statements and facilitated the participation of 1,371 perpetrators in community reconciliation hearings.[135]

5.4.3 UNMIK / EULEX War Crimes Panels in Kosovo

In the aftermath of a Serb-led attack on Kosovar Albanians in 1998-1999 approximately 10,000 individuals were killed and approximately one million displaced.[136] Following the end of hostilities, the UN stepped in to govern the turbulent region through the United Nations Interim Administration Mission in Kosovo (UNMIK). Deriving its authority from the Security Council's Chapter VII powers, UNMIK maintained a broad mandate, including re-establishing the rule of law. Accordingly, UNMIK established a Kosovo court system, which included the maintenance of civil law and order and the protection and promotion of human rights.[137] Foremost among one of UNMIK's tasks included the apprehension and prosecution of those believed responsible for the commission of war crimes.[138] Administered through the Special Representative of the Secretary-General,[139] UNMIK Regulations became the governing law in Kosovo.

UNMIK soon realized, however, that the number of available local judges or lawyers decreased substantially because Serbian judges and lawyers had fled or refused to take part and many of the non-Serbians lacked the required experience given the fact that ethnic Albanians had, for years, been barred from the judiciary.[140] Added to this predicament was the fact that many of the Albanian judges did not have the required independence and impartiality to oversee trials, particularly those trials concerned with war crimes.[141] As a result, UNMIK appointed international judges to

134 See Pigou, P., Crying without Tears: In Pursuit of Justice and Reconciliation in Timor Leste, Report for the International Center for Transitional Justice, August 2005; see also Reiger, C. and Wierda, M., The Serious Crimes Process in Timor-Leste: In Retrospect, Report for the International Center for Transitional Justice, March 2006, pp. 34-35.

135 Stanley (2009) at 111, noting that community reconciliation programs were focused on less serious offenses and did not include, for example, the crime of torture.

136 Bassiouni (2003) at 553.

137 UNSC Res. 1244, UN Doc. S/Res/1244 (1999), par. 10.

138 See Betts, et al. (2001).

139 Report of the Secretary-General on the United Nations Interim Administration Mission in Kosovo (Report of the Secretary-General), UN Doc. S/1999/779 (1999), par. 39.

140 Strohmeyer (2001) at 49-50 and 53.

141 Sending war crimes cases to the ICTY, however, was not an option because the then Prosecutor made clear that the ICTY would only prosecute cases of significant gravity, see Del Ponte, C., Prosecutor of the ICTY, Statement on the Investigation and Prosecution of Crimes Committed in Kosovo, The Hague, PR/P.I.S./437-E, 29 September 1999.

work together with domestic judges and international prosecutors to work alongside domestic lawyers.

The Kosovo court system is based partly on Regulation 1999/24 and partly on the Constitutional Framework.[142] The Constitutional Framework provides that there shall be the Supreme Court of Kosovo, District Courts, Municipal Courts and Minor Offense Courts.[143] The court system has no fixed internationalized court or panel. Instead, international judges sit on panels throughout Kosovo on a case-by-case basis.[144] Moreover, unlike the other internationalized jurisdictions mentioned above, the Kosovo court system is not required to directly apply international law. Rather, the courts apply international criminal law through pre-existing Yugoslav legislation.[145] As for procedural law they were meant to apply domestic law, which initially was the former Yugoslav Criminal Procedure Code,[146] but beginning in 2003 the new Provisional Criminal Code was used. All procedural codes reflect the civil law system whereby victims are afforded participatory roles other than as witnesses.

Within the Kosovo court system victims have extensive participatory rights, similar to those provided for under domestic proceedings found in many civil law systems. In this sense, in addition to submitting complaints and acting as witnesses, victims are free to act as civil parties (referred to as injured parties), subsidiary prosecutors, or private prosecutors. The term "injured party" refers to a person whose personal or property rights were violated or endangered by a criminal offense.[147] Thus, the property rights of a victim are emphasized. The term "subsidiary prosecutor" refers to an injured party who undertakes prosecution of those criminal offenses which are prosecuted *ex officio*.[148] Finally, the term "private prosecutor" means an injured party who conducts the prosecution of criminal offenses for which the criminal law requires a private charge such as the crime of insult.[149] In cases of serious crimes, victims, therefore, can be viewed as parties to the proceedings whether acting as an injured party or as a subsidiary prosecutor.

Article 78 of the Criminal Procedure Code (Kosovo CPC) explicitly provides that the "[t]he competent authority conducting the criminal proceedings shall at all stages of the proceedings consider the reasonable needs of the injured parties, especially of

142 See UNMIK Reg. 1999/24, 12 December 1999 and Constitutional Framework.

143 Constitutional Framework, section 9.4.4.

144 For the background to this development and resulting problems, see Cerone, J. and Baldwin, C., Explaining and Evaluating the UNMIK Court System, 48-57 and Cady, J.C. and Booth, N., Internationalized Courts in Kosovo: An UNMIK Perspective, 59-78, in Romano, et al. (2004).

145 International human rights law, however, was directly applicable by UNMIK Regulations, see Cerone, J. and Baldwin, C., Explaining and Evaluating the UNMIK Court System, 44, in Romano, et al. (2004).

146 However, some changes were made, bringing the rights of accused up to international human rights standards, see Cady, J.C. and Booth, N., Internationalized Courts in Kosovo: An UNMIK Perspective, 70, in Romano, et al. (2004).

147 New Provisional Criminal Procedure Code for Kosovo (Kosovo CPC), Art. 151.

148 *Ibid.*, Art. 151.

149 *Ibid.*, Art. 151.

children, elderly persons, persons with a mental disorder or disability, physically ill persons and victims of sexual or gender related violence." Interestingly, it appears that the Kosovo CPC favors victims representing themselves but that legal representation is also permitted.[150] If represented by legal counsel, the authorized representative has a duty to safeguard the rights of the victim and especially to protect his or her integrity during proceedings and to file property claims.[151] Victim Advocates working within the Victim Advocacy Unit are meant to be available to assist victims and, where appropriate, represent them.[152]

The injured party/auxiliary prosecutor may call attention to all facts and to propose evidence which has a bearing on establishing the criminal offense or on establishing his or her property claims.[153] Therefore, victims may participate on issues of guilt as well as their property claims. In addition, injured parties may file civil claims outside of the criminal process. During the investigation the injured party/auxiliary prosecutor may apply to the public prosecutor to collect certain evidence. If the public prosecutor rejects the application to collect evidence, the injured party may appeal such decision to the pre-trial judge.[154] At trial, the injured party/auxiliary prosecutor may propose evidence, put questions to the defendant and the witnesses, and make oral remarks and written submissions.[155] Moreover, victims have the right to access the case file and all objects that will serve as evidence, and importantly shall be informed of all of their rights existing under the Code.[156] Like many civil law jurisdictions, the injured party or auxiliary prosecutor must bear the costs of the criminal trial if the defendant is acquitted or the charges are rejected by the Court.[157]

From available records it appears that the number of victims participating as injured parties in war crimes or related cases is relatively low. However, as victim-witness protection improves and as victims groups become more organized a larger number of victims are beginning to act as injured parties. The Humanitarian Law Center, a human rights organization based in Belgrade and Kosovo, has played an important role in trial monitoring and the filing of victim complaints and victim compensation lawsuits.[158] According to their most recent Annual Report from 2008, injured parties have played an important role in a number of war crimes and related cases.[159] But calls for greater protection and access to justice remain.

150 *Ibid.*, Art. 79 and 81. Art. 82 prescribes when a representative must be provided.
151 *Ibid.*, Art. 81(3) and Art. 67; costs may even be covered by the Court.
152 *Ibid.*, Art. 81(4).
153 *Ibid.*, Art. 80.
154 *Ibid.*, Art. 239.
155 *Ibid.*, Art. 80(3); Art. 61.
156 *Ibid.*, Art. 80(4) and (5); Art. 61.
157 *Ibid.*, Art. 103.
158 Humanitarian Law Center, Annual Report (2008), p. 9.
159 See Humanitarian Law Center, Report: Trials for war crimes and ethnically and politically motivated crimes in post-Yugoslav countries (2008), pp. 113-123.

In April 2009 the European Union Rule of Law Mission in Kosovo (EULEX) took over the operational role of UNMIK with regard to the area of rule of law, with specific emphasis on the police, judiciary and customs.[160] As a result UNMIK completed the handover of war crimes cases to EULEX in December 2009. EULEX is now fully responsible for all war crimes and related cases.[161] The number of victims participating in war crimes trials, however, has not significantly increased under EULEX control.

5.4.4 Special Tribunal for Lebanon

On 14 February 2005 a car bomb exploded in Lebanon killing the former Lebanese Prime Minister Rafiq Hariri and 22 others. Eliciting international condemnation,[162] this event would eventually lead to the withdrawal of Syrian troops from Lebanese territory and calls for accountability. However, in the aftermath of the blast Lebanese authorities carried out a flawed and largely inept investigation which led to impunity concerns being raised.[163] As a result, the UN Security Council unanimously adopted Resolution 1595 establishing the United Nations International Independent Investigation Commission (UNIIIC) to assist Lebanese authorities in their investigation of the terrorist act.[164]

By the end of 2005, the Lebanese Prime Minister Fouad Siniora sent a letter to the UN Security Council asking about the possibilities of establishing a tribunal of an international character to deal with this event as well as similar crimes.[165] Shortly thereafter the Security Council unanimously adopted Resolution 1644, extending the mandate of the UNIIIC and requesting the Secretary-General to look into the request for the establishment of an international tribunal.[166] Lebanese authorities had, by this time, placed 10 individuals in detention in relation to the car bombing while UNIIIC investigations continued,[167] and discussions about the tribunal began. It was clear from

160 Council of the European Union, Joint Action 2008/124/CFSP on the European Union Rule of Law Mission in Kosovo, EULEX Kosovo, 4 February 2008; Kosovo, Law No. 03/L-053 "On the Jurisdiction, Case Selection and Case Allocation of EULEX Judges and Prosecutors in Kosovo;" Kosovo, Law No. 03/L-052 "On the Special Prosecution Office of the Republic of Kosovo."

161 Report of the Secretary-General on the United Nations Interim Administration Mission in Kosovo, UN Doc. S/2009/149, 17 March 2009.

162 See Statement by the President of the Security Council, UN Doc. S/PRST/2005/4, 15 February 2005.

163 UNSC Res. 1595, UN Doc. S/Res/1595, 7 April 2005, p. 1; Report of the Fact-Finding Mission to Lebanon Inquiring into the Causes, Circumstances and Consequences of the Assassination of former Prime Minister Rafiq Hariri, UN Doc. S/2005/203, 24 March 2005, para. 26-27.

164 See UNSC Res. 1595, UN Doc. S/Res/1595, 7 April 2005.

165 Letter dated 13 December 2005 from the Chargé d'affaires a.i. of the Permanent Mission of Lebanon to the United Nations addressed to the Secretary-General, UN Doc. S/2005/783, 13 December 2005.

166 UNSC Res. 1644, UN Doc. S/Res/1644, 15 December 2005.

167 These individuals were held for a number of years without proper charges being brought by Lebanese authorities. Once the STL was set up the Prosecutor examined the status of these individuals and recommended their release to the Pre-Trial Judge, see STL, Submission of the Prosecutor to the Pre-Trial Judge Under Rule 17 of the Rules of Procedure and Evidence, CH/PTJ/2009/004, 29 April 2009.

the outset that the Special Tribunal for Lebanon (STL) was not going to be either fully national or fully international and after over a year of negotiations the Secretary-General presented his conclusions on the matter.[168] On 30 May 2007, acting under its Chapter VII powers, the UN Security Council adopted Resolution 1757, which included the agreement between the UN and Lebanon for the establishment of the Special Tribunal for Lebanon (STL).[169]

As with the SCSL, international Judges at the STL outnumber national Judges and the prosecutor, Registrar and Pre-Trial Judge are international.[170] Created to help with investigations surrounding the terrorist attack, the UNIIIC has transitioned to become the Office of the Prosecutor. And in order to ensure the principle of equality of arms, the STL has set up a Defense Office as an organ of the court.[171] The STL will have jurisdiction over "all persons responsible for the attack of 14 February 2005,"[172] and will be the first international tribunal to deal with crimes of terrorism, albeit under Lebanese law. Interestingly, none of the crimes falling under the court's jurisdiction are international crimes. Instead, they are domestic crimes under Lebanese law that will be combined with internationally developed modes of responsibility,[173] making the STL "the only international tribunal exercising jurisdiction exclusively over crimes defined under national laws."[174] Nevertheless, the crime of terrorism, defined under Lebanese domestic law,[175] implies a notion of mass victimization and is generally seen as rising to the level of international significance because of its affect on international political stability. The limited mandate of the STL, however, means that it is likely to only deal with a very limited number of cases and may only carry out a handful of trials.[176]

The Pre-Trial Judge agreed and ordered the release of those remaining in custody, see STL, Order Regarding the Detention of Persons Detained in Lebanon in Connection with the Case of the Attack against Prime Minister Rafiq Hariri and Others, CH/PTJ/2009/06, 29 April 2009, par. 33.

168 Report of the Secretary-General on the establishment of a Special Tribunal for Lebanon, UN Doc. S/2006/893, 15 November 2006.

169 UNSC Res. 1757, Attachment to the Annexed Agreement to Resolution 1757, Statute of the Special Tribunal for Lebanon, UN Doc. S/RES/1757, 30 May 2007 [hereinafter STL Statute]. Originally a negotiated treaty between Lebanon and the UN, the treaty could not be ratified due to internal political problems. Thereafter, a majority of parliament signed a petition to the UNSC asking the agreement to be put into force.

170 Report of the Secretary-General on the establishment of a Special Tribunal for Lebanon, UN Doc. S/2006/893, 15 November 2006, par. 27.

171 Report of the Secretary-General on the establishment of a Special Tribunal for Lebanon, UN Doc. S/2006/893, 15 November 2006, par. 30.

172 STL Statute, Art. 1.

173 See Milanovic (2007).

174 Aptel (2007) at 1108.

175 In February 2011 the Appeals Chamber of the STL found in an interlocutory decision that recourse could also be made to an international definition of terrorism.

176 The prosecutor has filed an indictment under seal but as of the end of January 2011 this indictment has not been confirmed by the Pre-Trial Judge.

The procedural framework of the STL is notable in a number of respects.[177] First, the STL Statute provides Judges with roles that resemble those of Judges in inquisitorial systems, allowing the Judges leeway to control the proceedings, but incorporating elements from adversarial systems. The Statute provides for a single, independent Pre-Trial Judge whose job it is to review and confirm an indictment if the prosecutor has established a *prima facie* case against a suspect.[178] Although not an investigating judge, the Pre-Trial Judge may also issue orders concerning the investigation and is generally responsible for effective and efficient pre-trial administration. The Statute further allows the Trial Judges to be the first to pose questions to witnesses, followed by the parties, although this is to be decided based on the information made available to the Trial Chamber by the Pre-Trial Judge. And while the Judges will have access to case documents so that they are well informed about the case against an accused, the STL does not work off a dossier system. Therefore the Judges will not be in a position to direct the examination of witnesses as is common in civil law systems.[179]

Second, the procedural framework allows for the participation of victims throughout all stages of proceedings, including sentencing, but only after the issuance of an indictment. Article 17 of the Statute mirrors the language found in Article 6(b) of the Victims' Declaration and reproduces, verbatim, the language found in Article 68(3) of the Rome Statute:

> Where the personal interests of the victims are affected, the Court shall permit their views and concerns to be presented and considered at stages of the proceedings determined to be appropriate by the Court and in a manner which is not prejudicial to or inconsistent with the rights of the accused and a fair and impartial trial.

In accordance with Article 17, the Rules of Procedure and Evidence (STL Rules), adopted on 20 March 2009, further provide for rights of victims participating in proceedings. However, the Judges drafting the Rules were guided by the necessity to ensure fair and expeditious trials and had the opportunity to learn from the experiences of the ICC and ECCC (discussed in detail in Chapters 6 and 7). For this reason, although victims have broad participatory rights on paper, these rights are limited in a number of ways.

The Statute and Rules allow victims to remain informed about all procedural developments;[180] make opening and closing statements;[181] call witnesses;[182] lead

177 In addition to the role of judges and the participation of victims, the STL created a Defense Office as an official organ of the court (see STL Statute, Article 7) and allows for trials *in absentia* (see STL Statute, Article 22).
178 STL Statute, Art. 18.
179 Aptel (2007) at 1119.
180 STL RPE, Rule 168(A).
181 *Ibid.*, Rules 143 and 147.
182 *Ibid.*, Rules 87(B) and 146(B)(ii).

evidence;[183] question witnesses,[184] including the accused;[185] file motions and briefs;[186] receive all documents filed by the parties as well as the case file transferred from the Pre-Trial Judge to the Trial Chamber (unless restrictions are imposed).[187] In addition, victims will be able to participate during the sentencing phase of proceedings, which have been bifurcated from the guilt determination phase. In this respect, victims may convey their suffering so that Judges may evaluate the gravity of the crimes.[188] However, they will not be authorized to make any observations on the sentence to be imposed. This remains within the prerogative of the prosecutor.

Although these rights seem extremely broad, the STL has sought to limit these rights so as to ensure fair and effective as well as efficient proceedings. First, the STL has made a distinction between the concept of 'victim' and the definition of a 'victim participating in proceedings'.[189] A 'victim' is defined as "a natural person who has suffered physical, material or mental harm as a direct result of an attack within the Tribunal's jurisdiction," whereas a 'victim participating in the proceedings' is defined as a person "who ha[s] been granted leave by the Pre-Trial Judge to present his views and concerns at one or more stages of proceedings after an indictment has been confirmed."[190] The definitions adopted by the STL and subsequent comments made about them are restrictive in a number of ways. The definition only allows natural persons to be recognized as victims and therefore organizations or institutions will not qualify. In addition, victims suffering indirect harm will not qualify.[191] It was believed that allowing indirect victims the opportunity to participate would overburden the court or infringe upon the rights of the accused given the broad participatory rights available. Furthermore, victims may only participate after the confirmation of an indictment against an accused. This limitation will ensure that participation relates to the crimes contained in the indictment. In this regard, unlike in domestic practice, victims may not initiate criminal proceedings or direct investigations in a certain direction. Another departure from domestic practice is the fact that victims will not be able to claim reparations directly through the court. Instead, they may use the judgments of the court to claim reparations in domestic proceedings, though it is still unclear how exactly this will work in practice.

Additional safeguards and limitations imposed by the court on participation in order to ensure that participation is not prejudicial to or inconsistent with the rights of the accused include the following:

---

183 *Ibid.*, Rule 87(B).
184 *Ibid.*
185 *Ibid.*, Rule 144(B).
186 *Ibid.*, Rule 87(B).
187 *Ibid.*, Rule 87(A).
188 De Hemptinne (2010) at 178.
189 STL RPE, Rule 2.
190 *Ibid.*
191 STL, President's Explanatory Memorandum of the Rules of Procedure and Evidence, 10 June 2009, section 18.

- The Pre-Trial Judge, Trial Chamber or Appeals Chamber must authorize all participation;[192]
- The number of victims addressing the court may be limited by the Judges;[193]
- Victims are meant to participate through legal counsel and may only address the court themselves if permitted by the Pre-Trial Judge or relevant Chamber;[194]
- The Judges may group multiple victims with one or more common legal representatives, taking care to avoid conflicts of interest;[195]
- Unlike the questioning of witnesses, any questioning of the accused must go through the Judges;[196] and
- At trial, when victims are permitted to call evidence, the Court will decide upon their disclosure obligations.[197]

Many details about participation, however, are still unknown. For example, it is not clear whether victims will have access to confidential or *ex parte* material or the evidentiary threshold they will need to meet in order to be granted victim status. Regardless of these uncertainties the STL has sought to provide greater clarity than that provided for at other international courts employing victim participation. Although the victim participation framework adopted by the STL does not view victims as *parties civiles* as they would be viewed in Lebanese domestic procedures, they are, nevertheless, participants with important procedural rights. However, the court has sought to limit the rights so as to protect the rights of accused and ensure an effective and efficient trial.

5.5 Conclusion

Modern international criminal justice was borne out of prosecutions following WWII. Established as military tribunals, the IMT and IMTFE sought to prosecute those believed to be responsible for grave crimes while at the same time providing statutory fair trial rights. Although the fair trial rights afforded to defendants at these tribunals have been rightfully criticized, the recognition of these rights should not be dismissed. This recognition helped herald in a new era of human rights discourse promoting the rights of defendants in criminal proceedings.

Noticeably absent from the governing documents of the *Ad Hoc* Tribunals are references to the rights of victims. In terms of participation, victims were only permitted to participate as witnesses and they were not permitted to attach claims for damages to the criminal trials. Though victim impact statements were submitted on their

192 STL RPE, Rule 87(B).
193 *Ibid.*, Rule 86(C).
194 *Ibid.*
195 *Ibid.*
196 *Ibid.*, Rule 144(B).
197 *Ibid.*, Rule 112bis.

behalf by the prosecution, no victims were called before the Judges to publically express the impact of the crimes. The fact that victims could only actively participate as witnesses was largely due to the fact that the United States played a prominent role in establishing both tribunals. As a result, the procedures, in many ways, resembled what Damaška would phrase as a contest between two parties, making the inclusion of victims somewhat more difficult.

Paving the way for later international criminal courts, a preference for the adversarial approach would remain for some time, and although improvements in terms of defense rights have been introduced, the basic adversarial approach, with limited victim participation, endured at the SCSL. Accordingly, victims associated with these courts have not always felt that they were treated with dignity and respect, they were not individually notified and informed of important case developments, they did not receive psychological support or protection unless they also participated as witnesses, they were not permitted to be directly heard by the chambers unless called as witnesses, they could not attach reparations claims to the trials and the courts did not provide legal assistance. For the vast majority of victims not acting as witnesses, the option to participate was nonexistent. For a lucky few, their written statements could be used to provide information and express the impact of the crimes, with perhaps some consultation taking place with the prosecutor's office. However, overall, participation can, at best, be said to rise to the level of tokenism given the fact that prosecutors were under no positive obligation to consider the victims' views. When looking at Edward's typology, it appears that victims only participated as information-providers and by way of expression. The prosecutors and Judges were under no obligation to seek out and apply or consider victim preferences.

Calls for a greater procedural role for victims did, however, exist. These calls for a greater role for the victim in the justice process, while not successful in changing the role of the victim at these courts, prompted many to support the creation of non-judicial or quasi-judicial mechanisms which would supplement criminal prosecutions and allow victims to provide their stories in narrative form. These mechanisms sought to treat victims with dignity and respect, provide forms of victim support, and allow victims to be 'heard' by authorities. As a result, both the SCSL and the courts in East Timor worked alongside truth and reconciliation commissions as a way of engaging the wider community.

Unlike the ICTY, ICTR and SCSL the hybrid courts in East Timor and Kosovo as well as the STL have provided for greater victim participation in the criminal process. The greater role for victims at these courts reflects the domestic practices of the relevant domestic jurisdictions. However, at the SPSC and Kosovo war crimes panels it does not appear that victims have taken full advantage of their potential procedural status. The fact that victims have chosen not to actively participate in most of the trials is likely the result of many factors, including but not limited to the availability of the courts to the population; the resources at the disposal of the courts for victim services such as legal aid; the limitations placed on civil claims for damages; and (in the case of Kosovo) the requirement that the injured party pays for the criminal process if the accused is acquitted. Thus, despite governing documents that appear to provide victims with the opportunity to be kept informed about case developments, to be 'heard' in the criminal process, and to seek reparations, in practice, participation continued to be limited. Moreover, the authorities were still under no obligation to seek out and apply or consider victim preferences although they certainly sought information from victims. Nevertheless, if victims did participate as civil parties or auxiliary prosecutors, they would have had some decision-making control.

Drafters of the statutes and rules of all of the courts discussed in this chapter have had to decide on the best approach for the specific context in which the court operates. At the A*d Hoc* Tribunals, the Judges ultimately concluded that it would not benefit overall court operation to expand the mandate of the criminal process and as a result rejected proposals to increase victim participation with regard to reparations. Other courts opted to include victim participation provisions but tailored them to meet the realities facing the courts on the ground. This meant that no legal aid was available to victims at the SPSC, that in Kosovo the injured party could be responsible for costs, and at the STL it has been necessary to narrowly interpret the definition of victims. As such, the governing documents and practices of all the courts point in one direction: there are a variety of ways in which courts seek to acknowledge the rights of victims to some form of participation while focusing primarily on recognizing the rights of accused as evidenced by the detailed provision on fair trial rights. The forms of victim participation range from very limited access such as the submission of victim impact statements at the discretion of the prosecutor to acting as private or auxiliary prosecutors in trial.

Unfortunately, an examination into the SPSC, Kosovo war crimes panels and STL is only of limited value due to the fact that either few victims have taken advantage of the procedural roles available or, in the case of the STL, there are no trials ongoing at the moment. Therefore, although it is useful to examine what the governing documents provide, they reveal little about how participation could work in practice if a significant number of victims were to avail themselves of the participation provisions. For this reason, a study of the two courts in which victims have taken advantage of their participatory rights is necessary. Chapter 6 will examine victim participation at the ECCC which carried out the first international trial where victims participated as parties in the proceedings and Chapter 7 will examine victim participation at the only permanent international criminal court, the ICC, which was the first international court to recognize the rights of victims to participate in the criminal process.

CHAPTER 6
VICTIM PARTICIPATION AND THE EXTRAORDINARY CHAMBERS IN THE COURTS OF CAMBODIA

6.1 INTRODUCTION

From 17 April 1975 – 7 January 1979 roughly one quarter to one third of the population of Cambodia, estimated as roughly 1.5 to 2 million people, died as the result of starvation, disease and murder.[1] Under the control of the Communist Party of Kampuchea, also known as the Khmer Rouge, Pol Pot and others sought to turn Cambodia and its people into an extreme agrarian, communist state. Following the fall of the Khmer Rouge, a long period of instability and impunity reigned,[2] and it is only recently that an accountability process has taken shape. Long delayed and with many flaws, in 2006, the Extraordinary Chambers in the Courts of Cambodia (ECCC or Court) began trying individuals accused of serious crimes committed during the Khmer Rouge regime.[3]

The ECCC is a hybrid criminal tribunal, established and jointly operated by the UN and Royal Government of Cambodian. Presently, five former top Khmer Rouge officials are in the custody of the Court. The defendant in Case 001, Kaing Guek Eav, etter known as Duch, was the chief of the infamous S-21 security office in Phnom Penh.[4] Under his direction thousands of individuals were interrogated, tortured and killed. Duch surrendered himself to Cambodian authorities in May 1999. He was later detained, without formal charges against him, for eight years by the Cambodian Military Court. Only after the agreements on the ECCC were finalized was Duch transferred to the custody of the Court in 2007. Duch remained in detention throughout his trial, which began in February 2009 and concluded in July 2010. The other defendants in the custody of the Court will be jointly tried in Case 002. These individuals

1 Ciorciari, J.D., Introduciton, 14, in Ciorciari and Heindel (2009); Yesberg (2009) at 556. For more on the history of Cambodia during the Khmer Rouge, see Kiernan (1996); Chandler (1991) and (1999).

2 The fact that Western nations continued to recognize the Khmer Rouge as the official Cambodian government contributed to the instability of the country.

3 Specifically the Court has personal jurisdiction over senior leaders of Democratic Kampuchea and those most responsible for the crimes and serious violations of Cambodian penal law, international humanitarian law and custom, and international conventions recognized by Cambodia that were committed between 17 April 1975 to 6 January 1979. See Agreement between the United Nations and the Royal Government of Cambodia Concerning the Prosecution under Cambodian Law of Crimes Committed during the Period of Democratic Kampuchea [hereinafter UN-Cambodia Agreement], 6 June 2003, Art. 1-2; on the history of discussions between Cambodia and the United Nations see Donovan (2003).

4 His trial also concerned the detention facility known as S-24 which was an adjunct facility used as a re-education/work camp.

include Nuon Chea, Ieng Sary, Khieu Samphan, and Ieng Thirith.[5] They were all high-level members of the Communist Party of Kampuchea, holding important positions in the regime. They have all been in provisional detention since 2007 with their trial expected to start in the spring of 2011.[6] Cases 003/004 are currently under investigation and involve five additional senior Khmer Rouge leaders, all of whom have not yet been officially named. It is unclear whether these cases will move forward, however, as Cambodian officials have continuously tried to halt any progress on these additional trials.[7]

To be sure, Cambodian society is divided over its support for the Court.[8] Nevertheless, expectations are high that the Court will benefit Cambodians by bringing the most senior leaders of the Khmer Rouge to justice, facilitate reconciliation amongst Cambodians and serve as a model for the domestic legal system which is widely known for its corruption.[9] Its approach towards victims has certainly made the ECCC stand out amongst international criminal courts. The inclusion of victims as part of the criminal process, while an afterthought initially, is now heralded as one of its achievements.[10] However, the incorporation of victims into the proceedings has not been without its challenges. This chapter examines the scope and content of victim participation at the ECCC and explore the challenges encountered by the Court, the prosecution, the defense and the victims themselves.

6.2 Negotiating History and Framework of the ECCC

Attempts to create a legitimate accountability process first developed in the mid 1990s with the UN Commission on Human Rights' adoption of Resolution 1997/49.[11] The Resolution called upon the UN Secretary-General to examine requests for assistance

5 All of these individuals are older. At the time of writing their ages range from 77 to 84 years-old.

6 See *Case 002*, Closing Order, Co-Investigating Judges, 15 September 2010.

7 The Prime Minister and other high-level officials have repeatedly called for the closure of the Court following Case 002, See, e.g., Perter, Z. and Bopha, P., No more Khmer Rouge Trials, Premier Tells Ban, *Cambodia Daily*, 28 October 2010; Sokha, C. and O'Toole, J., Hun Sen Shoots from the Lip: Cases after 002 Face Embargo, *Phnom Penh Post*, 28 October 2010; Sokheng, V., Inquiries could sink ECCC: PM, *Phnom Penh Post*, 10 September 2009; Sokha, C. and Corey-Boulet, R., ECCC Ruling Risks Unrest: PM, *Phnom Penh Post*, 8 September 2009; Pheaktra, N. and Wilkins, G., Judges should Focus on Current KR Suspects: Gov't, *Phnom Penh Post*, 12 March 2008.

8 Chhang, Y., Forward, 10, in Ciorciari and Heindel (2009). A number of surveys on public attitudes towards the Court suggest broad support for criminal prosecutions, Mahon (2009) at 748, footnote 82; Pham, et al. (2009). Importantly these surveys are of the general population and not specifically of civil parties participating in the proceedings.

9 Acquaviva (2008) at 132.

10 Statement by the Victims Unit, Historic Achievement in International Criminal Law: Victims of Khmer Rouge crimes fully involved in proceedings of the ECCC, 4 February 2008.

11 U.N. High Commissioner for Human Rights, Situation of Human Rights in Cambodia, U.N. Hum. Rts. Comm'n Res. 1997/49, 11 April 1997. For a detailed chronology of events leading to the creation of the ECCC see Yale University, Cambodian Genocide Program, Chronology, 1994-2004.

in responding to past serious violations of law "as a means of bringing about national reconciliation, strengthening democracy and addressing the issue of individual accountability."[12] Soon thereafter the Cambodian Prime Minister, Hun Sen, and high-ranking UN Officials announced that Cambodia would seek a means of bringing Khmer Rouge leaders to justice without compromising the relative stability of the country.[13] A group of experts appointed by the UN Secretary-General to investigate options for bringing former Khmer Rouge leaders to justice soon issued a report. The report explored retributive and non-retributive options, including the possibility of creating a truth and reconciliation commission as a means of addressing the crimes of the Khmer Rouge.[14] However, according to the report few Cambodians attending the consultation meetings supported the creation of such a commission. Moreover, the political situation in Cambodia made such a commission unlikely given the fact that many individuals within the current government were at one time members of the Khmer Rouge. Therefore, negotiations between the Cambodian government and the UN began to focus on a more retributive model of justice.

Ultimately the Cambodian government and the UN would work towards the establishment of a criminal court. This would prove to be a "slow and painful process."[15] Original conceptions of a court were modeled almost entirely on the *Ad Hoc* Tribunals but any proposals that did not give a larger role to Cambodian nationals were rejected by the Cambodian government.[16] For this reason, negotiators turned their attention to a hybrid model. Yet, disputes still arose over the proper balance-of-influence between the UN and the Cambodian government, substantive legal issues, jurisdiction, and procedural rules. Nevertheless, in 2003 UN and Cambodian officials worked out an agreement on the establishment of the Court (Framework Agreement),[17] and a year later the Cambodian National Assembly enacted legislation establishing the Court (ECCC Law).[18]

The Framework Agreement, ECCC Law, and existing domestic procedural codes were to make up the legal foundations of the Court. However, it soon became apparent to those involved that a number of important procedural questions still remained, including the role of victims in proceedings dealing with mass crimes. In addition,

12 U.N. High Commissioner for Human Rights, Situation of Human Rights in Cambodia, U.N. Hum. Rts. Comm'n Res. 1997/49, 11 April 1997, par. 12.

13 See Dobbs, L., UN Official Calls for Cambodian Truth Commission, *Reuters News*, 6 February 1997; see also, Donovan (2003).

14 Report of the Group of Experts for Cambodia established pursuant to General Assembly Resolution 52/135, UN Doc. A/53/850, 16 March 1999.

15 Ciorciari, J.D., Introduction, 22, in Ciorciari and Heindel (2009).

16 Etcheson, C., The Politics of Genocide Justice in Cambodia, 199, in Romano, et al. (2004).

17 Ironically, on the same day that it approved the Framework Agreement the UN General Assembly passed a Resolution expressing concern about the functioning of the Cambodian judiciary "resulting from [...] corruption and interference by the executive with the independence of the judiciary." See UNGA Res. 57/225, UN Doc. A/RES/57/225, 18 December 2002, part II(2).

18 Law on the Establishment of the Extraordinary Chambers in the Courts of Cambodia for the Prosecution of Crimes Committed During the Period of Democratic Kampuchea [ECCC Law] (2004).

there was confusion over successive domestic codes of criminal procedure and the well-known fact that Cambodian judicial institutions have an appalling reputation for unfairness, widespread corruption and susceptibility to political pressure.[19] As a result of the concerns over clarity, fairness, corruption and usurpation of the judicial process, the newly sworn-in Judges of the Court went about drafting a set of Internal Rules. The Internal Rules, together with the Framework Agreement, ECCC Law and the domestic criminal procedural code (CPC) now form the procedural structure for the Court.[20]

It is this framework that recognizes the distinctive role of victims in the proceedings as well as a number of other innovative approaches to international trial operation. Unlike the *Ad Hoc* Tribunals the ECCC is based almost exclusively on a civil law-based system. Thus, unique to the ECCC model is the reliance on Co-Investigating Judges, one Cambodian and one international. Their role illustrates the strong reliance on the French, inquisitorial model, upon which the domestic Cambodian legal system is based.[21] Although the co-prosecutors initiate investigations, the bulk of investigations are meant to be judicial in nature rather than driven by the Prosecutors. The rationale being that a neutral authority better serves justice by uncovering inculpatory as well as exculpatory evidence.

After receiving an Introductory Submission from the co-prosecutors the Co-Investigating Judges investigate the facts laid out therein.[22] The investigation is not public and those involved are obliged to maintain this confidentiality. Though the Co-Investigating Judges carry out the bulk of the investigations they are not permitted to extend their investigations beyond the facts found in the Introductory or Supplementary Submissions. They do have the power, however, to charge individuals regardless of whether they are identified in the Introductory Submission or Supplementary Submissions.[23] In addition to their charging powers and having the ability to interview persons they deem useful in ascertaining the truth, they also have the power to grant protective measures for victims and witnesses. Throughout the investigation stage, all

---

19 Acquaviva (2008) at 132.

20 In its 25 February 2009 decision the Pre-Trial Chamber determined, against the wishes of the civil parties, that the Internal Rules take precedence over the Cambodian Criminal Procedural Code, see *Case of Nuon Chea (Case 002)*, Decision on Civil Party Co-Lawyers' Joint Request for Reconsideration, Pre-Trial Chamber, 25 February 2009. As of the end of January 2011 the Internal Rules have been revised six times. In Case 002 the successive versions of the revised Rules have applied but the Judges determined that the trial in Case 001 was too far advanced to impose new Rules. See ECCC, Internal Rules, Rule 114(3) (Rev. 5), adopted 9 February 2010, providing that "[a]mendments concerning Civil Party participation adopted at the 7th Plenary Session shall be applicable to those ECCC cases for which, at the date of adoption, a closing order has not been issued." Therefore all references to the Internal Rules related to Case 001 concern the 3rd Revision promulgated on 6 March 200; reference to the most recent Internal Rules as of the time of writing, the 6th Revision promulgated on 17 September 2010, is indicated with "(Rev. 6)." When no indication is made the Rule has not been amended and is the same in both Rev. 3 and Rev. 6.

21 Acquaviva (2008) at 135.

22 ECCC Internal Rules, Rule 55(2) and (3).

23 *Ibid.*, Rule 55(4).

parties have the opportunity to request the Co-Investigating Judges to undertake investigations on their behalf. The Co-Investigating Judges must explain any denial of an investigation request,[24] and when the Co-Investigating Judges conclude with an investigation, all parties must be notified.[25]

In addition to the Co-Investigating Judges, the ECCC is made up of three judicial chambers: a five-judge Pre-Trial Chamber, a five-judge Trial Chamber and a seven-judge Supreme Court Chamber.[26] In contrast with the SCSL, Special Panels in East Timor and war crimes courts in Kosovo, where international judges comprise the majority on each bench, at the ECCC the majority of judges in all of the chambers are Cambodian; as is the presiding judge of each Chamber.[27] However, due to fears of government interference or undue influence,[28] it was agreed that all decisions must be based on a super-majority formula, meaning that at least one of the international judges must agree in every decision.[29] The Pre-Trial Chamber plays an important role in early stages of the process because they handle disputes that arise between the co-prosecutors as well as the Co-Investigating Judges before a Closing Order is issued.[30] The Pre-Trial Chamber is also responsible for appeals against orders and decisions handed down by the Co-Investigating Judges,[31] including orders concerning the provisional detention of charged persons.[32] Once the Closing Order is issued, which contains the charges against an accused, the Trial phase begins. Importantly, decisions by the Pre-Trial Chamber are not binding upon the Trial Chamber. The Trial Chamber is responsible for the management of trial proceedings. At the close of the trial it rules on the guilt of the accused as well as on all civil claims submitted by victims. Appeals lodged at trial and against the final judgment are handled by the Supreme Court Chamber.

Unlike previous international and domestic court organization, the ECCC has two co-prosecutors, one Cambodian and one international, who have exclusive competence

---

24 *Ibid.*, Rule 55(10).

25 *Ibid.*, Rule 66(1), providing that all parties shall have 15 days to request further investigations; Rule 66(2) and (3), providing that a denial of further investigations may be appealed to the Pre-Trial Chamber.

26 ECCC Law, Art. 9.

27 *Ibid.*, Art. 9

28 Meijer, E.E., The Extraordinary Chambers in the Courts of Cambodia for Prosecuting Crimes Committed by the Khmer Rouge: Jurisdiction, Organization, and Procedure of an Internationalized National Tribunal, 208, in Romano, et al. (2004).

29 See De Bertodano (2006).

30 ECCC Internal Rules, Rule 71.

31 See Statement of the Co-Prosecutors, deciding to appeal the Closing Order of 8 August 2008 indicting Kaing Guek Eav for crimes, *available at*: http://www.eccc.gov.kh/english/cabinet/courtDoc/121/2008-08-21_OCP_Statement.pdf.

32 ECCC Internal Rules, Rule 63(1), which provides that Co-Investigative Judges may, after an 'adversarial hearing' between the charged person and the co-prosecutors (but not civil parties), issue orders concerning the provisional detention of charged persons.

to initiate the prosecution of crimes on the basis of a complaint or *proprio motu*.[33] The co-prosecutors carry out preliminary investigations to determine whether crimes were committed under the Court's jurisdiction and identify potential suspects and witnesses.[34] Once they complete their preliminary investigations they then send their information to the Co-Investigating Judges by way of an Introductory Submission together with the case file.[35] The co-prosecutors have an obligation to turn over exculpatory evidence to the Co-Investigative Judges and may add to their Introductory Submission by way of Supplementary Submissions.[36] At trial the co-prosecutors carry the burden of proof and must prove beyond a reasonable doubt each element of the crimes charged in order to secure a conviction of an accused.[37]

The governing documents of the Court provide that all individuals accused of crimes falling under the jurisdiction of the Court are entitled to fair trial rights,[38] including the right to a fair and public hearing; to be presumed innocent until proven guilty; to engage a counsel of their choice; to have adequate time and facilities for the preparation of their defense; and to examine or have examined the witnesses against them. Like the prosecution, defense teams are comprised of Cambodian and international lawyers. Each team is also assisted by a legal consultant and a case manager. Additionally, defense teams receive support from the Defense Support Section (DSS). The DSS is a permanent office set up to aid the accused in selecting a lawyer of their choosing. For those individuals who cannot afford a lawyer the Court will cover the costs. The DSS also provides legal and administrative support to defense legal teams and represents 'the defense' at outreach events. The work of the DSS helps ensure fair trials for defendants though the office may not submit independent legal arguments in the form of amicus briefs on defense issues.[39]

After a great deal of lobbying by victims' advocates,[40] victims are also recognized in the Court's governing documents. Supported by independent legal counsel and the Victim Support Section (VSS), formerly the Victims Unit, victims of the Khmer Rouge have the opportunity to take full advantage of fairly broad rights in the criminal process such as rights to participation, protection and reparation. Similar to the functions of the DSS the VSS is mandated to maintain a list of lawyers to represent civil parties. The VSS assists victims in filing complaints and submitting civil party applications and provides information to victims in order to facilitate effective partici-

33 *Ibid.*, Rule 49.
34 *Ibid.*, Rule 50.
35 *Ibid.*, Rule 53(1) and (2).
36 *Ibid.*, Rule 53(2) and (4).
37 *Ibid.*, Rule 87(1).
38 Framework Agreement, Art. 12(2) and 13; ECCC Law, Art. 33new, 34new, and 35new; Internal Rules, Rule 21.
39 See *Case of Kaing Guek Eav (Case 001)*, Decision on DSS Request to Submit an Amicus Curiae Brief to the Supreme Court Chamber, Supreme Court Chamber, 9 December 2010.
40 Bair (2008-2009) at 519.

pation.[41] Amendments made to the Internal Rules in 2010 expanded the mandate of the VSS to include the implementation of non-legal programs aimed at addressing victims' interests and concerns. As a result, the VSS also focuses on victim outreach and other non-legal projects. The inquisitorial nature of the proceedings, while not making the inclusion of victims necessarily easy, has certainly made it less difficult than it would be in proceedings that are more adversarial in nature. However, the inclusion of victims has not been without its challenges.

6.3 Victims and the ECCC

Despite victim-involvement being one of the most important features of the Court, questions about the inclusion of victims were some of the last issues addressed by Judicial Officers when drafting the Internal Rules and almost no mention was made of victims in the Framework Decision or ECCC Law.[42] This prior omission, particularly with regard to civil party participation and claims for reparation, may have to do with the fact that domestic Cambodian law provides for participation, either as an initiator of a complaint, a witness for the Court or as a civil party. Because domestic criminal procedures were originally meant to apply it is conceivable that the omission of any mention of direct civil party participation in the two founding documents of the Court is not a gross oversight. However, this is unlikely because one would think that a casual mention of participation or reparation would have been included in these documents given its importance. Regardless, it soon became apparent to the newly elected Judges that the domestic victim provisions would not work at the ECCC due to the potentially large number of victims (virtually most of Cambodian society) and the complexity of the crimes. Therefore, the Judges crafted a unique victim-oriented approach based on domestic practice, international trends and the unique context of the Court. At least on paper, victims have the benefits of participation, reparation and protection – the long, sought-after rights of the victims' movement. These rights, however, are limited in order to reflect the realities of international criminal prosecutions.

6.3.1 Participation

As with domestic procedures, the Internal Rules allow victims to participate in one of three ways: as a complainant, a civil party or as a witness. Each of these roles offers

---

41 ECCC Internal Rules, Rule 12, 12*bis* (Rev. 6).

42 Acquaviva (2008) at 140. Article 23 of the Framework Agreement only mentions the protection of victims and witnesses, Article 23 of the ECCC Law casually mentions the ability of the Co-Investigating Judges to question suspects, victims and witnesses, Article 33(new) of the ECCC Law mentions respect for the protection of victims and witnesses, and Article 36(new) of the ECCC Law generally mentions how the Supreme Court Chamber is responsible for appeals made by accused, victims or co-prosecutors against the decision of the trial court.

varying degrees of opportunities to assist the Court. However, the drafters of the Internal Rules sought to create a workable approach to victim participation for mass crimes, thereby departing from domestic practice when deemed necessary to ensure the efficiency of proceedings and preserve the right to a fair trial. By and large, this workable approach required that the rights of victims be limited or curtailed.

Victim Complainant

The Internal Rules define 'victim' as referring to a natural person or legal entity that has suffered harm as a result of the commission of any crime within the jurisdiction of the Court.[43] Victims, like other individuals, may file complaints with the Court so that the co-prosecutors can be made aware of particular crimes. In practice this means that the victims check a box on an application form, detailing their complaints and prompting the co-prosecutors to be informed about alleged offenses. The complaints do not require specificity but may contain general statements such as "a massacre happened in my village; the Court should come look here."[44] If the co-prosecutors find the complaint useful they may seek further information (possibly sending a supplementary submission to the Co-Investigating Judges to carry out investigations) and may seek to have the complainant act as a witness. An important difference between victims and civil parties is that victims interviewed by the Co-Investigating Judges do not have a right to have counsel present at these meetings.[45] Thus, victim-complainants are not afforded as many rights and safeguards as victims given civil party status. Unlike in Cambodian domestic proceedings, if the co-prosecutors choose not to take action regarding a complaint, victim-complainants are in no position to initiate prosecutions or force the co-prosecutors or Co-Investigating Judges to undertake an investigation.[46]

Civil Party

In addition to acting as complainants, victims may constitute themselves as civil parties in the criminal case if their harm suffered is a direct result of one of the crimes found in the Introductory Submission, Supplementary Submissions or Closing Order. A 'civil party' is therefore defined as a victim whose application to become a civil party has been declared admissible by the Court.[47] Victims wishing to participate as civil parties must apply for, and be granted, civil party status.[48] As with domestic practice, becoming a civil party allows victims to participate throughout the criminal

43 ECCC, Internal Rules, glossary.
44 Bair (2008-2009) at 521; See ECCC, Practice Direction on Victim Participation, Art. 2 (2008).
45 ECCC, Internal Rules, Rule 55(5)(a).
46 Cf. Cambodian Code of Criminal Procedure (2007), Art. 138-142.
47 ECCC, Internal Rules, glossary.
48 The application is four pages in length.

process and attach a claim for reparations. Again, however, the Court shaped civil party participation to fit the specific needs of the Court and civil party participation differs in practice from that at the domestic level.

Importantly, Rule 23(1) of the Internal Rules states that the purpose of a civil party action is to participate in the proceedings "against those responsible by supporting the prosecution" and to allow victims to "seek moral and collective reparations."[49] The wording of this provision is interesting. First, it presupposes the guilt of the accused by failing to include the word 'allegedly' before 'responsible'. Second, the phrase "by supporting the prosecution" has a number of important consequences. The wording suggests the possibility that civil parties may support the prosecution similar to the way an auxiliary prosecutor supports the public prosecutor in many national systems, such as through submitting evidence on the guilt of the accused and that participation is not limited to their interest in reparations. The wording also suggests that victims joining as civil parties must be aligned on the same side as the prosecution. In other words, civil parties must seek the conviction of the accused. Victims calling for a dismissal of charges, for example in the name of national reconciliation, would likely not fit this criterion. Finally, the wording relating to reparations is important because it recognizes that victims are entitled to redress and that, together with supporting the prosecution, this is a primary interest of their participation. Because there is no trust fund established with the Court, which could potentially allow victims to claim reparations without acting as civil parties, victims wishing to receive reparations must attach claims to the criminal proceedings. Thus, while it is not necessary that all civil parties seek reparations, it is necessary for all those victims wishing to seek reparations to join as civil parties.

In addition to supporting the prosecution generally and reparation claims, the Pre-Trial Chamber in Case 002 has stated that "a victim's interest in participating in pre-trial proceedings stems from two core rights – the right to truth and the right to justice."[50] Though neither of these rights is explicitly mentioned in any of the Court's governing documents, the Judges appear to recognize these human rights concepts as they apply to victims' rights. Unfortunately the Court has never elaborated on these inherent rights. Nevertheless, the dual purposes of participation found in the Internal Rules are far more specific than the general purpose of sharing views and concerns as prescribed by the Victims' Declaration. And, together with the recognition of a victim's right to truth and justice, this specificity has enabled civil party lawyers to base their arguments about the scope of participation on the concrete reasons given for participation.

In contrast with victims acting as complainants, civil parties have a number of important participatory rights. They are entitled to five days' notice before an inter-

49 ECCC Internal Rules, Rule 23(1).

50 *Case of Ieng Sary (Case 002)*, Directions on Unrepresented Civil Parties' Rights to Address the Pre-Trial Chamber in Person, Pre-Trial Chamber, 29 August 2008, par. 5.

view with the Co-Investigating Judges takes place.[51] During this time, the lawyer for the civil party may consult the case file. Moreover, unlike victim-complainants, civil parties may not be questioned by the Judicial Police but must be questioned by one of the Co-Investigating Judges in the presence of their lawyer.[52] During the pre-trial stage civil parties may request investigations and may appeal decisions by the Co-Investigating Judges not to investigate to the Pre-Trial Chamber. At trial, a civil party, like the accused, does not testify under oath,[53] and, through their lawyers, are granted a number of rights. These include the right to have full access to the case file,[54] to make limited pre-trial and trial appeals,[55] to make legal and factual submissions, to attend hearings, to request witnesses,[56] to question witnesses,[57] to question the accused,[58] to make closing arguments,[59] to rebut the closing statements of the accused,[60] and to request reparations.[61]

The role played by the lawyers for civil parties is vital in exercising the rights of victims. In Case 001 four teams of independent lawyers represented the interests of victims in the trial proceedings. Recognizing the importance of this participation but acknowledging that certain problems from the first trial had to be addressed the Judges at the Court have repeatedly revised the Internal Rules with regard to participation in an attempt to ensure fair and efficient proceedings. As of January 2011 the Internal Rules have been revised six times with further revisions expected later in the year. In February 2010 the Judges made the most significant revisions concerning participation. Arguing that the changes "strengthen the participation of the victims,"[62] the amendments to the Internal Rules have created two civil party lead co-lawyers.[63] At trial in Case 002 these lead co-lawyers will be responsible for the bulk of the advocacy, strategy and in-court presentation on behalf of all civil parties. In addition to the lead co-lawyers representing civil parties at trial civil parties will continue to be represented during the pre-trial stage and behind the scenes during the trial stage by independent legal counsel. Civil parties will therefore still be able to choose their own legal representative and although not leading the advocacy in the courtroom, the civil

51 ECCC, Internal Rules, Rule 59(1).

52 *Ibid.*, Rule 62(3)(b); and in accordance with Internal Rule 24(2) any relative of the civil party must also only be interviewed by the Co-Investigating Judge.

53 *Ibid.*, Rule 24(2).

54 *Ibid.*, Rule 86.

55 *Ibid.*, Rule 23(a) and Rule 74(f).

56 *Ibid.*, Rule 139

57 *Ibid.*, Rule 91.

58 *Ibid.*, Rule 90.

59 *Ibid.*, Rule 94.

60 *Ibid.*, Rule 94(2).

61 *Ibid.*, Rule 23 *quinquies* (Rev. 6).

62 Kong, S., Tribunal Judges Consider Duch Verdict, *Voice of America (VOA)*, Khmer, 2 February 2010, noting that in their opening statement Judges Kong Srim and Sylvia Cartwright said a representative model would "strengthen the participation of the victims."

63 ECCC, Internal Rules, Rule 12 *ter* (Rev. 6).

party lawyers will nevertheless continue to play an important role by submitting requests for investigations during the pre-trial stage and providing support to the lead co-lawyers at trial.

During trial the lead co-lawyers will need to seek the views of the independent civil party lawyers in order to coordinate on strategy and advocacy. Because this new arrangement will only come into play in the trial of Case 002 it is still unclear how it will work in practice. It is likely that some internal procedures or policies will need to be developed particularly when tensions between the different legal teams will inevitably arise. Importantly, the lead co-lawyers will be located within a separate section of the Court in order to safeguard their independence from other departments handling victim issues such as the VSS.[64]

Witness

Because direct victims are generally in the best position to provide investigating and prosecuting authorities with information on various aspects of an alleged crime it is clear that one of the most important roles of the victim is as a witness.[65] Accordingly, victim-witnesses act as valuable information providers. However, as with Cambodian domestic procedures at the ECCC a victim may not simultaneously act as both a civil party and a witness. The rationale behind this policy is the recognition that a civil party may have something to gain, financially or otherwise, by the conviction of an accused. Although this limitation is a disadvantage of constituting oneself as a civil claimant because in theory more weight is given to statements made under oath, it is meant as a way of preserving the integrity of the judicial process and fair proceedings. In domestic proceedings, however, an individual who wishes to attach a claim for damages and act as a witness first testifies as a witness and after doing so applies to participate as a civil party. This practice is possible because Cambodian criminal procedure allows victims to join a criminal case as civil parties up until the close of the prosecution's case. At the ECCC, however, it is not possible to first act as a witness and then as a civil party because the deadlines imposed for submitting civil party applications are set before the start of trial.[66] Therefore, a direct victim in a case will need to decide whether to participate as a witness (if approached by one of the parties) or as a civil party.

6.3.2 Reparation

Undoubtedly, seeking reparations is a primary interest of victims whether in domestic or international proceedings, but the drafters of the Internal Rules qualified the right

64 *Ibid.*
65 Handbook on Justice for Victims, Chapter II, D-8-(d).
66 See also, ECCC, Internal Rules, Rule 23(4) (Rev. 6).

to seek redress.[67] Unlike in domestic practice where victims may claim individual monetary reparations, upon handing down a judgment, the Judges at the ECCC may only award reparations to civil parties in the form of 'collective and moral reparations,' which are to be borne by a convicted defendant.[68] According to the Internal Rules (Rev. 3), these moral and collective reparations could take one of several forms. The Court could order that the judgment be published in any appropriate news or other media at the expense of the convicted person. The Court could order the convicted person to finance a non-profit activity or service designed to benefit the victims. And, finally, the Court could order any other appropriate or comparable form of reparation.[69] Assumedly, an appropriate and comparable form of reparation could have included the erection of monuments or the establishment of educational programs – all had to be paid for by the convicted defendant. A 2010 amendment to the Internal Rules, which will apply in Case 002, now requires the lead co-lawyers to make a single claim for collective and moral reparations on behalf of the consolidated civil parties.[70] Therefore, separate requests by individual civil party legal teams will not be entertained. Moreover, the amendments specify that collective and moral reparations are to (a) acknowledge the harm suffered by civil parties as a result of the commission of the crimes for which an accused is convicted and (b) provide benefits to the civil parties which address this harm.[71] Given that all the defendants who have appeared before the Court have been found to be indigent, it is unlikely that civil parties will ever receive moral and collective reparations beyond the most minimal available that the Court itself can implement such as the dissemination of judicial findings.

6.3.3 Protection

The Framework Agreement, ECCC Law, Internal Rules and Practice Direction issued by the Court all place high importance on ensuring the protection of victims. Internal Rule 29 holds that the Court shall ensure the protection of victims whether they participate as complainants, civil parties or witnesses. Protective measures include keeping a third-party address on file, using a pseudonym, non-disclosure of their identity to the public, voice or physical distortion, and relocation to a safe residence in Cambodia or abroad. Moreover, the relevant Chamber may order proceedings to be held in camera, and the Rules stipulate that communication with civil parties should, when appropriate, be made through their lawyers or Victims' Association. The Court also has a Witness and Expert Support Unit (WESU) that is set up to provide a variety of support services to witnesses and civil parties, including bringing witnesses to the trial, preparing them for the experience of testifying, and providing monetary allow-

---

67 Mahon (2009) at 744-745.
68 ECCC, Internal Rules, Rule 23(11) (Rev. 3); Rule 23 *quinquies* (Rev. 6).
69 ECCC, Internal Rules, Rule 23(11) and (12) (Rev. 3).
70 ECCC, Internal Rules, Rule 23 *quinquies* (2) (Rev. 6).
71 *Ibid.*, Rule 23 *quinquies* (1).

ances for their time. Importantly, WESU also provides tailored witness protection services and consults with judges as to what, if any, protective measures are necessary.

6.4 Participation in Practice

The participation of victims before the ECCC has been both hailed and criticized.[72] It has been hailed because for the first time a significant number of victims were able to actively participate as civil parties in an international trial, many have been able to sit inside the courtroom and face those individuals they hold responsible, and almost two dozen have had the opportunity to address the Court directly. It has been criticized because their participation has been perceived as unnecessarily delaying proceedings and infringing upon the rights of the accused. Moreover, through no fault of their own, their participation has inevitably raised their expectations about the outcomes of trial. These expectations were greatly let down following the final judgment in the *Duch* trial when many victims openly lamented about being re-victimized by the Court due to what they viewed as an inappropriate sentence, unjust reparations award and unfair revocation of civil party status qualifications.

To be sure, the participation of victims at the ECCC can be characterized as a cumbersome legal experiment. The relatively simple trial of Case 001 and the pre-trial proceedings of Case 002 have been the Petri dish where the Judges could determine the best approach for the larger, more significant trial of Case 002. After some initial, encouraging decisions recognizing the importance of civil party participation and providing victims with specific participatory rights, it soon became apparent that such a favorable approach would not continue. Facing prolonged proceedings and accusations of unfairness Judges became reluctant to recognize civil parties as equal parties to the prosecution and defense. Instead, the Court has sought, on the one hand, to acknowledge the importance of participation by providing for specific participatory rights, and, on the other hand, to limit participation in an attempt to ensure fair and efficient proceedings.

6.4.1 Application Process

In Case 001 the third revision of the Internal Rules applied. This set of the Rules was only moderately clear with regard to the criteria victim applicants had to meet in order to be accorded civil party status. Rule 23(2) (Rev. 3) provided that:

> The right to take civil action may be exercised by Victims of a crime coming within the jurisdiction of the ECCC, without any distinction based on criteria such as current

72 See, e.g., Statement by the Victims Unit, Historic Achievement in International Criminal Law: Victims of Khmer Rouge crimes fully involved in proceedings of the ECCC, 4 February 2008; Thomas, S. and Chy, T., Including the Survivors in the Tribunal Process, 214-293, in Ciorciari and Heindel (2009); Staggs Kelsall, et al. (December 2009); Bair (2008-2009); Yesberg (2009).

residence or nationality. In order for Civil Party action to be admissible, the injury must be: (a) physical, material or psychological; and (b) the direct consequence of the offence, personal and have actually come into being.

This provision was one of only a few guidelines from the Court's governing documents that helped instruct victims wishing to become civil parties on the criteria they would need to meet in their applications. In addition to laying out the criteria victims had to meet in order to gain civil party status the Rules also explain that civil party applicants need to provide sufficient information to allow verification of their claims by attaching any evidence of their injury suffered or evidence tending to show the guilt of the accused.[73]

Thus, first, civil party applicants had to have suffered harm as the result of a crime coming under the Court's jurisdiction.[74] When determining whether the events described by each applicant constituted a crime within the Court's jurisdiction, the Judges examined whether the harm alleged fell within both the subject-matter and temporal jurisdiction of the Court. The temporal jurisdiction of the Court is from 17 April 1975 to 6 January 1979.[75] Any complaints falling outside of this time frame have been denied. Crimes falling under the subject-matter jurisdiction of the Court include the national crimes of homicide, torture and religious persecution, and the international crimes of genocide, crimes against humanity and grave breaches of the Geneva Conventions of 1949.[76] Applications asserting harm suffered as a result of crimes other than those provided for in the governing documents have been denied. Second, the injury suffered by the victim-applicant had to be (i) physical, (ii) material or (iii) psychological. Hence, unlike victims appearing before other war crimes courts, such as the war crimes panels in Kosovo, emotional harm would suffice to support an application.[77] By explicitly providing for the definition of harm in the Internal Rules it was unnecessary for the parties to submit arguments on this issue, thereby saving the Court and parties valuable time and resources. Third, the injury or harm had to be the direct consequence of the offense, personal and it must have actually come into being. The Court determined that this criterion meant that a victim could only become a civil party if his or her harm arose as a result of the factual situation surrounding the case

73 ECCC, Internal Rules, Rule 23(5) (Rev. 3).

74 The ECCC has jurisdiction over genocide, crimes against humanity, grave breaches of the Geneva Conventions of 1949, the destruction of cultural property during armed conflict pursuant to the 1954 Hague Convention for the Protection of Cultural Property in the Event of Armed Conflict and crimes against internationally protected persons pursuant to the Vienna Convention of 1961 on Diplomatic Relations. See ECCC Law, Art. 2, 4, 5, 6, 7, and 8.

75 *Ibid.*, Art. 2.

76 *Ibid.*, Art. 3, 4, 5 and 6.

77 However, the Court later determined that emotional harm arising out of the witnessing of crimes would not be enough to support an application for civil party status. See *Case of Kaing Guek Eav (Case 001)*, Judgment, Trial Chamber, 26 July 2010, para. 640-643.

against an accused.[78] Although the wording of Rule 23(2) implies that only direct victims of the Khmer Rouge may participate, the Court granted both direct and indirect victims civil party status. Moreover, despite the fact that the injury suffered must be 'personal' the Trial Chamber found, in part on domestic practice, that under certain conditions a claim may be pursued by a deceased applicant's successors not on the harm they suffered as a result of their own loss but on behalf of the deceased victim.[79]

Together with the criteria found in the Internal Rules, on 17 February 2009 at the Initial Hearing in Case 001 the Trial Chamber laid out additional criteria for the evaluation of the admissibility of a civil party application. The Trial Chamber found that sufficient proof-of-identity of the applicant would be required,[80] though no mention of this is made in the Rules. The Court seemed to adopt a flexible approach, specifying that "the degree of proof required will be assessed by the Chamber on a case-by-case basis based on the materials before it."[81] However, the Court also noted that "[i]f the Chamber is to permit an Applicant to participate in criminal proceedings and to seek collective and moral reparations as provided in Rule 23(2), the identity of that person must be *unequivocal*."[82]

In general, in Case 001, few issues arose concerning the proof-of-identity of applicants. The lack of controversy likely stemmed in part from the fact that the conflict ended over thirty years ago and in contrast with conflict regions in Africa where many victims are unable to procure some form of proof-of-identity, in Cambodia most victims have documents proving their identity. Although the Chamber recognized the difficulties of some victims in obtaining proof-of-identity it nevertheless determined that some form of proof is required.[83] Though proof-of-identity issues have not been great concerning the identities of civil party applicants, issues have arisen regarding proof of a connection between indirect and direct victims.[84] In many cases, no documents exist that prove an indirect victim's relationship to a direct victim,

78 *Case of Kaing Guek Eav (Case 001)*, Transcript [hereinafter T], 17 February 2009, p. 26: "when reviewing the civil party applications received in this case the Chamber must satisfy itself, from the information provided, that it is possible to consider whether the applicant has indeed suffered damage, and whether this damage is the direct consequence of an offence under the jurisdiction of the Chamber." Note that it is not whether the damage is the direct consequence of an offense under the jurisdiction of the Court.

79 *Case of Kaing Guek Eav (Case 001)*, Judgment, Trial Chamber, 26 July 2010, par. 641; The Trial Chamber cited *Case of Kaing Guek Eav (Case 001)*, Decision on Motion Regarding Deceased Civil Party, Trial Chamber, 13 March 2009, para. 10-12, allowing a widower to continue the civil party action of his wife after she had passed away before the start of trial.

80 *Case of Kaing Guek Eav (Case 001)*, T, 17 February 2009, p. 33.

81 *Ibid.* at 33-34.

82 ECCC Law, Art. 2; *Case of Kaing Guek Eav (Case 001)*, Decision of the Trial Chamber Concerning Proof of Identity for Civil Party Applicants, Trial Chamber, 26 February 2009, par. 6 (emphasis added).

83 *Ibid.* at para. 6-8.

84 In Case 001, there was one instance where proof-of-identity issues arose concerning the identity of a civil party and a known detainee from S-21. See *Case of Kaing Guek Eav (Case 001)*, Judgment, Trial Chamber, 26 July 2010, par. 647.

and the defense argued that when no such proof exists an application should fail. Importantly, victims have never had to show how their personal interests are affected in order to participate as civil parties.[85] There is no requirement to show any special interest in any stage of the proceedings.[86]

Because little to no guidance could be found in the Internal Rules on how the Court should go about granting requests for civil party status, the Co-Investigating Judges, who were the first to review civil party applications, decided to apply a *prima facie* standard of review when assessing applications. In other words, they were simply assessing whether an application was more likely to be true than not. Similarly, when Case 001 was sent to the Trial Chamber, the Trial Chamber Judges also initially assessed applications using a *prima facie* standard of review.[87] Accordingly, in Case 001 the Judges granted 93 victims civil party status and allowed them the opportunity to exercise their participatory rights by supporting the prosecution and claiming reparations. However, in its final judgment the Trial Chamber confusingly laid out additional criteria that civil parties would need to meet in order to retain their status. The Trial Chamber found that "once declared admissible in the early stages of the proceedings, civil parties must satisfy the Chamber [at trial] of the existence of wrongdoing attributable to the accused which has a direct causal connection to a demonstrable injury personally suffered by the Civil Party."[88] The Court then went on to specifically recognize the nature of familial relationships within Cambodian culture and found that, in exceptional circumstances, in addition to a direct victim a direct victim's extended family may qualify as civil parties. However, in order to qualify the Trial Chamber held that "applicants" must submit proof of (1) the alleged kinship and (2) the existence of circumstances giving rise to special bonds of affection or dependence on the deceased.[89] It is these additional criteria created by the Trial Chamber which are nowhere to be found in the Internal Rules, prior decisions of the Trial Chamber or Practice Directives on participation. Ultimately the Trial Chamber revoked the civil party status from almost two dozen civil parties and, as will be discussed in the Trial Stage section, the approach taken by the Judges has had unfortunate consequences for victims and accused.

In many ways Case 001 acted as a testing ground for Case 002, which involves a higher number of accused, a more complex factual situation and a far greater number

85 Cf. ICC, Rome Statute, Art. 68(3).

86 *Case of Nuon Chea*, Decision on Civil Party Participation in Provisional Detention Appeals, Pre-Trial Chamber, 20 March 2008, par. 49.

87 *Case of Kaing Guek Eav (Case 001)*, T, 17 February 2009, p. 38, Judge Lavergne stated: "Having carefully reviewed each one of the latest applications, and having applied a *prima facie* standard of proof for the existence of criteria for the evaluation of the civil party application, and having heard the comments from the other parties, the Chamber declares that apart for applicants E2/69, 74, 87, all other remaining civil party applicants who do not have interim recognitions are admitted as civil parties in the case against the accused."

88 *Case of Kaing Guek Eav (Case 001)*, Judgment, Trial Chamber, 26 July 2010, par. 639.

89 *Ibid.* at par. 643.

of victims. Almost 4,000 individuals have applied to participate as civil parties in Case 002 with over 30 lawyers representing them. Although a relatively small number of individuals had been granted civil party status in Case 002 from as early as 2008, the Co-Investigating Judges reserved the bulk of their assessments until after the final judgment had been issued in Case 001. After the judgment was issued, the Co-Investigating Judges finally spelled out their approach to application determinations. In order to systematically process the large number of requests, the Co-Investigating Judges decided to issue the orders on admissibility based on the current residence of the applicant.[90]

Similar to the findings in Case 001, the Co-Investigating Judges found that civil parties must demonstrate specific standing or *locus standi*. As a guiding principle the Judges held that a civil action is open to all victims who are able to demonstrate, "in a plausible manner," that they have suffered physical, material or psychological harm as a direct consequence of one of the crimes alleged against the charged person.[91]

With regard to the level of proof and sufficiency of information provided, the Co-Investigating Judges referred to the Internal Rules (Rev. No. 5) noting that they must be "satisfied that facts alleged in support of the [civil party] application are more likely than not to be true."[92] The Judges made clear that the level of proof is specific to the admissibility of civil party applications and distinct from sufficiency of evidence criteria found in Internal Rule 67.[93] The Judges are not, they found, in a position to make final determinations concerning the harm suffered. Instead, final determinations are to be made by the Trial Chamber in its Judgment. Accordingly the Co-Investigating Judges make only a *prima facie* determination granting or denying civil party status.[94] The Judges acknowledged the difficulty (as well as the occasional impossibility) of substantiating claims with documentary evidence and therefore decided to adopt a flexible approach.[95] This flexible approach means that for applicants alleging psychological harm based on their relationship to a direct victim the Judges, where appropriate, applied a presumption of kinship based on the applicant's Victim Information Form and available supporting documents. Relying in part on decisions from the regional human rights courts, the Judges found that there is a presumption of psycho-

90 Orders on admissibility have been issued for applicants residing in Phnom Penh, in the provinces of Kandal, Svay Rieng, Prey Veng, Kompot, Pursat, Kampong Chhnang, Kampong thom, Kampong Cham, Battambang, Banteay Meanchey, Kratie, Kampong Speu, Koh Kong, Oddar Meanchey, Preah Sihanouk, Takeo, Rattanakiri, Pailin, Mundulkiri, kep, Preah Vihear, Stung Treng and those residing outside of Cambodia.

91 See, e.g., *Case 002*, Order on the Admissibility of Civil Party Applicants from Current Residents of Prey Veng Province, Co-Investigating Judges, 9 September 2010, par. 8. Beginning in September 2010, all orders on admissibility of civil party applications provide the same guidelines.

92 ECCC, Internal Rules, Rule 23bis.

93 *Case 002*, Order on the Admissibility of Civil Party Applicants from Current Residents of Prey Veng Province, Co-Investigating Judges, 9 September 2010, par. 9.

94 *Ibid.* at par. 10.

95 *Ibid.* at para. 11-12.

logical harm for immediate family members of direct victims.[96] The Judges further found that the presumption is determinant when the direct victim is deceased or has disappeared as a direct consequence of the facts under investigation, when the direct victim has been forcibly moved and separated from the immediate family as a direct consequence of facts under investigation, and when direct victims have been forcibly married.[97] The Co-Investigating Judges concurred with the approach of the Trial Chamber in the *Duch* final judgment and concluded that only "a relative presumption" exists for extended family members.[98] In these cases, the Judges will, on a case-by-case basis, determine whether there are "sufficient elements to presume bonds of affection or dependency" between the applicant and the direct victim. Consequently, non-immediate family members alleging psychological harm will find it more difficult in cases not dealing with the death or disappearance of another individual.[99] The Judges emphasized that psychological harm has a "character distinct from the emotional distress that may be regarded as inevitably caused to witnesses of crimes" and that applications asserting psychological harm for witnessing a crime will be rejected unless they witnessed "events of an exceedingly violent and shocking nature."[100]

Prior to the Rule changes in early 2010, the Victims Unit would send processed applications either to the Co-Investigating Judges or the Trial Chamber, depending on the stage of proceedings, for a determination of status. Following the Rule changes, all civil party determinations are to be made by the Co-Investigating Judges before a case is sent to the Trial Chamber. Thus, in Case 002 the Co-Investigating Judges will carry out the first assessment and either grant or deny civil party status. Neither the Internal Rules nor the Practice Direction on Victim Participation requires a reasoned order by the Co-Investigating Judges when admitting or denying a civil party application.[101] Victims may, however, appeal decisions denying civil party status to the Pre-Trial Chamber.[102] Those civil party applications that are rejected are nonetheless very often placed on the case file as complaints.

The two-tier approach first adopted by the Judges in Case 001 and later adopted by the Co-Investigating Judges in Case 002 certainly allow the Court to make quick, initial assessments of applications.[103] The backlog of applications perhaps required such an approach. However, it also means that victims will be granted civil party status and reap the benefits of all the rights that stem from such a determination. Many

96 *Ibid.* at par. 15.
97 *Ibid.*
98 *Ibid.*
99 *Ibid.*
100 *Ibid.*
101 *Case of Nuon Chea (Case 002)*, Decision on Civil Party Participation in Provisional Detention Appeals, Pre-Trial Chamber, 20 March 2008, par. 17.
102 ECCC, Internal Rules, Rule 23(3) and (4) (Rev. 3); Rule 23*bis* (2) (Rev. 6).
103 In civil law jurisdictions, courts usually allow a victim to attach a claim for civil damages and at a later stage review that claim to see whether the civil party was in fact a victim of the offense. However, this process is generally ill-suited for trials for mass crimes where the number of victims is so large.

victims will be able to exercise their participatory rights at trial only later to have their civil party status revoked in the final judgment. As will be discussed below, this is exactly what happened in Case 001. The problems resulting from this approach are many, including the disillusionment experienced by victims, the cost on the Court to review applications twice and, most importantly, it requires the defense to essentially face accusations at trial from individuals and their legal teams who did not have standing to participate, not to mention the time it takes a defense team to review thousands of civil party applications.

6.4.2 Pre-Trial Proceedings: Case 001 and 002

Throughout the pre-trial stages of both Case 001 and 002 numerous investigations have been carried out and many proceedings have taken place. In both cases, victims, granted civil party status, have exercised a number of important participatory rights during the pre-trial stage. They have gained access to the case file, submitted requests for specific investigations, been called upon to confront the accused, made written and oral interventions in pre-trial proceedings and have appealed decisions to the Pre-Trial Chamber. Additionally, the Co-Investigating Judges and Pre-Trial Chamber have issued important decisions on law and procedure. After an early favorable decision recognizing the importance of civil party participation, however, it became apparent that the Pre-Trial Chamber Judges were reluctant to recognize civil parties as equal parties to the prosecution and defense.

Access to the Case File

Once victims gain civil party status, one of the most important participatory rights afforded to victims during the Pre-Trial stage is their right to consult and examine the case file. Due to the fact that the proceedings more closely resemble those found in civil law jurisdictions the court uses a dossier or case file system. Thus, all of the parties, the prosecution, defense and civil parties have access to the case file. There is no system of disclosure between the parties, such as that which exists at the *Ad Hoc* Tribunal. Instead, it is up to each legal team to be familiar with the materials on file with the Court.

Investigations

Once gaining access to the information in the case file, the civil parties are then in a better position to exercise another important right: the right to request the Co-Investigating Judges to carry out specific investigations on their behalf.[104] Neither the defense nor the civil parties have the right to have their own investigators. Instead, they rely

104 ECCC, Internal Rules, Rule 59(5).

on the investigations carried out by the Co-Investigating Judges who in turn shape their investigation on the various submissions provided to them by the co-prosecutors. The opportunity to request specific investigations is a powerful right. In many ways it allows civil parties to help shape the case against an accused, including what crimes may ultimately be included in the Closing Order (which acts as an indictment). However, the Co-Investigating Judges must confine all investigations to the parameters of the Introductory Submission together with any Supplementary Submissions provided by the co-prosecutors. Therefore although civil parties may request specific investigations, these investigations must still relate to the submissions of the co-prosecutors. For example, the Judges have denied investigative requests for allegations of alleged attacks against culture because they had not been specifically referred to in the Introductory Submission by the co-prosecutors.[105]

Investigation requests, which may include requests for a particular witness to be interviewed, that a specific location be visited, or that a certain expert witness be approached,[106] have been submitted by civil parties. Fewer investigation requests were submitted by civil parties in Case 001 than in Case 002. The smaller number of requests is due, in part, to the fact that many of the victims did not join as civil parties until just before the start of trial and the investigations into Duch's criminal responsibility were relatively narrow in comparison to the factual situation in Case 002. Civil parties in Case 002, however, have taken advantage of the long investigation stage and have submitted a number of important investigation requests. These include requests for investigations into instances of forced marriage, enforced disappearance, attacks against culture and the financial situation of the defendants.[107] More specifically, the requests for investigative actions into forced marriage and enforced disappearance sought interviews with identified individuals and the appointment of experts on the topic to help with the investigation, namely the appointment of trained female investigators to interview female victims who suffered from sexually-related crimes.[108] The requests for investigative actions into attacks against culture included matters relating to courtship practice, birth and death rituals, imagination, the human spirit, identity of

105 *Case 002*, Order on Request for Investigative Action by the Civil Parties Concerning the Charge of Attack Against Culture, Co-Investigating Judges, 15 March 2010, par. 3, denying investigations into these matters because they had not been specifically referred to them by the Co-Prosecutors.

106 ECCC, Internal Rules, Rule 59(5).

107 See, e.g., *Case 002*, Co-Lawyers of Civil Parties' Investigative Request Concerning the Crimes of Enforced Disappearance, Co-Investigating Judges, 30 June 2009; Second Request for Investigative Actions Concerning Forced Marriages and Forced Sexual Relations, Co-Investigating Judges, 15 July 2009; Co-Lawyers for the Civil Parties' Fourth Investigative Request Concerning Forced Marriages and Sexually Related Crimes, Co-Investigating Judges, 4 December 2009.

108 *Case 002*, Second Request for Investigative Actions Concerning Forced Marriages and Forced Sexual Relations, Co-Investigating Judges, 15 July 2009, par. 31(c); Co-Lawyers for the Civil Parties' Fourth Investigative Request Concerning Forced Marriages and Sexually Related Crimes, Co-Investigating Judges, 4 December 2009, par. 8(b).

time and place and the exercise of language.[109] Despite limited success in having their investigative requests acted upon,[110] many have been rejected by the Co-Investigating Judges and then again on appeal to the Pre-Trial Chamber.[111] The denials of requests from the Pre-Trial Chamber have been based on a variety of reasons ranging from the fact that specific individuals had already been interviewed by investigators to avoidance of undue delay of proceedings. The right to appeal against denials of investigation requests can at times take a toll on the Court because "[e]very request to question witnesses, collect evidence, or order expertise that the civil party feels is necessary to his or her case is subject to appeal, even in situations where such evidence may not necessarily aid the goals of the prosecution."[112] This expansive right to appeal undoubtedly has the potential of causing undue delay and the Court seems keenly aware of this.

Confrontations

In addition to gaining access to the case file and submitting requests for investigations, civil parties may be called by the Co-Investigating Judges to confront the charged person.[113] In civil law systems it is common for investigating authorities to arrange for 'confrontations' between witnesses, civil parties and accused as a way in which to test the credibility of evidence. Although an accused may invoke his right to silence, in many civil law systems this can give rise to an unfavorable inference since the accused is regarded as an important source of information for revealing the truth.[114] If a confrontation with the accused takes place at the ECCC, with the permission of the Co-Investigating Judges the lawyers for the civil party may ask questions to the charged person (in theory even the civil parties themselves may be permitted to ask),

109 *Case 002*, Order on Request for Investigative Action by the Civil Parties Concerning the Charge of Attack Against Culture, Co-Investigating Judges, 15 March 2010, par. 3 (denying investigations into these matters because they had not been specifically referred to them by the Co-Prosecutors).

110 *Case 002*, Order on Civil Party Request for Investigative Action Concerning Enforced Disappearance, Co-Investigating Judges, 21 December 2009, par. 12, granting the request to conduct investigations into persons disappearing throughout the crime scenes invoked in the Introductory and Supplementary Submissions.

111 ECCC Internal Rules, Rule 59(5); *Case 001*, Order Concerning Requests for Investigative Actions, Co-Investigating Judges, 4 June 2008; *Case 002*, Order on Request for Investigative Action by the Civil Parties Concerning the Charge of Attack Against Culture, Co-Investigating Judges, 15 March 2010; Decision on Appeal of Co-Lawyers for Civil Parties Against Order Rejecting Request to Interview Persons Named in the Forced Marriages and Enforced Disappearance Requests for Investigative Action, Pre-Trial Chamber, 21 July 2010; *Case of Ieng Thirith (Case 002)*, Public Decision on Appeal of Co-Lawyers for Civil Parties Against Order on Civil Parties' Request for Investigative Actions Concerning All Properties Owned by the Charged Persons, Pre-Trial Chamber, 4 August 2010.

112 Bair (2008-2009) at 527, referencing ECCC, Internal Rules, Rule 74(4).

113 ECCC, Internal Rules, Rule 58(4).

114 Vanderpuye (2010) at 520.

and any refusal of a question will be noted in the written record.[115] Certainly, the right of the civil party to pose questions to a charged person during the investigation stage is significant symbolically and may well be significant substantively. In Case 001, the investigative judges arranged for a re-enactment to take place at S-21, with Duch, his lawyers, and a handful of surviving victims present. Afterwards, confrontation-interviews took place and were later referred to in the Closing Order.[116] Duch's cooperation with the Court certainly facilitated this confrontation situation.

Attending and Participating in Pre-Trial Proceedings

In addition to providing information and requesting investigations, civil parties may also participate in pre-trial proceedings through written and oral interventions. Nevertheless, at the pre-trial or investigative stage civil parties are not permitted to participate in all hearings. For example, Internal Rule 63(1) on Provisional Detention makes clear that at a hearing on provisional detention the Co-Investigating Judges shall only hear from the co-prosecutors and the charged person and his or her lawyer. Whether or not the judges would allow civil parties to participate in an appeal related to provision detention was up for debate.

In early February 2008 the Pre-Trial Chamber held its first hearing on an appeal against provisional detention by Nuon Chea. One week prior to the hearing the Pre-Trial Chamber was made aware that four civil parties had appointed lawyers and wanted to participate, which the Pre-Trial Chamber was willing to allow. At the hearing the lawyers for Nuon Chea challenged the participation of civil parties, arguing that their participation was not provided for in the Internal Rules and that their participation would infringe upon the right of the accused to a fair hearing because they had not been permitted to participate at the hearing before the Co-Investigating Judges. Moreover, they argued that the civil parties failed to inform the defense and prosecution of their interests in advance of the hearing.

Despite these objections, the Pre-Trial Chamber allowed the civil parties the opportunity to address the Court, with one civil party doing so directly. This civil party does not fit the mold of a prototypical victim.[117] She is an American trained lawyer, a civil society leader in Cambodia and somewhat of a media celebrity.[118] Her emotional presentation addressed Nuon Chea directly and failed to stick to the issue at hand – at one point using the opportunity to publicize a book put together by her NGO.[119] She openly questioned, "If Nuon Chea claimed he was not responsible, then

115 ECCC, Internal Rules, Rule 58(5).

116 *Case of Kaing Guek Eav (Case 001)*, Closing Order, Co-Investigating Judges, 12 August 2008, footnotes 63, 175, 177, 200, 226, 370 and 371.

117 Mahon (2009) at 752.

118 *Ibid.*

119 After offering a copy of the book to Nuon Chea the Judges actually ordered the bailiff to hand him the copy she brought with her. *Ibid.*

who was for the loss of my parents and other victims' loved ones?"[120] Her comments seemed to visibly upset Nuon Chea. Later, when another lawyer for civil parties informed the Court about harms suffered by his clients Nuon Chea requested a recess.

As a result of the emotionally charged proceeding, the Court seemed to recognize that such participation could potentially harm the rights of charged persons. Therefore, the Court sought submissions from *amici curiae* on the balance of rights between charged persons and civil parties.[121] Four amicus briefs were submitted by well-known victim advocacy groups and individuals working for such groups arguing for broad participation.[122] Only one amicus brief, submitted by a criminal law professor, cautioned against extensive participatory rights.[123]

In March 2008 the Pre-Trial Chamber determined that civil parties did in fact have a right to participate in appeals against detention orders even though they are barred from participating in the hearing on provisional detention before the Co-Investigating Judges.[124] The Judges emphasized that "Civil Parties have active rights to participate starting from the investigative stage of the procedure"[125] and that "the inclusion of Civil Parties [...] is in recognition of the stated pursuit of national reconciliation."[126] The Pre-Trial Chamber found that the text of Internal Rule 23(1)(a) was unambiguous and that victims can participate in all criminal proceedings, except for those proceedings in which they are explicitly barred. Noting that it wished to avoid an overly prescriptive procedure as that adopted by other courts,[127] the Chamber declared that civil parties should file submissions in advance of their participation in order to make it possible for the charged person to respond to the issues raised.[128]

Welcomed by victim advocates, this decision suggested that civil parties would be granted fairly broad participatory rights, while at the same time recognizing the rights of the charged person to be made aware in advance of the proceedings of civil party interests and given a chance to respond. However, only a short time later, the Pre-Trial Chamber seemed to reassess its support of a strong (and more prominent) civil party

120 Thomas, S. and Chy, T., Including the Survivors in the Tribunal Process, 261, in Ciorciari and Heindel (2009).

121 *Case of Nuon Chea (Case 002)*, Public Order on the Filing of Submissions on the Issue of Civil Party Participation in Appeals against Provisional Detention Order and an Invitation to Amicus Curiae, Pre-Trial Chamber, 12 February 2008.

122 The four briefs supporting broad participation were submitted by Anne Heindel (in her individual capacity though she works for DC-Cam), REDRESS/FIDH/ASF, ADHOC and the Khmer Institute of Democracy.

123 See, *Case 002*, Amicus brief by Christoph Safferling on the issue of Civil Party participation, Pre-Trial Chamber, 22 February 2008.

124 See *Case of Nuon Chea (Case 002)*, Decision on Civil Party Participation in Provisional Detention Appeals, Pre-Trial Chamber, 20 March 2008.

125 *Ibid.* at par. 36.

126 *Ibid.* at par. 38.

127 *Ibid.* at par. 43.

128 *Ibid.*

presence. The Pre-Trial Chamber sought to restrict what many viewed as an inherent right of civil parties; namely, the right to address the Court directly.

Prior to the provisional detention appeals of Khieu Samphan and Ieng Thirith the Court informed civil parties that only their lawyers would be permitted to make oral submissions. Citing the need to ensure expeditious proceedings, avoid disruptions, and take defense rights into account, the Pre-Trial Chamber found that "[t]he Internal Rules should […] be read to provide that civil parties who have elected to be represented by a lawyer shall make their brief observations related to the application or appeal through their lawyers."[129] The Chamber further based this decision on Internal Rules 23(7), 77(4) and 77(10), which refer to the participation by civil parties through their lawyers and noted (once again) that the defense should be made aware of the contents of the civil parties' oral submissions in advance of the hearing. During the hearing on the provisional detention of Khieu Samphan, however, one of the civil parties proceeded to directly address the Court, causing some confusion as to whether this sort of participation would be permitted. After some discussion the parties agreed that she could make a brief remark, but once again her comments went beyond the issues before the Chamber.[130] The Court had had enough.

When the issue of direct participation arose once more in Ieng Sary's hearing on provisional detention the Pre-Trial Chamber denied a request made by civil party lawyers that civil parties be allowed to speak in person even when represented by a lawyer.[131] When the same civil party, who directly addressed the Court in Nuon Chea's hearing and who requested to speak at the Khieu Samphan and Ieng Thirith hearings, sought a reconsideration of the decision denying her right to address the Court in person, a majority of the Court reiterated that "in the interests of ensuring expeditious proceedings and relevant submissions, and to avoid disruptions to the hearing" civil parties must participate through their lawyers and that it is appropriate to require civil parties to inform defense about their submissions ten days prior to any scheduled hearing.[132]

During these attempts to directly address the Court, the civil party in question dismissed her lawyer in order to get around the Court's ruling, raising the issue of the rights of unrepresented civil parties to directly speak to the Court. On this issue, the Pre-Trial Chamber recognized that civil parties have the possibility to address the Court in person when providing evidence, whether or not represented by a lawyer,[133] but stressed that lawyers for civil parties are in a better position to assist the Court for all other matters.[134] For this reason, the Chamber emphasized the need to find legal

---

129 *Ibid.* at para. 1, 4-5.

130 Bair at 548.

131 *Case of Ieng Sary (Case 002)*, Decision of 1 July 2008 on the Civil Party's request to Address the Court in Person, Pre-Trial Chamber, 1 July 2008, par. 3.

132 *Ibid.* at par. 7.

133 *Ibid.* at par. 5.

134 *Ibid.* at par. 7.

representation for civil parties. The Chamber pointed out that it is the lawyers who have access to the case file,[135] make submissions and who have the legal training necessary to assist the Court.[136] Nonetheless, the Court held that a legitimately unrepresented civil party, claiming a right to address the Court at a scheduled hearing, can make a written request to do so ten days prior to the hearing, explaining the content and relevance of his or her proposed submissions.[137] In practice there will be very few unrepresented civil parties in a position to file such a request. Thus, the Pre-Trial Chamber, with a minor exception, confirmed that civil parties represented by a lawyer may not speak in person during pre-trial appeals and that any civil party or civil party lawyer addressing the Court will need to give notice of his or her submissions to the defense prior to the scheduled hearing.[138]

Revisions made to the Internal Rules in March 2009 further support the early Pre-Trial Chamber decisions regarding the role of civil party lawyers and victim participation before the Court. The revisions, applying at the pre-trial and trial stages, stipulate "that where civil parties are represented by a lawyer, it is the lawyer and not the civil parties themselves who must make legal submissions before the Court."[139] In practice, it appears that the requirement of having civil parties make oral submissions through their lawyers promotes the efficient operation of the proceedings with a goal to ensuring that proceedings are conducted "within a reasonable time" as required by the Internal Rules. Indeed, as the numbers of civil parties increase, the importance of representation through legal counsel becomes apparent.[140]

Finally, observing that the prosecution, defense and civil parties have different positions in the criminal process, the Court's pre-trial decisions determined that the modalities of participation for victims do not need to be the same as those exercised by the other parties.[141] Accordingly, civil parties were given less time to make oral submissions in the hearing on Ieng Sary's appeal against provisional detention – though added together the time allotted to victims exceeded that of the defense.

135 *Case of Nuon Chea (Case 002)*, Decision on Civil Party Participation in Provisional Detention Appeals, Pre-Trial Chamber, 20 March 2008, par. 3.

136 *Ibid.*

137 *Case of Ieng Sary (Case 002)*, Decision of 1 July 2008 on the Civil Party's Request to Address the Court in Person, Pre-Trial Chamber, 1 July 2008, par. 11.

138 See *Case of Ieng Thirith (Case 002)*, Directions on Civil Party Oral Submissions during the hearing of the Appeal against Provisional Detention Order, Pre-Trial Chamber, 20 May 2008; see also *Case of Ieng Sary (Case 002)*, Decision of 1 July 2008 on the Civil Party's Request to Address the Court in Person, Pre-Trial Chamber, 1 July 2008.

139 ECCC, Fifth Plenary Session of Judicial Officers, Closing Press Statement, 6 March 2009.

140 Despite the important role played by legal representatives, Mahon notes that civil parties often find the legal process and meetings with their lawyers "boring and often incomprehensible." Mahon (2009) at 760.

141 *Case of Ieng Sary (Case 002)*, Decision on Preliminary Matters Raised by the Lawyers for the Civil Parties in Ieng Sary's Appeal against Provisional Detention Order, Pre-Trial Chamber, 1 July 2008, par. 4; see also *Case of Ieng Sary (Case 002)*, Directions on Unrepresented Civil Parties' Rights to Address the Pre-Trial Chamber in Person, Pre-Trial Chamber, 29 August 2008, par 5.

Undoubtedly, during the pre-trial stage, the Chamber continuously made clear that civil parties, while having certain rights, are not equal to the defense and prosecution. In response to an argument put forward by civil party lawyers that all parties should be treated equally, the Pre-Trial Chamber stressed that "no such general principle exists with respect to the length of oral submissions. Even if it did, such a principle would simply mean that as far as their position is equal, civil parties should be treated in the same way."[142] The Chamber further emphasized that "[t]he Parties have different positions in the criminal proceedings and these positions even vary in the different stages of the proceedings."[143] Therefore, although civil parties are in theory full parties in the proceedings the Court determined early in its jurisprudence that the parties have different roles to play in the proceedings and the manner and scope of the participation must reflect these differences.

The desire and enthusiasm of the victims to take full advantage of their participatory rights during pre-trial has never been in doubt; however, it is very likely that their passionate and often extraneous statements damaged the acceptance of broad participation in proceedings.[144] One commentator noted that the shift in attitude towards participation is attributable to the Judges' disinclination to hear from the civil party mentioned above rather than upon a correct reading of the Internal Rules or notions of the rights of charged persons.[145] It appears that civil party participation was viewed by the Court as unpredictable and something that needed to be controlled and limited.

6.4.3 Trial Stage: Case 001, The *Duch* Trial

Just over thirty years after the fall of the Khmer Rouge, on 26 July 2010 the Trial Chamber handed down its final judgment against Kaing Guek Eav. Based on the evidence presented at trial, the Court found him individually criminally responsible for crimes against humanity (including the crimes of murder, extermination, enslavement, imprisonment, torture (including rape), persecution on political grounds and other inhumane acts) and for grave breaches of the Geneva Conventions of 1949 (including willful killing, torture, inhumane treatment, willfully causing great suffering or serious injury to body or health, willfully depriving a prisoner of war or civilian of the rights of fair and regular trial and unlawful confinement of a civilian).[146] He received a sentence of 35 years' imprisonment.[147]

142 *Case of Ieng Sary (Case 002)*, Decision on Preliminary Matters Raised by the Lawyers for the Civil Parties in Ieng Sary's Appeal against Provisional Detention Order, Pre-Trial Chamber, 1 July 2008, par. 4.

143 *Ibid.* at par. 3.

144 Mahon (2009) at 754.

145 Thomas, S., Civil Party Participation at the ECCC, *IntLawGrrls blogspot*, 15 July 2008.

146 *Case of Kaing Guek Eav (Case 001)*, Judgment, Trial Chamber, 26 July 2010, para. 567 and 677.

147 *Ibid.* at para. 680-681.

In addition to two victims participating as witnesses,[148] the trial against Duch marked the first international(ized) trial where victims actively participated as civil parties. Operating before the 2010 revisions to the Internal Rules, which created the Lead Co-Lawyers, four civil party legal teams represented 93 direct and indirect victims.[149] Each civil party legal team was comprised, at a minimum, of one national lawyer and one international lawyer. Throughout the proceedings it became apparent that the four teams, while sharing a common goal, had difficulty working together. The lawyers for the civil parties disagreed on a number of legal issues and advocacy tactics. The disagreements ranged from whether to support the prosecution's arguments for the use of Joint Criminal Enterprise as a mode of criminal responsibility, whether victims could participate with regard to sentencing issues, whether to seek individual monetary reparations to whether the victims should boycott the proceedings after a number of unfavorable decisions. Regardless of these differences, the civil parties in the *Duch* trial exercised, through their lawyers, a number of important participatory rights. The civil parties had access to the case file, attended proceedings, including non-public proceedings, made written and oral submissions throughout trial, proposed witnesses and documents to the Court, questioned witnesses, challenged evidence, made closing arguments,[150] and sought reparations. In addition, despite the fact that the Trial Chamber initially forgot to include civil party testimony in its trial schedule, prompting some to believe that the Court may bifurcate the trial and reparation proceedings,[151] twenty-two civil parties were eventually permitted to address the Court directly without taking an oath.[152]

The majority of these participatory rights at the trial stage are explicitly provided for in the Internal Rules. The specific provision of participatory rights in the Rules saved the Court time and resources when deciding on the manner and scope of victim participation. It also provided much-needed clarity to the parties as well as some consistency to proceedings, though it did, at times, restrict participation more so than in the domestic system. However, the exact parameters of participation were still unclear and it was left to the Trial Chamber to define the proper scope of participation. Grappling with the need to oversee a unique trial for mass crimes with three parties

148 One of the victims chose to participate as a witness rather than a civil party because he did not wish to be associated with victims who want to profit from their suffering. See Mahon (2009) at 765; the other victim who participated as a witness had sought to participate as a civil party but filed his application past the deadline and was therefore not conferred civil party status.

149 During the pre-trial stage the Co-Investigative Judges granted 28 individuals civil party status. An additional 66 applications were submitted before the 2 February 2009 deadline set by the Trial Chamber. Sixty-five of these applications were granted by the Trial Chamber. Three of the civil parties later withdrew their claims, bringing the total number of civil parties participating at trial to 90. See *Case of Kaing Guek Eav (Case 001)*, Judgment, Trial Chamber, 26 July 2010, para. 637-638.

150 *Case of Kaing Guek Eav (Case 001)*, Direction on making a brief Opening Statement during the Substantive Hearing, Trial Chamber, 10 March 2009, par. 4.

151 *Case of Kaing Guek Eav (Case 001)*, T, 31 March 2009.

152 *Case of Kaing Guek Eav (Case 001)*, Direction on the Scheduling of the Trial, Trial Chamber, 20 March 2009.

participating and the rights of the accused to a fair and expeditious proceeding,[153] the Trial Chamber sought to demarcate the scope of participation and introduced a number of measures aimed at addressing expediency and efficiency concerns.

Supporting the Prosecution

One of the first questions relating to participation that arose dealt with whether a civil party lawyer could extract inculpatory evidence/information, not otherwise elicited by the co-prosecutors, during the questioning of witnesses so as to contribute to the establishment of the guilt of the accused. Contrary to the arguments of the civil parties, the defense argued that civil party questioning of witnesses should be limited to matters concerning reparations and harm suffered as is the case in many national systems. More specifically, the defense argued that the civil parties could not act as second prosecutors by attempting to draw out inculpatory information from the accused because this role belonged solely to the co-prosecutors.[154] Duch's very able defense counsel, Francois Roux, quoting French criminal procedural texts, submitted that civil parties have an inferior role in the proceedings to "defend their own positions, their own interests in relation to their own suffering, to the damage that they have suffered, but never [...] having the civil parties in charge of prosecution."[155] Throughout trial the defense would continue to argue that the victim's role should be clearly distinct from that of the prosecution. However, relying upon Internal Rule 23(1), the Chamber agreed with the civil parties. The Judges found that civil parties are entitled to pose questions "in support of the prosecution," so long as they are not repetitious, long-winded or outside the confines of the topic.[156] Essentially, this ruling allowed civil parties to elicit evidence to help establish the guilt of the accused. Civil party legal teams felt vindicated, having had this right secured by the Chamber, but within a couple of months the Chamber's approach toward participation would become more restrictive.

Sentencing and Character Witnesses

When issues surrounding the scope of participation arose in relation to sentencing, this time the Chamber limited participatory rights rather than securing them. The Chamber determined that civil party lawyers had no standing to make any submissions related to sentencing, finding that sentencing falls within the exclusive prerogative of the

153 See ECCC, Internal Rules, Rule 79(7), which refers to the Trial Chamber's role in facilitating 'fair and expeditious' proceedings.
154 *Case of Kaing Guek Eav (Case 001)*, T, 22 June 2009, p. 92.
155 *Ibid.* at 94-96.
156 *Ibid.* at 98.

prosecutor.[157] In particular, the Chamber directed the civil parties to refrain from making any submissions on a sentence to be imposed; making submissions relevant to sentencing; and making submissions on or an evaluation of factors underlying a decision on sentencing.[158] Even though the purpose of civil party participation is to 'support the prosecution' the Trial Chamber held that any understanding of the phrase 'supporting the prosecution' "must be interpreted restrictively, and does not confer a general right of equal participation with the Co-Prosecutors."[159]

On the same day as making this decision on sentencing, the Chamber also concluded that civil party lawyers were prohibited from posing questions to the accused and expert witnesses on issues related to the accused's character. Despite arguments put forward by both the prosecution and civil parties that domestic procedure allows civil parties to question all witnesses, including those testifying on an accused's character and that up until this late stage of the trial civil parties had already testified themselves or questioned the accused and others about his character,[160] the chamber agreed with the defense that character evidence is directly related to sentencing and has no relevance towards the guilt of the accused or reparations.[161]

Although one of the two international Judges dissented on both issues,[162] largely echoing the arguments made by the prosecution and civil parties, these two decisions signaled a marked shift in how the Chamber approached civil party participation. It appears that the Chamber sought to reign in participation for the final phases of the trial in an attempt to address defense concerns about fairness and expediency. However, there is nothing in the Internal Rules or Cambodian Code of Criminal Procedure which limits the participatory rights of civil parties once they join a criminal proceed-

157 *Case of Kaing Guek Eav (Case 001)*, T, 27 August 2009, pp. 41-42. This decision should have come as no surprise given the fact that the court had declined to hear expert witness testimony on sentencing proposed by civil party group one at the beginning of trial. See also, *Case of Kaing Guek Eav*, Decision on Civil Party Co-Lawyers' Joint Request for a Ruling on the Standing of Civil Party Lawyers to Make Submissions on Sentencing and Directions Concerning the Questioning of the Accused, Experts and Witnesses Testifying on Character, Trial Chamber, 9 October 2009.

158 *Case of Kaing Guek Eav (Case 001)*, T, 27 August 2009, p. 42.

159 *Case of Kaing Guek Eav*, Decision on Civil Party Co-Lawyers' Joint Request for a Ruling on the Standing of Civil Party Lawyers to Make Submissions on Sentencing and Directions Concerning the Questioning of the Accused, Experts and Witnesses Testifying on Character, Trial Chamber, 9 October 2009, par. 25

160 For instance, Judge Lavergne asked a civil party about an encounter she had with Duch during her time at the work camp. The Judge noted that although the meeting occurred after events for which the court has jurisdiction, her account was relevant to the issue of Duch's character. *Case of Kaing Guek Eav (Case 001)*, T, 24 August 2009, p. 26.

161 *Case of Kaing Guek Eav (Case 001)*, T, 27 August 2009, pp. 43-66, 74.

162 See *Case of Kaing Guek Eav*, Decision on Civil Party Co-Lawyers' Joint Request for a Ruling on the Standing of Civil Party Lawyers to Make Submissions on Sentencing and Directions Concerning the Questioning of the Accused, Experts and Witnesses Testifying on Character, Dissenting Opinion of Judge Lavergne, Trial Chamber, 9 October 2009, par. 8, finding the majority rulings inconsistent with the applicable law, and referring to them as a misrepresentation of the role and meaning of civil party participation, creating greater legal uncertainty.

ing.[163] Nevertheless, the Judges, who have wide discretion to shape the scope of participation, believed it necessary to limit the participatory rights of civil parties. At least some of the Judges likely had the looming trial of Case 002 in the back of their minds. These two rulings had a demoralizing effect on the civil parties, prompting 28 of the civil parties to boycott later proceedings. At a press conference, these civil parties argued that truth and justice were illusionary if they were not given the chance to understand the motivations of the accused.[164]

Having not had an opportunity to participate with regard to the sentence, victims were disillusioned when, in its final judgment, the Judges sentenced Duch to 35 years. This sentence will be reduced by approximately 11 years for the time served since his first detention,[165] and an additional five years will be taken off the sentence for the "violation of the Accused's rights occasioned by his illegal detention by the Cambodian Military Court between 10 May 1999 and 30 July 2007."[166] The idea that Duch may someday walk free has been difficult for many victims to handle.[167]

Reparations

Despite all of the disagreements amongst civil party legal teams, they joined together in order to file a joint claim for reparations.[168] The joint submission emphasized the rights of victims of gross human rights violations to reparation and requested: the compilation and dissemination of statements of apology made by Kaing Guek Eav throughout the trial acknowledging the suffering of victims, including comments by the civil parties; access to free medical care (both physical and psychological), including free transportation to and from medical facilities; funding of educational programs which inform Cambodians of the crimes committed under the Khmer Rouge regime and at S-21 in particular; erection of memorials and pagoda fences at S-21 (Choeung Ek and Prey Sar) as well as in the local communities of the civil parties; and inclusion of the names of the civil parties in Case 001 in the final judgment, along with a description of their connection to S-21.[169] Believing that an additional hearing would need to be held in order to work out the specifics,[170] the requests were only generally

163 Cambodian Code of Criminal Procedure (2007), Art. 326.

164 Saliba, M., Civil Parties Boycott Start of Character Witness Testimony while Experts Offer Psychological Assessment of Duch, *Cambodia Tribunal Monitor*, 31 August 2009.

165 *Case of Kaing Guek Eav (Case 001)*, Judgment, Trial Chamber, 26 July 2010, par. 633.

166 *Ibid.* at par. 632.

167 Mydans, S., Anger in Cambodia follows Khmer Rouge Sentence, *New York Times*, 26 July 2010.

168 In addition to the joint submission some civil party legal teams made subsequent requests for reparations in their final submissions, See *Case of Kaing Guek Eav (Case 001)*, Judgment, Trial Chamber, 26 July 2010, para. 654-657.

169 *Ibid.* at par. 652. The requests for reparations did in fact originate from the victims themselves and were not simply ideas submitted by the lawyers. I attended a number of individual as well as group meetings with victims on what reparations they wanted to request from the Court.

170 ECCC, Internal Rules, Rule 100(1) (Rev. 3), Rule 100 (Rev. 6) provides that "the Chamber may adjourn its decision on Civil Party claims to a new hearing."

worded and no specifics as to exact costs or logistics were provided. The joint submission further requested the Court to find a way around the provision in the Internal Rules that stipulates that reparation awards can only be borne by the convicted defendant.[171] This provision essentially nullifies any opportunity for victims to receive reparations because all defendants before the Court are receiving legal aid and are therefore deemed to be indigent. Knowing this limitation in the Rules, together with the fact that the Trial Chamber declined to call any expert witness on the issue of reparations, some civil party legal teams prepared their clients for a disappointing result.[172]

In its final judgment, the Trial Chamber found that it had no authority to award individual monetary reparations (as requested in the final submission of some civil party legal teams) and specifically noted that reparations were "intended to be essentially symbolic (aimed at conferring official recognition upon the victims, and assisting to restore dignity and preserve the collective memory) rather than compensatory."[173] In addition, the Court somberly noted that it had no authority to enforce its reparation awards, which fell instead to the domestic Cambodian judicial system.[174] Moreover, the Trial Chamber stressed that its hands were essentially tied, making it difficult to get around the limitations in the Internal Rules by stating that it had no authority over Cambodian officials not party to the proceedings and that it could "merely encourage national authorities, the international community and other potential donors to show solidarity with the victims by providing financial and other forms of support that contributes to their rehabilitation, reintegration, and restoration of dignity."[175]

With regard to the 'moral and collective' reparation claims, the Trial Chamber only granted two of the reparation requests. First, it granted the request that the names of civil parties be included in the judgment. Yet, the publication of the names of civil parties is hardly satisfactory to those civil parties who later had their civil party status revoked by the Chamber. Second, it granted the request that Duch's statements of apology be compiled, published and disseminated. The Chamber chose not to include accompanying statements made by civil parties "on grounds that such statements are distinct from apologies made by [Duch], and as their content has not been speci-

171 *Case of Kaing Guek Eav (Case 001)*, Judgment, Trial Chamber, 26 July 2010, par. 653.

172 Unfortunately, not all civil party legal teams adequately explained to their clients the unlikelihood of receiving anything more than symbolic reparations, leading many Civil Parties to be angry and frustrated with the result.

173 *Case of Kaing Guek Eav (Case 001)*, Judgment, Trial Chamber, 26 July 2010, par. 661, footnote 1144; many victims had a difficult time understanding how so much money could be spent on funding the Court with no individual compensation offered, see Mahon (2009) at 761.

174 *Case of Kaing Guek Eav (Case 001)*, Judgment, Trial Chamber, 26 July 2010, par. 661; *Case of Ieng Thirith*, Public Decision on Appeal of Co-Lawyers for Civil Parties Against Order on Civil Parties' Request for Investigative Actions Concerning All Properties Owned by the Charged Persons, Pre-Trial Chamber, 4 August 2010, par. 25 ("The ECCC legal framework does not grant any organ of the Court jurisdiction to enforce a reparation award").

175 *Case of Kaing Guek Eav (Case 001)*, Judgment, Trial Chamber, 26 July 2010, para. 663-664.

fied."[176] Every other request submitted by civil parties was denied, almost always on the basis of a lack of specificity. In this regard, the Chamber denied requests for the publication of portions of the final judgment (although later the Court would publish and disseminate the judgment in its outreach efforts),[177] denied requests for individual monetary awards,[178] denied requests for the establishment of a trust fund,[179] denied requests for measures by the Cambodian government such as instituting a national day of remembrance,[180] denied requests to erect memorials or pagodas,[181] denied requests to preserve archives, paintings or historical sites,[182] denied requests for free medical care,[183] and denied requests for education measures.[184]

In connection with the request for the erection of a memorial or pagoda, the Trial Chamber grounded its denial on the fact that "[n]o information has been provided, for example, regarding the identity of the owners of all proposed sites, whether they consent to the construction of each proposed memorial, or whether additional administrative authorizations such as building permits would be necessary to give effect to each measure."[185] Similarly, requests for the preservation of historical sites or archives were rejected because it had "no particulars regarding the current legal ownership of these sites, archives or items, or whether their owners or possessors consent to proposals that they be accessed or altered, or the reallocation of revenues derived from them to Civil Parties."[186] Thus, the Chamber rejected the request for lack of specifics but never afforded civil parties the opportunity to provide additional information. Civil party lawyer Karim Khan said the reparations ruling was "really the most minimal, most conservative, and perhaps it's fair to say unimaginative that could have been ordered"[187] Needless to say, many victims felt completely let down by the Court's approach to reparation requests.

Revocation of Civil Party Status

Undeniably, "tensions arise when victims are conferred (or denied) legal standing as civil parties."[188] Therefore, in addition to the disappointment in the sentence and reparation award, the final judgment dealt a huge blow to victims when the Judges

176 *Ibid.* at par. 668.
177 *Ibid.* at par. 669.
178 *Ibid.* at par. 670.
179 *Ibid.*
180 *Ibid.* at par. 671.
181 *Ibid.* at par. 672.
182 *Ibid.*
183 *Ibid.* at par. 674.
184 *Ibid.*
185 *Ibid.* at par. 672.
186 *Ibid.*
187 O'Toole, J., Reparation remain a key issue, *Phnom Penh Post*, 27 July 2010.
188 Mahon (2009) at 766.

revoked the civil party status of 22 individuals. The invalidation of their status illustrates the complexities of integrating a large number of victims into a criminal trial for mass crimes, and unfortunately serves as an example of how a court should not approach standing determinations.

At the start of the trial proceedings, the Trial Chamber ruled on civil party applications. At the Initial Hearing on 17 February 2009 the Chamber determined that, in accordance with Internal Rule 23(4), the 28 civil parties, who had been granted interim status during the Pre-Trial phase, were not required to renew their applications before the Trial Chamber. Accordingly, the Chamber found that these 28 individuals "remain as civil parties in the case against the accused person."[189] It further declared that with the exception of three applicants the remaining civil party applicants who did not have interim recognition were "admitted as civil parties in the case against the Accused."[190] In a subsequent written decision, the Chamber explicitly found that one of the three applicants who had previously not received civil party status had submitted sufficient proof-of-identity and granted that individual civil party status.[191] Eventually 93 individuals were granted civil party recognition.

None of the decisions granting civil party status informed victims that they were only conditionally being granted civil party status pending the satisfaction of additional criteria that they would learn about at a later stage. One of the only indications about a later review of applications was from Judge Lavergne at the Initial Hearing in response to comments made by defense counsel regarding claims by civil party applicants with the S-21 detention center. Judge Lavergne stated that "[i]t is perfectly clear that during the substantive proceedings [the judges] shall examine each of the applications to be perfectly certain that the alleged harm did in fact occur."[192] Months later, the defense challenged the admissibility of a number of civil party applications. First, the defense argued that friendship to a victim of S-21 is insufficient to give standing to a civil party.[193] Second, the defense argued that many of the civil party applications lacked sufficient documentary evidence to either prove that they were a direct victim or to link them with a direct victim.[194] The defense submitted that proof of a victim being detained at S-21 could be offered by way of a photograph from the prison, a confession or a name on the prisoners' list.[195]

Civil party lawyers objected to these challenges, stating that they could no longer be made given the fact that these individuals had already been accepted by the court

189 *Case of Kaing Guek Eav (Case 001)*, T, 17 February 2009, p. 34.

190 *Ibid.* at 50 (emphasis added).

191 *Case of Kaing Guek Eav (Case 001)*, Decision on Civil Party Status of Applicants E2/36, E2/51 and E2/69/Public, Trial Chamber, 4 March 2009.

192 *Case of Kaing Guek Eav (Case 001)*, T, 17 February 2009, p. 42.

193 *Case of Kaing Guek Eav (Case 001)*, T, 25 August 2009, p. 67.

194 See *Ibid.* for challenges to a number of civil party applications for failure to provide sufficient documentary evidence.

195 *Case of Kaing Guek Eav (Case 001)*, T, 26 August 2009, p. 12.

as civil parties and many had already testified before the court.[196] They further argued that since many documents from S-21 had been destroyed in the years after the fall of the Khmer Rouge and that so many Cambodians themselves destroyed evidence of links to family members who had been arrested, the Trial Chamber should not view documentary evidence, or the lack thereof, as conclusive with regard to proving civil party status.[197] Rather, it was argued that a liberal evidentiary standard should be applied. Both the civil parties and prosecutors argued that the chamber should consider the coherency and logic of statements and to assess their statements within their historical context.[198] Finally, they argued that just as the accused benefits from the presumption of innocence, civil parties should benefit from a presumption of good faith.[199]

Ultimately, in its final judgment, the Trial Chamber recognized four categories of civil parties, including: (1) Civil Parties claiming to be direct survivors of S-21 or S-24, (2) civil parties claiming to be the immediate family member of a victim of S-21 or S-24, (3) extended family members of a victim of S-21 or S-24, and finally (4) the successor of a deceased civil party applicant.[200] The acceptance of direct and indirect victims as civil parties finds support both in the Internal Rules, in Article 13 of the 2007 Cambodian Code of Criminal Procedure and in international law.[201] The Trial Chamber, however, limited the notion of an "indirect victim" to familial relationships, and in exceptional circumstances, extended family, provided the victim can prove (i) kinship and (ii) the existence of circumstances giving rise to special bonds of affection or dependence on the deceased.[202]

As to the first category, the Trial Chamber determined that only four of the eight direct victims substantiated their claims establishing Duch as responsible for their harms suffered.[203] Therefore the remaining four individuals, who could not supply sufficient evidence that they had been imprisoned at S-21, had their civil party status revoked.[204] As to the second and third category of civil parties, namely those individuals who claim to have lost a loved one imprisoned under the control of the accused, the Trial Chamber revoked the civil party status of 19 individuals. The Chamber determined that these individuals were "unable to establish the existence of immediate

196 *Case of Kaing Guek Eav (Case 001)*, T, 25 August 2009, pp. 74-77.
197 *Case of Kaing Guek Eav (Case 001)*, T, 26 August 2009, p. 7-10.
198 The civil parties also argued that applications based on friendship should be upheld, submitting that all that is required is a close relationship and that there is no requirement that a civil party be a direct family member, see *Ibid.* at 6.
199 *Case of Kaing Guek Eav (Case 001)*, T, 27 August 2009, p. 18.
200 *Case of Kaing Guek Eav (Case 001)*, Judgment, Trial Chamber, 26 July 2010, para. 641-642;
201 *Ibid.* at 221, footnote 1076.
202 *Ibid.* at par. 643.
203 *Ibid.* at par. 645. The four survivors who were successful as civil parties were Bou Meng, Chum Mey, Chum Neou, and Chin Met.
204 *Ibid.* at par. 647.

victims to the required standard"[205] or failed to "provide [...] proof of kinship or special bonds of affection or dependency in relation to immediate victims of S-21 or S-24."[206] Essentially the claims of these 19 civil parties were denied for their failure to produce tangible evidence or because the civil party could not demonstrate a special bond of affection or dependency.

For civil parties Jeffrey James and his brother Joshua Rothschild the new criteria were devastating. These two individuals were admitted as civil parties in the case at the Initial Hearing.[207] Both could positively show that their uncle James W. Clark was imprisoned and executed at S-21. Despite being able to prove their kinship with a direct victim, they had their civil party status revoked because the Trial Chamber determined that they were unable to show a special bond of affection or dependency in relation to their uncle. The Court appeared to hold that in order to show a special bond of affection the family member had to have lived with the direct victim.[208] No other circumstances were considered by the Court that could also qualify as special bonds of affection. Instead the Trial Chamber took special note of the expert testimony of Sotheara Chhim in which he explained the historical tendency of Cambodian families to live together with extended family members and the likelihood of strong bonds between grandparents, cousins, uncles and aunts.[209] The Trial Chamber used this standard (based on the Cambodian context) to determine whether or not Jeffrey James and Joshua Rothschild had a special bond with their uncle without acknowledging that outside of the Cambodian context extended family members can still maintain special bonds of affection without necessarily living with one another – particularly in societies where living with extended family is less common. It did not matter that the brothers, together with their mother, are the only living relatives of their uncle and that in his civil party application James specifically mentioned the frequent visits made by their uncle to the family home when they were growing up, and he wrote in his application that he and his uncle "were very close."[210] The approach adopted by the Court not only seems unfair, promoting one civil party lawyer to state "It's as if the court, late in the day, is rejecting [the victims'] loss and tragedy,"[211] because it had not been articulated previously, but it was also completely avoidable.

205 *Ibid.* at par. 648.

206 *Ibid.* at par. 649.

207 *Case of Kaing Guek Eav (Case 001)*, T, 17 February 2009, p. 50.

208 *Case of Kaing Guek Eav (Case 001)*, Judgment, Trial Chamber, 26 July 2010, par. 650, acceptance of Toch Monin as a civil party for the loss of his cousin with whom he was raised and of whom he is the only surviving relative; acceptance of Sin Sinet for the loss of her grandfather in whose house she had lived; acceptance of Yun Chhoeun for the loss of his nephew who lived in his house until the age of 15 and acceptance of Sek Siek for the loss of her cousin and fiancé who was living in the family home.

209 *Ibid.* at 221, footnote 1077, citing T, 25 August 2009, pp. 36-37, 48.

210 *Case of Kaing Guek Eav (Case 001)*, Group 1 – Civil Parties' Co-Lawyers' Immediate Appeal of Civil Party Status Determinations from the Final Judgment, Supreme Court Chamber, 14 September 2010, par. 78.

211 O'Toole, J., Reparation remain a key issue, *Phnom Penh Post*, 27 July 2010.

There are of course instances where a Court may decide to revoke an individual's civil party status, such as when evidence comes to light that an individual manufactured or fabricated evidence supporting his or her application. However, in Case 001, this was simply not the case. The revocation of civil party status from those individuals who had already participated throughout the entire trial makes little sense. The continuation of these individuals as civil parties at the final stage of the Duch trial did not prejudice the accused to the extent that it warrants the revocation of their status, particularly when they had already fully participated in proceedings and no real reparations were awarded. After extensive participation, the revocation of their civil party status only served to re-victimize these individuals and disillusion others with the process. Undoubtedly the victims participating in Case 001 invested a great deal of time and emotional well-being into the trial process. They recounted either their own or their family's stories numerous times,[212] and they attended day after day of hearings where they heard about the horrors suffered by those at S-21 and S-24. They nevertheless decided to take part believing that they were assisting in the documenting of the truth and contributing to the overall justice process.

Moreover, the prejudice to the accused is significant. The Court erroneously allowed individuals who ultimately did not qualify as civil parties to participate throughout the trial proceedings. These individuals had (through their lawyers) access to the case file, attended all proceedings, proposed witnesses, questioned witnesses and the accused, and made closing arguments. The civil parties were specifically allowed to submit and adduce evidence on the guilt of the accused. Issues of standing should arguably have been resolved prior to the commencement of proceedings so as to avoid a waste of resources, undue delay and an infringement of the rights of parties. Instead the Court placed itself in the position where it spent its time hearing and reading evidence from individuals who were later deemed ineligible to participate. Determining standing in advance of trial would make trial proceedings shorter and more efficient. Indiscriminately allowing in any type of 'evidence', regardless of its relevance or reliability, only prolongs trials and makes them more complex. The irrelevant or potentially fabricated 'evidence' is put in the record and requires the judges to shift through even more evidential material at the end of trial to arrive at the truth. Moreover, the defense must invest a great deal of their limited resources combing through applications and responding to evidence that in fact should not have been part of the case against the accused.

The concerns that dogged Case 001, particularly those relating to the length and fairness of the proceedings, will undoubtedly continue to be at issue in Case 002 where approximately 4,000 civil parties have applied to participate. Despite the rule changes instituting the positions of lead co-lawyers and imposing strict time limits the partici-

212 Each victim would generally have to recount his or her story at least twice: first when filing out an application and then when being interviewed by his or her lawyer. In practice most victims would recount their story to multiple lawyers or NGOs. In addition twenty-two victims addressed the Court directly.

pation of victims will once again prove troublesome. The two-tiered assessment of applications will require the defense and the Court to comb through thousands of applications at trial. Another approach could avoid such measures.

6.4.4 Appeals

Decisions and judgments from the Trial Chamber may be appealed to the Supreme Court Chamber. Its decisions are final and as with the other judicial chambers a decision by the Supreme Court Chamber requires a super-majority vote. The Supreme Court Chamber may hear appeals on two grounds, either an error on a question of law invalidating a judgment or decision or an error of fact that has occasioned a miscarriage of justice.[213] The Chamber may examine existing evidence as well as call new evidence when making its decision. Interlocutory appeals that have the effect of terminating the proceedings, such as appeals on decisions relating to detention and bail, protective measures, interference with the administration of justice, and decisions declaring a civil party application inadmissible may be appealed during proceedings.[214] The Trial Chamber does not have the authority to grant leave to appeal decisions falling outside of these issues. All decisions other than those listed above must be appealed at the same time as an appeal against the final judgment.

All of the parties filed appeals against the final judgment in Case 001. The defense appealed against the conviction, arguing that the Court had no personal jurisdiction over Duch due to the fact that he was not a senior leader of the Khmer Rouge or someone who could be held most responsible for the crimes that occurred.[215] In his appeal Duch echoed the request made at closing arguments and asked for immediate release.[216] The co-prosecutors filed an appeal against the sentence, calling it "plainly unjust" and "manifestly inadequate."[217] And, finally, unable to appeal the sentence, once the prosecution filed its notice of appeal,[218] the civil parties had two appealable issues they could raise. The first dealt with the revocation of civil party status determinations and the second dealt with the order for reparations.[219] Of the four civil party

213 ECCC, Internal Rules, Rule 104(1).

214 *Ibid.*, Rule 104.

215 See *Case of Kaing Guek Eav (Case 001)*, Appeal Brief by the Co-Lawyers for Kaing Guek Eav alias "Duch" against the Trial Chamber Judgment of 26 July 2010, Supreme Court Chamber, 18 November 2010.

216 *Ibid.* at par. 101.

217 *Case of Kaing Guek Eav (Case 001)*, Co-Prosecutors' Appeal against the Judgment of the Trial Chamber in the Case of Kaing Guek Eav alias "Duch", Supreme Court Chamber, 13 October 2010, para. 5 and 8.

218 ECCC, Internal Rules, Rule 105(1)(d) (sic) (Rev. 3); Rule 105(1)(c) (Rev. 6).

219 Though the Internal Rules were entirely unclear about the procedures to follow for appeals concerning civil party status determinations handed down in the final judgment, the Supreme Court Chamber decided that appeals against both issues would be considered as appeals against the judgment; see *Case of Kaing Guek Eav (Case 001)*, Decision on Characterization of Group 1 – Civil Party Co-Lawyers'

legal teams, Groups 1, 2 and 3 filed appeals, with one of the lawyers from Group 4 joining the Group 2 filing. Group 1 only filed an appeal against the revocation of civil party status from its clients.[220] Group 2 filed appeals against the rejection of civil party status from its clients and against the judgment on reparations.[221] Finally, Group 3 filed an appeal against the rejection of civil party status of its clients and against the order on reparations.[222] The appeals decision is expected at the end of March 2011.

6.5 Procedural Issues Arising Out of Participation

Undeniably victims participating in ECCC proceedings are taking full advantage of their procedural rights, and there are certain benefits arising from the participation of victims. One of the most notable contributions from civil parties came in Case 002. It was the facts found in complainant and civil party application forms that prompted the Co-Investigating Judges to request a Supplementary Submission from the co-prosecutors on the topic of forced marriage so that they could open investigations into these alleged crimes.[223] Notwithstanding this noteworthy instance, the participation of victims before the ECCC has not been without its challenges.

One major challenge posed by civil party participation has been the frequent criticism that their participation prolonged proceedings even more than necessary.[224] Similar to the requirements at other international and hybrid courts, ECCC proceedings are to be conducted in an expeditious manner. Internal Rule 79(7) refers to the Chamber facilitating the "fair and expeditious conduct of the proceedings," reflecting the right of the accused to be tried without delay.[225] Given the narrow factual allegations in Case 001 and the fact that Duch appeared to admit his guilt to the charges and sought forgiveness, it seemed remarkable that trial proceedings would last approximately ten months. However, it should be noted that although Duch admitted to his role in the crimes charged he contested his individual responsibility on the basis that he operated within a strict command structure and that failure to follow orders would

---

Immediate Appeal of Civil Party Status Determinations in the Trial Judgment, Supreme Court Chamber, 30 September 2010.

220 See *Case of Kaing Guek Eav (Case 001)*, Group 1 – Civil Parties' Co-Lawyers' Immediate Appeal of Civil Party Status Determinations from the Final Judgment, Supreme Court Chamber, 14 September 2010.

221 See *Case of Kaing Guek Eav (Case 001)*, Appeal against Rejection of Civil Party Applicants in the Judgment (Civil Party Group 2), Supreme Court Chamber, 22 October 2010; Appeal against Judgment on Reparations (Civil Party Group 2), Supreme Court Chamber, 2 November 2010.

222 See *Case of Kaing Guek Eav (Case 001)*, Appeal of the Co-Lawyers for the Group 3 Civil Parties against the Judgment of 26 July 2010, Supreme Court Chamber, 5 October 2010.

223 *Case 002*, Decision on Appeal of Co-Lawyers for Civil Parties against Order Rejecting Request to Interview Persons Named in the Forced Marriage and Enforced Disappearance Requests for Investigative Action, Pre-Trial Chamber, 21 July 2010, para. 1-2.

224 See, e.g., MacDonald, L., Chamber and Parties Seek an Expeditious Trial, But at What Cost? *Cambodia Tribunal Monitor*, 23 June 2009.

225 ECCC Law, Art. 35(c).

have resulted in his death. Moreover, since there is no mechanism for pleading guilty a full trial is required. Delays, however, certainly occurred and the participation of civil parties added to the delays.[226] A second major problem posed by participation was the fact that the defense, time and again, argued that the participation of civil parties infringed upon the rights of the accused. The defense argued that the civil parties improperly acted as second prosecutors and unjustly burdened the defense because they were required to face multiple accusers.

6.5.1 Disclosure Issues

Unlike at the *Ad Hoc* Tribunals, the SCSL, and the ICC, where disclosure between the defense and prosecution remains an ongoing issue,[227] the ECCC's dossier or case file system dictates that all materials pertinent to the trial are made available to all the parties, including civil parties. It is up to each legal team to comb through the numerous documents on the case file to prepare their cases. Because of the Court's recourse to the case file system very few, if any, arguments over access to information arose in the *Duch* trial. To be sure, the case file system seemed to aid in the efficient operation of proceedings. However, it could be envisioned that the defense may be placed at a great disadvantage with the case file system if the civil party lawyers coordinated their work. For example, a defense team, including consultants and case managers, has approximately four or five members whereas there are over thirty lawyers listed as civil party lawyers in Case 002. Such an imbalance is certainly a cause for concern from the defense perspective.

6.5.2 Evidentiary Issues

The Internal Rules vest the Trial Chamber with wide discretion to shape the proceedings by hearing the civil parties, witnesses and experts in the order it considers most useful.[228] As a result the Trial Chamber in the *Duch* trial adopted a unique approach. Rather than hearing evidence within a framework of the 'prosecution case' and the 'defense case', the Trial Chamber decided that it would hear evidence 'topic-by-topic'.[229] In its decision on the conduct of proceedings the judges listed seven topics, organized chronologically. Thus, the Chamber first heard evidence on 'Issues relating to M-13', followed by broadly labeled topics, including 'Armed conflict', 'Establishment of S-21 and the Takmao prison', and 'Functioning of S-21 including Choeng

226 Delays occurred due to the additional filings and oral interventions, debates about the proper scope of participation and the repetitive questioning on the part of civil parties.

227 Higgins (2007) at 395.

228 ECCC, Internal Rules, Rule 91(1).

229 See *Case of Kaing Guek Eav (Case 001)*, Direction on the Scheduling of the Trial, Trial Chamber, 20 March 2009.

Ek.'[230] With each topic the Chamber would hear evidence from witnesses and the accused. As with most civil law-based systems, the Internal Rules lay down very few rules of evidence. Internal Rule 87(1) provides, in part, that unless provided otherwise, all evidence is admissible and Rule 87(4) allows the Trial Chamber to admit "any new evidence which it deems conducive to ascertaining the truth." There is no requirement that the evidence be both relevant and probative.[231] In Case 001, the Court heard evidence from 13 witnesses and 22 civil parties.

6.5.2.1 Witnesses, Civil Parties and Dual Status

In the *Duch* trial, a handful of direct victims who potentially could have provided sworn testimony on the guilt of the accused opted instead to participate as civil parties. As civil parties they testified without taking an oath, were able to attend all proceedings and could claim reparations. Two direct victims testified as witnesses. One of these individuals sought to participate as a civil party but filed his application too late. The other individual chose to be a witness.

In theory, since civil party testimony is not given under oath it should therefore carry less weight than evidence given under oath since unsworn evidence is considered less persuasive than sworn testimony. In addition, when determining the weight to be given to evidence, the Judges should take into account the fact that civil parties, unlike witnesses, are able to attend all closed and public hearings before they address the Court, which could impact the information they provide. In practice, the Judges treated civil party testimony, especially testimony by direct victims, as witness testimony. The judges and parties frequently referred to civil parties as witnesses and there was no indication in its final judgment that the Court gave less weight to unsworn testimony on the part of the accused or civil parties.[232] Moreover, individuals testifying acknowledged that they based some of their knowledge of facts on previous testimony heard before the Court.[233] Tailoring one's story to fit with what one has previously heard at Court is a real concern, and one that may detract from the credibility of any such statements given. Although the Court has provisions in the Rules for preventing witnesses from viewing proceedings prior to giving testimony, no such provision applies to civil parties given that they have the right to be present at all proceedings. Civil parties are therefore in a position where they may, knowingly or unknowingly, bolster their testimony with facts previously unknown to them but learned from trial.

---

230 *Case of Kaing Guek Eav (Case 001)*, T, 22 April 2009, p. 69.

231 *Case of Ieng Thirith*, Co-Prosecutors' Response to Ieng Thirith's Defense Request for Exclusion of Evidence Obtained by Torture dated 11 February 2009, Co-Investigating Judges, 30 April 2009, para. 15-16.

232 See, e.g., *Case of Kaing Guek Eav (Case 001)*, T, 1 July 2009, pp. 9, 73.

233 See e.g., *Case of Kaing Guek Eav (Case 001)*, T, 21 July 2009, p. 40: "Q. How could you recall the name of the female medic Nam Mon? A. The name Nam Mon, the female medic, I recalled her name when she came to testify in this Chamber."

6.5.2.2 Familiarization and Proofing

Witness proofing, or the preparation of witnesses by parties for testimony at trial, has been a controversial issue at other international courts.[234] The dispute over proofing arises, in part, because witness proofing is a regular occurrence in some common law countries whereas it is prohibited in almost all civil law countries. In place of proofing, international courts have adopted witness familiarization whereby court personnel familiarize all witnesses with court procedure and protocol in order to prepare them for their testimony. Familiarization entails walking the witness through the layout of the court, the sequence of events that is likely to occur and duties of the participants. At the ECCC, which follows a markedly civil law procedural framework and where witnesses are seen as witnesses called by the Court and not by parties, the parties were not permitted to proof witnesses. Instead, WESU was responsible for familiarizing witnesses with proceedings and preparing them for their testimony. However, when civil parties appeared before the Court the Judges expected their lawyers to have fully prepped them for their testimony. In one situation when a civil party was confused about questions posed, the judges chastised the civil party lawyer for failing to properly prepare his client.[235] In another instance a Judge specifically stated that she expected better preparation of civil parties in the future.[236] Therefore, it appears that civil parties lawyers are not only free to proof their clients before they testify in Court but are actually required to do so.

6.5.2.3 Proposing Witnesses

Civil parties may request and propose witnesses both during the pre-trial and trial stages. For example, in situations where the Co-Investigating Judges consult an expert to aid in the investigation, a civil party has the right to request that additional experts be consulted if the first expert opinion was unfavorable.[237] At trial, like the prosecution and defense, civil parties may propose witnesses to the Court.[238] The right to propose witnesses who might highlight issues that are of particular concern to victims is significant.

There is a danger, however, that the proposed witnesses may not fit with the prosecution's case and could cause some confusion in cases that are dealing with complex crimes. It is therefore up to the Court to decide upon any proposed witnesses as it is the Court that calls witnesses and not the parties. Case 001 illustrated how the Court was not willing to entertain even the most basic of witnesses proposed by civil parties. Of the numerous witnesses proposed by the civil parties, the Court was willing

---

234 See Jordash (2009); Karemaker, et al. (2008).
235 *Case of Kaing Guek Eav (Case 001)*, T, 6 July 2009, pp. 55-56; 9 July 2009, pp. 50-51.
236 *Case of Kaing Guek Eav (Case 001)*, T, 6 July 2009, p. 56.
237 ECCC, Internal Rules, Rule 74(e) and 31(10).
238 *Ibid.*, Rule 80(2).

to call two, both of whom would testify about trauma. Eventually, only one of these expert-witnesses testified. Indeed, the Court rejected requests to call expert-witnesses on reparation options or sentencing. Nevertheless, the expert who testified about the psychological trauma suffered by victims explained that the vast majority of the Cambodian population suffers from psychological trauma resulting from the period of Khmer Rouge rule. He noted that his research suggests that 40 percent of Cambodian adults live with post-traumatic stress disorder and that their trauma is often transferred to the younger generations.[239] The expert testified that several factors could help alleviate the trauma suffered by victims, including better medical and psychiatric services, a sincere apology on the part of the accused, and the establishment of truth and holding the accused responsible.[240] He testified that truth and justice must be established before victims will be ready to forgive.[241] All of his testimony was centered on the victims and much of his testimony was referred to in the final judgment.

6.5.2.4 Questioning of Witnesses and Accused

It is with the questioning of witnesses and accused where the civil parties made a significant impact on proceedings. Their participation in this regard brought real emotion into the courtroom, personalizing the horrible crimes that took place. However, the questioning of witnesses and accused by civil parties also raised a number of concerns. First, there were constant problems with repetitive and irrelevant questions, prompting the imposition of time limits. Second, there were initiatives by the defense to limit the parameters of civil party questioning over fears that they were becoming second prosecutors. Finally, at times, the questioning by civil party lawyers undermined strategies of the prosecution. Though less of a concern in the Duch trial due to his cooperation with the Court, this could have a far more negative consequence in other cases.

In the *Duch* trial, the four civil party legal teams each had their own strategies in court. One group usually questioned witnesses in an attempt to show that Duch had discretion when making the choices he made;[242] other groups generally asked questions to highlight the suffering of the victims. At times, the questioning could become very emotional, particularly when the civil parties were searching for answers to specific questions about loved ones. One civil party lawyer's questions to a former guard proceeded as follows:

> Q. Today, here in the courtroom, could you tell today Mr. Bou Meng [one of her civil party clients] what happened to his wife; where she was killed and where she is buried?

239 *Case of Kaing Guek Eav (Case 001)*, T, 25 August 2009, p. 17.
240 *Ibid.* at 25.
241 *Ibid.* at 31.
242 *Case of Kaing Guek Eav (Case 001)*, T, 20 July 2009, pp. 27-33.

> A. When the detainees were taken away to be killed, of course, they were executed at Choeung Ek.
> Q. I asked not in general. I ask – I've asked you to tell Mr. Bou Meng, who is sitting here in the courtroom -- maybe you might, if you have a look and turn your head left, you will see him and to respond to him where -- about the fate of his wife and not a general answer that people were killed in Choeung Ek. That is well-known and also Mr. Bou Meng knows this.
> A. I don't actually know who is who or who was the wife of who because, normally, if a person was -- after being interrogated then he would or she would be taken away to be executed, and I only can confirm that the wives of those detainees were executed at Choeung Ek.
> Q. Mr. Him Huy, you told the Chamber already that you checked the lists at Choeung Ek; that means that you went through the name lists of prisoners to check if everybody who should be sent to Choeung Ek is present for to be killed. I would like to tell you the name of Mr. Bou Meng's wife; maybe that is helpful. This is Mrs. Ma Yoeun alias Thy. Could you now respond to my question?[243]

Given the fact that thousands of individuals were killed at S-21 and that thirty years have passed since the crimes occurred, it is questionable whether the civil party lawyer actually expected an answer for her client or whether she was simply trying to make the proceedings more dramatic. Regardless of her intentions, she succeeded in making the proceedings more emotional, which may make for interesting viewing but it does not necessarily aid the judges in determining the guilt of the accused.

Without a doubt, the civil parties noticeably asked questions off topic.[244] Time and again the Court had to remind them to ask relevant questions.[245] Moreover, even when asking relevant questions, questioning could drag on and on. One reason for the slower pace of trial undoubtedly had to do with the fact that each witness was first questioned by the five judges, followed by the co-prosecutors, four civil party legal teams and finally the defense. In addition, the Judges allowed Duch to comment upon a witness' testimony prior to questioning by the defense. It is no surprise, then, that repetitive questions became a big issue with so many lawyers in the courtroom, but with four legal teams comprised of up to two lawyers each, repetitive questions posed by civil parties were particularly concerning.

In response to concerns over the slow pace of the proceedings (and therefore the rights of the accused to an expeditious trial), the Chamber imposed a system of time limits within which the parties were allowed to question witnesses and the accused. Under the new time limits, the defense was generally allotted time equal to that given to the civil parties (combined) and the prosecution was allotted a time slightly less than that allotted to the defense and civil parties despite the fact that they carry the burden

243 *Ibid.* at 38-39.
244 *Case of Kaing Guek Eav (Case 001)*, T, 10 June 2009, p. 49.
245 *Case of Kaing Guek Eav (Case 001)*, T, 29 June 2009, pp. 88-90.

of proving the crimes charged.[246] At other times, the defense would be allotted time which was slightly more than that given to both the prosecution and civil parties but never equaling the combined total. For instance, when questioning the accused on the topic of the functioning of S-21, the co-prosecutors were given three hours, the defense were allocated four hours and the civil party legal teams were each given 45 minutes.[247] This meant that the three hours given to civil parties together with the three hours of the prosecution amounted to six hours in total. The inequality quickly adds up. The defense continuously objected to this allocation based on the argument that the defense should be given time equal to that of all its opponents.[248] They argued that the imbalance amounted to a violation of the rights of the accused and allowed the civil parties to act as a "super-prosecution."[249]

The Chamber did not agree. It acknowledged the objections of the defense and the need to preserve an equality of arms but nonetheless held fast to its time limit allocations.[250] The judges took note of the fact that the defense had never requested additional time but on a case-by-case basis would consider a request if posed in the future.[251] In fact, the judges vigorously enforced their time limits when it came to questioning witnesses. They would cut short the parties as soon as their designated time limit was reached.[252] Civil party lawyers often sought ways to extend the time allotted to them for questioning witnesses. One civil party lawyer proposed that they could submit unasked questions to the judges to pose themselves but this request was rejected.[253] In fact, only after long debates by the bench did the judges grant any extension of time limits.[254] Overall, requests for an extension of the time limits were regularly denied.[255]

Although the speed of the trial noticeably increased,[256] the strict adherence to the time limits affected the trial substantively. This is because without regard to whether

246 Thus, for full-day witnesses, the prosecution was generally allotted 30 to 45 minutes and the civil parties and defense allotted 40 to 60 minutes; for two-day witnesses, 60 minutes were given to the prosecution, 80 minutes to the civil parties and 80 minutes to the defense. For half-day witnesses, 15 minutes were allotted to the prosecution, 20 minutes to the civil parties and 20 minutes to the defense. See *Case of Kaing Guek Eav (Case 001)*, T, 29 June 2009.

247 *Case of Kaing Guek Eav (Case 001)*, T, 16 June 2009, pp. 2-3.

248 *Ibid.* at 8: "I don't think I can understand that if the Co-Prosecutors and the civil parties have six hours to question, in turn, the accused, why then the defence would have only four hours, that is to say, slightly more than half of the overall time allotted to the Co-Prosecutors and civil parties. The defence should at the very least, and by way of principle, have the same speaking time as all its opponents together." See also, *Case of Kaing Guek Eav (Case 001)*, T, 9 July 2009, p. 3.

249 *Case of Kaing Guek Eav (Case 001)*, T, 16 June 2009, p. 11.

250 *Case of Kaing Guek Eav (Case 001)*, T, 27 July 2009, p. 32.

251 *Ibid.* at 33.

252 See, e.g., *Case of Kaing Guek Eav (Case 001)*, T, 22 July 2009, p. 45.

253 *Ibid.* at 106-109; *Case of Kaing Guek Eav (Case 001)*, T 27 July 2009, p. 29.

254 *Case of Kaing Guek Eav (Case 001)*, T, 22 June 2009, pp. 75-78.

255 *Case of Kaing Guek Eav (Case 001)*, T, 1 July 2009, pp. 86, 87

256 Gibson and Rudy (2009) at 1020.

a party was pursuing a relevant line of questioning that could assist the Court, the Judges would end the questioning, losing the opportunity to hear potentially relevant evidence in the case. In addition, it did not seem as though the Court took into account the fact that many of the witnesses were direct victims or former guards who would often require time to compose themselves after recounting traumatic experiences. Providing a civil party legal team with 10 minutes to question a victim-witness, coupled together with serious interpretation issues, meant that lawyers for civil parties were often unable to fully examine witnesses. Moreover, the strict time-limit approach did little to stop repetitive questioning between the prosecution and civil parties as well as amongst the civil parties. Due to the fact that the civil party legal teams had different court strategies they rarely used their allotted time as a consolidated group. Instead, each team took their allocated time to pose their own questions, which were often very similar. Finally, even though the defense may not have ran over time with their questioning the precedent set by the Court of giving the defense less time than that equal to the prosecution and civil parties combined is potentially dangerous. The Court could have easily provided this time to the defense, not least for the perception of fairness. It matters little whether the defense would not use all of its allotted time.

Another issue the defense encountered with regard to civil party questioning of witnesses had to do with the parameters of their participation. In an attempt to restrict their line of questioning the defense argued that civil parties should not be permitted to question Duch or other witnesses on topics that do not directly relate to their clients' harm. For instance, when one of the civil party lawyers was questioning Duch on medical experiments he sabotaged the defense objected to this line of questioning, arguing that none of the civil parties were directly affected by the issue since none of the civil parties were injured or harmed in the situation under examination.[257] He insisted that questions about this topic should be asked by the prosecution and that the civil parties should not take over the role of the prosecution but should focus instead on relating to the court the harm they have suffered when relevant. The defense argued that the role of civil parties should be "completely distinct" from that of the prosecution.[258] Three separate civil party lawyers fired back, arguing that the Internal Rules place no restrictions on their line of questioning and that there are no limits on the topics they are permitted to touch upon. Although the Chamber allowed the civil parties to ask their questions, which they determined supported the prosecution,[259] perhaps unsurprisingly, two months later they would greatly restrict the rights of civil parties to post questions relating to sentencing.

Though they were prohibited from questioning expert witnesses on sentencing and the character of the accused, civil party lawyers did have the opportunity of questioning a number of other expert witnesses. Importantly they were able to contest asser-

257 *Case of Kaing Guek Eav (Case 001)*, T, 22 June 2009, p. 91.
258 *Ibid.* at 94.
259 *Ibid.* at 98.

tions by one expert that Duch could be considered as both a victim and a perpetrator given the high levels of fear within Khmer Rouge ranks.[260] They were also able to contest the assertion that S-21 was not unique within Cambodia at the time and that other prisons were far worse in terms of the number of deaths.[261] Notwithstanding the benefits to civil parties of being able to pose questions, their questioning added little to that already broached by the co-prosecutors.

Finally, despite the fact that there were a handful of times when civil party questioning reinforced the prosecution's case against the accused the opposite was also true. In one instance, a civil party lawyer questioning a victim-witness argued that his testimony contradicted previous statements on record with the Court, thereby pointing out potentially inconsistent statements on the part of the victim-witness.[262] It is unclear why the civil party lawyer did so, but it definitely seemed a strange tactic. On another occasion, another civil party lawyer may have undermined the prosecution's efforts when she decided to use the time she had been allotted to question a witness to instead pose questions to the accused.[263] During her questioning of Duch he pointed out fabrications in the witness' testimony.[264] And later under examination by the defense, the witness admitted that some of the details in his testimony did in fact come to him after watching previous witnesses testify on television.[265] On yet another occasion, during the questioning of a former guard, a civil party legal team established that this guard, like Duch, worked under extreme pressure and fearful conditions.[266] The defense was without a doubt pleased by these mishaps.

6.5.2.5 Civil Party Testimony

In addition to witness testimony the Trial Chamber in Case 001 heard testimony from 22 civil parties.[267] Those who testified were direct victims of S-21 as well as wives, husbands, brothers, sisters, children, cousins and family-in-law of direct victims. Their accounts were tragic and compelling, and were a reminder about the harm suffered by all victims.

The Court first heard testimony from direct victims and later in trial from indirect victims. In attendance every day, Chum Mey was one of the few survivors from S-21 participating and the first civil party to address the court. His testimony was emotional and even angry at times. In response to a question from the defense, Chum Mey confirmed that it made him happy to hear Duch's apology and see him shed tears at

---

260 *Case of Kaing Guek Eav (Case 001)*, T, 14 September 2009, pp. 105-118.
261 *Ibid.* at 105-118.
262 *Case of Kaing Guek Eav (Case 001)*, T, 29 June 2009, p. 93-94.
263 Jackson, C., Challenges to Witness' Credibility Continue, *Cambodia Tribunal Monitor*, 22 July 2009.
264 *Case of Kaing Guek Eav (Case 001)*, T, 22 July 2009, pp. 34, 37-39.
265 *Ibid.* at 71.
266 *Case of Kaing Guek Eav (Case 001)*, T, 28 July 2009, p. 57.
267 One civil party even testified via video conference from France, see *Case of Kaing Guek Eav (Case 001)*, T, 20 August 2009, p. 55.

an S-21 re-enactment in 2008 because he had waited thirty years for it. However, he said that a few tear-drops could not wash away the suffering of millions who died. He said, "Only the court can help to wash away the suffering."[268] Throughout his testimony Chum Mey broke down several times. Each time, the court instructed him to "compose himself."[269] The Court's lack of perceived compassion would later draw criticism but the Judges soon improved their approach towards civil party testimony. During another victim's particularly emotional testimony, the President, while continuing to remind the civil party to console himself, did so in a more sympathetic manner. He kindly reminded the civil party that he had waited for this opportunity to speak for so long and that this was the only chance he had to tell his story in court.[270] He also stated that if he was too emotional he might forget details.

Procedure allowed Duch to respond to civil party testimony after the judges, prosecution and civil party lawyers had questioned the civil party but before the defense began its questioning. The Chamber also allowed the civil party to put questions to Duch through the president of the chamber.[271] When the one direct victim testified the Court allowed an exchange to take place that was one of the more memorable moments of trial. Bou Meng first detailed the horrors he suffered at S-21 after which the Chamber allowed Bou Meng to ask Duch (through the judges) a question which illustrates the flexibility and uniqueness of the proceedings. In a very powerful exchange Bou Meng stated, "I would like to ask him where did he smash my wife.[272] He said that he just wanted to be able to pick up some soil so he could finally put his wife to rest. Duch stood to provide his response, stating that he was especially moved by Bou Meng's testimony but that he was not able to provide an answer to his question. He stated that he presumed she was killed at Choeung Ek where many prisoners had been taken to be killed. He then expressed his "highest respect and regards toward the soul of [Bou Meng's] wife."[273] Following their exchange Bou Meng broke down in tears. On another occasion, another civil party posed the following questions to Duch:

> Who made the decision to kill my father on the 6th of July 1977 or a little bit after that? At S-21, the prisoners were not allowed to die naturally, especially in the case of my father.

268 *Case of Kaing Guek Eav (Case 001)*, T, 30 June 2009, p. 87.

269 *Case of Kaing Guek Eav (Case 001)*, T, 1 July 2009, p. 17, 19.

270 *Ibid.* at 14.

271 See, e.g., *Case of Kaing Guek Eav (Case 001)*, T, 1 July 2009, testimony of Bou Meng; T, 13 July 2009, testimony of Nam Mon.

272 *Case of Kaing Guek Eav (Case 001)*, T, 1 July 2009, p. 90.

273 The Court had to remind the accused to control his emotions and to listen to the testimony of the survivors, see *Ibid.* at 92.

> What types of tortures were inflicted upon my father; the person who had a progressive idea, who based the judgment on justice and who had dignity and who held the ideology of democracy with his contradicting to the policy of the Khmer Rouge?
>
> Who made a decision to transfer him to S-21? It was said that S-21 came to take him from Psa Daem Thkov. That is the statement of Chanphal Norng (phonetic) and Ham Ham Keng (phonetic) that he was taken from Psa Daem Thkov at that time.[274]

The accused was unable to address directly any of these questions but stressed that like the civil parties, he too sought the truth.[275]

In mid-August 2009 the civil parties who were not direct victims were permitted to address the court in order to share their stories of harm suffered. They told stories of their despair over the loss of their loved ones and of having to rebuild their lives and families. They told of their families' pain and anger, of the reverberations of the tragic events that occurred at S-21 and of the resulting psychological problems that followed. One individual who addressed the Court was two years old when her father died. She described her experiences of growing up in France without a father and that the images of S-21 continue to haunt her.

Given that it was the first time most of the civil parties had testified in Court and the events over which they were speaking took place three decades prior, many civil parties had trouble understanding questions and recalling events.[276] Consequently, some of their statements contradicted those they made previously.[277] The testimony of Nam Mon reflects the difficulties of the process. Nam Mon testified that she personally saw Duch beat two of her uncles to death, despite no other evidence presented at trial that Duch had personally killed anyone.[278] Moreover, she previously testified that she had never seen anyone beaten or killed at S-21. She testified to children being bayoneted to death but had never mentioned this detail in her civil party application or in earlier testimony.[279] Her government-issued identification card stated she was almost ten years younger than she claimed to be.[280] Her civil party application referred to one of her siblings as a cousin.[281] One photo attached to her application was labeled sibling but was actually her father,[282] and she referred to her god-brother as a brother,[283] creating a great deal of confusion. Her justification for this confusion was that she was

274 *Case of Kaing Guek Eav (Case 001)*, T, 19 August 2009, pp. 60-63.
275 *Ibid.* at 60-63.
276 See e.g., *Case of Kaing Guek Eav (Case 001)*, T, 6 July 2009, testimony of Ly Hor, T, 7-8 July 2009, testimony of Phaok Khan; T, 1 July 2009, pp. 12, 24, 28, 29, 42, 56, 67 and 97.
277 *Case of Kaing Guek Eav (Case 001)*, T, 8 July 2009, pp. 35-36.
278 *Case of Kaing Guek Eav (Case 001)*, T, 13 July 2009, pp. 31-32.
279 *Ibid.* at 75.
280 *Ibid.* at 2.
281 *Ibid.* at 19.
282 *Ibid.* at 20.
283 *Ibid.* at 23.

scared at the time she filled out the application.[284] Needless to say, a good deal of time was spent on trying to get the facts straight, though they were never clearly resolved.

Very often the civil parties strayed from the relevant facts when giving testimony, meaning that they did not testify about their injuries suffered or their family links. Time and again the court had to remind them to refocus their testimony.[285] For instance, one civil party began his testimony by describing in detail his forced evacuation from Phnom Penh when the Khmer Rouge first arrived in the city. The defense objected several minutes into his testimony arguing that these events were outside the scope of the present case.[286]

Civil parties used their time to inform the Court that they did not believe in Duch's remorse.[287] Others simply stated that there would be no forgiveness for Duch.[288] Although the civil parties and their lawyers often asserted that they do not seek vengeance or revenge,[289] this did not necessarily mean that they are ready to forgive Duch for his actions.[290] Despite being barred from speaking about sentencing, a number of the civil parties requested the court to impose the maximum sentence.[291]

Often the civil parties would run over their allotted time. However, "[t]he judges as well as the attorneys [were] cognizant of the fact that a major purpose of civil party participation in these proceedings is to help them deal with their tragic losses."[292] Accordingly, the judges often allowed civil party testimony to run longer than the time allotted.[293] And although some civil parties had the opportunity to tell their stories in narrative form most were continuously interrupted by the Chamber to answer questions, ranging from the broad to the very specific.[294] Nevertheless, one commentator wrote, "After listening to the accounts of unbearable suffering that the witnesses have dealt with as a result of the deaths of their family members, it is impossible not to feel sympathy for them, and hope that this process provides them with at least some sense that justice is being achieved."[295]

A number of times the defense took issue with civil party testimony. In one instance when a civil party openly criticized Duch's conversion to Catholicism the

284 *Ibid.* at 43.

285 *Case of Kaing Guek Eav (Case 001)*, T, 20 August 2009, pp. 26-29; T, 24 August 2009, p. 97.

286 *Case of Kaing Guek Eav (Case 001)*, T, 24 August 2009, p. 97.

287 *Case of Kaing Guek Eav (Case 001)*, T, 20 August 2009, p. 29.

288 *Ibid.* at 63, 76.

289 See, e.g., *Case of Kaing Guek Eav (Case 001)*, T, 23 November 2009, pp. 5, 55; Cf. Mahon (2009) at 738-739, noting that in interviews with civil parties a number of them expressed feelings of hatred and a desire for violent revenge but that this is not what the ECCC "wished to hear."

290 See, e.g., *Case of Kaing Guek Eav (Case 001)*, T, 18 August 2009, p. 34.

291 See, e.g., *Case of Kaing Guek Eav (Case 001)*, T, 17 August 2009, pp. 31, 67.

292 Saliba, M., Civil Parties Boycott Start of Character Witness Testimony while Experts Offer Psychological Assessment of Duch, *Cambodia Tribunal Monitor*, 31 August 2009.

293 *Ibid.*

294 *Case of Kaing Guek Eav (Case 001)*, T, 1 July 2009, pp. 22-24.

295 Saliba, M., Civil Parties Boycott Start of Character Witness Testimony while Experts Offer Psychological Assessment of Duch, *Cambodia Tribunal Monitor*, 31 August 2009.

defense had to interrupt in order to ask the Judges to remind the civil party to speak only about the facts related to his case and not to disparage the accused.[296] On other occasions the defense questioned whether or not specific civil parties had standing before the Court. Duch refuted the testimony of at least five alleged direct victims of S-21, acknowledging their suffering but asserting that no evidence existed that their suffering occurred at S-21 and not another prison.[297] Even the Court seemed skeptical of some of the testimony provided by these individuals. On another occasion, before one civil party testified about the loss of her brother-in-law the defense argued that it was questionable whether the civil party's brother-in-law was in fact detained at S-21.[298] The President, however, decided to hear the testimony and that the Court would later decide on the veracity of the statements made, stating that after she gives her statement the judges can then conclude "whether the statement is genuinely true or not."[299] Ultimately this civil party had her civil party status revoked for failing to support her claim.[300]

Certainly there were times when the questioning of civil parties by the defense became aggressive, prompting the civil party lawyer to ask the judges to remind the defense to be more respectful.[301] In this regard, the civil party lawyers played an important role in protecting their client's interests in trial. Many times it was the civil party lawyers requesting breaks so that their clients could compose themselves or reminding the Court to treat the civil parties with compassion. On one occasion a civil party lawyer interceded on behalf of her client when the Chamber requested the civil party to remove his shirt in public session to show his scars.[302] After a short break, the President decided this was not the best course of action and requested photographs to be taken instead.

The common element from the testimony of the civil parties was that they sought, through the judicial process, broad notions of truth and justice. They desperately wanted answers to help explain how and why their loved ones were killed, and they all emphasized that their harms suffered were ongoing. The emotional impact of their testimony cannot be denied.

6.6 Victim Assistance

The VSS or Victims Unit was belatedly created by the passage of the Internal Rules in June 2007, and formally established in January 2008. However, because of an initial

296 *Case of Kaing Guek Eav (Case 001)*, T, 20 August 2009, pp. 25-26.
297 These include Lay Chan, Ly Hor, Phork Khan, Nam Mon, and Norng Chan Phal (who was not a civil party but instead participated as a witness)
298 *Case of Kaing Guek Eav (Case 001)*, T, 18 August 2009, p. 74.
299 *Ibid.*
300 *Case of Kaing Guek Eav (Case 001)*, Judgment, Trial Chamber, 26 July 2010, par. 648
301 *Case of Kaing Guek Eav (Case 001)*, T, 13 July 2009, p. 62.
302 *Case of Kaing Guek Eav (Case 001)*, T, 1 July 2009, pp. 35-36.

lack of support, it only became fully operational in 2010. Originally intended to serve as an administrative section to process victim-complaints and civil party applications, it soon developed into a full-service unit determined to improve the position of victims at the Court. The VSS interpreted its mandate broadly and found that provisions in the Rules instructing it to "assist Victims" should incorporate everything from designing outreach programs to holding trainings for civil party lawyers to organizing the logistical assistance necessary to bring victims to the Court.[303] However, the lack of financial support for a strong VSS undoubtedly affected the participation of victims. The backlog of complaints was perhaps the most glaring problem. At one point, the average processing time of applications was over one year, substantively affecting the right of victims to participate in the investigative stage in Case 002.

For many reasons, the functioning of the VSS could not have occurred without the support of numerous civil society organizations. Though civil society groups welcomed the new amendments made to the Internal Rules in 2010 expanding the mandate of the VSS,[304] they are nevertheless fearful that adequate funding will not be made available due to the budgetary problems faced by the Court, leaving NGOs to step in and do work that should arguably be done by the Court. One of the most important partnerships the VSS has established with an outside organization is its relationship with the Transcultural Psychosocial Organisation (TPO), a local NGO. TPO works together with WESU and the VSS to provide a wide variety of psychological services. The services include on-site psychological support during the ECCC proceedings to intense psychological and psychiatric follow-up care and awareness-raising activities on mental health.

6.7 Legal Representation

As a basic rule, civil parties before the ECCC have the right to be represented by a lawyer of their choice. As with the defense, this allows victims to ensure that their individual views and concerns are well-represented. However, bearing in mind the context of trials for mass crimes, the Court has the option of grouping civil parties together under common legal representation so as to make civil party participation more manageable.[305] Victims may also group together under Victims Associations, whereby the association would serve as an umbrella organization for a large group of victims with common legal representation.[306]

In Case 001, no such association existed and the forced grouping of civil parties was not necessary as only 93 civil parties participated and each victim chose his or her legal team based on advice received from either the Victims Unit or a civil society

303 Bair (2008-2009) at 530.
304 Cambodian Human Rights Action Committee Press Release, New Directions for Victim Participation at the ECCC, 26 February 2010.
305 ECCC, Internal Rules, Rule 23*ter* (3) (Rev. 6).
306 *Ibid.*, Rule 23*quarter* (Rev. 6); Practice Direction on Victim Participation, Art. 5.9.

organization operating in Cambodia. In Case 002 an Association of Khmer Rouge Victims in Cambodia was recognized in June 2010 and now represents a large number of victims. The Association not only collectively represents its members before the Court it also monitors Court developments and lobbies for the rights of victims. Also, due to the large number of civil parties in Case 002 the Court has resorted to forced grouping. For instance, non-represented civil parties in Case 002 have been grouped by Co-Investigating Judges based on provincially-oriented representation.[307] The lawyers assigned to these individuals will remain until such time as the individuals sign new power-of-attorney forms with other legal representatives. Other victims have opted to group themselves so as to avoid the Court doing it for them. Some victims are grouped by geographic region whereas others have decided to form groups based on their ethnic community such as a group of Cham Muslims. There are even those who have grouped themselves based on a harm suffered. For instance, there is a group of war orphans. Thus far the Court has not had to intervene in these groupings.

Case 001 illustrated the difficulties of managing the representation of less than one hundred victims. Knowing that Case 002 would have thousands of civil party participants, the Judges revised the Internal Rules in order to help facilitate effective and efficient participation. As mentioned above, the revisions now provide that beginning at the trial stage civil parties will comprise a "single, consolidated group" whose interests will be represented at trial by lead co-lawyers.[308] The benefits of having two lead co-lawyers is that the representation in trial proceedings should be more focused with less repetition and undue delays because these lawyers will make all submissions and filings on behalf of all civil parties in the case. It will certainly be easier for the prosecution and defense to respond to the civil parties and easier for the Court to control. The drawbacks of this obligatory coordination are that it fails to account for the inevitable diverging views of victims and their right to have lawyers of their choosing represent their interests at trial. In Mahon's view "the ECCC's legal process regards victims as having a collective story, a unitary, bounded and unchanging narrative of trauma that reduces and incorporates all that is essential into the 'story of the victim.'"[309] Consequently, the Court is reluctant to tolerate victims who do not fit their preferred victim mold or who believe that his or her story is unique and deserving

307 See *Case 002*, Order on the Organization of Civil Party Representation under Rule 23ter of the Rules, Co-Investigating Judges, 2 August 2010.

308 ECCC Internal Rules, Rule 23(3) (Rev. 6). The civil party lead co-lawyers are described in Rule 12*ter* (Rev. 6).

309 Mahon (2009) at 739. After comparing the stories of two civil parties Mahon noted that "Each arrogates centrality for his/her individual pain and claim to victimhood. Each feels he/she suffered more than the others did. This is not a phenomenon peculiar to these victims, but a trait common to many other victims I interviewed as well. Each individual story, and claim to victimhood, is separate from the next. Interestingly, I found that even victims who have suffered a similar plight in the same site subscribe to very different values, and have very different identities, views and desires for vindication." Mahon (2009) at 762.

of special attention.[310] There is no question that victims will not always share the same views on how to approach their participation at trial. Whether the lead co-lawyers will be able to represent the diverging views of individual victims and their lawyers is still unknown. More likely, representation will focus on the collective interests of victims generally.

6.8 Legal Aid

The effective representation of civil parties necessitates the assistance of effective legal counsel. However, unlike charged persons or accused, victims in Case 001 and victims participating in the pre-trial stage of Case 002 did not have the same rights to representation. A charged person or accused will have his legal expenses paid for if he is unable to afford such representation himself.[311] He is entitled to a national lawyer, an international lawyer, a case manager and a legal consultant. In contrast, the ECCC has no formal legal aid system for civil parties in need of legal representation. Despite the vast amounts of funding for the Court,[312] the expense necessary for a legal aid scheme for victims was never envisioned. Given the fact that the vast majority of Cambodians live in poverty, the lack of financial assistance means that without the work of many of the civil party lawyers who either work on a voluntary basis or are funded by outside donors and civil society groups most victims would not be able to participate.[313]

Though efforts have recently been undertaken to ensure that all civil parties have access to legal representation even when they are unable to afford it, the responsibility still largely falls to civil society groups. In Case 001, for example, the international lawyers for Group 1 worked on a *pro bono* basis and the Cambodian lawyer was funded by the British Embassy. Group 2's international and national lawyers were funded by the German Development Corporation (DED) and Cambodian Defenders' Project (CDP). Group 3's lawyers were funded by Advocats Sans Frontiers (ASF) and Group 4's international lawyer was funded by the Paris Bar Association and its

310 *Ibid.* at 740.

311 ECCC, Internal Rules, Rule 22(1)(a) (Rev. 3), referencing defense specifically and Rule 22(1)(a) (Rev. 6), making no direct reference to defense and therefore also potentially applicable to others.

312 The revised budget of the ECCC from 2005-2011 for the national side is approximately 39,000,000 USD. ECCC, National Side of the Budget, Summary of Expenditures and Budget Proposal by Years, 2006-2011, *available at*: http://old.eccc.gov.kh/english/finances_expenditures.aspx, *last visited* 28 March 2011; The budget for the UN-administered side of the court for 2006-2010 was approximately 80,000,000 USD. UNAKRT Finances, *available at*: http://www.unakrt-online.org/09_Finances.htm, *last visited* 28 March 2011; Together the revised budgets far exceed the original expected costs of 57,000,000 USD (combined Cambodian and UN sides) for three years of trials. See also Skilbeck (2008) at 7.

313 *Case of Ieng Sary (Case 002)*, Joint Civil Parties' Co-Lawyers' Observations on Application for Reconsideration of Civil Party's Right to Address the Chamber, Pre-Trial Chamber, 17 July 2008, par. 15, arguing that it is unfair to require participation through legal counsel when such legal representation is not paid for by legal aid.

national lawyer by the CDP (which in turn relied on a grant from the DED). Without the financial support of these civil society groups and the ability of a handful of international lawyers to work *pro bono* victim participation would have been as ineffective as in East Timor. Undoubtedly the role played by civil society groups was invaluable, though not without controversy.

6.9 Civil Society Groups

At its inception, the Court, and the VSS in particular, lacked the capacity to offer any type of services to victims. As such, the VSS had minimal to no funding in order to educate Cambodians about Court operation and their ability to participate in the process. Indeed, very little resources were provided to even process applications. For this reason the VSS had to depend upon outside assistance. Accordingly, throughout the Court's operation, the VSS and the various victims' legal teams have closely collaborated with civil society organizations that long before the Court began operating had begun working with victims in Cambodia. The civil society groups most active in Cambodia include the Documentation Center of Cambodia (DC-Cam), which for decades had been collecting evidence and statements from victims, the Khmer Institute of Democracy, the Cambodia Defenders' Project, and multiple organizations falling under the umbrella of the Cambodia Human Rights Action Committee (CHRAC). All of these groups have encouraged the Cambodian population to support the Court and have carried out significant work related to the criminal process.

For instance, the VSS has worked together with civil society to bring international experts on victims' rights to train staff at the Court on issues of participation and reparations or hold conferences on the importance of participation. More significantly, these groups have helped to fund or support legal teams representing civil parties. The VSS has also had to depend upon civil society groups for a majority of their outreach activities. This includes informing Cambodian society about the Court and correcting any commonly held misconceptions about the judicial process. Inevitably it also includes the managing of expectations.

Reliance on civil society to carry out these tasks is useful in many ways. Because civil society has been operating in Cambodia far longer than the Court they have the trust of local populations and the logistical know-how to receive input from local communities and individual victims. Moreover, it removes a burden on the Court's already strained budget because civil society organizations foot the bill for the outreach, conferences, logistical operations, and general support of legal teams.

Reliance to such a high degree on civil society can, however, also cause some problems. First, it can unwittingly embroil the VSS into the politics of Cambodian civil society organizations, which are known to have their own distinct visions and approaches to handling victim outreach and support. There was no shortage of tensions between victims' legal teams and the civil society organizations backing them, each with their own agenda and territorial 'claims'. The VSS must walk a fine line between the major players and not be seen as favoring one group over another, which is easier said than done. Second, the VSS loses control over exactly what information is given out and to whom, making the business of managing expectations all the more difficult. Third, it allows the Court to become complacent with regard to funding for victims. If the Court knows that civil society will take up the slack there is no incentive for the Court to make funding for victims a priority. Finally, the work of the civil society groups may not be up to the standards required by judicial institutions, which can ultimately harm the case for victims. For instance, many initial statements of victims were taken by volunteers working for civil society organizations. These volunteers had little experience in taking statements to be used in Court and almost no experience in drafting documents for use in court. There was an obvious lack of detail in statements and civil party applications. Though the lawyers for civil parties would re-interview the victims, their original statements were included in the case file and often their in court statements contradicted their initial interviews.

6.10 Conclusion

Many of the hard fought-after goals of the victims' rights movement have been achieved at the ECCC. The court makes every effort to treat victims with dignity and respect, victims are notified and informed of developments at the Court, they receive victim support in terms of psychological care, protective measures are available if necessary, they may attend and participate in proceedings, their right to reparations is recognized (though very limited) and if they qualify for civil party status they may receive legal assistance throughout the criminal process (though not directly funded by the Court). With regard to their participation, civil party status at the ECCC allows victims to have access to the Court in order to support the prosecution and to claim reparations. Unlike at the courts discussed in Chapter 5, civil parties before the ECCC have fully exercised their participatory rights. They have retained lawyers to represent their interests, submitted investigation requests, confronted the accused during the investigation stage, proposed witnesses for trial, questioned witnesses at trial, questioned the accused at trial, addressed the Court directly or in writing, made oral and written submissions on law and fact, given closing arguments, requested reparations and submitted appeals on decisions and the final judgment.

The participation of civil parties can be categorized as everything from maintaining the *status quo* (non-participation on Arnstein's ladder) to tokenism to decision-making powers, such as having the ability to deicide which questions to pose in trial proceeding. Over the course of the operation of the Court, the Internal Rules have evolved and now require that Court authorities assist victims in providing information to the Court and provide them the opportunity to express themselves. Moreover, the lead co-lawyers are required to seek the views of civil party lawyers and consider and apply their preferences in trial proceedings; though the Judges themselves are not required to do so. Instead, the Judges are only required to balance the rights of all the parties. Therefore participation is still non-dispositive. Importantly, despite adopting the label *civil parties*, the participation of victims before the ECCC is markedly different both from Cambodia's domestic system as well as other international criminal courts. Their participation was far more limited than that of civil parties participating elsewhere.

Nevertheless, the active participation of victims as civil parties in the proceedings has certainly been a hallmark of the Court, though there has been a steep learning curve for the Court as well as for all parties. In many ways the participation of victims has proven to be more symbolic than substantive. On the one hand, victims have succeeded in pushing for the inclusion of specific gender-related crimes such as rape and forced marriage in Case 002. And the participation of victims has engaged the wider Cambodian community, particularly in the provinces. On the other hand, the final judgment from the *Duch* trial illustrates how the participation of victims essentially resulted in no substantial benefits to the civil parties themselves. Only a limited number were permitted to address the Court in person and of these some later had their civil party status revoked. The civil parties were unhappy with the sentence imposed on the accused and could make no official comment on punishment. They were equally dissatisfied with the reparations ordered by the Trial Chamber, which rejected almost all of their requests. Chum Mey, a direct victim of S-21, summed up the views of many victims following the final judgment when he stated, "We are victims two times, once in the Khmer Rouge time and now once again."[314] According to one commentator their participation achieved no more than those victims who testified as witnesses.[315] Thus, despite the hugely significant symbolic benefits of participation, which itself has not been proven, its practical benefits are questionable. Moreover, the inability of the civil party lawyers to cooperate and the repetitive questioning at trial further added to frustrations with the participation scheme at the Court. In addition, the most serious concern about participation had to do with the impairment of the fair trial rights of the accused, most notably by making the accused face a multiplicity of opponents.[316]

Undoubtedly it is often difficult to reconcile the rights of victims with the rights of the accused. The Internal Rules require the Court to preserve "a balance between the rights of the parties,"[317] but soon after the first pre-trial hearings the Judges seemed to conclude that active victim participation may not be conducive to adequately preserving the balance of rights in proceedings. The trial in Case 001 solidified this apprehension towards participation. Accordingly, the Judges took action, limiting participatory rights at trial and amending the Internal Rules in an attempt to preserve the fair trial rights of the accused and ensure effective and efficient proceedings.

---

314 Mydans, S., Anger in Cambodia follows Khmer Rouge Sentence, *New York Times*, 26 July 2010.

315 Wojcik (2010) at 30.

316 *Case 002*, Joint and Several Submission on Civil Party Participation in Appeals related to Provisional Detention, Pre-Trial Chamber, 22 February 2008, par. 29, where the Defense teams argue that "extensive civil-party participation at every stage of the proceedings threatens to place an unjust burden on the accused to respond to a multiplicity of opponents."

317 ECCC, Internal Rules, Rule 21(1)(a).

At trial, the rejection of a request to allow victims to give opening statements, the imposition of time limits when questioning witnesses, and the prohibition on participation related to sentencing and the character of the accused all suggest that the judges were well aware of the need to adopt a participation regime that accommodates an international trial for mass crimes within the specific context of Cambodia. While not all of the measures were necessarily decisive, they were an attempt to recognize the increasing number of issues arising at trial. Additional measures taken through amendments to the Internal Rules include the creation of a single team of lawyers representing the collective interests of victims at trial, the early assessment of civil party applications prior to the start of trial, and the strengthening of the mandate of the VSS to include service-related rights. The ability of the judges to react to issues arising in proceedings through the amendment of the Internal Rules has undoubtedly assisted the Court pursuing a process whereby the core objectives of the criminal process are emphasized while at the same time additional objectives can also be realized.

Further actions or measures the Court may want to explore with regard to participation at trial include (i) restricting civil party interventions that neither contribute to the truth nor relate to the charges against an accused or the civil interests of the victims; and (ii) bifurcating the judgment and sentencing phase of trial so that civil parties can submit (both written and oral) victim impact statements on how the crimes have affected them. Such an approach would allow the active participation of victims with regard to the gravity of the crimes and the harms suffered without prejudicing the accused at trial. As Lord Hewart has poignantly stated, "it is not merely of some importance but is of fundamental importance that justice should not only be done, but should manifestly and undoubtedly be seen to be done."[318] Outside of the trial framework, the Court may want to consider (i) developing a policy plan to facilitate the work of the independent lawyers representing civil parties and the lead co-lawyers; and (ii) increasing the institutional support (through adequate funding and staffing) for the VSS so that it can carry out its new mandate related to service-related rights for victims. One commentator has aptly posited that "No one in the courtroom dares to deny the importance of the civil parties, but no one has been able to articulate clearly what their role is."[319] Thus far, the judges have borrowed from the national, regional and international levels when shaping victim measures and there is no denying that they grappled with ensuring respect for fair trial rights and the efficient conduct of proceedings when approaching issues related to the role of the victim in the criminal process. One thing is clear, however, the judges are adopting a wholly unique approach to participation that best reflects the specific characteristic of the ECCC.

318 *R v. Sussex Justices ex parte McCarthy*, 1 KB 256 (1924).

319 MacDonald, L., Chamber and Parties Seek an Expeditious Trial, But at What Cost? *Cambodia Tribunal Monitor*, 23 June 2009.

CHAPTER 7
VICTIM PARTICIPATION AT THE INTERNATIONAL CRIMINAL COURT

7.1 INTRODUCTION

The Preamble to the Rome Statute provides that States Parties are "mindful that during this century millions of children, women and men have been victims of unimaginable atrocities that deeply shock the conscience of humanity."[1] In recognition of this suffering the International Criminal Court (ICC or Court) became the first international criminal tribunal to endorse active victim participation in its proceedings. The Rome Statute (Statute), Rules of Procedure and Evidence (Rules) and Regulations of the Court (Regulations),[2] which constitute the Court's governing documents, award victims the right to participate, other than as witnesses called by either the prosecution or defense, in Court proceedings providing their participation is not prejudicial to or inconsistent with the rights of an accused and a fair and impartial trial. In addition to the right to claim reparations and greater protective measures, the right of participation is a significant departure from previous international practice.

The procedural rights afforded to victims have been heralded and praised by many commentators,[3] and five years since the handing down of its first major decision on victim participation,[4] the Court's jurisprudence on victims' participatory rights is mounting. However, it is unclear whether the increasing amount of case law provides greater clarification about the procedural rights of victims. Moreover, it is uncertain whether the Judges have been able to find the most appropriate way to afford victims participatory rights in the proceedings without affecting the Court's primary goals of investigation, prosecution and punishment as well as without adversely affecting the rights of the accused. Thus, although the victim participation scheme was a well-intentioned attempt to address perceived shortcomings from previous international tribunals, it is necessary to examine whether or not the incorporation of victims as participants in the proceedings has been managed effectively and efficiently.

---

1 Rome Statute, Preamble.

2 Although the Statute and Rules were largely drafted by state representatives the Regulations of the Court were drafted by the Judges and adopted at the 5th Plenary Session on 26 May 2004.

3 Cassese (1999) at 167-168; Fernández de Gurmendi, S., Definition of Victims and General Principles, 427, in Lee (2001); Jorda, J. and De Hemptinne, J., The Status and Role of the Victims, 1390, in Cassese, et al. (2002); Haslam, E., Victim Participation at the International Criminal Court: A Triumph of Hope Over Experience? 315, in McGoldrick, et al. (2004).

4 *Situation in Democratic Republic of Congo [hereinafter DRC]*, No. ICC-01/04-101-tEN-Corr, 17 January 2006.

In order to properly appreciate the scope of victim participation at the ICC it is important to understand what the Statute, Rules and Regulations provide. Likewise, it is essential to look at the practical effects of the Court's jurisprudence on shaping victim participation. Thus, using the same structure as that applied in Chapter 6, this chapter examines the current procedural status of the victim both in theory and in practice, and explore how participation has affected the operation of the Court.

7.2 Negotiating History and Framework of the ICC

In July of 1998 the UN Conference of Plenipotentiaries on the Establishment of an International Criminal Court was held in Rome, Italy. The purpose of the Rome Diplomatic Conference, which it came to be known as, was to draft and adopt the Statute of the ICC.[5] A total of 160 states and many other international organizations participated. The complexity of the undertaking is highlighted by the original draft statute submitted to the Conference which had numerous options with over 1,400 brackets indicating disagreement among the delegates. Almost all the victim participation provisions were bracketed.[6] Five weeks of intense negotiations followed, and through working groups, negotiations, and numerous heated debates a delicately balanced text emerged, merging elements from the two prominent Western legal traditions, the civil law and common law.

During the drafting of the ICC Rules "[d]elegations were often tempted to push discussions in a certain direction in order to obtain [...] an interpretation of the Statute that would alter the balance in favor of a particular view or particular legal system."[7] Although the ICC has adopted a mixed procedural approach to its proceedings, there is more of an emphasis on the adversarial approach associated with common law jurisdictions. As noted by Cassese:

> It is clear from even a cursory examination of the Rome Statute that states have opted for the common law approach. No investigating judge or chamber has been instituted,

5 Shortly after the UN Security Council created the ICTY in 1994, the International Law Commission (ILC), already working for decades on the possibility of an international criminal court, prepared a set of 60 draft articles and commentary for such a court. Meanwhile, in accordance with General Assembly Resolution 49/53 of 9 December 1994, the UN Ad Hoc Committee on the Establishment of an International Criminal Court convened in April and August of 1995. In December of 1995, the General Assembly, based on the Ad Hoc Committee's recommendations, created the Preparatory Committee on the Establishment of an International Criminal Court pursuant to GA Resolution 50/46. The Preparatory Committee met in December 1995, March-April and August of 1996, February, August and December of 1997 and March-April of 1998 in order to prepare a draft text for the court to be used at a proposed diplomatic conference.

6 Coalition for an International Criminal Court Diplomatic Conference on the Establishment of an International Criminal Court, Report of the Victims' Rights Working Group, Rome, Italy, 15 July – 17 July 1998, p. 3.

7 Fernández de Gurmendi, S.A., Elaboration of the Rules and Procedure of Evidence, 235 in Lee, et al. (2001).

> and the investigations and prosecution are entrusted to the prosecutor, to whom it falls to search for and collect the evidence and prosecute the case before the Court. In addition, one can discern in the Statute the typical feature of adversarial proceedings, namely the fact that the evidence, instead of being submitted to the court by an investigating judge, is presented in oral proceedings and exhibits tendered by each party to the trial are admitted into evidence if and when it is so decided by the Court.[8]

Nevertheless, a number of civil law elements have been incorporated, including greater victim participation. Thus, the procedural law applied at the ICC is based upon unique compromises reached during the drafting of the Statute and Rules, leaving a great deal of discretion to the judges.[9] The procedural law is neither based on a pure adversarial model nor on a pure inquisitorial model. In fact, it is also not based on mixed procedural models existing at the domestic level. Instead, it is based on what Kress refers to as the *fundamental compromise formula*, where the judges will need to determine the ultimate balance between competing adversarial and inquisitorial elements.[10]

On 17 July 1998 the Rome Statute was adopted. Because the Conference was of limited duration a Preparatory Commission was established in order to develop documents that would ensure a smooth transition from paper to operation and to "discuss ways to enhance the effectiveness and acceptance of the Court."[11] In addition, a number of other conferences took place to finalize the Rules of Procedure and Evidence and to hammer out other details of the Court's operation.[12]

The International Criminal Court is the only permanent international court with jurisdiction to try individuals believed to be responsible for serious international crimes. The Court has jurisdiction with respect to the crime of genocide, crimes against humanity, war crimes and the crime of aggression.[13] However, it only has jurisdiction with respect to these crimes after 1 July 2002, when the Rome Statute entered into force, or once a state becomes a Party to the Statute.[14] Moreover, jurisdiction is not universal. Rather, the Court's jurisdiction is limited to the nationals or

8 Cassese (1999) at 168.

9 Kress (2003) at 604.

10 *Ibid.*

11 Resolution adopted by the UN General Assembly on the establishment of an international criminal court, Res. 53/105, A/RES/53/105, 26 January 1999, par. 4.

12 For instance, in April 1999, France hosted a seminar on victims' access to the ICC, referred to as the Paris Seminar. Further, in February of 2000 Italy hosted an informal meeting on the Rules, known as the Siracusa Meeting, and in April-May of 2000, Canada hosted the inter-sessional meeting at Mont Tremblant where delegates prepared a set of draft Rules. Debates at these meetings all contributed to the final version of the Rules. See Bitti, G. and Friman, H., Participation of Victims in the Proceedings, 456-459, in Lee, et al. (2001).

13 Rome Statute, Art. 5; Following the Review Conference of the Rome Statute that took place in May-June 2010, the Assembly of States Parties (ASP) adopted by consensus amendments to the Statute which included a definition for the crime of aggression and the jurisdictional conditions attached thereto. The Court will not be able to exercise jurisdiction over the crime of aggression until after 1 January 2017 when a decision is taken by the States Parties to activate jurisdiction.

14 *Ibid.*, Art. 11.

territories of the States Parties, States accepting jurisdiction on an *ad hoc* basis, or when the UN Security Council acting pursuant to its Chapter VII powers refers a situation to the prosecutor.[15] The principle of complementarity directs the relationship between the Court and all states over which it has jurisdiction. Essentially a case will be admissible if a state is inactive, or, in other words, has failed to initiate any investigation.[16] A case will also be admissible if a state is unwilling or unable to genuinely carry out an investigation or prosecution.[17] In all respects, the Court is meant to complement national prosecutions and is generally a Court of last resort.

The Court is composed of four organs, namely the Presidency, the Judicial Divisions, the Office of the Prosecutor and the Registry.[18] The Presidency comprises the President and first and second Vice Presidents, who help manage the Court, and who also sit as judges. The Judicial Divisions are comprised of a Pre-Trial Division, a Trial Division and an Appeals Division. All Judges are required to be independent in the performance of their functions.[19]

At the time of writing, there are currently seven judges assigned to the Pre-Trial Chamber with three judges sitting at any one time, as well as some functions being carried out by a single judge.[20] The Pre-Trial Chamber has, under certain circumstances, the power to authorize an investigation sought by the Prosecutor pursuant to his *proprio motu* powers;[21] the power to review the Prosecutor's decision not to proceed with an investigation or prosecution upon a referral by a State Party or the Security Council;[22] the power to deal with issues of admissibility;[23] and the power to take testimony from witnesses or examine, collect or test evidence for the purpose of trial in relation to a "unique investigative opportunity."[24] The Pre-Trial Chamber is responsible for issuing arrest warrants and summonses to appear if there are reasonable grounds to believe that the person committed a crime falling under the Court's jurisdiction.[25] After a confirmation of charges hearing the Pre-Trial Chamber may then confirm the charges against an individual if there is sufficient evidence to establish

---

15 *Ibid.*, Art. 12-13.

16 *Ibid.*, Art. 17. *The Prosecutor v. Thomas Lubanga Dyilo [hereinafter Lubanga]*, No. ICC-01/04-01/06-8-US-Corr, 24 February 2006, par. 29; *the Prosecutor v. Germain Katanga and Mathieu Ngudjolo Chui [hereinafter Katanga/Ngudjolo]*, No. ICC-01/04-01/07-1497, 25 September 2009, par. 78; see also Stahn (2010) at 313, 316.

17 Rome Statute, Art. 17. *The Prosecutor v. Lubanga*, No. ICC-01/04-01/06-8-US-Corr, 24 February 2006, par. 29; *The Prosecutor v. Katanga/ Ngudjolo*, No. ICC-01/04-01/07-1497, 25 September 2009, par. 78; see also Stahn (2010) at 313, 316.

18 Rome Statute, Art. 34.

19 *Ibid.*, Art. 40.

20 *Ibid.*, Art. 39(2).

21 *Ibid.*, Art. 15(4)

22 *Ibid.*, Art. 53(3)

23 *Ibid.*, Art. 17-18

24 *Ibid.*, Art. 56.

25 *Ibid.*, Art. 58.

substantial grounds to believe that the person committed the crimes charged.[26] The case is then referred to the Trial Chamber.[27]

The Trial Chamber is responsible for ensuring a "fair and expeditious" trial "with full respect for the rights of the accused and due regard for the protection of victims and witnesses."[28] It has wide discretion in adopting the applicable procedures,[29] and may rule on the relevancy and admissibility of evidence at any point during the proceedings.[30] In order to convict the Trial Chamber must be convinced of the guilt of the accused beyond a reasonable doubt.[31] The final decision shall contain a full and reasoned statement of the Chamber's findings on the evidence.[32] In addition to determinations on the guilt of the accused, the Trial Chamber is also responsible for awarding reparations to victims.[33] Reparation awards may be included in the final decision or may be made subsequent to a finding of guilt.

The prosecution and defense may appeal final decisions on guilt as well as the sentence whereas victims may only appeal orders for reparations.[34] Therefore, the Appeals Chamber is vested with the authority to hear appeals against decisions of acquittal or conviction, sentence and reparation orders. It may reverse or amend the decision or sentence or even order a new trial before the Trial Chamber.[35] In addition, the Appeals Chamber may hear interlocutory appeals concerning a decision with respect to jurisdiction or admissibility, a decision granting or denying the release of the person being investigated or prosecuted, a decision of the Pre-Trial Chamber to act on its own initiative in relation to unique investigative opportunities, and a decision that involves an issue that would significantly affect the fair and expeditious conduct of the proceedings or the outcome of the trial, and for which an immediate resolution may materially advance the proceedings.[36]

One of the four organs of the Court, the Office of the Prosecutor (OTP), is responsible for receiving referrals and other information on crimes falling under the Court's jurisdiction and has the duty to investigate and prosecute these crimes.[37] The prosecutor may initiate investigations *proprio motu* and if the Prosecutor concludes that there is a reasonable basis to proceed with an investigation he must request authorization from the Pre-Trial Chamber.[38] Tasked with establishing the truth, the OTP is responsi-

26 *Ibid.*, Art. 61(7).
27 *Ibid.*, Art. 61(7)(a) and (11).
28 *Ibid.*, Art. 64(2).
29 *Ibid.*, Art. 64(3).
30 *Ibid.*, Art. 69(4).
31 *Ibid.*, Art. 66(3).
32 *Ibid.*, Art. 74(5).
33 *Ibid.*, Art. 75.
34 *Ibid.*, Art. 81 and Art. 82(4).
35 *Ibid.*, Art. 83.
36 *Ibid.*, Art. 82(1).
37 *Ibid.*, Art. 42(1).
38 *Ibid.*, Art. 15 and Art. 53.

ble for investigating both incriminating and exonerating evidence.[39] At any time after the initiation of an investigation the prosecutor may seek the issuance of an arrest warrant or summons to appear if he concludes there are reasonable grounds that the person committed a crime within the jurisdiction of the Court.[40] At the confirmation of charges hearing the prosecutor must support each charge brought against a suspect with sufficient evidence, and, at trial, the onus is on the prosecutor to prove the guilt of the accused beyond a reasonable doubt.[41]

In contrast with previous international criminal tribunals, the ICC divides its work into *situations* and *cases*.[42] Although this delineation is not explicitly apparent in the documents comprising the framework of the Court,[43] the Court has held that situations are "generally defined in terms of temporal, territorial and in some cases personal parameters," and are investigated to see whether specific criminal investigations should arise and whether individuals should be charged with a criminal offense under the jurisdiction of the Court.[44] Cases, on the other hand, are comprised of specific incidents falling under the jurisdiction of the Court and include proceedings that follow the issuance of an arrest warrant or a summons to appear.[45] The Court may deal with a number of situations at any given time and within these situations may try a number of cases and accused.

At the time of writing, the OTP is investigating six situations and prosecuting twelve cases. The situations that were state referrals include the situation in Northern Uganda (the cases include *The Prosecutor v. Joseph Kony, Vincent Otti, Okot Odhiambo and Dominic Ongwen*); the situation in Democratic Republic of Congo (DRC) (the four cases include *The Prosecutor v. Thomas Lubanga Dyilo*; *The Prosecutor v. Bosco Ntaganda*; *The Prosecutor v. Germain Katanga and Mathieu Ngudjolo Chui*; *The Prosecutor v. Callixte Mbarushimana*); and the situation in Central African Republic (the case includes *The Prosecutor v. Jean-Pierre Bemba Gombo*). The situations that were referred to the Court by the UN Security Council include the situation in Darfur, Sudan (the four cases include *The Prosecutor v. Ahmad Muhammad Harun "Ahmad Harun" and Ali Muhammad Ali Abd-Al-Rahman "Ali Kushayb"*; *The Prosecutor v. Omar Hassan Ahmad Al Bashir*; *The Prosecutor v. Bahr Idriss Abu Garda*; and *The Prosecutor v. Abdallah Banda Abakaer Nourain and Saleh Mohammed Jerbo Jamus*) and the situation in the Libyan Arab Jamahiriya (no suspects have been named). Finally, the only situation started under the prosecutor's *proprio motu*

39 *Ibid.*, Art. 54(1)(a).
40 *Ibid.*, Art. 58.
41 *Ibid.*, Art. 61(5) and 66(2).
42 Olásolo (2005) at 43, stating that the distinction made between situations and cases by drafters was out of "fear of the initiation of politically motivated investigations."
43 See, however, Olásolo (2005) at 40-47, arguing that such delineation was envisioned.
44 *Situation in DRC*, No. ICC-01/04-101-tEN-Corr, 17 January 2006, par. 65; *Situation in the Republic of Kenya*, No. ICC-01/09-19-Corr, 31 March 2010, para. 41-45.
45 *Situation in DRC*, No. ICC-01/04-101-tEN-Corr, 17 January 2006, par. 65; *the Prosecutor v. Joseph Kony et al.*, No. ICC-02/04-01/05-377, 10 March 2009, par. 14.

powers is the situation in Kenya (*The Prosecutor v. William Samoeiruto, Henry Kiprono Kosgey and Joshua Arap Sang*; and *The Prosecutor v. Francis Kirimimuthaura, Uhuru Muigaikenyatta and Mohammed Hussein Ali*). Additionally, the OTP is conducting preliminary examinations in a number of countries including Afghanistan, Georgia, Guinea, Côte d'Ivoire, Colombia, Honduras, Korea, Nigeria and Palestine.

In addition to the Presidency, the Judicial Divisions and the OTP, the fourth organ of the Court is the Registry. The Registry is responsible for the non-judiciary aspects of the Court's administration as well as a myriad of other services, including those related to the defense and victims. Aiming to be a model judicial administration,[46] the ICC has created an Office of Public Counsel for Defense (OPCD), which operates within the Registry.[47] The OPCD helps ensure that the fair trial rights of the accused are protected at all times "in order to reinforce the equality of arms and to enable a fair trial within the meaning of the Rome Statute."[48] More specifically, the OPCD represents defense rights at initial stages of an investigation, provides legal research and advice to the independent defense counsel, and acts as *ad hoc* counsel when necessary. The OPCD, together with independent defense counsel, help ensure that the Court upholds the due process rights of suspects and accused.

In addition to the OPCD, the Registry is also concerned with victims. The Victims and Witnesses Unit (VWU), the Victim Participation and Reparation Section (VPRS) and the Office of Public Counsel for Victims (OPCV) also fall within the Registry. The VWU is mandated to provide protection, support and other appropriate assistance to witnesses and victims who appear before the Court. The VPRS is responsible for receiving and processing victim application forms as well as assisting victims with the organization of their legal representation before the Court. If a victim or a group of victims is/are unable to afford legal counsel they may request legal aid from the Court. The OPCV provides support and assistance to the legal representatives for victims by providing legal research and advice. The OPCV may also appear before the Court on behalf of victims on specific issues,[49] and can be appointed by the Court as the legal representative of victims.[50] All of these departments within the Registry aim to assist victims in exercising their rights to protection, reparation and participation under the governing documents of the Court.

46 Rome Statute, Art. 67 provides for the rights of the accused, including, *inter alia*, the right to have adequate time and facilities for the preparation of the defense, to be tried without undue delay, to have the assistance of legal counsel, to examine witnesses against him and to obtain the attendance and examine witnesses on behalf of the defense, the right to remain silent, the right to submit an unsworn oral or written statement, the right to disclosure of information, and the right not to have imposed any reversal of the burden of proof or any onus of rebuttal.

47 ICC, Regulations of the Court, Reg. 77.

48 ICC website, *available at*: http://www.icc-cpi.int/Menus/ICC/Structure+of+the+Court/Defence/Office+of+Public+Counsel+for+the+Defence/, *last visited* 2 June 2011.

49 ICC, Regulations of the Court, Reg. 81(4).

50 *Ibid.*, Reg. 80(2).

In addition to the OPCV and OPCD the Court also has a Counsel Support Section (CSS), which is tasked with providing administrative and logistical support and assistance to both defense teams and to legal representatives of victims. The CSS liaises with the two Offices of Public Counsel in order to ensure quality legal services to victims and suspects/accused. However, the participation of victims in the proceedings will generally take place through independent legal representatives for victims, who like the independent defense counsel are not affiliated with an organ of the Court.[51] Though nothing in the Statute or Rules obliges victims to retain legal representation, the Court has implicitly stressed the importance of such representation by ensuring that victims are at all times represented in proceedings through the assignment of counsel.

7.3 Victims and the ICC

Although the Rome Statute expressly provides for a role for victims in the proceedings, more specificity was needed in the Rules of Procedure and Evidence (Rules) in order for the rights of victims to be made less ambiguous. Thus, as part of the many additional meetings which took place after the Rome Conference, in order to finalize the Rules, in April 1999 France hosted a seminar on victims' access to the ICC referred to as the Paris Seminar. Subsequently, in February of 2000 Italy hosted an informal meeting on the Rules, known as the Siracusa Meeting, and in April-May of 2000, Canada hosted the inter-sessional meeting at Mont Tremblant where delegates prepared a set of the draft Rules. Debates at these meetings all contributed to the final version of the Rules and the role of victims in proceedings.

Inspired by the Victims' Declaration and other domestic and regional developments related to the rights of victims, the Rules further elaborate the rights of victims with regard to participation, reparation and protection. But who exactly qualifies as a victim? The drafters of the Rules opted to create a new, broader definition than that found in the Rules of Procedure and Evidence of the *Ad Hoc* Tribunals.[52] Thus, Rule 85 provides:

> (a) 'Victims' means natural persons who have suffered harm as a result of the commission of any crime within the jurisdiction of the Court;
> (b) Victims may include organizations or institutions that have sustained direct harm to any of their property which is dedicated to religion, education, art or science

---

51 Defense lawyers and legal representatives for victims must have established competence in international or criminal law and meet the relevant criteria found in ICC RPE, Rule 22 and Regulations of the Court, Regulation 67.

52 In both the ICTY and ICTR RPE, Rule 2 (Definitions), a victim is defined as "A person against whom a crime over which the Tribunal has jurisdiction has allegedly been committed." During drafting negotiations, it had been argued by victims' rights groups and others that the ICTY/ICTR definition was too limited in that it is worded in the singular and it does not include family members or institutions.

orcharitable purposes, and to their historic monuments, hospitals and other places and objects for humanitarian purposes.[53]

In contrast with the definition from the *Ad Hoc* Tribunals, Rule 85 links the status of victims to the commission of a crime within the Court's jurisdiction rather than defining victims in relation to proceedings against a specific individual in respect to specific conduct.[54] The drafters of Rule 85 sought to adopt a definition that would be in agreement with the definition of victims found in the Victims' Declaration. However, despite NGO lobbying efforts for acceptance of a definition mirrored on the Victims' Declaration,[55] the ICC definition, while not a replica of the Declaration's definition, does closely resemble it.[56] A definition reproducing the one found in the Victims' Declaration proved too difficult to build a consensus around and instead a similar but slightly different definition surfaced.[57]

What does the definition mean for the practical operations of the Court? First, the broad definition of victims potentially allows for a greater number of victims to participate in proceedings. The definition is not limited to direct victims or even immediate family members. Moreover, despite many delegations' opposition out of fear of potential misuse by multinational companies or a drain on the Court's re-

---

53 For a detailed description of the development of the drafting of a definition see Fernández de Gurmendi, S., Definition of Victims and General Principle, 427-433, in Lee, et al. (2001); Heikkila (2004) at 17.

54 Stahn, et al. (2006) at 222.

55 Fernández de Gurmendi, S., Definition of Victims and General Principle, 430, in Lee, et al. (2001); see also, Human Rights Watch Commentary, Third Preparatory Commission Meeting on the International Criminal Court: Elements of Crimes and Rules of Evidence and Procedure, November 1999.

56 Donat-Cattin, Article 68: Protection of Victims and Witnesses and their Participation in the Proceedings [hereinafter Article 68], 884, in Triffterer (1999). See also, Victims' Declaration; the Victims' Declaration definition reads in part: (1) "Victims" means persons who, individually or collectively, have suffered harm, including physical or mental injury, emotional suffering, economic loss or substantial impairment of their fundamental rights, through acts or omissions that are in violation of criminal laws operative within Member States, including those laws proscribing criminal abuse of power. (2) A person may be considered a victim, under this Declaration, regardless of whether the perpetrator is identified, apprehended, prosecuted or convicted and regardless of the familial relationship between the perpetrator and the victim. The term "victim" also includes, where appropriate, the immediate family or dependants of the direct victim and persons who have suffered harm in intervening to assist victims in distress or to prevent victimization.

57 Fernández de Gurmendi, S., Definition of Victims and General Principle, 432, in Lee, et al. (2001): "Delegations objected to the inclusion or expressed the need to clarify the meaning of such terms used in the definition as 'collectively' and 'emotional suffering.' Some considered the phrase 'substantial impairment of their fundamental rights' to be too broad. Others objected to the reference to 'immediate family or dependents.' Some wanted to restrict the beneficiary to direct victims or to immediate family or dependents or to those cases where the victim was deceased and the family was intervening on his or her behalf. Some delegations wanted to define 'family.' Some opposed broadening the definition to those 'who have suffered harm in intervening to assist victims in distress or to prevent victimization.' Above all, there was a major and fundamental division between those who wanted a definition of victims confined to natural persons and those who wanted to include legal entities as well."

sources,[58] even legal entities may qualify as victims. Second, the status of victim is not linked to an individual defendant, which reinforces the argument that victims should be able to participate even before a specific suspect has been named.

7.3.1 Participation

Throughout the negotiations on the Statute and Rules, delegates presented different, and at times competing, ideas concerning victim participation.[59] Fernández de Gurmendi, currently a Judge at the ICC and previously a member of the Working Group for the Rules of Procedure and Evidence relating to Part 4: Composition and Administration of the Court, noted that, "the crafting of the regime on victims was probably the most challenging task undertaken by the Preparatory Commission," due to the fact that delegates came from different legal traditions.[60] The momentum in favor of participation was mitigated by concerns "equally widely considered and shared – that victims' participation should not occur to a degree or in a manner that would undermine the core ICC mission of trying perpetrators of mass crimes."[61] Delegates at the drafting of both the Statute and the Rules sought to devise a realistic system that would, on the one hand, include victims and, on the other, would not jeopardize the primary function of the Court.[62] Thus, the participatory rights found in the Statute and Rules, while broader than those existing in previously established international criminal tribunals, were deliberately made more restrictive than those found in domestic systems.[63]

In order to fully acknowledge the role of the victim in the criminal process, the Statute and Rules provide for victim participation at each stage of the proceedings – from pre-trial, through trial, to post-trial. In general victims have three ways of participating in the criminal trial. Victims may (1) submit a communication to the Court complaining about an offense; (2) participate as a victim participant in proceed-

58 *Ibid.* at 433; see also, Baumgartner (2008) at 420, footnote 66-67, taking note of the role churches played in the Rwandan Genocide and highlighting the fact that concerns over organizations, institutions or companies processing claims was not unfounded given the past history of the United Nations Compensation Commission, established by the UN Security Council to process claims and pay compensation for losses resulting from Iraq's invasion and occupation of Kuwait, where 5800 claims of corporations and other private legal entities alleged damages of over US $80 billion.

59 Bitti, G. and Friman, H., Participation of Victims in the Proceedings, 457, in Lee, et al. (2001). During negotiations, the Australian proposal contemplated only one rule dealing with victims and legal representatives, whereas the French proposals had a number of rules dealing with all aspects of participation. The French specifically stressed the need to have victims participate at all stages of the proceedings because of victims' interests in reparations.

60 Fernández de Gurmendi, S., Elaboration of the Rules of Procedure and Evidence, 256, in Lee, et al. (2001).

61 Chung (2008) at 464.

62 Fernández de Gurmendi, S., Definition of Victims and General Principle, 429, in Lee, et al. (2001).

63 For example, victims under the ICC system are referred to as *participants* rather than *parties*. Only the prosecution and defense are considered parties to the proceedings.

ings (including submitting requests for reparation); and (3) act as a victim-witness. In addition to their participation in relation to the criminal trial, victims may also participate in hearings on reparation, which are likely to occur following a conviction of an accused, without having participated in pre-trial or trial proceedings.[64]

Victim Complainant

Victims, like other individuals or organizations, have the opportunity to participate in a limited way by submitting communications to the OTP about potential cases falling under the Court's jurisdiction.[65] The filing of a communication is similar in many ways to the filing of a complaint. The prosecutor is obligated to evaluate all materials received.[66] After conducting a preliminary examination of the information, which can take as long as the prosecutor deems necessary, the prosecutor must then decide whether to authorize the initiation of an investigation or seek authorization from the Pre-Trial Chamber for the commencement of an investigation and a subsequent prosecution. At the time of writing the OTP has received over 8,800 communications.[67]

Victim Participant

With regard to direct participation in the criminal proceedings,[68] the Rome Statute provides for three explicit instances when victims may participate. First, pursuant to Article 15(3), victims may make representations to the Pre-Trial Chamber when the prosecutor, acting pursuant to his *proprio motu* powers, requests the authorization of an investigation from the Pre-Trial Chamber. Second, pursuant to Article 19(3), victims may submit observations to the Court when a challenge to the jurisdiction of the Court or the admissibility of a case arises. Finally, pursuant to Article 68(3), victims may express their views and concerns in other proceedings so long as their participation does not infringe upon the rights of the accused and a fair trial.

64 In regard to any issue before it, ICC RPE, Rule 93 allows the Trial Chamber to seek the views of non-participating victims, as appropriate.

65 Although some victims' groups argue that the ability to present complaints is not a specific right of victims to participate since it is available to all individuals, the Court characterizes it as the first instance of when victims can participate, see ASP, Report of the Court on the strategy in relation to victims, No. ICC-ASP/8/45, 18-26 November 2009, pp. 2, 4; see also, Office of the Prosecutor, Policy Paper on Victims' participation under Article 68(3) of the ICC Statute, April 2010.

66 Rome Statute, Art. 53(1)

67 ICC website, *available at*: http://www.icc-cpi.int/Menus/ICC/Structure+of+the+Court/Office+of+the+Prosecutor/Comm+and+Ref/, *last visited* 2 June 2011; approximately half of these communications were found to be manifestly outside the jurisdiction of the Court.

68 Hence, not including the submission of complaints or participation in reparation proceedings.

By far the most far-reaching provision dealing with victim participation, Article 68(3) provides:[69]

> Where the personal interests of the victims are affected, the Court *shall* permit their views and concerns to be presented and considered at stages of the proceedings determined to be appropriate by the Court and in a manner which is not prejudicial to or inconsistent with the rights of the accused and a fair and impartial trial. Such views and concerns may be presented by the legal representatives of the victims where the Court considers it appropriate, in accordance with the Rules of Procedure and Evidence (RPE). (Emphasis added).

The original draft of Article 68(3) developed out of an NGO proposal,[70] and it reproduces text found in Article 6(b) of the Victims' Declaration.[71] The New Zealand delegation at the Rome Conference then worked on the NGO draft language and formally submitted it for inclusion in the ICC Draft Statute.[72] However, the reference to legal representation of the victims, found in the second sentence of Article 68(3), derives from a French proposal.[73] As mentioned in previous chapters, the French system, like many other civil law systems, recognizes the right of victims to obtain legal representation for their civil claims attached to criminal proceedings and many drafters saw this right as necessary to ensure effective participation due to the technical procedures inherent in criminal trials. However, as indicated previously, the scope of victim representation is strikingly dissimilar between the French system and the ICC.

69 Donat-Cattin, D., Article 68, 871, in Triffterer (1999); on the development of the drafting of Article 68, see Donat-Cattin, D., Article 68, 874, in Triffterer (1999), where he writes that the current drafting stemmed from Article 43 of the International Law Commission Draft Statute of 1994 dealing with the Protection of the accused, victims and witnesses. This draft contained similar provisions to Article 22 of the ICTY Statute and Article 21 of the ICTR Statute. Later, in 1997, an important discussion took place during the UN ICC Preparatory Committee, the result of which included the addition of nine paragraphs dealing with victims to draft Article 43. Those nine paragraphs were re-elaborated upon in the so-called Zutphen text of January 1998 (then Article 61). A second draft with minor modifications then became Article 68 of the Draft Statute transmitted by the Preparatory Commission to the Diplomatic Conference in 1998.

70 *Ibid.* at 881, footnote 42.

71 Article 6(b) of the Victims' Declaration reads: The responsiveness of judicial and administrative processes to the needs of victims should be facilitated by: Allowing the views and concerns of victims to be presented and considered at appropriate stages of the proceedings where their personal interests are affected, without prejudice to the accused and consistent with the relevant national criminal justice system.

72 Proposal by New Zealand on Article 43 [later to become Article 68], UN/ICC Preparatory Committee, Non-Paper/WG.4/No.19, 13 August 1997; Donat-Cattin, D., Article 68, 881, footnote 42, in Triffterer (1999).

73 Draft Statute for an International Criminal Court – Working Paper submitted by France, UN/ICC Preparatory Committee, UN Doc. A/AC.249/L.3, 12-30 August 1996; Donat-Cattin, D., Article 68, 881, in Triffterer (1999).

Negotiations at the Rome Conference focused a great deal on whether the article should be limited to trial proceedings.[74] Many delegates at the Rome Conference feared that victim participation, as granted under Article 68(3), would have a crippling effect on the proceedings, particularly on the due process and fair trial rights of the accused.[75] In order to allay any concerns during the drafting process, the Dutch delegation recommended that the drafters 'safeguard' the article by inserting text which states that participation shall take place *in a manner which is not prejudicial to or inconsistent with the rights of the accused and a fair and impartial trial.*

In addition to Article 68(3), Rule 86 from the Rules, entitled "General Principle," provides:

> A Chamber in making any direction or order, and other organs of the Court in performing their functions under the Statute or Rules, *shall* take into account the needs of all victims and witnesses in accordance with article 68, in particular, children, elderly persons, persons with disabilities and victims of sexual or gender violence. (Emphasis added).

Rule 86, like Article 68(3), makes it mandatory for the Court to recognize victims. Originating from the Siracusa Seminar on protection of victims, Rule 86 requires the Court to consider the needs of victims when making any direction or order. If read carefully, the rule makes no distinction between issues affecting the personal interests of victims and those that do not. Therefore, Rule 86 requires a Chamber to take victims' concerns into account even when making decisions on matters that may or may not deal directly with victim issues.

In addition to Rule 86, Rule 93 allows the Court to seek the views of participating victims pursuant to Rules 89-91 on any issue, *inter alia*, in relation to an amendment to the charges (Rule 128), joint and separate trials (Rule 136), and assurances made by the Court (Rule 191). Rule 93 suggests that victims, through a request from the Court, have the potential to participate with regard to any issue arising in proceedings. Moreover, victims or their legal representatives may also seek to participate by requesting leave under Rule 103 to submit, in writing or orally, any observation on any issue that a Chamber deems appropriate.

In order to meaningfully exercise their participatory rights victims have the right to choose a legal representative.[76] In accordance with Rule 91, legal representatives may attend and participate in proceedings unless the relevant Chamber believes their interventions should be confined to written observations; they may be permitted to make opening and closing statements,[77] present their views and concerns;[78] make

74 Donat-Cattin, D., Article 68, 873, in Triffterer (1999).

75 Mekjian and Varughese (2005) at 19; Bitti, G. and Friman, H., Participation of Victims in the Proceedings, 457, in Lee, et al. (2001).

76 ICC RPE, Rule 90.

77 *Ibid.*, Rule 89(1).

78 Rome Statute, Art. 68(3); ICC RPE, Rule 89.

representations in writing to the Pre-Trial Chamber concerning a request for the authorization of an investigation;[79] submit observations concerning challenges to the jurisdiction of the Court or the admissibility of a case;[80] request protective measures;[81] and apply to the Court to question witnesses.[82] Their ability to participate is directly related to their right to be informed about proceedings and developments in a case pursuant to Rule 92. In order to ensure the fairness of proceedings, the prosecutor and the defense have the opportunity to reply to any oral or written observation submitted by victims.[83] Despite what might appear as a litany of participatory rights, many participatory rights are not explicitly provided for in the governing documents. Accordingly, the various Chambers, each with their own wide discretion to shape proceedings, were left to decide upon the proper modalities of participation.[84]

Victim-Witness

In addition to appearing before the Court as a victim participant an individual may also appear as a victim-witness. In this sense, a victim may be called as a witness by the prosecution, defense or the relevant Chamber (at the request of participating victims for example). In contrast with victim participants, victim-witnesses do not share their views and concerns but instead give evidence,[85] usually by answering questions posed. In many cases they are not represented by legal counsel and do not take part in all proceedings but instead are called at specific times to testify. However, unlike at the ECCC, victims participating before the ICC may hold the dual status of both a victim participant and a victim-witness.[86] In both the pre-trial stage and trial stage there have been a number of victims who held this dual status.

79 *Ibid.*, Art. 15(3); ICC RPE, Rule 50(3).
80 *Ibid.*, Art. 19(3).
81 *Ibid.*, Art. 68(1) and 88(1).
82 ICC RPE, Rule 91(3).
83 *Ibid.*, Rule 91(2).
84 *Ibid.*, Rule 89(1), "The Chamber shall [...] specify the proceedings and manner in which participation is considered appropriate."
85 Rome Statute, Art. 68 and 69; See also, Booklet: Victims Before the International Criminal Court, A Guide for the Participation of Victims in the Proceedings of the Court (available through the Court), pp. 10 and 28, defining a 'witness' as "a person who gives evidence before the Court by testimony. A witness is normally called by the Prosecutor, who is trying to prove the criminal case against an accused, or the defense, who is defending the accused against the accusation. A witness may also be called by a victim or by a Chamber."
86 *The Prosecutor v. Katanga/ Ngudjolo*, No. ICC-01/04-01/07-632, 23 June 2008, para. 18-19; *The Prosecutor v. Lubanga*, No. ICC-01/04-01/06-1119, 18 January 2008, para. 133-134; *The Prosecutor v. Katanga/ Ngudjolo*, No. ICC-01/04-01/07-1788-tENG, 22 January 2010, par. 110.

7.3.2 Reparation

In recognition of a victim's right to redress and in accordance with the Basic Principles, the Statute provides for the possibility for the Court to grant victims reparations. Article 75 states that "the Court may, either upon request or on its own motion in exceptional circumstances, determine the scope and extent of any damage, loss and injury to, or in respect of, victims [...]." In so doing, the Court may make an order directly against a convicted person or order that the award be made through the Trust Fund for Victims (Trust Fund). The Trust Fund is administered by the Registry but is independent of the Court. In addition to implementing reparation awards ordered by the Court the Trust Fund may also finance other projects for the benefit of victims.[87]

Reparation awards may be individual or collective and may be monetary.[88] Victims are authorized to appeal a decision on reparations.[89] Before issuing a reparations award the Court may invite the victims, convicted person(s), experts and other interested parties to share their views and concerns.[90] As mentioned above, victims wishing to claim reparations are not required to participate in trial proceedings. Instead, they may simply submit a claim for reparations and participate in any special hearings on reparations without being required to participate in hearings on the guilt of the accused. Undoubtedly, the provisions on reparations are unique among international criminal courts and go a long way to recognizing the rights of victims of crime.

7.3.3 Protection

As with other international criminal courts, the ICC takes the issue of protection seriously. Article 68 obliges the Chambers, as well as the prosecutor, to take appropriate measures to protect the safety, physical and psychological well-being, dignity and privacy of victims and witnesses.[91] Moreover, the Judges acknowledge that the personal interests of victims are affected by the adoption of protective measures, or the failure thereto. The Pre-Trial Chamber, for example, is mandated "[w]here necessary, [to provide] for the protection and privacy of victims and witnesses" and to "[s]eek the cooperation of States to take protective measures for the purpose of forfeiture, in particular for the ultimate benefit of victims."[92] The VWU is the main department assigned to assist victims and witnesses and advise the Judges on protective measures.[93] Protective measures may include, among other things, in camera proceed-

87 Rome Statute, Art. 79, ICC RPE, Rule 98.
88 ICC RPE, Rule 97.
89 Rome Statute, Art. 82(4).
90 *Ibid.*, Art. 75, ICC RPE, Rule 97.
91 Protection also extends to family members of witnesses. See also ICC RPE, Rule 87.
92 Rome Statue, Art. 57; see also *Situation in Uganda*, No. ICC-02/04-101, 10 August 2007, par. 98, pp. 37-38.
93 Rome Statute, Art. 43; *The Prosecutor v. Lubanga*, No. ICC-01/04-01/06-1379, 5 June 2008, para. 52-78.

ings, using a pseudonym, voice and face distortion, or redacting identifying information from Court documents.[94] In principle, protective measures may not prejudice or be inconsistent with the rights of an accused and a fair and impartial trial.

7.4 Participation in Practice

Both the Statute and Rules left many gaps with regard to participation provisions, believing the Judges would be in the best position to provide greater clarification. For this reason, the Judges have wide discretion in shaping victim participation in practice. This has not been an easy task. From the beginning the Judges have undoubtedly struggled with interpreting the above-mentioned provisions concerning the procedural rights of victims. The lack of harmonization between the various Chambers becomes all too evident when one begins to examine their diverse approaches to participation. In addition, many of the approaches adopted by the Court arguably infringe upon the fair trial rights of the accused.

7.4.1 Application Process

If a victim of a crime falling under the Court's jurisdiction wishes to participate in the criminal process as a victim participant he or she must apply to do so. Again, the application process for victim participants is not connected to applications seeking reparations though victim participants may also seek reparations.[95] Victims wishing to apply generally use the standard application form provided by the Court.[96] The VPRS developed a standard 17-page application form in 2005 in order to facilitate participation.[97] In addition, a booklet explaining how to complete the form was made available. However, after a number of complaints, in 2009, the Court undertook a review of both the participation and reparation application forms. New forms were introduced in 2010, which consolidate the two forms in a 7-page document. The prosecution and defense are entitled to reply to any application for participation.[98] Victim-applicants may not reply to the observations of the prosecution or defense.[99] Nor may victims request leave to appeal decisions denying victim participant status

94 ICC RPE, Rule 87.

95 *Situation in Darfur, Sudan [hereinafter Darfur]*, No. ICC-02/05-110, 3 December 2007, par. 6.

96 However, there is no requirement that victims use this standard application form so long as they provide all of the relevant information found in Regulation 86(2), *Situation in DRC*, No. ICC-01/04-101-tEN-Corr, 17 January 2006, par. 102. Additionally, victims do not need to exhaust domestic remedies before applying to participate or seek reparations. See *Situation in Darfur*, No. ICC-02/05-110, 3 December 2007, par. 12.

97 A separate form for reparations has also been used.

98 See ICC RPE, Rule 89(1); *Situation in DRC*, No. ICC-01/04-73, 21 July 2005, p. 2

99 *Situation in DRC*, No. ICC-01/04-418, 10 December 2007, para. 16-17; *The Prosecutor v. Lubanga*, No. ICC-01/04-01/06-1119, 18 January 2008, p. 3.

because they do not have standing before the Court in order to do so.[100] Instead, they may simply reapply.

The VPRS collects completed applications, prepares a Report on them and sends both to the relevant Chamber. An application is complete when it includes the identity of the applicant, including proof-of-identity; the date of the crime(s); the location of the crime(s); a description of the harm suffered as a result of the commission of any crime within the jurisdiction of the Court; the express consent of the victim if another person is acting on their behalf; proof of kinship or legal guardianship if the application is made on a person on behalf of another; and a signature or thumb-print of the applicant.[101] As a rule, the Court does not disclose the VPRS Report to the parties or participants.[102] The Report is meant to be neutral on its face and generally contains: (i) summaries of the matters contained in the original applications, set out on an applicant-by-applicant basis in narrative summaries, along with a grid or a series of boxes dealing with formal matters; (ii) a grouping of applications in one report when there are links founded on such matters as time, circumstance or issue; (iii) any other information which may be relevant to the Chamber's decision on the application such as information supplied by States, the prosecutor and intergovernmental or non-governmental organizations pursuant to Regulation 86(4); and (iv) any other assistance the VPRS can give to assist the Chamber in its task of assessing the merits of the applications, while refraining from expressing any views on the merits of the applications.[103] For those individuals who submit incomplete applications, the VPRS requests additional information from them. However, after a reasonable period of time it will also submit the incomplete applications (if no additional information is provided) together with a Report to the relevant Chamber for consideration.

Irrespective of the stage of the proceedings in which the victim-applicant wishes to participate Rule 85 provides the criteria that must be met in order to gain victim participant status. Judges determining victim status for an individual ask (i) whether the identity of the applicant as a natural person appears duly established; (ii) whether

100 *Situation in DRC*, No. ICC-01/04-418, 10 December 2007, para. 16-17; ICC-01/04-437, *The Prosecutor v. Lubanga,* No. ICC-01/04-01/06-1119, 18 January 2008, pp. 3-4.

101 *Situation in DRC*, No. ICC-01/04-374, 17 August 2007, par. 12; *Situation in Darfur*, No. ICC-02/05-111-Corr, 14 December 2007, para. 24 and 26; *Situation in DRC*, No. ICC-01/04-505, 3 July 2008, par. 17; *The Prosecutor v. Bahar Idriss Abu Garda [hereinafter Abu Garda]*, No. ICC-02/05-02/09-255, 19 March 2009, par. 4. If the applicant is a minor and the person acting on his or her behalf is neither related nor a legal guardian, the application must contain the consent of the next-of-kin or legal guardian. The consent of the minor to have a third-party apply on his or her behalf is insufficient, see *Situation in DRC*, No. ICC-01/04-505, 3 July 2008, par. 31.

102 *Situation in DRC*, No. ICC-01/04-374, 17 August 2007, par. 38; *Situation in Darfur*, No. 02/05-93, 21 August 2007, p. 4; and, *The Prosecutor v. Omar Hassan Ahmad Al Bashir [hereinafter Al Bashir]*, No. ICC-02/05-01/09-62, 10 December 2009, para. 16-18. See also, *The Prosecutor v. Lubanga*, No. ICC-01/04-01/06-1022, 9 November 2007, para. 25-27, noting that in some circumstances the Court may decide to disclose the report subject to confidential measures.

103 Regulations of the Court, Reg. 86(5); *The Prosecutor v. Lubanga*, No. ICC-01/04-01/06-1022, 9 November 2007, para. 19-20.

the events described by each applicant constitute a crime within the jurisdiction of the Court;[104] (iii) whether the applicant claims to have suffered harm; and (iv) whether such harm appears to have arisen as a result of the event constituting a crime within the jurisdiction of the Court for situations or as a result of the crimes brought against an accused for cases.[105] Similarly, organizations or institutions must meet the criteria found in Rule 85(b) in order to be granted victim status, but they must show both that property they owned suffered direct harm and that such property was dedicated to religion, education, art or science or other charitable purpose.[106] Importantly, the Court has stated that "a decision to grant an Applicant a procedural status in the proceedings in no way predetermines any factual findings that could be made by a Chamber in any judgment on the merits."[107] However, the language found in some of the decisions granting victim status hint that factual determinations are in fact being made. For instance, in a decision granting victim status the Trial Chamber in *Lubanga* determined that similarities in applications were unsurprising given the "broad context of the systematic conscription of children under the age of 15 into the military forces of the UPC" [...].[108] The wording of the decision seems unfortunate even if such determinations are not made in the final judgment.

104 *Situation in DRC*, No. ICC-01/04-101-tEN-Corr, 17 January 2006, para. 83-93; *Situation in DRC*, No. ICC-01/04-177-tENG, 31 July 2006, p. 14; *Situation in DRC*, No. ICC-01/04-374, 17 August 2007, par. 5; *Situation in DRC*, No. ICC-01/04-423-Corr-tENG, 31 January 2008, par. 37.

105 See, e.g., *Situation in DRC*, No. ICC-01/04-101-tEN-Corr, 17 January 2006, para. 66 and 79; *Situation in DRC*, No. ICC-01/04-177-tENG, 31 July 2006, p. 7; *The Prosecutor v. Lubanga*, No. ICC-01/04-01/06-228, 28 July 2006, p. 7; *The Prosecutor v. Lubanga*, No. ICC-01/04-01/06-601-tEN, 20 October 2006, p. 9; *Situation in DRC*, No. ICC-01/04-374, 17 August 2007, par. 4; *Situation in DRC*, No. ICC-01/04-423-Corr-tENG, 31 January 2008, par. 36; *The Prosecutor v. Joseph Kony et al.*, No. ICC-02/04-01/05-282, 14 March 2008, par. 8; *The Prosecutor v. Katanga/ Ngudjolo*, No. ICC-01/04-01/07-357, 2 April 2008, p. 8.; see also *Situation in Uganda*, No. ICC-02/04-101, 10 August 2007, par. 12; *The Prosecutor v. Lubanga*, No. ICC-01/04-01/06-1119, 18 January 2008, para. 84-86.

106 ICC RPE, Rule 85(b). For instance, in the DRC situation an application was submitted by the headmaster of a school on behalf of the school. The Court accepted that the applicant had *locus standi* to act on behalf of the school and ultimately granted the school victim status as an institution in accordance with the Rules, see *Situation in DRC*, No. ICC-01/04-423-Corr-tENG, 31 January 2008, para. 139-143; *Prosecutor v. Lubanga*, No. ICC-01/04-01/06-1556-Corr-Anx1, 15 December 2008; *Prosecutor v. Lubanga*, No. ICC-01/04-01/06-1563, 19 December 2008; and *Prosecutor v. Lubanga*, No. ICC-01/04-01/06-1861, 8 May 2009. Cf., *The Prosecutor v. Abdallah Banda Abakaer Nourain and Saleh Mohammed Jerbo Jamus [hereinafter Banda/Jerbo]*, No. ICC-02/05-03/09-89, 29 October 2010, para. 41-50, where the Pre-Trial Chamber rejects an application filed on behalf of the Nigerian Army for (i) failing to establish that the person acting on behalf of the Nigerian Army had the authority to do so, and (ii) failing to establish that the property in question (property used in a peacekeeping mission) referred to objects for humanitarian purposes. It held that "an ancillary humanitarian use of the property in question would not be sufficient to ground an application for participation" under Rule 85(b).

107 *Situation in DRC*, No. ICC-01/04-505, 3 July 2008, par. 30.

108 *The Prosecutor v. Lubanga*, No. ICC-01/04-01/06-2509, 29 June 2010; Redacted version of the Corrigendum of Decision on the applications by 15 victims to participate in the proceedings, No. ICC-01/04-01/06-2659-Corr-Red, 8 February 2011, par. 29 (the original decision was issued on 13 December 2010), quoting [arguably out of context] No. ICC-01/04-01/06-1556-Corr-Anx1, 15 December 2008, par. 103.

The time it takes the Court to process victim participation applications has been a serious concern. For years, some victims had to wait over one year before they would receive a definitive answer on their status determination. The screening process has also been detrimental for defense teams. Nowhere is this detriment more apparent than in the *Bemba* trial where over 1000 individuals have sought to participate. The six-member defense team has had to assign no less than three individuals to comb through the 17-page forms for each victim-applicant. The Trial Chamber notifies the parties of the applications in rolling batches of up to 300 applications at one time, giving the parties ten days to file their observations.[109] In addition to the difficulties of responding to these applications, they have had to do this at the beginning of trial proceedings when they should arguably be dedicating their "limited time and resources to reviewing prosecution disclosure, conducting any necessary investigations concerning upcoming prosecution witnesses, and preparing its cross-examination strategy."[110] Instead, they have become so entangled in studying the victims' applications, arguing for the dismissal of vague applications that do not sufficiently specify the context of the events giving rise to their harm and arguing for greater disclosure of exculpatory material found therein.[111]

The various Chambers have adopted divergent approaches concerning cut-off dates for the submission of applications. The Trial Chamber in *Lubanga* has not set deadlines and was granting applications as late as December 2010.[112] In contrast, the Trial Chamber in *Bemba* set a deadline for applications to be submitted prior to the start of trial. The rationale for doing so likely had to the do with the very high number of victim applications submitted during the pre-trial stage.

Natural Person and Proof-of-Identity

The first criterion to be met by victims is to establish their identity as a natural person. The Court's case law on this issue has evolved so that it now accepts that conditions on the ground may not facilitate what traditionally would be required to prove identity in a court of law. However, there is a concern that allowing too broad an array of options for proof-of-identity may open the Court up to potential fraud.[113]

109 *The Prosecutor v. Jean-Pierre Bemba Gombo [hereinafter Bemba],* Transcipt [hereinafter T], 24 September 2010, pp. 23-24.

110 *The Prosecutor v. Bemba*, No. ICC-01/05-01/08-1053, 26 November 2010, par. 5.

111 See, *The Prosecutor v. Bemba*, No. ICC-01/05-01/08-1053, 26 November 2010.

112 See *The Prosecutor v. Lubanga*, No. ICC-01/04-01/06-2509, 29 June 2010; Redacted version of the Corrigendum of Decision on the applications by 15 victims to participate in the proceedings, No. ICC-01/04-01/06-2659-Corr-Red, 8 February 2011 (the original decision was issued on 13 December 2010).

113 This concern was raised in a number of interviews with court staff, particularly those working on defense legal teams.

The Single Judge in the Ugandan situation originally required victims to produce documents that proved extremely difficult to obtain.[114] He found that proof-of-identity of a victim applicant can be confirmed if the document stating the identity of the applicant: (i) has been issued by a recognized public authority; (ii) states the name and the date of birth of the holder, and (iii) includes a photograph of the holder.[115] If applicants could not provide appropriate proof-of-identity their application assessment would be deferred until they could submit adequate proof-of-identity or until the VPRS submitted a Report on the identity documents available in the specific region, shedding light on the difficulties of providing such proof.[116] Due, in part, to the difficulties of meeting these rather stringent proof-of-identity requirements, only two of the forty-nine applicants were originally granted victim status.[117] The majority of applications were deferred until they could submit additional information. In March 2008, however, the Single Judge reassessed the deferred applications and decided to "lower" the proof-of-identity requirements and to accept a broader range of documents.[118] Based on the VPRS Report, the new requirements took into account the realities on the ground in northern Uganda and the difficultly victim-applicants had in meeting the original requirements.[119]

Similarly, other Pre-Trial Chambers have acknowledged that it is inappropriate for the Court to expect applicants from post-conflict areas to be able to provide the same forms of proof-of-identity as those living under more normal circumstances.[120] Accordingly they have allowed (i) national identity card, passport, birth certificate, death certificate, marriage certificate, family registration booklet, will, driving license, card from a humanitarian agency; (ii) voting card, student identity card, pupil identity card, letter from local authority, camp registration card, documents pertaining to medical treatment, employee identity card, baptism card; (iii) certificate/attestation of loss of

114 *Situation in Uganda*, No. ICC-02/04-101, 10 August 2007, para. 16-21; Cf. *Situation in DRC*, No. ICC-01/04-374, 17 August 2007, par. 15, providing a broader list of documents that can be considered at the investigation phase as proof of identity, including: (i) national identity card, passport, birth certificate, death certificate, marriage certificate, family registration booklet, will, driving license, card from a humanitarian agency; (ii) voting card, student identity card, pupil identity card, letter from local authority, camp registration card, documents pertaining to medical treatment, employee identity card, baptism card; (iii) certificate/attestation of loss of documents (loss of official documents), school documents, church membership card, association and political party membership card, documents issued in rehabilitation centers for children associated with armed groups, certificates of nationality, pension booklet; or (iv) a statement signed by two witnesses attesting to the identity of the applicant or the relationship between the victim and the person acting on his or her behalf, providing that there is consistency between the statement and the application. If the latter proof of identity is provided, the Statement should be accompanied by proof of identity of the two witnesses.

115 *Situation in Uganda*, No. ICC-02/04-101, 10 August 2007, para. 16-21.

116 *Ibid.*

117 *Ibid.* at par. 61.

118 See *Situation in Uganda,* No. ICC-02/04-125, 14 March 2008.

119 *Ibid.* at para. 4-6.

120 *Situation in DRC*, No. ICC-01/04-374, 17 August 2007, para. 13-14; *The Prosecutor v. Katanga/ Ngudjolo*, No. ICC-01/04-01/07-579, 10 June 2008, par. 37

documents (loss of official documents), school documents, church membership card, association and political party membership card, documents issued in rehabilitation centers for children associated with armed groups, certificates of nationality, pension booklet; or (iv) a statement signed by two witnesses attesting to the identity of the applicant or the relationship between the victim and the person acting on his or her behalf, providing that there is consistency between the statement and the application.[121] Moreover, the statement should be accompanied by the proof-of-identity of the two witnesses.[122] In addition to these forms of identification, Pre-Trial Chamber II has also accepted driving permits, graduated tax ticket, and certificates of amnesty.[123]

When establishing the proof-of-identity for an applicant at trial, the Trial Chamber in *Lubanga* noted that it will "seek to achieve a balance between the need to establish an applicant's identity with certainty, on the one hand, and the applicant's personal circumstances, on the other."[124] Consequently, the Trial Chamber considered, *inter alia*, (i) official identification documents, such as a national identity card, a passport, a birth certificate, a death certificate, a marriage certificate, a family registration booklet, a will, a driving license or a card from a humanitarian agency; (ii) non-official identification documents, such as a voting card, a student identity card, a pupil identity card, a letter from a local authority, a camp registration card, documents relating to medical treatment, an employee identity card or a baptism card; or (iii) other documents, such as a certificate or attestation of loss of specified official documents, school documents, a church membership card, an association or political party membership card, documents issued in rehabilitation centers for children associated with armed groups, certificates of nationality or a pension booklet.[125] If an applicant was unable to produce any of the above listed documents the Trial Chamber also considered "a statement signed by two credible witnesses attesting to the identity of the applicant," their relationship with one another and proof-of-identity of the two witnesses.[126] Finally, if an applicant was still unable to provide documented proof of his or her

121 See *Situation in DRC*, No. ICC-01/04-374, 17 August 2007, par. 15; *The Prosecutor v. Katanga/ Ngudjolo*, No. ICC-01/04-01/07-579, 10 June 2008, par. 46; *The Prosecutor v. Abu Garda*, No. ICC-02/05-02/09-121, 25 September 2009; *The Prosecutor v. Banda/ Jerbo*, No. ICC-02/05-03/09-89, 29 October 2010.

122 See *Situation in DRC*, No. ICC-01/04-374, 17 August 2007, par. 15; *The Prosecutor v. Katanga/ Ngudjolo*, No. ICC-01/04-01/07-579, 10 June 2008, par. 46.

123 *The Prosecutor v. Kony et al.*, No. ICC-02/04-01/05-282, 14 March 2008, par. 6. In *Bemba* the Pre-Trial Chamber accepted the following: (i)certificat de nationalité, (ii) permis de conduire, (iii) passeport, (iv) livret de famille, (v) extrait d'acte de mariage, (vi) acte de mariage, (vu) extrait d'acte de décès, (viii) acte de décès, (ix) jugement supplétif, (x) extrait d'acte de naissance», (xi) «acte de naissance», (xii) «nouvelle carte d'identité, (xiii) ancienne carte d'identité qui n'est plus en vigueur, (xiv) carte professionnelle, (xv) carte d'association, (xvi) récépissé de dépôt de demande de carte nationale d'identité, (xvii) carte de commission d'emploi, (xviii) carte de député, (xix) déclaration de naissance, (xx) carte d'identité pastorale, (xxi) testament, and (xxii) livret de pension, see *The Prosecutor v. Bemba*, No. ICC-01/05-01/08-320, 12 December 2008, par. 36.

124 *The Prosecutor v. Lubanga*, No. ICC-01/04-01/06-1119, 18 January 2008, par. 87.

125 *The Prosecutor v. Lubanga*, No. ICC-01/04-01/06-1119, 18 January 2008, para. 87-89.

126 *Ibid.* at par. 88.

identity, he or she could also provide an explanation for the absence of identifying documents.[127] With regard to organizations or institutions applying to participate as victims, pursuant to Rule 85(b), the Trial Chamber in *Lubanga* considered any document establishing it in accordance with the law of the relevant country.[128] The Trial Chambers in *Katanga/Ngudjolo* and *Bemba* took similar approaches.[129]

Despite the importance of acknowledging that victims of post-conflict and conflict regions will not have access to traditional forms of proof-of-identity usually accepted in courts of law, there is a legitimate concern that the Court has gone too far in accepting any document with a name attached. Often even the names on applications differ from the names on documents submitted as proof-of-identity. At the confirmation stage of proceedings, defense teams are unable to challenge the validity of most victims' applications based either on insufficient or not credible proof-of-identity because all of the identifying information in the applications provided to defense teams is redacted. However, subsequently, in all the cases before the Court that have proceeded to the trial stage, defense teams have been able to successfully challenge the identity of victim participants after they have been accepted to participate by the Court. This suggests that it may be desirable to have a better screening process in place prior to their being granted victim status by the Judges or allow challenges to applications prior to the start of trial. This should be done, if for no other reason than to protect the integrity of the proceedings and the role played by those victims who can legitimately provide proof-of-identity. A better screening process for participation purposes does not need to affect proof-of-identity determinations for the purposes of reparation awards coming from the Trust Fund. A lower standard of proof may even be desirable so as to provide reparation to a wider community.

Jurisdiction of the Court

The second criterion that must be met by victim-applicants is whether the events described in their application for participation constitute a crime within the jurisdiction of the Court. The term 'jurisdiction' refers to the *ratione materiae*, *ratione temporis* and *ratione personae or loci*.[130] In other words, the crime must be included in Article 5

---

127 *Ibid.* at par. 113.
128 *Ibid.* at par. 89.
129 *The Prosecutor v. Katanga/Ngudjolo*, No. ICC-01/04-01/07-933-tENG, 26 February 2009, par. 30. The Trial Chamber in *Bemba* adopted the approach of its Pre-Trial Chamber and allowed a wide array of proof-of-identity documents, including: (i)certificat de nationalité, (ii) permis de conduire, (iii) passeport, (iv) livret de famille, (v) extrait d'acte de mariage, (vi) acte de mariage, (vu) extrait d'acte de décès, (viii) acte de décès, (ix) jugement supplétif, (x) extrait d'acte de naissance», (xi) «acte de naissance», (xii) «nouvelle carte d'identité, (xiii) ancienne carte d'identité qui n'est plus en vigueur, (xiv) carte professionnelle, (xv) carte d'association, (xvi) récépissé de dépôt de demande de carte nationale d'identité, (xvii) carte de commission d'emploi, (xviii) carte de député, (xix) déclaration de naissance, (xx) carte d'identité pastorale, (xxi) testament, and (xxii) livret de pension, *The Prosecutor v. Bemba*, No. ICC-01/05-01/08-699, 22 February 2010, para. 35-36.
130 *The Prosecutor v. Lubanga*, No. ICC-01/04-01/06-228, 28 July 2006, p. 14.

of the Statute (genocide, crimes against humanity, war crimes or the crime of aggression), the crime must have occurred after 1 July 2002 in accordance with Article 11 and the preconditions to the exercise of jurisdiction, found in Article 12, must be met.[131] Interestingly, when it comes to detailing the crimes in the application the controversial role played by intermediaries when helping victims fill out participation forms is evident. For instance, when multiple forms (often in the same handwriting) allege that the said event violated the Geneva Conventions it is likely that the intermediary had a hand not only in helping the victim fill in the form but also in influencing the content of the form itself.[132]

Harm Suffered

Once the Trial Chamber has determined that the applicant is a natural or legal person, it will then consider if there is evidence that the applicant suffered any harm as a result of the commission of a crime within the jurisdiction of the Court. The term 'harm' is not defined in either the Statute or the Rules. During the drafting history of Rule 85, the draft definition explicitly mentioned types of harm, including physical or mental injury, emotional suffering, economic loss or substantial impairment of their fundamental rights.[133] These explicit references, however, were deleted and never included in the final definition. Instead, it was left to the various Chambers to decide what type of harm constitutes harm under Rule 85.

In the DRC situation, Pre-Trial Chamber I determined that it would interpret the word 'harm' on a case-by-case basis in light of Article 21(3), according to which "the application and interpretation of law pursuant to this article must be consistent with internationally recognized human rights."[134] Ultimately, the Judges, together with other Pre-Trial Chambers, concluded that 'harm' includes economic loss, physical suffering and emotional suffering.[135] Similarly, the Trial Chamber in *Lubanga* used Principle 8 of the Basic Principles as a reference to establish that the harm suffered by a victim may be suffered individually or collectively, and may include physical, mental, emotional, and economic harm or may consist in a substantial impairment of his or her

131 *Situation in DRC*, No. ICC-01/04-101-tEN-Corr, 17 January 2006, para. 83-93; *Situation in DRC*, No. ICC-01/04-177-tENG, 31 July 2006, p. 14; *The Prosecutor v. Katanga/Ngudjolo*, No. ICC-01/04-01/07-4, 6 July 2007, par. 11; *Situation in DRC*, No. ICC-01/04-374, 17 August 2007, par. 5; *Situation in DRC*, No. ICC-01/04-423-Corr-tENG, 31 January 2008, par. 37.

132 This information was obtained through a number of conversations with Court personnel.

133 See Rule on the Definition of Victims, Working Document, Proposal of the Coordinator, ICC Preparatory Works, Preparatory Commission, UD/PCNICC/2000/WGRPE(6)/IP, 29 March 2000, referencing proposal in footnote 8 of L.5/Rev.1/Add.1

134 *Situation in DRC*, No. ICC-01/04-101-tEN-Corr, 17 January 2006, para. 81-82; see also *Situation in DRC*, No. ICC-01/04-545, 4 November 2008.

135 *Situation in Darfur*, No. ICC-02/05-111-Corr, 14 December 2007, para. 30 and 38-50; *The Prosecutor v. Lubanga*, No. ICC-01/04-01/06-1432, 11 July 2008, par. 1.

fundamental rights.[136] In the context of conscripting child soldiers, Trial Chamber I in *Lubanga* has also held that psychological harm to a direct victim includes instances when that individual becomes aware that an *attempt* is being made to conscript, enlist or to use children actively to participate in hostilities.[137]

With respect to the issue of "collective" harm, the Appeals Chamber seemed to disregard its value for the purposes of the definition of a victim under the Rules. As a result the Appeals Chamber held that "[t]he fact that harm is collective does not mandate either its inclusion or exclusion in the establishment of whether a person is a victim before the Court. The issue for determination is whether the harm is personal to the individual victim. The notion of harm suffered by a collective is not, as such, relevant or determinative."[138] In all other respects the Appeals Chamber has generally agreed with the definitions of harm promulgated by the various Chambers, adding that victims may be direct or indirect victims because "harm suffered by one victim as a result of the commission of a crime within the jurisdiction of the Court can give rise to harm suffered by other victims."[139] The Appeals Chamber made specific reference to scenarios where there is a close personal relationship such as between a child soldier and his or her parents but otherwise the Chamber offered no further guidance as to whether extended family members or close friends would suffice. Although no Chamber has yet to grant an application based on friendship,[140] the Single Judge in the DRC situation has granted the status of victim to an extended family member such as a nephew of a direct victim.[141] In the context of the situations before the Court the acceptance of extended family members may be important.

136 *The Prosecutor v. Lubanga*, No. ICC-01/04-01/06-1119, 18 January 2008, para. 91-92; in his dissent, Judge Blattmann rejected the majority's reliance on the Basic Principles as a source of authoritative law. He argued that the drafters had referenced the draft Basic Principles and rejected their use. *The Prosecutor v. Lubanga*, No. ICC-01/04-01/06-1119, 18 January 2008, para. 4-5.

137 *The Prosecutor v. Lubanga*, No. ICC-01/04-01/06-1813, 8 April 2009, par. 51.

138 *The Prosecutor v. Lubanga*, No. ICC-01/04-01/06-1432, 11 July 2008, par. 35.

139 *Ibid.* at para. 1, 32, and 107.

140 In *Abu Garda*, the Single Judge at the Pre-Trial stage (citing the Appeals Chamber decision in *The Prosecutor v. Kony et al.*, No. ICC-02/04-01/05-371, 23 February 2009, par.32) appeared to accept that friends of a direct victim could, in principle, qualify as indirect victims, see *The Prosecutor v. Abu Garda*, No. ICC-02/05-02/09-255, 19 March 2010, para. 26-32. With respect to the particular application before the Chamber, the Single Judge rejected, without prejudice, the application submitted by the individual claiming to be a close friend of a direct victim due to insufficient evidence supporting the claim. The Single Judge held that for applications submitted by non-immediate family members emotional harm is less apparent and therefore requires more information and/or evidence to substantiate the claim.

141 *Situation in DRC*, No. ICC-01/04-423-Corr-tENG, 31 January 2008, par. 15. The Single Judge in the Pre-Trial Chamber of *Abu Garda* indicated that applications submitted by aunts, uncles, cousins, nephews, nieces and even second cousins may be considered but that additional information and/or evidence will need to be submitted in order to support a claim of emotional harm resulting from the death of the direct victim, see *The Prosecutor v. Abu Garda*, No. ICC-02/05-02/09-255, 19 March 2010, para. 26-32.

As a result of these decisions, the harm suffered by a direct victim as a result of a crime falling under the Court's jurisdiction can give rise to harm suffered by other (indirect) victims. In a later decision the Trial Chamber in *Lubanga* also reaffirmed what the Pre-Trial Chamber in *Lubanga* previously found: persons who have suffered harm whilst intervening to help direct victims as well as those that prevent potential direct victims from becoming victims may also be considered victims in the case.[142] In the context of conscripting child soldiers, an attempt to prevent the conscription may qualify an individual to participate as an indirect victim.[143] In addition, the Appeals Chamber in *Kony et al.* confirmed victim status for victims who suffered psychological harm on account of witnessing events of an exceedingly violent nature.[144]

Causal Link

The final criterion to be met is whether the alleged harm appears to have arisen as a result of the event constituting a crime within a situation under the jurisdiction of the Court or as a result of the crimes brought within a case against a suspect or accused.[145] It was not always clear, however, that victims would need to link their harms suffered with the specific charges alleged against a suspect or accused.

Although the Pre-Trial Chamber in *Lubanga* had determined that victim-applicants would need to show a causal link between their harms suffered and the charges brought against a suspect, the Trial Chamber in *Lubanga* opted to take a different approach. It concluded that since Rule 85 does not expressly restrict participation in a case to the crimes contained in the Charging Document that doing so would unnecessarily introduce a limitation not found in the framework of the Court. Instead, the Trial Chamber found that so long as the harm suffered was a result of a crime within the jurisdiction of the Court the causal link requirement would be fulfilled.[146] This ruling would essentially allow a far greater number of victims to participate in trial proceedings. The Appeals Chamber, however, disagreed with the Trial Chamber's broad approach. It unequivocally found that "[f]or the purposes of participation in the trial proceedings, the harm alleged by a victim and the concept of personal interests under article 68(3) of the Statute must be linked with the charges confirmed against the accused."[147] This judgment of the Appeals Chamber once and for all determined that

142 *The Prosecutor v. Lubanga*, No. ICC-01/04-01/06-1556, 15 December 2008, par. 108; *The Prosecutor v. Lubanga*, No. ICC-01/04-01/06-1813, 8 April 2009, par. 51

143 *The Prosecutor v. Lubanga*, No. ICC-01/04-01/06-1813, 8 April 2009, par. 51.

144 *The Prosecutor v. Kony, et al.*, No. ICC-02/04-01/05-324, 27 October 2008, para. 11-14.

145 *The Prosecutor v. Lubanga*, No. ICC-01/04-01/06-172-tEN, 29 June 2006, p. 6; *Situation in DRC*, No. ICC-01/04-423-Corr-tENG, 31 January 2008, par. 38; *The Prosecutor v. Lubanga*, No. ICC-01/04-01/06-172-tEN, 29 June 2006, pp. 7-8; *The Prosecutor v. Lubanga*, No. ICC-01/04-01/06-601-tEN, 20 October 2006, p. 9.

146 *The Prosecutor v. Lubanga*, No. ICC-01/04-01/06-1119, 18 January 2008, para. 93-94.

147 *The Prosecutor v. Lubanga*, No. ICC-01/04-01/06-1432, 11 July 2008, para. 2, 64.

only those victims who can show a causal link between the harm and the charges against an accused can participate in trial proceedings.

In a later decision on whether victim-applicants who are the victims of crimes committed by direct victims, such as victims who suffered harm resulting from acts committed by persons conscripted or enlisted as children, can also be considered "indirect victims" the Trial Chamber in *Lubanga* decided to set limits on participation. The Chamber reaffirmed its earlier finding that there are two categories of victims who may participate: (1) direct victims whose harm is the result of the commission of a crime within the jurisdiction of the Court and (2) indirect victims who suffer harm as a result of the harm suffered by the direct victims.[148] Accordingly, indirect victims must establish that their harm has occurred as a consequence of their relationship with the direct victim and the harm suffered by the direct victim.[149] The Judges found that the purpose of trial proceedings, as stated by the Appeals Chamber, is the determination of the guilt or innocence of the accused for the crimes charged against him, and therefore only victims of the crimes charged may participate.[150] Those individuals who suffer harm as the direct result of the conduct of direct victims are excluded from being considered victims in the case.[151] In practical terms, this means, for example, that women and girls who were raped by child soldiers allegedly conscripted by the accused cannot participate in proceedings against the accused. This decision highlights the importance of the charges against an accused and effectively results in the prosecution (and to a limited extent the Pre-Trial Chamber) deciding on the potential category of victims able to participate. If a narrow line of charges are pursued, for example because of evidentiary, logistical or political reasons, the possibility for broad victim participation is negated.

Minors

Due in part to the fact that the Court has been handling cases that involve the enlistment and conscription of child soldiers it has had to address a number of issues involving the participation of minors. Rule 89(3) of the Rules provides for the possibility of a person acting with the consent of a victim on his or her behalf in the case of a victim who is a child or who is disabled. For those victims who may not be in a position to participate themselves this provision allows them to have someone act on their behalf. The Trial Chamber in *Lubanga* concluded that the person acting on someone else's behalf does not need to be a relative or legal guardian given that Rule 89(3) made no such restrictions.[152] However, the Chamber retained the right to disallow participation under 89(3) if it determined, on a case-by-case basis, that the

148 *The Prosecutor v. Lubanga*, No. ICC-01/04-01/06-1813, 8 April 2009, par. 44.
149 *Ibid.* at par. 49.
150 *Ibid.* at par. 52.
151 *Ibid.* at par. 51.
152 *The Prosecutor v. Lubanga*, No. ICC-01/04-01/06-1556, 15 December 2008, par. 67.

arrangement for participation was unsuitable.[153] In contrast, the Pre-Trial Chamber in *Katanga/Ngudjolo* explicitly required that those acting on behalf of a minor provide proof of kinship or legal guardianship.[154]

The Chambers also split when it came to the question of whether or not a minor would be required to have someone act on his or her behalf. Pre-Trial Chamber I in the DRC situation has not allowed minors to apply on their own behalf.[155] In contrast, the Trial Chamber in *Lubanga* noted that although it would normally expect a person to act on behalf of a minor, the wording of Rule 89(3) "coupled with the absence of any provision denying children the opportunity of applying to participate without an intermediary, creates, at the very least, the opportunity for a child to apply on his or her own behalf to participate in the proceedings, depending always on their individual circumstances (viz. the age and the apparent maturity of the child) and the interests of justice overall."[156] Similarly, Trial Chamber II in *Katanga/Ngudjolo* has permitted minors to apply in their own capacity with determinations made on a case-by-case basis taking into account their maturity and powers of discernment.[157]

Often, because of the long time in which it takes for the Court to process applications (sometimes up to two or more years), it has happened that an applicants were underage when they had someone apply on their behalf but later when their applications are being considered by the Court they are adults. The Trial Chamber in *Lubanga* needed to consider the consequences of this change of circumstances. In doing so, the Chamber concluded that "it would be onerous and against the interests of justice to require applicants, when they turn 18, to furnish the Court with a fresh document formally authorizing the person who has represented them hitherto to remain in that role."[158] Instead, the Court will infer that when the applicant becomes an adult he continues to consent to the person acting on his behalf unless the victim otherwise informs the Court.[159]

Submitting on Behalf of Deceased Persons

As mentioned above Rule 89(3) of the Rules provides for the possibility of a person acting with the consent of a victim on his or her behalf in the case of a victim who is a child or who is disabled. There are no provisions, however, in the Statute, Rules or Regulations that address the submission of an application for participation on behalf of a deceased person. Moreover, there is nothing in the Court's drafting history that suggests that this issue had been discussed. Therefore it was left to the Chambers to

153 *Ibid.* at par. 72
154 *The Prosecutor v. Katanga/Ngudjolo*, No. ICC-01/04-01/07-579, 10 June 2008, par. 44.
155 *Situation in DRC*, No. ICC-01/04-545, 4 November 2008, par. 33.
156 *The Prosecutor v. Lubanga*, No. ICC-01/04-01/06-1556, 15 December 2008, para. 94, 96.
157 *The Prosecutor v. Katanga/Ngudjolo*, No. ICC-01/04-01/07-1491-Red, 23 September 2009, par. 98.
158 *The Prosecutor v. Lubanga*, No. ICC-01/04-01/06-1556, 15 December 2008, par. 78.
159 *Ibid.* at par. 78.

determine whether victims would be permitted to submit victim applications on behalf of deceased individuals and the jurisprudence has not been consistent.[160]

On the basis that Rule 85 refers to natural persons and pointing to the impossibility of obtaining the consent of and knowing the views and concerns of a deceased individual, the Pre-Trial Chambers in *Lubanga* and *Katanga/Ngudjolo*, the Trial Chambers in *Lubanga* and *Katanga/Ngudjolo* and the Appeals Chamber have found victims may not submit applications for participation on behalf of a deceased person.[161] Accordingly, relatives of deceased persons may only submit applications for participation in their own names for mental or material harm personally suffered as a result of the death of their relative.

However, when a victim-applicant or victim participant dies these same Chambers have allowed their successors to continue with their participation. For instance, Trial Chamber II in the *Kantaga/Ngudjolo* case held that in the case of successors of deceased persons, the close relative of the victim can take over the application on behalf of the deceased victim but only within the limits of the views and concerns expressed by the deceased victim in his initial application.[162] Similarly, in *Bemba* Pre-Trial Chamber III, taking into account the jurisprudence of the Inter-American Court of Human Rights, concluded that there is nothing to stop the rights of a deceased individual from being exercised during the proceedings by his or her successors if they have been granted the status of victims participating in the proceedings.[163] The Trial Chamber in *Bemba* likewise determined that the "death of a victim should not extinguish the opportunity for the Chamber to consider his or her views and concerns," and decided to allow "an appropriate individual (not necessarily a relative) to provide the Chamber with relevant information (reflecting the views and concerns of the victim who died), whether through counsel or otherwise."[164] Both the deceased applicant/participant and the person acting on his behalf may be treated as victims who suffered personal harm.

160 Olásolo and Kiss (2010) at 128.

161 *The Prosecutor v. Katanga/Ngudjolo*, No. ICC-01/04-01/07-1491-Red, 23 September 2009, par. 52; *The Prosecutor v. Lubanga*, No. ICC-01/04-01/06-1432, 11 July 2008, par. 38 and *The Prosecutor v. Lubanga*, No. ICC-01/04-01/06-1813, 8 April 2009, par. 44; *Situation in DRC*, No. ICC-01/04-545, 4 November 2008, par. 19, 68; *Situation in DRC*, No. ICC-01/04-423-Corr-tENG, 31 January 2008, par. 24.

162 *The Prosecutor v. Katanga/Ngudjolo*, No. ICC-01/04-01/07-1737, 22 December 2009 [No English translation available], par. 30.

163 *The Prosecutor v. Bemba*, No. ICC-01/05-01/08-320, 12 December 2008, para. 44 and 47.

164 *The Prosecutor v. Bemba*, No. ICC-01/05-01/08-807-Corr, 12 July 2010, para. 83-85; *The Prosecutor v. Bemba*, No. ICC-01/05-01/08-320, 12 December 2008, para. 39-40; *The Prosecutor v. Bemba*, No. ICC-01/05-01/08-424, 15 June 2009, para. 71, 72 and 210-212.

Redactions

Due to serious security risks in the regions under investigation by the Court, the Judges adopt protective measures for victims and witnesses.[165] The most commonly used protective measure is that of redactions which are often the only feasible and appropriate protective measure available to the Court. Redactions protect the anonymity of a victim or witness by expunging information that could potentially place an individual in harm's way. Accordingly, the Judges redact identifying information, including information related to the place and time in which they were victimized. The Chambers regularly authorize redactions for the: (i) name of the applicant; (ii) name of the parents; (iii) place of birth; (iv) exact date of birth (year of birth shall not be redacted); (v) tribe or ethnic group; (vi) occupation; (vii) current address; (viii) phone number and email address; (ix) name of other victims of, or of witnesses to, the same incident; (x) identifying features of the injury, loss or harm allegedly suffered; and (xi) name and contact details of the intermediary assisting the victim in filing the application.[166]

Before ordering redactions the Court must take into account its obligations under Article 57(3)(c) concerning the protection and privacy of victims and witnesses, Rule 86 concerning the obligation to take into account the needs of victims and witnesses together with its obligation to ensure fair trials and Rule 89(1) concerning the right of the prosecution and defense to reply. Thus, the Court should approach redactions cautiously and to use them only when strictly necessary.[167] In the pre-trial stage of proceedings there is generally no problem allowing victims to remain anonymous so long as their participatory rights do not infringe upon the rights of the accused. However, leading up to the first trial both the prosecution and defense argued that

---

165 Citing fears of retaliation and concerns over safety for themselves and their families, many victims request that their identity not be disclosed to the prosecution, defense, States Parties or general public. See, *The Prosecutor v. Lubanga*, No. ICC-01/04-01/06-1308, 6 May 2008, para. 19-20; *The Prosecutor v. Bemba*, No. ICC-01/05-01/08-699, 22 February 2010, para. 27 and 33; *The Prosecutor v. Katanga/Ngudjolo*, No. ICC-01/04-01/07-933-tENG, 26 February 2009, para. 49 and 51-52; *The Prosecutor v. Katanga/Ngudjolo*, No. ICC-01/04-01/07-1094, 4 May 2009, para. 6-7; *The Prosecutor v. Katanga/Ngudjolo*, No. ICC-01/04-01/07-1129, 12 May 2009, para. 6-7; *The Prosecutor v. Katanga/ Ngudjolo*, No. ICC-01/04-01/07-1151, 19 May 2009, par. 8; *The Prosecutor v. Katanga/Ngudjolo*, No. ICC-01/04-01/07-1206, 12 June 2009, para. 11 and 13.

166 *The Prosecutor v. Lubanga*, No. ICC-01/04-01/06-1308, 6 May 2008, par. 28; *The Prosecutor v. Bemba*, No. ICC-01/05-01/08-699, 22 February 2010, para. 27 and 33; *The Prosecutor v. Katanga/ Ngudjolo*, No. ICC-01/04-01/07-933-tENG, 26 February 2009, para. 49 and 51-52; *The Prosecutor v. Katanga/Ngudjolo*, No. ICC-01/04-01/07-1094, 4 May 2009, para. 6-7; *The Prosecutor v. Katanga/ Ngudjolo*, No. ICC-01/04-01/07-1129, 12 May 2009, para. 6-7; *The Prosecutor v. Katanga/Ngudjolo*, No. ICC-01/04-01/07-1151, 19 May 2009, par. 8; *The Prosecutor v. Katanga/Ngudjolo*, No. ICC-01/04-01/07-1206, 12 June 2009, para. 11 and 13.

167 *Situation in DRC*, No. ICC-01/04-374, 17 August 2007, para. 20, 21, 28, 29 and 31; *Situation in DRC*, No. ICC-01/04-73, 21 July 2005, pp. 3-5; *The Prosecutor v. Lubanga*, No. ICC- 01/04-01/06-494-tEN, 29 September 2006, p. 3; *The Prosecutor v. Bemba*, No. ICC-01/05-01/08-320, 12 December 2008, par. 79; *The Prosecutor v. Al Bashir*, No. ICC-02/05-01/09-62, 10 December 2009, par. 12.

victims should not be able to remain anonymous.[168] The Trial Chamber disagreed, however, finding that anonymous victims could participate but that their participation would be more limited than those who have disclosed their identities.[169] Other Trial Chambers have followed this approach,[170] with the Trial Chamber in *Katanga/Ngudjo lo* stating that anonymous "victims cannot be authorized to participate actively in the proceedings, since such participation would be inconsistent with the rights of the defense, the fairness of the proceedings and equality of arms."[171] This approach appears to be consistent with Article 64(2) which requires the Trial Chambers to "ensure that a trial is fair and expeditious and is conducted with *full respect* for the rights of the accused and *due regard* for the protection of victims and witnesses."[172]

With the fair trial rights of accused in mind, a number of the Chambers have determined that in order to preserve the principle of equality of arms, the redactions should apply equally to the prosecution and defense.[173] However, this may not be the best approach to ensure the fair trial rights of the accused. The defense in *Bemba* complained that it is impossible to respond to claims made by victims seeking participation and asking for reparation when they are not given the dates and place-names related to alleged crimes.[174] The defense team has repeatedly requested that un-redacted applications be provided to the prosecution,[175] particularly when the majority of the applicants never requested their identities to be withheld from the parties and the prosecution in particular. The prosecution not only has the resources to process the information in the applications, but they also have duty to disclose exculpatory information or information which is material to the preparation of the defense.

Although for other reasons, Pre-Trial Chamber I adopted the approach advanced by defense counsel in *Bemba*, it has held that a victim-applicant's identity can be provided to the prosecution via un-redacted applications.[176] The rationale for doing so is because (i) the prosecution is an organ of the Court; (ii) the prosecution is mandated to protect victims and witnesses; and (iii) in accordance with Regulation 86(4) of the

168 *The Prosecutor v. Lubanga*, No. ICC-01/04-01/06-1119, 18 January 2008, par. 130.

169 *Ibid.* at par. 130.

170 *The Prosecutor v. Katanga/Ngudjolo*, No. ICC-01/04-01/07-1788-tENG, 22 January 2010, par. 21; *The Prosecutor v. Bemba*, No. ICC-01/05-01/08-699, 22 February 2010, par. 24; *The Prosecutor v. Lubanga*, No. ICC-01/04-01/06-824, 13 February 2007, par. 42.

171 *The Prosecutor v. Katanga/Ngudjolo*, No. ICC-01/04-01/07-1788-tENG, 22 January 2010, par. 21.

172 Emphasis added.

173 *The Prosecutor v. Lubanga*, No. ICC-01/04-01/06-1308, 6 May 2008, par. 30; *The Prosecutor v. Kony, et al.*, No. ICC-02/04-01/05-134, 1 February 2007, para. 24-25; *The Prosecutor v. Kony, et al.*, No. ICC-02/04-01/05-312, 17 September 2008, pp. 6-7; *The Prosecutor v. Bemba*, No. ICC-01/05-01/08-253, 15 November 2008, para. 11-13.

174 *The Prosecutor v. Bemba*, T, 27 April 2010, p. 7; see also, *The Prosecutor v. Bemba*, No. ICC- 01/05-01/08-945, 11 October 2010; No. ICC- 01/05-01/08-968, 22 October 2010, para. 7-12.

175 See, e.g., *The Prosecutor v. Bemba*, No. ICC- 01/05-01/08-945, 11 October 2010; No. ICC- 01/05-01/08-968, 22 October 2010, para. 13-17; No. ICC-01/05-01/08-1053, 26 November 2010, par. 10.

176 *The Prosecutor v. Abu Garda*, No. ICC-02/05-02/09-68, 27 August 2009, p. 4; *The Prosecutor v. Abu Garda*, No. ICC-02/05-02/09-106, 16 September 2009, p. 5; *The Prosecutor v. Abu Garda*, No. ICC-02/05-02/09-240, 29 January 2010, p. 4.

Regulations of the Court, the Registrar may request the prosecution to provide "additional information" about an applicant.[177] Thus, although not for the same reasons as those argued by the defense counsel in *Bemba*, at least one Pre-Trial Chamber has seen the added value of providing un-redacted applications to the prosecution.

In a November 2010 decision from *Lubanga* the Trial Chamber ordered the VPRS to lift redactions in victims' applications related to exculpatory information or information material to the preparation of the defense.[178] The Trial Chamber acknowledged that in balancing security concerns with the right of the defense to receive Article 67(2) and Rule 77 information the "mere assertion that someone is in danger" does not necessarily mean that is the case.[179] The decision indirectly recognized the need to continuous review previously authorized redactions in order to ensure the rights of the accused.[180]

Standard of Review

The Statute and Rules are silent with regard to the standard to apply when assessing victim applications, leaving it to the Judges to determine the appropriate standard of review. Thus, the Chambers have broad discretion in making their assessments of applications. In making their decisions, the Chambers first look to the application and VPRS Report and then to the observations filed by the prosecution and defense. They generally view the applications in a light which is most favorable to the applicants who have the burden of proving the elements in support of their applications.[181] In making their assessments, the Judges may directly infer material, including moral and contextual elements of the crimes within the jurisdiction of the Court.[182]

Pre-Trial Chamber I in the DRC situation reasoned that the "grounds to believe" standard mentioned in Article 55(2) concerning the rights of persons during an investigation comprises a less demanding standard, which is appropriate to assess victim applications for the investigative phase of the pre-trial stage.[183] Therefore, the Judges assessed applications based on whether there were grounds to believe that the applicants suffered harm as a result of a crime which falls within the jurisdiction of the Court, and that such a crime had been committed within temporal, geographical and,

177 *The Prosecutor v. Abu Garda*, No. ICC-02/05-02/09-68, 27 August 2009, p. 4; *The Prosecutor v. Abu Garda*, No. ICC-02/05-02/09-106, 16 September 2009, p. 5; *The Prosecutor v. Abu Garda*, No. ICC-02/05-02/09-240, 29 January 2010, p. 4.

178 *The Prosecutor v. Lubanga*, No. ICC-01/04-01/06-2586-Red, 23 November 2010.

179 *Ibid.* at par. 6.

180 *Ibid.* at par. 4; see also, *The Prosecutor v. Katanga/Ngudjolo*, No. ICC-01/04-01/07-476, 13 May 2008, par. 64: "Even if non-disclosure is authorized, this determination must be kept under review and altered should changed circumstances make that appropriate. [...] The overriding principle is that full disclosure should be made."

181 *Situation in Uganda*, No. ICC-02/04-101, 10 August 2007, par. 13.

182 *Situation in DRC*, No. ICC-01/04-505, 3 July 2008, par. 29.

183 *Situation in DRC*, No. ICC-01/04-101-tEN-Corr, 17 January 2006, para. 99-100.

if appropriate, personal parameters which define the situation at stake.[184] The Judges noted that, at the early stages, they were only determining whether the criteria found in Rule 85 are met *prima facie*, and not *stricto sensu* and alluded to the fact that a more stringent assessment would be required at a later stage.[185]

The Single Judge of the Pre-Trial Chamber in *Katanga/Ngudjolo*, however, did not adopt the language used in the 17 January 2006 Decision. Instead, the Single Judge opted for a test requiring "intrinsic coherence" of the claim asserted by the victim-applicant. When assessing documents the Single Judge embraced a "pragmatic, strictly factual approach, whereby the alleged harm would be held as 'resulting from' the alleged incident when the spatial and temporal circumstances surrounding the appearance of the harm and the occurrence of the incident seem to overlap, or at least to be compatible and not clearly inconsistent."[186] The fact of the matter is that many victim-applicants will not be in a position to fully substantiate their claims. Therefore, the Court has determined that as a general principle of law, "indirect proof (i.e. inferences of fact and circumstantial evidence) is admissible" if the applicant can show how he or she was hampered by objective obstacles from obtaining direct proof to support his or her claim.[187] Thus, applications will be assessed by the Chamber on the merits of their intrinsic coherence together with available information.

The Trial Chambers in *Lubanga*, *Katanga* and *Bemba* adopt a similar approach to that of both the Pre-Trial Chambers touched upon above. They carry out only *prima facie* assessments. Moreover, the Trial Chamber in *Katanga* confirmed that "only a blatant contradiction between the information in an application for participation and that appearing in the documents in support thereof can justify a decision to dismiss the application."[188] Along the same lines, the *Lubanga* Trial Chamber has held that similarities among applications are "unsurprising and do not in any way undermine their credibility."[189]

Two, Three and Four-Tier Approach

A decision granting victim participant status taken during the pre-trial stage continues to apply at the trial stage, meaning there is no need to reapply so long as the victim

---

184 *Situation in DRC*, No. ICC-01/04-101-tEN-Corr, 17 January 2006, para. 99-100; *Situation in DRC*, No. ICC-01/04-423-Corr-tENG, 31 January 2008, par. 4.

185 *Situation in Darfur*, No. ICC-02/05-111-Corr, 14 December 2007, par. 5; *Situation in Darfur*, No. ICC-02/05-110, 3 December 2007, par. 8.

186 *Situation in Uganda*, No. ICC-02/04-101, 10 August 2007, par. 14.

187 *Ibid.* at par. 15; see also *Situation in Uganda*, No. ICC-02/04-172, 21 November 2008, par. 7.

188 *The Prosecutor v. Katanga/Ngudjolo*, No. ICC-01/04-01/07-1491-Red, 23 September 2009, par. 32.

189 See, e.g., *The Prosecutor v. Lubanga*, No. ICC-01/04-01/06-2509, 29 June 2010; redacted version of the Corrigendum of Decision on the applications by 15 victims to participate in the proceedings, No. ICC-01/04-01/06-2659-Corr-Red, 8 February 2011, par. 29 (the original decision was issued on 13 December 2010).

stated in his application that he wished to participate in all stages of the proceedings.[190] However, since only a cursory assessment was made at the pre-trial stage, it was uncertain whether the Trial Chamber would conduct another assessment of applications at the trial stage.

The Trial Chambers have differed on their approach to this issue.[191] The Trial Chamber in *Lubanga*, using a *prima facie* standard of review, found that it was obliged to reassess the four applications for participation of those victims who participated in the confirmation of charges hearing.[192] One reason for doing so is, for instance, to confirm that the harm allegedly suffered was still the result of at least one of the crimes confirmed in the confirmation of charges. Trial Chambers II and III adopted another approach. These Chambers did not review those applications granted by the Pre-Trial Chamber unless contested by one of the parties on the basis of new material or information emerging since the original decision was taken.[193] This approach requires the parties to spend a great deal of time reevaluating victim applications. Moreover, Trial Chamber III has likewise required VPRS to review each application rejected by the Pre-Trial Chamber to establish whether it should be reconsidered by the Trial Chamber.[194]

Regardless of the approach adopted victims' applications must go through a two, three or four-tiered review process, depending upon the stage of proceedings when their application was first assessed. Victims in the DRC situation could have their application reviewed by the Pre-Trial Chamber in the context of the situation. They would then have their application reviewed by the Pre-Trial Chamber in the context of the case. After the confirmation of charges, and depending upon the approach adopted by the Trial Chamber, they could have their application reviewed once again. All of these "early" assessments are made under a *prima facie* standard of review. Finally, if the accused is convicted, it is expected that a more stringent standard may apply when evaluating the applications – as was the case at the ECCC. A stricter standard may be particularly important if the convicted individual is required to pay reparations.

7.4.2 Article 68(3) Requirements

The granting of victim status is required for a victim-applicant to participate in proceedings. However, the extent of the participation must then subsequently be

190 Regulations of the Court, Reg. 86(8). However, a Chamber may modify a previous ruling in accordance with Rule 91(1).

191 Olásolo and Kiss (2010) at 139-140.

192 *The Prosecutor v. Lubanga*, No. ICC-01/04-01/06-1119, 18 January 2008, par. 12 and *The Prosecutor v. Lubanga*, No. ICC-01/04-01/06-1556, 15 December 2008, para. 54-59; See also, *Situation in DRC*, No. ICC-01/04-101-tEN-Corr, 17 January 2006, par. 67; *The Prosecutor v. Lubanga*, No. ICC-01/04-01/06-172-tEN, 29 June 2006, p. 6.

193 *The Prosecutor v. Katanga/Ngudjolo*, No. ICC-01/04-01/07-933-tENG, 26 February 2009, para. 10-11; *The Prosecutor v. Bemba*, No. ICC-01/05-01/08-699, 22 February 2010, para. 17-18.

194 *The Prosecutor v. Bemba*, No. ICC-01/05-01/08-699, 22 February 2010, par. 20.

determined by the relevant Chamber. Therefore, subsequent to finding that an individual meets the criteria to be a victim participant pursuant to Rule 85, the Judges will then determine whether participation in proceedings is consistent with Article 68(3). Accordingly, if the interests of the victim participant are affected by a certain stage of the proceedings, a Chamber will determine if participation is appropriate and consistent with the rights of the defense to a fair and expeditious trial.[195] Once a Chamber determines participation is consistent with Article 68(3) the Judges will lay out a set of procedural rights, or modalities of participation, for victim participants. Inconsistent approaches to Article 68(3) determinations as well as to the appropriate modalities of participation have plagued the Court throughout its operation.[196]

Systematic Approach

The Single Judge in *Katanga/Ngudjolo* found that victims have a core interest in the determination of the facts, the identification of those responsible, and the declaration of their responsibility.[197] These interests were found to be at the root of a well-established right to truth.[198] And, when the right to truth is satisfied through criminal proceedings victims have a general interest in the outcome of the proceedings because such proceedings bring clarity about what happened and "close possible gaps between the factual findings resulting from the criminal proceedings and the actual truth."[199] The issue of guilt or innocence, the Single Judge found, is inherently linked to the right to truth and that the search for truth can only be satisfied if those responsible are declared guilty and those not responsible are acquitted so that the search for those who are criminally liable can continue.[200] Moreover, the Single Judge found that the interests of victims go beyond the determination of what happened and the identification of those responsible. The interests of victims extend to securing a certain degree of punishment for those found criminally responsible.[201] Thus, identification, prosecution and punishment are all "at the root" of the right to justice for victims of serious violations of human rights and are independent from an interest in reparation.[202] The

195 Rome Statute, Art. 68(3); *The Prosecutor v. Lubanga*, No. ICC-01/04-01/06-1119, 18 January 2008, par. 104; see also, *The Prosecutor v. Katanga/Ngudjolo*, No. ICC-01/04-01/07-1491-Red, 23 September 2009; *The Prosecutor v. Bemba*, No. ICC-01/05-01/08-699, 22 February 2010.

196 See Olásolo (2009) and Olásolo and Kiss (2010) at 140-144.

197 *The Prosecutor v. Katanga/Ngudjolo*, No. ICC-01/04-01/07-474, 13 May 2008, par. 32.

198 *Ibid.*

199 *Ibid.* at par. 34.

200 *Ibid.* at para. 35-36.

201 *Ibid.* at par. 38.

202 *Ibid.* at par. 39; *The Prosecutor v. Kony, et al.*, No. ICC-02/04-01/05-252, 10 August 2007, para. 9-11. Similar to the Pre-Trial Chamber in *Katanga*, the Pre-Trial Chamber in *Abu Garda* found that the personal interests of victims may include (i) the right to truth, i.e., the desire to have a declaration of truth by a competent body; (ii) the right to justice, i.e., their desire to identify, prosecute and punish those responsible for their harm; and (iii) the right to reparation, see *The Prosecutor v. Abu Garda*, No. ICC-02/05-02/09-121, 25 September 2009, par. 3.

Single Judge therefore concluded that victims have a personal interest in the outcome of the pre-trial stage of a case which determines whether there is sufficient evidence providing substantial grounds to believe that the suspect(s) are responsible for the crimes charged.[203]

Essentially when carrying out an Article 68(3) determination the Single Judge concluded that those individuals who meet the criteria of Rule 85 and who are granted victim status in the case will always have a personal interest in participating in all pre-trial proceedings. In other words, the determinations of whether a victim's personal interests are affected were carried out with respect to all victims collectively rather than on an individual basis. Furthermore, this assessment was carried out in relation to the pre-trial stage of proceedings rather than in relation to specific proceedings arising during the pre-trial stage or specific pieces of evidence. As a result, the confirmation of charges hearing was automatically considered to be appropriate for the views and concerns of victims to be shared.

Viewing the pre-trial proceedings in a broad context, the Single Judge then laid out the manner and scope of participation for all victims in all proceedings during the pre-trial stage. The approach adopted by the Single Judge in the *Katanga/Ngudjolo* case builds upon previous case law from the pre-trial stage of the *Lubanga* case.[204] It attempts to provide an 'easy-to-apply' set of procedural rights for victims. This broad approach has also been followed in the *Bemba* pre-trial stage,[205] and, to some extent, acknowledged in the *Katanga/Ngudjolo* trial stage.[206] The benefit of such an approach is that the parties and the legal representatives of victims know in advance what their rights are and can prepare better for hearings. The drawback of this approach is that it essentially invalidates the personal interest precondition found in Article 68(3).

Piecemeal Approach

Contrary to the systematic approach, the Trial Chamber in *Lubanga* implemented a piecemeal, or casuistic, approach when carrying out Article 68(3) determinations.[207] Although the Trial Chamber acknowledged that victims share several general interests like those identified by the Pre-Trial Chamber in *Katanga/Ngudjolo* such as the right

---

203 *The Prosecutor v. Katanga/Ngudjolo*, No. ICC-01/04-01/07-474, 13 May 2008, par. 43.

204 See *Situation in DRC*, No. ICC-01/04-101-tEN-Corr, 17 January 2006 and *The Prosecutor v. Lubanga*, No. ICC-01/04-01/06-228, 28 July 2006.

205 See *The Prosecutor v. Bemba*, No. ICC-01/05-01/08-320, 12 December 2008.

206 See *The Prosecutor v. Katanga/Ngudjolo*, No. ICC-01/04-01/07-1788-tENG, 22 January 2010.

207 See *The Prosecutor v. Lubanga*, No. ICC-01/04-01/06-1119, 18 January 2008. The Pre-Trial Chamber in the Uganda situation and *Kony et al.* case also adopted a piecemeal approach. The Single Judge determined that regardless of whether or not the victim had been granted a general right to participate during the investigation phase, the victim would need to show how his or her personal interests are affected by participation in a specific proceeding; see *Situation in Uganda*, No. ICC-02/04-101, 10 August 2007, par. 89.

to truth and justice,[208] it nevertheless determined that an Article 68(3) analysis requires a determination of the specific personal interests of individual victims in relation to specific issues.[209] Thus, in order to exercise their participatory rights, the Trial Chamber determined that victims must: (i) file a discrete written application to the Chamber; (ii) give notice to the parties; (iii) demonstrate how their personal interests are affected by the *specific* proceedings; and (iv) comply with disclosure obligations and protection orders.[210] Hence, victims' legal representatives will need to show how specific proceedings at trial affect their clients' personal interests rather than the trial generally as was the case in the pre-trial stage both in *Lubanga* and *Katanga/Ngudjolo*. In practice, this requires victims' legal representatives to demonstrate how the testimony of witness X or the admission of evidence Y affects the personal interests of one of their clients before they are granted participatory rights beyond basic access to public documents or attendance at public hearings. The Trial Chamber considered the piecemeal approach as the most suitable way to determine the appropriateness of participation so that the participation would be consistent with Article 68(3) and the rights of the accused and a fair trial.[211]

Once the Trial Chamber concludes that a victim's personal interests are affected by a specific matter, it will then determine the specific modalities of participation, such as questioning the witness or submitting a document.[212] The Trial Chamber emphasized that victims are not parties to the proceedings and made very clear that victims do not have an unfettered right to participate, particularly in a manner similar to that of the prosecution and defense. Rather, victims were afforded a number of party-like rights that are neither automatic nor unconditional.

An 11 July 2008 Appeals Chamber judgment appears to support the Trial Chamber's piecemeal approach.[213] The Appeals Chamber concluded that the Trial Chamber correctly identified the procedure for determining victim participation under Article 68(3).[214] This judgment suggests that many Judges at the Court are apprehensive of affording "across-the-board" participatory rights regardless of whether or not such rights can be limited on a case-by-case basis. The Trial Chamber in *Katanga/Ngudjolo* found that the recognition of victim status would automatically imply the recognition of the personal interests of the victims at the trial stage of the case. However, it held that it could require more information in situations where the link between the intervention requested and the personal interests were not readily clear.[215] In practice, both in *Katanga/Ngudjolo* and *Bemba* the Trial Chambers have adopted a de facto piece-

208 *The Prosecutor v. Lubanga*, No. ICC-01/04-01/06-1119, 18 January 2008, par. 97.
209 *Ibid.* at par. 96.
210 *Ibid.* See also, *The Prosecutor v. Lubanga*, No. ICC-01/04-01/06-1432, 11 July 2008, par. 4.
211 See *The Prosecutor v. Lubanga*, No. ICC-01/04-01/06-1119, 18 January 2008; see also, *The Prosecutor v. Lubanga*, No. ICC-01/04-01/06-1432, 11 July 2008.
212 *The Prosecutor v. Lubanga*, No. ICC-01/04-01/06-1119, 18 January 2008, par. 104.
213 *The Prosecutor v. Lubanga*, No. ICC-01/04-01/06-1432, 11 July 2008. Cf. Olásolo (2009) at 527.
214 *The Prosecutor v. Lubanga*, No. ICC-01/04-01/06-1432, 11 July 2008, par. 104.
215 *The Prosecutor v. Katanga/Ngudjolo*, No. ICC-01/04-01/07-1788-tENG, 22 January 2010, para. 61-62.

meal approach, requiring victims to file discrete written applications detailing how their personal interests are affected by a specific witness or piece of evidence before being permitted to participate.[216]

The prerequisite for victims' legal representatives to file discrete written applications pertaining to specific matters arising at trial, such as the testimony of a specific witness or a hearing on a specific piece of evidence, is undoubtedly onerous. Yet, such an approach is arguably consistent with the requirements of Article 68(3) and the need to ensure a fair trial. Those victims who can demonstrate how their personal interests are affected by a specific matter may be given a greater opportunity to participate. This, however, has not been evident when examining the participation in practice.

7.4.3 Pre-Trial Stage

Without a doubt the duration of trials has long been a problem for international criminal tribunals. In response to the criticism over the length of trials at the *Ad Hoc* Tribunals, the drafters of the Statute created a formal Pre-Trial Chamber. In addition to providing judicial oversight over investigations, drafters hoped that a Pre-Trial Chamber would be able to deal with procedural issues arising prior to the actual commencement of trial, thereby speeding up the trial process as a whole.[217] In accordance with the Statute proceedings are to be held in public, including proceedings that take place during the pre-trial stage, unless special circumstances require otherwise.[218] The pre-trial stage includes three phases: (1) the preliminary examination phase; (2) the investigation phase; and (3) the confirmation of charges phase. Although it is highly debatable whether the Pre-Trial Chambers at the ICC have sped up the criminal process it did provide a forum to flesh out the new procedures for victim participation at the early stages of the proceedings.

7.4.3.1 Preliminary Examination Phase

The preliminary examination phase takes place once a situation has been referred to the OTP, upon receipt of information by the prosecutor about a situation through a communication, or once the Prosecution decides to closely follow a situation on its own on the basis of information on crimes within the jurisdiction of the Court.[219] Referrals may only be made by a State Party or the UN Security Council, acting to address a threat to international peace and security. However, as mentioned previously, individuals (including victims) may "prior to and irrespective of whether a situation

216 The Chambers have found personal interests may range from helping to establish the truth to having a personal interest in the contextual elements of the crimes charged against the accused, see, e.g., *The Prosecutor v. Bemba,* T, 1 December 2010, p. 44.

217 Khan, K.A.A., Article 34: Organs of the Court, 592, in Triffterer (1999).

218 Rome Statute, Art. 64(7).

219 *Ibid.*, Art. 15.

or a case is pending [...], [and] with the view of triggering the exercise of the prosecutor's *proprio motu* powers," submit communications and complaints to the Court.[220] To date the OTP has received three referrals from States Parties,[221] two referrals from the UN Security Council,[222] and thousands of communications from individuals or groups.[223]

Initiation and Authorization of an Investigation

At the *Ad Hoc* Tribunals, the decision of whether to initiate an investigation fell exclusively within the discretionary power of the prosecutor. Neither the Court nor victims had any control over what investigations the prosecutor carried out.[224] This process was significantly changed in the Statute and Rules of the ICC. Victims may communicate their interest in the initiation of an investigation, the Pre-Trial Chamber taking victims' concerns into consideration pursuant to Rule 86 is given more oversight over the actions of the prosecutor, and victims have a limited opportunity to participate in proceedings when the prosecutor seeks authorization for an investigation pursuant to his *proprio motu* powers.

In deciding whether to initiate an investigation, the ICC prosecutor is required to consider whether the information available provides a reasonable basis to believe that a crime falling under the Court's jurisdiction has been or is being committed, and the admissibility of a potential case under Article 17; all the while taking into account the gravity of the crimes and the interests of victims and whether justice would be served through an investigation.[225] Regulation 16 of the Regulations of the Office of the prosecutor further provides that "The Office shall, in coordination with the Victims Participation and Reparations Section of the Registry, as appropriate, seek and receive the views of the victims at all stages in order to be mindful of and take into account their interests."[226] So long as the initiation of an investigation is based on a referral the prosecutor retains his discretionary power to proceed without oversight from the

220 *Situation in Uganda*, No. ICC-02/04-101, 10 August 2007, para. 90-92.
221 The three referrals by States Parties have come from Uganda, the Democratic Republic of Congo (DRC) and the Central African Republic (CAR), each referring situations in their own territories.
222 UN SC Res. 1593 (2005), UN Doc. S/RES/1593, 31 March 2005; UN SC Res. 1970 (2011), UN Doc. S/RES/1970, 26 February 2011.
223 ICC website, *available at*: http://www.icc-cpi.int/Menus/ICC/Structure+of+the+Court/Office+of+the+Prosecutor/Comm+and+Ref/, *last visited* 2 June 2011.
224 Once a prosecution team completes its investigations, it submits a report to the chief prosecutor, who then evaluates the evidence and determines whether there is enough evidence to indict a suspect. If the chief prosecutor determines there is enough evidence for an indictment, the prosecutor drafts an indictment and forwards it to the Registry for confirmation by a judge. Nowhere in this process did victims have a chance to officially share their views and concerns with either the prosecutor or the Court with regard to investigations carried out and charges brought by the prosecutor.
225 Rome Statute, Art. 53(1)
226 Regulations of the Office of the Prosecutor, Reg. 16.

Court.[227] Therefore, the decision to initiate an investigation is not reviewable by the Pre-Trial Chamber unless the investigation was initiated *proprio motu*.

If the prosecutor initiates an investigation *proprio motu* then victims have the explicit statutory right to present their views and concerns to the Court and the Pre-Trial Chamber has the power to review the prosecutor's decision. Article 15(3) provides:

> If the Prosecutor concludes that there is a reasonable basis to proceed with an investigation, he or she shall submit to the Pre-Trial Chamber a request for authorization of an investigation, together with any supporting material collected. Victims may make representations to the Pre-Trial Chamber, in accordance with the Rules of Procedure and Evidence.

Article 15(3) explicitly recognizes one of the earliest opportunities for victims to participate in actual court proceedings. At present the prosecutor has sought authorization for an investigation pursuant to his *proprio motu* powers on one occasion – with regards to the post-election violence in Kenya. The Rules lay out the procedure the prosecutor should follow when seeking an authorization for an investigation. In accordance with Rule 50, the prosecutor must first inform any victims known to him or the VWU when seeking authorization of an investigation.[228] Under Rule 50(3), after victims have been notified, they may make representations in writing to the relevant Pre-Trial Chamber. The Pre-Trial Chamber then has the discretion to request any additional information from the victims who made representations and may also deem it necessary to hold a hearing pursuant to Rule 50(4) in order to hear their views and concerns. But again, victims only have the statutory right to participate in regard to an initiation of an investigation if the prosecutor acts pursuant to his *proprio motu* powers and seeks authorization for an investigation.

The Pre-Trial Chamber in the Kenya situation, mindful of their need to ensure expeditious proceedings, provided for a limited scope of participation confined to the prosecutor's request for authorization of an investigation. In this regard it requested VPRS to: (1) identify community leaders of the affected groups to act on behalf of those victims who may wish to make representations (collective representation); (2) receive victims' representations (collective and/or individual); (3) conduct an assessment of whether the conditions set out in Rule 85 of the Rules have been met; and (4) summarize victims' representations into one consolidated report with the original representations annexed thereto.[229]

In its determination of whether or not to authorize an investigation pursuant to Article 15, the Pre-Trial Chamber also concluded that it would consider Article 15

227 However, once the prosecutor brings charges against an individual the Pre-Trial Chamber retains supervisory powers during the confirmation of charges hearing where it has the power to authorize and confirm the charges alleged by the prosecutor.

228 ICC RPE, Rule 50(1), 50(4) and Rule 92(2).

229 *Situation in the Republic of Kenya*, No. ICC-01/09-4, 10 December 2009, para. 5-9.

together with Article 53 (initiation of an investigation). Although Article 53 refers to the admissibility of a 'case' and not a 'situation', the Chamber decided to construe it in its broader context and essentially substitute the word 'situation' for 'case'.[230] In this way, the Chamber was able to then carry out an admissibility assessment of the situation (or of potential cases) and therefore address the issues of both complementarity and gravity.[231] In both of these assessments the Chamber used representations of victims to support their ultimate findings.

With regard to complementarity, the Chamber cited the VPRS Report on Victims' Representations which presented victim observations attesting to the fact that Kenyan authorities did not appear willing to investigate alleged crimes.[232] Ultimately the Chamber found that the principle of complementarity was not infringed. When assessing the gravity threshold, the Chamber stated that it would consider several factors, including (i) the scale or intensity of the alleged crimes; (ii) the nature of the unlawful behavior or of the crimes allegedly committed; (iii) the manner in which the alleged crimes were committed; and (iv) the impact of the crimes and the harm caused to victims and their families.[233] In this respect, the Chamber found that the representations submitted by the victims' representations would be of significant guidance for its assessment. Accordingly, although the Chamber relied a great deal on NGO and UN Reports, it also specifically took note of the VPRS Report as well as other specific victim representations.[234]

In his dissent, Judge Hans-Peter Kaul (Germany) emphasized that after carefully going through the prosecution's submissions and the submissions by victims' legal representatives he cannot authorize the commencement of an investigation into the post-conflict violence in Kenya. What is striking in his dissent is his personal comment made to victims. He writes:

> I wish to thank all victims and victims' representatives in the Republic of Kenya who have come forward to provide Pre-Trial Chamber II with their representations, their testimony and their accounts of the events pertaining to what is often referred to as the post-election violence of 2007-2008. I was, as a human being, deeply moved by these accounts. My feelings and all my sympathy are with the victims and their families. Likewise, I have studied with anguish and deep sorrow in particular the reports of the Commission of Inquiry into Post-Election Violence ("CIPEV" or "Waki Commission") and the Kenyan National Commission of Human Rights ("KNCHR") who have investi-

230 *Situation in the Republic of Kenya*, No. ICC-01/09-19, 31 March 2010, para. 41-52.

231 *Ibid.* at par. 59: the Chamber defined "the parameters of a potential case by way of reference to: (i) the groups of persons involved that are likely to be the object of an investigation for the purpose of shaping the future case(s); and (ii) the crimes within the jurisdiction of the Court allegedly committed during the incidents that are likely to be the focus of an investigation for the purpose of shaping the future case(s)."

232 *Ibid.* at par. 186, footnote 273.

233 *Ibid.* at par. 62.

234 *Ibid.* at par. 196.

> gated in the field over a prolonged period of time and gathered testimonies from victims, those who may have been involved in the violence and State authorities alike.[235]

His sentiments are noteworthy for the openly apologetic tone he takes towards those victims who have participated but for whom he does not believe can have access to the ICC as a forum with jurisdiction to adjudicate the crimes which have allegedly taken place. Indeed, Judge Kaul did not grant victims further access to the Court because he believed that the Court lacked jurisdiction over the alleged crimes.

Decision by the Prosecutor Not to Initiate an Investigation, Seek Authorization of an Investigation or Initiate a Prosecution

What happens when the prosecutor decides not to initiate an investigation, seek authorization for an investigation or initiate a prosecution? During negotiations over the Rules, some delegates, mainly from France, argued that the general right of victims to have access to justice suggests that they have a right to review a prosecutor's decision *not* to investigate a certain situation.[236] In contrast, other delegates felt that any review of the prosecutor's discretion not to initiate an investigation would unjustifiably usurp the prosecutor's independence and that judges would have too much power if given the power of review.[237] Ultimately, a compromise was reached and it appears that the prosecution retains some discretion while the judges have some supervisory role.

If the prosecutor determines that there is no reasonable basis to proceed with an investigation, the prosecutor must inform the Pre-Trial Chamber and the State Party making the referral or the Security Council depending upon the referral situation of the reasons for not proceeding.[238] In accordance with Rule 49, where a decision was taken not to initiate an investigation on the basis of communications received, the prosecutor typically informs senders of the communication of the reasons for not taking further action. If the prosecutor decides not to proceed with an investigation referred by a State Party or the Security Council and that determination is based solely on the fact that an investigation would not serve the interests of justice, the Pre-Trial Chamber may not only review the decision but must confirm the prosecutor's decision not to proceed and the Court is required to take victims' concerns into account when making that decision.[239] Pre-Trial review is not the case, however, when the prosecution decides not to proceed on the basis of a communication.

235 *Situation in the Republic of Kenya*, No. ICC-01/09-19 (Judge Kaul), 31 March 2010, par. 7.
236 Stahn, et al., at 230; see also Friman, H., Investigation and Prosecution, 497 in Lee, et al. (2001); Olásolo (2005).
237 Stahn, et al, at 230; see also Friman, H., Investigation and Prosecution, 497 in Lee, et al. (2001); Olásolo (2005) at 65.
238 Rome Statute, Art. 53(2)
239 *Ibid.*, Art. 53(3)(b)

While Article 53(3) makes no express mention of victim involvement when reviewing the prosecutor's decision not to initiate an investigation, this does not necessarily mean that victims will not have an opportunity to share their views and concerns. The Pre-Trial Chamber can rely on Rule 93, which allows the Court to "seek the views of victims or their legal representatives...*on any issue*" in relation to requests for review under Article 53(3)(a) and in relation to review by the Pre-Trial Chamber under Article 53(3)(b) (emphasis added). Moreover, if a Chamber does not seek the views of victims, victims are still free to request for leave to submit observations under Rule 103, dealing with amicus curiae.[240] Although no individual victim has, as of yet, sought to submit observations through the amicus curiae provision, victims' rights NGOs, such as the Women's Initiative for Gender Justice, have attempted to do so.[241] A January 2011 decision by the Pre-Trial Chamber in the Kenya situation may, however, limit the ability of victims to submit observations via Rule 103.[242] In this decision, the Pre-Trial Chamber held that the "core rationale underlying an *amicus curiae* submission is that the Chamber be assisted in the determination of the case by an independent and impartial intervener having no other standing in the proceedings."[243] Accordingly, the Chamber rejected the request by a person under the Prosecutor's investigations to submit observations (he was named by the Prosecutor in a request for a summons to appear). If this reasoning is extended to victims, it is unclear whether only participating victims would be excluded under this Rule or whether any individual with a clear interest in the outcome of the case would also be excluded.

Despite the fact that a number of victims' rights groups argue that victims should be allowed to initiate court investigations in their own right, as is the case in a number of domestic civil law jurisdictions, victims at the ICC may do no such thing. This form of participation would prove unworkable in regard to the Court's operation given the number of potential victims and potential cases. In 2010 victims in the DRC situation did, however, attempt to initiate a review of the prosecutor's failure to open a formal investigation into crimes allegedly committed by Bemba in the DRC.[244] Two of the first ever recognized victims requested the Pre-Trial Chamber in the DRC situation to review what they considered to be a decision by the Prosecutor not to proceed against Bemba with respect to crimes allegedly committed in the DRC.[245] Both the OPCD and

240 Rule 103 provides that a Chamber can grant anyone leave to submit, in writing or orally, any observation on any issue that it deems appropriate.

241 The Women's Initiative for Gender Justice sought to submit an amicus brief in the case of *The Prosecutor v. Lubanga* but the Pre-Trial Chamber denied their request for leave to submit observations. Instead, they were invited to re-file their request for leave to submit observations in the record in the DRC situation.

242 See *Situation in the Republic of Kenya*, No. ICC-01/09-35, 18 January 2011.

243 *Ibid.* at par. 6.

244 At the time of writing, Bemba is only charged with crimes occurring in the CAR.

245 See *Situation in DRC*, No. ICC-01-04-564, 28 June 2010.

the OTP responded, requesting the Chamber to dismiss the request.[246] The Chamber declared that since the prosecution has made no decision based on the grounds of "interests of justice" there is no decision to review under Article 53(3)(b).[247] This decision left the victims little alternative in having a decision not to proceed reviewed, but should the prosecutor make such a decision based on the grounds of "interests of justice" it is likely that the victims could successfully seek a review by the Pre-Trial Chamber.

7.4.3.2 Investigation Phase

The investigation phase starts with the initiation or authorization of an investigation into a particular situation. This phase does not end when the confirmation of charges phase of a case begins. On the contrary, the investigation phase into a situation may continue for an unlimited number of years.[248] For example, the investigation into the DRC situation will continue well after the conclusion of the *Lubanga* case. Unlike in the preliminary examination phase where victim participation is limited to submitting information for examination by the prosecutor or taking part in Article 15(3) proceedings, victims may have broader rights during the investigative phase of a situation to participate.

Can Victims Participate During the Investigation Phase? The 17 January 2006 Decision

Following the referral of the situation in the DRC, the OTP officially announced its decision to open the first investigation of the Court, and the President assigned the DRC situation to Pre-Trial Chamber I. Shortly thereafter, the International Federation for Human Rights (FIDH) submitted applications for participation of victims designated VPRS 1-6 and authorized a legal representative to represent them.

Although there was no suspect as of yet the Court assigned an *ad hoc* defense counsel to the situation in order to oversee defense issues. The *ad hoc* defense counsel filed a response to the victim applications.[249] Notably, he did not challenge the applicability of Article 68(3) to the investigation of a situation or the participation of victims in this early phase, prior to the naming of a suspect. Although it is not clear why he did not do so, it is presumably because he had a civil law background and was familiar

---

246 See *Situation in DRC*, No. ICC-01/04-566, 15 July 2010 and No. ICC-01/04-581, 29 September 2010.

247 See *Situation in DRC*, No. ICC-01/04-583, 25 October 2010.

248 *The Prosecutor v. Callixte Mbarushimana*, No. ICC-01/04-01/10-1, 28 September 2010, par. 6: "it is only within the boundaries of the situation of crisis for which the jurisdiction of the Court was activated that subsequent prosecutions can be initiated. Such a situation can include not only crimes that had already been or were being committed at the time of the referral, but also crimes committed after that time, in so far as they are sufficiently linked to the situation of crisis referred to the Court as ongoing at the time of the referral."

249 For the procedural history see *Situation in DRC*, No. ICC-01/04-101-tEN-Corr, 17 January 2006.

with early victim participation in a national setting. Instead, the *ad hoc* defense counsel focused his response on challenging the individual applications for not meeting the required criteria and for vagueness. Meanwhile, the prosecutor filed a motion to oppose the victim applications, arguing that the Statute did not envision victim participation at such an early stage. The OTP further argued that the objectivity of the proceedings could be placed in jeopardy, as well as the integrity of the prosecutor's office if the Court were to allow a third party to intervene so early in the process.[250]

The central question arising at this point in the proceedings was whether victims have a right to participate during the investigation of a situation prior to the naming of a suspect. There are different rationales for involving victims at this early stage of proceedings. First, it is argued that victims, in general, have the best information about the nature and extent of alleged crimes and therefore their input could be invaluable in helping to shape charges that can later be brought against an accused. Second, some commentators suggest that victim involvement can add "objectivity" to the proceedings by "ensuring a view other than the Prosecutor's."[251] The rationale for not allowing victims to participate at this early stage centers on the fact that investigations at the ICC are driven by the OTP and not by a judicial magistrate. It is the prosecution's right to direct investigations and victims, it is argued, are free to submit information to the prosecutor. Needless to say, the extent to which victims would be able to participate during the pre-trial stage generated lengthy discussions during the drafting of the Rules. At the negotiations on the Rules, some delegations wanted victims to act as full parties at this stage, whereas other delegations felt that victim participation would negatively affect the efficiency of pre-trial proceedings.[252]

In answering the above question of whether victims would have the right to participate during the investigation phase, the Pre-Trial Chamber responded with a definitive *yes*. Despite the fact that the right to participate during this phase is not expressly foreseen in the Statute's text, the Court found that the broad approach to victim participation during this phase was supported by the Statute and Rules generally, as well as a number of human rights documents.[253] Addressing the arguments in a terminological, contextual and teleological approach, Pre-Trial Chamber I looked at a number of different issues when making its decision.

First, the Judges examined whether the Statute, Rules and Regulations of the Court allow for early victim participation. The Court first looked to Article 68(3) and determined that, although Article 68(3) is located in the "Trial" section of the Statute, because it does not specifically stipulate a stage of the proceedings for victim involvement, participation can take place during the pre-trial stage before the identification

250 De Hemptinne and Rindi (2006) at 343.

251 Stahn, et al. (2006) at 226.

252 Holmes, J.T., Jurisdiction and Admissibility, 332, in Lee, et al. (2001).

253 The Chamber cited cases from the ECtHR, including *Oğur v. Turkey*, App. No. 21594/93, 20 May 1999 and *Kelly and Others v. United Kingdom*, App. No. 30054/96, 4 August 2001, both of which are discussed in Chapter 4.

of a suspect or the initiation of an investigation.[254] Arguments submitted by the prosecution, maintaining that there is a clear distinction between court proceedings – as referred to in Article 68(3) – and the investigation phase of the pre-trial stage, fell on deaf ears. The Judges determined that victims could participate during the investigation phase because "victims are affected *in general* at the investigation stage, since the participation at this stage can serve to clarify the facts, to punish the perpetrators of crimes and to request reparations for the harm suffered."[255]

Second, in looking at the overall objectives of the Court, the Judges concluded that early victim participation was a laudable goal of the drafters as evidenced by the various references to victim participation in the Statute and Rules. In particular, the Judges took note of the fact that the Court was created in a context where international human rights law and international humanitarian law were placing more and more emphasis on the role of victims in criminal proceedings.[256] Along these lines, the Judges used jurisprudence from the European Court of Human Rights and the Inter-American Court of Human Rights to bolster its decision allowing victims participatory rights prior to the naming of a suspect.[257] The Chamber cited numerous cases from the ECtHR in support of its finding.[258] However, none of these cases were directly pertinent to the issue before the Court, namely the rights of victims to participate during the investigation phase. Instead, the cases from the ECtHR provide that when the domestic law allows for victims to join their civil claim to a criminal proceeding the victim has a right to have the criminal proceeding conducted within a reasonable time.[259] Similarly, the reference to the case law of the IACtHR falls short of supporting its finding that Article 68(3) gives victims the right to participate during the investigation phase and "in the fight against impunity."[260] The Court found that the IACtHR "decided that it was clear from the terms of article 8 of the Convention that victims of human rights violations or their relatives are entitled to take steps during the criminal proceedings, from the investigation stage and prior to confirmation of the charges, to have the facts clarified and the perpetrators prosecuted, and are entitled to request reparations for the harm suffered."[261] However, unlike in the jurisdictions over which the IACtHR has

254 Rome Statute, Art. 15(3); ICC RPE, Rules 50(1), 50(3), 92(2) and 107(5)

255 *Situation in DRC*, No. ICC-01/04-101-tEN-Corr, 17 January 2006, par. 63; see also *Situation in Darfur*, No. ICC-02/05-111-Corr, 14 December 2007, para. 11 and 14.

256 *Situation in DRC*, No. ICC-01/04-101-tEN-Corr, 17 January 2006, par. 50. Before being appointed as a Judge at the ICC (and one of the three judges on the Pre-Trial Chamber that issued the 17 January 2006 decision on victim participation), Claude Jorda wrote that victims "may not participate in the investigation undertaken by the Proseuctor…." See Jorda, J. and de Hemptinne, J., The Status and Role of the Victims, 1406 in Cassese, et al. (2002).

257 *Situation in DRC*, No. ICC-01/04-101-tEN-Corr, 17 January 2006, para. 51-53.

258 Including, *inter alia*, ECtHR, *Acquaviva v. France*, App. No. 19248/91, 21 November 1995; *Tomasi v. France*, App. No. 12850/87, 27 August 1992; *Perez v. France*, App. No. 47287/99, 12 February 2004, all of which are discussed in Chapter 4.

259 Manning (2007) at 824.

260 *Situation in DRC*, No. ICC-01/04-101-tEN-Corr, 17 January 2006, par. 53.

261 *Ibid.*

heard cases, the ICC does not allow victims to insist upon prosecutions or to pursue prosecutions when the prosecutor declines to do so. In fact, taking into account the specific characteristics of international criminal law, the drafters specifically declined to grant victims the right to pursue private prosecutions commonly found in domestic systems. Finally, little consideration is given to the differences in the nature of the documents expounding rights or explanation provided as to the applicability of regional instruments and the decisions from regional courts with regard to crimes committed in an African state.[262]

This decision ultimately envisioned victims participating in a number of proceedings taking place at the investigation phase of the pre-trial stage, including proceedings related to protection measures, preservation of evidence, and investigations generally.[263] When interpreting the obligations arising under Article 68(3) to deny participation when participation would be inconsistent with the rights of a fair trial, the Judges seemed to dismiss the notion. They concluded that "the participation of victims during the stage of investigation of a situation does not *per se* jeopardize the appearance of integrity and objectivity of the investigation, nor is it inherently inconsistent with basic considerations of efficiency and security."[264] Instead, the Judges found that the extent of participation, and not participation generally, may impact the investigation. They held that any prejudice to a future suspect or the fairness and efficiency of the proceedings could be regulated on a case-by-case basis by the Chamber.[265]

The result of the decision was to grant six victim-applicants the right to participate in pre-trial proceedings during the investigation phase (the victims had not requested to participate in any specific proceeding). After granting the applicants victim status, the Court then had to determine the proper modalities of participation. However, because the victim-applicants had not requested to participate in any specific proceeding, the Judges simply determined that the victims would have access to all public documents. In this sense the Judges restricted access to any non-public document contained in the record of the situation.[266]

When the first case arose under the DRC situation with the arrest and transfer of Thomas Lubanga Dyilo in March of 2006, Pre-Trial Chamber I invited submissions on whether the six victims should also be granted the right to participate in the case.[267] The six victims of the situation subsequently failed to meet the criteria for obtaining victim status in the case due to the fact that their harms suffered did not relate to the charges alleged against Lubanga, raising serious issues about heightening the expectations of victims so early in the process.

262 Sheppard (2010) at 49.
263 *Situation in DRC*, No. ICC-01/04-101-tEN-Corr, 17 January 2006, para. 71, 73-74.
264 *Ibid.* at par. 57.
265 *Ibid.* at para. 57, 70.
266 *Ibid.* at par. 76.
267 See *The Prosecutor v. Lubanga*, No. ICC-01/04-01/06-172-tEN, 29 June 2006.

In many ways the Pre-Trial Chambers handling the situations in Uganda and Darfur followed the precedent set by the 17 January 2006 Decision, finding that victims have a general right to participate in investigations.[268] Despite repeated attempts by the prosecutor to appeal these decisions, the Pre-Trial Chambers were generally reluctant to have their decisions appealed. Any requests by the prosecutor seeking leave to appeal on the issue of victim participation were initially denied.[269]

Revisiting Victim Participation during the Investigation Phase

As early as the 17 January 2006 Decision, the OTP objected to the finding of the Pre-Trial Chamber that the Statute grants a procedural status of victim or a general right to participate during the investigation phase.[270] The prosecutor also objected to the finding that questions about fairness and efficiency should be dealt with when deciding on the modalities of participation and not when deciding on participation itself.[271] The prosecution consistently argued that whether an applicant's personal interests are affected within the meaning of Article 68(3) would need to be determined in relation to a 'proceeding' within the meaning of Article 68(3) and that an 'investigation' should not be equated with a 'proceeding'.[272] It further argued that Article 68(3) was meant to limit broad participation. If the Court were to permit the participation of victims without taking into the account the requirements found in Article 68(3), the Judges would violate the principle of treaty interpretation.[273] Moreover, the prosecution claimed that the Court's interpretation of the Statute went far beyond the system agreed to in Rome, which, for example, did not adopt a system in which victims would have broad access to the Court during investigations.

In accordance with the Statute, the prosecutor argued that the active participation of victims during the investigation phase is permitted under Article 15(3) (presenting views when the prosecutor seeks authorization for an investigation *proprio motu*) and under Article 19(3) (submitting observations in jurisdiction and admissibility hearings). In addition, the prosecutor noted that under Article 53 and Rule 92(2) the Court must inform victims or their legal representatives who have already participated in proceedings or who have communicated with the Court in respect to a situation or case when the prosecutor decides not to initiate an investigation or prosecution. A general

---

268 See *Situation in Uganda*, No. ICC-02/04-101, 10 August 2007; See *Situation in Darfur*, No. ICC-02/05-111-Corr, 14 December 2007, p. 3-5, 22-23, para. 45-47.

269 See *Situation in DRC*, No. ICC-01/04-103, 23 January 2006 and No. ICC-01/04-141, 24 April 2006; see also *Situation in Uganda*, No. ICC-02/04-103, 20 August 2007.

270 *Situation in DRC*, No. ICC-01/04-84, 15 August 2005, para. 11-17; *Situation in Uganda*, No. ICC-02/04-85, 28 February 2007, par. 22.

271 *Situation in DRC*, No. ICC-01/04-103, 23 January 2006, par. 22.

272 *Situation in DRC*, No. ICC-01/04-84, 15 August 2005, para. 11-17; *Situation in Uganda*, No. ICC-02/04-85, 28 February 2007, par. 22.

273 *Situation in DRC*, No. ICC-01/04-84, 15 August 2005, par. 25; *Situation in Uganda*, No. ICC-02/04-85, 28 February 2007, par. 29.

right to participate in the investigation phase would make these provisions unnecessary. The prosecution also maintained that early victim participation would negatively affect the independence of the prosecutor and its duty to carry out investigations as well as the overall efficiency of the Court.

The prosecutor further contended that the Court was wrong when saying that participation generally is fair and expeditious, and that questions about fairness and efficiency should be dealt with when deciding on the modalities of participation rather than when deciding on participation itself. It warned of a bottleneck of procedures whereby the Court could potentially have to deal with thousands of victims from the conflicts under investigation and only a small percentage of those victims would later be permitted to participate in the case proceedings. The raising of false expectations, it contended, was damaging to victims. Finally, the prosecutor asserted that the fairness of the proceedings was at stake because victims would be permitted to participate in investigations and in theory to present facts to the Chambers without having the duty to disclose this information to the *ad hoc* defense or the duty to investigate exculpatory material – two fair trial principles enshrined in the Statute.[274]

It was not until 2008 when, two years after the 17 January 2006 Decision, the Pre-Trial Chambers in the Darfur situation and the DRC situation eventually granted leave to appeal the issue. Ultimately the Appeals Chamber agreed, in part, with the arguments of the prosecutor. The Appeals Chamber, in its 19 December 2008 Judgment on victim participation, reversed the 3 December 2007 Pre-Trial Chamber I decision in the Darfur situation and the 24 December 2007 Pre-Trial Chamber I decision in the DRC situation. These earlier decisions found that individuals accorded the status of victim, notwithstanding any specific proceedings being conducted in the framework of such an investigation, could present their views and concerns and file documents pertaining to the relevant investigation. The Appeals Chamber disagreed with this approach, finding that "[t]he article of the Statute that confers power upon a victim to participate in any proceedings is article 68 (3)," and that "participation can take place only within the context of judicial proceedings."[275] It went on to find that investigations are not judicial proceedings but rather are inquiries conducted by the prosecutor into the alleged commission of crimes and the identification of those responsible.[276] The Appeals Chamber noted that pursuant to Article 42, the "authority for the conduct of investigations vests in the Prosecutor" and that acknowledgement by the Pre-Trial Chamber of a right of victims to participate in the investigations contravenes the

274 *Situation in DRC*, No. ICC-01/04-103, 23 January 2006, para. 10, 13-22; *Situation in Uganda*, No. ICC-02/04-85, 28 February 2007, para. 32-33, 38-39; *Situation in Uganda*, No. ICC-02/04-103, 20 August 2007, para. 13-14.

275 *Situation in DRC*, No. ICC-01/04-556, 19 December 2008, par. 45; see also *Situation in Darfur*, No. ICC-02/05-177, 2 February 2009.

276 *Situation in DRC*, No. ICC-01/04-556, 19 December 2008, par. 45; see also *Situation in Darfur*, No. ICC-02/05-177, 2 February 2009.

Statute by reading into it a right that it does not provide.[277] Thus the Appeals Chamber eventually came around to finding, in at least two situations, that broad participatory rights in the investigative phase do not exist. Instead, victims will need to show how their personal interests are affected by a specific procedural matter in this phase.

In its November 2010 decision on victims' participation in proceedings related to the Kenya situation, Pre-Trial Chamber II followed the guidance of the Appeals Chamber.[278] The Judges concluded that applicants must link their requests to participate with an issue which forms the subject-matter of the judicial proceeding.[279] In other words, the Pre-Trial Chamber adopted the piecemeal approach to Article 68(3) determinations.

One rationale for this approach is that by equating an entire phase of the criminal process to a proceeding under Article 68(3) and then finding that the personal interests are affected by an entire phase effectively negates the personal interests provision. Moreover, the original position taken by the Pre-Trial Chambers, namely, that victims had a general interest in participating during the investigation phase and could therefore theoretically have participatory rights, proved problematic. Victims would gain victim status but would later be denied any actual participatory rights at specific proceedings, begging the question of whether such a status carried any substance or whether it only led victims to feel disillusioned by the system.

7.4.3.3 Confirmation of Charges Phase

Up until this point in the process, the confirmation of charges phase of the Pre-Trial stage provides the most comprehensive rights for victim participation. This comes as no surprise since the confirmation of charges phase of the pre-trial stage envisions the naming of a suspect. The confirmation of charges phase begins with the warrant of arrest or the summons to appear and only ends after the confirmation of charges and the setting of a trial date.

Warrant of Arrest or Summons to Appear

Warrants of arrest and summonses to appear before the Court are the two ways in which to inform a suspect of the pending charges against him. An arrest warrant issued on behalf of the Court authorizes the arrest and detention of an individual while a judicial summons is addressed to an individual suspected of crimes requesting his presence and surrender before the Court. At any time after the initiation of an investigation, the prosecutor may initiate a prosecution by applying to the Pre-Trial Chamber

277 *Situation in DRC*, No. ICC-01/04-556, 19 December 2008, par. 52; see also *Situation in Darfur*, No. ICC-02/05-177, 2 February 2009.
278 See *Situation in the Republic of Kenya*, No. ICC-01/09-24, 3 November 2010.
279 *Ibid.* at par. 16.

for the issuance of an arrest warrant for an individual or a summons to appear.[280] Before issuing the arrest warrant or summons to appear, the Court must be satisfied there are reasonable grounds to believe that the person committed a crime within the jurisdiction of the Court and the arrest of the person appears necessary.[281]

The arrest warrants issued thus far by the Court make no reference to the victims being heard in relation to the Prosecutor's applications for the arrest warrants. Moreover, because the arrest warrants are generally issued under seal it is unlikely that any victims participated in hearings on the issue.[282] This means that although victims can indirectly influence the charges found in arrest warrants, for example, by providing information to the prosecutor, they have little direct influence over the initial charges brought against a suspect. Instead, victims have greater influence during the confirmation of charges – but only if the crimes they allege they suffered are included in the charges brought against that suspect.

When victims' groups learned of the narrow charges found in the arrest warrant brought against Lubanga they condemned the prosecutor's approach,[283] and were frustrated that they did not have the opportunity to directly influence the charges at the early stage of the process. None of the six victims granted participatory rights in the DRC situation had the opportunity to raise any concerns surrounding the arrest warrant. Moreover, these victims did not have an opportunity to raise concerns in future hearings because the Pre-Trial Chamber determined that no sufficient causal link was established between the harm suffered by these victim participants of the situation and the crimes specified in the arrest warrant since their harms suffered did not relate to the charges brought against Lubanga.[284] This example illustrates the inability of victims to have a greater influence on the charges brought against suspects that they may have in domestic systems.

---

280 Rome Statute, Art. 58(2): The application for the arrest warrant must contain the name of the person, specific reference to the crimes under the Court's jurisdiction and a concise statement of the facts which are alleged to constitute the crimes, a summary of evidence and the reasons why the Prosecutor believes that an arrest is necessary.

281 *Ibid.*, Art. 58(1). Necessity may stem from the assurance that the person will appear at trial, the assurance that the person will not obstruct or endanger the investigation or the prevention of the continuation of crimes by that individual.

282 However, a number of victims and two amici curiae have been allowed to participate in appeals related to applications for arrest warrants, see *Situation in Darfur*, No. ICC-02/05-01/09-48, 23 December 2009.

283 See, e.g., Joint Letter from ASF, Center for Justice and Reconciliation, DRC Coalition for the ICC, FIDH, HRW, REDRESS, and the Women's Initiative for Gender Justice to Luis Moreno Ocampo, Chief Prosecutor, ICC, on the Narrow Scope of the Charges Brought Against Mr. Lubanga, 31 July 2006, *on file with the author*.

284 See *The Prosecutor v. Lubanga*, No. ICC-01/04-01/06-172-tEN, 29 June 2006.

Challenges to the Jurisdiction and Admissibility of a Case

In the Statute and Rules there is a clear difference between jurisdiction and admissibility. Jurisdiction is whether the Court has legal competence over the acts in question. Admissibility "seeks to establish whether matters over which the Court properly has jurisdiction should be litigated before it."[285] Articles 17, 18 and 19 of the Statute deal with admissibility and jurisdiction issues.[286] Admissibility and jurisdiction questions are inherently connected to the principle of complementarity. The principle of complementarity obliges the Court to defer jurisdiction to a national authority unless that authority is unwilling or unable to investigate or prosecute a case.[287] Persons charged or States that could potentially have jurisdiction may challenge the admissibility or jurisdiction of a case, and victims have the right to express their views and concerns.[288] Under Article 19(3) victims are expressly authorized to participate in challenges to jurisdiction or the admissibility of a case. Article 19(3) reads as follows:

> The Prosecutor may seek a ruling from the Court regarding a question of jurisdiction or admissibility. In proceedings with respect to jurisdiction or admissibility, those who have referred the situation under article 13, as well as victims, may also submit observations to the Court.

Rule 59, the counterpart to Article 19, provides that the Registrar shall notify victims or their legal representatives about challenges to jurisdiction. Those victims can then make observations in writing to the competent Chamber. However, victims may not necessarily be limited to written observations if the Chamber seeks the view of victims under Rule 93 through oral submissions. Again, the amount of victim participation depends upon the discretion of the Judges.

Article 18 deals with preliminary rulings regarding admissibility. Unlike Articles 15 and 19, which explicitly allow for victim participation during the pre-trial stage, Article 18 does not expressly allow for the involvement of victims. The absence of an express provision is due, in large part, to negotiations during drafting. Delegates expressed concern about giving victims too many opportunities to participate, thereby affecting the speed of the proceedings.[289] The drafting history supports the argument that victims are not permitted to participate in Article 18 proceedings concerning a

---

285 Schabas (2004) at 68.

286 See *The Prosecutor v. Lubanga*, No. ICC-01/04-01/06-8-US-Corr, 24 February 2006. States Parties may challenge the jurisdiction of the Court or the admissibility of a situation during the investigative phase of the pre-trial stage; however, most challenges to jurisdiction and admissibility will arise once a suspect has been named. Therefore, this chapter will discuss the issues surrounding victim participation and challenges to jurisdiction and admissibility during this phase.

287 See Fairlie (2005); Delmas-Marty (2005).

288 Rome Statute, Art. 19(2). A State from which acceptance of jurisdiction is required under Article 12 may also challenge the admissibility of a case.

289 Holmes, J.T., Jurisdiction and Admissibility, 343, in Lee, et al. (2001).

State's challenge to admissibility and jurisdiction; however, some commentators suggest that Article 19(3) is drafted so broadly that it allows victims involvement even in Article 18 proceedings.[290] Ultimately, it is left to the Judges to decide upon the scope and manner of victim involvement. In general, the Judges have allowed victims to file observations following a challenge to jurisdiction or to admissibility.[291]

Pre-Trial Detention and the Conditional Release of a Suspect

During or just after the initial Pre-Trial proceedings a suspect who is in the custody of the Court is entitled to request interim release.[292] The ability to request interim release is a fair trial right found in a number of human rights instruments and the Statute of the ICC.[293] Article 60(2) states that "[a] person subject to a warrant of arrest may apply for interim release pending trial." In line with the fundamental rights to individual liberty and the presumption of innocence, pre-trial detention at the national level is generally the exception rather than the rule. However, this is usually not the case at the international level. If the criteria found in Article 58(1) are satisfied then detention may continue.[294] These criteria include (i) concluding that there are reasonable grounds to believe that the person has committed a crime under the Court's jurisdiction; (ii) ensuring the person's appearance at trial; (iii) ensuring that the person does not obstruct or endanger the investigation or court proceedings; and (iv) preventing the person from continuing with the commission of that crime or a related crime falling within the jurisdiction of the Court.[295] While recognizing the seriousness of the crimes alleged against a suspect or accused, the Court must balance the rights of that individual to be presumed innocent and therefore free from detention prior to trial with the interests of society to ensure the presence of that individual before the Court.

If the Pre-Trial Chamber finds that the criteria of Article 58(1) are not satisfied then it may grant interim release, with or without conditions attached.[296] As a further safeguard against unreasonable detention, Article 60(4) states that "[t]he Pre-Trial Chamber shall ensure that a person is not detained for an unreasonable period prior to trial due to inexcusable delay by the Prosecutor." Delays in general, those caused by the defense, legal representatives for victims, or excusable delays caused by the prosecutor, will not affect the Court's assessment of interim release. When deciding on the conditional release of a suspect or accused Rule 119(3) specifically requires the Pre-Trial Chamber to seek the views of victims who have communicated with the

290 Hall, C.K., Article 19, 412, in Triffterer (1999).

291 See, e.g., *The Prosecutor v. Lubanga*, No. ICC-01/04-01/06-349-tEN, 24 August 2006; *The Prosecutor v. Katanga/Ngudjolo*, No. ICC-01/04-01/07-1060, 16 April 2009.

292 Rome Statute, Art. 60; ICC RPE, Rule 118(1)

293 See ICCPR, Art. 9 and ECHR, Art. 5.

294 Rome Statute, Art. 58(1).

295 *Ibid.*, Art. 58(1).

296 *Ibid.*, Art. 60(2) and ICC RPE, Rule 119.

Court on a particular case and with whom the Chamber considers at risk as a result of conditional release.

In Lubanga's pre-trial detention appeal,[297] the issue over whether victims would be able to automatically participate in appeals concerning the conditional release of a suspect or accused arose. Article 82(1)(b) states that either *party* may appeal a decision granting or denying the release of a person being investigated or prosecuted. It makes no mention of participants. Nevertheless, a majority of the Appeals Chamber found that victims would be permitted to participate in these types of appeals, but in order for victims to participate in an appeal under Article 82(1)(b) the victim must file an application seeking leave to participate.[298] Victims, therefore, do not have an automatic right to participate in this type of appeal even though Rule 119 requires the Pre-Trial Chamber to seek the views of victims on this issue. In their application victims must indicate how their personal interests are affected and why it would be appropriate for the Appeals Chamber to permit their views and concerns to be presented.[299] In contrast, the dissenting opinion of Judge Song argues that victims should not need to file an application to participate in appeals because he argues that such a right is granted to all participants to the proceedings that gave rise to the appeal.[300] After the hearing, in which victims were permitted to participate, the Appeals Chamber confirmed the decision of the Chamber to reject the defense request.[301]

Although it is likely that the Pre-Trial Chamber and Appeals Chamber would have continued Lubanga's detention even without the observations put forward by the victims due to the fact that the detention of suspects and accused at the international level appears to be the norm rather than the exception, symbolically, the participation of victims in these types of proceedings is significant. It is the victims themselves who can inform the Court about safety concerns without having to rely on the prosecutor to do this on their behalf. Substantively, the victims' observations may in fact have had an impact on the Court's decisions in denying Lubanga's request for conditional release. In the least, it allowed the victims the opportunity to express their views and concerns on the topic.

The Confirmation of Charges Hearing

The purpose of a confirmation of charges hearing is to establish whether there is enough evidence to put a suspect on trial for the crimes alleged in the Charging

297 See *The Prosecutor v. Lubanga*, No. ICC-01/04-01/06-586-tEN; 18 October 2006 and No. ICC-01/04-01/06-594; 20 October 2006.

298 *The Prosecutor v. Lubanga*, No. ICC-01/04-01/06-925, 13 June 2007, par. 23.

299 *Ibid.* See also *The Prosecutor v. Lubanga*, No. ICC-01/04-01/06-824, 13 February 2007, para. 1 and 38.

300 *The Prosecutor v. Lubanga*, No. ICC-01/04-01/06-824, 13 February 2007, par. 3.

301 See *Ibid.* One day later, Pre-Trial Chamber I relied on the Appeals Chamber judgment to decide that Thomas Lubanga should remain in detention.

Document.[302] In many civil law systems, the confirmation of charges is an established procedure to oversee the investigating magistrate or prosecutor. In the words of the Court, "it is designed to protect the rights of the defense against wrongful or wholly unfounded allegations."[303] Because the hearing is not a trial in the strict sense the Prosecutor may rely on summary or documentary evidence in addition to witness testimony.[304] In turn, the suspect charged may challenge the evidence presented and present additional evidence.[305] In other words, although it is not a trial in the strict sense, it has the potential of turning into a mini-trial.

Following the hearing, the Pre-Trial Chamber may make one of several decisions: (1) confirm one or more charges and send the case to trial; (2) refuse to confirm one or more charges, to which the prosecutor may re-submit the charge or charges for confirmation based on additional evidence; (3) adjourn the hearing and request the prosecutor to consider providing additional evidence or consider conducing further investigations; or (4) adjourn the hearing and request the prosecutor to consider amending a charge to better reflect the evidence.[306] While a confirmation hearing differs from other pre-trial hearings and the trial itself, victims will almost always have an interest in participating.[307] Although the Statute does not explicitly state that victims have a right to participate in these types of hearings, a number of Rules support the argument in favor of participation. For instance, Rules 89 to 91 apply to confirmation of charges proceedings; therefore, there is a presumption in favor of participation. In addition, pursuant to Article 93, the Chamber may also seek the view of other victims on any issue, *inter alia*, in relation to Rule 125 dealing with the confirmation hearing in the absence of the person concerned.[308] Likewise, under Rule 92(3) the Court is required to notify victims of confirmation hearings so that they can submit applications for participation in accordance with Rule 89.[309] Finally, the Rules require the Registrar under Rule 92(8) to give "adequate publicity" of the confirmation hearing proceedings so that victims are aware of their ability to apply to participate. At the time of writing,

302 Notably, the issuance of an arrest warrant at the *Ad Hoc* Tribunals was, for the most part, an immaterial aspect of the proceedings. Once the prosecutor determines that sufficient evidence exists to indict a suspect, he prepares an indictment and forwards it to the Registry for confirmation by a judge. Once the indictment is confirmed, it is made public unless ordered by the judge to remain sealed. The indictment is then served on the suspect at the time of arrest. As such, the issuance of an arrest warrant at the *Ad Hoc* Tribunals is distinct from the confirmation of charges before the ICC.

303 *The Prosecutor v. Lubanga,* T, 29 January 2007, p. 9.

304 Rome Statute, Art. 61(5).

305 *Ibid.*, Art. 61(6). One concern for defense counsel regarding the confirmation of charges is the fact that a defense team can essentially fight the charges, challenging the evidence and proposing a new theory, but a decision by the Pre-Trial Chamber does not qualify for the *ne bis in idem* principle (the double jeopardy principle).

306 *Ibid.*, Art. 61(7); see *The Prosecutor v. Bemba*, No. ICC-01/05-01/08-388, 3 March 2009, para. 38-39, stating that Article 61(7)(c) does not allow the Chamber to order the prosecutor to provide additional evidence or to amend the charges.

307 Bitti, G., and Friman, H. Participation of Victims in the Proceedings, 470, in Lee, et al. (2001).

308 Stahn, et al. (2006) at 235.

309 *Ibid.*

victims have participated in all confirmation of charges hearings that have taken place at the Court. However, the modalities of participation have differed and the impact of participation has also varied.

The *Lubanga* case illustrates the numerous issues surrounding victim participation and the confirmation of charges process. Being the first case to reach the confirmation of charges stage, the issues that arose caused a great deal of conflict between the interests of all Court actors. Prior to the confirmation hearing, there were numerous filings by the prosecution, defense and legal representatives for victims concerning which victims could participate (if at all) and the arrangements for participation. The Pre-Trial Chamber ultimately concluded that having met the criteria under Rule 85 as well as Article 68(3) victims could participate in the confirmation of charges hearing,[310] and granted four victims, represented by four separate legal representatives, participatory rights.

After granting the right to participate the Pre-Trial Chamber then had to determine the modalities of participation. The Chamber concluded that pursuant to Rule 89(1) the victims would have the opportunity to make opening and closing statements, and that the legal representatives for victims would be able to request leave to intervene in the proceedings. The Chamber found that legal representatives may, in their opening and closing statements, amongst other things, address any point of law, including the legal characterization of the modes of liability with which the prosecutor charged the suspect.[311] However, their participation would be limited to the charges brought against Lubanga.[312] In addition, participation was also limited to (i) access to only the public documents in the record of the case (and not to the DRC situation generally); and (ii) attendance at only the public hearings due to the fact that the victims wanted to participate anonymously (including status hearings and the confirmation of charges hearing).[313]

The Court found that the fundamental principle prohibiting anonymous accusations would be violated if anonymous victims were permitted to add any point of fact or evidence to the case file. To this end, the victims in the *Lubanga* case were neither permitted to question witnesses pursuant to Rule 91(3) nor eligible to give evidence or call witnesses.[314] The Court noted that only if the victims agreed to disclose their identities to the defense would the Chamber consider broadening their participatory rights in the case against Lubanga.[315] Furthermore, they were not permitted to discuss factual issues not put forward by the prosecutor because otherwise this could be viewed as making an anonymous accusation against the suspect.[316]

310 See *The Prosecutor v. Lubanga*, No. ICC-01/04-01/06-462-tEN, 22 September 2006.
311 *The Prosecutor v. Lubanga*, No. ICC-01/04-01/06-678, 7 November 2006, p. 7.
312 Victims a/0001/06, a/0002/06 and a/0003/06 were given permission to participate on 22 June 2006. For the procedural history, see *The Prosecutor v. Lubanga*, No. ICC-01/04-01/06-601-tEN, 20 October 2006.
313 See *The Prosecutor v. Lubanga*, No. ICC-01/04-01/06-462-tEN, 22 September 2006.
314 *Ibid.* at 6-7.
315 *Ibid.* at 7-8.
316 *Ibid.*

The confirmation hearing itself was extensive. The proceedings, a first in international criminal law, lasted from 9 November 2006 to 28 November 2006. The topics touched upon covered diverse issues ranging from disclosure obligations, evidentiary concerns, equality of arms and, most importantly, the alleged individual criminal responsibility of Lubanga. Of the four victims permitted to participate all exercised their right to remain anonymous. Therefore, none of the four victims were present during the hearing. With the exception of their opening and closing statements, victims' legal representatives made observations almost exclusively on legal matters, including on issues concerning the principle of legality, the probative value of evidence, the admissibility of evidence, proof-of-age of child soldiers and the criminal liability of Lubanga.[317]

The opening statements of the four legal representatives were hugely symbolic. Acknowledging the historic moment, the one legal representative stated, "Today for the first time in the history of international criminal justice, victims can express their viewpoints and concerns through their counsel. [...] Today, they can express themselves."[318] He presented the background of the case, argued that Lubanga was responsible for the abduction and conscription of many children, and explained how the Congolese justice system was ill-prepared to handle these types of cases.[319] He then informed the Court that his clients are unable to attend school anymore and are haunted by what they experienced. He further highlighted the fact that entire families are affected by these crimes and not just the former child soldiers.[320] He reminded the Court that the proceedings are not meant to be an intellectual exercise but that the lives of thousands of youth should be at the center of discussions.[321] Another legal representative similarly asserted that his client holds Lubanga criminal responsible and that his client, as a victim, deserves dignity, respect and recognition from the Court and from the world.[322] He then went on to lament about the limited rights afforded to victims in the process.

During the hearing the prosecution called one witness, an expert on issues relating to children in the Ituri region of the DRC. During the defense's cross-examination of the expert-witness, one of the legal representatives informed the Chamber that he would like to pose a question. Later that day, the Court heard the proposed question, which related to whether the witness took notes when interviewing parents of child soldiers.

In addition to the opening statements, one question posed and two document requests, the legal representatives made closing statements. But before they began the

317 See *The Prosecutor v. Lubanga*, No. ICC-01/04-01/06-750, 4 December 2006 and No. ICC-01/04-01/06-745, 1 December 2006.

318 *The Prosecutor v. Lubanga*, T, 9 November 2006, p. 76.

319 *Ibid.* at 76, 77, 79.

320 *Ibid.* at 81.

321 *Ibid.* at 93.

322 *Ibid.* at 96.

presiding Judge remarked, "We are listening to you very carefully, because what you have to say is perhaps what is most important, especially in view of the Statute of the ICC."[323] One legal representative began her closing arguments, outlining the background of events leading to the recruitment and enlistment of child soldiers in the DRC, characterizing the situation in the DRC as an international armed conflict and then specifically discussing the enlistment of her client.[324] Another legal representative touched upon a search and seizure carried out in the DRC, which may become an issue at trial, procedural provisions of the Statute related to summaries of witness interviews, and the rights of victims to remain anonymous, and another explained how his clients did not voluntarily join the UPC militia and argued that the victims are not motivated by financial compensation but rather want the truth to be established.[325]

On 29 January 2007, Pre-Trial Chamber I confirmed the charges against Lubanga, sending his case to trial. The Chamber found sufficient evidence establishing substantial grounds to believe he is criminally responsible as a co-perpetrator for all three charges brought against him, including (1) enlisting children under the age of fifteen; (2) conscripting children under the age of fifteen; and (3) using children under the age of fifteen to participate actively in hostilities. However, the Chamber substituted "internal armed conflict" war crimes under Article 8(2)(e)(vii) with "international armed conflict" war crimes under Article 8(2)(b)(xxvii) – something the legal representatives maintained throughout the hearings.[326] The decision was 134 pages in length – far more than anyone expected.

The representative for victims filed observations in response to both the prosecution and defense applications seeking leave to appeal, asking the Court to reject both of them.[327] Acknowledging that the issues raised by the defense *did not directly concern victims*, their observations nonetheless stressed that the requests for leave to appeal slowed down the proceedings thereby prejudicing victims' interests that justice be done.[328] The Pre-Trial Chamber rejected both the prosecution and defense's requests to appeal the confirmation of charges. Despite the fact that the Chamber could have allowed for an appeal, the Chamber remarked that the Statute intentionally excluded a direct right to appeal decisions confirming charges. Additionally, the Chamber found that the authorization of such an appeal would cause avoidable delay affecting the rights of the accused.[329] No explicit mention was made of the rights of victims to a trial without undue delay. With the requests for leave to appeal rejected, Lubanga's case was referred to the Trial Chamber.

---

323 *The Prosecutor v. Lubanga*, T, 28 November 2006, p. 45.
324 *Ibid.* at 47, 49, 51.
325 *Ibid.* at 73-74.
326 See *The Prosecutor v. Lubanga*, No. ICC-01/04-01/06-806, 5 February 2007.
327 See *The Prosecutor v. Lubanga, No. ICC-01/04-01/06-839, 26 February 2007.*
328 See *Ibid.*
329 *The Prosecutor v. Lubanga*, No. ICC-01/04-01/06-915, 24 May 2007, para. 29-30.

The next case to hold a confirmation of charges hearing was the joint case of Germain Katanga and Mathieu Ngudjolo Chui. The Single Judge in this case embraced the systematic approach granting all victims the same procedural rights throughout pre-trial proceedings, with only a distinction being made between anonymous and non-anonymous victims.[330] The participation of victims, she contended, is not only meant to have an impact on the case but a "substantial" impact.[331] As a result, she divided the specific procedural rights for victim participants into six groups,[332] noting, however, that all of the procedural rights could "be limited by the Chamber *proprio motu*, or at the request of the parties, the Registry or any other participant, if it is shown that the relevant limitation is necessary to safeguard another competing interest protected by the Statute and the Rules – such as national security, the physical or psychological well-being of victims and witnesses, or the Prosecution's investigations."[333] Nevertheless, the scope of any such limitation would need to be carefully delimited on the basis of the principle of proportionality.[334]

The first group of procedural rights comprised the right to have access to, prior to and during the confirmation hearing, the record of the case kept by the Registry, including to the evidence filed by the prosecution and the defense pursuant to Rule 121 (Proceedings before the confirmation hearing). However, the right to have access to the evidence was limited to the format, such as un-redacted versions, redacted versions or summaries, in which the evidence is made available to the party which has not proposed it.[335] The first group of procedural rights also included the right to have access to the transcripts of both public and closed hearings, with the exception of *ex parte* transcripts.[336] Access to documents or hearings, however, did not include the right to access filings and decisions classified as *ex parte*.[337] There was no right of access to non-public filings and decisions from the situation to which the relevant case relates.[338] Importantly, the Court determined that victims' access rights could by no means exceed the access rights granted by the Statute and the Rules to the defense. The first group further included the right to be notified in the same way as the prosecution and the defense of all decisions, requests, motions, responses and other procedural documents which are filed in the record of the case and are not classified 'ex parte'.[339]

The Single Judge determined that the second group of rights included "the rights (i) to make submissions on all issues relating to the admissibility and probative value of the evidence on which the prosecution and the defense intend to rely at the confir-

330 *The Prosecutor v. Katanga/Ngudjolo*, No. ICC-01/04-01/07-474, 13 May 2008, para. 44-45.
331 *Ibid.* at par. 157.
332 *Ibid.* at par. 127.
333 *Ibid.* at para. 147-148.
334 *Ibid.* at par. 148.
335 *Ibid.* at par. 132.
336 *Ibid.* at par. 130.
337 *Ibid.* at para. 127-128.
338 *Ibid.* at par. 133.
339 *Ibid.* at par. 129.

mation hearing; and (ii) to examine such evidence at the confirmation hearing."[340] However, the victims did not have the right to introduce additional evidence.[341] The Court stressed that the introduction of additional evidence on which neither the prosecutor nor the defense intend to rely on by victims would infringe upon the rights of the suspects due to the potential to prolong proceedings.[342] The third group of procedural rights dealt with the examination of witnesses. So long as the victim participant is not an anonymous victim, the victim will have the right to examine, at the confirmation hearing, any witness called by the prosecution or defense.[343] If the victim participant is anonymous the principle of prohibiting anonymous accusations nullifies this right. The Court also found that victims exercising this right should examine witnesses after the prosecution but before the defense and within the time allocated by the Chamber. Furthermore, the victims, like the prosecution and defense, are not required to file the list of questions they intend to pose prior to the examination of the witness.[344]

The fourth group of procedural rights was comprised of the right to attend all public and closed session hearings leading up to and during the confirmation of charges hearing. However, the fourth group does not include the right to attend *ex parte* hearings.[345] The fifth group of procedural rights included the right to participate by way of oral motions, responses and submissions. Victims were permitted to orally participate in: (i) all hearings in which those granted the procedural status of victim have the right to attend; and (ii) in relation to all matters other than those in which their intervention has been excluded by the Statute and Rules. This exclusion may include, for example, matters relating to inter-party disclosure or any discussion of the evidence which aims at extending the factual basis contained in the Prosecution Charging Document (PCD).[346] Nonetheless, victims would be permitted to try to extend the legal characterization of the facts contained in the PCD to the point where the Court could ask the Prosecution to consider amending the PCD to include a different crime.[347]

The sixth and last group of procedural rights included the right to file written motions, responses and replies in accordance with Regulation 24 concerning all matters other than those in which the victim's legal representative has been excluded by the Statute and Rules. This group of rights included the right to file written submissions on evidentiary and legal issues to be discussed at the confirmation of charges hearing and to raise objections or make observations in regard to issues related to the proper conduct of the proceedings prior to the confirmation hearing in accordance with Rule 122(3). However, this group of rights did not include the right to make challenges

340 *Ibid.* at par. 134.
341 *Ibid.* at par. 111.
342 *Ibid.* at para. 111-113.
343 *Ibid.* at par. 137.
344 *Ibid.* at para. 135 and 137-138.
345 *Ibid.* at par. 140.
346 *Ibid.* at par. 141.
347 *Ibid.* at para. 122-123.

to, or raise issues relating to, the jurisdiction of the Court or the admissibility of a case pursuant to Article 19(2) and (3) of the Statute and Rule 122(2).[348]

The confirmation of charges hearing began on 27 June 2008 and concluded on 18 July 2008.[349] Katanga and Ngudjolo were alleged to have committed three counts of crimes against humanity and six counts of war crimes in Ituri,[350] a territory in eastern DRC, from January to March 2003. The allegations against the two suspects focused in particular on one attack against the village of Bogoro on 24 February 2003.

Four legal representatives, representing 56 victims (38 of whom were anonymous), gave opening statements.[351] Sharing the two hours they were allotted, the legal representatives touched upon the importance of participation and questioned those who would oppose it. One legal representative asked, "Who might hesitate to allow the participation of victims unless this person has something to hide."[352] Focusing largely on the unimaginable harms suffered by their clients,[353] legal representatives also emphasized the gravity of their participation by stating, "We represent hope, the hope for justice, the hope in justice."[354] Another stated that despite the perceived inconvenience of participation "this is the only framework available to victims to express their pain, to express their hope, to express their despair."[355] In addition, the victims' legal representatives emphasized their belief that the attack took place within a wider international conflict. One legal representative argued that together with Katanga and Ngudjolo "there is complicity or active coercion on the part of the Ugandan and Rwandan governments who are liable for the massacres in Bogoro in the guise of an ethnic conflict."[356] The opening comments were at times emotional and relevant and at other times unrelated and redundant.

Throughout the confirmation hearings the victims' legal representatives made submissions on important aspects of the case, including on the joint nature of the attack, the specific crimes charged, the responsibility of the accused, the applicable modes of liability and most importantly on the harm suffered by their clients.[357] Wishing to broaden their role, at one point during the proceedings a legal representative for victims attempted to introduce evidence (though he argued it was not evidence as such but only a document that could shed light on the background of the attack). The Pre-Trial Chamber declined. Instead, the Chamber emphatically stated, "we

348 *Ibid.* at para. 141-144.

349 Initially scheduled on 28 February 2008 and then on 21 May 2008, the hearing was postponed twice by the Chamber to afford more preparation time to the parties.

350 The alleged criminal acts included murder, inhumane acts, inhuman or cruel treatment, the use of child soldiers, sexual slavery, wilful killing, intentional attacks against the civilian population and pillage.

351 Some legal representatives were not present at the opening hearing.

352 *The Prosecutor v. Katanga/Ngudjolo,* T, 27 June 2008, p. 42.

353 See, e.g., *Ibid.* at 59-60.

354 *Ibid.* at 45.

355 *Ibid.* at 55.

356 *Ibid.* at 61.

357 See *The Prosecutor v. Katanga/Ngudjolo,* T, 15 July 2008.

cannot allow a second Prosecutor in this process."[358] The Pre-Trial Chamber seemed steadfast in its attempt to try to clearly define the proper role for victims in its proceedings as participants and not as parties. In September 2008 the Pre-Trial Chamber confirmed the charges in a 226-page decision, sending the case to trial. [359]

The third case to reach the confirmation of charges hearing was the case of Jean-Pierre Bemba Gombo in the CAR situation. In *Bemba*, prior to the confirmation of charges hearing, the Pre-Trial Chamber issued a number of decisions on victim participation in an effort to provide much needed guidance to parties and participants. Its "Fourth decision on victims' participation" of 12 December 2008 lays out the modalities for participation, including for the confirmation of charges hearing.

The Single Judge found that victims, both anonymous and non-anonymous, would have access to all public decisions, documents, transcripts and evidence contained in the record of the case and be able to attend all public hearings.[360] However, this right to access documents/transcripts does not extend to those that are confidential or *ex parte*.[361] The Judge held that no differentiation should be "made between victims whose identity is known to the Defense and those for whom anonymity has been granted by the Chamber."[362] He reasoned that an anonymous victim should not face "detriment[al]" treatment due to their request for protective measures.[363] Importantly, the Court concluded that since victims are not parties to the proceedings they do not assume the role of accuser.[364]

Victims' legal representatives were also permitted to make opening and closing statements (20 minutes for each legal team), and have notification rights.[365] The Judge also determined that victims' legal representatives would be able to make succinct written submissions on specific issues of law and fact if (i) victims prove first by way of application that their interests are affected by the issue under examination and (ii) it is deemed appropriate by the Chamber.[366] Unlike in previous cases, the Single Judge did not find it necessary to pronounce upon the right to question witnesses as no witnesses were being called at the confirmation of charges hearing.[367] Finally, the parties and victims were permitted to file written submissions at the end of the confirmation of charges hearing.[368]

This decision essentially curtails the rights of non-anonymous victims in that they would no longer have access to confidential filings and closed hearings which non-

358 *Ibid.* at 70.
359 See *The Prosecutor v. Katanga/Ngudjolo*, No. ICC-01/04-01/07-717, 30 September 2008.
360 *The Prosecutor v. Bemba*, No. ICC-01/05-01/08-320, 12 December 2008, par. 101.
361 *Ibid.* at para. 103-105.
362 *Ibid.* at par. 99.
363 *Ibid.*
364 *Ibid.*
365 *Ibid.* at para. 106-107.
366 *Ibid.* at para. 103, 110.
367 *Ibid.* at par. 109.
368 *Ibid.* at par. 110.

anonymous victims in previous pre-trial proceedings in *Lubanga* and *Katanga/ Ngudjolo* enjoyed. On the flip side, anonymous victims would now have a right to make submissions on both law and fact, which did not exist previously. As a result, anonymous victims seemed to gain rights while non-anonymous victims seemed to lose rights exercised by similarly situated victims in other cases.

In practice, however, the distinctions made between anonymous and non-anonymous victims in *Lubanga* and *Katanga/Ngudjolo* make little practical difference. Neither of these cases group victims amongst representatives on the basis of their anonymity. Legal representatives simultaneously represent anonymous and non-anonymous victims. Thus, Defense counsel are unable to challenge the participatory rights exercised on behalf of anonymous victims because they can also be legitimately raised on behalf of non-anonymous victims.

At the hearings the two legal representatives for victims, one of whom was the Principal Counsel of the OPCV, represented a total of 54 victims. The two legal representatives made very "clear and concise" opening statements,[369] stressing their right to truth and emphasizing the harms suffered by the clients. In closing arguments, the OPCV spoke directly on the elements of the crimes and, like the prosecutor, went into the criminal responsibility of the accused as well as the applicable mode of liability.[370] She concluded by stating that there were substantial grounds to believe Bemba was responsible for the crimes charged.[371] Though the presentation by the independent legal representative was not as clear and focused as that by the Principal Counsel of the OPCV, she too spoke generally about the suffering of her clients but focused more on the guilt of the accused. As far as confirmation of charges hearings are concerned their participatory role was by far the most targeted than in previous hearings although one could easily argue that their participation overlapped a great deal with the role assigned to the prosecution. On 15 June 2009 Pre-Trial Chamber II handed down its decision,[372] confirming the charges of murder and rape as crimes against humanity as well as the charges of murder, rape and pillaging as war crimes, and declining to confirm charges for torture and outrages upon personal dignity.[373]

The case against Bahar Idriss Abu Garda was the fourth case to make it to the confirmation of charges stage. Victims seemed to play a large role in the pre-trial proceeding of this case, making up the majority of decisions leading up to the hearing. The Chamber outlined four sets of participatory rights that would apply to victims, including: access to the public record of the case; attendance at and participation in hearings; questioning of witnesses; and the filing of documents.[374]

369 *The Prosecutor v. Bemba*, T, 12 January 2009, p. 38.
370 *The Prosecutor v. Bemba*, T, 15 January 2009, pp. 88-90.
371 *Ibid.* at 91.
372 See *The Prosecutor v. Bemba*, No. ICC-01/05-01/08-424, 15 June 2009.
373 See *Ibid.*
374 See *The Prosecutor v. Abu Garda*, No. ICC-02/05-02/09-136, 6 October 2009.

Under the heading of 'access to the public record of the case' the Chamber found that victims or their legal representatives have, prior to and during the confirmation of charges hearing, the right to: (i) access all public filings and public decisions; (ii) notification of all public requests, submissions, motions, responses and other documents filed as public; (iii) notification of the decisions of the Chamber; (iv) access the transcripts of the public hearings; (v) notification of all public proceedings and the date of delivery of decisions; and (vi) access the public evidence filed by the prosecution and defense (subject to a format in which it is made available to the non-proposing party).[375] Access to confidential filings would only be available at the discretion of the Chamber and would be decided upon on a case-by-case basis.[376]

With regard to attendance and participation at hearings, the Chamber found that victims would have the right to attend and participate in all public session hearings.[377] The Chamber, however, retained the ability to limit the right by confining participation to written observations and submissions. Victims' legal representatives would be able to participate by way of oral motions, responses and submissions. Furthermore, victims' legal representatives would be able to make opening and closing statements at the confirmation of charges hearing.[378] Concerning the questioning of witnesses, the Chamber concluded that in accordance with the principle of prohibiting anonymous accusations victims granted anonymity would not be entitled to examine witnesses.[379] Therefore, if victims decided to disclose their identities to the parties they would be permitted to question witnesses at the confirmation hearing.[380] With the filing of documents the Chamber determined that victims' legal representatives would be permitted to file written motions, responses and replies in relation to all matters unless the Statute or Rules prohibit them from doing so or the Chamber has decided to limit their participation in this respect.[381] Finally, the parties and victims were allowed to submit written observations following the confirmation of charges hearing.[382]

Prior to the hearing the defense challenged a number of victim applications that related to villagers alleging harm which did not relate to the charges in the Charging Document. Abu Garda was alleged to have committed war crimes in the context of an attack on personnel and installations of the African Union peacekeeping mission in Darfur (AMIS) and was therefore responsible for the resulting loss of life, injury and pillaging. The Chamber agreed with the challenges by the defense and found that a number of the applicants were unable to show that they suffered harm as a result of the crimes which were allegedly committed during the attack on AMIS on 29 September

375 *Ibid.* at par. 13.
376 The Chamber did allow victims to have some access to confidential documents, see *The Prosecutor v. Abu Garda*, T, 20 October 2009, pp. 13-14
377 *The Prosecutor v. Abu Garda*, No. ICC-02/05-02/09-136, 6 October 2009, par. 17.
378 *Ibid.* at par. 19.
379 *Ibid.* at par. 22.
380 *Ibid.* at para. 23-24.
381 *Ibid.* at par. 25.
382 See *The Prosecutor v. Abu Garda*, No. ICC-02/05-02/09-236, 23 November 2009.

2007.[383] Nevertheless, at the confirmation of charges hearing four lawyers representing 78 victims took part. The victims included former members of the African Union peacekeeping mission and the family members of those peacekeepers who had died as a result of the attack on the mission's headquarters.[384]

The four legal representatives were given one hour amongst them to make opening statements. They chose to each speak for 15 minutes. The first lawyer to speak focused part of his statement on the material harm suffered by his clients, emphasizing the loss of cameras, clothing, computers, uniforms, shoes, and other goods that were looted in the attack.[385] This same legal representative also claimed that his clients suffered "moral and professional" injury due to the loss of credibility of the mission following the attack.[386] Other legal representatives brought attention to the dependents of the soldiers killed and the difficulties they face.[387] In addition to opening statements the legal representatives were permitted to question witnesses and give closing statements.[388] In general, and in contrast with the closing statements given in *Bemba*, the closing arguments were generally vague and repetitive.[389]

The defense in *Abu Garda* was without a doubt the most deferential to victims than in any other case.[390] Time and again the defense counsel extended courtesies to victims and victims' legal representatives in order to contribute to the smooth operation of the case. For instance, the defense counsel did not object to a victim-witness who applied late for victim status to be granted such status,[391] and at times offered to share his unused presentation time with victims' legal representatives.[392] Moreover, both the suspect and defense legal counsel time and again expressed their sincere condolences to the victims. And on more than one occasion the defense counsel grouped his client with victims by proclaiming that they both "deserved better" from the prosecution and that they deserved the truth.[393] Ultimately, on 8 February 2010, the Pre-Trial Chamber declined to confirm charges against Abu Garda.[394] The prosecutor sought leave to appeal,[395] but this request was denied.[396]

---

383 *The Prosecutor v. Abu Garda*, No. ICC-02/05-02/09-147-Red, 9 October 2009, par. 138.

384 The peacekeepers hailed from a number of African countries, including, amongst others, Senegal, Mali, and Nigeria.

385 *The Prosecutor v. Abu Garda*, T, 19 October 2009, p. 28.

386 *Ibid.* at 28-29.

387 *Ibid.* at 31-32.

388 *The Prosecutor v. Abu Garda*, T, 28 October 2009, p. 31.

389 See *The Prosecutor v. Abu Garda*, T, 30 October 2009.

390 Abu Garda's defense counsel, Karim A.A. Khan, has also represented civil parties before the Extraordinary Chambers in the Courts of Cambodia.

391 See *The Prosecutor v. Abu Garda*, T, 20 October 2009.

392 See, e.g., *The Prosecutor v. Abu Garda*, T, 28 October 2009, p. 56.

393 *Ibid.* at 68.

394 See *The Prosecutor v. Abu Garda*, No. ICC-02/05-02/09-243-Red, 8 February 2010.

395 See *The Prosecutor v. Abu Garda*, No. ICC-02/05-02/09-252-Red, 15 March 2010.

396 *The Prosecutor v. Abu Garda*, No. ICC-02/05-02/09-267, 23 April 2010.

The fifth confirmation of charges hearing was that of Abdallah Banda Abakaer Nourain (Banda) and Saleh Mohammed Jerbo Jamus (Jerbo) in the Darfur, Sudan situation. The Pre-Trial Chamber largely followed the precedent set in *Abu Garda* with regard to the modalities of victim participation; however, some novel issues arose in this case.

Just prior to the confirmation of charges hearing, the prosecution and defense separately objected to the representation of two victims by their legal representatives and requested the Pre-Trial Chamber to assign other counsel in the case.[397] The OTP and defense alleged that the two legal representatives, who represent two victims in the proceedings, also represent the Sudan International Defense Group (SIDG) and the Sudan Workers Trade Unions Federation (SWTUF), both of which are alleged to be proxies for the Sudanese Government and more specifically for President Al Bashir (an individual over whom the Court has issued an arrest warrant). The SIDG and SWTUF attempted to intervene in a number of proceedings related to the situation in Darfur, Sudan, but the various Chambers largely limited such interventions.[398] However, the SIDG and SWTUF now pay the legal fees of the two legal representatives to act as legal counsel for two victims in the *Banda/Jerbo* case. As such, these legal representatives informed the Court that they planned on contesting the legitimacy and appropriateness of the Court's exercise of jurisdiction.[399] The prosecution and defense submitted that legal counsel are using the two victims "as a front for the Government of Sudan and President Al Bashir" in order to subvert the legal process.[400] The parties argued that the confirmation of charges hearing is meant to determine whether or not a case proceeds to trial and nothing beyond that limited scope should be entertained, particularly interventions made with political motivations in mind. The legal representatives objected to the requests, arguing that their clients are well aware who pays for their legal fees and that their clients are free to hold whatever opinions they like, whether or not they support the exercise of jurisdiction by the Court.[401] Ultimately the Pre-Trial Chamber rejected the requests made by the OTP and defense team because no concrete evidence had been submitted substantiating their claims.[402] Nonetheless, the Judges strictly confined the participation of the legal representatives. They prohibited interventions that would go beyond the spatial and temporal parameters of the case

---

397 *The Prosecutor v. Banda/Jerbo*, No. ICC-02/05-03/09-110, 6 December 2010 and No. ICC-02/05-03/09-113, 6 December 2010. The two legal representatives in question are Sir Geoffrey Nice, QC and Rodney Dixon. Sir Geoffrey Nice worked as a prosecutor at the ICTY where both Rodney Dixon and the defense attorney for the two accused worked as defense counsel. All three individuals are affiliated with Temple Garden Chambers in the United Kingdom.

398 *The Prosecutor v. Banda/Jerbo*, No. ICC-02/05-03/09-110, 6 December 2010, par. 2.

399 *The Prosecutor v. Banda/Jerbo*, T, 8 December 2010, pp. 4-7.

400 *The Prosecutor v. Banda/Jerbo*, No. ICC-02/05-03/09-113, 6 December 2010, par. 1.

401 *The Prosecutor v. Banda/Jerbo*, No. ICC-02/05-03/09-115, 7 December 2010. Interestingly, in this filing the legal representatives noted that unlike the prosecution and defense teams, which are unable to visit Darfur to carry out investigations, they have visited Darfur to meet with their clients and plan to do so again.

402 *The Prosecutor v. Banda/Jerbo*, T, 8 December 2010, pp. 4-7.

and the personal interest of the clients (as determined by the Chamber), such as issues related to the admissibility of the case.[403]

In addition, issues over the expeditiousness of proceedings also arose. For the purposes of the confirmation of charges hearing the OTP and the defense, through a joint filing, agreed to the facts contained in the OTP's Document Containing the Charges.[404] The OTP informed the Chamber that it would not call any witnesses and the defense stated that it would not contest the charges or present its own evidence. Under these circumstances, and with a view to expediting proceedings, the parties suggested that the participation of victims could be limited to written submissions.[405] However, after hearing the views of the legal representatives on the matter, the Trial Chamber determined that victims would in fact be able to make oral submissions at the hearing.[406] Nevertheless, the confirmation hearing was completed in one day with the victims' legal representatives making oral statements.[407] Two of the legal teams representing victims chose to make very brief statements in line with the general expeditious approach adopted by the parties.[408] However, one legal representative chose to make more detailed remarks emphasizing the emotional and psychological impact of the crimes on her clients.[409] Despite the record speed at which the parties and participants concluded the hearing, however, the Court prolonged the pre-trial stage against the wishes of the prosecution and defense by allowing parties and participants to file written observations following the confirmation hearing.[410] The prosecution, defense and a majority of the legal representatives for victims informed the Court that they would not file written observations.[411] However, one legal representative stated that she would in fact file final observations, prompting the defense to express their disappointment at the Court's decision. Noting the opportunity of victims to make oral arguments and emphasizing that no substantive submissions were made by the prosecution or defense, he emphasized that "one of the driving forces, [...] in relation to [the] joint filing, was to have matters expedited. The consequence of allowing the proceedings to stay open, to allow written submissions, is yet again to delay. It is to frustrate the attempts of the Defence to have a fair and expeditious trial."[412] In response, the Chamber made absolutely no acknowledgement of the right of the defense

403 *Ibid.* at 4-7.

404 *The Prosecutor v. Banda/Jerbo*, No. ICC-02/05-03/09-80, 19 October 2010.

405 *Ibid.* at par. 11.

406 *The Prosecutor v. Banda/Jerbo*, No. ICC-02/05-03/09-103, 17 November 2010.

407 One hour was allotted to the OTP and defense team whereas each legal team for victims was given 10 minutes.

408 For instance, one legal representative simply requested the Court to confirm the charges against the accused. See *The Prosecutor v. Banda/Jerbo*, T 8 December 2010, p. 38.

409 *Ibid.* at 43.

410 *Ibid.* at 50.

411 *Ibid.* at 50-51.

412 *Ibid.* at 51.

to an expeditious trial (given that the accused are detained) and simply confirmed their decision.[413]

The participation of victims at the prosecution phase of the pre-trial stage, while not without its difficulties, has proven to be more meaningful and substantive than at earlier stages of proceedings. The opening and closing statements of victims in the various confirmation of charges hearings highlight the importance victims attach to such participation rights. When examining the transcripts, one can easily delineate a clear difference in the way victims' legal representatives choose to participate. Without a doubt, successful and effective participation largely depends on the legal representatives in the proceedings. At times participation was meant to contribute by clarifying facts. Other times participation was meant to bring in a more emotional aspect to the proceedings by focusing on the harms suffered by victims. There have been times when victims simply remind the Court about their right to truth and justice and they do not necessarily comment upon the alleged guilt of the suspect. Unquestionably, however, victims have tried to do far more than simply clarify facts or discuss their harms suffered. They have very often commented upon the guilt of the suspect and have at times tried to elicit evidence that goes towards establishing that there are substantial grounds to believe the suspect was responsible for the charges brought against him. The myriad of approaches adopted at the pre-trial stage underscores the numerous challenges encountered by the Court concerning participation. The trial stage would prove no less challenging.

7.4.4 Trial Stage

Article 64(3) allows Trial Chambers to adopt such procedures as they deems necessary to facilitate the fair and expeditious conduct of proceedings. As a result the different Chambers are free to adopt procedures that other Chambers may or may not have adopted. By way of an example, in the *Bemba* confirmation of charges hearing the Pre-Trial Chamber heard the evidence by topic rather than in relation to a prosecution case and defense case. In contrast, the Trial Chambers have all adopted an approach whereby the prosecution presents its case first, followed by the defense, and allowing flexibility where the judges wish to call a certain witness (such as witnesses proposed by the victims). Another example is how Trial Chambers I and III adopted the terms and phrases commonly associated with common law legal systems, including 'examination-in-chief,' 'cross-examination' and 're-examination,'[414] whereas these

413 *Ibid.*

414 The Court stated that "The purpose of the 'examination-in-chief' is 'to adduce by the putting of proper questions relevant and admissible evidence which supports the contentions of the party who calls the witness.' It follows from this purpose that the manner of such questioning is neutral and that leading questions (*i.e.* questions framed in a manner suggestive of the answers required) are not appropriate. However, it needs to be stressed that there are undoubted exceptions to this approach, for instance when leading questions are not opposed. In contrast, the purpose of 'cross-examination' is to raise relevant or pertinent questions on the matter at issue or to attack the credibility of the witness. In this context,

terms and phrases were deemed not to be useful by Trial Chamber II, which instead adopted an entirely different set of terminology. As with terminology, and similar to pre-trial proceedings, each Trial Chamber has adopted its own approach to participation. The Trial Chamber in *Katanga/Ngudjolo* acknowledged these differences by recognizing that "the regime governing victim participation may [...] vary from case to case" depending upon the specific circumstances before the Court.[415] Nevertheless, the modalities of participation at trial are similar to those that were afforded to victims during the pre-trial stage. With that said, however, participation at trial is meant to be more substantive given that proceedings at trial are on the determination of the guilt of the accused.

In respect to a victim's right to notification, in accordance with the Rules of all Chambers, through the Registry, notify participating victims of submissions and proceedings in the case.[416] Without such notification victims would not be in a position to fully exercise their rights at trial. In addition, at the trial stage, participating victims are permitted to attend all public hearings. With the exception of *ex parte* hearings, the Trial Chambers for *Katanga/Ngudjolo* and *Bemba* have extended this right to include closed sessions as well.[417] In contrast, the *Lubanga* Trial Chamber only stated that, at its discretion, it may allow victims to attend and participate in closed and *ex parte* hearings.[418] In practice, the *Lubanga* Trial Chamber allows victims to attend almost all public and closed hearings.[419]

With regard to filings, in all Chambers victims have access to public filings. However, some Chambers have chosen to limit access to confidential filings. Generally, in the *Lubanga* trial proceedings, legal representatives of victims have had access to public filings only. However, if the legal representatives can show that confidential filings are of material relevance to their client's personal interests, they may also have access to these filings so long as this access will not breach other protective measures that need to remain in place.[420] The *Katanga/Ngudjolo* and *Bemba* Trial Chambers

---

it is legitimate that the manner of questioning differs, and that counsel are permitted to ask closed, leading or challenging questions, where appropriate." *The Prosecutor v. Lubanga*, No. ICC-01/04-01/06-2127, 16 September 2009, para. 20-30; see also *The Prosecutor v. Bemba*, No. ICC-01/05-01/08-807-Corr, 12 July 2010, para. 38-40.

415 *The Prosecutor v. Katanga/Ngudjolo*, No. ICC-01/04-01/07-1788-tENG, 22 January 2010, par. 54, noting that the crimes charged and the number of victims may influence the approach adopted.

416 ICC RPE, Rule 92(5) and (6).

417 *The Prosecutor v. Katanga/Ngudjolo*, No. ICC-01/04-01/07-1788-tENG, 22 January 2010, par. 71. In *Bemba* no decision touched directly upon this issue but in practice Trial Chamber III has followed the *Katanga/Ngudjolo* approach.

418 *The Prosecutor v. Lubanga*, No. ICC-01/04-01/06-1119, 18 January 2008, par. 113.

419 In *Lubanga* the defense argued that the legal representatives for victims should be precluded from attending closed session proceedings during the testimony of a defense witness. The Chamber rejected this request, finding that legal representatives may remain in the courtroom. Otherwise, they found, the ability to discharge their professional obligations would be undermined. See *The Prosecutor v. Lubanga*, No. ICC-01/04-01/06-2340, 11 March 2010, par. 39.

420 *The Prosecutor v. Lubanga*, No. ICC-01/04-01/06-1119, 18 January 2008, par. 106; see also ICC RPE, Rule 131(2).

explicitly held that legal representatives have access to both public and confidential filings, but not to *ex parte* filings.[421]

All Chambers allow victims' legal representatives the opportunity to submit requests to question witnesses, including experts and accused. They follow the Appeals Chamber judgment in this regard which confirmed the approach first adopted by the *Lubanga* Trial Chamber.[422] However, the way in which the Chambers approach the scope of questioning differs and will be discussed below.

All Chambers also allow victims the opportunity to participate by way of both oral and written submissions (including *ex parte* filings).[423] Such submissions include commenting on matters of admissibility and the relevance of evidence.[424] Additionally, the Trial Chambers often give victims the opportunity to comment upon a wide range of procedural matters. For instance, in *Katanga/Ngudjolo* the Court requested the views of victims on issues such as the order of appearance of witnesses, the manner of refreshing the memory of witnesses, hearsay, and the admissibility of evidence.[425] The Trial Chamber in *Katanga/Ngudjolo* made clear that only when an intervention by a legal representative is not related to the personal interests of the victims represented by that counsel will the Chamber not allow the participation.[426]

Oral submissions may also include making opening and closing statements at trial.[427] The opening statements of victims at trial, while not considered evidence, are nonetheless an important part of trial and participation. The different approaches taken by legal representatives are interesting in this regard. Many legal representatives emphasized victims' rights to truth and justice as well as the cathartic and restorative value of their inclusion in the criminal process.[428] Others spoke directly of their clients

421 *The Prosecutor v. Katanga/Ngudjolo*, No. ICC-01/04-01/07-1788-tENG, 22 January 2010, par. 121; *The Prosecutor v. Bemba*, No. ICC-01/05-01/08-807, 30 June 2010, par. 47.

422 *The Prosecutor v. Katanga/Ngudjolo*, No. ICC-01/04-01/07-1665, 20 November 2009, para. 84-89; *The Prosecutor v. Bemba*, No. ICC-01/05-01/08-807, 30 June 2010, par. 102; see *The Prosecutor v. Lubanga*, No. ICC-01/04-01/06-1432, 11 July 2008.

423 *The Prosecutor v. Lubanga*, No. ICC-01/04-01/06-1119, 18 January 2008, para. 114, 118; see also *The Prosecutor v. Katanga/Ngudjolo*, No. ICC-01/04-01/07-1665, 20 November 2009; *The Prosecutor v. Katanga/Ngudjolo*, No. ICC-01/04-01/07-1788-tENG, 22 January 2010; *The Prosecutor v. Bemba*, No. ICC-01/05-01/08-807, 30 June 2010. Upon request by the parties or victims or upon its own motion, the Trial Chamber in *Lubanga* may, depending upon the circumstances, permit victims to file confidential or *ex parte* written submissions. Indeed, there is nothing in the Court's statutory and regulatory provisions which prohibits victims from filing requests or applications to the Chamber whenever an issue arises that affects their personal interests; *The Prosecutor v. Lubanga*, No. ICC-01/04-01/06-1119, 18 January 2008, para. 114, 118.

424 *The Prosecutor v. Lubanga*, No. ICC-01/04-01/06-1119, 18 January 2008, par. 109.

425 *The Prosecutor v. Katanga/Ngudjolo*, T, 3 November 2009, p. 27; T, 27 November 2009, p. 23; T, 08 July 2010, pp. 38-41; T, 23 August 2010, pp. 52-56; T, 08 July 2010, pp. 38-41; T, 23 August 2010, pp. 52-56.

426 *The Prosecutor v. Katanga/Ngudjolo*, No. ICC-01/04-01/07-1788-tENG, 22 January 2010, par. 58.

427 *The Prosecutor v. Lubanga*, No. ICC-01/04-01/06-1119, 18 January 2008, par. 117.

428 See *The Prosecutor v. Lubanga*, T, 26 January 2009, pp. 37-41 and 47-48; *The Prosecutor v. Bemba,* T, 22 November 2010, pp. 40-41.

and the harms they suffered.[429] Some spoke about reparations or protection.[430] Most legal representatives decided not to speak directly about the individual criminal responsibility of the accused. However, a handful of legal representatives did in fact make comments implicating the accused, which mirrored comments presented by the prosecution.[431]

In one of the more controversial interventions, one of the legal representatives for victims in *Lubanga* stated in her opening that she wished "to reserve the right to request from [the] Chamber a classification of the crime of sexual slavery against the accused Thomas Lubanga."[432] The defense immediately responded to this request in its statements, emphasizing that one of their main concerns about a fair trial is in relation to the participation of victims.[433] They voiced their alarm over the emphasis on rape and sexual slavery in the opening statements by victims as well as the call for adding new charges.[434] Quoting Robert Badinter, the defense stated, "Justice is not vengeance, and it is not about compassion towards victims."[435]

New Charges against the Accused?

The charges confirmed against Thomas Lubanga Dyilo relate to offenses falling under Articles 8(2)(b)(xxvi) and 8(2)(e)(vii) of the Rome Statute concerning the conscription, enlistment and use of child soldiers. However, those working with victims have long voiced their annoyance and indignation over these narrow set of charges, arguing that they do not fully reflect the experiences suffered by victims.[436] In particular, victims' advocates protested that rape and other sexual crimes should have been

---

429 See *The Prosecutor v. Lubanga*, T, 26 January 2009, pp. 45, 47, 49, and 52-54; *The Prosecutor v. Katanga/Ngudjolo*,T, 24 November 2009, p. 40; interestingly, there were a number of occasions when legal representatives made no mention of their clients.

430 *The Prosecutor v. Lubanga*, T, 26 January 2009, pp. 59, 67; *The Prosecutor v. Katanga/Ngudjolo*, T, 24 November 2009, p. 46.

431 *The Prosecutor v. Bemba*, T, 22 November 2010, p. 43; See *The Prosecutor v. Lubanga*, T, 26 January 2009, p. 55. For instance, in *Lubanga*, one legal representative stated that "the responsibility of Thomas Lubanga Dyilo in particular should be recognized [...]."

432 *The Prosecutor v. Lubanga*, T, 26 January 2009, p. 57

433 *The Prosecutor v. Lubanga*, T, 27 January 2009, p. 16

434 *Ibid.* at 18.

435 *Ibid.* at 19.

436 See *The Prosecutor v. Lubanga*, No. ICC-01/04-01/06-1891, 22 May 2009; see also, e.g., Joint Letter from ASF, Center for Justice and Reconciliation, DRC Coalition for the ICC, FIDH, HRW, REDRESS, and the Women's Initiative for Gender Justice to Luis Moreno Ocampo, Chief Prosecutor, ICC, on the Narrow Scope of the Charges Brought Against Mr. Lubanga, 31 July 2006, *on file with the author*; Vélez, S., Victims raise their voice in the Lubanga case, Aegis Trust, 23 October 2009, citing OPCV Principal Counsel, Paolina Massidda, as saying "The majority of Victims if not all of female victims, represented by the Legal representatives were actually recruited to became sexual slaves or forced wives to commanders. [...] This was an essential component of the recruitment. And it is important for victims that their story is told in the way it happened. They want that the truth and the facts are qualified as they were in the context of the charges."

included. In response, in what many feel was an attempt by the OTP to appease victims, rape and other sexual offenses were explicitly mentioned in its opening statements. In addition, many of the prosecution witnesses testified about repeated rapes and other sexual offenses carried out by UPC commanders so that such acts would be recognized in the record of the case.[437] But recognition of these crimes on the record was not enough to appease victims in the case. They wanted Lubanga charged for these crimes.

Thus, after giving notice in their opening statements of their intention to have the charges broadened through a re-characterization of the facts,[438] on 22 May 2009, victims' legal representatives filed a joint motion requesting the Trial Chamber to consider adding the legal characterization of sexual slavery as a crime against humanity and war crime and of cruel and/or inhuman treatment as a war crime to the facts of the case pursuant to Regulation 55 of the Regulations of the Court.[439] Regulation 55 provides, in part, that the Chamber has the authority to change the legal characterization of facts to fit with new charges "without exceeding the facts and circumstances described in the charges and any amendments to the charges."[440] More specifically, Regulation 55(2) permits the Chamber to change the legal characterization of the facts at any time during trial and Regulation 55(3) compels the Court to guarantee that the defense has adequate time and facilities to prepare its defense. This many include, for example, carrying out further investigations or recalling witnesses to re-examine them with regard to the new charges. In reply to the request submitted by victims, the defense argued that the request exceeds the facts as laid out in the indictment and that any re-characterizing of facts at so late a stage of the proceedings (the conclusion of the prosecution's case) would infringe upon the rights of the accused to a trial without undue delay. The prosecution also argued against the reclassification, citing reasons of unfairness.

Despite their objections, a majority of the Trial Chamber found that it would consider the legal re-characterization of the facts requested by the victims' legal representatives.[441] Moreover, the majority decision seemed to conclude that the Judges may even add new charges based on facts that came to light during trial but that are not explicitly mentioned in the charging document. However, the Trial Chamber later clarified that facts coming to light at trial must still be connected with those facts

437 *The Prosecutor v. Lubanga*, No. ICC-01/04-01/06-1891, 22 May 2009, para. 32-36; *The Prosecutor v. Lubanga*, T, 06 March 2009, pp. 30-31; T, 13 March 2009, p. 49.

438 As noted by Judge Fulford in his minority opinion, the expression 'legal characterization of the facts' stems from Regulation 52 on the Document containing the charges. As such, a charge brought against an accused "is, in essence, a combination of a 'statement of facts' and the 'legal characterization' of those facts." See *The Prosecutor v. Lubanga*, No. ICC-01/04-01/06-2054 (Judge Fulford), 17 July 2009, para. 7-8. However, this minority decision leaves it open whether a modification of the legal characterization of facts would entail *ipso facto* amending the charges, par. 18.

439 See *The Prosecutor v. Lubanga*, No. ICC-01/04-01/06-1891, 22 May 2009.

440 Regulations of the Court, Reg. 55(1).

441 See *The Prosecutor v. Lubanga*, No. ICC-01/04-01/06-2049, 14 July 2009.

found in the charging document.[442] In his dissenting opinion, Judge Fulford strongly disagreed with the majority decision, arguing that victims should not be able to use court regulations to add new charges against the accused.

On appeal, both parties argued that an expansion of the factual basis of the crimes would require the parties to re-investigate and re-plead new facts. The delay, they argued, would infringe upon the rights of the accused to a speedy trial. But even the filing significantly delayed proceedings for over three months until the Appeals Chamber, on 8 December 2009, unanimously reversed the Trial Chamber's decision. The Appeals Chamber held that Trial Chamber I erred in law when it found that Regulation 55 has two separate procedures, which in essence, allowed the Court under Regulation 55(2) and (3) to include additional facts and circumstances not described in the charging document.[443]

Despite the unanimous decision, on 15 December 2009, the victims' legal representatives filed observations on the Appeals Chamber judgment, requesting the Trial Chamber to interpret the judgment as not preventing a new legal characterization of the facts as described in the charges.[444] In other words, they were again asking the Trial Chamber to use its authority under Regulation 55 to modify the legal characterization of facts (found in the charging document) in order to include additional charges.[445] At the re-commencement of trial, the Trial Chamber indicated that no further discussion on the issue would be entertained. Nevertheless, there is a chance that facts of sexual violence will be acknowledged in the final decision and may even be viewed as an aggravating factor for purposes of sentencing should the accused be convicted. In any case, one of the legal representatives stated in an interview that their initiative to broaden the charges was not futile because through their request they were able to open the debate about the crimes initially brought by the prosecutor.[446]

Supporting the Prosecution: Divergent Approaches on the Scope of Participation

In addition to the controversy surrounding the attempt to broaden the charges against Lubanga further questions surrounding the proper role of victims and the scope of their participation have arisen. More specifically, the issue of whether victims would be permitted to lead and challenge evidence on the guilt of the accused at trial similar to the prosecution was particularly contentious. This issue was especially delicate given that no agreement between the drafters of the Rome Statute could be reached on the matter and the Statute only acknowledges the rights of the parties to tender evidence

442 See *The Prosecutor v. Lubanga*, No. ICC-01/04-01/06-2093, 27 August 2009.

443 See *Prosecutor v. Lubanga*, No. ICC-01/04-01/06-2205, 8 December 2009.

444 See *The Prosecutor v. Lubanga*, No. ICC-01/04-01/06-2211, 15 December 2009.

445 The defense responded, arguing that the Appeals Chamber judgment ends any attempts to re-characterize the facts and modify the charges, see *The Prosecutor v. Lubanga*, No. ICC-01/04-01/06-2214, 18 December 2009.

446 Wakabi, W., Q&A with Luc Walleyn, Lawyer for Victims in Lubanga's Trial, *LubangaTrial.org Commentary*, 13 January 2010.

and the Court to request evidence. Article 69(3), which relates to evidence, provides that:

> The parties may submit evidence relevant to the case, in accordance with article 64. The Court shall have the authority to request the submission of all evidence that it considers necessary for the determination of the truth.

The wording of Article 69(3) is significant. The first part seems to implicitly recognize the partiality and subjectivity of the adversarial parties in that it only requires the presentation of their evidence to be relevant. There is no requirement that their evidence assists the Court in determining the truth. In contrast, the second part seems to recognize the Court as an objective and impartial truth-seeker and implies that the evidence it requests will (at least in the Judges' view) aid in the determination of the truth. Undeniably, the inclusion of the second part of this provision was to ensure that the Court was not restricted in its evaluation of a case to the extent that it could only review evidence provided by the parties.[447] However, no one could have foreseen that it would be used as the means through which victims would regularly tender and elicit evidence – often on the guilt of the accused.

When this issue first arose in the *Lubanga* case, both the prosecution and defense argued that victims did not have a right to lead and challenge evidence. The defense argued that if the Court were to grant victims the same rights as those traditionally reserved for the parties, they would be violating the principle of equality of arms and prejudicing the rights of the accused by having the defense face two accusers.[448] Nevertheless, the Trial Chamber held that victims did, in fact, have the right to lead and challenge evidence.[449] Although the Chamber noted that the primary responsibility for the presentation and challenging of evidence lies with the parties, victims, it concluded, should also be able to do so if it assists the Chamber in the determination of the truth and if the Court has in some way "requested" the evidence.[450] A majority of the Appeals Chamber agreed,[451] and further added that "if victims were generally

---

447 The phrasing "for the determination of the truth" was submitted by the German delegate and although the power of the Court to call evidence is often associated with civil law jurisdictions, in fact, such authority exists in common law jurisdictions as well. In practice, however, due to the adversarial nature of proceedings judges from common law systems rarely exercise this right. See Piragoff, D.K., Article 69 Evidence, 1304, in Triffterer (1999).

448 See *The Prosecutor v. Luganga*, No. ICC-01/04-01/06-1220, 10 March 2008, para. 51-52.

449 *The Prosecutor v. Lubanga*, No. ICC-01/04-01/06-1119, 18 January 2008, par. 109.

450 *Ibid.* at par. 108.

451 Disagreeing with the Appeals Chamber judgment, Judge Pikis dissented, arguing instead that according to the Statute and Rules victims can neither adduce evidence on the guilt or innocence of the accused nor challenge the admissibility or relevance of evidence. By examining what the Statute and Rules actually provide he reasoned that these documents do not "permit the participation of anyone in the proof or disproof of the charges other than the Prosecutor and the accused," and that in the Statute the prosecution has "exclusive responsibility [...] for the investigation of a case, the collection of evidence, the arrest of the person, the substantiation of the charges at the confirmation hearing, and their proof

and under all circumstances precluded from tendering evidence relating to the guilt or innocence of the accused and from challenging the admissibility or relevance of evidence, their right to participate in the trial would potentially become ineffectual."[452] Therefore, although Article 66(2) states that the onus is on the prosecutor to prove the guilt of the accused, the Appeals Chamber concluded that Trial Chambers may permit victims to tender and elicit evidence if it will assist in the determination of the truth and the Court "requests" the evidence in accordance with Article 69(3).[453] Accordingly, Trial Chambers may consider the issue of the guilt of the accused as a subject that affects the personal interests of victims and may authorize legal representatives to question witnesses on the issue of guilt.[454] Before granting such a request, the Chambers must bear in mind the limitations of article 68(3), 69(3) and the need to ensure a fair and expeditious trial conducted with full respect for the rights of the accused, including the right to have adequate time and facilities for preparation of the defense.[455] The Chambers, however, have approached this idea that victims' evidence is related to the broader purpose of the court to determine the truth in dramatically different ways.

The *Lubanga* and *Bemba* Trial Chambers view the scope of participation broadly. In this sense they regularly allow victims' legal representatives to question witnesses on the guilt of the accused, linking this right with helping the Court to determine the truth.[456] When questioning prosecution witnesses, legal representatives have not had to confine their questions to the context of crimes, the harm suffered by their clients or reparation issues. Instead, legal representatives often attempted to establish the guilt

at the trial." He further submitted that victims are not parties in the proceedings and that they are not able to proffer or advance anything other than their views and concerns. See *The Prosecutor v. Lubanga*, No. ICC-01/04-01/06-1432 (Partly Dissenting opinion of Judge G.M. Pikis), 11 July 2008, para. 4-6; Similarly, Judge Kirsch, who also dissented from the judgment, and agreed with Judge Pikis on this point, referred to Article 69(3), dealing with evidence at trial, to argue that the Statute is unambiguous. Article 69(3) clearly states that "the parties may submit evidence relevant to the case" and not by any other participant, such as the victims. Judge Kirsch also referred to Article 69(4) and argued that it is for the parties to challenge admissibility or relevance and not victim participants. See *The Prosecutor v. Lubanga*, No. ICC-01/04-01/06-1432-Anx (Partly Dissenting Opinion of Judge Philippe Kirsch), 23 July 2008, para. 21, and 35-37.

452 *The Prosecutor v. Lubanga*, No. ICC-01/04-01/06-1432, 11 July 2008, par. 97.

453 *The Prosecutor v. Lubanga*, No. ICC-01/04-01/06-1119, 18 January 2008, par. 108; *The Prosecutor v. Katanga/Ngudjolo*, No. ICC-01/04-01/07-1788-tENG, 22 January 2010, para. 81-84; *The Prosecutor v. Bemba*, No. ICC-01/05-01/08-807-Corr, 12 July 2010, para. 29-37; and *The Prosecutor v. Katanga/Ngudjolo*, No. ICC-01/04-01/07-2288, 16 July 2010, para. 37-40; *The Prosecutor v. Lubanga*, No. ICC-01/04-01/06-1432, 11 July 2008, par. 94.

454 *The Prosecutor v. Lubanga*, No. ICC-01/04-01/06-2127, 16 September 2009, par. 25; see also *The Prosecutor v. Katanga/Ngudjolo*, No. ICC-01/04-01/07-2288, 16 July 2010, par. 48.

455 *The Prosecutor v. Katanga/Ngudjolo*, No. ICC-01/04-01/07-2288, 16 July 2010, para. 43-48.

456 *The Prosecutor v. Lubanga*, No. ICC-01/04-01/06-2127, 16 September 2009, par. 27.

of the accused, similar to the attempts of the prosecution.[457] For instance, legal representatives in *Lubanga* questioned a number of witnesses about the funding of the UPC in an attempt to link Lubanga to such financial support in order to help establish his role in the UPC leadership structure.[458] In another instance, the legal representatives asked questions of a witness, who worked with the child protection unit of MONUC, about specific contact she had with the accused and his knowledge of the use of child soldiers in an attempt to establish his knowledge of the crimes.[459] Notably, in this situation no objections were raised by the defense that the role of victims overlapped with that of the prosecutor. Generally, when objections are raised the Court allows questioning to clarify facts or elicit additional facts even in relation to the guilt of the accused.[460]

One the one hand, this approach acknowledges the partiality of the victims and their desire to have the accused convicted. On the other hand, their interventions, unlike those of the other parties, are linked with the notion of assisting the Court in establishing the truth, which implies some sort of objectivity. Another problem with this approach is that it essentially allows for multiple accusers in the courtroom.

In contrast with *Lubanga* and *Bemba*, the *Katanga/Ngudjolo* Trial Chamber greatly limits the scope of participation and takes a different approach to the link made between victims' evidence and the concept of assisting the Court in its determination of the truth. In this regard, the Trial Chamber in *Katanga/Ngudjolo* found that "the only legitimate interest the victims may invoke when seeking to establish the facts which are the subject of the proceedings is that of contributing to the determination of

457 It is not necessary for the prosecution to show that Lubanga enlisted and recruited child soldiers himself. Rather, he can be held criminally responsible for being part of a group that did. In other words, the prosecution must show that Lubanga was part of a group of persons that had a "common plan." The group's common plan does not need to be criminal in nature but it must involve the commission of the alleged crime. Thus, the prosecution argues that Lubanga, as a high-ranking figure of the UPC, had a common plan to further the UPC war effort and in doing so enlisted and recruited children. It is not necessary to show that they specifically targeted children. The fact that the UPC accepted young people was a risk that they allegedly accepted when carrying out their common plan. The recruitment and enlistment of children was therefore a risk that they knew of and accepted when implementing their common plan. The prosecution must also show that Lubanga had an essential task in carrying out the common plan and that he was aware of his essential role. 'Essential' generally means that if he did not carry out his part of the plan the plan would fail. The Pre-Trial Chamber characterized his essential task as having direct and ongoing contact with other members of the common plan, inspecting military training camps to encourage new recruits and helping to garner funds and financial backing for the implementation of the common plan. Finally, the prosecution must show that Lubanga and other participants in the common plan were aware that the recruitment and enlistment of soldiers involved children under the age of 15 and either accepted it or condoned it.

458 *The Prosecutor v. Lubanga*, T, 12 February 2009, p. 73; T, 24 March 2009, pp. 83-88; T, 06 May 2009, pp. 8-9; T, 02 July 2009, p. 2.

459 *The Prosecutor v. Lubanga*, T, 09 July 2009, pp. 24-25.

460 *The Prosecutor v. Lubanga*, No. ICC-01/04-01/06-2127, 16 September 2009, para. 20-30; *The Prosecutor v. Bemba*, No. ICC-01/05-01/08-807-Corr, 12 July 2010, para. 38-40. These decisions stress a preference for a neutral form of questioning but do not prohibit questions that seek to clarify facts or elicit facts on the guilt of the accused so long as they aid the Chamber in its determination of the truth.

the truth by helping the Chamber to establish what exactly happened."[461] In this way they can provide background to the case or draw the Court's attention to relevant information. The Trial Chamber held that as a matter of general principle questioning by legal representatives of victims must have as its main aim the ascertainment of the truth. It found that victims are not parties to the proceedings. Nor do victims have a role to support the case of the prosecution. Rather, their local knowledge and socio-cultural background are seen as assets in that they may help the Court to better understand contentious issues arising at trial.[462]

As a result, the Judges of Trial Chamber II have rarely allowed victims to question witnesses about the guilt of the accused. The Judges have frequently reminded legal representatives to remain within the framework of their representation.[463] In this sense, the presiding Judge reminded the legal representatives that they "are not objective or subjective allies of the prosecutor. They are simply seeking to better inform themselves within the framework of the representation of the interests of their clients."[464] To be sure, more than in any other trial the Trial Chamber in *Katanga/Ngudjolo* consistently reminds legal representatives that they are not there to "reinforce the Prosecution team,"[465] often stating that the legal representatives are not supplemental prosecutors or "part two of the Prosecution,"[466] and warning legal representatives not to put questions to the witness which would end up providing some form of assistance, direct or indirect, to the prosecution team.[467] In one of the few instances where legal representatives tried to ask specifically about the individual criminally responsibility of one of the accused in the case, one of the defense teams objected and the Judge reformulated the question finding it was inappropriate for victims to ask.[468] The benefit of this approach is that the defense teams in *Katanga/Ngudjolo* rarely have to face multiple accusers and the roles of the prosecution and victims are more clearly delimited. The drawback is that when victims make interventions the Court rarely recognizes their partiality and instead views them as objective aiders in determining the truth.

Whichever approach future Chambers favor, though defense teams likely favor the latter approach, it is clear that 'views and concerns' may, at the discretion of the Chamber, relate to more than the personal experiences or personal emotions concerning the harm suffered or comments on the efficiency of trial proceedings. Sharing 'views and concerns' now may entail the possibility to tender and challenge evidence

461 *The Prosecutor v. Katanga/Ngudjolo*, No. ICC-01/04-01/07-1788-tENG, 22 January 2010, par. 60.

462 *The Prosecutor v. Katanga/Ngudjolo*, No. ICC-01/04-01/07-1665, 20 November 2009, para. 82-91. See also, *The Prosecutor v. Lubanga*, No. ICC-01/04-01/06-1119, 18 January 2008, para. 108-111; *The Prosecutor v. Bemba*, No. ICC-01/05-01/08-807-Corr, 12 July 2010, para. 30-40.

463 *The Prosecutor v. Katanga/Ngudjolo*, T, 22 March 2010, p. 24; T, 12 July 2010 p. 15.

464 *The Prosecutor v. Katanga/Ngudjolo*, T, 31 March 2010, p. 41.

465 *The Prosecutor v. Katanga/Ngudjolo*, T, 30 November 2009, p. 26.

466 *Ibid.* at 33.

467 *The Prosecutor v. Katanga/Ngudjolo*, T, 23 June 2010, p. 20.

468 *The Prosecutor v. Katanga/Ngudjolo*, T, 14 May 2010, p. 28-34.

on the guilt of the accused, which in turn can fundamentally affect the fair trial rights of the accused.[469]

Sentencing

Following a trial resulting in a conviction the Trial Chamber, pursuant to Article 78(1), must determine the appropriate sentence. In accordance with Rule 145 the Chamber is obliged to take into account mitigating and aggravating factors. Mitigating factors include, *inter alia*, substantially diminished mental capacity, duress, efforts of the convicted individual to compensate victims, and cooperation with the Court. Aggravating factors include, *inter alia*, abuse of power or official capacity, particularly defenseless victims and multiple victims.

In accordance with Rule 143 victims may request an additional hearing and participate in the hearing on issues related to sentencing. Judges may allow victims the opportunity to address the Court either in writing or in person regarding the impact of the crime and Rule 86 requires a Chamber in making any direction or order to take into account the needs of all victims. Therefore, in addition to oral interventions, another way in which the legal representatives for victims or the OPCV may wish to address the Court is through the submission of victim impact statements. As mentioned in previous chapters a victim impact statement is a statement submitted into the record "during sentencing to inform the judge […] of the financial, physical, and psychological impact of the crime on the victim and the victim's family."[470] At the discretion of the Court, victim impact statements may include the right of victims to give their view on what should be done with regard to addressing their harm. In this sense, although controversial, a Chamber may permit victims to make a sentencing recommendation.

Reparations Hearings

A traditional rationale for "allowing questioning by the legal representative was that certain evidence important also for a later determination of reparations could be obtained already in the criminal proceedings. This would avoid repeated appearances of witnesses before the Court."[471] Moreover, Regulation 56 allows the Trial Chamber to hear witnesses and examine evidence for the purposes of a decision on reparations.

469 The ability to tender evidence also relates to documentary evidence. Viewed as a means of expressing their 'views and concerns' the ability to tender documentary evidence was found to assist the court in its search for the truth. See *The Prosecutor v. Katanga/Ngudjolo*, No. ICC-01/04-01/07-1788-tENG, 22 January 2010, para. 98-100. In *Lubanga*, when questioning the UN court-appointed expert on the pillaging of natural resources in the DRC one of the legal representatives introduced a report of the UN Secretary-General to the UN Security Council relating to the final report of the expert group on the illegal exploitation of natural resources in the DRC, see *The Prosecutor v. Lubanga*, T, 18.06.09, p. 14.

470 Black's Law Dictionary, 7th Ed., West Publishing Company (1999).

471 Bitti, G. and Friman, H., Participation of Victims in the Proceedings, 467, in Lee, et al. (2001); Regulations of the Court, Reg. 56.

Accordingly, the Chambers have allowed legal representatives to question witnesses with regard to reparation issues. However, they have also concluded that it would not be appropriate or fair to consider all evidence related to reparations during the trial stage,[472] suggesting that all of the Chambers will likely hold separate hearings on reparations.

Special provisions in the Statute provide for separate reparation proceedings. Article 76(3) insinuates that if a separate sentencing hearing takes place then reparations could be dealt with at this hearing or alternatively at a completely separate hearing on reparations. According to the Rules,[473] reparation proceedings would be open to victims who did not necessarily participate in the trial.[474] During this 'reparations phase,' the Statute and Rules grant participating victims additional procedural rights. For example, there are no restrictions on the questioning of witnesses, and victims are free to submit relevant supporting documentation.[475] Thus, in most cases, the reparation hearing will strive to establish injury, harm or loss, which resulted from the crimes for which the accused was convicted. The Statute and Rules do not stipulate what standard-of-proof would apply but at least one Pre-Trial Chamber has suggested that the standard-of-proof for the element of causation will be higher for reparation purposes than for the granting of participation generally.[476]

For the purposes of reparation, the prosecution "favours a wider approach to allow participation of victims and representations from or on behalf of victims and other interested persons who suffered harm as a result of crimes other than those included in the charges selected for prosecution."[477] As a result of this position, the prosecution will support the participation of a broader range of victims than those victims permitted to participate at trial, which would effectively turn the Court into a mini claims commission. Despite the issues that this potentially raises for a convicted defendant, who could be made to bear the costs of reparations, a powerful victims' rights group, REDRESS, expressed concern about the process of the Court having to make additional findings on liability if victims, whose harm is not related to the charges for which the accused is convicted, were permitted to participate.[478] There is no doubt that the proceedings could become very drawn out.

---

472 See, e.g., *The Prosecutor v. Lubanga*, No. ICC-01/04-01/06-1119, para. 119-122; *The Prosecutor v. Bemba*, No. ICC-01/05-01/08-807, 30 June 2010, par. 28.

473 ICC RPE, Rule 143.

474 In fact, many victims participating at trial have refrained from filing reparation applications until a later stage. One benefit of waiting to file a reparation claim is that they cannot be accused of having a financial interest in the outcome of the case.

475 ICC RPE, Rule 91(4) and Rule 94(1)(g).

476 *The Prosecutor v. Kony, et al.*, No. ICC-02/04-01/05-252, 10 August 2007, par. 14.

477 Office of the Prosecutor, Policy Paper on Victims' participation under Article 68(3) of the ICC Statute, April 2010, p. 9.

478 REDRESS, Comments on the OTP Policy Paper on Victims' Participation Under Article 68(3) of the ICC Statute, February 2010, pp. 2-3.

7.4.5 Appeals

The Appeals Chamber at the ICC "is the only permanently constituted appellate body in international criminal law."[479] As a result, it is uniquely positioned to develop a body of law that is not only applicable to the various Chambers at the Court but which will also be heavily persuasive outside the Court.[480] At the time of writing, the Appeals Chamber has yet to review a final decision, sentence or order for reparations. However, it has reviewed a number of high-profile issues arising in proceedings, including the manner and scope of victim participation.

Appeals of Judgment / Sentence / Reparation Orders

Article 81 governs appeals against the final decision for acquittals, convictions or sentences. It provides that the prosecution (on its behalf or on the convicted person's behalf) and defense may appeal on the grounds of procedural error, error of fact, and error of law. Moreover, the convicted person (or the prosecutor on that person's behalf) may appeal on any other ground that affects the fairness or reliability of the proceedings or decision. With regard to sentence determinations, the parties may appeal on the ground of disproportion between the crime and the sentence imposed. The Appeals Chamber may also independently decide to review the merits of a conviction or sentence if one or the other is appealed. The Appeals Chamber has all of the powers of the Trial Chamber when reviewing an appeal. In this sense, it may remand a factual issue back to the Trial Chamber, it may call evidence that it deems necessary to determine the truth, it may modify a sentence, it may reverse or amend a decision, and it may order a new trial before a different Trial Chamber.[481]

Victims do not have the right to appeal a final decision or sentence due to the fact that they are not parties to the proceedings. Nonetheless, they may appeal against an order for reparations.[482] In this regard, the Appeals Chamber may confirm, reverse or amend a reparation order made pursuant to Article 75.[483] In is unclear, however, whether victims will be able to appeal when no reparation order is awarded. While Manning believes this may be possible,[484] Hoel posits that the Statute and Rules only allow victims to appeal the *content* of a reparation order but not a *refusal* to make a reparation order.[485]

479 Manning (2007) at 805.

480 Decisions of the Appeals Chamber are not *per se* binding on Chambers other than the Chamber from which the appeal arises. However, Article 21(2) of the Statute stipulates that "The Court may apply principles and rules of law as interpreted in its previous decisions."

481 Rome Statute, Art. 83.

482 *Ibid.*, Art. 82(4).

483 ICC RPE, Rule 153(1).

484 Manning (2007) at 813.

485 Hoel (2007) at 286.

Interlocutory Appeals

Interlocutory appeals are appeals on matters that arise before a final determination of a case.[486] In general the Appeals Chamber is limited in its power of review against decisions other than final decisions.[487] When deciding whether or not an issue is appropriate for an interlocutory appeal raised in relation to Article 82(1)(d) the Chambers have articulated the general standard, by finding that the relevant Chamber should determine whether there is an identifiable topic requiring a resolution and not merely disagreement on an issue.[488] Article 82(1)(d) provides that the *parties* may appeal a decision that involves an issue that would significantly affect the fair and expeditious conduct of the proceedings or the outcome of the trial and for which an immediate resolution by the Appeals Chamber would materially advance the proceedings. Rule 155 similarly only mentions parties with regard to interlocutory appeals requiring leave from the Court. Nevertheless, Regulation 65 mentions the right of participants to file responses for leave to appeal and substantive appeals and a limited right to orally be heard if the relevant Chamber ordered an immediate hearing on an application seeking leave to appeal. Moreover, although the Statute and Rules generally support arguments for broad participation it can be argued that the drafters purposefully restricted access to interlocutory appeals because they have the potential of causing undue delay, thereby infringing upon the rights of the accused. Thus, the Statute, Rules and Regulations are not entirely clear about whether victims have the automatic right to participate in interlocutory appeals. Although the governing documents specify that victims "have no right of appeal and cannot, on that basis, present [...] arguments against the accused to the Appeals Chamber," it was less certain when victims would nonetheless be able to share their views and concerns with the Appeals Chamber when a request for leave to appeal is granted to one of the parties.[489]

When the issue arose with regard to an appeal filed by Lubanga against a decision denying interim release, the Appeals Chamber interpreted Regulation 65 as providing victims the right to participate in interlocutory appeals but stopped short of finding an

486 Black's Law Dictionary, 7th Ed., West Publishing Company (1999).

487 See Rome Statute, Art. 82, which states that either party may appeal a decision with respect to jurisdiction and admissibility; a decision granting or denying release of the person being investigated or prosecuted; a decision of the Pre-Trial Chamber to act on its own initiative under Article 56(3); and a decision that involves an issue that would significantly affect the fair and expeditious conduct of the proceedings or the outcome of trial [...]. See also, *The Prosecutor v. Kony, et al.*, No. ICC-02/04-01/05-209, 20 February 2007, p. 4.

488 *Situation in DRC*, No. ICC-01/04-168, 13 July 2006, para. 9-10; see also *Situation in Darfur*, No. ICC-02/05-33, 22 November 2006, p. 5; *Situation in Darfur*, No. ICC-02/05-52, 21 February 2007, pp. 4-5; *Situation in Darfur*, No. ICC-02/05-70, 27 March 2007, p. 3; and *Situation in Uganda*, No. ICC-02/04-112, 19 December 2007, para. 19-21.

489 Jorda, J. and de Hemptinne, J., The Status and Role of the Victim, 1406, in Cassese, et al. (2002).

automatic right of victims to appeal.[490] Therefore, victims wishing to participate in an appeal under Article 82(1)(d) must file an application seeking leave to participate. The application must demonstrate that (i) the challenged decision involves an issue that would significantly affect the fair and expeditious conduct of the proceedings or the outcome of the trial, and (ii) the challenged decision requires an immediate resolution by the Appeals Chamber in order to materially advance proceedings. Using Article 68(3), the Appeals Chamber will examine each application for participation in light of the issue on appeal, and determine: (i) whether the individuals seeking participation are victims in the case (or situation); (ii) whether they have personal interests which are affected by the issues on appeal; (iii) whether their participation is appropriate; and finally (iv) that the manner of participation is not prejudicial to or inconsistent with the rights of the accused and a fair and impartial trial.[491] The Appeals Chamber will not carry out Rule 85 assessments; therefore, those victims who have yet to be granted victim status will be denied the right to participate in an appeal.[492] Thus, the Appeals Chamber has consistently found that even those victims who have previously participated in the specific issue underlying the appeal must file an application seeking leave to participate in the appeal and that only those victims who can show how their personal interests are affected by the issue on appeal will be permitted to participate.[493]

Judge Song, in his separate opinions, continuously argues that if victims participated in the proceedings at the pre-trial or trial level that gave rise to the appeal then their participation on appeal is appropriate.[494] More recently, another Judge, Judge Van

490 *Situation in DRC*, No. ICC-01/04-503, 30 June 2008, par. 34. Although Article 82 concerning 'appeals against other decisions,' and Rule 155 dealing with 'appeals that require leave of the Court' only make mention of parties and not participants, the Appeals Chamber affirmed for trial proceedings that victims could in fact participate. The Appeals Chamber determined in its 16 May 2008 decision that the 13 February 2007 Appeals Chamber decision from the pre-trial stage, which held that victims need to file an application seeking leave to participate in Article 82(1)(b) appeals, is equally applicable to appeals under Article 82(1)(d). See *The Prosecutor v. Lubanga*, No. ICC-01/04-01/06-1335, 16 May 2008, par. 13

491 For participation during the investigation phase, see *Situation in DRC*, No. ICC-01/04-503, 30 June 2008, par. 89. For participation during the confirmation of charges phase and trial stage, see *The Prosecutor v. Lubanga*, No. ICC-01/04-01/06-1335, 16 May 2008, para. 35-36; see also *The Prosecutor v. Lubanga*, No. ICC-01/04-01/06-824, 13 February 2007, par. 43; *Situation in Darfur*, No. ICC 02/05-138, 18 June 2008, para. 23, 49, 51, and 53-59; *Situation in DRC*, No. ICC-01/04-503, 30 June 2008, para. 88-98; *Situation in DRC*, No. ICC-01/04-450, 13 February 2008, par. 1; *Situation in Darfur*, No. ICC-02/05-129, 29 February 2008, par. 1; *Situation in DRC*, No. ICC-01/04-480, 29 February 2008, par. 1; *The Prosecutor v. Lubanga*, No. ICC-01/04-01/06-1239, 20 March 2008, par. 1; and *The Prosecutor v. Lubanga*, No. ICC-01/04-01/06-1452, 6 August 2008, para. 7-8.

492 *Situation in DRC*, No. ICC-01/04-503, 30 June 2008, par. 93.

493 *The Prosecutor v. Lubanga*, No. ICC-01/04-01/06-824, 13 February 2007, para. 38, 45; *Situation in Darfur*, No. ICC 02/05-138, 18 June 2008, par. 49; *Situation in DRC*, No. ICC-01/04-503, 30 June 2008, par. 88; *The Prosecutor v. Bemba*, No. ICC-01/05-01/08-566, 20 October 2009, para. 13-14.

494 *The Prosecutor v. Lubanga*, No. ICC-01/04-01/06-824 (dissenting opinion by Judge Song), 13 February 2007, para. 2-8; *The Prosecutor v. Lubanga*, No. ICC-01/04-01/06-1335 (dissenting opinion by Judge Song), 16 May 2008, para. 3-7; *Situation in Darfur*, No. ICC 02/05-138 (partly dissenting opinion by Judge Song), 18 June 2008, par. 3; *Situation in DRC*, No. ICC-01/04-503 (partly dissenting opinion by

den Wyngaert, agreed with Judge Song's approach and similarly began to argue that victims have a right to make submissions under Regulation 65(5) because they participated in proceedings giving rise to the appeal. Thus, both Judges argue that there is no need for victims to apply to participate in the interlocutory appeal.[495]

In order to ensure fair and expeditious proceedings, the Appeals Chamber has emphasized that it will limit the observations filed by participating victims in interlocutory appeals to the extent that they must be specifically relevant to the issues arising in the appeal which affect their personal interests.[496] In addition, taking note of the similarity, number and complexities of issues in one interlocutory appeal, the Appeals Chamber has required the legal representatives of victims to file consolidated briefs.[497]

Revision Proceedings

Article 84 and Rules 159-161 deal with revision of conviction or sentence and lay out the basic procedures that need to be followed. The revision scheme at the Court is provided only for revision of a conviction or sentence. It does not provide for revision of a decision to acquit an accused as this would violate the principle of *ne bis in idem*. An exceptional remedy, revision is only permitted if new evidence is discovered and had it been available at trial could have resulted in a different verdict; the non-availability of the evidence is not attributable to the party making the application; heavily relied on evidence taken into account at trial proves to be false or forged; or one or more of the judges who participated either in the judgment or confirmation of charges committed serious misconduct or a breach of duty of sufficient gravity to warrant removal. Persons who can seek revision include the convicted person, the prosecutor on the convicted individual's behalf, or after the death of the convicted person, his or her immediate family or authorized individual.

It was initially unclear who should be able to participate in revision proceedings. Although the French delegation argued that all participants from the trial should be able to participate,[498] the final wording of Rule 159 states that notification of a decision on an application for revision shall be sent to all the *parties* who participated in the proceedings. Further, Rule 161 provides that the relevant Chamber shall communicate

---

Judge Song), 30 June 2008, para. 1 and 2; *The Prosecutor v. Lubanga*, No. ICC-01/04-01/06-1452 (separate opinion of Judge Song), 6 August 2008, par. 1; *The Prosecutor v. Bemba*, No. ICC-01/05-01/08-623 (dissenting opinion of Judge Song), 27 November 2009, para. 3-4 and *The Prosecutor v. Katanga/Ngudjolo*, No. ICC-01/04-01/07-2124 (separate opinion of Judge Song), 24 May 2010, p. 8.

495 *The Prosecutor v. Lubanga*, No. ICC-01/04-01/06-2205 (separate opinion of Judge Song and Judge van der Wyngaert), 8 December 2009, p. 43.

496 *Situation in Darfur*, No. ICC 02/05-138, 18 June 2008, para. 60 and 62; *Situation in DRC*, No. ICC-01/04-503, 30 June 2008, par. 101; *The Prosecutor v. Lubanga*, No. ICC-01/04-01/06-1452, 6 August 2008, par. 12; *The Prosecutor v. Lubanga*, No. ICC-01/04-01/06-1453, 6 August 2008, par. 11; *The Prosecutor v. Lubanga*, No. ICC-01/04-01/06-1335, 16 May 2008, par. 50.

497 *Situation in DRC*, No. ICC-01/04-503, 30 June 2008, para. 101-102.

498 Brady, H., Appeal and Revision, 600-602, in Lee, et al. (2001).

to the applicant and to all those who received notification whether the conviction or sentence should be revised. Given that victims are not parties to the proceedings related to guilt, these provisions suggest that victims will not need to be notified of an application for revision or able to participate in a hearing on revision. However, it is not unlikely that should revision proceedings occur, the Court would, under its own authority, notify victims and seek their views and concerns given the fact that the Judges are required to take into account the needs of all victims in accordance with Rule 86 before making any direction or order.

7.5 Procedural Issues Arising Out of Participation

As with the ECCC, victims at the ICC are taking full advantage of their procedural rights, and their participation has clearly made an impact on proceedings. For example, it is undeniable that the initiative by legal representatives to expand the charges against Lubanga brought to the forefront issues about charging crimes of a sexual nature. Additionally, victims' contributions have, on a handful of occasions, aided the Court when examining a case. One example was when victims' legal representatives proposed the calling of expert witnesses on the use of names in the DRC. Their knowledge of the use of names in that region, which is dissimilar to other regions around the world, triggered the Court to gain better insight into the context of the events. However, these notable instances aside, the participation of victims before the ICC has, at times, been challenging.

A major challenge generated by victim participation has been the recurrent complaint that participation unnecessarily prolongs proceedings.[499] The Statute and Rules require that the Court ensure that proceedings are fair and expeditious.[500] It is therefore concerning that the narrow set of charges against *Lubanga* were confirmed in early 2007 and his trial is still ongoing. Although the delays are due, for the most part, to the two stay-of-proceedings related to the refusal by the prosecutor to disclose certain information to the Court,[501] the delay caused by the legal representatives' request to broaden the charges further added to the trial interruptions. In other cases, concerns have arisen with regard to the number of victim-applicants, the time it takes a defense team to process and respond to the applications,[502] and the motives behind those representing victims in proceedings.[503] Rather than giving the defense more time to

499 See, e.g., *The Prosecutor v. Banda/Jerbo*, T, 8 December 2010, pp. 51-52, where the defense counsel objected to a decision by the Pre-Trial Chamber to allow victims to file written submissions following the confirmation of charges hearing, arguing the right to an expeditious hearing.

500 Rome Statute, Art. 60(4), 64, and 67; see also ICC RPE, Rules 84, 91, 101, 132 and 162.

501 *The Prosecutor v. Lubanga*, No. ICC-01/04-01/06-1401, 13 June 2008; No. ICC-01/04-01/06-1487, 21 October 2008; No. ICC-01/04-01/06-2517-Red, 8 July 2010; No. ICC-01/04-01/06-2583, 8 October 2010.

502 Concerns were raised in interviews with the author.

503 See *The Prosecutor v. Banda/Jerbo*, No. ICC-02/05-03/09-110, 6 December 2010 and No. ICC-02/05-03/09-113, 6 December 2010.

deal with these applications, the Court has instead allowed victim-applicants to have limited participatory rights until final determinations on their applications are made, which, in turn, may disadvantage the accused further. Related to this is another challenge brought about by participation; namely, that victims operate as second prosecutors, unjustly encumbering the defense by making them face multiple accusers. The following sections will touch upon these concerns.

7.5.1 Disclosure Issues

Unlike the ECCC, which operates using a dossier system familiar to civil law jurisdictions, the ICC operates using a disclosure system more familiar to common law jurisdictions. The disclosure of information is of vital importance to the parties as well as to victims' participating in the proceedings. Without access to information, particularly exculpatory information, the accused would be unable to adequately prepare a defense. Similarly, for victims, without access to information meaningful participation would be negligible.

Formal disclosure at the ICC only involves the prosecution and defense, and should, in principle, take place prior to the commencement of trial.[504] Accordingly, prior to the confirmation of charges hearing, the prosecutor is obliged to disclose all evidence it intends to use at that hearing.[505] Following the confirmation of charges, the Trial Chamber must "[p]rovide for disclosure of documents or information not previously disclosed, sufficiently in advance of the commencement of the trial to enable adequate preparation for trial."[506] Further, the Trial Chamber must ensure that the prosecutor discloses, prior to the commencement of trial, any evidence not previously disclosed during the pre-trial phase of the case. However, as indicated above, Article 69(3) allows the Trial Chamber to request the submission of evidence that it considers necessary for the determination of the truth. And since the Trial Chamber may not know in advance of trial what this may be, it may order the production of evidence during the course of trial. Thus, there may be circumstances when the disclosure of evidence takes place after the commencement of trial. In addition to the disclosure obligations of the OTP, the defense also has disclosure obligations. Pursuant to Rule 79, the accused must communicate to the prosecution any specific defense he attends to raise and the names of witnesses who will be called to testify at trial – though the accused is not obliged to disclose previous statements taken by those witnesses on matters related to his legal strategy.

More than any other case, the trial in *Lubanga* has been particularly plagued with disclosure issues, ranging from late disclosure of information to withholding exculpatory material on the basis that the material is confidential. The Judges in *Lubanga* twice ordered a stay of the proceedings and the unconditional release of the accused

504 *The Prosecutor v. Katanga/Ngudjolo*, No. ICC-01/04-01/07-2288, 16 July 2010, par. 43.
505 Rome Statue, Art. 61(3); ICC RPE, Rule 121(3) and (5).
506 *Ibid.*, Art. 64(3)(c).

in response to the failure of the prosecution to acknowledge the fundamental right of the accused to have access to exculpatory material in its possession in order to prepare a defense.[507] However, in addition to these very serious concerns regarding the disclosure of information under the control of the prosecution which arose in *Lubanga*, defense teams in all the trials have struggled with gaining access to material from the victims.

Due to the fact that formal disclosure in the Statute and Rules does not involve victims one Chamber has found that "[t]hose granted the procedural status of victim cannot be part of the disclosure process [...], and thus they have neither disclosure rights nor disclosure obligations."[508] The Appeals Chamber similarly held that there is no general obligation on victims to disclose to the accused all evidence in their possession, whether incriminating or exculpatory.[509] It held that such an obligation would disregard the limited role victims play in presenting their views and concerns. Thus, there is no obligation on victims to disclose exculpatory evidence in their possession to the defense.

Instead, the Appeals Chamber held that when a victim's application for participation indicates that he or she may possess potentially exculpatory information, the OTP is responsible for investigating such information in the victim's possession.[510] Such information should then be disclosed to the defense. Moreover, it found that there may be specific instances when the Trial Chamber may require disclosure such as when the information is available and would contribute to the determination of the truth.[511] In addition, the Appeals Chamber has indicated that disclosure obligations could apply to victims who are granted the right to introduce evidence at trial.[512] The procedures for doing so would be determined by the Trial Chamber.

A situation in which victims were in possession of potentially exculpatory material arose in *Katanga/Ngudjolo*, and the legal representatives did indeed inform the prosecution of the potentially exculpatory information. The prosecution began investigating that information but would not inform the defense about the nature of the investigation until the investigation was complete. In the meantime, the Trial Chamber held that the legal representatives were free, as a courtesy, to provide the information to the defense.[513] However, given the general tensions between the defense and victims, the legal representatives declined to do so.

507 The Appeals Chamber reversed both decisions on the release of the accused. See *The Prosecutor v. Lubanga*, No. ICC-01/04-01/06-1401, 13 June 2008 and No. ICC-01/04-01/06-1418, 2 July 2008; see also, *The Prosecutor v. Lubanga*, No. ICC-01/04-01/06-1487, 21 October 2008; No. ICC-01/04-01/06-2517-Red, 8 July 2010; No. ICC-01/04-01/06-2583, 8 October 2010; T, 15 July 2010, pp. 17-22.

508 *The Prosecutor v. Katanga/Ngudjolo*, No. ICC-01/04-01/07-474, 13 May 2008, par. 114.

509 *The Prosecutor v. Katanga/Ngudjolo*, No. ICC-01/04-01/07-2288, 16 July 2010, para. 71-72 and 75.

510 *Ibid.* at par. 81.

511 *Ibid.* at par. 71.

512 *The Prosecutor v. Lubanga*, No. ICC-01/04-01/06-1432, 11 July 2008, para. 100 and 104.

513 *The Prosecutor v. Katanga/Ngudjolo*, T, 07 September 2010, p. 10.

Although formal disclosure only concerns the parties, the Trial Chamber in *Lubanga* did set out a procedure in which any materials within the prosecution's possession that are relevant to the personal interests of the victims may be provided to victims who have been granted the right to participate.[514] A similar practice was adopted in *Katanga/Ngudjolo* and *Bemba*. First, in a discrete written application to the Court the legal representative of the victim will need to identify the victim's personal interest and the nature of the information they seek, which may be within the control of the prosecution.[515] The material sought must be identified with precision in writing and may include information relating to a particular event at a specific time or location.[516] The legal representatives for victims and the prosecution should deal with the provision of this material *inter se*. However, should disagreements arise one of the parties may bring the disagreement to the Court's attention.[517] Thus, using the public documents as a starting point, including the detailed descriptions of the charges and lists of evidence the prosecutor intended to present at the confirmation of charges hearing, the legal representatives can start to file discrete written applications seeking additional information in the control of the prosecution. In contrast, with regard to information under the control of the defense, the victims are in a more tenuous position.

Similar to complaints raised by the defense with regard to the disclosure of information from victims,[518] victims' legal representatives have often complained about their access to documents and the disclosure practices by the defense.[519] Though victims have a general right to access the public record of a case, they do not have unfettered acces to non-public documents. As such, they depend upon the Court and other parties for access to information.[520] The general guidelines for defense disclosure to victims are as follows: (i) the Defense is to provide the Chamber, the prosecution and victims with a list of witnesses they intend to call seven days in advance of testimony; (ii) simultaneously, the defense should provide the Chamber, the prosecution and victims with a list of documents and other objects that may arise in the course of the evidence presented; and (iii) victims must then show how their personal interests are affected by the evidence or issue.[521] The defense should then consider the position of the victim(s) making the request and whether or not to disclose the relevant material if there is a prima facie basis for concluding that the Judges would allow the victim(s) to question the witness. If the defense does not believe that disclosure should take place it is left to the Chamber to resolve the dispute.[522]

---

514 *The Prosecutor v. Lubanga*, No. ICC-01/04-01/06-1119, 18 January 2008, par. 138.
515 *The Prosecutor v. Lubanga*, No. ICC-01/04-01/06-1368, 2 June 2008, par. 30.
516 *Ibid.* at para. 31, 111.
517 *Ibid.* at par. 34.
518 *The Prosecutor v. Katanga/Ngudjolo*, T, 3 November 2009, p. 36.
519 *The Prosecutor v. Lubanga*, T, 20 February 2009, p. 54.
520 Olásolo and Kiss (2010) at 155.
521 *Ibid.* at footnote 120, citing transcripts from the *Lubanga* trial.
522 *Ibid.* at 156, footnote 120, citing transcripts from the *Lubanga* trial.

In *Katanga/Ngudjolo* the defense had interviewed an individual who later turned out to be a victim in the case. At the time of the interview the defense alleged that it did not know the individual was a victim because the identity of anonymous victims had not been disclosed. The victim's legal representative requested from the defense the statement it took from the individual. When the defense was reluctant to provide the statement the Court asked the legal representatives to get a copy from their client. If that was not possible then another approach to the defense would be appropriate, emphasizing that courtesy should govern relations between counsel. However, the defense again declined, arguing that just as there is no provision requiring legal representatives to disclose information to the defense, there is likewise no obligation on the defense to disclose information to the victims.[523]

Ultimately, the Chamber held that if the defense sought to call this victim then it would be required to disclose the statement or a summary of the main points of the statement at least two weeks prior to the commencement of the defense case,[524] and therefore ordered the defense to transmit a document encompassing the key points addressed during the interview.[525] On another occasion in *Bemba*, though Rule 59 only allows victims to have a summary of the grounds on which the admissibility of the case is challenged, the Judges asked the defense to provide more than a summary and to give the victims a suitably redacted application.[526] It appears that the Court is generally in favor of legal representatives having access to information so as to ensure the smooth operation of proceedings.

7.5.2 Evidentiary Issues

Evidence presented in criminal proceedings is fundamentally linked with arguing a case to be determined by the court. The aim of the evidence is to prove, disprove or cast doubt upon a matter under examination. Thus, in principle, the introduction of evidence is therefore the primary right of the parties, namely those who bring and must answer a case before the court.[527] With regard to the hearing of evidence, the Statute and Rules provide for a liberal system. Generally, the parties may submit evidence relevant to the case and the Court has the authority to request evidence that it considers necessary for the determination of the truth.[528] The Court may rule on the relevance or admissibility of any evidence, taking into account its probative value and potential prejudice.[529] Thus far, the various Chambers at the Court have agreed that victim applications are not part of the evidence in a case regardless of whether or not they are

---

523 *The Prosecutor v. Katanga/Ngudjolo*, T, 24 November 2010, p. 80.
524 *Ibid.* at 81.
525 *Ibid.* at 82.
526 *The Prosecutor v. Bemba*, T, 08 March 2010, pp. 4-5.
527 Friman (2009) at 492.
528 Rome Statute, Art. 69(3)
529 *Ibid.*, Art. 69(4).

also witnesses.[530] Similarly, the Trial Chambers have thus far held that if victims wish to address the Court and have their views and concerns taken into account as evidence they must do so as a witness under oath.[531]

7.5.2.1 Witnesses, Civil Parties and Dual Status

As mentioned in the previous chapter, there are two concerns that arise when a victim has the dual role of victim-witness. First, a victim-witness could be in a position where he or she would provide evidence to the Court after gaining access to the confidential part of the case file, thereby enabling that victim-witness to conform or adjust his/her testimony to the available evidence on which the prosecution intends to rely. Second, the credibility of the victim-witness could be questioned due to his/her financial interests in the outcome of the proceedings, providing an incentive for the victim-witness to modify his/her testimony. For these reasons, the Court has sought to take important steps to minimize any potential problems with the rights of the accused.

When the issue of dual status for victim-witnesses arose in the *Katanga/Ngudjolo* case the Single Judge thought it prudent to impose procedural safeguards with the aim of preserving the admissibility and probative value of the evidence that the victim-witness may provide. To this end, she thought it best to (i) prevent the victim-witness from having access to the confidential part of the case record, which includes the bulk of the evidence on which the parties intend to rely at the confirmation hearing, including the statements of the other witnesses; and (ii) prevent the victim-witness from attending any hearing of a witness in the present case, even if such hearing is public. The procedural safeguards were to remain in effect until such point when the victim-witness no longer remained an anonymous victim.[532]

The Trial Chamber in *Lubanga* has never set out the parameters of the rights for victims with dual status as witnesses. However, the Chamber has rejected the notion that victims appearing before the Court should automatically be treated as witnesses.[533] When considering applications for participation by victims who are also witnesses the Court will determine whether having dual status could adversely affect the rights of the defense at a particular stage in the case and reserved the right to restrict the modalities of participation.[534] Importantly, the Trial Chamber noted that when "an

530 *The Prosecutor v. Abu Garda*, T, 20 October 2009, p. 14. See also *The Prosecutor v. Katanga/ Ngudjolo*, No. ICC-01/04-01/07-717, 30 September 2008, para 229-232; Cf. *The Prosecutor v. Lubanga*, No. ICC-01/04-01/06-1637, 21 January 2009.

531 See, e.g., *The Prosecutor v. Lubanga*, No. ICC-01/04-01/06-2032 and its Annex No. ICC-01/04-01/06-2032-Anx, 9 July 2009, Annex, par. 25; *The Prosecutor v. Katanga/Ngudjolo*, No. ICC-01/04-01/07-1788-tENG, 22 January 2010, par. 86.

532 *The Prosecutor v. Katanga/Ngudjolo*, No. ICC-01/04-01/07-632, 23 June 2008, para. 31-32.

533 *The Prosecutor v. Lubanga*, No. ICC-01/04-01/06-1119, 18 January 2008, par. 132.

534 *Ibid.* at para. 132, 134.

individual has dual status [this] does not grant him or her rights in addition to those of someone who is only a victim or a witness."[535]

Unsurprisingly, issues arose at trial related to appropriate protective measures for victim-witnesses and the rights of the accused to a fair trial, and to the disclosure of exculpatory material in the possession of the prosecution and VPRS. The defense requested the Court to order the Registry to provide the defense with un-redacted victim application forms for those victims holding dual status. In approaching this issue the Trial Chamber highlighted the right to a fair trial, emphasized the need to protect the safety, physical and psychological well-being, dignity and privacy of victims and witnesses and stressed the fact that the prosecution has an obligation to disclose exculpatory material, including copies of statements made by witnesses it intends to call.[536] The Court further noted that only the prosecution has a positive obligation to disclose exculpatory material and that this obligation cannot be imposed on other Court organs.[537] In taking into account the various interests, the Court concluded that when victims have dual status, the prosecution will likely need to disclose their prior statements, including their victim application forms, but first the prosecution must notify the legal representative of that victim so that objections to the disclosure may be raised.[538]

Finally, in *Lubanga* and *Bemba* the parties, victims and Judges have agreed to the following: when a legal representative of victims becomes aware that his client has dual status, they should provide the prosecution with the name, date of birth and other identifying information, to the extent possible, of that individual.[539] The prosecution should then confirm in writing whether or not the individual in fact has dual status and whether it intends to make an application for protective measures.[540] Similar procedures operate with regard to the defense. Alternatively, the legal representative may ask the Court to verify whether his client is in the ICC protection program.[541] If the individual in question has dual-status, the Court, through the Registry, will communicate with the individual to seek his consent to share this fact with the legal representative.[542] If one of the parties wishes to contact a victim-witness, it should do so through the legal representative. If a victim-witness wishes to communicate with one of the

535 *The Prosecutor v. Lubanga*, No. ICC-01/04-01/06-1379, 5 June 2008, par. 52(b).

536 *The Prosecutor v. Lubanga*, No. ICC-01/04-01/06-1637, 21 January 2009, par. 9.

537 *Ibid.* at par. 10.

538 *Ibid.* at para. 12-13.

539 A victim's legal representative must have the victim's consent to disclose his or her identity to the prosecution. See *The Prosecutor v. Lubanga*, No. ICC-01/04-01/06-1379, 5 June 2008; *The Prosecutor v. Bemba*, No. ICC-01/05-01/08-807-Corr, 12 July 2010.

540 *The Prosecutor v. Lubanga*, No. ICC-01/04-01/06-1379, 5 June 2008, para. 52-78; *The Prosecutor v. Bemba*, No. ICC-01/05-01/08-807-Corr, 12 July 2010, para. 50-54.

541 *The Prosecutor v. Lubanga*, No. ICC-01/04-01/06-1379, 5 June 2008, para. 52-78; *The Prosecutor v. Bemba*, No. ICC-01/05-01/08-807-Corr, 12 July 2010, para. 50-54.

542 *The Prosecutor v. Lubanga*, No. ICC-01/04-01/06-1379, 5 June 2008, para. 52-78; *The Prosecutor v. Bemba*, No. ICC-01/05-01/08-807-Corr, 12 July 2010, para. 50-54.

parties, the VWU will facilitate the contact.[543] As a general rule, legal representatives may contact their clients who have dual status. However, legal representatives who represent a victim with dual status may not discuss their testimony with them in advance and often must meet their clients while supervised by an agent of the Court.[544] Nonetheless, legal representatives may request access to materials related to their client and be present during interviews of the victim-witness, provided consent is given by that individual.[545]

7.5.2.2 Familiarization and Proofing

Very early in the Court's operation, the Pre-Trial Chamber in *Lubanga* barred the prosecution from "witness proofing," which is the substantive preparation of witnesses prior to giving evidence.[546] Other Chambers have adopted this approach.[547] However that same decision did allow what it referred to as "witness familiarization," which is to take measures to better acquaint witnesses with the layout of the Court, the procedures to expect and the roles and functions of the parties and participants. Witness familiarization is to be carried out by the VWU and not by the parties calling the witness.

Once victim-witnesses arrive in The Hague the *Lubanga* Trial Chamber has determined that there should be no contact between victim-witnesses and their legal representative without the express consent of the Court. The rationale behind this approach is the principle "that witnesses to a crime are the property neither of the prosecution nor of the defense and that they should therefore not be considered as witnesses of either party, but as witnesses of the Court."[548] The only exceptions to this general rule are for the courtesy meetings and consent meetings. In *Katanga/Ngudjolo*, the Court held that victims' legal representatives may take part in the familiarization process but only with regard to the victims' safety concerns. In other words, the legal representative may not answer questions related to the victim's testimony.[549] In addition to the familiarization process, legal representatives have been permitted to participate in courtesy meetings arranged by the Court in order to meet with their clients after arrival in The Hague.[550]

543 *The Prosecutor v. Lubanga*, No. ICC-01/04-01/06-1379, 5 June 2008, para. 52-78; *The Prosecutor v. Bemba*, No. ICC-01/05-01/08-807-Corr, 12 July 2010, para. 50-54.

544 *The Prosecutor v. Abu Garda*, T, 20 October 2009, pp. 8-9, 95.

545 The parties may contest the presence of the legal representative and inform the Court of their position. This became apparent through interviews with Court personnel.

546 See *The Prosecutor v. Lubanga*, No. ICC-01/04-01/06-679, 8 November 2006. The approach adopted stands in contrast to the approach taken by the *Ad Hoc* Tribunals and the SCSL.

547 *The Prosecutor v. Lubanga*, No. ICC-01/04-01/06-1049, 30 November 2007; cf. *The Prosecutor v. Lubanga*, No. ICC-01/04-01/06-1069, 10 December 2007, allowing parties to jointly or separately instruct expert witnesses.

548 *The Prosecutor v. Lubanga,* T, 25 January 2010, p. 11.

549 *The Prosecutor v. Katanga/Ngudjolo*, No. ICC-01/04-01/07-1788-tENG, 22 January 2010, para. 79-80.

550 *The Prosecutor v. Katanga/Ngudjolo,* T, 23 February 2010, p. 72.

7.5.2.3 *Proposing Witnesses*

The legal representatives of victims do not have an unfettered right to call witnesses. However, they may identify persons in addition to their clients who they would like to have give evidence that is pertinent to the personal interests of victims.[551] The Chamber may then decide to call the witness on its own motion in accordance with Articles 64(6)(b), (d) and 69(3) and may allow the legal representative who proposed the witness to pose questions either before or after the Chamber poses questions.[552] The most notable example of when legal representatives successfully proposed a witness other than their clients was in *Lubanga* when one of the legal representatives proposed two expert witnesses on the use of names in the DRC.[553]

7.5.2.4 *Questioning Witnesses*

When their personal interests are affected, Rule 91(3) permits victims to question witnesses with the leave of the relevant Chamber. This right includes the questioning of fact witnesses, character witnesses, expert witnesses and the defendant if the defendant testifies.[554] Though originally included as a way in which victims could elicit evidence in relation to reparations,[555] it no longer has such limited value. Indeed, though questioning by victims' legal representatives started off slowly in the *Lubanga* trial with relatively few questions being put to witnesses, including witnesses who were alleged former child soldiers and expert witnesses,[556] the questioning of witnesses has become one of the most significant rights exercised by victims through their legal representatives. At times emotional,[557] victims' legal representatives have generally focused on the conditions under which their clients suffered,[558] and the physical and

551 *The Prosecutor v. Katanga/Ngudjolo*, No. ICC-01/04-01/07-1665, 20 November 2009, para. 45-48.

552 *Ibid.* at para. 45-48.

553 See *The Prosecutor v. Lubanga*, No. ICC-01/04-01/06-1896, 25 May 2009.

554 *The Prosecutor v. Lubanga*, No. ICC-01/04-01/06-1119, 18 January 2008, par. 108; *The Prosecutor v. Katanga/Ngudjolo*, No. ICC-01/04-01/07-1788-tENG, 22 January 2010, para. 72-78; *The Prosecutor v. Bemba*, No. ICC-01/05-01/08-807-Corr, 12 July 2010, para. 38-40. Victims' legal representatives also questioned the age-determination experts in *Lubanga*, see *The Prosecutor v. Lubanga,* T, 12 May 2009, pp. 76-83, T, 08 June 2009, and on the questioning of UN experts on the origin and causes of the conflict in the DRC, see *The Prosecutor v. Lubanga*, T, 18 June 2009, pp. 2-7.

555 Mekjian and Varughese (2005) at 28; Bitti, G. and Friman, H., Participation of Victims in the Proceedings, 467, in Lee, et al. (2001).

556 In *Lubanga*, the legal representatives did not seek to pose any questions to the expert who testified on the Hema-Lendu conflict, see *The Prosecutor v. Lubanga*, T, 26 March 2009; see also, *The Prosecutor v. Lubanga*, T, 09 July 2009, p. 44.

557 In fact, in some cases the legal representatives were cautioned against using emotive language, see, e.g., *The Prosecutor v. Katanga/Ngudjolo,* T, 06 October 2010, p. 45.

558 *The Prosecutor v. Katanga/Ngudjolo,* T, 30 November 2010, pp. 68-70; *The Prosecutor v. Bemba,* T, 2 December 2010, p. 21 (on rapes committed for example).

psychological effects and consequences of their experiences.[559] Nevertheless, the questioning has also raised a number of concerns. The defense and the Court have had to intervene on numerous occasions because of irrelevant, repetitive or leading questions. In addition, concerns have been raised about victims acting as second prosecutors.

The procedure for authorizing questions by victims' legal representatives is, for the most part, the same in all three Trial Chambers. When a legal representative wishes to pose a question to a witness on matters related to a potential order on reparations in accordance with Article 75 that legal representative shall make a written application to that effect. The application must include the questions to be posed as well as an explanation of the precise purpose and scope of the question and any relevant documents that will be used for questioning. The application must be filed early enough for the defense to submit observations (namely, seven days before the witness' appearance).[560] If the Chamber grants the request, it will do so under Regulation 56, which allows questions related to reparations to be asked during trial.

When legal representatives know in advance that they wish to pose specific questions outside the topic of reparations they shall request to do so in a discrete written application, notified to the Judges and prosecution, at least seven days before the witness appears in Court.[561] The application must include the proposed questions and how they relate to the interests of the victims represented. If the Chamber feels that the defense should submit observations it will notify the defense of the request and the defense will have three days to file its observations.[562] If, after an examination-in-chief by the party calling the witness, the Chamber believes that the matters raised by the proposed questions have not been sufficiently addressed it will allow the legal representative to put the questions to the witness before the cross-examination begins.

When requesting leave to ask questions in addition to those filed in the discrete written application, following the direct-examination, the legal representatives file further applications (usually via email) to either withdraw, rephrase or add to their

---

559 See, e.g., *The Prosecutor v. Katanga/Ngudjolo,* T, 23 June 2010, p. 26; *The Prosecutor v. Lubanga*, T, 04 February 2009, pp. 38-39; T, 25 February 2009, pp. 54-57; T, 06 March 2009, pp. 28-31; T, 18 June 2009, pp. 9-10; *The Prosecutor v. Bemba,* T, 2 December 2010, pp. 17-18. Answers to these questions varied but most responses focused on the delay or abandonment of schooling, physical ailments, nightmares and an overall sense of unimaginable loss, see, e.g., *The Prosecutor v. Lubanga*, T, 04 February 2009, pp. 39-40; T, 10 February 2009, p. 31.

560 *The Prosecutor v. Katanga/Ngudjolo*, No. ICC-01/04-01/07-1665, 20 November 2009, para. 82-91; *The Prosecutor v. Lubanga*, No. ICC-01/04-01/06-1119, 18 January 2008, para. 108-111; *The Prosecutor v. Bemba*, No. ICC-01/05-01/08-807-Corr, 12 July 2010, para. 30-40.

561 See *The Prosecutor v. Bemba*, No. ICC-01/05-01/08-1005, 10 November 2010 and No. ICC-01/05-01/08-1023, 19 November 2010. In *Bemba* the Court had to remind legal representatives about the numerous decisions laying out the procedures for questioning a witness, see, e.g., *The Prosecutor v. Bemba,* T, 24 November 2010, p. 53.

562 *The Prosecutor v. Katanga/Ngudjolo*, No. ICC-01/04-01/07-1665, 20 November 2009, para. 82-91; *The Prosecutor v. Lubanga*, No. ICC-01/04-01/06-1119, 18 January 2008, para. 108-111; *The Prosecutor v. Bemba*, No. ICC-01/05-01/08-807-Corr, 12 July 2010, para. 30-40.

previous list of proposed questions. The Chamber will take into consideration the rights of the accused, the interests of the witness, the need for a fair, impartial and expeditious trial and the need to ensure the participation of victims in accordance with Article 68(3). The Chambers have indicated that when giving consideration to the rights of the accused they must take into account the timing of the intervention as well as the overall effect of the questioning.[563] If the Court feels that it is inappropriate for the legal representatives to pose a particular question, the Chamber may decide to pose the proposed question itself.[564] When legal representatives wish to pose unanticipated questions, during examination-in-chief by the party calling the witness, the legal representative may submit the proposed question to the Chamber, usually via email. The Chamber may then decide upon the request.[565]

Without a doubt, the list of questions submitted in advance to the Trial Chambers helped avoid repetitive questions because the Judges could inform the legal representatives which questions or topics were permissible to cover.[566] As a result, the Chambers were in a position to reject a number of proposed questions by the legal representatives for victims,[567] commenting that a question "doesn't seem to be necessary" or "seems to be far too leading."[568] By and large, the Chambers have frowned upon overly broad requests. When one legal representative in *Lubanga* included a category of "other questions" in his application the Judges did not accept such a submission, pointing out that they accept specific questions (or topics) so long as they are proposed in advance – even if only orally shortly before questioning commences.[569] In general, the Chambers have been flexible when allowing victims' legal representatives to ask unexpected and spontaneous questions.[570] This flexibility is necessary because very often the questions filed beforehand lose their relevance or become repetitive.[571]

As mentioned previously the proper scope of questioning varies between Chambers. The Trial Chamber in *Katanga/Ngudjolo* has found that questions should, in principle, be limited to those that have as their purpose to clarify or complement previous evidence given by the witness.[572] Nevertheless, on a number of occasions this

563 *The Prosecutor v. Lubanga*, No. ICC-01/04-01/06-2340, 11 March 2010, para. 34-35; *The Prosecutor v. Bemba*, No. ICC-01/05-01/08-807-Corr, 12 July 2010, par. 25.

564 *The Prosecutor v. Katanga/Ngudjolo*, No. ICC-01/04-01/07-1665, 20 November 2009, para. 82-91; *The Prosecutor v. Lubanga*, No. ICC-01/04-01/06-1119, 18 January 2008, para. 108-111; *The Prosecutor v. Bemba*, No. ICC-01/05-01/08-807-Corr, 12 July 2010, para. 30-40.

565 *The Prosecutor v. Katanga/Ngudjolo*, No. ICC-01/04-01/07-1665, 20 November 2009, para. 82-91; *The Prosecutor v. Lubanga*, No. ICC-01/04-01/06-1119, 18 January 2008, para. 108-111; *The Prosecutor v. Bemba*, No. ICC-01/05-01/08-807-Corr, 12 July 2010, para. 30-40.

566 *The Prosecutor v. Katanga/Ngudjolo*, T, 03 March 2010, p. 43.

567 See, e.g., *The Prosecutor v. Katanga/Ngudjolo*, T, 22 March 2010, p. 17; T, 12 July 2010, p. 15.

568 *The Prosecutor v. Katanga/Ngudjolo*, T, 06 October 2010, pp. 34-35.

569 *The Prosecutor v. Lubanga*, T, 08 June 2009, p. 43.

570 See, e.g., *The Prosecutor v. Katanga/Ngudjolo*, T, 22 March 2010, p. 24; see also, *The Prosecutor v. Katanga/Ngudjolo*, No. ICC-01/04-01/07-1665, 20 November 2009.

571 *The Prosecutor v. Katanga/Ngudjolo*, T, 23 June 2010, p. 19.

572 *The Prosecutor v. Katanga/Ngudjolo*, T, 25 February 2010, p. 22.

Chamber, as well as the others, has allowed legal representatives to ask questions beyond matters raised during examination-in-chief so long as the questions are not duplicative or repetitive and are limited to matters in controversy between the parties or are directly relevant to the interests of victims represented.[573] With regard to the manner or mode of questioning, the Trial Chambers have generally agreed that unless specifically authorized to do so, legal representatives should conduct their questioning in a neutral manner and avoid leading and closed questions.[574]

On the whole, at the time of writing, the Trial Chamber in *Lubanga* has allowed victims to ask about (i) factors contributing to the conscription and enlistment of children, including the vulnerability of children; (ii) the living conditions of the child soldiers, including acts of sexual violence; (iii) the difficulties encountered by children when reintegrating into their families and communities and the difficulties they continue to face as a result of their victimization.[575] Similarly, the Judges in *Katanga/Ngudjolo* have allowed legal representatives to ask about the context of the crimes, the role played by child soldiers, the training received, difficulties encountered and overall living conditions.[576] Legal representatives were able to draw the Court's attention to the effects of fighting and the difficulties faced when reintegrating into society.[577] For example, when questioning the expert clinical psychologist about post-traumatic stress disorder the legal representatives focused their questions on how trauma impacts the personal development of children.[578] In *Bemba* victims oddly chose not to question the expert on post-traumatic stress disorder.[579]

Many times, the Court thanked legal representatives for their interventions such as in *Katanga/Ngudjolo* when a legal representative asked a witness about how he evaluated the age of those he saw in the training camps.[580] The Judges indicated that had the question not been asked by the legal representatives they would have posed the question. Likewise in *Lubanga*, following the testimony of the first of the three victims called by the Court, the presiding Judge remarked that the questioning by his legal representative was "extremely focused and helpful."[581] The reverse, at least for the

573 *The Prosecutor v. Katanga/Ngudjolo*, No. ICC-01/04-01/07-1665, 20 November 2009, para. 82-91; *The Prosecutor v. Lubanga*, No. ICC-01/04-01/06-1119, 18 January 2008, para. 108-111; *The Prosecutor v. Bemba*, No. ICC-01/05-01/08-807-Corr, 12 July 2010, para. 30-40.

574 *The Prosecutor v. Katanga/Ngudjolo*, No. ICC-01/04-01/07-1665, 20 November 2009, para. 82-91; *The Prosecutor v. Lubanga*, No. ICC-01/04-01/06-1119, 18 January 2008, para. 108-111; see also *The Prosecutor v. Lubanga*, No. ICC-01/04-01/06-2127, 16 September 2009; *The Prosecutor v. Bemba*, No. ICC-01/05-01/08-807-Corr, 12 July 2010, para. 30-40.

575 *The Prosecutor v. Lubanga*, T, 07 January 2010, p. 25; see also, e.g., *The Prosecutor v. Lubanga*, T, 06 March 2009, pp. 32-39; T, 18 June 2009, p. 38; T, 02 July 2009, pp. 6-13.

576 *The Prosecutor v. Katanga/Ngudjolo*, T, 23 June 2010, p. 19; T, 17 November 2010, p. 72; T, 30 November 2009, p. 26.

577 *The Prosecutor v. Katanga/Ngudjolo*, T, 12 July 2010, pp. 16-48; T, 13 July 2010, pp. 2-11;

578 *The Prosecutor v. Lubanga*, T, 07 April 09, pp. 60-78.

579 *The Prosecutor v. Bemba*, T, 29 November 2010 and T, 30 November 2010.

580 *The Prosecutor v. Katanga/Ngudjolo*, T, 31 March 2010, p. 54; T, 20 April 2010, p. 33

581 *The Prosecutor v. Lubanga*, T, 12 January 2010 p. 31.

prosecution, is also true. There have been a number of instances when the questioning on the part of victims' legal representatives negatively impacted the case of the prosecution.[582] One instance in *Katanga/Ngudjolo* involved a legal representative asking the witness, a former soldier, whether the looting and destruction of homes was part of the plan of attack – a question specifically avoided by the prosecution.[583] The witness responded that no such plan existed.[584] Though relatively minor, there are numerous examples highlighting why, at times, the prosecution opposes broader participation.

More often, though, it is the defense that is disadvantaged by an overly active victims' bench. The defense in *Lubanga* would regularly object to the phrasing of questions posed by legal representatives. Specifically the defense would object to leading questions,[585] or repetitive questions that had already been asked by the prosecution.[586] However, only occasionally did the defense object to the scope of the questioning. For instance, the defense did not object to questions posed about the pillaging of natural resources in the DRC, which is only broadly related to the enlistment and conscription of child soldiers and arguably more within the purview of the prosecution.[587] Most importantly, the defense did not object to questions specifically posed to criminally implicate the accused.

In contrast, in *Katanga/Ngudjolo*, the defense repeatedly raised objections both to leading questions and to the scope of questioning, arguing time and again that victims are not there as "substitute and ancillary prosecutors."[588] The defense in *Katanga/Ngudjolo* were particularly adamant that the legal representatives for victims "should not be viewed, as it were, as performing the same function as the man who follows the Lord Mayor's show and comes behind with his brush to sweep up after the horses and everyone else [who] has passed."[589] In one instance, during the questioning of a witness by a legal representative on the subject of rape, the defense objected. The defense argued that the prosecution had not asked the witness about rape and therefore objected to the attempt by the legal representatives to expand the scope of the testimony.[590] The defense argued that they should not be placed in a position after the prosecution has finished their examination, where the legal representatives open up new subjects. They submitted that this might lead to the situation where the defense

582 See, e.g., *The Prosecutor v. Katanga/Ngudjolo*, T, 06 October 2010, p. 52.

583 *The Prosecutor v. Katanga/Ngudjolo*, T, 27 May 2010, p. 24.

584 *Ibid.*

585 *The Prosecutor v. Lubanga*, T, 18 February 2009, pp. 88-89; T, 06 May 2009, pp. 13-14.

586 *The Prosecutor v. Lubanga*, T, 06 March 2009, pp. 34-35.

587 See *The Prosecutor v. Lubanga*, T, 18 June 2009, p. 15. One of the first instances when the defense began objecting to the scope of questions asked by either the prosecution or legal representatives was in early 2010, see *The Prosecutor v. Lubanga*, T, 12 January 2010 p. 38; however it was pointed out to the Court that no such objections had previously been raised.

588 *The Prosecutor v. Katanga/Ngudjolo*, T, 30 November 2009, p. 32; T, 31 March 2010, p. 45; T, 23 June 2010, p. 21; T, 22 June 2010, p. 73; T, 23 June 2010, pp. 39-42; T, 17 November 2010, p. 48.

589 *The Prosecutor v. Katanga/Ngudjolo*, T, 30 November 2009, p. 32.

590 *Th e Prosecutor v. Katanga/Ngudjolo*, T, 17 November 2010, p. 62-63.

would need to seek an adjournment to investigate.[591] The Judges agreed and advised the legal representatives to stick to the transcript from the direct examination of the prosecutor.[592] In another instance, the defense successfully argued that victims should be confined to questions of contention in the case and therefore should not be able to ask questions about forced recruitment which was not a matter of contention but which could have a prejudicial effect on the accused.[593]

The defense teams in *Katanga/Ngudjolo* regularly objected because they viewed it improper for the victims' legal representatives to pose questions, for instance on the guilt of the accused, but not necessarily to the questions themselves. In other words, the defense stated that it would not object if the Court or the prosecution asked the proposed questions but that allowing the victims to do so would be inappropriate if for no other reason than for the sake of appearance.[594] On occasion the Judges agreed, and in one instance told the defense that either they may pose the question or the Court would do so themselves but that it would be inappropriate for the victims to do so.[595] Interestingly, at one point in the trial, even the victims acknowledged their limited role saying "I do not even want to talk about Mr. Katanga because this is not my role when it comes to liability [...]."[596] Again, this stands in stark contrast with the proceedings in *Lubanga* and *Bemba* where victims regularly elicit evidence that goes to the specific guilt of the accused and overlaps with the role traditionally assigned to the prosecution.

Often, even when the defense failed to state an objection, the Court would intervene and suggest that the question be rephrased to avoid leading questions or because the scope of the question was too broad or inappropriate.[597] More commonly, however, the Judges in *Lubanga* simply let the legal representatives pose questions without interruption. At one point during trial, the presiding Judge stated that "rather than interrupting counsel in every question, unless you have strenuous objections, I think it would be better to let this run. But I undertake and reassure you that we will separate, as I say, the relevant from the irrelevant."[598] There is no doubt that the parties will comb through final decisions to scrutinize on what evidence the Trial Chamber ultimately relied upon to support its final decision. For now, they can only hope that the Chambers are capable of separating, as it were, the relevant from the irrelevant.

591 *Ibid.* at 69.

592 *Ibid.* at 63.

593 *The Prosecutor v. Katanga/Ngudjolo,* T 07 December 2010, p. 28.

594 *The Prosecutor v. Katanga/Ngudjolo*, T, 30 November 2009, p. 32.

595 *Ibid.* at 35, 45.

596 *The Prosecutor v. Katanga/Ngudjolo*, T, 23 June 2010, p. 41.

597 *The Prosecutor v. Lubanga*, T, 18 June 2009, p. 37; T, 07 January 2010, pp. 4-5; T, 08 January 2010, p. 3; *The Prosecutor v. Katanga/Ngudjolo*, T, 25 February 2010, p. 25; T, 22 June 2010, p. 65.

598 *The Prosecutor v. Lubanga*, T, 07 January 2010, p. 39.

7.5.2.5 Victim Testimony

On 2 April 2009 one of the legal representatives for victims in *Lubanga* requested that three victims be allowed to address the Court and give evidence on four 'discrete' issues which included presenting their individual histories within the context of the charges faced by the accused, discussing the harm they individually experienced, sharing their views on the approach to be taken with regard to reparations, focusing on relevant facts not yet covered in trial, and speaking about the issue of child recruitment.[599] Both the prosecution and defense objected to the request.[600]

In assessing whether or not to grant the application the Chamber took a number of things into account. It began by stating that the presumption is that those participating will do so through their legal representatives. However, for those victims wishing to participate in person, they will have to show powerful reasons for why the Court should make an exception to the general rule. The Court emphasized that such participation could destabilize proceedings and that it would need to take into account a variety of factors including the rights to a fair trial. In view of this position, the Chamber noted that it must ensure that presentations made by victims are not unnecessarily repetitive.[601] By way of example, the Chamber noted that it would be mindful if a victim first makes a personal presentation of his or her views and concerns, and this is then repeated by them in evidence and finally addressed on a third occasion by their legal representatives in submissions. Overall the Chamber concluded that victim participation must be proportionate and consistent with a fair trial and that fact-specific decisions are required, taking into account the trial proceedings as a whole. The Chamber surmised that if all the participating victims sought to personally present their views and concerns the fair trial rights of the accused could be infringed.[602]

Ultimately the Trial Chamber granted the request, concluding that the three victims would be permitted to give evidence under oath.[603] In this sense, the victims would be called as witnesses pursuant to Article 69(3) which provides the Chamber with the authority to request the submission of all evidence that it considers necessary for the

599 When a victim wishes to testify at trial, his legal representative must file a written application to do so before the completion of the prosecution's case. The application must include a signed statement by the victim and a comprehensive summary of the testimony to be given. This summary will then be disclosed to the parties. The filing in this case was confidential. See *The Prosecutor v. Lubanga*, No. ICC-01/04-01/06-2032 and its Annex No. ICC-01/04-01/06-2032-Anx, 9 July 2009, Annex, par. 1.

600 Both objections were filed confidentially but reference is made to them in filings and transcripts. See, e.g., *The Prosecutor v. Lubanga*, No. ICC-01/04-01/06-2032 and its Annex No. ICC-01/04-01/06-2032-Anx, 9 July 2009, Annex, para. 2-3.

601 *Ibid.* at par. 26.

602 *Ibid.* at par. 27.

603 *Ibid.* At the beginning of trial Lubanga had a clear view of the victim-witness. However, after the first victim-witness recanted his earlier statements and withdrew his initial testimony the Court began to shield victim-witnesses from Lubanga's direct line of vision. All former child soldiers testified with curtains pulled across the side of their witness box though Lubanga could watch them via the video screen.

determination of the truth. In its decision the Court made a distinction between "expressing their views and concerns" and "giving evidence."[604] Expressing views and concerns, they found, does not form part of the evidence at trial.[605] Instead, it is meant as a way of aiding the Judges in their approach to the evidence. If the victims sought to give evidence they would need to take an oath before testifying. After which the Chamber determined that it would allow the victims the opportunity to express their views and concerns personally (not under oath).[606] The Judges rejected submissions by the prosecution that the evidence of the former child soldiers would duplicate previous testimony. The Judges stated that "the account of each former child soldier is unique," adding that they would discuss an area not previously covered by the prosecution.[607]

The Chamber determined that victims giving evidence should do so after the prosecution's case but before the defense's case in order to give the defense the opportunity to present its case once all the evidence alleged against it has been heard.[608] When testifying the Court permitted the victims to refresh their memories with their own victim applications and any other previous statements but they were not permitted to have access to other individuals' applications or statements.[609] In addition, although the order of questioning was arranged so that the legal representatives questioned the victims first, followed by the prosecution and finally by the defense, the Court could have also allowed the victims to tell their stories in narrative form which it had allowed with other victim-witnesses.[610]

The first of three victims to testify in *Lubanga* was a schoolmaster at the time when his students were allegedly forcibly enlisted in the UPC. He had tried to intervene to help the children and suffered harm as a result. Though much of his testimony, which spanned three days, was in private session, he informed the Court that he wanted the world to know about the crimes committed against his community and that he sought reparations.[611] In his testimony he sought to directly implicate Lubanga,[612] and he emphasized that in his opinion the narrow charges against Lubanga were "insignificant" compared with the experiences suffered by victims, including murders, sexual slavery and sexual violence.[613] His testimony marked the first time a victim appeared

604 *Ibid.* at par. 25.
605 *Ibid.*
606 *Ibid.* at par. 40.
607 *Ibid.* at par. 37.
608 *Ibid.* at par. 44.
609 See *The Prosecutor v. Lubanga*, T, 08 January 2010.
610 Whether testifying as prosecution witnesses or witnesses called by the Court, very often the Chamber would allow the victim to testify in narrative form without prompting questions or interruptions, see *The Prosecutor v. Lubanga*, T, 10 February 2009, p. 3; T, 05 March 2009, p. 3.
611 *The Prosecutor v. Lubanga*, T, 12 January 2010, p. 31.
612 *Ibid.* at 20.
613 *Ibid.* at 31.

before the Court as a witness called by the Judges and not as a witness called by the parties.

The second victim to testify in *Lubanga* similarly implicated the accused by naming him as the head of the UPC.[614] He also testified that girl soldiers of 13 and 14 years-old were sexually abused by commanders in the militia.[615] He gave details about his living conditions in the camp and how his commander tortured him.[616] When asked what his hopes for the future were he replied that he wished to remain in school.[617] However, after a number of leading questions posed by the legal representative, the Judge warned that the value of the evidence "will simply be less if his answers are merely the product of questions that have been asked in a leading way."[618]

The third victim to testify before the *Lubanga* Trial Chamber testified about his abduction and forced enlistment in the UPC militia.[619] Like the other victims, much of his testimony was in private session. Nevertheless, in public session he testified that no one had ever asked his age and explained the living and training conditions he experienced as a child soldier.[620] Like the others he stated that Lubanga was the head of the UPC. All three victims testified with their voices and faces distorted in order to shield their identities from the public and all three shared horrific stories of murder, sexual slavery and inhumane treatment. None of the three victims gave their views and concerns outside the framework of testifying under oath.

In its cross-examination the defense undermined many of their previous statements given to prosecutors, getting one to admit that he had given false information.[621] Later, during the defense case, the defense would claim that although their applications were accepted by the ICC two of these victims falsely used the names and identities of two defense witnesses. Subsequently the defense presented various documents to the Court showing that at least seven victim-witnesses, who claimed to be former child soldiers, may have lied about their identities and the schools they attended.[622] If the allegations made by the Defense are true, it is concerning that individuals falsely testifying before the Court as victims had not only been previously accepted by the Judges to participate as victims but were also called by the Judges as witnesses to give evidence that they considered necessary to the determination of the truth.

As in *Lubanga*, the common legal representative in *Katanga/Ngudjolo* sought to have victims testify in their own right and not as witnesses for one of the parties. After

614 *The Prosecutor v. Lubanga*, T, 14 January 2010, p. 62.
615 *Ibid.* at 61.
616 *Ibid.* at 57-58; *The Prosecutor v. Lubanga*, T, 15 January 2010, pp. 9-10.
617 *The Prosecutor v. Lubanga*, T, 14 January 2010, p. 71.
618 *Ibid.* at 63.
619 *The Prosecutor v. Lubanga*, T, 21 January 2010, p. 36.
620 *Ibid.* at 43, 47 and 49.
621 *The Prosecutor v. Lubanga*, T, 22 January 2010, p. 31.
622 See *The Prosecutor v. Lubanga*, T, 25 May 2010.

carrying out a "rigorous selection"[623] one of the legal representatives requested that the Judges allow four of his 365 clients to testify before the Court in order to share their views and concerns.[624] The *Katanga/Ngudjolo* Trial Chamber held that when evaluating applications for participation by giving oral testimony it will take into account the relevancy of the testimony, the repetitiveness of the testimony, whether the testimony is typical of or reflects the experiences of a larger group of participating victims and whether the testimony will bring to light new information relevant to the charges against the accused.[625]

Agreeing with Trial Chamber I, Trial Chamber II in *Katanga/Ngudjolo* believed it would be contrary to the obligations of the Court to establish the truth if it were to exclude the possibility of hearing the testimony of participating victims. Although it noted that in the domestic legal systems that provide victims with an active role at trial, they usually testify without taking an oath. However, the approach of Trial Chamber II, like that of Trial Chamber I, would be different. Victims testifying would need to do so under oath,[626] essentially giving them the status of a victim-witness. This approach would, according to the Trial Chamber, allow "the Defence to cross-examine him or her, which acts as a safeguard and makes the said victim liable to prosecution under article 70(1)(a) of the Statute if he or she gives false testimony."[627] If there are potential doubts as to the credibility of the victim's testimony, the Chamber may decide to disallow the victim from testifying under oath.[628]

It determined that it will only grant applications for giving oral testimony from those victims whose testimony could make a genuine contribution to the ascertainment of the truth. Bearing in mind the need to ensure fair and expeditious proceedings, the Chamber emphasized that it would not allow victims to turn into auxiliary prosecutors and it would not permit victims to testify anonymously.[629] Furthermore, the Chamber stressed that the defense must have time to prepare for the testimony and respond adequately. Legal representatives were therefore permitted to call their clients only after the prosecution concluded its case insofar as it would not undermine the integrity of the proceedings. As of 1 February 2011, the victims have not testified. However, as in *Lubanga*, the defense teams in *Katanga/Ngudjolo* have contested the allegations made by victim-witnesses called by the prosecution claiming to be child soldiers and

623 *The Prosecutor v. Katanga/Ngudjolo*, T, 09 July 2010, p. 23; indeed, when one of the legal representatives responded that it is difficult to contact all 354 victims he represents, the Court was generally unsympathetic.

624 *The Prosecutor v. Katanga/Ngudjolo*, No. ICC-01/04-01/07-2517, 9 November 2010. The Court further noted that the overall time used by legal representatives to question the victims should not exceed 12 hours and that each party would be given a maximum of two hours to question each victim, see *The Prosecutor v. Katanga/Ngudjolo*, T, 29 November 2010, p. 21.

625 *The Prosecutor v. Katanga/Ngudjolo*, No. ICC-01/04-01/07-1665, 20 November 2009, para. 19-30.

626 *Ibid.* at par. 19; *The Prosecutor v. Katanga/Ngudjolo*, No. ICC-01/04-01/07-1788-tENG, 22 January 2010, par. 86

627 *The Prosecutor v. Katanga/Ngudjolo*, No. ICC-01/04-01/07-1788-tENG, 22 January 2010, par. 88.

628 *Ibid.* at par. 91.

629 *Ibid.* at para. 92-93.

are likely to do the same to victims testifying in their own behalf.[630] Overall, these defense teams have been successful in getting former child soldiers to admit that many of their earlier statements were untrue.[631] While inconsistencies are common in international criminal proceedings, they underscore the importance of giving oral testimony and allowing the defense to examine statements made by witnesses against them.

7.6 Victim Assistance

It is clear from looking at the filings, decisions and transcripts that the roles played by the various departments dealing with victims are crucial. The VPRS serves as the first point of contact and in addition to its outreach activities it must process the thousands of applications received by the Court. The OPCV not only supports the independent legal representatives but also represents victims in a number of proceedings. In this role, the Office, unlike a number of the independent legal representatives, makes sure that it visits and consults with each and every one of its clients throughout the proceedings. Finally, the VWU is responsible for all of the protective measures issued for victims and it is responsible for the well-being of victims when testifying.[632]

However, the smooth functioning of these various departments has not always been easy. The most notable concern has to do with the time it takes the VPRS to process applications for participation though improvements are being made. For a large number of victims, the process has taken over one year from the time they submitted the application and when they received a decision by the Court.[633] Another concern with regard to applications is the fact that little pre-screening is carried out by the VPRS. Therefore, the Judges, who only carry out a *prima facie* assessment based on the applications and the VPRS Report have admitted many victims who it has later been shown should likely have gone through a more rigorous screening before being able to participate and seek reparations. Whether this should be done by the VPRS is a matter of debate but the Court has been placed in the precarious and embarrassing position where it has granted victim status to applicants who likely lied when filling out their applications or grossly exaggerated their damages. In order to address some

630 *The Prosecutor v. Katanga/Ngudjolo*, T, 08 June 2010, pp. 1-34.

631 See, e.g., *The Prosecutor v. Katanga/Ngudjolo*, T, 22 November 2010 pp. 55-59. See also Combs (2009) and (2010).

632 When legal representatives in *Katanga* sought to intervene in situations in which a victim-witness' demeanor changed due to a rather contentious cross-examination, the Court was reluctant to allow legal counsel to do so. Instead, the Court held that it was the role of the VWU to handle issues related to the well-being of the victim when testifying, see *The Prosecutor v. Katanga/Ngudjolo*, T, 11 June 2010, pp. 27-30. At one point during the testimony of the three victims appearing in *Lubanga*, the VWU requested the Court to allow the victims to have social contact with one another in order to help their psychological well-being. For humanitarian reasons, the Judge allowed this but held that the VWU had to be present during the meeting and would need to advise the victims not to discuss their testimony, see *The Prosecutor v. Lubanga*, T, 15 January 2010, pp. 61-62.

633 Chung (2008) at 501.

of the concerns associated with the various departments working on victims, the Registry has recently announced a major reshuffling of its victim services.[634] It is hoped that this reshuffling will better streamline the Registry's work with victims.[635]

7.7 Legal Representation

Early in the Court's operation, the Judges needed to address a number of issues concerning the issue of legal representation. Is legal representation mandatory? Should victims have access to legal representation during the time between filing an application and the Court's assessment of the application? Will victims always be able to choose their legal representative?

In answering these questions the Court acknowledged that the Statute and Rules nowhere require victims to be represented by legal counsel.[636] The Court recognized that victims could be granted participation rights, for instance in the form of opening and closing statements, without the assignment of legal counsel. Accordingly, the Pre-Trial Chamber in *Kony, et al.* concluded that victims are free to choose a legal representative or not.[637] Those choosing to forgo legal representation may, however, have more limited rights of participation.[638] Thus, the participation of victims in proceedings is not conditional upon their representation by legal counsel but fully exercising their participatory rights would likely require victims to obtain legal representation. And in light of this, there is no absolute or unconditional right to have access to legal representation prior to a decision on the merits of an application.[639] With the exception of the *Bemba* Trial Chamber, which allowed victim-applicants to be represented by the OPCV and participate in proceedings pending a final determination of their status,[640] all other Chambers have not allowed victim-applicants standing in proceedings.

The Court's Strategy on Victims emphasizes the importance of victims being able to a have a lawyer of their choice or at least a lawyer from their own community or

634 ASP, 9th session, para. 213-214, *available at*: http://www.icc-cpi.int/iccdocs/asp_docs/ASP9/OR/ICC-ASP-9-20-Vol.II-ENG.pdf, *last visited* 2 June 2011.

635 *Ibid.*

636 See for example, Rome Statute, Art. 68(3) and the choice of the term "may" in relation to legal representatives; ICC RPE, Rule 89-93.

637 *The Prosecutor v. Kony, et al.*, No. ICC-02/04-01/05-134, 1 February 2007, para. 2-12.

638 ICC RPE, Rule 91.

639 *The Prosecutor v. Kony, et al.*, No. ICC-02/04-01/05-134, 1 February 2007, para. 2-12.

640 In *Bemba*, the Trial Chamber had yet to process and decide upon all of the victim applications prior to the start of trial but in order not to prejudice the victim-applicants allowed them not only to be represented at trial pending a decision on their application but also to make opening statements. It noted, however, that such statements are not considered evidence for the purposes of trial, and declined to allow them to put questions to witnesses. See *The Prosecutor v. Bemba*, No. ICC-01/05-01/08-1023, 19 November 2010, para. 22-23.

country.[641] The Strategy stresses that these lawyers have a contextual knowledge that others do not and that their participation promotes the Rome Statute at the national level. The belief is that when these lawyers do not have the necessary skill or knowledge of international law or legal precedent, which many of them do not, the OPCV can assist the legal teams and provide specialist legal research. In practice, however, the quality and experience (or the lack thereof) of the lawyers is readily apparent in the courtroom. Nevertheless, the OPCV, does as much as it can to assist the legal representatives with its limited staff and resources.

In the *Lubanga* trial around 120 victims are represented by seven lawyers as well as the OPCV.[642] The relatively low number of victims participating allowed victims to have the lawyer of their choice. However, the high number of legal representatives in the proceedings has, on occasion, meant that some victims are questioned first by the prosecution and then by at least four separate legal representatives before the defense even begins its examination. It is a testament to the Judges and the legal teams representing victims that more delays have not occurred. As a whole, the legal representatives have not sought to question every witness and have limited the number of questions posed.

In contrast to the *Lubanga* proceedings, when a larger numbers of victims participate the Judges may decide to group victims under common legal representation. As such, Rule 90(2) allows the Chamber to *request* victims to choose a common legal representative "for the purposes of ensuring the effectiveness of the proceedings." If victims are unable to choose a common legal representative the Chamber may request the Registrar to choose one.[643] Rule 90(4) stresses that conflicts of interest are to be avoided.

Due to the larger number of victims participating in *Katanga/Ngudjolo* as well as the growing number of legal representatives the Trial Chamber decided to group victims under common legal representation. Thus, in order to ensure procedural efficiency, the Chamber divided the 300 plus victims, represented by over ten different legal teams, into two groups.[644] The first group includes all victims except for former child soldiers. The second, smaller group includes former child soldiers. The groups each have one common legal representative, two assistants and one case manager.[645]

641 ASP, Report of the Court on the strategy in relation to victims, ICC-ASP/8/45, 18-26 November 2009, p. 10; Rule 90(6) requires legal representatives of victims to have the qualifications set forth in Rule 22(1) which are the same qualifications required for the legal counsel for the defense; Legal representatives must have at least ten years experience working as a criminal lawyer, judge or prosecutor and be fluent in one of the Court's working languages.

642 In contrast with other cases, the Trial Chamber in *Lubanga* has not set a deadline for victim applications. As recently as December 2010, see *The Prosecutor v. Lubanga*, No. ICC-01/04-01/06-2659-Corr-Red, 8 February 2011. Therefore, the trial started with just over 90 victims and, at the time of writing, 120 victims have thus far been admitted to participate.

643 ICC RPE, Rule 90(3).

644 See *The Prosecutor v. Katanga/Ngudjolo*, No. ICC-01/04-01/07-1328, 22 July 2009.

645 In other cases, each victim's legal team has one head legal representative, one co-counsel, one legal assistant and one intern in addition to the assistance they receive from the OPCV.

The grouping by the harm suffered allowed the legal representatives to formulate more targeted questions. Accordingly, the legal representative for former child soldiers confined his questions to issues related directly to child soldiers,[646] whereas the other legal representative asked questions related to civilians, property destruction, pillaging, rape and other crimes.[647] This legal representative frequently asked about the importance and value attached to cattle in the region,[648] or specifically asked the names of the owners of shops or houses that had been destroyed.[649] Unlike the questions posed by the prosecution, who would not necessarily touch upon these issues, these interventions will likely help a potential case for a reparations award.

As in *Katanga/Ngudjolo*, the Trial Chamber in *Bemba* sought to group victims under common legal representation. But the unprecedented number of victims participating (over one thousand have applied to participate) did not persuade the Court that additional representation was necessary. Thus, just like in *Katanga/Ngudjolo*, the Trial Chamber determined that for the purpose of trial only two common legal representatives from the CAR would represent the victims in the case.[650] The OPCV, which had represented victims during the confirmation of charges hearing, would no longer represent victims but could be called upon by the Chamber to appear with respect to specific issues.[651] Additionally, the OPCV was called upon to represent those victims who were permitted to participate at trial pending a decision on their application, but once a decision would be made on their application one of the two independent legal representatives would be assigned.[652]

However, unlike in *Katanga/Ngudjolo*, the Trial Chamber in *Bemba* opted not to group victims by the harm suffered but instead decided that victims would be grouped according to the geographical location of the crimes. The Women's Initiatives for Gender Justice criticized this approach, arguing that groupings based on geographic region may not be in the best interests of victims, particularly for victims of sexual violence.[653] It is feared that disagreements or conflicts of interest may arise.

When disagreements between victims arise, the legal representative will need to equitably represent the divergent positions. When conflicts of interest arise the Chamber should take appropriate measures, for example, by appointing the OPCV to

646 *The Prosecutor v. Katanga/Ngudjolo*, T, 25 February 2010, pp. 25-27; T, 16 March 2010, pp. 56-59; T, 22 March 2010, p. 26; T, 20 April 2010, p. 28; T, 14 May 2010, p. 23; T, 22 June 2010, beginning on p. 66; T, 15 September 2010, p. 94; T, 20 October 2010, p. 6; T, 18 November 2010, pp. 12-13

647 *The Prosecutor v. Katanga/Ngudjolo*, T, 25 February 2010, p. 31; T, 03 March 2010, pp. 51-53; T, 16 March 2010, p. 63; T, 22 March 2010, p. 20; T, 12 May 2010, pp. 53-54; T, 27 May 2010, pp. 21-24; T, 23 June 2010, pp. 33-34; T, 06 October 2010, p. 63; T, 20 October 2010, p. 16; T, 18 November 2010, pp. 9, and 13-14; and T, 30 November 2010, p. 67.

648 *The Prosecutor v. Katanga/Ngudjolo*, T, 03 March 2010, p. 46; T, 30 November 2010, pp. 63, 67.

649 *The Prosecutor v. Katanga/Ngudjolo*, T, 20 April 2010, pp. 25-26.

650 See *The Prosecutor v. Bemba*, No. ICC-01/05-01/08-1005, 10 November 2010.

651 *The Prosecutor v. Bemba*, No. ICC-01/05-01/08-1005, 10 November 2010, par. 29.

652 *The Prosecutor v. Bemba*, No. ICC-01/05-01/08-651, 9 December 2009, par. 18.

653 Statement by the Women's Initiatives for Gender Justice on the Opening of the ICC Trial of Jean-Pierre Bemba Gombo, Women's Initiatives for Gender Justice, 22 November 2010.

represent one of the conflicting groups of victims. Overall, disagreements and conflicts of interest will be difficult to avoid when representing a large amount of victims in a case though some lawyers may be keen on downplaying any conflicts. To be sure, lawyers for victims in the Sudanese situation and cases have acknowledged the challenges, stating, "We have found conflicts of interests amongst victims in the Diaspora, let alone conflicts between those in the US and those still in Darfur."[654]

7.8 LEGAL AID

Rule 90(5) of the Rules provides that when victims are indigent the Court may fund their legal representation and in most circumstances the Court does in fact try to do so. In 2010 the Court's program budget was approximately 104,000,000 EUR,[655] with portions of this allocated to the various victim sections, including the OPCV, VPRS, VWU, as well as the costs of legal aid for external legal counsel. Unlike at the ECCC, the Statue and Rules provide that when victims are indigent the Court may fund their legal representation. Nevertheless, as of 2010, the process of declaring a victim indigent is cumbersome. For instance, although minors are considered indigent, other victims claiming indigence will need to complete the same 12-page form as that used for a defendant. The questionnaire asks about gross and net income, assets, bank accounts, cars and other property. Victims' rights groups argue that victims find the form to be time-consuming, confusing and humiliating and that the vast majority of victims will not be able to fund a legal representative working on their behalf at the Court. As an alternative, victims' groups submit that unless there are suspicions of significant assets, victims should instead be presumed indigent, without having to fill in any additional forms or undertake a sworn statement.[656] As of yet, the Court has not sought to change its procedures.

A report of the court on legal aid, presented to the Assembly of State Parties (ASP) at its Eighth session, signaled that legal aid for victims was of critical importance to ensure that victims may effectively exercise their rights.[657] The report noted that many of the principles underlying the legal aid for the defense, namely objectiveness, transparency, continuity and economy, are also applicable to legal aid for victims. According to the report, the principle of equality of arms, which is perhaps the most important principle underlying the legal aid scheme for the defense, applies only to the parties and not the participants. Nevertheless, the court found that the principle of

---

654 Sudan Victim Lawyers recount their experiences with the ICC so far, Interview with Attorneys Raymond M. Brown and Wanda M. Akin Brown, Victims' Rights Working Group Bulletin, Summer/Autumn 2007, Issue 9, p. 7.

655 ICC website, *available at*: http://www.icc-cpi.int/NR/rdonlyres/5134EE4B-97FE-48B8-93EC-92AC9C0EED8E/281815/TheCourtTodayEngWeb.pdf, *last visited* 2 August 2010.

656 REDRESS, Victims central role in fulfilling the ICC's mandate, paper prepared for the 8th Assembly of States Parties, 18-26 November 2009, p. 6.

657 ICC, Report of the Court on legal aid: Legal and financial aspects of funding victims' legal representation before the Court, Eighth session, The Hague, ICC-ASP/8/25, 18-26 November 2009, p. 2.

equality of arms may appropriately be replaced by the principle that victims must be assured of the possibility of playing in full the role accorded to them in proceedings.[658] The report further concluded that despite the different role played by victims' legal representatives and legal counsel for the defense, representatives for victims should continue to be remunerated at the P-5 level. In other words, victims' legal representatives, from pre-trial through reparations proceedings, should receive the highest pay, equal to that of lead defense counsel.[659]

7.9 Civil Society Groups and Intermediaries

Intermediaries play a number of important roles in the relationship with the Court. The OTP relies upon intermediaries to help carry out investigations in the field by, for example, identifying and facilitating access to potential witnesses. Unquestionably, the collection of evidence in the field would be impossible without the assistance of intermediaries. In addition to assisting the OTP, intermediaries also assist the various victim departments operating at the Court. The VPRS relies upon intermediaries to inform victims about their participatory rights and helping victims apply to exercise these rights. The OPCV also relies on intermediaries to make contact and correspond with participating victims in order to know their views and concerns on particular matters. Intermediaries also play a key role in the Court's outreach activities. Thus it is clear that intermediaries assisting victims play an especially noteworthy role and the Court is in many ways reliant upon their support.[660] Without their assistance, often at great personal expense to themselves, victims would not play such a prominent role in proceedings.

However, an overreliance upon the intermediaries also poses some problems because of the potential for abuse. Issues and concerns related to intermediaries first arose in the *Lubanga* trial.[661] First, the defense raised concerns about the role played by intermediaries after noticing that a number of applications were similarly written – often using language that an uneducated, former child soldier would not use. The Chamber called on the Registry to remind intermediaries that their role is to assist victims when filling out applications and not to influence the actual context of statements.[662] Second, the defense began finding numerous inconsistencies between the information in victims' applications for participation, their statements to investigators (if interviewed) and their testimony in Court (if they gave testimony). In one instance, a prosecution witness who was a former child soldier was called to testify by the defense where he admitted to never serving in the UPC and claimed that an intermedi-

658 *Ibid.* at 3-4.

659 *Ibid.* at 7.

660 *Situation in DRC*, No. ICC-01/04-545, 4 November 2008, par. 25; *The Prosecutor v. Katanga/Ngudjolo*, No. ICC-01/04-01/07-1491-Red, 23 September 2009, para. 42-43.

661 *The Prosecutor v. Lubanga*, No. ICC-01/04-01/06-2434-Red2, 31 May 2010, para. 138-139.

662 *The Prosecutor v. Katanga/Ngudjolo*, No. ICC-01/04-01/07-1491-Red, 23 September 2009, para. 42-43.

ary working with prosecution investigators fed him lies.[663] Finally, through its own investigations, the defense was able to bring to light the potential influence and pressure some intermediaries exerted on victims by alleging having them lie about their identities. The defense alleged that a number of intermediaries bribed and coached witnesses and therefore requested that the names of a number of intermediaries relied upon by the prosecution be disclosed to the defense to carry out further investigations.

The issues that arose in *Lubanga* are similar in all the trials at the Court and they raise concerns not only about fair trial rights but also about reparations. In the *Bemba* trial, if the accused is convicted and his millions of dollars of assets are made available to victims claiming reparations then fraudulent claims become important – not least of which because they would divert reparations from actual victims making truthful claims. Despite the many glaring problems, defense teams are generally not in a position to investigate these matters due to the fact that for the most part intermediary identities are still withheld from defense teams for security concerns.

7.10 Conclusions

In November 2009 the ASP took note of the Court's Strategy in Relation to Victims.[664] This strategy document states that "[a] key feature of the system established in the Rome Statute is the recognition that the ICC has not only a punitive but also a restorative function."[665] It then goes on to outline seven broad principles which underpin the Court's strategy on victims, including:

(a) A recognition of the importance of the victim and the need to take account of their needs and interests;
(b) A commitment to communicate with victims both in order to provide information so that the Court's mandate on victims is widely understood by victims and in order to listen to victims;
(c) A recognition that victims should be enabled to have a voice throughout all stages of the proceedings, subject to the rights of the defense and a fair and impartial trial, starting at the preliminary examination stage and to seek reparations in the event of a conviction;
(d) A commitment to providing victims with equal and effective access to the Court, including effective representation of their interest by qualified counsel;
(e) A commitment to enable victims to interact with the Court with maximum security, consistent with the Rome Statute, and without suffering further harm as a result of this interaction;

663 *The Prosecutor v. Lubanga*, T, 17 March 2010, pp. 15, 33.
664 See ASP, Resolution ICC-ASP/8/Res.3, par. 35, referring to the Report of the Court on the strategy in relation to victims, ICC-ASP/8/45, 18-26 November 2009.
665 ASP, Report of the Court on the strategy in relation to victims, ICC-ASP/8/45, 18-26 November 2009, p. 1.

(f) A commitment to transparency and clarity in conducting relations with third parties; and
(g) A commitment to serving as a catalyst for improving the realization of the rights of victims of genocide, crimes against humanity and war crimes worldwide.[666]

A key objective of the Court's Strategy is to "ensure that victims are able to fully exercise their right to participate in ICC proceedings, in a manner that is sensitive to their rights and interests and consistent with the rights of the defense and the need to ensure a fair trial."[667] Most importantly, the strategy document emphasizes that victim participation is a right and not a privilege. Therefore, it is clear that the ASP is committed to many of the goals articulated by the victims' rights movement, and, in fact, the rights to participation, reparation and protection seem to be solidified. The Court makes every effort to treat victims with dignity and respect, victim participants are notified and informed about case developments, they have access to psychological support and protection measures, in theory they may attend proceedings and be 'heard' (though this is usually done through legal counsel), they may request reparations regardless of whether or not they participate and they have access to legal assistance.

Particularly with respect to participation, victims have made a substantial impact on the Court. They have participated in every pre-trial and trial stage of a case. Through their lawyers their views and concerns have been presented, although this is usually done collectively rather than on an individual basis.[668] Through their submissions they have highlighted their desire for the Court to focus on gender-based crimes and they have time and again emphasized their right to truth and justice. Notwithstanding the unique label the Court attaches to victims participating in proceedings, i.e. *victim participants*, the participatory rights afforded to victims at the ICC appear to reflect many of the features commonly associated to those of a civil party and auxiliary prosecutor (from Chapter 3). Although the adversarial nature of the proceedings makes the inclusion of victims wishing to actively participate somewhat difficult, participation can be categorized as ranging anywhere from therapy (non-participation) to consultation (tokenism) to informing (tokenism) to potentially partnership (citizen power). The Judges are required to seek and consider victim preferences and information, and are required to provide victims the opportunity to share their views and concerns so long as this does not infringe upon the rights of the accused. Nevertheless, participation remains non-dispositive.

---

666 *Ibid.* at 3-4.
667 *Ibid.* at 8.
668 In her opening statement, the Principal Counsel of the OPCV emphasized both the individual and the collective nature of participation: "If the choice of victims to request part in the proceedings is an individual choice, above all, which allows each and every victim through the intermediary of their counsel to tell part of their story and share part of their knowledge of the events, the choice to participate is also sometimes a group experience. It reunites neighbors and families that can sometimes be separated by a wall of silence." See *The Prosecutor v. Bemba,* T, 22 November 2010, p. 49.

Despite the positive impact victims have made, the participatory regime at the ICC has posed significant challenges for the Court. To be sure, "[n]o single legal issue [...] has garnered as much attention as the manner in which the ICC judges have interpreted the right of victims to participate in the proceedings."[669] Each Chamber has had to decide how to best implement the victim participation provisions found in the Statute, Rules and Regulations. They have attempted to provide victims (through their legal representatives) with access to proceedings so that their collective participation is meaningful and effective, but considerable problems continue to surface. In 2007 the War Crimes Research Office of American University's Washington College of Law published a Report which found that the Court's management of effective participation and the efficiency of proceedings were unfavorable.[670] One year later, Chung, a former Senior Trial Attorney in the OTP, characterized the process of participation as follows:

> [...] the true nature of the right being provided to individuals seeking to participate in ICC proceedings is the entitlement to stand in a queue, for longer than a year, to obtain a theoretical participation privilege which most likely will never be converted to an actual right to express views and concerns in court proceedings.[671]

In 2009 the IBA noted that "The participation rights of victims, while a significant achievement of the Rome Statute, are difficult to implement in practice."[672] Court commentators echoed these concerns in 2010.[673] Everyone from judges, prosecutors, defense counsel and even victims' representatives have expressed doubt about the current system in place.[674] Certainly there are clear benefits to participation but as of yet there has been a mismanagement with its implementation.

The system that is in place at the ICC complicates matters more than necessary. Time and again, each Pre-Trial Chamber and Trial Chamber must (re)address the same issues. And given the fact that the Chambers have a great deal of discretion over applicable procedures, they often interpret the same issue in very different ways. It means that victims in one case are treated differently than in another case. For instance, a child victim in case X will need to participate through someone acting on their behalf whereas a child victim in case Y can participate in their own right. Along the same lines, a defendant in one case will need to face two accusers when victims are

---

669 Chung (2008) at 459.

670 War Crimes Research Office, American University, Washington College of Law, Victim Participation Before the International Criminal Court, November 2007, p. 5.

671 Chung (2008) at 462.

672 International Bar Association, First Challenges: An Examination of recent landmark developments at the ICC, June 2009, p. 20.

673 See Zappalá (2010); Johnson (2009-2010).

674 For the perspective of victims' legal representatives see Sudan Victim Lawyers recount their experiences with the ICC so far, Access: Victims' Rights Before the International Criminal Court, (Victims' Rights Working Group), Issue No. 9, Summer/Autumn 2007, at 7. In interviews carried out between the author and victims' legal representatives a number of lawyers indicated that victim participation is often more for the lawyers than for the victims.

able to adduce evidence at trial going to the guilt of the accused whereas in another case the interventions by victims will be limited to their personal interests such as the gravity of the harm and the effect of the harm. Likewise, in case X where neither the prosecution nor the defense are provided with un-redacted victim applications during the pre-trial stage the ability to contest standing to participate, test the credibility of a victim or gain access to potentially exculpatory information is negated until trial begins. In contrast, in case Y, where un-redacted victim application forms are given to the prosecution, the defense can at least rely upon the prosecutor's duty to disclose exculpatory material in its possession. The lack of harmonization and the failure to clarify these and other important issues affecting Court operation seriously compromise the integrity of the proceedings – both for victims and for accused. As a whole, it appears that the Court has little conceptual understanding of and agreement on how to approach victim participation in international criminal proceedings.[675]

The Court may want to consider taking the following actions, whether independently in each Chamber or through the Court-wide adoption of clarifying regulations. First, it is apparent that issues with the assessment of victims' applications continue to beleaguer the parties and the Court. It is advisable that an early and more thorough assessment is made of victim applications. This assessment should look into irregularities in the applications, such as when unusual similarities in applications continue to arise. This can be done by a department in the Registry that is not necessarily dedicated to the victims *per se*, but rather is mandated to protect the efficiency and integrity of the proceedings. When irregularities are detected, informal or formal investigations can be carried out to enquire into the factual circumstances surrounding the filing of the applications. Also, once these more thorough assessments have been made and the Court or administrative body grants victim status, un-redacted victim applications should be provided to the prosecution. Despite arguments based on the principle of equality of arms, the defense is in a position where it depends upon the prosecution (with its greater resources) to process, investigate potentially exculpatory information found therein and disclose relevant information. If this is not done, the defense is placed in a position where it has far fewer resources to go through the applications just prior to or during trial when it should arguably be focusing its efforts on other matters.

With regard to victims participating in the proceedings, the Court needs to do better in protecting the due process and fair trial rights of the accused. There is no need to wait until a fundamental right has been violated. The potential of such a violation should be enough to warrant certain measures to be taken. As such, despite all of the rhetoric against protecting accused from anonymous accusations, the Court has done little to actually ensure that anonymous victims (through those acting on their behalf) do not get to pose questions going to the guilt of the accused, for example. It is therefore advisable to group anonymous and non-anonymous victims separately in order to properly reflect the modalities of participation assigned to both groups.

675 See Wemmers (2010) at 643, finding "there is no singular view of what participation at the ICC is or should be."

Likewise, the participation of victims should be limited to interventions which contribute to the truth by clarifying facts or relate to the personal interests of the victims. Victims can make great contributions in this regard. Accordingly, victims should not take over the role of the prosecutor and attempt to establish elements going towards the guilt of the accused. A clear delimitation should be made between the role of the prosecutor and the role of victims' legal representatives. Moreover, Judges should be weary of using evidence adduced by victims when making findings of the guilt of the accused. It is the prosecutor who has the burden of proving the guilt beyond a reasonable doubt and he should not be relieved of this burden. Instead, evidence adduced by victims should contribute to aggravating or mitigating factors for sentencing determination. These minimal steps will go a long way to acknowledging the additional burden placed on the defense with regard to victim participation and will help to ensure that their fundamental rights in the criminal process are respected while at the same time recognizing the rights of victims to participate.

CONCLUSION

CHAPTER 8
CONCLUSIONS AND RECOMMENDATIONS

8.1 INTRODUCTION

This study began by focusing on the French trial of former Vichy government agent Paul Touvier for crimes against humanity. His trial, like other former Vichy government officials prosecuted in France, involved the participation of a large number of victims. As civil parties the victims in his trial were represented by no less than 30 lawyers; one of whom sought to present a theory of the case which stood in direct contrast with that of the prosecution and other civil parties. The *Touvier* trial is noteworthy because although it involved a limited number of possible victims, took place within the inquisitorial legal tradition familiar to all participating, and only included symbolic claims for reparation, numerous issues concerning the participation of victims still arose. As a result, the case brings to light the difficulties that arise in criminal proceedings when a large number of victims participate in complex criminal trials for mass crimes, and, at the same time, it suggests that such participation is possible.

Bearing in mind the potentially larger number of victims, the unfamiliar, mixed procedural system and the added element of reparation claims, it is unsurprising, then, that the mass participation of victims in international criminal proceedings has similarly raised a number of serious issues. Building upon the previous chapters, this chapter addresses the research question of this study and provide recommendations for how best to approach the participation of victims in international criminal proceedings.

8.2 PARTICIPATION AS A HUMAN RIGHTS STANDARD?

Tied to substantive human rights such as the right to life and the right to a remedy, two of the most important rights of victims that have emerged from the jurisprudence of human rights bodies are the *right to truth* and the *right of access to justice*.[1] As with many human rights, these terms are vague and apply to a variety of concepts. In the criminal justice construct, they generally recognize an obligation of states to investigate, prosecute and punish individuals believed to be responsible for serious violations of human rights and humanitarian law.[2] Principle 19 of the Impunity Principles describes the right to justice as follows:

1 Doak (2008) at 180.
2 Sorochinsky (2009) at 185.

> States shall undertake prompt, thorough, independent and impartial investigations of violations of human rights and international humanitarian law and take appropriate measures in respect of the perpetrators, particularly in the area of criminal justice, by ensuring that those responsible for serious crimes under international law are prosecuted, tried and duly punished.[3]

Former UN Special Rapporteur, Theo van Boven has underscored these rights by finding that "only the complete and public revelation of the truth will make it possible to satisfy the basic requirements of the principles of justice."[4] Accordingly, human rights bodies have emphasized the need to ensure victims' procedural rights in order to make certain that states carry out effective investigations and prosecutions. In order to help ensure a state's compliance with its obligations, the right to truth and the right of access to justice have been interpreted as including an obligation on states to provide victims with the opportunity to participate in the criminal process by presenting their views and concerns at appropriate stages and by providing a forum where victims may seek reparation for their harm suffered.[5] Thus, while not an explicitly recognized human right as such, the right to participate in criminal proceedings (to receive information, to provide information, and to seek redress) is undoubtedly linked with important human rights standards.

Based on these notions, the catalogue of victims' rights that should be recognized as minimum standards by criminal institutions include the right to respect and dignity, the right to receive information, the right to provide information, the right to protection, the right to reparation and the right to legal and general support.[6] Many of these rights are interrelated with the right to participation. At a minimum, the right to participation provides that states should allow the views and concerns of victims to be presented and considered at appropriate stages of the proceedings where their personal interests are affected, without prejudice to the accused and consistent with the relevant

3 Updated Set of Principles for the Protection and Promotion of Human Rights Through Action to Combat Impunity, Report of the independent expert Diane Orentlicher delivered to the Commission on Human Rights, UN Doc. E/CN.4/2005/102/Add. 1, 8 February 2005, Principle 19. These Principles were viewed by the UN Commission on Human Rights as guidelines "to assist States in developing effective measures for combating impunity." See Commission on Human Rights Resolution 2005/81, UN Doc. E/CN.4/RES/2005/81, 21 April 2005, par. 20.

4 Study concerning the right to restitution, compensation and rehabilitation for victims of gross violations of human rights and fundamental freedoms, Final report submitted by Mr. Theo van Boven, Special Rapporteur, UN Doc. E/CN.4/SUB.2/1993/8 (1993).

5 The Declaration of Basic Principles of Justice for Victims of Crime and Abuse of Power, UN Doc. A/Res/40/34/Annex (1985) [hereinafter Victims' Declaration]; Basic Principles and Guidelines on the Right to a Remedy and Reparation for Victims of Gross Violations of International Human Rights Law and Serious Violations of International Humanitarian Law, UN Doc. A/RES/60/147 (2005) [hereinafter Basic Principles].

6 Groenhuijsen, M., Victims' Rights and the International Criminal Court: The Model of the Rome Statute and Its Operation, 301-302, in Van Genugten, et al. (2009).

national criminal justice system.[7] However, the extent of the right to participation is necessarily limited by the procedural frameworks adopted by states. States may interpret the right to participation broadly or narrowly depending upon its procedural approach and adopt an appropriate corresponding participation model.

When interpreting this right to participation human rights bodies have emphasized two main areas where participation is most critical. First, human rights bodies have stressed the participation of victims during the investigation stage of a criminal process. Participation at this stage allows victims to both receive information and provide information that may be critical to help ensure a state's obligations to investigate, prosecute and punish perpetrators. Second, participation at a stage of proceedings in which victims may claim reparation or seek redress for harms suffered has also been underscored. However, the ability to seek redress through reparation claims can also be sought outside of the criminal context depending upon the domestic procedures in place.

Human rights standards, like those touched upon above, have played an important part in the promotion of a set of common procedural norms at international criminal tribunals directed towards victims. There is no doubt that embracing international human rights standards at the international criminal law level is important. International institutions must be seen as the embodiment of these standards and emphasize their universal character. As such, it is generally uncontested that international criminal institutions should fully respect internationally recognized human rights. However, should the same emphasis on investigations and reparations, which applies at the domestic level, apply within the international criminal law context? Or are more active participatory rights in trial more appropriate? Is the exercising of the right to participation in international criminal procedures somehow different from the domestic level?

8.3 Victim Participation in International Criminal Proceedings

Beginning with the Nuremberg military trials, the participation of victims has, to varying degrees, been incorporated in all international criminal institutions. From what Arnstein refers to as token roles to more decision-making positions victims continue to exercise a number of participatory functions. Thus, using the participatory models examined in Chapter 3, whether participating as complainants, witnesses, civil parties, auxiliary prosecutors or impact statement providers, victims are involved in and have impacted international criminal justice processes. The extent of their participation, however, has varied, and none of their participatory roles has been dispositive. Calls for a more prominent position for victims in international criminal proceedings have been answered by the ECCC and ICC and given the fact that these institutions have now developed a fair amount of practice with regard to victim participation it seems

7 See Victims' Declaration.

an appropriate time for an evaluation of the implementation and management of their respective victim participation schemes.

8.3.1 Uneasy Transplantation

The unique characteristics associated with international criminal tribunals often mean that domestic procedures (and the rationales behind them) do not translate well at the international level. As noted by Mégret, "To literally transpose the standards of domestic criminal trials to those of mass atrocities might [...] be inappropriate and difficult to justify."[8] This is particularly relevant with regard to victim participation issues. As such, the justifications supporting victim participation at the domestic level should not just be wholeheartedly accepted at the international level. Many of these arguments in favor of participation do not correlate with the realities of international criminal justice due to the unique context in which international criminal courts operate.[9] The rationales for participation should therefore be scrutinized and examined in light of the specific characteristics of international criminal proceedings. Below four of the general justifications will be examined.

(1) Participation helps avoid 'secondary victimization' and contributes to the restoration of the victim

It is submitted by victim advocates that the act of addressing the court can, for many victims, be therapeutic.[10] For example, victims may "find meaning in being heard, in having a witness who affirms that [their abuse] did happen, that it was terrible, [and] that it was not their fault."[11] The process of addressing the court, in their own words, often allows victims to receive validation of their experiences and begin the healing process.[12] In addition, and particularly when victims feel the prosecution is not looking after their interests, having a role in the prosecution may allow victims to reclaim some control of their lives by ensuring that their voices are heard.[13] The participation is justified based on the fact that the process becomes more democratic,[14] it increases victim satisfaction with the criminal justice process,

8 Mégret (2009) at 65.
9 Trumbull (2008) at 780; War Crimes Research Office, American University, Washington College of Law, Victim Participation at the Case Stage of Proceedings, February 2009, p. 41.
10 Haslam, E., Victim Participation at the International Criminal Court: A Triumph of Hope over Experience? 315-316, in McGoldrick, et al. (2004).
11 O'Connell (2005) at 330; Trumbull (2008) at 802.
12 Haslam, E., Victim Participation at the International Criminal Court: A Triumph of Hope over Experience? 315, in McGoldrick, et al. (2004); Mahon (2009) at 748, footnotes 79-81.
13 Danieli (2004) at 6.
14 Henderson (1985) at 1003.

and provides a cathartic process for the victim.[15] Finally, those participating in proceedings may feel particular acknowledgment and validation if the trial (as a symbol of authority) is viewed as society's condemnation of the acts in question.[16]

Before even looking to the international level, it must first be noted that it has been questioned whether victim participation in criminal trials is in fact therapeutic.[17] The UN Handbook on Justice for Victims warns that giving victims a decision-making role "may lead to even greater harassment and intimidation by the defendant and may otherwise cause the victim anxiety."[18] Lurgio and Resick have likewise noted that "victim participation in the prosecution of cases has been commonly regarded as stressful and disruptive to victims' recovery."[19] At the international level, there have been no empirical studies specifically conducted on the rehabilitative aspect of victim participation in international criminal proceedings. However, the reaction of victims following the first trial at the ECCC has not been an encouraging sign.[20] Victims in the *Duch* trial have expressed their outrage over the sentence imposed, the reparations awarded and the revocation of civil party status of fellow victims. One prominent victim lamented, "I feel like I was a victim under the Khmer Rouge, and now I'm a victim again."[21] Without empirical data it remains unclear whether active participation circumvents secondary victimization.[22]

If secondary victimization in the criminal process is linked to feelings of indifference, inability to find counseling or medical treatment, inappropriate questioning by law enforcement officials, threats by the defendant, inappropriate questioning during trial or violations of privacy by the media,[23] then means other than direct and active participation at trial may be more appropriate to contribute to the rehabilitation of the victim. Protection provisions, service-related reforms, and sensitivity training for court personnel are but a few of the ways in which some courts have chosen to address these issues.

15 However, there are relatively no articles or books in English focusing on the psychological effects of trials of perpetrators of human rights violations on victims, see O'Connell (2005) at 298-299; however, for studies on the potentially cathartic aspects of participation in domestic criminal proceedings, see Kilpatrick and Otto (1987) and Rubel (1986).

16 Jorda, C. and De Hemptinne, J., The Status and the Role of the Victim, 1389, in Cassese, et al. (2002).

17 Mohan (2009); cf. Women's Caucus for Gender Justice, Victims and Witnesses in the ICC Report of Panel Discussions on Appropriate Measures for Victim Participation and Protection in the ICC, July 26-August 1999.

18 Handbook on Justice for Victims, p. 36.

19 Lurgio, A.J. and Resick, P., Healing the Psychological Wounds of Criminal Victimization: Prediction Postcrime Distress and Recovery, 60, in Lurigio, et al. (1990).

20 See Mohan (2009); also supported by the author's own experiences at the ECCC.

21 Neilan, T., Outrage at Cambodian Holocaust's Killer's Sentence, *AOL news*, 26 July 2010.

22 Haslam, E., Victim Participation at the International Criminal Court: A Triumph of Hope over Experience? 317, in McGoldrick, et al. (2004); Henderson (1985) at 1010.

23 Trumbull (2008) at 805.

(2) Participation can lead to more successful prosecutions by providing information to the court

It is commonly asserted that victim participation in the criminal process can help lead to more successful prosecutions.[24] Advocates of participation often argue that participation can help clarify facts and fight against impunity,[25] and as 'information-providers' victims may have important information to share with the court about the crime or about the harm suffered.

It is clear that victims may be in a position to provide information to court authorities about alleged crimes, which may lead to more successful prosecutions. Especially when participating as complainants or witnesses victims play important roles as information providers. However, outside of these roles, the participation of a large number of victims with conflicting interests may actually frustrate the role of the prosecution as it attempts to prove its theory of the case beyond a reasonable doubt.[26] Victims participating as civil parties or auxiliary prosecutors may unknowingly present evidence that calls into question the credibility of witnesses or undermine evidence presented by the prosecution.[27] At the domestic level, the *Touvier* trial is one example where an active role for victims may in fact jeopardize a successful prosecution. This concern is only exacerbated in international trials because of their inherent complexity, their geopolitical nature and the potentially large number of victim participants.

(3) Participation in trial with regard to a victim's right to seek reparations is more efficient than a separated process

The right to participation is often linked with the right to claim reparations. Advocates of victims' participatory rights argue that participation is a necessary corollary of the right to seek reparations. International human rights courts have certainly made this link and it is distinct from the role of the prosecutor to secure a conviction. Participation therefore becomes important because it enables courts to fulfill a legal duty to provide redress to victims.

Although the right to reparations is widely acknowledged in international law the nature of international criminal trials and the crimes falling under their jurisdictions often means that reparations must be dealt with through other mechanism – most notably state mechanisms. The fact of the matter is that international courts will only prosecute and convict a small number of individuals for crimes of mass victimization. This means that a very large number of victims will seek reparation from a single

24 Bassiouni (2006) at 205-206.

25 ICC, *Situation in Uganda*, No. ICC-02/04-106, 31 August 2007, par. 23.

26 Jorda, J. and De Hemptinne, J., The Status and Role of the Victims, 1412, in Cassese, et al. (2002); Jouet (2007) at 275-76.

27 Jouet (2007) at 276.

defendant or a handful of defendants.[28] However, because most accused are determined indigent and will be unable to provide reparation, victims will be left empty-handed unless they also have recourse to state courts, a claims commission or trust funds.

If a trust fund has been established, and this has only been the case with the ICC, it may be desirable to institute an administrative-based claims commission process for reparations rather than through the criminal process. Such a process has proven successful in the past for processing large amounts of claims and it would allow victims to meet a lower standard of proof than that usually required in traditional legal settings. Additionally, collective reparation awards, such as those carried out by the Trust Fund, are attractive alternatives to individual reparations attached to a criminal process at the international level.

(4) Participation in criminal proceedings keeps a check on state authorities to comply with human rights standards

Victims may act as a check on prosecuting authorities who fail to adequately investigate, prosecute or punish crimes. The regional human rights courts place special emphasis on the role of victims as a sort of watch guard over the process.

Unlike at the domestic level where human rights courts have consistently found that victims should have a say during the investigative stage so as to inform courts about possible charges and to keep the state authorities in check, the same rationale for participation does not fully apply at the international criminal law level. International courts were designed, in part, because they counter biases that may exist in domestic settings such as judges or prosecutors receiving undue influence from other government agencies or protecting defendants who work for the government. To be sure, allowing too great a role for victims in investigations could hinder the progress of international investigations by infringing upon the role assigned to the prosecutor.

The specific characteristics of international criminal law, including the mass victimization aspect to the trials, the make-up and structure of the courts and the financial and practical constraints faced by the courts dictate that participation at the international level must be different than at the domestic level. As noted by Heikkila, the collective nature of victim participation in international criminal proceedings may in fact lessen the therapeutic effect for many victims because their participation will almost always be limited.[29] The conflicting interests of victims cannot be taken into account with any specificity. Instead, the effective operation of the courts largely requires that personal interests go unrepresented.[30] In this sense, the individual memories and experiences of victims are diminished and conflated into collective narratives. Victims, therefore, largely lack any individualized decision-making ability that

28 Keller (2007) at 211.
29 Heikkila (2004) at 163.
30 Mohan (2009) at 767-769.

participation at the domestic level was designed, in part, to provide.[31] Moreover, the make-up and structure of the courts, as young systems, applying a mixture of procedural approaches, complicates attempts to include the active participation of victims. The experiment of directly borrowing procedures from domestic systems and approaching procedural issues from a myriad of mindsets has proven problematic. There is an inherent difficulty in transplanting processes and procedures from one legal tradition to another. Institutional constraints and cultural resistance may diminish the intended impact.[32] Damaška has warned that mixing procedures can produce less satisfactory results than in their pre-transplanted form.[33] Finally, the practical and financial constraints mean that international criminal institutions cannot be all things to all people. They must decide how, within their abilities, best to meet the minimum human rights standards applicable to both victims and accused within the construct of the criminal process.

8.3.2 Areas of Concern Arising Out of Increased Participation: Fair Trial Rights of Accused

The liberal human rights values hold that a fair trial necessitates that convictions are based on sound evidence and requires that defendants have the ability to mount a defense before an impartial tribunal. There can be no foregone conclusions of individual guilt for offenses charged, and each crime must be proven beyond a reasonable doubt by the prosecuting authority. However, a shift from liberal values focused on the defendant to a more victim-oriented focus, which has already occurred within the human rights system (most notably in the Inter-American system), is steadily occurring within the international criminal law system. Looked at in isolation the various fair trial standards affected by participation may seem less problematic, but rather it is the combined effect of the edging away of these rights and values that matters most.

The edging away of liberal values is alarming not least of which because international courts have already witnessed the 'relaxing' of procedural and evidentiary rules that negatively affect the rights of an accused to a fair trial.[34] The ability of the prosecutor to continuously amend and add to charges against an accused throughout trial,[35] the admission of statements going to acts and conduct of an accused without cross-examination taking place,[36] and the admission of anonymous testimony[37] are only a

31 Trumbull (2008) at 806.
32 Jackson, J., Transnational Faces of Justice: Two Attempts to Build Common Standards beyond National Boundaries, 223, in Jackson, et al. (2008).
33 Damaška (1997) at 852.
34 Knoops (2005) at 1576-1577; Mundis (2001) at 378.
35 See Jordash and Martin (2010).
36 ICTY RPE, Rule 92*quater*.
37 The *Tadić* case at the ICTY was the first case in which anonymous witness testimony was used against a defendant, see, ICTY, *Prosecutor v. Tadić*, Case No. IT-94-1, Decision on the Prosecutor's Motion Requesting Protective Measures for Victims and Witnesses, Trial Chamber, 10 August 1995, stressing

handful of examples of complaints made by defense teams against the institutions set up and designed to investigate, prosecute and punish individuals for serious international crimes.

Additionally, a recent study has revealed that international criminal courts face severe impediments to accurate fact-finding, which has led to doubts about the legitimacy of the courts' factual determinations.[38] In her groundbreaking study of court transcripts and judgments from the ICTR, SCSL and SPSC, Combs found that the reliability of eye-witness testimony was highly questionable and that testimony provided in court is often inconsistent with previous pre-trial statements.[39] Her study found that "90 percent of cases featured at least one example of diametrically opposed testimony between one or more witnesses,"[40] with many cases having numerous examples. The reasons for the false or inconsistent testimony are numerous, ranging from group-based loyalties, ethnic divisions, financial incentives, or honest mistakes. Prosecutors often invoke educational, cultural and linguistic factors for why testimony may appear deficient. Often witnesses have hidden behind these deficiencies as a means of concealing a lie or weakness in their testimony.[41] Regardless of the reasons for the inconsistencies, vague testimony introduced by the prosecution is more difficult, if not impossible, to rebut by the defense.

Given that almost all evidence in international criminal trials comes in the form of witness testimony, Combs' findings are alarming. In addition to concerns about unreliable witness testimony, her study indicates that because the international courts fail to require prosecutors or witnesses to specify facts, defendants could be put into a position where they are prevented from presenting alibis or otherwise mounting meaningful challenges, denying them the opportunity to mount a meaningful defense.[42] In their judgments, judges often fail to even mention testimonial deficiencies and when acknowledged they are found to not have impacted a witness' credibility.[43] Combs

the unique character of international tribunals and 'balancing' the rights of the accused with the rights of victims and witnesses. The Trial Chamber afforded the maximum protection to the victims and witnesses at the expense of the fundamental rights of the accused. Indeed, Witness L, who was permitted to testify anonymously, subsequently lied; see Scharf (1997-1998) at 179. Through the independent investigations of the prosecution, the Court learned that the witness who had been provided full anonymity lied about the death of his father and admitted that he was trained by the Bosnian government to testify against the accused, see DeFrancia (2001) at 1416. The inability of the defense to test the witness' credibility hindered the accused's right against anonymous accusations. The decision allowing anonymous testimony has since been criticized by commentators and has not been wholeheatedly followed by other chambers.

38 Combs (2009) at 239; see also Combs (2010)

39 Combs (2009) at 239.

40 *Ibid.* at 256.

41 *Ibid.* at 254-256.

42 *Ibid.* at 243.

43 Murphy argues that international courts must do more to protect against polluting the evidentiary record. He suggests that the use of some exclusionary rules of evidence, which are generally associated with the common law tradition, would make international criminal trials fairer, shorter, and more

determined that the cavalier approach taken by the judges reflects the fact that they give prosecution witnesses the benefit of the doubt, without similar treatment of defense witnesses.[44] Overlooking the impact of these testimonies on the defense, Combs found a pro-conviction bias at the courts she studied, which she argues is inconsistent with the 'beyond a reasonable doubt' standard of proof required by the governing documents. She found that their factual determinations are more closely aligned with a preponderance of the evidence standard, and that the judges largely draw inferences from the defendant's experiences to determine whether or not he is responsible for the crimes charged.[45] Her findings support what Amann refers to as the *impartiality deficit* of international criminal institutions.[46] The impartiality deficit has to do with an international criminal court's compulsion to convict and downplay the rights of the accused so as to fulfill its mandate of ending impunity and providing justice to victims.

Due to the fact that the vast majority of defendants who are tried by international criminal courts are convicted,[47] one must wonder whether these facts are concerning. Or perhaps, precisely because of this high conviction rate these facts should be troubling. Either way, when the courts assert that they provide for robust fair trial rights of the accused and then continue to further undermine these rights, alarm bells should ring. It appears that historically and presently, international courts have hid behind the rhetoric of upholding strict fair trial rights while at the same time slowly undermining such rights.[48]

This study cautions that adding the element of active victims' participation into proceedings of international criminal trials may further contribute to the edging away of defendants' rights. As argued by Zappalà, there is no requirement that participation must actually create prejudice.[49] Instead, an abstract conflict is sufficient in order to question forms of participation. In other words, even when there is a substantial risk that an accused's rights may be violated the court should look to rigorously protect the fair trial rights of an accused and limit active participation in trial. The sections below

efficient. He further argues that the civil law assumptions that rules of evidence (1) are of relevance only to jury trials; and (2) hinder the search for the truth, are incorrect. Instead, he submits that the present system of 'free proof' in the context of international criminal law is a judicial failure in the exercise of due discretion by indiscriminately admitting any material claimed to be 'evidence', regardless of its reliability and with little inquiry as to possible perjury or fabrication. This practice makes trials longer and more complex than they need be, and it poisons the record, making it more difficult for judges to later assess the weight of the evidence and arrive at the truth. See Murphy (2010).

44 Combs (2009) at 264.

45 *Ibid.* at 267.

46 Amann, D.M., Impartiality Deficit and International Criminal Judging, 208, in Schabas (2007).

47 The SCSL has a 100 percent conviction rate, the SPSC have a 97 percent conviction rate, and the ICTR has an 85 percent conviction rate.

48 Mégret (2009) at 71.

49 Zappalà (2010) at 143.

will highlight potential risks as well as existing concerns about the impact that participation has on the rights of accused.

Presumption of Innocence

The presumption of innocence has long historical roots and is found in all major human rights and international criminal law documents.[50] The right to be presumed innocent simply means that although there are suspicions as to guilt (otherwise the accused would not be before the court), the court will withhold findings of guilt unless and until such time as the prosecuting authority has proven guilt beyond a reasonable doubt in fair and efficient proceedings.[51] Indeed, according to Van Sliedregt, the presumption of innocence is a procedural and evidentiary principle that essentially supports the placing of the burden of proof on the prosecuting authority.[52]

The participation of victims in the criminal process is certainly not *per se* in conflict with an accused's right to be presumed innocent. However, one concern that arises with regard to this fundamental fair trial right has to do with the terminology adopted by international courts in their governing documents as well as the terminology adopted by judges in their decisions. Terms and phrases used in governing documents and decisions should unequivocally preserve this principle. Unfortunately, that is not always the case. At the ECCC, for example, Internal Rule 23(1) states that the purpose of a civil party action is to participate "*against those responsible for crimes* within the jurisdiction of the ECCC by supporting the prosecution."[53] The wording implies that the accused is already responsible for the crimes falling under the Court's jurisdiction. It should instead say 'against those allegedly responsible', 'against those believed to be responsible', or deleting the clause altogether. At the ICC, the Trial Chamber in the *Lubanga* case has used questionable language in its decisions granting applicants victim status. The Judges have held that they accept broad similarities in victim applications and find the similarities unsurprising given the "broad context of the systematic conscription of children under the age of 15 into the military forces of the UPC."[54] The statement is intricately connected to the context of the crimes charged against the accused, and as such, the prosecution has the burden of establishing this fact. Yet it appears that well before the end of the trial the Judges have already accepted it as true for the purposes of accepting victim applications. Moreover, the statement is even more unfortunate given the fact that the defense in *Lubanga* actively contests this allegation. Instead, the Judges could easily have stated that they believe the similarities are unsurprising given the 'broad context of the

50 Trechsel (2005) at 154-155; Van Sliedregt (2008) at 6.
51 Trechsel (2005) at 155.
52 Van Sliedgregt (2008) at 2, 10.
53 Emphasis added.
54 ICC, *The Prosecutor v. Lubanga*, No. ICC-01/04-01/06-1556, 15 December 2008, par. 103.

allegations of systematic conscription of children under the age of 15 into military forces in the region'. Regrettably, time again, this is overlooked.

The problem posed by the above examples is that in criminal trials an accused is not responsible to prove his innocence. Instead, the prosecuting authority must establish (i) the facts of a crime and (ii) the culpability of the accused. However, when victims are granted victim status and permitted to participate in the proceedings, the court is, on some level (at a minimum a *prima facie* level), accepting that certain events, namely the crimes in question, did in fact take place and that certain individuals, namely the victims participating, were harmed. In many cases this will not be a problem because all sides will agree that certain events occurred and that certain individuals were harmed. However, in some cases, the defense will likely contest allegations made by the prosecution and victims as to whether or not certain individuals were in fact harmed by a certain event. Likewise, it may even contest whether or not an event took place. As a result, in these situations, there is a danger that either the court accepts certain allegations as true (or at least seems to do so through the choice of language used) or that the burden of proof may be shifted, leaving it up to the defense to prove that something is in fact not true. The courts should therefore be cautious not to assume the factual basis of the events in question when such facts are contested. Accordingly, the choice of language becomes very important. The language adopted by the court should refrain implying guilt or accepting contested facts as true. As stated by Judge Song of the ICC, "If we really want to protect the rights of accused persons who are prosecuted at the ICC then we need to vocally maintain the presumption of innocence throughout the proceedings."[55]

Adequate Time and Facilities

Often linked with adversarial proceedings and the principle of equality of arms, the right to have adequate time and facilities is a fundamental right of accused in criminal trials.[56] If the defense lacks the means or opportunity to properly prepare a defense then fair trial rights have been violated. Although there will always be a degree of inequality of resources between the defense and prosecution, defense teams must be given a genuine opportunity to prepare their case.

One of the most serious concerns has to do with the processing of and responding to victim applications. This has been particularly problematic in a number of cases, most notably in Case 002 at the ECCC and in *Bemba* at the ICC where thousands of victims have sought to participate. Problems arise because the evaluation of applications is, as noted by the prosecution, a "resource-intensive and extremely time consuming exercise."[57] If, for example, each application is approximately 10 pages in length

---

55 IBA-ICC Film, *In the Dock: Defense Rights at the International Criminal Court*, May 2011, *available at*: www.ibanet.org, *last visited* 2 June 2011.

56 Temminck Tuinstra (2009) at 153-154.

57 ICC, *The Prosecutor v. Lubanga*, No. ICC-01/04-01/06-1136, 28 January 2008, par. 11.

and 1,000 victims seek to participate, a legal team, which on average is composed of six individuals (including interns), must process 10,000 pages of documents on top of the documents that relate to the charges against an accused. The sheer magnitude of this processing places a great burden on the limited resources of defense teams and needs to be taken seriously by courts.

Once admitted to participate, the inclusion of victims inevitably creates an increase in workload. Therefore, it is no surprise that both the ECCC and ICC have faced an abundance of litigation concerning the issue of victim participation. While the ECCC has arguably spent less time litigating victim issues due to their more detailed rules of procedure, issues nonetheless included: whether successors of civil party applicants could qualify as civil parties, whether victims were required to be represented by legal counsel, what criteria victims need to meet in order to be granted civil party status, whether victims could participate with regard to sentencing issues, and whether victims could question character witnesses of the accused. At the ICC, where the Statute and Rules are less detailed, litigation of victim issues has been continuous. The various issues dealt with by the chambers have included, *inter alia*: how to define and interpret 'personal interests' in Article 68(3); how to define harm; whether the harm suffered needs to relate to charges brought against an accused; whether victims can participate during the investigation phase of the pre-trial stage; whether victims can represent themselves or whether they must have legal representation; whether victim-applicants are entitled to protective measures; whether and at what time the identity of victim-applicants needs to be made available to the parties and participants; how to define the duties of the departments working with victims, including the prosecution, OPCV, VPRS and VWU; whether victims should have access to confidential information in a situation or case; whether victims should be able to lead and challenge evidence; whether victims cannot maintain their anonymity and how this will affect the rights of the accused; whether victims must disclose exculpatory evidence to the defense; whether common legal representation should be arranged, and, if so, how to handle conflicts of interest amongst victims; and whether victims should be presumed indigent so that the Court bears the responsibility to pay for their legal representation. All of the issues mentioned above have required the filing of written briefs (and responses) by the defense, prosecution and victims, and often the hearing of oral arguments.

The amount of working hours and resources that the parties and participants put into these issues is enormous. Defense teams have complained that they often do not have the resources to dedicate to all of these procedural issues while at the same time having to examine documents and allegations going to the substantive charges brought by the prosecutor.[58] This is especially problematic in light of the complex charges or factual allegations faced by accused. It is also problematic in light of the fact that some accused will not be deemed indigent and may place a high priority on assessing victim

58 Learned through interviews with members of various members of defense teams at the ICC.

applications. The right to adequate time and facilities to conduct a defense is a fundamental human right of accused in criminal trials. However, the overly burdensome nature of processing applications coupled with the excessive litigation related to victims' issues seriously threatens to violate this right.

Right to an Expeditious Trial

One of the major criticisms of international criminal law has been the unseemly length of proceedings,[59] which can impact upon a defendant's right to an expeditious trial. The potential violation of the right to an expeditious trial is of particular concern because most defendants in international trials remain in custody throughout the criminal process.

Article 64 of the Rome Statute requires the Trial Chambers to ensure that proceedings are conducted in "a manner that is fair and expeditious." Article 67 requires fair and impartial hearings and trial without undue delay, and Rule 101 further requires that the "Court shall have regard to the need to facilitate fair and expeditious proceedings, bearing in mind in particular the rights of the defense and victims." Similarly, at the ECCC, Article 33(new) of the Framework Agreement provides that "The Extraordinary Chambers of the trial court shall ensure that trials are fair and expeditious and are conducted in accordance with existing procedures in force, with full respect for the rights of the accused and for the protection of victims and witnesses," and Article 35(new) lists trial without undue delay as a right of the accused. Rule 37(d) of the Internal Rules likewise provides that "The Chambers may also order suspension of public broadcasts of the trial and any other measures that they consider necessary for the conduct of fair and expeditious proceedings." Rule 79 references the Trial Chamber's need to facilitate fair and expeditious proceedings, and the recently enacted Rule 12*ter* requires the lead co-lawyers to ensure the need for fair and expeditious proceedings. Finally, Rule 85 provides that "In consultation with the other judges, the President may exclude any proceedings that unnecessarily delay the trial, and are not conducive to ascertaining the truth."

However, despite statutory references to the need to ensure an expeditious trial, the courts have, at least initially, been reluctant to limit the active participation of victims in order to curb delays to the proceedings. At the ECCC, the Trial Chamber originally allowed the participation of four teams of civil party lawyers to participate and was reluctant to group victims into more manageable teams. It was only after the participation proved repetitive that the Judges amended the Internal Rules and created lead co-lawyers to help ensure expeditious proceedings at trial for Case 002. At the ICC, the example in *Banda/Jerbo* where the Pre-Trial Chamber both allowed victims to make oral submissions at the confirmation of charges hearing and allowed them to file written observations following the hearing was directly at odds with the wishes of the

59 Knoops (2005) at 1570.

parties to carry out an expeditious pre-trial stage. It also meant that the suspects would spend additional time in detention.

Although Judge Song of the ICC Appeals Chamber has found in a separate opinion that delays in the proceedings due to victim participation did not violate the rights of the accused because they were a *mere consequence* of their participation authorized under the Statute,[60] his statement is hard to reconcile with the fact that although participation is authorized it is only permitted when not inconsistent with the rights of the accused, including the right to an expeditious trial. Therefore, criminal proceedings may not be unreasonably long regardless of whether and to what extent victims participate. If proceedings are prolonged due, in part, to the participation of victims the courts have an obligation to limit the participation if participation detrimentally affects the rights of the accused to a fair and expeditious trial. For example, the courts can group victims under more manageable legal teams or on certain issues they can limit submissions to written observations.

Right to be Tried by an Independent and Impartial Court

International courts must not only be independent and impartial but they must be seen to be independent and impartial. This means that although judges have a truth-seeking role, they should be cautious about becoming investigators, prosecutors or additional accusers intent on following up a certain theory of the case presented by one of the parties in trial.

At the ICC, before being able to call a witness or introduce evidence, victims must receive the permission of the Chamber. There are no provisions providing for victims to introduce evidence directly. As a result, when victims call a witness or introduce evidence, it is actually the Chamber *requesting* the evidence pursuant to Article 64(6)(d). The authority of the Chamber to request evidence is undisputed. However, it is submitted that it would be inappropriate for a Chamber to use this provision predominantly as a means through which victims can directly lead evidence. If the Judges exercise this power without restraint they can unnecessarily change into bias participants appearing to push a certain theory of the case.

There is a difference in exercising this power at the behest of victims versus requesting certain evidence at their own initiative. When done repeatedly at the victims' request Judges can be seen as less objective. Zappalà asks whether it is desirable for the prosecution's burden of proof to be shared by the prosecution, the victims and the judges collectively.[61] It is certainly more difficult for the defense to challenge evidence requested by the Judges, who would undoubtedly argue they are requesting the evidence as an impartial tribunal even when on behalf of victims, than

60 ICC, *The Prosecutor v. Lubanga*, No. ICC-01/04-01/06-925 (separate opinion of Judge Song), 13 June 2007, par. 27.

61 Zappalá (2010) at 148.

evidence requested by the prosecution. Instead, it would be preferred that the Judges use their powers to request evidence either in favor of the accused, who is arguably in an unequal position at trial to that of the prosecution (as well as victims), or only in very limited circumstances on behalf of victims.

In addition to concerns with judges taking too active a role in pushing one theory of a case, the nature of the harm suffered by the victims and the emotional impact this may have on the proceedings could also interfere with the rights of an accused if not properly controlled by the judges.[62] This is particularly true in mass atrocity cases where the harms suffered are extreme. Damaška has noted that "emotionally-charged stories of massive atrocities can easily generate an atmosphere of revulsion and anger, in which judges could – consciously or subconsciously – neglect alternative explanations of events, attribute blame more easily, or in greater measure than warranted, and might even lower the postulated standard of proof sufficiency."[63] For this reason judges will need to exercise great care in ensuring the objectivity of the court, otherwise the "extensive interpretation of victims' rights could conflict with two cardinal principles which are vital to the work and functioning of the Court: the function of the Court as a judicial institution, and the imperative of impartiality."[64]

Equality of Arms

In addition to the explicit rights of the accused listed in governing documents the principle of equality of arms is often invoked when speaking of fair trial rights. Adherence to the principle of equality of arms between the defense and the prosecution is arguably viewed as "the single most important criterion in evaluating the fairness of a trial."[65] Thus, although there is no specific reference to equality of arms in the governing documents of either the ECCC or ICC it is nevertheless recognized as a fundamental aspect of a fair trial – if not the most essential aspect of a fair trial.[66]

Commentators have concluded that the intervention of victims, especially with regard to their ability to lead and challenge evidence, can affect the principle of equality of arms.[67] Doak notes that when a system is set up in such a way that there is a "delicate balance of power achieved through the clear delineation of roles of the prosecution and defense, the system could be perceived as appearing 'out of balance' if another party were involved in the case that could actively work against the interests of the defense."[68] At both courts, defense teams must be prepared to be confronted

62 De Hemptinne (2007) at 412.
63 Damaška (2009) at 29, citing psychological studies of this phenomenon.
64 Stahn, et al. (2006) at 221.
65 Lawyers Committee for Human Rights, What is a Fair Trial? A Basic Guide to Legal Standards and Practice, 12, March 2000.
66 Trechsel (2005) at 94.
67 Doak (2005) at 298; Zappalà (2010) at 149-150.
68 Doak (2005) at 298.

with accusations not only from the prosecution but also from victims. Chung argues that the mere fact that the defense teams must prepare to meet additional evidence risks prejudicing their rights.[69] The prejudice results from having to meet multiple accusers. The effect of multiple accusers against an accused impacts not only the time and resources of defense counsel in having to respond to multiple arguments but also relieves part of the burden of proof from the prosecution.

The Trial Chamber in *Lubanga* acknowledged that although its decision on victim participation in the trial proceedings "does not have the effect *per se* of shifting the burden of proof," it "could lead, in particular circumstances and in some degree, to such an effect, and this could significantly affect the fairness of the proceedings pursuant to Article 67(1)(i)," which provides that the defense shall not have imposed on him any reversal of the burden of proof or any onus of rebuttal.[70] In a separate, concurring Appeals Chamber opinion, Judge Pikis underscored the tension between the rights of the accused and the rights of victims to lead evidence at trial, stating that "[e]quality of arms is another element of a fair trial, which in the context of the Statute, putting the burden of proof on the Prosecutor, means that the defendant cannot be required to confront more than one accuser."[71] With this statement in mind, the approach taken by the *Katanga/Ngudjolo* Trial Chamber is most desirable. In that case, the Judges limit the participation of victims by generally not allowing them to adduce evidence on the guilt of the accused. Finding that such a role is inappropriate, they may instead request the Court or the prosecutor to follow a certain line of questioning. At the ECCC, defense counsel for Duch continuously argued that when the defense must face 10 lawyers from both the prosecution and civil parties, all attempting to illicit evidence on the guilt of the accused, he is facing multiple accusers. Though the Internal Rules have brought the number of civil party lawyers at trial down to two, the complaint of having to face multiple accusers remains.

Interestingly, victims have also sought to claim rights under the principle of equality of arms, leading to questions of whether the principle in fact applies to them in criminal proceedings. Arguably the principle only applies to the individual facing a disadvantage vis-à-vis the prosecuting authority. However, the ECtHR has found that the principle applies to victims in relation to their civil claim for damages when participating as parties in a criminal case. Both the ICC and ECCC have been reluctant to recognize such a right. At the ICC victims are not parties to the proceedings and thus it is difficult to justify why the principle should apply to non-parties. At the ECCC, where victims participate as parties, the Judges have nonetheless been unwilling to apply the principle of equality of arms outside of the reparations context. In response to an argument put forward by the civil party lawyers in Case 002 before the ECCC that all parties should be treated equally the Pre-Trial Chamber stressed that "no

69 Chung (2008) at 519, footnote 242.

70 ICC, *The Prosecutor v. Lubanga*, No. ICC-01/04-01/06-1191, 26 February 2008, par. 42.

71 ICC, *The Prosecutor v. Lubanga*, No. ICC-01/04-01/06-925 (separate Opinion of Judge Pikis), 13 June 2007, par. 19.

such general principle exists with respect to the length of oral submissions. Even if it did, such a principle would simply mean that as far as their position is equal, civil parties should be treated in the same way."[72]

Legal (Un)Certainty

The multi-faceted principle of legal certainty is closely associated with the right to a fair trial.[73] Although it has not been precisely defined in law or legal literature,[74] it is recognized as a general principle of law common to most legal systems.[75] Related to the principle of legitimate expectation, the notion of predictability and the rule of law, the principle of legal certainty refers to the requirement that legal rules be sufficiently clear and precise, and that situations and legal relationships remain foreseeable.[76]

While many of the provisions in the governing documents on victims' participation are laudable since they aim to address the needs and concerns of victims, the vagueness of the procedural rules together with the lack of harmonization by the various chambers within a judicial institution have created a great deal of legal uncertainty. Zappalà notes that "[t]he proper understanding of the position and role of victims in international criminal proceedings suffers from inextricable uncertainty relating to the procedural model chosen for international criminal courts and tribunals, and the ambiguities of some crucial provisions of their constitutive instruments."[77] This legal uncertainty is damaging to all parties and participants and significantly affects smooth court operation.

Although the ECCC appears to provide for more comprehensible procedural rules for victim participation than the ICC, both courts have faced challenges in properly delimiting the role of victims in proceedings. The case-by-case approach adopted by the courts was undoubtedly necessary at the outset and has to some extent been beneficial to the development of the law, but at this point in time it creates difficulties with regularity and certainty. The system that is in place at the ICC complicates matters more than is necessary. Each Pre-Trial Chamber and each Trial Chamber must address the same issues over and over, with the Chambers often interpreting the same issue in very different ways. The lack of harmonization of decisions has led to uncertainty and a delay of the proceedings due to re-litigation on the same issues. This has a particularly damaging effect on the defense given their limited resources in facing the charges brought by the prosecution. At the ECCC, there had also been a great deal

72 ECCC, *Case of Ieng Sary (Case 002)*, Decision on Preliminary Matters Raised by the Lawyers for the Civil Parties in Ieng Sary's Appeal against Provisional Detention Order, Pre-Trial Chamber, 1 July 2008, par. 4.
73 See Zappalá (2010); Emmerson, et al. (2007) at 401.
74 Raitio (2003) at 125.
75 *Ibid.*
76 *Ibid.* at 126.
77 Zappalá (2010) at 138.

of ambiguity surrounding victim-related issues but the smaller number of cases coupled with the Judges' ability to revise the Internal Rules has helped provide greater clarity for future cases.

8.4 What is the Proper Scope and Content of Victim Participation in International Criminal Proceedings?

In light of the specific characteristics of international criminal law and the concerns raised with regard to human rights, what should the proper scope and content of victim participation be in international criminal proceedings? Unfortunately, there is no one-size-fits-all answer to this question. There is no clear benchmark against which current practice can easily be measured because so much depends upon the specific context of the criminal institution. International criminal institutions are intricate organizations, each with their own self-contained spheres of influence. Nevertheless, this study of victim participation in international criminal proceedings has shown that the right to participation is linked to human rights and state/institutional obligations. It has further shown that like domestic jurisdictions, international criminal courts have adopted a wide range of participation models, but that participation in international criminal proceedings is decidedly different from participation in domestic proceedings due in large part to the unique characteristic of international criminal proceedings.

The case studies evaluated in this research, viewed together with the practice of other international courts, suggest that there is little consensus on what the extent of participation should be. However, due to the number of concerns arising out of participation from the ECCC and ICC, it is argued that human rights standards relating to the traditional liberal model should receive greater consideration when determining the scope and content of participation. By using a human rights-based approach while at the same time taking into account the unique characteristics of international criminal law, courts will be a better position to delimit the participatory rights of victims while at the same time safeguarding the fair trial rights of the accused and recognizing victims' rights. As such, when courts are deciding upon the proper scope and content of participation, the following points should act as guidelines: (i) give sufficient regard for the core objectives of the criminal process; (ii) reject the balancing consciousness and recognize the primacy of the rights of accused; (iii) focus on services for victims; and (iv) embrace pluralism taking into account the specific characteristics of the court.

8.4.1 Give Sufficient Regard for the Core Objectives of the Criminal Process

Once it was acknowledged that ensuring justice requires more than just punishing offenders, it became acceptable to broaden the list of goals and objectives of international criminal institutions.[78] The laundry list of goals now includes deterrence, adding to the historical record, maintenance of peace, bringing justice to victims, promoting reconciliation, providing restoration to victims, as well as ending impunity for serious violations of human rights and humanitarian law.[79] Whether international criminal institutions do in fact ensure justice (broadly speaking, of course) beyond the narrow parameters of investigation, prosecution and punishment is outside the scope of this study. However, many scholars have openly questioned the ability of these institutions to meet the plethora of goals assigned to them.[80]

Despite the long list of articulated goals, there is no getting around the fact that international criminal courts are first and foremost retributive-based institutions with their primary role and function being the investigation and prosecution of individuals for the most serious crimes of concern to the international community, in fair and efficient proceedings.[81] A key aspect of criminal justice systems is the notion that wrongdoers should be punished because they have violated certain legal and moral standards.[82] At the international level those found guilty of international crimes are believed to be deserving of punishment because they have violated standards agreed upon by the international community. The search for truth related to the individual criminal responsibility of an accused in fair trials with due process protections is therefore the main goal of international justice institutions. All other goals, while important, are ancillary, including deterrence, maintenance of peace, communication of the wrongdoing,[83] and victim-oriented measures.

Damaška has observed a paradox in international criminal law: the courts deal with crimes of unusual complexity while at the same time aspiring to achieve goals that are more ambitious than those faced by national criminal justice systems. He views this paradox as an alarming discrepancy between promise and achievement and argues that international criminal institutions "cannot afford to disregard the attainability of the goals they profess to pursue" because the "viability of professed goals is a close cousin of legitimacy."[84] Unlike domestic systems, international criminal institutions often have more complex procedural frameworks, more demanding and arduous investigations, and little to no enforcement powers. These institutions are expected to adjudicate crimes involving a mass number of victims and a large number of perpetrators. The

78 See Groenhuijsen, M., Victims' Rights and the International Criminal Court: The Model of the Rome Statute and Its Operation, 300, in Van Genugten, et al. (2009); see generally Drumbl (2007).

79 Schabas (2006) at 67-73; Orentlicher (1991) at 2547, footnote 32, quoting Justice Robert Jackson, chief US prosecutor for the Nuremburg trials on the purpose of the proceedings; Mahon (2009) at 733-734, noting that the long list of ambitions are largely unproven by empirical research.

80 Mahon (2009) at 734; see also, Ku and Nzelibe (2006) and Stover (2005).

81 Dembour and Haslam (2004) at 152; Gallant (2001) at 21; Doak (2005) at 295; Jackson, J., Transitional Faces of Justice: Two Attempts to Build Common Standards beyond National Boundaries, 239, in Jackson, J., et al. (2008); see also, Boas (2001).

82 Hall (1990-1991) at 260.

83 Duff (1986) at 116.

84 Damaška (2009) at 20.

courts regularly have to deal with ongoing conflicts or with conflicts that took place decades earlier. Given these challenges, one would expect the goals of international criminal justice to be more modest than their national counterparts. However, that is not the case. Time and again, the courts strive to be all things to all people.

While it is a welcome development that courts begin to focus more on outreach and capacity building, within the construct of the criminal trial itself, courts need to focus on their primary objectives. Gilbert Bitti of the International Criminal Court once proudly professed that the proceedings at the ICC are not just criminal proceedings but in addition to being a criminal court, the ICC is also a claims commission and truth commission all rolled up into one convenient package. Adding a less positive spin, Jose Alvarez found that "the ICC is a cumbersome combination of technique for mobilization of shame/class action suit/truth commission/reparations process and criminal trial" and feared that "it may collapse under the weight of competing goals [...]."[85] His interpretation seems more apt, particularly in light of the fact that the procedural frameworks adopted by a handful of the courts make the realization of their primary goals far more difficult. The ICC and ECCC's procedural frameworks are made more complex with the inclusion of active participation at trial. Damaška's has therefore called for an "unburdening" of international criminal justice and this study reiterates this call.[86]

Because only a small number of victims will actually benefit from direct participation due to the mass victimization element of international crimes, it is instead better that in the actual proceedings the courts focus on their primary objectives of investigation, prosecution and punishment. By focusing on these narrow objectives courts "have the best chance of strengthening the sense of accountability for gross human rights violations, and are best positioned to spread the sense of empathy and compassion, crucial for the vitality of the evolving human rights culture."[87] Consequently, a more targeted focus would mean that criminal courts would not be simultaneously acting as claim commissions or truth commissions.

The courts would be concerned, first and foremost, with investigations, prosecutions and punishment. This would mean that the emphasis of proceedings is not necessarily on the harm suffered by the victims (though this is important to establish for purposes of sentencing) but rather on the crime committed and whether the accused should be held responsible. Participation going beyond this focus, such as participation trying to shame national governments or establish crimes other than those brought by the prosecutor, would need to be restricted. This is also true for the vast majority of interventions related to reparation claims. Most matters related to reparation should be dealt with separately. Just as many national jurisdictions decide to deal with reparations apart from criminal matters in complex cases, so too should international courts.

---

85 Alvarez (2000) at 135.

86 Damaška (2008) at 329-365; Damaška (2009) at 32.

87 Damaška (2009) at 33.

However, it is important to recognize that outside of the criminal trial process victims should be able to exercise greater rights in reparation proceedings or hearings. In reparation proceedings, victims should be full parties with all the rights that attach to that status.

8.4.2 Reject the Balancing Consciousness and Recognize the Primacy of the Rights of Accused

Although rights for victims are sometimes vaguely worded and not as explicit as rights afforded to accused, they do represent minimum standards that states should strive to meet. The same is true for international criminal institutions that strive to uphold human rights norms. When an international criminal court deviates from minimum human rights standards the court undermines existing human rights. Minimum rights "create a baseline below which a court cannot go without compromising fairness and effectiveness."[88] Taking away a right designated as a minimum guarantee compromises the entire criminal process and serves as a denial of justice.[89]

Once it is accepted that both victims and accused have minimum rights in the criminal process it is necessary to delimit those rights. Unfortunately, what has transpired is that courts have sought to expand or at least broadly interpret the rights of victims while narrowly interpreting the minimum rights of accused. Although minimum standards for both victims and accused should be maintained courts should caution against maximizing (or expanding) rights of victims while only holding to the very minimum rights for defendants (if not violating those rights altogether).

International human rights law, since the adoption of the UDHR, has recognized the due process and fair trial rights of the accused as intrinsic values underlying human rights instruments. These liberal values are related to the notion that human rights impose limits on what states can do to their own citizens. Whether formulated in general or specific terms, almost all basic human rights instruments recognize specific rights for a defendant in the criminal process. Ranging from the prohibition of arbitrary arrest to procedural guarantees at trial, these documents, as well as the statutes and rules of the various international criminal courts, explicitly provide for substantive and procedural fair trial guarantees for accused.[90] The rights of accused in criminal trials have been adopted across criminal procedural traditions, making them a "fundamental bedrock of modern criminal procedural law" regardless of whether a legal system leans more to the adversarial or inquisitorial approach.[91] The same specificity and underlying acceptance is not applicable to victims' participatory rights.

---

88 Stapleton (1998-1999) at 548.

89 Van Dijk, P., Universal Legal Principles of Fair Trial in Criminal Proceedings, 99, in Rosas and Helgesen (1990).

90 Trechsel (2005) at 38; Zappalá (2010) at 143.

91 Zappalá (2010) at 143-144.

Therefore, it is highly desirable that courts, both in their governing documents as well as in their jurisprudence, recognize that the minimum rights of accused must be preserved which may require a narrow interpretation of victims' minimum rights. This is particularly relevant with regard to victims' participation. As noted by Zappalá, "One should not confuse the panoply of rights granted to victims under various branches of international law with their procedural rights in the international criminal justice system."[92] The right to truth and access to justice and the right to share their views and concerns does not translate into a right to always make oral submissions or comment upon all issues arising at trial.

Tied to the argument of recognizing the primacy of the minimum rights of the accused is the important notion of rejecting what Porat refers to as the balancing consciousness. Porat's theory in the field of constitutional law posits whether the balancing of individual rights and interests must always take place.[93] He terms the widespread acceptance of the rhetoric of 'balancing' rights, or the view that every problem can and should be solved through balancing conflicting considerations, as the 'balancing consciousness.' The widespread acceptance of the notion of balancing, which he asserts is shared by legal and non-legal thinkers, is misleading. He argues that it distorts the weight that should be afforded to various interests in law. In fact, balancing at times unnecessarily *elevates* certain rights, and at other times, unnecessarily *lowers* them, depending on the specific circumstances at hand.[94]

As Kress noted, international courts are implementing a *fundamental compromise formula*, where the judges determine the ultimate balance between competing adversarial and inquisitorial elements.[95] With regard to victim participation, the courts seem to have adopted a similar formula. Although the ECCC endorses a more restrictive approach and the ICC a less restrictive approach, they nonetheless speak about balancing the interests of victims with those of the other parties. However, as this study has shown, this 'balancing' rhetoric is largely misplaced. Edwards correctly points out that "[t]o speak of 'balance' assumes a duality of positions in diametric opposition," and it is inappropriate to view the position of victims and defendants in this way.[96]

Of course the Judges will need to balance the rights and interests of all parties and participants throughout a trial. However, any balancing of the minimum rights between the victims and accused should be premised on the notion that a defendant's fair trial rights must take precedence over victims' minimum participatory rights.[97] It is unclear why, but jurisprudence to date suggests that the Judges are reluctant to acknowledge the primacy of the rights of the accused. Even when they mention the rights of accused

92 Zappalá (2010) at 144.
93 See Porat (2005-2006).
94 See Edwards (2004).
95 Kress (2003) at 605.
96 Edwards (2004) at 972.
97 Jouet (2007) at 250; Zappalá (2010) at 140, 143.

in their decisions they do so in connection with broader court interests, making it less clear that the minimum rights of the accused take precedence. By failing to unequivocally uphold the minimum rights of the accused the courts diminish the protection of these fundamental rights.

Moreover, although equalizing victim and defendant rights may sound appealing for political purposes given the fact that "in the criminal justice debate, concern for the interests of victims of crime constitutes an almost unassailable moral position,"[98] it fails to take into the account the values of criminal justice systems.[99] Unquestionably, victims' interests and circumstances differ greatly from those of defendants in criminal trials. Victims have often suffered unimaginable harm and in addition to reparation they desire to know the truth about the circumstances giving rise to their harms suffered and to hold those individuals who are responsible to account. Defendants are concerned with the deprivation of their liberty and property at the hands of some central authority which accuses them of having committed a criminal act. They are concerned with receiving a fair trial such that the outcome will be correct and fair. While the concerns of victims are very important, they are far more inchoate. In addition, criminal trials are retributive institutions focusing on the crime committed rather than the harm suffered. Therefore, very often the balancing of rights and calls for equal treatment are inappropriate.

Equal rights are about equal treatment of the *similarly situated* and victims and defendants are not similarly situated.[100] Instead, when matters affecting an accused's minimum rights are at stake, there is a better way of thinking about victim-oriented reforms than in terms of 'counterbalancing'. This means that while providing for victims' rights, these rights should be narrowly tailored in order to ensure the minimum rights of defendants.

8.4.3 Focus on Services for Victims

Though this study concentrates on the procedural rights of victims in the criminal process, these rights are closely connected with important service-related rights. International courts should remain focused on their core objectives, but at the same time, the rights of victims, vis-à-vis criminal justice institutions, nonetheless need to be recognized. However, because active participation may not provide additional benefits, when striving to meet the minimum standards required by human rights in relation to victims, it is advisable for courts to focus on service-related rights. These service-related rights include increased victim support in the form of protective measures or medical and psychological services as well as information services. It may also mean strengthening outreach efforts and working together with local, restorative

98 Miers (1992) at 496.
99 O'Hear (2006b) at 86.
100 O'Hear (2006b) at 86; Mettraux (2008) at 77.

justice mechanisms. Indeed, of the three avenues pursued by the victims' rights movement, namely (1) one which aims at ameliorating the situation for victims without hampering the existing functioning of criminal courts; (2) one which works on elevating the status of victims before criminal courts by granting them certain procedural rights which would affect the functioning of criminal courts; and (3) one which advocates non-criminal proceedings with victim-centered approaches,[101] at the international level the first and third options should be taken up.

Respecting the dignity of victims and addressing their needs and concerns is not antithetical to respecting the rights of the accused. By emphasizing service-related rights for victims outside of the criminal trial instead of focusing on procedural rights in trial, victims will remain informed about developments in a case, will still be able to provide information to the court about crimes, will have access to or information about medical and psychological services and will have access to information about reparation processes. Additionally, courts can ensure that secondary victimization is minimized by creating separate spaces for victims attending trial and listening to their views and concerns. If an accused is found guilty then victims could be able to present, either orally or in written form, victim impact statements to the court. Portions of these statements, with the consent of the victim, can then be published and circulated by the court together with the judgment. Furthermore, victims can receive guidance about how best to pursue reparation claims either directly through the court or by having the court facilitate contact between the victim and an NGO dedicated to such issues. It is crucial that the courts should be able to provide victims with information about health care services available in their area and put them into contact with voluntary organizations and NGOs that perform various tasks for victims and victim communities.

All of these services concern the international criminal justice system although they focus on support, assistance and respect for victims who are dealing with the often harsh and confusing demands of the criminal process. These steps will ensure that the rights of the accused are at all times protected during the criminal trial process. At the same time victims will maintain narrowly tailored procedural rights, such as the right to submit complaints to the prosecution during the investigation stage and may even be able to bring specific concerns before a relevant chamber. The holistic approach argued by Groenhuijsen which focuses on participation, protection and reparation is still possible but with greater emphasis on services rather than direct participation in trial proceedings.

8.4.4 Embrace Pluralism

International criminal courts employing staff from many different legal systems benefit when a single set of legal standards and precedents applies. Therefore, within each self-contained institution uniformity and harmonization are desirable. However, the

101 Heikkilä (2004) at 35.

case for uniformity amongst international criminal institutions, based in large part on the values of normative development, are convincing only to a certain extent. Thus, although the struggle for consistency and uniformity has its place with regard to certain substantive criminal law matters, pluralism with respect to procedural law should welcome divergent approaches that take into account the specific characteristics of that court so long as minimum human rights standards are upheld.

There is no reason justifying why one approach adopted by the ICC, for instance, should dictate the procedural approach applied at other international criminal courts. In this sense, just as is the case in domestic legal systems, it is perfectly fine for victims before one international criminal court to not be granted the same procedural rights as victims before another international criminal court. And as Part II of this study has shown there is great variation amongst international criminal courts concerning their approach to victims' rights. Many of these differences should be embraced.

The pluralism that exists at the international level is healthy and procedural hegemony impractical. International criminal procedure does not require uniformity in practice. Instead, pluralism with regard to international criminal procedure, and particularly with regard to victim participation, should be appreciated.[102] In fact, the search for uniformity may be misguided. Procedural approaches to victim participation should be court-specific rather than uniform across courts. This is because there are few authoritative sources in international law on the extent of participation and there is strong disagreement about the parameters of participation at the domestic level.

Although there are those who argue that international criminal law (and procedure) should aim to enhance normative development because the field should act as a sort of model or best practice for domestic courts and in this sense seek to influence and promote reform in domestic criminal law procedures, in the case of victim participation there is simply no 'best practice' model. Rather, criminal procedure largely depends upon the specific circumstances and characteristics of the institution. The diversity amongst similarly modeled domestic systems with regard to victim participation is evidence of the fact that international courts should not necessarily strive to promote uniformity in this area.

8.5 Final Observations

Hannah Arendt, in her book *Eichmann in Jerusalem: A Report on the Banality of Evil*, argued that those prosecuting Eichmann failed to concentrate on the primary purpose of the trial, namely the individual criminal responsibility of the accused.[103] Instead, she found that the parties allowed victims to recount events not directly related to the indictment because it was history at the center of trial not the individual criminal

102 Cf. Marsten Danner (2005) at 96-97.
103 Arendt (1963) 9-10, 19, 225.

responsibility of the accused.[104] Victim-witnesses produced stories that were 'calculated to shock the heart,'[105] not so much to decide the individual criminal responsibility of the accused but rather to serve the interests of victims, both individually and collectively. Thus, she concluded that the trial had less to do with the accused and more to do with the collectivity of the victims. Though she ultimately approved of the final judgment because the court, and more precisely the presiding judge, resisted the temptation to further broaden the scope of the trial,[106] her observations are valuable. International criminal courts would be wise to resist the temptation to expand the scope of international criminal proceedings beyond that which they can deliver. Because the legal process is not always compatible with the notions of personal narratives and social memory, non-legal mechanisms are generally better suited to provide victim-oriented or restorative measures.

The practice of international criminal courts has, regrettably, indicated that the courts are still struggling to find the most appropriate way to afford victims their participatory rights in proceedings without compromising the primary role of the courts, the decision-making of the prosecutor and the rights of the accused. Participation can be valuable and is an important means through which to realize the rights of victims. However, it cannot be ignored that participation has led to the lengthening of already long trials, raised concerns about fair trial protections and the perceived impartiality of judges, and brought up questions about the disparate treatment of similarly situated victims. Hence, although the incorporation of victims' rights in international criminal proceedings was a well-intentioned attempt to address the perceived shortcomings of previous tribunals that for one reason or other failed to properly address victims' concerns, its effective and efficient implementation has nonetheless proven problematic.

Undoubtedly, the proper role for victims in international criminal justice will continue to be debated. Simply stated, there is no one best practice. However, the challenge for international criminal courts is to develop fairer and more efficient procedures. The promise of procedural justice demands that these institutions comply with minimum human rights standards while recognizing the specific characteristics of international criminal law in order to best determine the proper procedural role for victims.

---

104 *Ibid.* at 19.
105 Osiel (2000) at 15-16.
106 Arendt (1963) at 9, 253.

SAMENVATTING

In de moderne strafrechtspleging gaat de aandacht meestal uit naar het delict en de verdachte, en wordt er nauwelijks rekening gehouden met de positie van het slachtoffer. De nadruk op de verdachte in de strafrechtelijke procedure komt voort uit het feit dat het strafproces als primaire doelstelling heeft onderzoek te doen naar personen die verantwoordelijk worden gehouden voor strafbare feiten en hen te vervolgen, en de personen die schuldig worden bevonden te bestraffen. Derhalve legt het strafrechtelijk paradigma meer nadruk op het misdrijf en op de vraag of een individu daarvoor verantwoordelijk kan worden gehouden en hoe deze kan worden gestraft. In de afgelopen vijftig jaar is er echter, ondanks de minimale rol die aan slachtoffers wordt toebedeeld, verandering gekomen in de bijna exclusieve focus op de verdachte. Het idee ontstond dat slachtoffers meer rechten moesten krijgen binnen het strafrechtssysteem. Sociale bewegingen die zich bezighielden met slachtoffers van misdrijven begonnen zich te mobiliseren en de notie dat er meer aandacht zou moeten komen voor de slachtoffers van misdaden ontwikkelde zich langzamerhand tot wat bekend werd als de slachtofferrechtenbeweging (*victims' rights movement*). Deze beweging benadrukt dat slachtoffers direct geraakt worden door strafrechtelijke procedures en dat strafrechtssystemen daarom moeten worden aangepast om beter tegemoet te komen aan hun behoeften en belangen.

De slachtofferrechtenbeweging is een van de meest succesvolle politieke en sociale bewegingen in de recente geschiedenis. De beweging zet zich algemeen in voor verbeterde service-gerelateerde en procedurele rechten in de vorm van sterkere bescherming van, participatie van en schadevergoeding voor slachtoffers. Onder service-gerelateerde rechten wordt onder andere verstaan de ondersteuning van slachtoffers in vorm van beschermende maatregelen, medische en psychologische hulp en informatievoorziening. Procedurele rechten bieden meer inspraak bij besluitvormingsprocessen en voorzien in de mogelijkheid om schadevergoeding te eisen. De slachtofferrechtenbeweging heeft vooral succes geboekt in het beïnvloeden van het strafrechtelijk beleid, waardoor de rechten van slachtoffers in toenemende mate worden opgevat als mensenrechten. Het succes van de beweging is enerzijds te te verklaren door de vele voorvechters van slachtofferrechten en anderzijds, door het gemakkelijk te aanvaarden beeld van 'goede' slachtoffers en 'slechte' verdachten, hetgeen leidt tot een sterkere vraag naar gelijke procedurele rechten voor verdachten en slachtoffers. Op nationaal niveau is er inderdaad opgeroepen tot een 'evenwichtige afweging' van de rechten van slachtoffers en verdachten in strafrechtelijke procedures. Er bestaan echter verschillende praktijken zowel op nationaal als op internationaal niveau en het is niet duidelijk wat de omvang van slachtofferrechten zou moeten zijn.

Het valt bovendien te betwisten of een evenwichtige verdeling van procedurele rechten tussen slachtoffers en verdachten wel juist is.

Begin 2006 riep de Hoge Commissaris voor de Rechten van de Mens (*Office of the High Commissioner for Human Rights*) op tot nader onderzoek naar internationale normen en naar de nationale en internationale rechtspraktijk betreffende de rol van slachtoffers in strafzaken. Geïnspireerd door deze oproep gaat dit onderzoek in op slachtofferparticipatie in internationale strafzaken. In tegenstelling tot het merendeel van het onderzoek dat is gewijd aan slachtoffers in het strafproces, wordt slachtofferparticipatie in dit onderzoek niet vanuit het perspectief van de slachtoffers benaderd, behalve voorzover hun participatierechten worden erkend als een vorm van mensenrechten. In plaats daarvan is het doel van dit onderzoek in te gaan op slachtofferparticipatie in internationale strafzaken vanuit het perspectief van mensenrechten en strafrecht, en niet vanuit het perspectief van slachtoffers. Deze benadering houdt rekening met de rol en de rechten van alle individuen die betrokken zijn in een internationaal strafrechtelijke procedure en leidt tot het onderscheiden van duidelijk aanwijsbare en toepasselijke normen. De centrale onderzoeksvraag is als volgt geformuleerd: binnen de karakteristieken van het internationaal strafrecht en de normen van de rechten van de mens, wat zou de juiste omvang en inhoud van slachtofferparticipatie in internationale strafzaken moeten zijn.

Het streven is dat de uitkomsten van dit onderzoek bij zullen dragen aan een beter begrip van de conflicterende rechten in het internationaal strafrecht, en dat de partijen die betrokken zijn bij het vormgeven van het internationaal strafrecht van een goed instrument worden voorzien om inzicht te verkrijgen in de participatierechten van slachtoffers. De drie doelstellingen van dit onderzoek zijn: (i) het beschrijven, uitleggen en verhelderen van de procedurele rol die slachtoffers hebben in internationale strafzaken; (ii) het evalueren of de huidige benaderingen van slachtofferparticipatie in internationale strafzaken stroken met de normen van de rechten van de mens; en (iii) het bepalen van de juiste reikwijdte en inhoud van slachtofferparticipatie in internationale strafzaken. Om de analyse te structureren, richt het onderzoek zich op twee centrale concepten: (i) de unieke eigenschappen van internationale strafzaken en (ii) de normen van de rechten van de mens. De dataverzameling voor dit onderzoek is gebaseerd op uiteenlopende bronnen van mensenrechten en internationale strafvordering. Aangezien dit onderzoek zicht richt op de procedures van internationale straftribunalen, is ten eerste een gedetailleerde analyse gemaakt van de statuten en regels van strafvordering en bewijsvoering van de verschillende tribunalen. Ten tweede zijn verdragen, conventies, internationaal gewoonterecht, algemene rechtsbeginselen, jurisprudentie en andere documenten uit de dossiers, evenals wetenschappelijke literatuur bestudeerd. Ten slotte zijn interviews gehouden en heeft observatie plaatsgevonden.

Als deel van het internationaal recht kan het internationaal strafrecht worden gedefinieerd als het rechtsgebied waarin individuele strafrechtelijke verantwoordelijkheid wordt vastgesteld bij ernstige inbreuken op het internationaal publiekrecht. Internationaal strafrecht wordt in het bijzonder ontwikkeld en gehandhaafd door internationale straftribunalen. Ingegeven door grove schendingen van de rechten van de mens en het humanitaire recht, zijn verschillende internationale tribunalen opgericht om straffeloosheid te bestrijden en individuen verantwoordelijk te stellen voor schendingen van het internationaal strafrecht. Hoewel deze straftribunalen in opzet verschillen, bestaat er een aantal karakteristieken die uniek zijn voor internationale strafzaken, waarmee ze zich onderscheiden van nationale strafzaken. Dit onderzoek richt zich op de volgende karakteristieken: het aspect van massa slachtofferschap in internationale strafzaken, de samenstelling en structuur van de internationale tribunalen en de financiële en praktische beperkingen waar deze tribunalen mee kampen. Het samenstel van deze factoren betekent meestal dat slechts een klein aantal zaken kan worden behandeld. Internationale straftribunalen zijn niet opgericht om een groot aantal individuen te berechten. Integendeel, het doel is om selectief vervolging in te stellen tegen diegenen die het meest verantwoordelijk worden geacht voor ernstige misdaden. Deze selectieve vervolging betekent dat niet alle klachten over misdaden tot vervolging kunnen leiden, wat weer betekent dat niet alle slachtoffers van ernstige misdaden zullen worden gehoord.

In combinatie met de karakteristieken van het internationaal strafrecht biedt het stelsel van mensenrechten een uitstekend interpretatie-instrument voor het verklaren en analyseren van de procedurele rechten van personen in internationale strafzaken. In het recht kan het gebruik van de term 'rechten van de mens' terug worden geleid naar het VN Handvest (*UN Charter*) en het begrip van de inherente menselijke waardigheid als fundamenteel en universeel recht, dat overheden ten aanzien van ieder individu dienen te respecteren en te beschermen. Sinds het vaststellen van het VN Handvest en de Universele Verklaring van de Rechten van de Mens van 1948 (*Universal Declaration of Human Rights*; *UDHR*) is een internationaal systeem ontstaan voor het bevorderen en beschermen van de rechten van de mens. Met name in strafprocedures, waarin individuen (zowel verdachten als slachtoffers) rechten hebben tegenover de overheid, is bescherming van de rechten van de mens van uitzonderlijk belang. Bovendien overstijgt, met de ontwikkeling van het internationaal strafrecht, de bescherming van de rechten van de mens in strafzaken de traditionele staat-individu verhouding.

Dit onderzoekt bestudeert welke algemeen geaccepteerde mensenrechtennorm met betrekking tot slachtofferparticipatie zou moeten worden toegepast door internationale straftribunalen en hoe participatie vorm gegeven zou moeten worden wanneer participatienormen botsen met andere mensenrechtennormen zoals het recht op een eerlijk proces. Deze analyse bouwt daarbij ook voort op de theorie van Iddo Porat op het gebied van het constitutioneel recht, waarin hij de vraag stelt of individuele rechten en belangen tegen elkaar moeten worden afgewogen. Hij verwijst naar de wijdverspreide acceptatie van de retoriek van het 'afwegen' van rechten als het '*balancing consciousness*' ('afwegende bewustzijn') of het standpunt dat ieder probleem kan en moet worden opgelost door tegengestelde aspecten af te wegen. Deze zienswijze, waarvan Porat stelt dat hij wordt gedeeld door zowel juristen als niet-juristen, is misleidend. *Balancing consciousness* verstoort het gewicht dat aan verschillende belangen in het recht dient te worden toegekend, waardoor bepaalde rechten soms onnodig *hoger* en soms onnodig *lager* worden geplaatst, afhankelijk van de zaak en het soort recht.

In dit onderzoek verwijzen mensenrechtennormen allereerst naar het recht op een eerlijk proces en daarvan afgeleide rechten zoals deze voorkomen in mensenrechteninstrumenten en in documenten van internationale strafrechttribunalen. Hoewel er niet één specifieke internationale conventie bestaat met betrekking tot internationale normen en beginselen van een eerlijk proces in strafzaken, bestaat er wel een verzameling internationale en regionale conventies die voorzien in garanties voor een eerlijk proces. De belangrijkste internationale mensenrechteninstrumenten, zowel bindend als niet-bindend, die expliciet voorzien in bescherming van een eerlijk proces zijn onder andere: de Universele Verklaring van de Rechten van de Mens (*Universal Declaration on Human Rights*; Art. 10, 11); het Internationaal Verdrag inzake Burgerrechten en Politieke Rechten (*International Covenant on Civil and Political Rights*; Art. 9, 14, 15); het Europees Verdrag tot Bescherming van de Rechten van de Mens en de Fundamentele Vrijheden (*European Convention on the Protection of Human Rights and Fundamental Freedoms*; Art. 5, 6, 7); het Amerikaans Verdrag inzake de Rechten van de Mens (*American Convention on Human Rights*; Art. 7, 8, 9); en het Afrikaans Handvest inzake de Rechten van de Mens en Volken (*African Charter on Human and People's Rights*; Art. 3, 6, 7). Deze internationale mensenrechteninstrumenten zijn gebaseerd op liberale theorieën en waarden. In het liberale model wordt de overheid gezien als vele malen machtiger dan haar burgers. De macht van de overheid dient te worden beperkt om rechten van burgers te garanderen. De noodzaak van deze beperkingen is met name van belang in het strafrecht, waarin overheden substantiële macht uitoefenen over het individu. Omdat een individu gemarginaliseerd en impopulair kan zijn, zullen strafrechtelijke procedures moeten voldoen aan strikte waarborgen voor een eerlijk proces, om zo de inherente machtsverschillen te verkleinen. Liberale waarden voorzien derhalve specifiek in rechten van de verdachte en bevorderen deze in de strafrechtelijke procedure.

Dit onderzoek richt zich op het principe van '*equality of arms*' en het rechtszekerheidsbeginsel, omdat deze aspecten van het recht op een eerlijk proces het meest botsen met het recht op participatie van slachtoffers. Hoewel ook andere rechtsbeginselen worden beïnvloed wanneer het slachtoffer betrokken is bij strafzaken, zijn deze twee beginselen nauw verwant aan mensenrechtennormen inzake eerlijkheid in de procedure en spelen ze een steeds prominentere rol in jurisprudentie en wetenschappelijke literatuur over slachtofferparticipatie. Bovendien verwijzen mensenrechtennormen ook naar participatierechten van slachtoffers in het strafrecht voor zover deze rechten kunnen worden beschouwd als een beschermd mensenrecht. Zoals geldt voor de rechten van de verdachte en garanties voor een eerlijk proces in strafzaken, richten mensenrechteninstrumenten zich ook op de relatie tussen slachtoffers en de overheid. Overheden hebben verplichtingen ten opzichte van slachtoffers en slachtoffers hebben in toenemende mate afdwingbare rechten in strafrechtelijke procedures. Zo worden staten in een aantal internationale en regionale documenten opgeroepen, zowel expliciet als impliciet, tot het versterken van de positie van slachtoffers in strafrechtelijke procedures en zelfs het verstrekken van procedurele rechten van slachtoffers in strafzaken.

Dit onderzoek bestaat uit twee hoofddelen. Deel I (hoofdstuk 2-4) behandelt de oorsprong en huidige rol van slachtoffers in de nationale rechtsgang en de ontwikkeling van hun procedurele rechten op nationaal en internationaal niveau. Deel II (hoofdstuk 5-7) gaat uitsluitend in de participatierechten van slachtoffers bij internationale strafrechtelijke instellingen. Hoofdstuk 8, ten slotte, presenteert conclusies en aanbevelingen.

Het onderliggende thema van dit onderzoek is het strafrecht in het algemeen en het internationaal strafrecht in het bijzonder. Strafrechtstheorieën vormen daarom een belangrijke achtergrond voor een goed begrip van de huidige (en toekomstige) rol van slachtoffers in strafzaken. Strafrechtstheorieën *verklaren* de doelstellingen van strafrechtelijke systemen en geven *vorm* aan de manier waarop strafrechtelijke systemen werken in de maatschappij. Hoofdstuk 2 verkent daarom de belangrijkste theoretische kaders van het strafrecht, die de rollen van verdachten en slachtoffers belichten.

Hoofdstuk 2 gaat allereerst in op de traditionele theorieën, waaronder de vergeldingstheorie en het utilitarisme. Vergeldingstheorieën stellen over het algemeen dat schuldig bevonden wetsovertreders dienen te worden gestraft, met het idee van het 'verdiende loon'. Om te garanderen dat alleen diegenen die straf verdienen ook worden gestraft, legt de vergeldingstheorie grote nadruk op de rechten van de verdachte op een eerlijk proces. Aanhangers van de vergeldingstheorie richten zich bovendien niet op het subjectieve lijden van de slachtoffers. De aandacht gaat juist naar de objectieve elementen van het delict, om te vermijden dat daders in vergelijkbare omstandigheden verschillende straffen krijgen. Ten gevolge hiervan krijgen slachtoffers geen prominente rol in rechtszaken, en functioneren zij alleen als hulp voor de rechters door informatie te verschaffen aan de hand waarvan de schuld van de verdachte kan worden vastgesteld. Het utilitarisme beschouwt het strafrecht als een geschikt middel voor een gerechtvaardigd doel en ziet afschrikking, preventie, correctie en/of gevangenisstraf als de voornaamste doelen van de strafrechtelijke procedure. In het utilitarisme mogen rechten van individuen voor het algemeen goed worden gemarginaliseerd. Slachtoffers spelen daarom niet per se een centrale rol in rechtszaken omdat de belangen van de maatschappij of zelfs de belangen van de dader boven die van het slachtoffer kunnen worden geplaatst.

In geen van de twee traditionele theorieën die de rechtspraktijk momenteel het sterkst beïnvloeden wordt een prominente plaats gegeven aan slachtoffers, wat heeft geleid tot vragen over het doel van het strafrecht en wie ervan dient te profiteren. Hoofdstuk 2 gaat daarom in op wat slachtoffers zelf wensen van het strafrechtelijk systeem en behandelt restoratieve strafrechtstheorieën, die ernaar streven in te gaan op de behoeften en belangen van slachtoffers. De restoratieve theorie verlegt de nadruk van de begane misdaden naar het berokkende leed, en streeft naar actieve participatie van slachtoffers, daders, gezinnen en gemeenschappen om de oorzaken en gevolgen van een misdaad effectief aan te pakken. Het restorativisme is veelomvattend en veel modellen zijn ontwikkeld op nationaal niveau, waaronder modellen die streven naar een combinatie van een vorm van de traditionele strafrechtstheorieën met modernere restoratieve praktijken. Nadruk wordt gelegd op het feit dat restoratieve strafrechtsprocedures bijna altijd alleen effectief kunnen werken nadat de verdachte schuldig is bevonden, de verdachte zijn schuld erkend heeft of de basale onderliggende feiten van de misdaad heeft aanvaard. Door deze onderliggende vooronderstelling, kan de autonome participatie van slachtoffers in rechtszaken een concrete manier bieden om emotioneel lijden te uiten, maar het maakt een procedure niet noodzakelijkerwijs restoratief. Het is daarom belangrijk onderscheid te maken tussen procedurele rechten van slachtoffers in strafzaken en een restoratieve rechtsprocedure. Met andere woorden, slachtoffers kunnen uitgebreide procedurele rechten krijgen binnen een traditioneel strafrechtssysteem zonder dat dit systeem meteen een restoratief systeem hoeft te zijn.

De theoretische basis van het strafrecht dient te worden bekeken tegen de achtergrond van wat er nou werkelijk plaatsvindt met betrekking tot de wetgeving in het strafrecht, de strafrechtelijke praktijk en de maatschappij waarin deze functioneren. Hoofdstuk 3 gaat daarom in op de dominante rechtstradities en strafvorderingsbenaderingen die internationale strafzaken het sterkst hebben beïnvloed. Dit hoofdstuk besteedt bovendien aandacht aan de verschillende benaderingen van academici aangaande het onderzoek naar verschillende rechtstradities, waaronder het invloedrijke werk van Herbert Packer, Mirjan Damaška en Richard Vogler. In dit hoofdstuk worden ook vormen van participatie zoals beschreven door Sherry R. Arnstein en Ian Edwards behandeld. Arnstein's participatieladder, de *Ladder of Citizen Participation*, die werd ontworpen in verband met stadsplanning, beschrijft een indeling van 'leeg ritueel' naar werkelijke beslisbevoegdheden. Edwards bouwt voort op haar werk en beschrijft een typologie van participatie in het strafrechtssysteem. Hij stelt dat rechtbanken slachtoffers een stem kunnen geven, informatie van slachtoffers kunnen inwinnen en in overweging nemen, voorkeuren van slachtoffers kunnen nagaan en overwegen, en voorkeuren van slachtoffers kunnen nagaan en toepassen. Participatie wordt daarom onderverdeeld in expressie (stem geven), informatie, raadpleging en beheersing. Vervolgens gaat Hoofdstuk 3 in op bestaande participatiemodellen. Dit onderzoek is geen studie naar bepaalde nationale rechtssystemen en de rol die slachtoffers daarin hebben, maar het legt de nadruk op de verschillende archetypen van participatie die in veel rechtssystemen bestaan. De participatiemodellen omvatten: het slachtoffer als (i) eiser; (ii) getuige; (iii) civiele partij; (iv) particuliere aanklager of hulpaanklager; en (v) verschaffer van een slachtofferverklaring. Verbonden met de belangrijkste procedurele benaderingen sluiten deze modellen elkaar niet onderling uit en kunnen zij elkaar complementeren. Bovendien zijn deze versimpelde modellen een illustratie van de grote variatie in participatierechten die slachtoffers kunnen hebben in nationale strafzaken.

Hoofdstuk 4 beschrijft de toenemende aandacht voor slachtofferparticipatie op internationaal niveau met betrekking tot participatie in nationale strafzaken. De nadruk op slachtofferparticipatie op internationaal niveau heeft voorzien in een ruime norm waaraan overheden en internationale straftribunalen zouden moeten proberen te voldoen. In 1985 hebben overheden consensus bereikt over de algemene rechten van slachtoffers in strafzaken door het vaststellen van de *United Nations Declaration of Basic Principles of Justice for Victims of Crime and Abuse of Power* (*Victims' Declaration;* VN Declaratie). De VN Declaratie was het eerste VN instrument dat uitsluitend was gewijd aan de rechten van slachtoffers en het eerste waarin werd opgeroepen tot slachtofferparticipatie in nationale strafzaken. De rechten die in deze niet-bindende verklaring worden erkend vertegenwoordigen zowel de service-gerelateerde als de procedurele rechten die de slachtofferrechtenbeweging nastreeft en houden verband met hun doelstelling om meer rechten te verwerven op het gebied van bescherming, participatie en schadevergoeding voor slachtoffers. Artikel 6(b) van de VN Declaratie roept overheden op ervoor te zorgen dat de standpunten en belangen van slachtoffers kunnen worden weergegeven en in overweging worden genomen in de relevante stadia van gerechtelijke procedures waarin hun persoonlijke belangen gemoeid zijn, zonder afbreuk te doen aan de rechten van de verdachte en in overeenstemming met het betreffende nationale strafrechtssysteem. In ruime bewoordingen dient Artikel 6(b) als herinnering aan overheden dat zij de plicht hebben om open te staan voor de behoeften en belangen van slachtoffers in gerechtelijke procedures. Net als de VN Declaratie, wijzen de *UN Basic Principles and Guidelines on the Right to a Remedy and Reparation for Victims of Gross Violations of International Human Rights Law and Serious Violations of International Humanitarian Law* (VN Richtlijnen inzake herstelmaatregelen), hoewel ze niet specifiek oproepen tot participatie, ook op het belang van participatie door nadruk te leggen op gelijke en effectieve toegang tot de rechter, adequate, effectieve en onmiddellijke schadevergoeding en het recht op de waarheid. Deze twee VN documenten illustreren samen het belang van het opnemen van slachtofferrechten in rechtssystemen.

In navolging van Artikel 6(b) van de VN Declaratie, is op regionaal niveau in Europa en Afrika gehoor gegeven aan de oproep om slachtoffers de kans te geven hun standpunten en belangen te presenteren in de relevante stadia van de strafzaak. De Raad van Europa en de Europese Unie hebben beide pogingen ondernomen om meer duidelijkheid te scheppen met betrekking tot de noodzaak slachtoffers een middel te verschaffen waarmee zij in de strafrechtelijke procedure kunnen participeren. Het EU Kaderbesluit (*European Union's Framework Decision*) is voor de lidstaten bindend en verplicht hen om hun strafvorderingswetgeving in overeenstemming te brengen met de op het slachtoffer gerichte hervormingen. Ook de Commissie van de Afrikaanse Unie (*African Commission on Human and Peoples' Rights*) streeft naar de bevordering van rechten van slachtoffers in strafzaken middels niet-bindende beginselen.

Naast de genoemde VN verklaringen en initiatieven op regionaal niveau, erkennen internationale mensenrechtenorganen verschillende rechten van slachtoffers van misdaden met de bijbehorende verplichtingen voor overheden. De regionale mensenrechtenverdragen, bevatten geen expliciete bepalingen over de rechten van slachtoffers, maar leggen juist specifiek nadruk op de rechten van de verdachte in de strafrechtelijke procedure. Sinds de opkomst van de slachtofferrechtenbeweging begin jaren zeventig, is er in de regionale mensenrechtensystemen een verschuiving gaande van de verdachte naar het slachtoffer. Een grote aanjager van deze verschuiving vormden de misdaden die door overheden in Latijns Amerika in de jaren tachtig zijn gepleegd. De context waarin deze misdrijven plaatsvonden stelde het liberale model op de proef. De nationale strafrechtssystemen beschermden vaak overheidsfunctionarissen die van misdaden werden beschuldigd, en boden de slachtoffers geen gerechtigheid. Verdachten werden niet politiek gemarginaliseerd, maar werden afgeschermd om onderzoek en vervolging door andere overheidsinstanties te voorkomen. Het Inter-Amerikaans Hof voor de Rechten van de Mens (*Inter-American Court of Human Rights*) nam de taak op zich dit misstand aan te pakken. Bij het uitvoeren van deze taak, heeft het Hof solide rechtspraak opgebouwd aangaande de rechten van slachtoffers.

Uit jurisprudentie van de verschillende mensenrechtenorganen blijkt dat de belangrijkste mensenrechtenverdragen voorzien in ruime rechten voor het individu en verplichtingen voor de overheid. Op basis van het recht op een effectief rechtsmiddel en het recht op toegang tot de rechter hebben de mensenrechtenorganen geconcludeerd dat overheden de plicht hebben om mensenrechtenschendingen te onderzoeken, te vervolgen en te bestraffen. Hoewel de plicht tot vervolging oorspronkelijk werd beschouwd als verplichting tegenover de gemeenschap en niet als een verplichting die door een individueel persoon kon worden afgedwongen, komt uit de jurisprudentie van deze instanties op dat punt een verschuiving naar voren. De mensenrechtenorganen hebben bepaald dat slachtoffers ruimere toegang dienen te krijgen tot de strafrechtelijke procedure om ervoor te zorgen dat onderzoek en vervolging effectief plaatsvinden. De door mensenrechtenorganen onderschreven procedurele rechten omvatten het recht op informatie, het recht om gehoord te worden (om opvattingen en bezorgdheid te uiten), het recht op juridische bijstand en het recht op schadevergoeding. De twee regionale systemen hebben ieder een eigen stijl, maar streven naar hetzelfde resultaat: rechtspraak die sterker slachtoffergeoriënteerd is. Het Inter-Amerikaanse Hof volgt een directe aanpak, en volgt hiermee de algemene tendens binnen de mensenrechten om meer nadruk te leggen op de rechten van slachtoffers, wat vaak ten koste gaat van de rechten van de verdachte. Het Europees Hof streeft er op zijn beurt naar conflicten met de liberale benadering (van een eerlijk proces) te vermijden, maar erkent ook uitgebreide rechten van slachtoffers in strafrechtelijke procedures. Als gevolg van deze verschuiving worden in de jurisprudentie van de regionale mensenrechtenorganen bepalingen zo geïnterpreteerd dat deze voor overheden de plicht behelzen slachtoffers participatierechten te geven in strafrechtelijke procedures. Hierbij ligt de nadruk op de rol van slachtoffers in het onderzoek en hun recht op het eisen van schadevergoeding.

Hoofdstuk 4 sluit af met de bevinding dat de toegenomen erkenning van procedurele en materiële rechten van slachtoffers verontrustend is, omdat deze rechten vaak botsen met het traditionele liberale mensenrechtenmodel dat de nadruk legt op de rechten van verdachten op een eerlijk proces. Hoewel het erkennen van rechten van slachtoffers in de mensenrechten positieve aspecten heeft, is het ook belangrijk om te erkennen dat inconsistenties de algemene indruk van rechtvaardigheid zullen ondermijnen.

Waar Deel I de nationale aspecten behandelt, beschrijft Deel II van dit onderzoek uitsluitend internationale strafrechtelijke instellingen. Zoals nationale systemen hun procedures, hetzij vooral inquisitoir hetzij accusatoir, hebben aangepast aan de toenemende rechten van slachtoffers, hebben ook internationale straftribunalen dat gedaan. Alvorens in te gaan op de twee voornaamste casestudies, beschrijft Hoofdstuk 5 de participatierechten die slachtoffers hebben bij veel van de internationale straftribunalen. Er wordt ingegaan op de militaire tribunalen van Neurenberg en Tokio, het Joegoslavië-tribunaal (*International Criminal Tribunal for the former Yugoslavia*; *ICTY)* en het Rwanda-tribunaal (*International Criminal Tribunal for Rwanda*; *ICTR*) (samen de ad hoc tribunalen), het Speciaal Hof voor Sierra Leone (*Special Court for Sierra Leone*; *SCSL*), het Tribunaal voor Oost-Timor (*Special War Crimes Panels in East Timor*; *SPSC*), de UNMIK/EULEX tribunalen in Kosovo en het Libanon-Tribunaal (*Special Tribunal for Lebanon*; *STL*).

Bij de militaire tribunalen van Neurenberg en Tokio traden slachtoffers alleen op als getuige. Voor het grootste deel geldt dit ook voor het ICTY, het ICTR en het SCSL, hoewel deze tribunalen sterker leunden op getuigenverklaringen dan de militaire tribunalen van Neurenberg en Tokio. Daarnaast dienden de aanklagers het bij de ad hoc tribunalen en het SCSL slachtofferverklaringen (*victim impact statements*) in, welke bij de strafbepaling kunnen worden gebruikt als vast onderdeel in de procedure, Het SCSL functioneerde bovendien naast de waarheids- en verzoeningscommissie van Sierra Leone die misschien een betere positie had om kennis te nemen van de verhalen van slachtoffers, als onderdeel van het overgangsproces in het rechtssysteem. Ondanks de vele grote successen van deze tribunalen bij het vervolgen van personen voor internationale misdaden, blijven twee belangrijke punten van kritiek steeds terugkeren. Het eerste draait om de rechten van de verdachte op een eerlijk proces, met name in relatie tot de duur van de procedure en de kosten die met langlopende rechtszaken gepaard gaan. Het tweede draait om de behandeling van slachtoffers door de tribunalen en het gebrek aan service-gerelateerde en procedurele rechten in de procedure.

Efficiëntie en eerlijke behandeling van de verdachte vormden de voornaamste reden om de rechten van slachtoffers bij de *ad-hoc* tribunalen in te perken. Deze beperkte rol lijkt op de rol van slachtoffers in traditioneel accusatoire rechtssystemen. Hoewel deze tribunalen ook inquisitoire elementen hanteerden, maakten hun algemeen accusatoire lijn het moeilijk om slachtoffers onderdeel te laten uitmaken van de procedure. Bij de hybride tribunalen die in Oost-Timor en Kosovo werden ingesteld lukte het echter wel om intensievere slachtofferparticipatie onderdeel te maken van hun werkwijze, deels doordat de procedures nauwer zijn afgestemd op inquisitoire systemen. Slechts weinig slachtoffers participeerden in de zaken bij deze tribunalen. Het minimale gebruik van slachtofferparticipatievoorzieningen bij deze tribunalen werd waarschijnlijk veroorzaakt door een aantal verschillende factoren, onder andere door een slecht begrip van of wantrouwen jegens de strafrechtelijke procedures, gebrekkige inspanningen vanuit de tribunalen om slachtoffers te bereiken en de angst een zaak te verliezen en op te draaien voor de proceskosten.

Net als de SPSC en de tribunalen in Kosovo, volgt het STL ook een grotendeels inquisitoire procedure en voorziet het in slachtofferparticipatie in zijn strafzaken. Het STL streeft er echter naar participatie zodanig te beperken dat eerlijkheid en efficiëntie in de rechtszaken gewaarborgd zijn. De behoedzame benadering van het STL is waarschijnlijk een reactie op problemen die zich voordeden bij het Cambodja-Tribunaal (*Extraordinary Chambers in the Courts of Cambodia*; *ECCC*) en het Internationaal Strafhof (*International Criminal Court*; *ICC*), die het STL voorgingen.

Anders dan de internationale tribunalen die in Hoofdstuk 5 worden beschreven, waar slachtoffers ofwel beperkte procedurele rechten kregen ofwel uitgebreide rechten kregen maar hiervan geen volledig gebruik maakten, worden in Hoofdstuk 6 en 7 uitgebreide casestudies gepresenteerd van de ECCC en ICC. Op basis van jurisprudentie (tot 1 februari 2011), illustreren deze casestudies de verschillende manieren waarop twee internationale tribunalen – verschillend in structuur en functioneren maar vergelijkbaar in de toepassing van ruime slachtofferparticipatievoorzieningen en beide met een groot aantal slachtoffers dat hun rechten wilde uitoefenen – slachtofferparticipatie hebben benaderd. De keuze om uitgebreid in te gaan op deze twee casestudies is ingegeven door de substantiële hoeveelheid jurisprudentie van deze tribunalen op het gebied van slachtofferparticipatie. Bovendien neemt de hoeveelheid wetenschappelijke literatuur over de tribunalen en de wijze waarop de tribunalen omgaan met slachtoffers toe, waardoor slachtofferparticipatie op internationaal niveau beter kan worden bestudeerd.

Het verantwoordingsproces dat in Cambodja vorm kreeg door het onderzoek naar en de vervolging van voormalige kopstukken van de Rode Khmer en anderen die de het meest verantwoordelijk worden gehouden voor ernstige misdaden is uniek ten opzichte van alle eerdergenoemde internationale strafrechtprocedures. De ECCC is een hybride straftribunaal dat nationale en internationale elementen combineert ten aanzien van toepasselijk recht en de medewerkers. Het duale karakter van het tribunaal, tussen de VN en de Cambodjaanse regering, heeft zeker een nieuwe dimensie toegevoegd aan de strafzaken, met twee *co-prosecutors* ('co-aanklagers'), twee *co-defence lawyers* ('co-verdedigers'), en recentelijk ook twee *co-lead lawyers* ('co-advocaten') die civiele partijen vertegenwoordigen in het proces. Door Cambodja's Frans-koloniale verleden, dat in de huidige nationale strafwetgeving nog steeds prominent aanwezig is, is het tribunaal grotendeels gebaseerd op een inquisitoire benadering van het strafproces. De ECCC is dan ook het eerste tribunaal waarin een groot aantal slachtoffers actief in de rechtszaak participeert als civiele partij.

De participatierechten van slachtoffers worden uiteengezet in de Interne Regels (*Internal Rules*), die door de rechters zijn opgesteld en voortdurend worden aangepast. Deze Regels vormen de meest gezaghebbende bron van procedureel recht bij het Cambodja-Tribunaal, en de bepalingen over de participatie van civiele partijen lijken erg op de bepalingen die normaal ook voorkomen in het Cambodjaanse nationale strafrechtssysteem. Op een aantal punten verschillen ze echter van de nationale praktijk, zoals in het soort schadevergoeding dat kan worden geëist en de mogelijkheid om een zelf gekozen raadsman in de rechtszaak te laten participeren. De verschillen tussen de procedures bij de ECCC en die in het nationale systeem zijn bedoeld om de rechtszaken efficiënt te laten verlopen door rekening te houden met de unieke eigenschappen van internationale strafzaken.

Zaak 001, ofwel de *zaak-Duch*, was de eerste internationale strafzaak waarin een groot aantal slachtoffers werd toegelaten als civiele partij. Onder de derde herziening van de Interne Regels mochten civiele partijen een aantal participatierechten uitoefenen. In het vooronderzoek konden civiele partijen een verzoek indienen bij de *Co-Investigating Judges* ('co-onderzoeksrechters') om specifiek onderzoek te verrichten, konden zij deelnemen aan de confrontaties met de verdachte of andere getuigen, en konden zij aanwezig zijn bij en participeren in hoorzittingen tijdens het vooronderzoek en beroepzittingen over bevelen tot bewaring. Tijdens de rechtszaak zelf hadden civiele partijen ook verscheidene rechten. Via hun advocaten mochten zij een lijst van getuigen indienen die door het Tribunaal zouden moeten worden opgeroepen (hoewel veel van de voorgestelde getuigen werden geweigerd), mochten zij door het Tribunaal gehoorde getuigen ondervragen, bewijs aanvoeren en betwisten aangaande de schuld van de verdachte en met betrekking tot schadevergoeding, konden zij geschriften indienen over wetgeving en feiten, civiele partijen oproepen om verklaring zonder eed af te leggen, eindpleidooi houden en collectieve en morele schadevergoeding eisen. Wat de civiele partijen echter niet was toegestaan was het houden van een openingpleidooi, het eisen van individuele schadevergoeding, het presenteren van conclusies ten aanzien van straftoemeting, of het ondervragen van karaktergetuigen van de verdachte. Ondanks deze beperkingen, die leidden tot een tijdelijke boycot van de zaak door een aantal van de slachtoffers, probeerden de vier juridische teams die uit Cambodjaanse en internationale advocaten bestonden en de 94 civiele partijen vertegenwoordigden, uitgebreid gebruik te maken van hun rechten. De rechter en andere waarnemers van de procesgang stelden echter vast dat actieve participatie van slachtoffers problemen veroorzaakte.

Het was duidelijk dat de vier juridische teams die de civiele partijen vertegenwoordigden verschillende opvattingen hadden over hun rol in de strafzaak. Dit verschil in benadering had grotendeels te maken met het feit dat de internationale advocaten verschillende achtergronden hadden. Naast het brede spectrum aan zienswijzen binnen de juridische teams voor de civiele partijen was er tijdens de rechtszaak zelf nog een ander terugkerend probleem: het repetitief ondervragen door de advocaten van de civiele partijen. Dit repetitief ondervragen was een van een aantal elementen die de strafzaak lang deed voortduren. Ook hieraan gerelateerd waren de klachten van de verdediging, die stelde dat de verdachte zich moest verdedigen tegenover meerdere aanklagers – een totaal van tien advocaten. Op het moment van de uitspraak, toen de Kamer van berechting aan twintig civiele partijen hun status als civiele partij ontnam, kwamen nog meer aspecten naar voren met betrekking tot de slachtofferparticipatie. Door het opstellen van nieuwe criteria voor het opnieuw beoordelen van participatie-aanvragen van civiele partijen, legde het Tribunaal bijzonder strenge eisen op; dit nadat de civiele partijen hun participatierechten al hadden uitgeoefend.

Nadat *Zaak 001* was afgerond, werden er opvallende veranderingen doorgevoerd aangaande de participatie van civiele partijen. De belangrijkste hiervan waren het aanstellen van twee *co-lead lawyers* om de collectieve belangen van civiele partijen tijdens de rechtszaak te behartigen en het instellen van de eis dat alle vaststellingen ten aanzien van civiele partijen plaatsvinden voordat de rechtszaak begint. Deze veranderingen waren ingegeven door de kennelijke tekortkomingen van *Zaak 001*, die anders een directe invloed zouden hebben gehad op *Zaak 002* die vele malen complexer is: met vier verdachten en meer dan vier duizend aanvragen voor participatie als civiele partij. Er wordt vanuit gegaan dat deze veranderingen de vertragingen tijdens de rechtszaak tot een minimum zullen beperken, en bovendien de onzekerheid zoals ervaren door de civiele partijen in *Zaak 001* en de problemen rond de eerlijkheid van het proces voor de verdediging zullen worden voorkomen. De herzieningen zijn een poging om de rechten van de slachtoffers en die van de verdediging met elkaar in overeenstemming te brengen, en tegelijkertijd een effectieve en efficiënte werking van het Tribunaal te bewerkstelligen. Toch, hoewel de herzieningen veel van de problemen die zich in *Zaak 001* voordeden trachten te voorkomen, bieden ze geen oplossing voor vele klachten van de verdediging over de reikwijdte van slachtofferparticipatie tijdens de rechtszaak. Daarom zullen de rechters in *Zaak 002*, net als in *Zaak 001*, de exacte parameters van participatie moeten vaststellen. Een andere zorg is dat de veranderingen ook geen oplossing bieden voor de bezorgdheid bij advocaten van civiele partijen aangaande hun recht op een effectieve uitoefening van de participatierechten waarvoor zij naar eigen zeggen meer ondersteuning nodig hebben.

De praktijk bij het ECCC maakt het aannemelijk dat de Interne Regels waarschijnlijk nog verder zullen worden herzien, omdat de rechters reageren en anticiperen op toekomstige uitdagingen die aan het soepel functioneren van het Tribunaal in de weg kunnen staan. De rechters kunnen en moeten meer duidelijkheid bieden over de omvang en inhoud van participatie van civiele partijen, zodat alle partijen helderheid hebben over de parameters van participatie voordat de rechtszaak begint. Voor effectieve en efficiënte participatie wordt aanbevolen dat het Tribunaal (i) interventies van civiele partijen beperkt voorzover deze niet bijdragen aan de waarheidsvinding of verband houden met de aanklachten tegen een verdachte of met de civiele belangen van de slachtoffers; en (ii) een splitsing aanbrengt tussen het stadium van de veroordeling en dat van de straftoemeting zodat civiele partijen slachtofferverklaringen kunnen indienen (zowel schriftelijk als mondeling) over wat voor effect de misdaden op hen hebben gehad. Bij deze aanpak kunnen slachtoffers actief participeren met betrekking tot de ernst van de misdaden en de schade die zij hebben geleden, zonder dat de verdachte wordt benadeeld. Buiten het kader van de strafzaak wordt aanbevolen dat het Tribunaal (i) een beleidsplan ontwikkelt ter ondersteuning van het werk van de onafhankelijke juristen die optreden namens civiele partijen en van het werk van co-advocaten voor civiele partijen; en (ii) de institutionele ondersteuning vergroot (door toevoeging van fondsen en medewerkers) voor de Afdeling Slachtofferondersteuning

(*Victim Support Section*), zodat deze zijn nieuwe mandaat wat betreft service-gerelateerde rechten van slachtoffers kan uitvoeren.

Hoofdstuk 7 is het meest omvangrijke hoofdstuk en behandelt de casestudie van het ICC. De vaststelling van het Statuut van Rome (*Rome Statute*) van het ICC in 1998 luidde een nieuw tijdperk in op het gebied van het international strafrecht, omdat voor het eerst slachtoffers ook participant zouden kunnen zijn (hoewel niet als civiele partij) in internationale strafzaken. Tijdens het onderhandelingsproces over Statuut en Regels (*Statute* en *Rules*) presenteerden gedelegeerden veel verschillende en tegengestelde ideeën over de juiste omvang en inhoud van slachtofferparticipatie in internationale strafzaken, veelal gebaseerd op hun eigen juridische cultuur en procedurele achtergrond. Het opzetten van het regime voor slachtofferparticipatie was zelfs een van de moeilijkste taken voor de opstellers van Statuut en Regels. Een breed gedragen overeenstemming werd echter bereikt, maar wel tegen een prijs. De bepalingen in Statuut en Regels zijn vaag en onduidelijk, waardoor de rechters de bepalingen zelf moeten interpreteren (en herinterpreteren).

Het Statuut en de Regels voorzien in een aantal manieren waarop slachtoffers kunnen participeren in rechtszaken, anders dan als getuige. Ten eerste mogen slachtoffers participeren door een klacht in te dienen bij het Hof over een misdaad en een verzoek tot voorlopig onderzoek naar vermeende misdaden. Ten tweede kunnen slachtoffers een eis tot schadevergoeding indienen. De mogelijkheid om een eis tot schadevergoeding in te dienen wordt beschouwd als belangrijk succes in het streven naar ruimere slachtofferrechten. Anders dan in de ECCC kunnen slachtoffers schadevergoeding eisen ongeacht of zij participeren in de rechtszaak. Ten derde kunnen slachtoffers direct in de rechtszaak participeren, meestal via hun advocaat.

Met betrekking tot directe participatie in de rechtszaak bieden Statuut en Regels een nodeloos ingewikkeld systeem. Ingevolge Artikel 15(3), kunnen slachtoffers verklaringen afleggen bij de *Pre-Trial Chamber* ('Kamer van Vooronderzoek') indien de aanklager, handelend op basis van zijn *proprio-motu* bevoegdheden, de *Pre-Trial Chamber* om goedkeuring van een onderzoek vraagt. Regel 50 verduidelijkt de procedure voor participatie in deze fase door te stellen dat slachtoffers op de hoogte dienen te worden gesteld wanneer de aanklager om goedkeuring heeft gevraagd en dat zij schriftelijke verklaringen mogen indienen. Naast Artikel 15(3) mogen slachtoffers in overeenstemming met Artikel 19(3) eigen waarnemingen indienen bij het Hof, als de rechtsmacht van het Hof of de ontvankelijkheid van een zaak wordt aangevochten. Dit participatierecht ontstaat nadat een verdachte bekend is gemaakt en geeft slachtoffers de kans aan te geven of een zaak naar hun mening zou moeten worden voorgezet. Artikel 75 voorziet ook in de participatie van slachtoffers in verband met het eisen van schadevergoeding zonder vast te stellen of participatie zou moeten plaatsvinden in een afzonderlijke hoorzitting of tijdens de rechtszaak. Hierdoor kan het recht op het eisen van schadevergoeding ook worden gezien tezamen met het recht om direct in de rechtszaak te participeren. Naast Artikel 15(3), 19(3) en 75, heeft het Hof krachtens Regel 93 de bevoegdheid om slachtoffers en hun juridisch vertegenwoordigers om hun opvatting te vragen aangaande ieder mogelijk onderwerp. En ten slotte, volgens de meest verstrekkende bepaling met betrekking tot de participatierechten van slachtoffers, *dient* het Hof, ingevolge Artikel 68(3), slachtoffers toe te staan om hun standpunten en bezorgdheid naar voren te brengen in een passende procedure zolang deze participatie geen afbreuk doet aan de rechten van de verdachte op een eerlijk en onpartijdig proces.

In navolging van de tekst in Artikel 6(b) van de VN Declaratie heeft de vage formulering van Artikel 68(3) ertoe geleid dat alle partijen die betrokken zijn bij de gerechtelijke procedures een aanzienlijke hoeveelheid tijd en middelen spenderen aan de discussie over hoe deze bepaling moet worden geïnterpreteerd. Bovendien zorgt het overnemen van de formulering van een document dat bedoeld is om nationale wetgevers te stimuleren tot het opstellen van slachtoffergeoriënteerde wetgeving in een strafvorderingsbepaling ervoor dat de ICC rechters deze bepaling voortdurend (opnieuw) moeten interpreteren. Het is vanzelfsprekend een grote uitdaging voor het ICC om hier helderheid in te scheppen. Tot op heden is de rechtspraak van het Hof fragmentarisch en inconsistent, met voorbeelden van gelijkgesitueerde slachtoffers die verschillend worden behandeld en gebrekkige bescherming van de rechten van de verdachte. Het lijkt erop dat de verschillende Kamers bij het ICC aan het touwtrekken zijn om te bepalen of participatiebepalingen strikt geïnterpreteerd moeten worden of dat zij ruim moeten worden opgevat.

Veel van de uitspraken die tot nu toe zijn gedaan, lijken de ruime benadering te volgen, waarbij gebruik wordt gemaakt van ontwikkelingen op het gebied van de mensenrechten en nationaal strafrecht om kracht bij te zetten aan de drang om de rechten van slachtoffers verder uit te breiden dan overeengekomen in Rome. De ICC rechters hebben de uitspraken van de mensenrechtenorganen en tekst van de VN Verklaringen meegenomen bij het trekken van conclusies ten aanzien van participatie. Zodoende werd participatie toegestaan tijdens het vooronderzoek of door middel van aanvoeren of betwisten van bewijs aangaande de schuld van de verdachte. Ten minste een van de *Trial Chambers* heeft echter erkend dat het noodzakelijk is om de rol van slachtoffers tijdens de rechtszaak nauwkeurig af te bakenen. Hierbij is gesteld dat, hoewel slachtoffers achtergrondinformatie kunnen leveren bij een zaak of de aandacht van het Hof kunnen vestigen op relevante informatie, als algemeen principe moet gelden dat ondervragingen door advocaten van slachtoffers als voornaamste doel het vaststellen van de waarheid dienen te hebben. Geconcludeerd werd dat slachtoffers geen partij zijn bij de procedure, en dat zij ook geen rol hebben in het leveren van steun aan de zaak van de aanklager. Hun lokale kennis en sociaal-culturele achtergrond worden eerder beschouwd als aanwinst in de zin dat zij het Hof kunnen helpen een beter begrip te krijgen van de twistpunten die tijdens de zaak kunnen voorkomen. In tegenstelling tot andere *Trial Chambers* heeft deze Kamer dus slechts zelden slachtoffers toegestaan om getuigen te ondervragen over de schuld van de verdachte.

Slachtoffers hebben ongetwijfeld een bijzonder grote invloed gehad op het Hof. Zij hebben geparticipeerd in alle stadia van vooronderzoek en berechting. Via hun advocaten zijn hun standpunten en bezorgdheid gepresenteerd, hoewel dit vaak op collectieve en niet op individuele basis gebeurde. Ook hebben ze de aandacht van het

Hof gevraagd voor gender-gerelateerde misdaden en hebben zij herhaaldelijk nadruk gelegd op hun recht op waarheid en op gerechtigheid. Ondanks deze successen heeft het participatieregime het ICC voor substantiële problemen gesteld. Het Hof moet beter presteren op het gebied van bescherming van de rechten van de verdachte op een eerlijk proces. Er hoeft niet te worden gewacht tot er een fundamenteel recht is geschonden. De kans op een dergelijke schending zou voldoende moeten zijn om maatregelen te treffen. De participatie van slachtoffers zou beperkt moeten worden tot interventies die bijdragen aan de waarheidsvinding door opheldering van feiten of die verband houden met de persoonlijke belangen van de slachtoffers. Slachtoffers zouden derhalve niet de rol van aanklager moeten overnemen en geen pogingen moeten doen om de schuld van de verdachte vast te stellen.

Hoofdstuk 8 is het afsluitende hoofdstuk en omvat analyses en aanbevelingen. Gesteld wordt dat de redenen die worden aangevoerd ter rechtvaardiging van slachtofferparticipatie op nationaal niveau niet zomaar moeten worden overgenomen op internationaal niveau. Veel van deze argumenten voor participatie sluiten niet aan bij de realiteit van het internationaal strafrecht, door de unieke context waarin internationale straftribunalen functioneren. De specifieke eigenschappen van internationaal strafrecht, waaronder het aspect van massa slachtofferschap, de samenstelling en structuur van de tribunalen, en de financiële en praktische beperkingen waarmee de tribunalen te maken hebben, maken het noodzakelijk dat participatie op internationaal niveau anders moet zijn dan participatie op nationaal niveau. Het is onmogelijk rekening te houden met de tegengestelde belangen van specifieke slachtoffers. Integendeel, voor een effectief functioneren van de tribunalen is het vereist dat persoonlijke belangen buiten de procedure worden gehouden. De individuele herinneringen en ervaringen van slachtoffers worden zo verkleind en samengebracht in collectieve verhalen. Slachtoffers hebben dus geen geïndividualiseerde besluitvormingsbevoegdheid die participatie op nationaal niveau, voor een deel, bedoelt te verschaffen. Bovendien maken de samenstelling en structuur van de nieuwe tribunalen, die een mengeling van procedurele benaderingen toepassen, de pogingen om actieve slachtofferparticipatie op te nemen in de procedures erg ingewikkeld. Het is vanzelfsprekend moeilijk om procedures en processen van de ene in de andere procesrechtelijke traditie over te nemen. Institutionele beperkingen en culturele weerstand kunnen het bedoelde effect verminderen. En ten slotte hebben de praktische en financiële beperkingen tot gevolg dat internationale strafrechttribunalen niet voor 'ieder wat wils kunnen bieden'. Zij moeten besluiten hoe zij, binnen hun mogelijkheden, het beste kunnen voldoen aan de minimum mensenrechtennormen die gelden voor zowel slachtoffers als verdachten in een strafzaak.

In het internationaal strafrecht vindt langzamerhand een verschuiving plaats die zich reeds binnen de mensenrechten heeft voorgedaan (met als goed voorbeeld het Inter-Amerikaanse systeem), namelijk van het liberale model met een focus op de verdachte naar een meer slachtoffergeoriënteerd model. Individueel bekeken lijkt de invloed van slachtofferparticipatie op de verschillende normen voor een eerlijk proces niet zo problematisch. Het is echter het gecombineerde effect van het afbrokkelen van deze rechten en waarden dat belangrijkst is. Het afbrokkelen van liberale waarden is bovendien alarmerend omdat internationale tribunalen al kennis hebben gemaakt met de 'versoepeling' van procedurele regels en regels van bewijsvoering die een negatieve invloed hebben op de rechten van een verdachte op een eerlijk proces. Dit onderzoek waarschuwt dat het toevoegen van actieve slachtofferparticipatie als element in internationale strafzaken verder afbreuk zal doen aan de rechten van de verdachte. De onschuldpresumptie, het recht op voldoende tijd en middelen om een verdediging voor te bereiden, het recht op een spoedig en onafhankelijk en onpartijdig proces, het recht op *equality of arms*, en het rechtszekerheidsbeginsel kunnen allemaal worden aangetast door het opnemen van ruimere participatierechten van slachtoffers.

Als antwoord op de centrale onderzoeksvraag is de conclusie van het onderzoek dat er geen *one-size-fits-all* antwoord bestaat. Internationale straftribunalen zijn complexe organisaties, die ieder hun eigen afgebakende invloedssferen hebben. Dit onderzoek naar slachtofferparticipatie in internationale strafzaken heeft aangetoond dat het recht op participatie verband houdt met de rechten van de mens en institutionele en/of overheidsverplichtingen. Er is verder aangetoond dat, net als nationale jurisdicties, internationale straftribunalen veel verschillende participatiemodellen hebben ontwikkeld, maar dat participatie in internationale strafzakken nadrukkelijk verschilt van participatie in nationale rechtszaken, vooral door de unieke karakteristieken van internationale strafzaken. De in dit onderzoek geanalyseerde casestudies, in samenhang met de praktijk van andere internationale tribunalen, laten zien dat er weinig consensus bestaat over de juiste omvang van slachtofferparticipatie. Doordat participatie in de procedures bij de ECCC en het ICC een aantal heikele kwesties heeft opgeleverd, wordt echter gesteld dat de mensenrechtennormen van het traditioneel liberale model meer aandacht zouden moeten krijgen bij het bepalen van de omvang en inhoud van slachtofferparticipatie. Door een op mensenrechten gebaseerde benadering (*human rights based approach*) te volgen en tegelijkertijd rekening te houden met de unieke eigenschappen van het internationaal strafrecht zullen internationale straftribunalen beter in staat zijn de participatierechten van slachtoffers af te bakenen en tegelijkertijd de rechten van de verdachte op een eerlijk proces te garanderen. Wanneer de straftribunalen dus voor beslissingen staan over de juiste omvang en inhoud van participatie, zouden de volgende punten als richtlijn moeten dienen: (i) houd voldoende oog voor de centrale doelstellingen van de strafprocedure; (ii) verwerp het 'afwegende bewustzijn' en erken de voorrang van de rechten van de verdachte; (iii) richt de aandacht op service voor slachtoffers; en (iv) neem pluralisme als uitgangspunt, waarbij rekening wordt gehouden met de specifieke eigenschappen van het tribunaal.

Ongetwijfeld zal er discussie blijven bestaan over de juiste rol van slachtoffers in de internationale strafrechtspleging. Het is echter de uitdaging voor internationale straftribunalen om eerlijkere en efficiëntere procedures te ontwikkelen. Volgens de belofte van procedurele rechtvaardigheid is het vereist dat deze tribunalen voldoen aan de minimum mensenrechtennormen en tegelijk ook de specifieke eigenschappen van het internationaal strafrecht in acht nemen, om zo de juiste procedurele rol van slachtoffers vast te stellen.

BIBLIOGRAPHY

Acquaviva, G., New Paths in International Criminal Justice? 6 *Journal of International Criminal Justice* 129 (2008).

Akhavan, P., Justice and Reconciliation in the Great Lakes Region of Africa: The Contribution of the International Criminal Tribunal for Rwanda, 7 *Duke Journal of Comparative & International Law* 325 (1997).

Aldana-Pindell, R., In Vindication of Justiciable Victims' Rights to Truth and Justice for State-Sponsored Crimes, 35 *Vanderbilt Journal of Transnational Law* 1399 (2002).

Aldana-Pindell, R., An Emerging Universality of Justiciable Victims' Rights in the Criminal Process to Curtail Impunity for State-Sponsored Crimes, 26 *Human Rights Quarterly* 605, (2004).

Alvarez, J.E., *Post International Criminal Court Challenges*, paper presented at the Joint Conference of the Australian and New Zealand Society of International Law and the American Society of International Law, 26-29 June 2000.

Ambos, K., International Criminal Procedure: "Adversarial," "Inquisitorial" or Mixed? 3 *International Criminal Law Review* 1 (2003).

Amnesty International, The International Criminal Court: Ensuring an Effective Role for Victims – Memorandum for the Paris Seminar (1999).

Anderson, R. and Otto, A., Perceptions of Fairness in the Justice System: A Cross-Cultural Comparison, 31 *Social Behavior and Personality* 557 (2003).

Andrews, J.A., ed., *Human Rights in Criminal Procedure: A Comparative Study*, Martinus Nijhoff Publishers (1982).

Aptel, C., Some Innovations in the Statute of the Special Tribunal for Lebanon, 5 *Journal of International Criminal Justice* 1107 (2007).

Arendt, H., *Eichmann in Jerusalem: A Report on the Banality of Evil*, Penguin Books (1963).

Arnstein, S.R., A Latter of Citizen Participation, 35 *AIP Journal* 216 (1969).

Ashworth, A., Some Doubts about Restorative Justice, 4 *Criminal Law Forum* 277 (1993).

Ashworth, A., *Sentencing and Criminal Justice*, Cambridge University Press (2005).

Bachrach, M., The Protection and Rights of Victims under International Criminal Law, 34 *International Law* 7 (2000).

Bacik, I., Maunsell, C. and Grogan, S., *The Legal Process and Victims of Rape*, Dublin Rape Crisis Center (1998).

Bagaric, M. and Morss, J., International Sentencing Law: In Search of a Justification and Coherent Framework, 6 *International Criminal Law Review* 191 (2006).

Bair, J.P., From the Numbers Who Died to Those Who Survived: Victim Participation in the Extraordinary Chambers in the Courts of Cambodia, 31 *University of Hawaii Law Review* 507 (2008-2009).

Barnett, R.E., Restitution: A New Paradigm of Criminal Justice, 87 *Ethics* 279 (1977).

Basch, F.F., The Doctrine of the Inter-American Court of Human Rights Regarding States' Duty to Punish Human Rights Violations and Its Dangers, 23 *American University International Law Review* 195 (2007).

Bassiouni, M.C., The Proscribing Function of International Criminal Law in the International Protection of Human Rights, 9 *Yale Journal of World Public Order* 193 (1982).

Bassiouni, M.C., ed., *International Protection of Victims*, Eres Publications (1988).

Bassiouni, M.C., Human Rights in the Context of Criminal Justice: Identifying International Procedural Protections and Equivalent Protections in National Constitutions, 3 *Duke Journal of Comparative International Law* 235 (1992-1993).

Bassiouni, M.C., *Introduction to International Criminal Law*, Transnational Publishers (2003).

Bassiouni, M.C., ed., *The Legislative History of the International Criminal Court: An Article-by-Article Evolution of the Statute, Vol. 2*, Transnational Publishers (2005).

Bassiouni, M.C., International Recognition of Victims' Rights, 6 *Human Rights Law Review* 203 (2006).

Baumgartner, E., Aspects of Victim Participation in the Proceedings of the International Criminal Court, 90 *International Review of the Red Cross* 409 (2008).

Bazemore, G. and Walgrave, L., *Restorative Juvenile Justice: Repairing the Harm of Youth Crime*, Criminal Justice Press (1999).

Beckett, K. and Sasson, T., *The Politics of Injustice: Crime and Punishment in America*, Sage Publications (2004).

Bekou, O., *Pre-Trial Procedures Before the International Criminal Court*, paper presented at the 20th International Conference of the International Society for the Reform of Criminal Law held in Brisbane, Australia from 2-6 July 2006.

Belli, M.M., Punitive Damages: Their History, Their Use and Their Worth in Present-Day Society, 49 *University of Missouri at Kansas City Law Review* 1 (1980-1981).

Beloof, D.E., The Third Model of Criminal Process: The Victim Participation Model, 1999 *Utah Law Review* 289 (1999).

Betts, W.S., Carlson, S.N. and Gisvold, G., The Post-Conflict Transitional Administration of Kosovo and the Lessons Learned in Efforts to Establish a Judiciary and the Rule of Law, 22 *Michigan Journal of International Law* 371 (2001).

Bianchi, H. and Van Swaaningen, R., eds., *Abolitionism: Towards a Non-Repressive Approach to Crime*, Free University Press (1986).

Boas, G., Creating Laws of Evidence for International Criminal Law: The ICTY and the Principle of Flexibility, 12 *Criminal Law Forum* 41 (2001).

Boas, G. and Schabas, W.A., eds., *International Criminal Law Developments in the Case Law of the ICTY*, Martinus Nijhoff Publishers (2003).

Bohlander, M., Boed, R. and Wilson, R., eds., *Defense in International Criminal Proceedings: Cases, Materials and Commentary*, Transnational Publishers (2006).

Boyle, D., The Rights of Victims: Participation, Representation, Protection, Reparation, 4 *Journal of International Criminal Justice* 307 (2006).

Bradley, C.M., *Criminal Procedure: A Worldwide Study*, Carolina Academic Press (1999).

Braithwaite, J., *Crime, Shame and Reintegration*, Cambridge University Press (1989).

Braithwaite, J. and Pettit, P., *Not Just Deserts*, Clarendon Press (1990).

Braithwaite, J. and Strang, H., eds., *Restorative Justice and Civil Society*, Cambridge University Press (2001).
Brienen, M.E. and Hoegen, E.H., *Victims of Crime in 22 European Criminal Justice Systems*, Wolf Legal Publishers (2000).
Brown, J.G., The Use of Mediation to Resolve Criminal Cases: A Procedural Critique, 43 *Emory Law Journal* 1247 (1994).
Butler, R.P., What Practitioners and Judges Need to Know Regarding Crime Victims' Participatory Rights in Federal Sentencing Proceedings, 19 *United States of America Federal Sentencing Reporter* 21 (2006).
Cape, E., ed., *Reconcilable Rights? Analysing the Tension between Victims and Defendants*, Legal Action Group (2004).
Cardenas, J., The Crime Victim in the Prosecutorial Process, 9 *Harvard Journal of Law & Public Policy* 357 (1986).
Cassese, A., On the Current Trends towards Criminal Prosecution and Punishment of Breaches of International Humanitarian Law, 9 *European Journal of International Law* 2 (1998).
Cassese, A., The Statute of the International Criminal Court: Some Preliminary Reflections, 10 *European Journal of International Law* 144 (1999).
Cassese, A., Gaeta, P. and Jones, J.R.W.D., eds., *The Rome Statute of the International Criminal Court: a Commentary*, Oxford University Press (2002).
Cassese, A., Report on the Special Court for Sierra Leone, submitted by the Independent Expert, 12 December 2006.
Chandler, D.P., *The Tragedy of Cambodian History*, Yale University Press (1991).
Chandler, D.P., *Brother Number One: A Political Biography of Pol Pot*, Silkworm Books (1999).
Chayes, S., The Trial of Paul Touvier: An Eyewitness Account, 34 *Michigan Quarterly Review* 334 (1995).
Christie, N., Conflicts as Property, 17 *British Journal of Criminology* 1 (1977).
Chung, C.H., Victims' Participation at the International Criminal Court: Are Concessions of the Court Clouding the Promise? 6 *Northwestern Journal of International Human Rights* 459 (2008).
Ciorciari, J.D. and Heindel, A., eds., *On Trial: The Khmer Rouge Accountability Process*, Documentation Center of Cambodia (2009).
Clayton, R. and Tomlinson, H., *Fair Trial Rights*, Oxford University Press (2001).
Coalition for an International Criminal Court, Diplomatic Conference on the Establishment of an International Criminal Court, Report of the Victims' Rights Working Group, Rome, Italy, 15-17 July 1998.
Coalition for an International Criminal Court, Draft Report on the Third Session of the Preparatory Commission November 29-December 17 1999 (2000).
Cockayne, J., Hybrids or Mongrels? Internationalized War Crimes Trials as Unsuccessful Degradation Ceremonies, 4 *Journal of Human Rights* 455 (2005).
Colquitt, J.A., On the Dimensionality of Organizational Justice: A Construct Validation of a Measure, 86 *Journal of Applied Psychology* 386 (2001).

Combs, N.A., Testimonial Deficiencies and Evidentiary Uncertainties in International Criminal Trials, 14 *University of California Los Angeles Journal of International Law and Foreign Affairs* 235 (2009).
Combs, N.A., *Fact-Finding Without Facts: The Uncertain Evidentiary Foundations of International Criminal Convictions*, Cambridge University Press (2010).
Commission for Reception, Truth and Reconciliation in East Timor (CAVR), Final Report (2006).
Coomans, F., Grünfeld, F. and Kamminga, M.T., eds., *Methods of Human Rights Research*, Intersentia (2009)
Cottingham, J., Varieties of Retribution, 29 *The Philosophical Quarterly* 238 (1979).
Cragg, W., *The Practice of Punishment: Towards a Theory of Restorative Justice*, Routledge Publishers (1992).
Crawford, A. and Goodey, J., eds., *Integrating a Victim Perspective within Criminal Justice*, Ashgate (2000).
Dadomo, C. and Ferran, S., *The French Legal System, 2nd Ed.*, Sweet & Maxwell (1993).
Damaška, M., *The Faces of Justice and State Authority: A Comparative Approach to the Legal Process*, Yale University Press (1986).
Damaška, M., The Uncertain Fate of Evidentiary Transplants: Anglo-American and Continental Experiments, 45 *American Journal of Comparative Law* 839 (1997)
Damaška, M., What is the Point of International Criminal Justice? 83 *Chicago Kent Law Review* 329 (2008).
Damaška, M., The International Criminal Court between Aspiration and Achievement, 14 *University of California Los Angeles Journal of International Law and Foreign Affairs* 19 (2009).
Danieli, Y., Victims: Essential Voices at the Court, Victims Rights Working Group Bulletin, September 2004.
David, R., *English Law and French Law: A Comparison in Substance*, Stevens Publisher (1980).
Davis, A., *Arbitrary Justice: The Power of the American Prosecutor*, Oxford University Press (2007).
De Bertodano, S., Problems Arising from the Mixed Composition and Structure of the Cambodian Extraordinary Chambers, 4 *Journal of International Criminal Justice* 285 (2006).
DeFrancia, C., Due Process in International Criminal Courts: Why Procedure Matters, 87 *Virginia Law Review* 1381 (2001).
De Hemptinne, J., The Creation of Investigating Chambers at the International Criminal Court: An Option Worth Pursuing? 5 *Journal of International Criminal Justice* 402 (2007).
De Hemptinne, J., Challenges Raised by Victims' Participation in the Proceedings of the Special Tribunal for Lebanon, 8 *Journal of International Criminal Justice* 165 (2010).
De Hemptinne, J. and Rindi, F., ICC Pre-Trial Chamber Allows Victims to Participate in the Investigation Phase of Proceedings, 4 *Journal of International Criminal Justice* 342 (2006).
Delgado, R., Goodbye to Hammurabi: Analyzing the Atavistic Appeal of Restorative Justice, 52 *Stanford Law Review* 751 (2000).

Delmas-Marty, M., Interactions between National and International Criminal Law in the Preliminary Phase of Trial at the ICC, 4 *Journal of International Criminal Justice* 2 (2005).
Delmas-Marty, M. and Spencer, J., eds., *European Criminal Procedures*, Cambridge University Press (2002).
Del Ponte, C., Prosecutor of the ICTY, Statement on the Investigation and Prosecution of Crimes Committed in Kosovo, The Hague, PR/P.I.S./437-E, 29 September 1999.
Del Ponte, C., Address by Chief Prosecutor Carla Del Ponte at the conference on "Establishing the truth about war crimes and conflicts," Zagreb, Croatia, 8-9 February 2007.
Dembour, M.B. and Haslam, E., Silencing Hearing? Victim-Witnesses at War Crimes Trials, 15 *European Journal of International Law* 151 (2004).
Dignan, J., *Understanding Victims and Restorative Justice*, Open University Press (2005).
Dill, F., Victims, Police, and Criminal Court Decisions: A Research Note on Witness Participation and Case Processing, 6 *Victimology: An International Journal* 345 (1981).
Doak, J., The Victim and the Criminal Process: an Analysis of Recent Trends in Regional and International Tribunals, 23 *Legal Studies* 1 (2003).
Doak, J., Victims' Rights in Criminal Trials: Prospects for Participation, 32 *Journal of Law and Society* 294 (2005).
Doak, J., *Victims' Rights, Human Rights and Criminal Justice*, Hart Publishing (2008).
Dobbs, L., UN Official Calls for Cambodian Truth Commission, *Reuters News*, 6 February 1997.
Donovan, D.K., Joint U.N.-Cambodia Efforts to Establish a Khmer Rouge Tribunal, 44 *Harvard International Law Journal* 551 (2003).
Doucet, G., ed., *Terrorism, Victims, and International Criminal Responsibility*, SOS Attentats (2003)
Drumbl, M., *Atrocity, Punishment and International Law*, Cambridge University Press (2007).
Dubber, M.D., The Victim in American Penal Law: A Systematic Overview, 3 *Buffalo Criminal Law Review* 3 (1999).
Dubber, M.D., Theories of Crime and Punishment in German Criminal Law, 53 *American Journal of Comparative Law* 679 (2005).
Duff, A., *Trials and Punishment*, Cambridge University Press (1986).
Duff, A., ed., *Philosophy and the Criminal Law: Principle and Critique*, Cambridge University Press (1998).
Duff, A., *Punishment, Communication and Community*, Oxford University Press (2001).
Duff, A., Farmer, L., Marshall, S. and Tadros, V., eds., *Calling to Account and Judgment*, Hart Publishing (2006).
Dworkin, R., *Taking Rights Seriously*, Harvard University Press (1977).
Edwards, I., An Ambiguous Participant: The Crime Victim and Criminal Justice Decision-Making, 44 *British Journal of Criminology* 967 (2004).
Emmerson, B., Ashworth, A. and Macdonald, A., *Human Rights and Criminal Justice*, Thomson Sweet & Maxwell (2007).
Erez, E., Who's Afraid of the Big Bad Victim? Victim Impact Statements as Victim Empowerment *and* Enhancement of Justice, 7 *Criminal Law Review* 545 (1999).

Fairlie, M., The Marriage of Common and Continental Law at the ICTY and its Progeny, Due Process Deficit, 4 *International Criminal Law Review* 243 (2004).
Fairlie, M., Establishing Admissibility at the International Criminal Court: Does the Buck Stop with the Prosecutor, Full Stop? 39 *International Lawyer* 817 (2005).
Fatić, A., *Punishment and Restorative Crime-Handling: A Social Theory of Trust*, Avebury Publishers (1995).
Fattah, E. and Parmentier, S., eds., *Victim Policies and Criminal Justice on the Road to Restorative Justice*, Leuven University Press (2001).
Fedorova, M. and Sluiter, G., Human Rights as Minimum Standards in International Criminal Proceedings, 3 *Human Rights and International Legal Discourse* 9 (2009).
Fernando, B., ed., *Problems Facing the Cambodian Legal System*, Asian Human Rights Commission (1998).
Field, S., Fair Trials and Procedural Tradition in Europe, 29 *Oxford Journal of Legal Studies* 365 (2009).
Findlay, M., Synthesis in Trial Procedures? The Experience of International Criminal Tribunals, 50 *International Comparative Law Quarterly* 26 (2001).
Findlay, M. and Henham, R., *Transforming International Criminal Justice: Retributive and Restorative Justice in the Trial Process*, Willan Publishing (2005).
Fischer, H., Kress, C. and Lüder, S.R., eds., *International and National Prosecution of Crimes under International Law: Current Developments*, BWV Berliner-Wissenschaft (2001).
Fletcher, G.P., What is Punishment Imposed For? 5 *Journal of Contemporary Legal Issues* 101 (1994).
Fletcher, G.P., The Place of Victims in the Theory of Retribution, 3 *Buffalo Criminal Law Review* 51 (1999-2000).
Francioni, F., ed., *Access to Justice as a Human Right*, Oxford University Press (2007).
Freedman, M.H., Our Constitutionalized Adversary System, 1 *Chapman Law Review* 57 (1998).
Frehsee, D., Restitution and Offender-Victim Arrangement in Germany Criminal Law: Development and Theoretical Implications, 3 *Buffalo Criminal Law Review* 235 (1999).
Frey, R.G. and Morris, C.W., eds., *Liability and Responsibility*, Cambridge University Press (1991).
Friedman, L.M., Legal Culture and Social Development, 4 *Law and Society Review* 29 (1969).
Friman, H., The International Criminal Court and Participation of Victims: A Third Party to the Proceedings? 22 *Leiden Journal of International Law* 485 (2009).
Fry, M., *Arms of the Law*, Gollancz (1951).
Galaway, B. and Hudson, J., eds., *Restorative Justice: International Perspectives*, Criminal Justice Press (1996).
Gallant, K.S., The Role and Powers of Defense Counsel in the Rome Statute of the International Criminal Court, 34 *International Law* 21 (2000).
Garkawe, S. Victims and the International Criminal Court: Three Major Issues, 3 *International Criminal Law Review* 345 (2003).
Garvey, S.P., Restorative Justice, Punishment and Atonement, 1 *Utah Law Review* 303 (2003).

Gibson, K. and Rudy, D., A New Model of International Criminal Procedure? The Progress of the *Duch* Trial at the ECCC, 7 *Journal of International Criminal Justice* 1005 (2009).
Gillin, J.L., *Criminology and Penology*, Vol. 1, Kessinger Publishing (1927).
Goldman, A.H., The Paradox of Punishment, 9 *Philosophy & Public Affairs* 42 (1979).
Goldstone, R., Conference Luncheon Address, 7 *Transnational Law & Contemporary Problems* 1 (1997).
Greenberg, J., Taxonomy of Organizational Justice Theories, 12 *Academy of Management Review* 9 (1987).
Griffen, J.B., A Predictive Framework for the Effectiveness of International Criminal Tribunals, 34 *Vanderbilt Journal of Transnational Law* 405 (2001).
Gromet, D.M. and Darley, J.M., Restoration and Retribution: How Including Retributive Components Affects the Acceptability of Restorative Justice Procedures, 19 *Social Justice Research* 395 (2006).
Hall, C.K., The First Proposal for a Permanent International Criminal Court, 332 *International Review of the Red Cross* 57 (1998).
Hall, D.J., Victims' Voices in Criminal Court: The Need for Restraint, 28 *American Criminal Law Review* 233 (1990-1991).
Harris, D., The Right to a Fair Trial in Criminal Proceedings as a Human Right, 16 *International & Comparative Law Quarterly* 352 (1967).
Hart, H.L.A., *Punishment and Responsibility: Essays in the Philosophy of Law*, Oxford University Press (1968).
Hayner, P., *Unspeakable Truths: Confronting State Terror and Atrocity*, Routledge (2001).
Heikkilä, M., *International Criminal Tribunals and Victims of Crime*, Åbo Akademi University Press (2004).
Henderson, L.N., The Wrongs of Victim's Rights, 37 *Standard Law Review* 937 (1985).
Henham, R. and Mannozzi, G., Victim Participation and Sentencing in England and Italy: A Legal and Policy Analysis, 11 *European Journal of Crime, Criminal Law and Criminal Justice*, 278 (2003).
Higgins, G., Fair and Expeditious Pre-Trial Proceedings, 5 *Journal of International Criminal Justice* 394 (2007).
Hodžić, R., Living the Legacy of Mass Atrocities: Victims' Perspectives on War Crimes Trials, 8 *Journal of International Criminal Justice* 113 (2010).
Hoel, A., The Sentencing Provisions of the International Criminal Court: Common Law, Civil Law, or Both? 33 *Monash University Law Review* 264 (2007).
Hudson, J. and Galaway, B., eds., *Restitution in Criminal Justice*, Lexington Books (1977).
Humanitarian Law Center, Report: Trials for War Crimes and Ethnically and Politically Motivated Crimes in post-Yugoslav Countries (2008).
Humanitarian Law Center, Annual Report (2008).
Human Rights Watch, Commentary, Third Preparatory Commission Meeting on the International Criminal Court: Elements of Crimes and Rules of Evidence and Procedure (1999).
International Bar Association (IBA), Human Rights Institute Report, International Criminal Court, April (2006).
International Bar Association (IBA), First Challenges: An Examination of Recent Landmark Developments at the ICC, June 2009.

International Crisis Group (ICG), The Special Court for Sierra Leone: Promises and Pitfalls of a New Model, Africa Briefing, 4 August 2003.
International Federation for Human Rights (FIDH), Victims in the Balance: Challenges Ahead for the International Criminal Tribunal for Rwanda, FIDH Report, No. 329/2, 25 October 2002.
International Federation for Human Rights (FIDH), Report: Supporting the Participation of Victims from DRC before the International Criminal Court (2006).
Jackson, C., Challenges to Witness' Credibility Continue, *Cambodia Tribunal Monitor*, 22 July 2009.
Jackson, J., The Effect of Human Rights on Criminal Evidentiary Processes: Towards Convergence, Divergence or Realignment? 68 *Modern Law Review* 737 (2005).
Jackson, J., Langer, M. and Tillers, P., eds., *Crime, Procedure and Evidence in Comparative and International Context*, Hart Publishing (2008).
Johnson, S.T., Neither Victims Nor Executioners: The Dilemma of Victim Participation and the Defendant's Right to a Fair Trial at the International Criminal Court, 16 *ISLA Journal of International and Comparative Law* 489 (2009-2010).
Jorda, C., The Major Hurdles and Accomplishments of the ICTY: What the ICC Can Learn from Them, 2 *Journal of International Criminal Justice* 572 (2004).
Jordash, W., The Practice of 'Witness Proofing' in International Criminal Tribunals: Why the International Criminal Court should prohibit the practice, 22 *Leiden Journal of International Law* 501 (2009).
Jordash, W. and Martin, S., Due Process and Fair Trial Rights at the Special Court: How the Desire for Accountability Outweighed the Demands of Justice at the Special Court for Sierra Leone, 23 *Leiden Journal of International Law* 585 (2010).
Jouet, M., Reconciling the Conflicting Rights of Victims and Defendants at the International Criminal Court, 26 *Saint Louis University Public Law Review* 249 (2007).
Joutsen, M., *The Role of the Victim of Crime in European Criminal Justice Systems: A Cross National Study of the Role of the Victim*, Helsinki Institute for Crime Prevention and Control (1987).
Joutsen, M., Listening to the Victim: The Victim's Role in European Criminal Justice Systems, 34 *Wayne Law Review* 95 (1987-1988).
Kaiser, G., Kury, H. and Albrecht, H.J., eds., *Victims and Criminal Justice: Legal Protection, Restitution and Support*, Max Planck Institute for Foreign and International Criminal Law (1991).
Kamatali, J.M., From the ICTR to ICC: Learning from the ICTR Experience in Bringing Justice to Rwandans, 12 *New England Journal of International and Comparative Law* 89 (2005).
Karemaker, R., Taylor III, B.D. and Pittman, T., Witness Proofing in International Criminal Tribuanls: A Critical Analysis of Widening Procedural Divergence, 21 *Leiden Journal of International Law* 683 (2008).
Keller, L.M., Seeking Justice at the International Criminal court: Victims' Reparations, 29 *Thomas Jefferson Law Review* 189 (2007).
Kermani Mendez, P., The New Wave of Hybrid Tribunals: A Sophisticated Approach to Enforcing International Humanitarian Law or an Idealistic Solution with Empty Promises? 20 *Criminal Law Forum* 53 (2009).

Kiernan, B., *The Pol Pot Regime: Race, Power, and Genocide in Cambodia under the Khmer Rouge, 1975-79*, Yale University Press (1996).

Kilpatrick, D.G. and Otto, R.K., Constitutionally Guaranteed Participation in Criminal Proceedings for Victims: Potential Effects on Psychological Functioning, 34 *Wayne Law Review* 7 (1987).

King, F.P. and La Rosa, A.M., The Jurisprudence of the Yugoslavia Tribunal: 1994-1996, 8 *European Journal of International Law* 123 (1997).

Kirchhoff, G.F., et al., eds., *International Debates of Victimology*, WSV Publishing (1991).

Klaming, L. and Giesen, I., Access to Justice: The Quality of Procedure, paper presented at the 18th Conference of the European Association of Psychology and Law July 2008, TISCO Working Paper Series on Civil Law and Conflict Resolution Systems No. 002/2008 (2008).

Knoops, G.G.J., The Dichotomy Between Judicial Economy and Equality of Arms Within International and Internationalized Criminal Trials: A Defense Perspective, 28 *Fordham International Law Journal* 1566 (2005).

Kong, S., Tribunal Judges Consider Duch Verdict, *Voice of America (VOA)*, Khmer, 2 February 2010.

Kool, R. and Moerings, M., The Victim Has the Floor: The Victim's Right to be Heard in Writing or Orally in the Dutch Courtroom, 12 *European Journal of Crime, Criminal Law and Criminal Justice* 46 (2004).

Koper, G., et al., Procedural Fairness and Self-Esteem, 23 *European Journal of Social Psychology* 313 (1993).

Kress, C., The Procedural Law of the International Criminal Court in Outline: Anatomy of Unique Compromises, 1 *Journal of International Criminal Justice* 603 (2003).

Kutnjak Ivkovic, S., Justice by the International Criminal Tribunal for the Former Yugoslavia, 37 *Stanford Journal of International Law* 255 (2001).

Ku, J. and Nzelibe, J., Do International Criminal Tribunals Deter or Exacerbate Humanitarian Atrocities, 84 *Washington University Law Review* 777 (2006).

Langer, M., The Rise of Managerial Judging in International Criminal Law, 53 *American Journal of Comparative Law* 835 (2005).

Langer, M., The Diplomacy of Universal Jurisdiction: The Political Branches and the Transnational Prosecution of International Crimes, 105 *American Journal of International Law* 1 (2011).

Laster, R.E., Criminal Restitution: A Survey of Its Past History and an Analysis of Its Present Usefulness, 5 *University of Richmond Law Review* 71 (1970).

Lawyers Committee for Human Rights, What is a Fair Trial? A Basic Guide to Legal Standards and Practice, March 2000.

Lee, R.S., et al., eds., *The International Criminal Court: Elements of Crimes and Rules of Procedure and Evidence*, Transnational Publishers (2001).

Lind, E.A. and Tyler, T.R. *The Social Psychology of Procedural Justice*, Springer (1988).

Linton, S., Rising from the Ashes: The Creation of a Viable Criminal Justice System in East Timor, 25 *Melbourne University Law Review* 122 (2001).

Luban, D., *Lawyers and Justice: An Ethical Study*, Princeton University Press (1988).

Luna, E., Punishment Theory, Holism, and the Procedural Conception of Restorative Justice, 1 *Utah Law Review* 205 (2003).

Lurigio, A.J., Skogan, W.G. and Davis, R.C., eds., *Victims of Crime: Problems, Policies and Programs*, Sage Publications (1990).
MacCarrick, G., *The Right to a Fair Trial in International Criminal Law (Rules of Procedure and Evidence in Transition from Nuremberg to East Timor)*, submitted at the 19th International Conference of the International Society for the Reform of Criminal Law held in Edinburgh, Scotland from 26-30 June 2005.
MacDonald, L., Chamber and Parties Seek an Expeditious Trial, But at What Cost? *Cambodia Tribunal Monitor*, 23 June 2009.
Mack, N., et al., Qualitative Research Methods: A Data Collector's Field Guide, Participant Observation, *available at*: http://www.fhi.org/nr/rdonlyres/ed2ruznpftevg34lxuftzjiho65asz7betpqigbbyorggs6tetjic367v44baysyomnbdjkdtbsium/participantobservation1.pdf.
Malsh, M., Lay Participation in the Netherlands Criminal Law System, presented at the International Society for the Reform of Criminal Law, Convergence of Criminal Justice Systems: Building Bridges—Bridging the Gaps, The Hague, Netherlands, 24-28 August 2003.
Manning, J., On Power, Participation and Authority: The International Criminal Court's Initial Appellate Jurisprudence, 38 *Georgetown Journal of International Law* 803 (2007).
Marshall, T.F., Restorative Justice: An Overview, a Report by the Home Office Research and Development Statistics Directorate (1999).
Marsten Danner, A. and Martinez, J.S., Guilty Associations: Joint Criminal Enterprise, Command Responsibility, and the Development of International Criminal Law, 93 *California Law Review* 75 (2005).
Mawby, R.I. and Walklate, S., *Critical Victimology: International Perspectives*, Sage Publications Limited (1994).
McGoldrick, D., Rowe, P. and Donnelly, E., eds., *The Permanent International Criminal Court: Legal and Policy Issues*, Hart Publishing (2004).
McGonigle, B., Two for the Price of One: Victim Participation and the ECCC, a Criminal Court and Reconciliation Commission in One, 22 *Leiden Journal of International Law* 127 (2009a).
McGonigle, B., Bridging the Divides in International Criminal Proceedings: An Examination into the Victim Participation Endeavor of the International Criminal Court, 21 *Florida Journal of International Law* 93 (2009b).
McIntyre, G., Equality of Arms: Defining Human Rights in the Jurisprudence of the ICTY, submitted at the 17th International Conference of the International Society for the Reform of Criminal Law in The Hague, Netherlands from 24-28 August 2003, *available at*: http://www.isrcl.org/Conference_Papers.htm.
McKay, F., Legal Officer REDRESS, Speech Regarding Redress on Behalf of the Victims Rights Working Group, delivered to the Rome Conference on June 17 1998, *available at*: http://www.un.org/icc/speeches/616mck.htm.
Mégret, F., Beyond 'Fairness': Understanding the Determinants of International Criminal Procedure, 14 *University of California Los Angles Journal of International Law and Foreign Affairs* 37 (2009).

Mekjian, G.J. and Varughese, M.C., Hearing the Victim's Voice: Analysis of Victims' Advocate Participation in the Trial Proceedings of the International Criminal Court, 17 *Pace International Law Review* 1 (2005).
Merchant, J., History, Memory and Justice: The Touvier Trial in France, 23 *Journal of Criminal Justice* 425 (1995).
Merino-Blanco, E., *The Spanish Legal System*, Sweet & Maxwell (1996).
Merryman, J.H., *The Civil Law Tradition: An Introduction to the Legal System of Western Europe and Latin America*, Stanford University Press (1969).
Mettraux, G., Foreword for Symposium on Victims' Participation in International Criminal Law, 8 *Journal of International Criminal Justice* 75 (2008).
Mibenge, C., *Show Me a Woman! Narratives of Gender and Violence in Human Rights Law and Processes of Transitional Justice*, Pennsylvania University Press (2011).
Miers, D., The Responsibilities and the Rights of Victims of Crime, 55 *Modern Law Review* 482 (1992).
Milanovic, M., An Odd Couple: Domestic Crimes and International Responsibility in the Special Tribunal for Lebanon, 5 *Journal of International Criminal Justice* 1139 (2007).
Minow, M., *Between Vengeance and Forgiveness: Facing History after Genocide and Mass Violence*, Beacon Press (1998).
Mohan, M., The Paradox of Victim-Centrism: Victim Participation at the Khmer Rouge Tribunal, 9 *International Criminal Law Review* 733 (2009).
Moore, M., *Placing Blame: A General Theory of the Criminal Law*, Clarendon Press (1997).
Moore, M., Victims and Retribution: A Reply to Professor Fletcher, 3 *Buffalo Criminal Law Review* 65 (1999-2000).
Morgan, T., L'Affaire Touvier: Opening Old Wounds, *New York Times Magazine*, 1 October 1989.
Morris, V. and Scharf, M.P., *An Insiders Guide to the International Criminal Tribunal for the Former Yugoslavia, Vol. 1*, Transnational Publishers (1995).
Morris, V. and Scharf, M.P., *The International Criminal Tribunal for Rwanda, Vol. 1*, Transnational Publishers (1998).
Mundis, D.A., From 'Common Law' Towards 'Civil Law': The Evolution of the ICTY Rules of Procedure and Evidence, 14 *Leiden Journal of International Law* 367 (2001).
Murphy, P., The Indiscriminate Admission of Evidence is a Serious Flaw in International Criminal Trials, 8 *Journal of International Criminal Justice* 539 (2010).
Musila, G.M., The Participation of Victims in the International Criminal Court and the Question of Reparations, presented at the seminar 'International Justice: the Challenge for Africa' organized by the Institute for War and Peace Reporting, Goethe Institute, 31 October 2006.
Mydans, S., Anger in Cambodia follows Khmer Rouge Sentence, *New York Times*, 26 July 2010.
Naqvi, Y., The Right to the Truth in International Law: Fact or Fiction? 88 *International Review of the Red Cross* 245 (2006).
Neilan, T., Outrage at Cambodian Holocaust's Killer's Sentence, *AOL news*, 26 July 2010.
Newton, M.A., Iraqi Special Tribunal: A Human Rights Perspective, 38 *Cornell International Law Journal* 863 (2005).

Nicola, H., Witness to Rape: The Limits and Potential of International War Crimes Trials for Victims of Wartime Sexual Violence, 3 International Journal of Transitional Justice 114 (2009).
Nowak, M., *U.N. Covenant on Civil and Political Rights, CCPR Commentary, 2nd Ed.*, N.P. Engel Publisher (2005).
Ntanda Nsereko, D.D., Prosecutorial Discretion before National Courts and International Tribunals, submitted at the 17th International Conference of the International Society for the Reform of Criminal Law held in The Hague, Netherlands from 24-28 August 2003.
O'Connell, J., Gambling with the Psyche: Does Prosecuting Human Rights Violators Console Their Victims? 46 *Harvard International Law Journal* 295 (2005).
O'Hara, E.A., Victim Participation in the Criminal Process, 13 *Journal of Law & Policy*, 229 (2005).
O'Hear, M.M., Punishment, Democracy and Victims, 19 *United States of America Federal Sentencing Reporter* 1 (2006a).
O'Hear, M.M., Victims and Criminal Justice: What's Next? 19 *United States of America Federal Sentencing Reporter* 83 (2006b).
O'Hear, M.M., Plea Bargaining and Procedural Justice, 42 *Georgia Law Review* 407 (2008).
Olásolo, H., *The Triggering Procedure of the International Criminal Court*, Martinus Nijhoff Publishers (2005).
Olásolo, H., Systematic and Casuistic Approaches to the Role of Victims in Criminal Proceedings before the International Criminal Court, 12 *New Criminal Law Review* 513 (2009).
Olásolo, H. and A. Kiss, The Role of Victims in Criminal Proceedings before the International Criminal Court, 81 *International Review of Penal Law* 125 (2010).
Oldenquist, A., An Explanation of Retribution, 85 *The Journal of Philosophy* 464 (1988).
Orentlicher, D.F., Settling Accounts: The Duty to Prosecute Human Rights Violations of a Prior Regime, 100 *Yale Law Journal* 2537 (1991).
Osiel, M., *Mass Atrocity, Collective Memory, and the Law*, Transaction Publishers (2000).
Othman, M., Peacekeeping Operations in Asia: Justice and UNTAET, 3 *International Law Forum* 114 (2001).
O'Toole, J., Reparation Remain a Key Issue, *Phnom Penh Post*, 27 July 2010.
Packer, H.L., *The Limits of the Criminal Sanction*, Stanford University Press, (1968).
Parlevliet, M., Considering Truth: Dealing with a Legacy of Gross Human Rights Violations, 16 *Netherlands Quarterly of Human Rights* 141 (1998).
Patel King, F. and La Rosa, A.M., International Criminal Tribunal for the Former Yugoslavia: Current Survey, 8 *European Journal of International Law* 123 (1997).
Perter, Z. and Bopha, P., No More Khmer Rouge Trials, Premier Tells Ban, *Cambodia Daily*, 28 October 2010.
Pfanner, T., Interview with Philippe Kirsch, President of the International Criminal Court, 88 *International Review of the Red Cross* 9 (2006).
Pham, P., et al., *So We Will Never Forget: A Population-Based Survey on Attitudes about Social Reconstruction and The Extraordinary Chambers in the Courts of Cambodia*, Human Rights Center, University of California, Berkeley (2009).

Pheaktra, N. and Wilkins, G., Judges Should Focus on Current KR Suspects: Gov't, *Phnom Penh Post*, 12 March 2008.
Pigou, P., Crying without Tears: In Pursuit of Justice and Reconciliation in Timor Leste, Report for the International Center for Transitional Justice, August 2005.
Pizzi, W.T., Victims' Rights: Rethinking Our "Adversary System," 2 *Utah Law Review* 349 (1999).
Pizzi, W.T. and Marafioti, L., The New Italian Code of Criminal Procedure: The Difficulties of Building an Adversarial Trial System on a Civil Law Foundation, 17 *Yale Journal of International Law* 1 (1992).
Pizzi, W.T. and Perron, W., Crime Victims in German Courtrooms: A Comparative Perspective on American Problems, 32 *Stanford Journal of International Law* 37 (1996).
Pointing, J. and Maguire, M., eds., *Victims of Crime: A New Deal*, Open University Press (1988).
Porat, I., The Dual Model of Balancing: A Model for the Proper Scope of Balancing in Constitutional Law, 27 *Cardozo Law Review* 1393 (2005-2006).
Raitio, J., *The Principle of Legal Certainty in EC Law*, Kluwer Academic Publishers (2003).
Ramji, J. and Van Schaack, B., eds., *Bringing the Khmer Rouge to Justice: Prosecuting Mass Violence before the Cambodian Courts*, Edwin Mellen Press (2005).
Rauschenbach, M. and Scalia, D., Victims and International Criminal Justice: A Vexed Question, 90 *International Review of the Red Cross* 441 (2008).
Rawls, J., *A Theory of Justice*, Harvard University Press (1971).
REDRESS, Comments and Recommendations Regarding Legal Representation for Victims, Ensuring the Effective Participation of Victims before the International Criminal Court (2005).
REDRESS, Victims Central Role in Fulfilling the ICC's Mandate, paper prepared for the 8th Assembly of States Parties, 18-26 November 2009.
REDRESS, Comments on the OTP Policy Paper on Victims' Participation Under Article 68(3) of the ICC Statute, February 2010.
Refshauge, R., Justice For All—Victims, Defendants, Prisoners and the Community, Victims Rights and the Role of the Prosecutor, presented at Reform of Criminal Law Conference in Brisbane, Australia (2006).
Reiger, C. and Wierda, M., The Serious Crimes Process in Timor-Leste: In Retrospect, Report for the International Center for Transitional Justice, March 2006.
Ripstein, A., *Equality, Responsibility and the Law*, Cambridge University Press (1999).
Roach, K., *Due Process and Victims' Rights: The New Law and Politics of Criminal Justice*, University of Toronto Press (1999).
Roberts, P., Comparative Criminal Justice Goes Global, 28 *Oxford Journal of Legal Studies* 369 (2008).
Robinson, P.H., Hybrid Principles for the Distribution of Criminal Sanction, 82 *Northwestern University Law Review* 19 (1987).
Robinson, P.H., Should the Victims' Rights Movement Have Influence Over Criminal Law Formulation and Adjudication? 33 *McGeorge Law Review* 749 (2002).
Roche, D., *Accountability in Restorative Justice*, Oxford University Press (2003).

Romano, C.P.R., Nollkaemper, A. and Kleffner, J.K., *Internationalized Criminal Courts and Tribunals*, Oxford University Press (2004).
Rosas, A. and Helgesen, J., eds., *Human Rights in a Changing East-West Perspective*, Pinter Publishers (1990).
Rubel, H.C., Victim Participation in Sentencing Proceedings, 49 *Federal Probation* 50 (1986).
Ryngeart, C., ed., *The Effectiveness of International Criminal Justice*, Intersentia (2009).
Sadat, L., Reflections on the Trial of Vichy Collaborator Paul Touvier for Crimes against Humanity in France, 20 *Law & Social Inquiry* 191 (1995).
Safferling, C.J.M., *Towards an International Criminal Procedure*, Oxford University Press (2001).
Saliba, M., Civil Parties Boycott Start of Character Witness Testimony while Experts Offer Psychological Assessment of Duch, *Cambodia Tribunal Monitor*, 31 August 2009.
Sanders, A., *Taking Account of Victims in the Criminal Justice System: A Review of the Literature, Social Work Research Findings, No. 32*, The Scottish Office (1999).
Schabas, W.A., *An Introduction to the International Criminal Court, 2nd Ed.*, 68, Cambridge University Press (2004a).
Schabas, W.A., Conjoined Twins of Transitional Justice? The Sierra Leone Truth and Reconciliation Commission and the Special Court, 2 *Journal of International Criminal Justice* 1082 (2004b).
Schabas, W.A., *The UN International Criminal Tribunals: The Former Yugoslavia, Rwanda and Sierra Leone*, Cambridge University Press (2006).
Schabas, W.A., Thakur, R. and Hughes, E., eds., *Atrocities and International Accountability: Beyond Transitional Justice*, United Nations University (2007).
Scharf, M., The Case for a Permanent International Truth Commission, 7 *Duke Journal of Comparative and International Law* 375 (1997).
Scharf, M., Trial and Error: An Assessment of the First Judgment of the Yugoslavia War Crimes Tribunal, 30 *New York University Journal of International Law and Policy* 167 (1997-1998).
Scheffer, D., Memorandum on the Application of International Standards of Due Process by the Extraordinary Chambers in the Courts of Cambodia, Open Society Justice Initiative, April 2006.
Schoeman, F.D., ed., *Responsibility, Character, and the Emotions: New Essays in Moral Psychology*, Cambridge University Press (1987).
Schwikkard, P.J., Does the Merging of Inquisitorial and Adversarial Procedures Impact on Fair Trial Rights? Submitted at the 17th International Conference of the International Society for the Reform of Criminal Law held in The Hague, Netherlands from 24-28 August 2003.
Sebba, L., *Third Parties: Victims and the Criminal Justice System*, Ohio State University Press (1996).
Shapland, J., Willmore, J. and Duff, P., *Victims in the Criminal Justice System*, Gower (1985).
Sheehan, A.V., *Criminal Procedure in Scotland and France*, H.M. Stationery Office (1975).
Shelton, D., *Remedies in International Human Rights*, Clarendon Press (1999).

Sheppard, D., The International Criminal Court and "Internationally Recognized Human Rights": Understanding Article 21(3) of the Rome Statute, 10 *International Criminal Law Review* 43 (2010).
Skilbeck, R., Funding Justice: The Price of War Crimes Trials, 15 *Human Rights Brief* 6 (2008).
Sluiter, G., Victims in International Criminal Proceedings: A Plea for a Cautious Approach, Special Symposium Edition *Merkourios* 31 (2006).
Sluiter, G. and Vasiliev, S., eds., *International Criminal Procedure: toward a coherent body of law*, Cameron May Publishers (2009).
Sokha, C. and Corey-Boulet, R., ECCC Ruling Risks Unrest: PM, *Phnom Penh Post*, 8 September 2009.
Sokha, C. and O'Toole, J., Hun Sen Shoots from the Lip: Cases after 002 Face Embargo, *Phnom Penh Post*, 28 October 2010.
Sokheng, V., Inquiries Could Sink ECCC: PM, *Phnom Penh Post*, 10 September 2009.
Sorochinsky, M., Prosecuting Torturers, Protecting "Child Molesters": Toward a Power Balance Model of Criminal Process for International Human Rights Law, 31 *Michigan Journal of International Law* 157 (2009).
Staggs Kelsall, M., Baleva, M.K.A., Nababan, A., Chou, V., Guo, R., Ehlert, C., Nget S. and Ph, S., Lessons Learned from the Duch Trial: a Comprehensive Review of the First Case before the Extraordinary Chambers in the Courts of Cambodia, 33, produced by the Asian International Justice Initiative's KRT Trial Monitoring Group, December 2009
Stahn, C., Accommodating Individual Criminal Responsibility and National Reconciliation: The UN Truth Commission for East Timor, 95 *American Journal of International Law* 952 (2001).
Stahn, C., Olásolo, H., and Gibson, K., Participation of Victims in the Pre-Trial Proceedings of the ICC, 4 *Journal of International Criminal Justice* 219 (2006).
Stahn, C., Perspectives on *Katanga*: An Introduction, 23 *Leiden Journal of International Law* 311 (2010).
Stanley, E., *Torture, Truth and Justice: The Case of Timor Leste*, Routledge (2009).
Stapleton, S., Ensuring a Fair Trial in the International Criminal Court: Statutory Interpretation and the Impermissibility of Derogation, 31 *New York University Journal of International Law & Policy* 535 (1998-1999).
Stover, E., *The Witnesses: War Crimes and the Promise of Justice in The Hague*, University of Pennsylvania Press (2005).
Strang, H., *Repair or Revenge: Victims and Restorative Justice*, Clarendon Press (2002).
Strohmeyer, H., Collapse and Reconstruction of a Judicial System: The United Nations Missions in Kosovo and East Timor, 95 *American Journal of International Law* 46 (2001).
Sullivan, D. and Tifft, L., eds., *Restorative Justice*, Routledge International (2006).
Summers, S.J., *Fair Trials: The European Criminal Procedural Tradition and the European Court of Human Rights*, Hart Publishing (2007).
Swart, B., Damaška and the Faces of International Criminal Justice, 6 *Journal of International Criminal Justice* 87 (2008).
Taylor, T., *The Anatomy of the Nuremberg Trials*, Little, Brown & Co. (1992).

Temminck Tuinstra, J., *Defense Counsel in International Criminal Law*, T.M.C. Asser Press (2009).
Ten, C.L., *Crime, Guilt and Punishment, A Philosophical Introduction*, Clarendon Press (1987).
Thibaut, J. and Walker, L., *Procedural Justice: A Psychological Analysis*, Lawrence Erlbaum (1975).
Thomas, S., Civil Party Participation at the ECCC, *IntLawGrrls blogspot*, 15 July 2008.
Tobolowsky, P.M., Victim Participation in the Criminal Justice Process: Fifteen Years After the President's Task Force on Victims of Crime, 25 *Criminal and Civil Confinement* 21 (1999).
Tochilovsky, V., Rules of Procedure for the International Criminal Court: Problems to Address in Light of the Experience of the ad hoc Tribunals, 2 *World Justice Information Network, The Rule of Law Series* 1, 10 July 2000.
Trechsel, S., *Human Rights in Criminal Proceedings*, Oxford University Press (2005).
Triffterer, O., ed., *Commentary on the Rome Statute of the International Criminal Court: Observers' Notes, Article by Article*, Nomos Verlagsgesellschaft (1999).
Trumbull, C.P., The Victims of Victim Participation in International Criminal Proceedings, 29 *Michigan Journal of International Law* 777 (2008).
Tyler, T.R., The Psychology of Procedural Justice: A test of the Group-Value Model, 57 *Journal of Personality and Social Psychology* 830 (1989).
Tyler, T.R., Psychological Models of the Justice Motive: Antecedents of Distributive and Procedural Justice, 67 *Journal of Personality and Social Psychology* 850 (1994).
Tyler, T.R. and Lind, E.A., A Relational Model of Authority, 25 *Advanced Experimental Social Psychology* 115 (1992).
Van den Bos, et al., Procedural and Distributive Justice: What is Fair Depends More on What Comes First than on What Comes Next, 72 *Journal of Personality and Social Psychology* 95 (1997a).
Van den Bos, et al., How Do I Judge My Outcome When I Do Not Know the Outcome of Others? The Psychology of the Fair Process Effect, 72 *Journal of Personality and Social Psychology* 1034 (1997b).
Vanderpuye, K., Tranditions in Conflict: The Internationalization of Confrontation, 43 *Cornell International Law Journal* 513 (2010).
Van Dijk, J.J.M., et al., eds., *Criminal Law in Action: An Overview of Current Issues in Western Societies*, Kluwer Law and Taxation Publishers (1986).
Van Dijk, J.J.M., van Kaam, R.G.H. and Wemmers, J.M., eds., *Caring for Crime Victims: Selected Proceedings of the 9th International Symposium on Victimology*, Criminal Justice Press (1999).
Van Dijk, P., *The Right of the Accused to a Fair Trial under International Law*, SIM Special Publication (1983).
Van Genugten, W., Van Gestel, R., Groenhuijsen, M. and Letschert, R., Loopholes, Risks and Ambivalences in International Lawmaking; The Case of a Framework Convention on Victims' Rights, 37 *Netherlands Yearbook of International Law* 109 (2006).
Van Genugten, W., Scharf, M. and Radin, S.E., eds., *Criminal Jurisdiction 100 Years After the 1907 Hague Peace Conference*, T.M.C. Asser Press (2009).

Van Ness, D., New Wine and Old Wineskins: Four Challenges of Restorative Justice, 4 *Criminal Law Forum* 251 (1993).
Van Sliedregt, E., *Tien tegen Één*, Oratie Vrije Universiteit Amsterdam, 19 September 2008, *available at*: http://www.advalvas.vu.nl/images/documenten/oratiesliedregt.pdf.
Vasiliev, S., Proofing the Ban on 'Witness Proofing': Did the ICC Get It Right? 20 *Criminal Law Forum* 193 (2009).
Vélez, S., Victims Raise Their Voice in the Lubanga Case, Aegis Trust, 23 October 2009.
Vidmar, N. and Miller, D.T., Social Psychological Processes Underlying Attitudes Toward Legal Punishment, 14 *Law & Society Review* 565 (1980).
Vogler, R., *A World View of Criminal Justice*, Ashgate (2005).
Vogler, R. and Huber, B., eds., *Criminal Procedure in Europe*, Duncker & Humblot (2008).
Von Hebel, H., et al., eds., *Reflections on the International Criminal Court: Essays in Honour of Adriaan Bos*, T.M.C. Asser Press (1999)
Von Hirsh, A., et al., eds., *Restorative Justice and Criminal Justice: Competing or Reconcilable Paradigms?* Hart Publishing (2003).
Wakabi, W., Q&A with Luc Walleyn, Lawyer for Victims in Lubanga's Trial, *LubangaTrial.org Commentary*, 13 January 2010.
War Crimes Research Office, American University, Washington College of Law, Victim Participation Before the International Criminal Court, November 2007.
War Crimes Research Office, American University, Washington College of Law, Victim Participation at the Case Stage of Proceedings, February 2009.
Weed, F.J., *Certainty of Justice: Reform in the Crime Victim Movement*, Aldine de Gruyter (1995).
Weissbrodt, D., *The Right to a Fair Trial Under the Universal Declaration of Human Rights and the International Covenant on Civil and Political Rights*, Martinus Nijhoff Publishers (2001).
Weitekamp, E., Reparative Justice: Towards a Victim Oriented System, 1 *European Journal of Criminal Policy Research* 70 (1992).
Welling, S.N., Victims in the Criminal Process: A Utilitarian Analysis of Victim Participation in the Charging Decision, 30 *Arizona Law Review* 85 (1988).
Wemmers, J., *Victims in the Criminal Justice System*, Kugler Publications (1996).
Wemmers, J., Victims' Rights and the International Criminal Court: Perceptions Within the Court Regarding the Victims' Right to Participate, 23 *Leiden Journal of International Law* 629 (2010).
Wenzel, M., et al., Retributive and Restorative Justice, 32 *Law and Human Behavior* 375 (2008).
Werle, G., *Principles of International Criminal Law*, T.M.C. Asser Press (2005).
Whiteley, D., The Victim and the Justification of Punishment, 17 *Criminal Justice Ethics* 42 (1998).
Wierda, M.L., What Lessons Can Be Learned From the Ad Hoc Criminal Tribunals? 9 *University of California Davis Journal of International Law & Policy* 13 (2002).
Willis, J.F., *Prologue to Nuremberg: The Politics and Diplomacy of Punishing War Criminals of the First World War*, Greenwood Publishing Group (1982).

Women's Caucus for Gender Justice, Victims and Witnesses in the ICC Report of Panel Discussions on Appropriate Measures for Victim Participation and Protection in the ICC (1999).

Wojcik, M.E., False Hope: the Rights of Victims Before International Criminal Tribunals, 28 *L'Observateur des Nations Unies* 16 (2010).

Wright, M., *Justice for Victims and Offenders: A Restorative Response to Crime*, Open University Press (1991).

Yesberg, K., Accessing Justice through Victim Participation at the Khmer Rouge Tribunal, 40 *Victoria University Wellington Law Review* 555 (2009).

Zahar, A. and Sluiter, G., *International Criminal Law*, Oxford University Press (2008).

Zappalá, S., *Human Rights in International Criminal Proceedings*, Oxford University Press (2003).

Zappalá, S., The Rights of Victims v. the Rights of the Accused, 8 *Journal of International Criminal Justice* 137 (2010).

Zegveld, L., Victims' Reparation Claims and International Criminal Courts: Incompatible Values? 8 *Journal of International Criminal Justice* 79 (2010).

Zehr, H., *Changing Lenses: A New Focus for Crime and Justice*, Herald Press (1990).

Zehr, H. and Toews, B., eds., *Critical Issues in Restorative Justice*, Criminal Justice Press (2004).

UN and Selected Documents

UN Documents

The Declaration of Basic Principles of Justice for Victims of Crime and Abuse of Power, UN Doc. A/Res/40/34/Annex (1985).

Study concerning the right to restitution, compensation and rehabilitation for victims of gross violations of human rights and fundamental freedoms, Final report submitted by Mr. Theo van Boven, Special Rapporteur, UN Doc. E/CN.4/SUB.2/1993/8 (1993).

Report of the Secretary General pursuant to par. 2 of Security Council Resolution 808, UN Doc. S/25704 (1993).

Preliminary Report of the Independent Commission of Experts established in accordance with SC Res. 935 (1994), UN Doc. S/1994/1125 (1994).

Report of the Commission on Human Rights on Its Third Special Session, UN Doc. E/1994/24/Add.2 (1994).

Resolution on Children as victims and perpetrators, adopted by the Ninth UN Congress on the Prevention of Crime and the Treatment of Offenders, UN Doc. A/CONF.169/16 (1995).

Draft Basic Principles and Guidelines on the Right to Restitution, Compensation, and Rehabilitation for Victims of Gross Violations of Human Rights and Fundamental Freedoms, UN Doc. E/CN.4/1997/104 (1997).

UN High Commissioner for Human Rights, Situation of Human Rights in Cambodia, UN Human Rights Comm'n Res. 1997/49 (1997).

UN Diplomatic Conference on Plenipotentiaries on the Establishment of an International Criminal Court, Preparatory Committee on the Establishment of an International Criminal Court, Report of the Preparatory Committee on the Establishment of an International Criminal Court, UN Doc. A/CONF.183/2/Add.1 (1998).

UN Diplomatic Conference of Plenipotentiaries on the Establishment of an International Criminal Court, Committee of the Whole, Working Group on Procedural Matters, Report of the Working Group on Procedural Matters, UN Doc. A/CONF.183/C.1/WGPM/ L.2/ADD.6 (1998).

Report of the Secretary-General on the United Nations Interim Administration Mission in Kosovo, UN Doc. S/1999/779 (1999).

Report of the Group of Experts for Cambodia established pursuant to UNGA 52/135, UN Doc. A/53/850 (1999).

UN Commission on Human Rights, The right to restitution, compensation and rehabilitation for victims of grave violations of human rights and fundamental freedoms, UN Doc. E/CN.4/RES/2000/41 (2000).

Draft Basic Principles and Guidelines on the Right to a Remedy and Reparation for Victims of Violations of International Human Rights and Humanitarian Law, UN Doc. E/CN.4/2000/62 (2000).

Principles on the Effective Investigation and Documentation of Torture and Other Cruel, Inhuman, or Degrading Treatment or Punishment, UN Doc. A/RES/55/89 (2000).

Working Paper: Offenders and Victims: Accountability and Fairness in the Criminal Justice Process, Tenth United Nations Congress on the Prevention of Crime and the Treatment of Offenders, UN Doc. A/CONF.187/8 (2000).

Letter from the permanent Representative of Sierra Leone to the United Nations to the President of the Security Council, UN Doc. S/2000/786 (2000).

Report of the Secretary General on the Establishment of a Special Court for Sierra Leone, UN Doc. S/2000/915 (2000).

Letter dated 2 November 2000 from the Secretary-General addressed to the President of the Council, UN Doc. S/2000/1063 (Annex) (2000).

Letter of 14 December 2000 from the Secretary General addressed to President of the Security Council, UN Doc. S/2000/1198 (2000).

Protocol to Prevent, Suppress and Punish Trafficking in Persons, Especially Women and Children, Supplementing the United Nations Convention Against Transnational Organized Crime, UN Doc. A/45/49 (Vol. I) (2001).

ACmHPR, Principles and Guidelines on the Right to a Fair Trial and Legal Assistance, UN Doc. DOC/05/(XXX)247 (2001).

UNSubCHR, Recognition of responsibility and reparation for massive and flagrant violations of human rights which constitute crimes against humanity and which took place during the period of slavery, colonialism and wars of conquest, UN Doc. E/CN.4/SUB.2/RES/2002/5 (2002).

ECOSOC, Basic Principles on the use of Restorative Justice Programs in Criminal Matters 2002/12, UN Doc. E/CN.15/2002/5/Add.1 (2002).

UN Commission on Human Rights, Question of enforced or involuntary disappearances, UN Doc. E/CN.4/RES/2002/41 (2002).

UN Commission on Human Rights, Draft basic principles on the right to a remedy and reparation for victims of violations of international human rights and humanitarian law, UN Doc. E/CN.4/2003/63 (2003).

UN Commission on Human Rights, Draft basic principles the right to a remedy and reparation for victims of violations of international human rights and humanitarian law, UN Doc. E/CN.4/2004/57 (2004).

Statement by the President of the Security Council, UN Doc. S/PRST/2005/4 (2005).

UN Commission on Human Rights, Draft basic principles on the right to a remedy and reparation for victims of violations of international human rights and humanitarian law - Note by the High Commissioner for Human Rights, UN Doc. E/CN.4/2005/59 (2005).

UN Commission on Human Rights, The right to truth, UN Doc. E/CN.4/RES/2005/66 (2005).

Basic Principles and Guidelines on the Right to a Remedy and Reparation for Victims of Gross Violations of International Human Rights Law and Serious Violations of International Humanitarian Law, UN Doc. A/RES/60/147 (2005).

Report of the Fact-Finding Mission to Lebanon Inquiring into the Causes, Circumstances and Consequences of the Assassination of former Prime Minister Rafiq Hariri, UN Doc. S/2005/203 (2005).

Report to the Secretary-General of the Commission of Experts to Review the Prosecution of Serious Violations of Human Rights in Timor-Leste (then East Timor) in 1999, UN Doc. S/2005/458 (Annex) (2005).

Letter dated 13 December 2005 from the Chargé d'affaires a.i. of the Permanent Mission of Lebanon to the United Nations addressed to the Secretary-General, UN Doc. S/2005/783 (2005).

Right to the truth, Commission on Human Rights Resolution 2005/66, UN Doc. E/CN.4/RES/2005/66 (2005).

Updated Set of Principles for the Protection and Promotion of Human Rights Through Action to Combat Impunity, Report of the independent expert Diane Orentlicher delivered to the Commission on Human Rights, UN Doc. E/CN.4/2005/102/Add. 1 (2005).

Report of the Secretary-General on the establishment of a Special Tribunal for Lebanon, UN Doc. S/2006/893 (2006).

Study on the right to the truth, Report of the Office of the United Nations High Commissioner for Human Rights, UN Doc. E/CN.4/2006/91 (2006).

Implementation of General Assembly Resolution 60/251 of 15 March 2006 entitled "Human Rights Council," Right to the truth, Report of the Office of the High Commissioner for Human Rights, UN Doc. A/HRC/5/7 (2007).

Report of the Court on legal aid: Legal and financial aspects of funding victims' legal representation before the Court, UN Doc. ICC-ASP/8/25 (2009).

Report of the Secretary-General on the United Nations Interim Administration Mission in Kosovo, UN Doc. S/2009/149 (2009).

2009 Report of the International Criminal Tribunal for the former Yugoslavia to the UN General Assembly, UN Doc. A/64/205-S/2009/394 (2009).

Human Rights Commission
UN Hum. Rights Commission Res. 1997/49 (1997).

Human Rights Committee
GC No. 32, UN Doc. CCPR/C/GC/32 (2007).

UNGA
UNGA Res. 53/105, UN Doc. A/RES/53/105 (1999).
UNGA Res. 57/225, UN Doc. A/RES/57/225 (2002).
UNGA Res. 147, UN Doc. A/RES/60/147 (2006).

UNSC
UNSC Res. 764, UN Doc. S/RES/764 (1992)
UNSC Res. 780, UN Doc. S/RES/780 (1992).
UNSC Res. 808, UN Doc. S/RES/808 (1993).
UNSC Res. 935, UN Doc. S/RES/935 (1994).
UNSC Res. 955, UN Doc. S/RES/955 (1994).
UNSC Res. 1244, UN Doc. S/RES/1244 (1999).
UNSC Res. 1272, UN Doc. S/RES/1272 (1999).
UNSC Res. 1595, UN Doc. S/RES/1595 (2005).
UNSC Res. 1644, UN Doc. S/RES/1644 (2005).
UNSC Res. 1757, UN Doc. S/RES/1757 (2007).
UNSC Res. 1970 UN Doc. S/RES/1970 (2011).

UNTAET
UNTAET Reg. 2000/11 (2000).
UNTAET Reg. 2000/15 (2000).
UNTAET Reg. 2000/30 (2000).
UNTAET Reg. 2001/10 (2001).
UNTAET Reg. 2001/25 (2001).

UNMIK
UNMIK Reg. 1999/24 (1999).

Miscelaneous
United Nations Office for Drug Control and Crime Prevention: Center for International Crime Prevention, Guide for Policy Makers on the Implementation of the United Nations Declaration of Basic Principles for Justice for Victims of Crime and Abuse of Power (1999).

United Nations Office for Drug Control and Crime Prevention: Center for International Crime Prevention, Handbook on Justice for Victims: On the Use and Application of the Declaration of Basic Principles of Justice for Victims of Crime and Abuse of Power (1999).

Office of the United Nations High Commissioner for Human Rights, *The Right to a Fair Trial: Part I – From Investigation to Trial...*, Human Rights in the Administration of Justice: A Manual on Human Rights for Judges, Prosecutors and Lawyers (2003).

Draft Convention on Justice and Support for Victims of Crime and Abuse of Power (2006).

Joint Letter from ASF, Center for Justice and Reconciliation, DRC Coalition for the ICC, FIDH, HRW, REDRESS, and the Women's Initiative for Gender Justice to Luis Moreno Ocampo, Chief Prosecutor, ICC, on the Narrow Scope of the Charges Brought Against Mr. Lubanga, 31 July 2006.

Statement by the Victims Unit, Historic Achievement in International Criminal Law: Victims of Khmer Rouge crimes fully involved in proceedings of the ECCC, 4 February 2008.

Special Tribunal for Lebanon (STL), President's Explanatory Memorandum of the Rules of Procedure and Evidence (2009)

ECCC, Fifth Plenary Session of Judicial Officers, Closing Press Statement, 6 March 2009.

Cambodian Human Rights Action Committee Press Release, New Directions for Victim Participation at the ECCC, 26 February 2010.

TABLE OF CASES

DECISIONS, JUDGMENTS AND FILINGS

Human Rights Committee

Torres Ramirez v. Uruguay, Comm. No. 4/1977, 26 January 1978.
Dante Santullo Valcada v. Uruguay, Comm. No. 9/1977, 26 October 1979.
Grille Motta v. Uruguay, Comm. No. 11/1977, 29 July 1980.
Bleier Lewenhoff and Valiño de Bleier v. Uruguay, Comm. No. 30/1978, 29 March 1982.
R.A.V.N. et al. v. Argentina, Comm. No. 343, 344 and 345/1988, 5 April 1990.
Laureano Atachahua v. Peru, Comm. No. 540/1993, 25 March 1996.
Vicente and Villafaqe Chaparro, Napolesn Torres Crespo, Marma Torres Arroyo and Hugues Chaparro Torres v. Colombia, Comm. No. 612/1995, 29 July 1997.
Chonwe v. Zambia, Comm. No. 821/1998, 25 October 2000.
Vaca v. Colombia, Comm. No. 859/1999, 25 March 2002.
Staselovich and Lyashkevich v. Belarus, Comm. No. 887/1999, 3 April 2003.
Sarma v. Sri Lanka, Comm. No. 950/2000, 31 July 2003.
Khalilov v. Tajikistan, Comm. No. 973/2001, 30 March 2005.
Aliboev v. Tajikistan, Comm. No. 985/2001, 18 October 2005.
Dudko v. Australia, Comm. No. 1347/2005, 29 August 2007.

European Court of Human Rights

Jespers v. Belgium, App. No. 8403/78, 14 December 1981.
Kaufman v. Belgium, App. No. 10938/84, 9 December 1986.
Brandstetter v. Austria, App. No. 11170/84; 12876/87; 13468/87, 28 August 1991.
Tomasi v. France, App. No. 12850/87, 27 August 1992.
Ruiz-Mateos v. Spain, App. No. 12952/87, 23 June 1993.
McCann and Others v. United Kingdom, App. No. 18984/91, 5 September 1995.
Acquaviva v. France, App. No. 19248/91, 21 November 1995.
Bulut v. Austria, App. No. 17358/90, 22 February 1996.
Hamer v. France, App. No. 19953/92, 7 August 1996.
Aksoy v. Turkey, App. No. 21987/93, 18 December 1996.
Foucher v France, App No. 22209/93, 18 March 1997.
Aydin v. Turkey, App. No. 23178/94, 25 September 1997.
Kaya v. Turkey, App. No. 22729/93, 19 February 1998.
Belziuk v. Poland, App. No. 23103/93, 25 March 1998.
Güleç v. Turkey, App. No. 21593/93, 27 July 1998.
Yasa v. Turkey, App. No. 22495/93, 2 September 1998.
Assenov and Others v. Bulgaria, App. No. 24760/94, 28 October 1998.
Oğur v. Turkey, App. No. 21594/93, 20 May 1999.

Çakici v. Turkey, App. No. 23657/94, 8 July 1999.
Tanrikulu v. Turkey, App. No. 23763/94, 8 July 1999.
Rowe and Davis v. United Kingdom, App. No. 28901/95, 16 February 2000.
Timurtas v. Turkey, App. No. 23531/94, 13 June 2000.
Salman v. Turkey, App. No. 21986/93, 27 June 2000.
Gül v. Turkey, App. No. 22676/93, 14 December 2000.
Hugh Jordan v. United Kingdom, App. No. 24746/94, 4 August 2001.
McKerr v. United Kingdom, App. No. 28883/95, 4 August 2001.
Kelly and Others v. United Kingdom, App. No. 30054/96, 4 August 2001.
Shanaghan v. United Kingdom, App. No. 37715/97, 4 August 2001.
Perez v. France, App. No. 47287/99, 12 February 2004.
Gorraiz Lizarraga and Others v. Spain, App. No. 62543/00, 27 April 2004.
Siliadin v. France, App. No. 73316/01, 26 July 2005.

European Court of Justice

Jokela and Pitkäranta, C-9/97 and C-118/97, 22 October 1998.

Inter-American Court of Human Rights

Velasquez Rodriguez v. Honduras, Judgment, 29 July 1988.
Godínez Cruz v. Honduras, Judgment, 20 January 1989.
Fairen Garbi and Solís Corrales v. Honduras, Judgment, 15 March 1989.
Neira Alegría v. Peru, Judgment, 19 January 1995.
Cabellero-Delgado and Santana v. Columbia, Judgment, 8 December 1995.
Genie Lacayo v. Nicaragua, Judgment, 29 January 1997.
Castillo Páez v. Peru, Judgment, 3 November 1997.
Blake v. Guatemala, Judgment, 24 January 1998.
Paniagua-Morales et al. v. Guatemala, Judgment, 8 March 1998.
Villagrán Morales et al. v. Guatemala, Judgment, 19 November 1999.
Durand and Ugarte v. Peru, Judgment, 16 August 2000.
Bámaca-Velásquez v. Guatemala, Judgment, 25 November 2000.
Barrios Altos v. Peru, Judgment, 14 March 2001.
Bulacio v. Argentina, Judgment (Merits, Reparations and Costs), 18 September 2003.
Myrna Mack Chang v. Guatemala, Judgment, 25 November 2003.
Tibi v. Ecuador, Judgment, 7 September 2004.
Gutiérrez Soler v. Colombia, Judgment, 12 September 2005.
Almonacid-Arellano, et al., v. Chile, Preliminary Objections, Merits, Reparations and Costs, 26 September 2006.
La Cantuta v. Peru, Judgment, 29 November 2006.
Albán-Cornejo v. Ecuador, Judgment, 22 November 2007.

African Court of Human and Peoples' Rights

Yogogombaye v. Republic of Senegal, App. No. 001/2008, Judgment, 15 December 2009.

African Commission on Human and Peoples' Rights

Amnesty International v. Zambia, Comm. No. 212/98, 5 May 1999.

International Criminal Tribunal for the former Yugoslavia
Prosecutor v. Tadić, Case No. IT-94-1, Decision on the Prosecutor's Motion Requesting Protective Measures for Victims and Witnesses, Trial Chamber II, 10 August 1995.

Prosecutor v. Tadić, Case No. IT-94-1, Order Denying Leave to Appear as *Amicus Curiae*, Trial Chamber II, 25 November 1996.

Prosecutor v. Blaškić, Case. No. IT-95-14, Orders Granting Leave to Appear as Amicus Curiae, Trial Chamber I, 11 April 1997.

Prosecutor v. Tadić, Case No. IT-94-1, Opinion and Judgment, Trial Chamber II, 7 May 1997.

Prosecutor v. Tadić, Case No. IT-94-1, Sentencing Judgment, Trial Chamber II, 14 July 1997.

Prosecutor v. Erdemović, Case No. IT-96-22, Judgment, Joint and Separate Opinion of Judge McDonald and Judge Vorah, Trial Chamber I, 7 October 1997.

Prosecutor v. Erdemović, Case No. IT-96-22, Sentencing Judgment, Trial Chamber I, 5 March 1998.

Prosecutor v. Furundžija, Case No. IT-95-17/1, Order Granting Leave to File *Amicus Curiae* Brief, Trial Chamber II, 10 November 1998.

Prosecutor v. Furundžija, Case No. IT-95-17/1, Order Granting Leave to File *Amicus Curiae* Brief, Trial Chamber II, 11 November 1998.

Prosecutor v. Mucić et al., Case No. IT-96-21, Judgment, Trial Chamber II quater, 16 November 1998.

Prosecutor v. Aleksovski, Case No. IT-95-14/1-A, Decision on Prosecutor's Appeal on Admissibility of Evidence, Appeals Chamber, 16 February 1999.

Prosecutor v. Tadić, Case No. IT-94-1, Sentencing Judgment (II), Trial Chamber II, 11 November 1999.

Prosecutor v. Tadić, Case No. IT-94-1, Judgment in Sentencing Appeals, Appeals Chamber, 26 January 2000.

Prosecutor v. Blaškić, Case No. IT-95-14, Judgment, Trial Chamber I, 3 March 2000.

Prosecutor v. Aleksovski, Case No. IT-95-14/1-A, Judgment, Declaration of Judge David Hunt, Appeals Chamber, 24 March 2000.

Prosecutor v. Furundžija, Case No. IT-95-17/1-A, Judgment, Declaration of Judge Patrick Robinson, Appeals Chamber, 21 July 2000.

Prosecutor v. Kunarac et al., Case. No. IT-96-23 & 23/1, Judgment, Trial Chamber II, 22 February 2001.

Prosecutor v. Kordić & Čerkez, Case No. IT-95-14/2, Judgment, Trial Chamber III, 26 February 2001.

Prosecutor v. Kvocka et al., Case No. IT-98-30/1, Decision on Interlocutory Appeal by the Accused Zoran Zigic against the Decision of Trial Chamber I dated 5 December 2000, Appeals Chamber, 25 May 2001.

Prosecutor v. Todorović, Case No. IT-95-9/1, Sentencing Judgment, Trial Chamber III, 31 July 2001.

Prosecutor v. Krstić, Case No. IT-98-33, Judgment, Trial Chamber I, 2 August 2001.

Prosecutor v. Kunarac et al., Case. No. IT-96-23 & 23/1, Appeal Judgment, Appeals Chamber, 12 June 2002.

Prosecutor v. Nikolic, Case No. IT-94-2, Decision on Defense Motion Challenging the Exercise of Jurisdiction by the Tribunal, Trial Chamber II, 9 October 2002.

Prosecutor v. Nikolic, Case No. IT-94-2-S, Sentencing Judgment, Trial Chamber II, 18 December 2003.

Prosecutor v. Bralo, Case No. IT-95-17, Sentencing Judgment, Trial Chamber III, 7 December 2005.

Prosecutor v. Krajišnik, Case No. IT-00-39-T, Reasons for Decision Denying Defense Motion Regarding Chamber Witnesses Biljana Plavšić and Branko Derić and Decision on Admission into Evidence of Biljana Plavšić's Statement and Book Extracts, Trial Chamber I, 14 August 2006.

International Criminal Tribunal for Rwanda
Prosecutor v. Akayesu, Case No. ICTR-96-4-T, Order Granting Leave for Amicus Curiae to Appear, Trial Chamber I, 12 February 1998.

Prosecutor v. Bagosora, Kibiligi, Ntabakuze and Nsengiyumva, Case No. ICTR-96-7-T, Decision on the amicus curiae application by the Government of the Kingdom of Belgium, Trial Chamber II, 6 June 1998.

Prosecutor v. Kambanda, Case no.: ICTR 97-23-S, Judgment and Sentence, Trial Chamber I, 4 September 1998.

Prosecutor v. Akayesu, Case. No. ICTR-96-4-T, Sentencing Judgment, Trial Chamber I, 2 October 1998.

Prosecutor v. Musema, Case No. ICTR-96-13-T, Decision on an application by African Concern for leave to appear as amicus curiae, Trial Chamber I, 17 March 1999.

Prosecutor v. Semanza, Case No. ICTR-97-20-T, Decision on the Kingdom of Belgium's Application to File an *Amicus Curiae* and on the Defense Application to Strike Out Observations of the Kingdom of Belgium Concerning the Preliminary Response by the Defense, Trial Chamber III, 9 February 2001.

Prosecutor v. Ntagerura, Bagambiki and Imanishimwe, Case No. ICTR-99-46-T, Decision on the Application to File an *Amicus Curiae* Brief According to Rule 74 of the Rules of Procedure and Evidence Filed on Behalf of the NGO Coalition for Women's Human Rights in Conflict Situations, Trial chamber III, 24 May 2001.

Prosecutor v. Bagosora, Kibiligi, Ntabakuze and Nsengiyumva, Case No. ICTR-98-41-T, Decision on Amicus Curiae Request by the Rwandan Government, Trial Chamber III, 13 October 2004.

Special Panels in East Timor (SPSC)
Prosecutor v. Cardoso Ferreira, Case No. 04c/2001, Judgment, (Dist. Ct. Dili) Trial Chamber, 4 May 2003.

Special Tribunal for Lebanon
Submission of the Prosecutor to the Pre-Trial Judge Under Rule 17 of the Rules of Procedure and Evidence, CH/PTJ/2009/004, 29 April 2009.

Order Regarding the Detention of Persons Detained in Lebanon in Connection with the Case of the Attack against Prime Minister Rafiq Hariri and Others, CH/PTJ/2009/06, 29 April 2009.

Extraordinary Chambers in the Courts of Cambodia
Case of Nuon Chea (Case 002), Public Order on the Filing of Submissions on the Issue of Civil Party Participation in Appeals against Provisional Detention Order and an Invitation to Amicus Curiae, Pre-Trial Chamber, 12 February 2008.

Case 002, Joint and Several Submission on Civil Party Participation in Appeals Related to Provisional Detention, Pre-Trial Chamber, 22 February 2008.

Case 002, Amicus Brief by Christoph Safferling on the Issue of Civil Party Participation, Pre-Trial Chamber, 22 February 2008.

Case of Nuon Chea (Case 002), Decision on Civil Party Participation in Provisional Detention Appeals, Pre-Trial Chamber, 20 March 2008.

Case of Ieng Thirith (Case 002), Directions on Civil Party Oral Submissions during the hearing of the Appeal against Provisional Detention Order, Pre-Trial Chamber, 20 May 2008.

Case of Kaing Guek Eav (Case 001), Order Concerning Requests for Investigative Actions, Co-Investigating Judges, 4 June 2008.

Case of Ieng Sary (Case 002), Decision of 1 July 2008 on the Civil Party's Request to Address the Court in Person, Pre-Trial Chamber, 1 July 2008.

Case of Ieng Sary (Case 002), Decision on Preliminary Matters Raised by the Lawyers for the Civil Parties in Ieng Sary's Appeal against Provisional Detention Order, Pre-Trial Chamber, 1 July 2008.

Case of Ieng Sary (Case 002), Joint Civil Parties' Co-Lawyers' Observations on Application for Reconsideration of Civil Party's Right to Address the Chamber, Pre-Trial Chamber, 17 July 2008.

Case of Kaing Guek Eav (Case 001), Closing Order, Co-Investigating Judges, 12 August 2008.

Case of Ieng Sary (Case 002), Decision on Application for Reconsideration of Civil Party's Right to Address Pre-Trial Chamber in Person, Pre-Trial Chamber, 28 August 2008.

Case of Ieng Sary (Case 002), Directions on Unrepresented Civil Parties' Rights to Address the Pre-Trial Chamber in Person, Pre-Trial Chamber, 29 August 2008.

Case of Nuon Chea (Case 002), Decision on Civil Party Co-Lawyers' Joint Request for Reconsideration, Pre-Trial Chamber, 25 February 2009.

Case of Kaing Guek Eav (Case 001), Decision of the Trial Chamber Concerning Proof of Identity for Civil Party Applicants, Trial Chamber, 26 February 2009.

Case of Kaing Guek Eav (Case 001), Decision on Civil Party Status of Applicants E2/36, E2/51 and E2/69/Public, Trial Chamber, 4 March 2009.

Case of Kaing Guek Eav (Case 001), Direction on Making a Brief Opening Statement During the Substantive Hearing, Trial Chamber, 10 March 2009.

Case of Kaing Guek Eav (Case 001), Decision on Motion Regarding Deceased Civil Party, Trial Chamber, 13 March 2009.

Case of Kaing Guek Eav (Case 001), Direction on the Scheduling of the Trial, Trial Chamber, 20 March 2009.

Case of Ieng Thirith (Case 002), Co-Prosecutors' Response to Ieng Thirith's Defense Request for Exclusion of Evidence Obtained by Torture dated 11 February 2009, Co-Investigating Judges, 30 April 2009.

Case 002, Co-Lawyers of Civil Parties' Investigative Request Concerning the Crimes of Enforced Disappearance, Co-Investigating Judges, 30 June 2009.

Case 002, Second Request for Investigative Actions Concerning Forced Marriages and Forced Sexual Relations, Co-Investigating Judges, 15 July 2009.

Case of Kaing Guek Eav (Case 001), Decision on Civil Party Co-Lawyers' Joint Request for a Ruling on the Standing of Civil Party Lawyers to Make Submissions on Sentencing and Directions Concerning the Questioning of the Accused, Experts and Witnesses Testifying on Character, Trial Chamber, 9 October 2009.

Case 002, Co-Lawyers for the Civil Parties' Fourth Investigative Request Concerning Forced Marriages and Sexually Related Crimes, Co-Investigating Judges, 4 December 2009

Case 002, Order on Civil Party Request for Investigative Action Concerning Enforced Disappearance, Co-Investigating Judges, 21 December 2009.

Situation in Darfur, Sudan, Decision On the Applications by Victims a/0443/09 to a/0450/09 to Participate in the Appeal against the "Decision on the Prosecution's Application for a Warrant of Arrest against Omar Hassan Ahmad Al Bashir" and on the Request for an Extension of Time, Appeals Chamber, No. ICC-02/05-01/09-48, 23 December 2009.

Case 002, Order on Request for Investigative Action by the Civil Parties Concerning the Charge of Attack against Culture, Co-Investigating Judges, 15 March 2010.

Case 002, Decision on Appeal of Co-Lawyers for Civil Parties against Order Rejecting Request to Interview Persons Named in the Forced Marriages and Enforced Disappearance Requests for Investigative Action, Pre-Trial Chamber, 21 July 2010.

Case of Kaing Guek Eav (Case 001), Judgment, Trial Chamber, 26 July 2010.

Case 002, Order on the Organization of Civil Party Representation under Rule 23ter of the Rules, Co-Investigating Judges, 2 August 2010.

Case of Ieng Thirith (Case 002), Public Decision on Appeal of Co-Lawyers for Civil Parties against Order on Civil Parties' Request for Investigative Actions Concerning All Properties Owned by the Charged Persons, Pre-Trial Chamber, 4 August 2010.

Case of Kaing Guek Eav (Case 001), Group 1—Civil Parties' Co-Lawyers' Immediate Appeal of Civil Party Status Determinations from the Final Judgment, Supreme Court Chamber, 14 September 2010.

Case 002, Closing Order, Co-Investigating Judges, 15 September 2010.

Case of Kaing Guek Eav (Case 001), Decision on Characterization of Group 1—Civil Party Co-Lawyers' Immediate Appeal of Civil Party Status Determinations in the Trial Judgment, Supreme Court Chamber, 30 September 2010.

Case of Kaing Guek Eav (Case 001), Appeal of the Co-Lawyers for the Group 3 Civil Parties against the Judgment of 26 July 2010, Supreme Court Chamber, 5 October 2010.

Case of Kaing Guek Eav (Case 001), Co-Prosecutors' Appeal against the Judgment of the Trial Chamber in the Case of Kaing Guek Eav alias Duch, Supreme Court Chamber, 13 October 2010.

Case of Kaing Guek Eav (Case 001), Appeal against Rejection of Civil Party Applicants in the Judgment (Civil Party Group 2), Supreme Court Chamber, 22 October 2010.

Case of Kaing Guek Eav (Case 001), Appeal against Judgment on Reparations (Civil Party Group 2), Supreme Court Chamber, 2 November 2010.

Case of Kaing Guek Eav (Case 001), Appeal Brief by the Co-Lawyers for Kaing Guek Eav alias "Duch" against the Trial Chamber Judgment of 26 July 2010, Supreme Court Chamber, 18 November 2010.

Case 002, Order on the Admissibility of Civil Party Applicants from Current Residents of Prey Veng Province, Co-Investigating Judges, 9 September 2010.

Case of Kaing Guek Eav (Case 001), Decision on DSS Request to Submit an Amicus Curiae Brief to the Supreme Court Chamber, Supreme Court Chamber, 9 December 2010.

International Criminal Court

Situation in Democratic Republic of the Congo, Decision on Protective Measures Requested by Applicants 01/04-1/dp to 01/04-6/dp, Pre-Trial Chamber I, No. ICC-01/04-73, 21 July 2005.

Situation in Democratic Republic of Congo, Prosecution's Reply on the Applications for Participation 01/04-1dp to 01/04-6/dp, Pre-Trial Chamber I, No. ICC-01/04-84, 15 August 2005.

Situation in Democratic Republic of the Congo, Decision on the Applications for Participation in the Proceedings of VPRS 1, VPRS 2, VPRS 3, VPRS 4, VPRS 5 and VPRS 6, Pre-Trial Chamber I, No. ICC-01/04-101-tEN-Corr, 17 January 2006.

Situation in Democratic Republic of Congo, Prosecution's Application for Leave to Appeal Pre-Trial Chamber I's "Decision on the Applications for Participation in the Proceedings of VPRS 1, VPRS 2, VPRS 3, VPRS 4, VPRS 5, and VPRS 6," Pre-Trial Chamber I, No. ICC-01/04-103, 23 January 2006.

Situation in the Democratic Republic of Congo, Observations of the Legal Representatives of VPRS 1 to VPRS 6 following the Prosecution's Application for Leave to Appeal Pre-Trial Chamber I's Decision on the Applications for Participation in Proceedings of VPRS 1 to VPRS 6, Pre-Trial Chamber I, 27 January 2006.

The Prosecutor v. Thomas Lubanga Dyilo, Decision concerning Pre-Trial Chamber I's Decision of 10 February 2006 and the Incorporation of Documents into the Record of the Case against Mr. Thomas Lubanga Dyilo, Pre-Trial Chamber I, No. ICC-01/04-01/06-8-US-Corr, 24 February 2006.

Situation in Democratic Republic of Congo, Prosecution's Application for Extraordinary Review of Pre-Trial Chamber I's 31 March 2006 Decision Denying Leave to Appeal, Appeals Chamber, No. ICC-01/04-141, 24 April 2006.

The Prosecutor v. Thomas Lubanga Dyilo, Decision on the Applications for Participation in the Proceedings Submitted by VPRS 1 to VPRS 6 in the Case the Prosecutor v. Thomas Lubanga Dyilo, Pre-Trial Chamber I, No. ICC-01/04-01/06-172-tEN, 29 June 2006.

Situation in Democratic Republic of Congo, Judgment on the Prosecutor's Application for Extraordinary Review of Pre-Trial Chamber I's 31 March 2006 Decision Denying Leave to Appeal, Appeals Chamber, No. ICC-01/04-168, 13 July 2006.

The Prosecutor v. Thomas Lubanga Dyilo, Decision on the Applications for Participation in the Proceedings of a/0001/06, a/0002/06 and a/0003/06 in the Case of the Prosecutor v. Thomas Lubanga Dyilo and of the Investigation in the Democratic Republic of the Congo, Pre-Trial Chamber I, No. ICC-01/04-01/06-228, 28 July 2006.

Situation in Democratic Republic of the Congo, Decision on the Applications for Participation in the Proceedings of a/0001/06, a/0002/06 and a/0003/06 in the Case of the Prosecutor v. Thomas Lubanga Dyilo and of the Investigation in the Democratic Republic of the Congo, Pre-Trial Chamber I, No. ICC-01/04-177-tENG, 31 July 2006.

The Prosecutor v. Thomas Lubanga Dyilo, Decision on the Arrangements for Participation of Victims a/0001/06, a/0002/06 and a/0003/06 at the Confirmation Hearing, Pre-Trial Chamber I, No. ICC-01/04-01/06-462-tEN, 22 September 2006.

The Prosecutor v. Thomas Lubanga Dyilo, Decision Authorizing the Filing of Observations on Applications for Participation in the Proceedings a/0072/06 to a/0080/06 and a/0105/06, Pre-Trial Chamber I, No. ICC- 01/04-01/06-494-tEN, 29 September 2006.

The Prosecutor v. Thomas Lubanga Dyilo, Decision on the Application for the Interim Release of Thomas Lubanga Dyilo, Pre-Trial Chamber I, No. ICC-01/04-01/06-586-tEN, 18 October 2006.

The Prosecutor v. Thomas Lubanga Dyilo, Defense Appeal against "Decision sur la demande de mise en liberté provisoire de Thomas Lubanga Dyilo," Appeals Chamber, No. ICC-01/04-01/06-594, 20 October 2006.

The Prosecutor v. Thomas Lubanga Dyilo, Decision on the Applications for Participation a/0004/06 to a/0009/06, a/0016/06 to a/0063/06, a/0071/06 to a/0080/06 and a/0105/06 in the Case of The Prosecutor v. Thomas Lubanga Dyilo, Pre-Trial Chamber I, No. ICC-01/04-01/06-601-tEN, 20 October 2006.

The Prosecutor v. Thomas Lubanga Dyilo, Decision on the Schedule and Conduct of the Confirmation Hearing, Pre-Trial Chamber I (Single Judge), No. ICC-01/04-01/06-678, 7 November 2006.

The Prosecutor v. Thomas Lubanga Dyilo, Decision on the Practices of Witness Familiarization and Witness Proofing, Pre-Trial Chamber I, No. ICC-01/04-01/06-679, 8 November 2006.

Situation in Darfur, Sudan, Décision relative à la requête sollicitant l'autorisation d'interjeter appel du conseil ad hoc pour la Défense, Pre-Trial Chamber I, No. ICC-02/05-33, 22 November 2006 [English translation not available].

The Prosecutor v. Thomas Lubanga Dyilo, Written Submission of the Legal Representative of Victim a/0105/06, Pre-Trial Chamber I, No. ICC-01/04-01/06-745, 1 December 2006.

The Prosecutor v. Thomas Lubanga Dyilo, Observations Made During the Confirmation Hearing on Behalf of Victims a/001/06, a/0002/06 and a/0003/06, Pre-Trial Chamber I, No. ICC-01/04-01/06-750, 4 December 2006.

The Prosecutor v. Joseph Kony, Vincent Otti, Okot Odhiambo and Dominic Ongwen, Decision on Legal Representation, Appointment of Counsel for the Defense, Protective Measures and Time Limit for Submission of Observations on Applications for Participation a/0010/06, a/0064/06 to a/0070/06, a/0081/06 to a/0104/06 and a/0111/06 to a/0127/06, Pre-Trial Chamber II (Single Judge), No. ICC-02/04-01/05-134, 1 February 2007.

The Prosecutor v. Thomas Lubanga Dyilo, Application for Leave to Appeal Pre-Trial Chamber I's 29 January 2007 "Décision sur la confirmation des charges," Pre-Trial Chamber I, ICC-01/04-01/06-806, 5 February 2007.

The Prosecutor v. Joseph Kony, Vincent Otti, Okot Odhiambo and Dominic Ongwen, Decision on "Prosecutor's Application to Attend 12 February Hearing," Pre-Trial Chamber II (Single Judge), No. ICC-02/04-01/05-155, 9 February 2007.

The Prosecutor v. Thomas Lubanga Dyilo, Judgment on the Appeal of Mr. Thomas Lubanga Dyilo against the Decision of Pre-Trial Chamber I Entitled "Décision sur la demande de mise en liberté provisoire de Thomas Lubanga Dyilo," Appeals Chamber, No. ICC-01/04-01/06-824, 13 February 2007.

The Prosecutor v. Joseph Kony, Vincent Otti, Okot Odhiambo and Dominic Ongwen, Decision on Prosecutor's "Application to Lift Redactions from Applications for Victims' Participation to be Provided to the OTP" and on the Prosecution's Further Submissions Supplementing Such Application, and Request for Extension of Time, Pre-Trial Chamber II (Single Judge), No. ICC-02/04-01/05-209, 20 February 2007.

Situation in Darfur, Sudan, Decision on the Ad Hoc Counsel for the Defense's Request for Leave to Appeal the Decision of 2 February 2007, Pre-Trial Chamber I, No. ICC-02/05-52, 21 February 2007.

The Prosecutor v. Thomas Lubanga Dyilo, Réponse à la demande de la Défense en autorisation d'interjeter appel de la Décision de la Chambre Préliminiare I du 29 janvier 2007, Pre-Trial Chamber I, ICC-01/04-01/06-839, 26 February 2007 [English translation no available].

Situation in Uganda, Prosecution's Reply under Rule 89(1) to the Applications for Participation of Applicants a/0010/06, a/00/64/06 to a/0070/06, a/0081/06 to a/0104/06 and a/0111/06 to a/0127/06 in the Uganda Situation, Pre-Trial Chamber II, No. ICC-02/04-85, 28 February 2007.

The Prosecutor v. Joseph Kony, Vincent Otti, Okot Odhiambo and Dominic Ongwen, Decision on the OPCV's "Request to Access Documents and Material," Pre-Trial Chamber II (Single Judge), No. ICC-02/04-01/05-222, 16 March 2007.

Situation in Darfur, Sudan, Decision on the Request for Leave to Appeal to the Decision Issued on 15 March 2007, Pre-Trial Chamber I, No. ICC-02/05-70, 27 March 2007.

Situation in Democratic Republic of the Congo, Decision Authorizing the Filing of Observations on Applications for Participation in the Proceedings, Pre-Trial Chamber I, No. ICC-01/04-329, 23 May 2007.

The Prosecutor v. Thomas Lubanga Dyilo, Decision on the Prosecutor and Defense Application for Leave to Appeal the Decision on the Confirmation of Charges, Pre-Trial Chamber I, No. ICC-01/04-01/06-915, 24 May 2007.

The Prosecutor v. Thomas Lubanga Dyilo, Decision of the Appeals Chamber on the Joint Application of Victims a/0001/06 to a/0003/06 and a/0105/06 Concerning "Directions and Decision of the Appeals Chamber," Appeals Chamber, No. ICC-01/04-01/06-925, 13 June 2007.

Situation in Democratic Republic of the Congo, Decision on Matters of Confidentiality and the Request for Extension of the Page Limit, Pre-Trial Chamber I (Single Judge), No. ICC-01/04-342, 19 June 2007.

The Prosecutor v. Germain Katanga and Mathieu Ngudjolo Chui, Decision on the Evidence and Information Provided by the Prosecution for the Issuance of a Warrant of Arrest for Germain Katanga, Pre-Trial Chamber I, No. ICC-01/04-01/07-4, 6 July 2007.

Situation in Uganda, Order to the Prosecutor and the Victims and Witnesses Unit to Submit Observations on the Unsealing of Certain Documents in the Record Both of the Situation and of the Case, Pre-Trial Chamber II (Single Judge), No. ICC-02/04-98, 12 July 2007.

Situation in Democratic Republic of the Congo, Decision Authorizing the Filing of Observations on Applications for Participation in the Proceedings, Pre-Trial Chamber I (Single Judge), No. ICC-01/04-358, 17 July 2007.

Situation in Uganda, Decision on Victims' Application for Participation a/0010/06, a/0064/06 to a/0070/06, a/0081/06 to a/0104/06 and a/0111/06 to a/0127/06, Pre-Trial Chamber II (Single Judge), No. ICC-02/04-101, 10 August 2007.

The Prosecutor v. Joseph Kony, Vincent Otti, Okot Odhiambo and Dominic Ongwen, Decision on Victims' Applications for Participation a/0010/06, a/0064/06 to a/0070/06, a/0081/06 to a/0104/06 and a/0111/06 to a/0127/06, Pre-Trial Chamber II (Single Judge), No. ICC-02/04-01/05-252, 10 August 2007.

Situation in Democratic Republic of the Congo, Decision on the Requests of the Legal Representative of Applicants on Application Process for Victims' Participation and Legal Representation, Pre-Trial Chamber I, No. ICC-01/04-374, 17 August 2007.

Situation in Uganda, Prosecution's Application for Leave to Appeal the Decision on Victims' Applications for Participation a/0010/06, a/0064/06 to a/0070/06, a/0081/06 to a/0104/06 and a/0111/06 to a/0127/06, Pre-Trial Chamber II, No. ICC-02/04-103, 20 August 2007.

Situation in Darfur, Sudan, Decision on the Requests of the OPCD and the Legal Representatives of the Applicants Regarding the Transmission of the Report of the Registry Under Rule 89 of the Rules of Evidence and Procedure, Pre-Trial Chamber I, No. 02/05-93, 21 August 2007.

Situation in Uganda, Response of Legal Representatives of Victims a/01119/06 to the Prosecutor's Application for Leave to Appeal the Decision on Victims' Applications for Participation a/0010/06, a/0064/06 to a/0070/06, a/0081/06 to a/0104/06, and a/0111/06 to a/0127/06, Pre-Trial Chamber II, No. ICC-02/04-106, 31 August 2007.

The Prosecutor v. Thomas Lubanga Dyilo, Decision on the Implementation of the Reporting System Between the Registrar and the Trial Chamber in Accordance with Rule 89 and Regulation of the Court 86(5), Trial Chamber I, No. ICC-01/04-01/06-1022, 9 November 2007.

The Prosecutor v. Thomas Lubanga Dyilo, Decision Regarding the Practices Used to Prepare and Familiarize Witnesses for Giving Testimony at Trial, Trial Chamber I, No. ICC-01/04-01/06-1049, 30 November 2007.

Situation in Darfur, Sudan, Decision on the Requests of the OPCD on the Production of Relevant Supporting Documentation Pursuant to Regulation 86(2)(e) of the Regulations of the Court and on the Disclosure of Exculpatory Materials by the Prosecutor, Pre-Trial Chamber I (Single Judge), No. ICC-02/05-110, 3 December 2007.

Situation in Democratic Republic of the Congo, Decision on the Requests of the OPCD on the Production of Relevant Supporting Documentation Pursuant to Regulation 86(2)(e) of the Regulations of the Court and on the Disclosure of Exculpatory Materials by the Prosecutor, Pre-Trial Chamber I (Single Judge), No. ICC-01/04-417, 7 December 2007.

Situation in Democratic Republic of Congo, Decision on the Requests of the OPCV, Pre-Trial Chamber I (Single Judge), No. ICC-01/04-418, 10 December 2007.

The Prosecutor v. Thomas Lubanga Dyilo, Decision on the Procedures to be Adopted for Instructing Expert Witnesses, Trial Chamber I, No. ICC-01/04-01/06-1069, 10 December 2007.

Situation in Darfur, Sudan, Corrigendum to Decision on the Applications for Participation in the Proceedings of Applicants a/0011/06 to a/0015/06, a/0021/07, a/0023/07 to a/0033/07 and a/0035/07 to a/0038/07, Pre-Trial Chamber I (Single Judge), No. ICC-02/05-111-Corr, 14 December 2007.

Situation in Uganda, Decision on the Prosecution's Application for Leave to Appeal the Decision on Victims' Applications for Participation a/0010/06, a/0064/06 to a/0070/06, a/0081/06 to a/0104/06 and a/0111/06 to a/0127/06, Pre-Trial Chamber II, No. ICC-02/04-112, 19 December 2007.

The Prosecutor v. Thomas Lubanga Dyilo, Decision on Victims' Participation, Trial Chamber I, No. ICC-01/04-01/06-1119, 18 January 2008.

The Prosecutor v. Thomas Lubanga Dyilo, Application for Leave to Appeal Trial Chamber I's January 18, 2008 Decision on Victims' Participation, Trial Chamber I, No. ICC-01/04-01/06-1136, 28 January 2008.

Situation in Democratic Republic of the Congo, Corrigendum to the "Decision on the Applications for Participation Filed in Connection with the Investigation in the Democratic

Republic of the Congo by a/0004/06 to a/0009/06, a/0016/06 to a/0063/06, a/0071/06 to a/0080/06 and a/0105/06 to a/0110/06, a/0188/06, a/0128/06 to a/0162/06, a/0199/06, a/0203/06, a/0209/06, a/0214/06, a/0220/06 to a/0222/06, a/0224/06, a/0227/06 to a/0230/06, a/0234/06 to a/0236/06, a/0240/06, a/0225/06, a/0226/06, a/0231/06 to a/0233/06, a/0237/06 to a/0239/06 and a/0241/06 to a/0250/06," Pre-Trial Chamber I (Single Judge), No. ICC-01/04-423-Corr-tENG, 31 January 2008.

Situation in Darfur, Sudan, Decision on the Requests for Leave to Appeal the Decision on the Application for Participation of Victims in the Proceedings in the Situation, Pre-Trial Chamber I (Single Judge), No. ICC-02/05-121, 6 February 2008.

Situation in Democratic Republic of the Congo, Decision on the Prosecution, OPCD and OPCV Requests for Leave to Appeal the Decision on the Applications for Participation of Victims in the Proceedings in the Situation, Pre-Trial Chamber I (Single Judge), No. ICC-01/04-444, 6 February 2008

Situation in Democratic Republic of the Congo, Decision of the Appeals Chamber on the OPCV's Request for Clarification and the Legal Representatives' Request for Extension of Time and Order of the Appeals Chamber on the Date of Filing of Applications for Participation and on the Time of the Filing of the Responses Thereto by the OPCD and the Prosecutor, Appeals Chamber, No. ICC-01/04-450, 13 February 2008.

The Prosecutor v. Thomas Lubanga Dyilo, Decision on the Defense and Prosecution Requests for Leave to Appeal the Decision on Victims' Participation of 18 January 2008, Trial Chamber I, No. ICC-01/04-01/06-1191, 26 February 2008.

Situation in Democratic Republic of the Congo, Order of the Appeals Chamber on the Date of Filing of Applications for Participation and on the Time of the Filing of the Responses Thereto by the OPCD and the Prosecutor, Appeals Chamber, No. ICC-01/04-480, 29 February 2008.

Situation in Darfur, Sudan, Decision of the Appeals Chamber on the OPCV's Request for Clarification and Order of the Appeals Chamber on the Date of Filing of Applications for Participation and on the Time of the Filing of the Responses Thereto by the OPCD and the Prosecutor, Appeals Chamber, No. ICC-02/05-129, 29 February 2008.

The Prosecutor v. Thomas Lubanga Dyilo, Decision on the Role of the Office of Public Counsel for Victims and its Request to Access to Documents, Trial Chamber I, No. ICC-01/04-01/06-1211, 6 March 2008.

The Prosecutor v. Thomas Luganga Dyilo, Defense Appeal against Trial Chamber I's 18 January 2008 Decision on Victims' Participation, Trial Chamber I, No. ICC-01/04-01/06-1220, 10 March 2008.

Situation in Uganda, Decision on Victims' Applications for Participation a/0010/06, a/0064/06 to a/0070/06, a/0081/06, a/0082/06, a/0084/06 to a/0089/06, a/0091/06 to a/0097/06, a/0099/06, a/0100/06, a/0102/06 to a/0104/06, a/0111/06, a/0113/06 to a/0117/06, a/0120/06, a/0121/06 and a/0123/06 to a/0127/06, Pre-Trial Chamber II (Single Judge), No. ICC-02/04-125, 14 March 2008.

The Prosecutor v. Joseph Kony, Vincent Otti, Okot Odhiambo and Dominic Ongwen, Decision on Victims' Applications for Participation a/0010/06, a/0064/06 to a/0070/06,a/0081/06, a/0082/06, a/0084/06 to a/0089/06, a/0091/06 to a/0097/06, a/0099/06,a/0100/06, a/0102/06 to a/0104/06, a/0111/06, a/0113/06 to a/0117/06, a/0120/06,a/0121/06 and a/0123/06 to a/0127/06, Pre-Trial Chamber II (Single Judge), No. ICC-02/04-01/05-282, 14 March 2008.

Situation in Uganda, Decision on Notification of the Trust Fund for Victims and on its Request for Leave to Respond to OPCD's Observations on the Notification, Pre-Trial Chamber II, No. ICC-02/04-126, 19 March 2008.

The Prosecutor v. Joseph Kony, Vincent Otti, Okot Odhiambo and Dominic Ongwen, Decision on Notification of the Trust Fund for Victims and on its Request for Leave to Respond to OPCD's Observations on the Notification, Pre-Trial Chamber II, No. ICC-02/04-01/05-283, 19 March 2008.

The Prosecutor v. Thomas Lubanga Dyilo, Order of the Appeals Chamber on the Date of Filing of Applications for Participation by Victims and on the Time of the Filing of the Responses Thereto by the Prosecutor and the Defense, Appeals Chamber, No. ICC-01/04-01/06-1239, 20 March 2008.

The Prosecutor v. Germain Katanga and Mathieu Ngudjolo Chui, Decision on the Application for Participation in the Proceedings of Applicants a/0327/07 to a/0337/07 and a/0001/08, Pre-Trial Chamber II, No. ICC-01/04-01/07-357, 2 April 2008.

The Prosecutor v. Germain Katanga and Mathieu Ngudjolo Chui, Fourth Decision on the Prosecution Request for Authorization to Redact Documents Related to Witnesses 166 and 233, Pre-Trial Chamber I (Single Judge), No. ICC-01/04-01/07-361, 3 April 2008.

The Prosecutor v. Thomas Lubanga Dyilo, Decision Inviting the Parties' Observations on Applications for Participation of a/0001/06 to a/0004/06, a/0047/06 to a/0052/06, a/0077/06, a/0078/06, a/0105/06, a/0221/06, a/0224/06 to a/0233/06, a/0236/06, a/0237/06 to a/0250/06, a/0001/07 to a/0005/07, a/0054/07 to a/0062/07, a/0064/07, a/0065/07, a/0149/07, a/0155/07, a/0156/07, a/0162/07, a/0168/07 to a/0185/07, a/0187/07 to a/0191/07, a/0251/07 to a/0253/07, a/0255/07 to a/0257/07, a/0270/07 to a/0285/07, and a/0007/08, Trial Chamber I, No. ICC-01/04-01/06-1308, 6 May 2008.

The Prosecutor v. Germain Katanga and Mathieu Ngudjolo Chui, Decision on the Set of Procedural Rules Attached to Procedural Status of Victim at the Pre-Trial Stage of the Case, Pre-Trial Chamber I (Single Judge), No. ICC-01/04-01/07-474, 13 May 2008.

The Prosecutor v. Germain Katanga and Mathieu Ngudjolo Chui, Judgment on the appeal of Mr. German Katanga against the Decision of Pre-Trial Chamber I Entitled "First Decision on the Prosecution Request for Authorization to Redact Witness Statements," Appeals Chamber, No. ICC-01/04-01/07-476, 13 May 2008.

The Prosecutor v. Thomas Lubanga Dyilo, Decision, *in limine*, on Victim Participation in the Appeals of the Prosecutor and the Defense against Trial Chamber I's Decision Entitled "Decision on Victims' Participation," Appeals Chamber, No. ICC-01/04-01/06-1335, 16 May 2008.

The Prosecutor v. Germain Katanga and Mathieu Ngudjolo Chui, Decision on Limitations of Set of Procedural Rights for Non-Anonymous Victims, Pre-Trial Chamber I (Single Judge), No. ICC-01/04-01/07-537, 30 May 2008.

The Prosecutor v. Thomas Lubanga Dyilo, Decision on the Legal Representative's Request for Clarification of the Trial Chamber's 18 January 2008 "Decision on Victims' Participation," Trial Chamber I, No. ICC-01/04-01/06-1368, 2 June 2008.

The Prosecutor v. Thomas Lubanga Dyilo, Decision on Certain Practicalities Regarding Individuals who Have the Dual Status of Witness and Victim, Trial Chamber I, No. ICC-01/04-01/06-1379, 5 June 2008.

The Prosecutor v. Germain Katanga and Mathieu Ngudjolo Chui, Public Redacted Version of the "Decision on the 97 Applications for Participation at the Pre-Trial Stage of the Case," Pre-Trial Chamber I (Single Judge), No. ICC-01/04-01/07-579, 10 June 2008.

The Prosecutor v. Thomas Lubanga Dyilo, Decision on the Consequences of Non-Disclosure of Exculpatory Materials Covered by Article 54(3)(e) Agreements and the Application to Stay the Prosecution of the Accused, Together with Certain Other Issues Raised at the Status Conference on 10 June 2008, Trial Chamber I, No. ICC-01/04-01/06-1401, 13 June 2008.

Situation in Darfur, Sudan, Decision on Victim Participation in the Appeal of the Office of Public Counsel for the Defense against Pre-Trial Chamber I's Decision of 3 December 2007 and in the Appeals of the Prosecutor and the Office of Public Counsel for the Defense against Pre-Trial Chamber I's Decision of 6 December 2007 (and partly dissenting opinion of Judge Sang-Hyun Song), Appeals Chamber, No. ICC-02/05-138, 18 June 2008.

Situation in Darfur, Sudan, Prosecution's Response to Legal Representative of Victim's Request to Participate in OPCD's Appeal against the 3 December 2007 Decision on Production and Disclosure of Material and in the Appeals of the Prosecution and OPCD against the 6 December 2007 Decision on the Victims' Applications for Participation in the Proceedings, Appeals Chamber, No. ICC 02/05-142, 23 June 2008.

The Prosecutor v. Germain Katanga and Mathieu Ngudjolo Chui, Decision on Victims' Requests for Anonymity at the Pre-Trial Stage of the Case, Pre-Trial Chamber I (Single Judge), No. ICC-01/04-01/07-628, 23 June 2008.

The Prosecutor v. Germain Katanga and Mathieu Ngudjolo Chui, Decision on the Application for Participation of Witness 166, Pre-Trial Chamber I (Single Judge), No. ICC-01/04-01/07-632, 23 June 2008.

Situation in Democratic Republic of the Congo, Decision on Victim Participation in the Appeal of the Office of Public Counsel for the Defense against Pre-Trial Chamber I's Decision of 7 December 2007 and in the Appeals of the Prosecutor and the Office of Public Counsel for the Defense against Pre-Trial Chamber I's Decision of 24 December 2007, Appeals Chamber, No. ICC-01/04-503, 30 June 2008.

The Prosecutor v. Thomas Lubanga Dyilo, Decision on the Release of Mr. Thomas Lubanga Dyilo, Trial Chamber I, No. ICC-01/04-01/06-1418, 2 July 2008.

Situation in Democratic Republic of the Congo, Decision on the Applications for Participation Filed in Connection with the Investigation in the Democratic Republic of Congo by Applicants a/0047/06 to a/0052/06, a/0163/06 to a/0187/06, a/0221/06, a/0225/06, a/0226/06, a/0231/06 to a/0233/03, a/0237/06 to a/0239/06, and a/0241/06 to a/0250/06, Pre-Trial Chamber I (Single Judge), No. ICC-01/04-505, 3 July 2008.

The Prosecutor v. Germain Katanga and Mathieu Ngudjolo Chui, Decision on the Provisional Separation of Legal Representative of Victims a/0015/08, a/0022/08, a/0024/08, a/0025/08, a/0027/08, a/0028/08, a/0029/08, a/0032/08, a/0033/08, a/0034/08 and a/0035/08, Pre-Trial Chamber I, No. ICC-01/04-01/07-660, 3 July 2008.

The Prosecutor v. Thomas Lubanga Dyilo, Judgment on the Appeals of The Prosecutor and The Defense against Trial Chamber I's Decision on Victims' Participation of 18 January 2008, Appeals Chamber, No. ICC-01/04-01/06-1432, 11 July 2008.

The Prosecutor v. Thomas Lubanga Dyilo, Judgment on the Appeals of The Prosecutor and The Defense against Trial Chamber I's Decision on Victims' Participation of 18 January 2008 (partly dissenting opinion of Judge Philippe Kirsch), Appeals Chamber, No. ICC-01/04-01/06-1432-Anx, 23 July 2008.

The Prosecutor v. Thomas Lubanga Dyilo, Decision on the Participation of Victims in the Appeal, Appeals Chamber, No. ICC-01/04-01/06-1452, 6 August 2008.

The Prosecutor v. Thomas Lubanga Dyilo, Decision on the Participation of Victims in the Appeal, Appeals Chamber, No. ICC-01/04-01/06-1453, 6 August 2008.

The Prosecutor v. Jean-Pierre Bemba Gombo, Decision on Victim Participation, Pre-Trial Chamber III (Single Judge), No. ICC-01/05-01/08-103-tENG-Corr, 12 September 2008.

The Prosecutor v. Joseph Kony, Vincent Otti, Okot Odhiambo and Dominic Ongwen, Decision on Legal Representation, Appointment of Counsel for the Defense, Criteria for Redactions of Applications for Participation, and Submission of Observations on Applications for Participation a/0014/07 to a/0020/07 and a/0076/07 to a/0125/07, Pre-Trial Chamber II (Single Judge), No. ICC-02/04-01/05-312, 17 September 2008.

The Prosecutor v. Germain Katanga and Mathieu Ngudjolo Chui, Decision on the Confirmation of Charges, Pre-Trial Chamber II, No. ICC-01/04-01/07-717, 30 September 2008.

The Prosecutor v. Thomas Lubanga Dyilo, Judgment on the Appeal of the Prosecutor against the Decision of Trial Chamber I Entitled "Decision on the Release of Thomas Lubanga Dyilo," Appeals Chamber, No. ICC-01/04-01/06-1487, 21 October 2008.

The Prosecutor v. Jean-Pierre Bemba Gombo, Second Decision on the Question of Victims' Participation Requesting Observations from the Parties, Pre-Trial Chamber III, No. ICC-01/05-01/08-184, 23 October 2008.

The Prosecutor v. Joseph Kony, Vincent Otti, Okot Odhiambo and Dominic Ongwen, Decision on the Participation of Victims in the Appeal, Appeals Chamber, No. ICC-02/04-01/05-324, 27 October 2008.

Situation in Uganda, Decision on the Participation of Victims in the Appeal, Appeals Chamber, No. ICC-02/04-164, 27 October 2008.

Situation in Democratic Republic of the Congo, Decision on the Applications for Participation Filed in Connection with the Investigation in the Democratic Republic of Congo by Applicants a/0189/06 to a/0198/06, a/0200/06 to a/0202/06, a/0204/06 to a/0208/06, a/0210/06 to a/0213/06, a/0215/06 to a/0218/06, a/0219/06, a/0223/06, a/0332/07, a/0334/ 07 to a/0337/07, a/0001/08, a/0030/08 and a/0031/08, Pre-Trial Chamber I (Single Judge), No. ICC-01/04-545, 4 November 2008.

The Prosecutor v. Jean-Pierre Bemba Gombo, Third Decision on the Question of Victims' Participation Requesting Observations from the Parties, Pre-Trial Chamber III (Single Judge) No. ICC-01/05-01/08-253, 15 November 2008.

Situation in Uganda, Decision on Victims' Applications for Participation a/0066/06, a/0067/06, a/0069/06, a/0070/06, a/0083/06, a/0088/06, a/0091/06, a/0092/06, a/0102/06, a/0114/06, a/0115/06, a/0125/06 and a/0126/06, Pre-Trial Chamber II (Single Judge), No. ICC-02/04-170, 17 November 2008.

Situation in Uganda, Decision on Victims' Applications for Participation a/0014/07 to a/0020/07 and a/0076/07 to a/0125/07, Pre-Trial Chamber II (Single Judge), No. ICC-02/04-172, 21 November 2008.

The Prosecutor v. Joseph Kony, Vincent Otti, Okot Odhiambo and Dominic Ongwen, Decision on Victim's Applications for Participation a/0014/07 to a/0020/07 and a/0076/07 to a/0125/07, Pre-Trial Chamber II, (Single Judge), No. ICC-02/04-01/05-356, 21 November 2008.

The Prosecutor v. Jean-Pierre Bemba Gombo, Fourth Decision on Victims' Participation, Pre-Trial Chamber III (Single Judge), No. ICC-01/05-01/08-320, 12 December 2008.

The Prosecutor v. Thomas Lubanga Dyilo, Decision on the Applications by Victims to Participate in the Proceedings, Trial Chamber I, No. ICC-01/04-01/06-1556, 15 December 2008.

The Prosecutor v. Jean-Pierre Bemba Gombo, Fifth Decision on Victims' Issues Concerning Common Legal Representation of Victims, Pre-Trial Chamber III (Single Judge), No. ICC-01/05-01/08-322, 16 December 2008.

The Prosecutor v. Thomas Lubanga Dyilo, Decision on the Applications by 3 Victims to Participate in the Proceedings, Trial Chamber I, No. ICC-01/04-01/06-1562, 18 December 2008.

Situation in Democratic Republic of the Congo, Judgment on Victim Participation in the Investigation Stage of the Proceedings in the Appeal of the OPCD against the Decision of Pre-Trial Chamber I of 7 December 2007 and in the Appeals of the OPCD and the Prosecutor against the Decision of Pre-Trial Chamber I of 24 December 2007, Appeals Chamber, No. ICC-01/04-556, 19 December 2008.

Prosecutor v. Thomas Lubanga Dyilo, Order issuing Annexes to the "Decision on the Applications by Victims to Participate in the Proceedings" of 15 December 2008, Trial Chamber I, No. ICC-01/04-01/06-1563, 19 December 2008.

The Prosecutor v. Jean-Pierre Bemba Gombo, Sixth Decision on Victims' Participation Relating to Certain Questions Raised by the Office of Public Counsel for Victims, Pre-Trial Chamber III (Single Judge), No. ICC-01/05-01/08-349, 8 January 2009.

The Prosecutor v. Thomas Lubanga Dyilo, Corrigendum to "Decision on the Applications by Victims to Participate in the Proceedings," Trial Chamber I, No. ICC-01/04-01/06-1556-Corr, 13 January 2009.

The Prosecutor v. Thomas Lubanga Dyilo, Decision on the Defense Application for Disclosure of Victims Applications, Trial Chamber I, No. ICC-01/04-01/06-1637, 21 January 2009.

Situation in Darfur, Sudan, Judgment on Victim Participation in the Investigation Stage of the Proceedings in the Appeal of the OPCD against the Decision of Pre-Trial Chamber I of 3 December 2007 and in the Appeals of the OPCD and the Prosecutor against the Decision of Pre-Trial Chamber I of 6 December 2007, Appeals Chamber, No. ICC-02/05-177, 2 February 2009.

The Prosecutor v. Germain Katanga and Mathieu Ngudjolo Chui, Decision on the Treatment of Applications for Participation, Trial Chamber II, No. ICC-01/04-01/07-933-tENG, 26 February 2009.

The Prosecutor v. Jean-Pierre Bemba Gombo, Decision Adjourning the Hearing Pursuant to Article 61(7)(c)(ii) of the Rome Statute, Pre-Trial Chamber III, No. ICC-01/05-01/08-388, 3 March 2009.

Situation in Uganda, Decision on Victims' Applications for Participation a/0192/07 to a/0194/07, a/0196/07, a/0200/07, a/0204/07, a/0206/07, a/0209/07, a/0212/07, a/0216/07, a/0217/07, a/0219/07 to a/0221/07, a/02228/07 to a/0230/07, a/0234/07, a/0235/07, a/0237/07, a/0324/07 and a/0326/07 under rule 89, Pre-Trial Chamber II (Single Judge), No. ICC-02/04-180, 10 March 2009.

The Prosecutor v. Joseph Kony, Vincent Otti, Okot Odhiambo and Dominic Ongwen, Decision on Victims' Applications for Participation a/0192/07 to a/0194/07, a/0196/07, a/0200/07, a/0204/07, a/0206/07, a/0209/07, a/0212/07, a/0216/07, a/0217/07, a/0219/07 to a/0221/07, a/02228/07 to a/0230/07, a/0234/07, a/0235/07, a/0237/07, a/0324/07 and a/0326/07 under rule 89, Pre-Trial Chamber II (Single Judge), No. ICC-02/04-01/05-375, 10 March 2009.

The Prosecutor v. Bahar Idriss Abu Garda, Decision on Applications a/0655/09, a/0656/09, a/0736/09 to a/0747/09, and a/0750/09 to a/0755/09 for Participation in the Proceedings at the Pre-Trial Stage of the Case, Pre-Trial Chamber I, No. ICC-02/05-02/09-255, 19 March 2009.

The Prosecutor v. Thomas Lubanga Dyilo, Redacted Version of "Decision on 'Indirect Victims,'" Trial Chamber I, No. ICC-01/04-01/06-1813, 8 April 2009.

The Prosecutor v. Germain Katanga and Mathieu Ngudjolo Chui, Decision Inviting the Parties to Submit Their Observations on Applications for Participation (Rule 89(1) of the Rules of Procedure and Evidence), Trial Chamber II, No. ICC-01/04-01/07-1094, 4 May 2009.

The Prosecutor v. Thomas Lubanga Dyilo, Order Issuing Public Redacted Annexes to the Decisions on the Applications by Victims to Participate in the Proceedings of 15 and 18 December 2008, Trial Chamber I, No. ICC-01/04-01/06-1861 (together with Annex A1 No. ICC-01/04-01/06-1861-AnxA1 and Annex A2 No. ICC-01/04-01/06-1861-AnxA2), 8 May 2009.

The Prosecutor v. Germain Katanga and Mathieu Ngudjolo Chui, Second Decision Inviting the Parties to Submit Their Observations on Applications for Participation (Rule 89(1) of the Rules of Procedure and Evidence), Trial Chamber II, No. ICC-01/04-01/07-1129, 12 May 2009.

The Prosecutor v. Germain Katanga and Mathieu Ngudjolo Chui, Third Decision Inviting the Parties to Submit Their Observations on Applications for Participation (Rule 89(1) of the Rules of Procedure and Evidence), Trial Chamber II, No. ICC-01/04-01/07-1151, 19 May 2009.

The Prosecutor v. Thomas Lubanga Dyilo, Joint Application of the Legal Representatives of the Victims for the Implementation of the Procedure under Regulation 55 of the Regulations of the Court, Trial Chamber I, No. ICC-01/04-01/06-1891, 22 May 2009.

The Prosecutor v. Thomas Lubanga Dyilo, Observations conjointes des représentants légaux des victimes sur les questions à poser au(x) expert(s) concernant l'attribution et les composantes du nom en République démocratique du Congo, Trial Chamber I, No. ICC-01/04-01/06-1896, 25 May 2009 [English translation not available].

The Prosecutor v. Germain Katanga and Mathieu Ngudjolo Chui, Fourth Decision Inviting the Parties to Submit Their Observations on Applications for Participation (Rule 89(1) of the Rules of Procedure and Evidence), Trial Chamber II, No. ICC-01/04-01/07-1206, 12 June 2009.

The Prosecutor v. Bahar Idriss Abu Garda, Decision on Issues Relating to Victims' Applications in the Case, Pre-Trial Chamber I (Single Judge), No.ICC-02/05-02/09-20, 12 June 2009.

The Prosecutor v. Jean-Pierre Bemba Gombo, Decision Pursuant to Article 61(7)(a) and (b) of the Rome Statute on the Charges of the Prosecutor against Jean-Pierre Bemba Gombo, Pre-Trial Chamber III, No. ICC-01/05-01/08-424, 15 June 2009.

The Prosecutor v. Thomas Lubanga Dyilo, Decision on the Request by Victims a/0225/06, a/0229/06 and a/0270/07 to Express their Views and Concerns in Person and to Present Evidence During the Trial, Trial Chamber I, No. ICC-01/04-01/06-2032 and its Annex No. ICC-01/04-01/06-2032-Anx, 9 July 2009.

The Prosecutor v. Thomas Lubanga Dyilo, Decision on the Applications by 7 Victims to Participate in the Proceedings, Trial Chamber I, No. ICC-01/04-01/06-2035, 10 July 2009.

The Prosecutor v. Thomas Lubanga Dyilo, Decision Giving Notice to the Parties and Participants that the Legal Characterization of the Facts may be Subject to Change in Accordance with Regulation 55(2) of the Regulations of the Court, Trial Chamber I, No. ICC-01/04-01/06-2049, 14 July 2009.

The Prosecutor v. Thomas Lubanga Dyilo, Minority Opinion on the "Decision Giving Notice to the Parties and Participants that the Legal Characterization of Facts may be Subject to Change in Accordance with Regulation 55(2) of the Regulations of the Court," Trial Chamber I (Judge Fulford), No. ICC-01/04-01/06-2054, 17 July 2009.

The Prosecutor v. Thomas Lubanga Dyilo, Decision on the Supplementary Information Relevant to the Applications of 21 Victims, Trial Chamber I, No.ICC-01/04-01/06-2063, 21 July 2009.

The Prosecutor v. Germain Katanga and Mathieu Ngudjolo Chui, Order on the Organization of Common Legal Representation of Victims, Trial Chamber II, No. ICC-01/04-01/07-1328, 22 July 2009.

The Prosecutor v. Thomas Lubanga Dyilo, Order Issuing Confidential and Public Redacted Versions of Annex A to the "Decision on the Applications by 7 Victims to Participate in the Proceedings" of 10 July 2009 (ICC-01/04-01/06-2035), Trial Chamber I, No.ICC-01/04-01/06-2065, together with Annex 2, No.ICC-01/04-01/06-2065-Anx2, 23 July 2009.

The Prosecutor v. Germain Katanga and Mathieu Ngudjolo Chui, Corrigendum du dispositif de la décision relative aux 345 demandes de participation de victimes à la procédure, Trial Chamber II, No. ICC-01/04-01/07-1347-Corr, 5 August 2009 [English translation not available].

The Prosecutor v. Omar Hassan Ahmad Al Bashir, Decision on the "Legal Representative's Request to Expedite the Consideration of Applications for Victim Status," Pre-Trial Chamber I (Single Judge), No. ICC-02/05-01/09-36, 27 August 2009.

The Prosecutor v. Bahar Idriss Abu Garda, Decision Ordering the Parties to Submit Their Observations on the Applications for Victims' Participation in the Proceedings, Pre-Trial Chamber I, No. ICC-02/05-02/09-68, 27 August 2009.

The Prosecutor v. Thomas Lubanga Dyilo, Clarification and Further Guidance to Parties and Participants in Relation to the "Decision Giving Notice to the Parties and Participants that the Legal Characterization of the Facts may be Subject to Change in Accordance with Regulation 55(2) of the Regulations of the Court," Trial Chamber I, No. ICC-01/04-01/06-2093, 27 August 2009.

The Prosecutor v. Jean-Pierre Bemba Gombo, Decision on the Participation of Victims in the Appeal against the "Decision on the Interim Release of Jean-Pierre Bemba Gombo and Convening Hearings with the Kingdom of Belgium, the Republic of Portugal, the Republic of France, the Federal Republic of Germany, the Italian Republic, and the Republic of South Africa," Appeals Chamber, No. ICC-01/05-01/08-500, 3 September 2009.

The Prosecutor v. Thomas Lubanga Dyilo, Decision on the Manner of Questioning Witnesses by the Legal Representatives of Victims, Trial Chamber I, No. ICC-01/04-01/06-2127, 16 September 2009.

The Prosecutor v. Bahar Idriss Abu Garda, Decision Ordering the Parties to Submit their Observations on the 52 Applications for Victims' Participation in the Proceedings, Pre-Trial Chamber I, No. ICC-02/05-02/09-106, 16 September 2009.

The Prosecutor v. Germain Katanga and Mathieu Ngudjolo Chui, Grounds for the Decision on the 345 Applications for Participation in the Proceedings Submitted by Victims, Trial Chamber II, No. ICC-01/04-01/07-1491-Red, 23 September 2009.

The Prosecutor v. Germain Katanga and Mathieu Ngudjolo Chui, Judgment on the Appeal of Mr. German Katanga against the Oral Decision of Trial Chamber II of 12 June 2009 on the Admissibility of the Case, No. ICC-01/04-01/07-1497, 25 September 2009.

The Prosecutor v. Bahar Idriss Abu Garda, Decision on the 34 Applications for Participation at the Pre-Trial Stage of the Case, Pre-Trial Chamber I (Single Judge), No. ICC-02/05-02/09-121, 25 September 2009.

The Prosecutor v. Bahar Idriss Abu Garda, Decision on Victims' Modalities of Participation at the Pre-Trial Stage of the Case, Pre-Trial Chamber I, No. ICC-02/05-02/09-136, 6 October 2009.

The Prosecutor v. Bahar Idriss Abu Garda, Public Redacted Version of "Decision on the 52 Applications for Participation at the Pre-Trial Stage of the Case," Pre-Trial Chamber I (Single Judge), No. ICC-02/05-02/09-147-Red, 9 October 2009.

The Prosecutor v. Bahar Idriss Abu Garda, Decision on the "Request in Respect of Information Relevant to Victim Participation on the Basis of the Decision on 52 Applications for Participation at the Pre-Trial Stage of the Case," Pre-Trial Chamber I (Single Judge), No.ICC-02/05-02/09-169, 14 October 2009.

The Prosecutor v. Jean-Pierre Bemba Gombo, Reasons for the "Decision on the Participation of Victims in the Appeal against the 'Decision on the Interim Release of Jean-Pierre Bemba Gombo and Convening Hearings with the Kingdom of Belgium, the Republic of Portugal, the Republic of France, the Federal Republic of Germany, the Italian Republic, and the Republic of South Africa,'" Appeals Chamber, No. ICC-01/05-01/08-566, 20 October 2009.

The Prosecutor v. Thomas Lubanga Dyilo, Decision on the Participation of Victims in the Appeals, Appeals Chamber, No. ICC-01/04-01/06-2168, 20 October 2009.

The Prosecutor v. Omar Hassan Ahmad Al Bashir, Decision On the Applications by Victims a/0443/09 to a/0450/09 to Participate in the Appeal against the "Decision on the

Prosecution's Application for a Warrant of Arrest against Omar Hassan Ahmad Al Bashir" and on the Request for an Extension of Time, Appeals Chamber, No. ICC-02/05-01/09-48, 23 October 2009.

The Prosecutor v. Thomas Lubanga Dyilo, Annex A to Order Issuing Public and Confidential Redacted Annex to the Decision on the Applications by 2 Victims to Participate in the Proceedings of 10 September 2009 (ICC-01/04-01/06-2115), Trial Chamber I, No. ICC-01/04-01/06-2115-AnxA-Red, 27 October 2009.

The Prosecutor v. Germain Katanga and Mathieu Ngudjolo Chui, Directions for the Conduct of the Proceedings and Testimony in Accordance with Rule 140, Trial Chamber II, No. ICC-01/04-01/07-1665, 20 November 2009.

The Prosecutor v. Bahar Idriss Abu Garda, Final Written Observations of Victims Represented by Akin Akinbote, Pre-Trial Chamber I, No. ICC-02/05-02/09-236, 23 November 2009.

The Prosecutor v. Germain Katanga and Mathieu Ngudjolo Chui, Dispositif de la deuxième décision relative aux demandes de participation de victimes à la procedure, Trial Chamber II, No. ICC-01/04-01/07-1669, 23 November 2009 [English translation not available].

The Prosecutor v. Jean-Pierre Bemba Gombo, Decision on the Participation of Victims in the Appeal against the "Decision on the Interim Release of Jean-Pierre Bemba Gombo and Convening Hearings with the Kingdom of Belgium, the Republic of Portugal, the Republic of France, the Federal Republic of Germany, the Italian Republic, and the Republic of South Africa" - Dissenting Opinion of Judge Sang-Hyun Song, Appeals Chamber, No. ICC-01/05-01/08-623, 27 November 2009.

The Prosecutor v. Thomas Lubanga Dyilo, Judgment on the Appeals of Mr. Lubanga Dyilo and the Prosecutor against the Decision of Trial Chamber I of 14 July 2009 Entitled "Decision Giving Notice to the Parties and Participants that the Legal Characterization of the Facts may be Subject to Change in Accordance with Regulation 55(2) of the Regulations of the Court," Appeals Chamber, No. ICC-01/04-01/06-2205, 8 December 2009.

The Prosecutor v. Omar Hassan Ahmad Al Bashir, Decision on Applications a/0011/06 to a/0013/06, a/0015/06 and a/0443/09 to a/0450/09 for Participation in the Proceedings at the Pre-Trial Stage of the Case, Pre-Trial Chamber I (Single Judge), No. ICC-02/05-01/09-62, 10 December 2009.

Situation in the Republic of Kenya, Order to the Victims Participation and Reparations Section Concerning Victims' Representations Pursuant to Article 15(3) of the Statute, Pre-Trial Chamber II, No. ICC-01/09-4, 10 December 2009.

The Prosecutor v. Thomas Lubanga Dyilo, Observations conjointes des Représentants Légaux des Victimes quant aux conséquences de l'arrêt de la Chambre d' appel du 8 décembre 2009, Trial Chamber I, No. ICC-01/04-01/06-2211, 15 December 2009 [English translation not available].

The Prosecutor v. Thomas Lubanga Dyilo, Réponse de la Défense aux "Observations conjointes des Représentants Légaux des Victimes quant aux conséquences de l'arrêt de la Chambre d' appel du 8 décembre 2009," datées du 15 décembre 2009, Trial Chamber I, No. ICC-01/04-01/06-2214, 18 December 2009 [English translation not available].

The Prosecutor v. Germain Katanga and Mathieu Ngudjolo Chui, Motifs de la deuxième décision relative aux demandes de participation de victimes à la procedure, Trial Chamber II, No. ICC-01/04-01/07-1737, 22 December 2009 [English translation not available].

The Prosecutor v. Germain Katanga and Mathieu Ngudjolo Chui, Decision on the Modalities of Victim Participation at Trial, Trial Chamber II, No. ICC-01/04-01/07-1788-tENG, 22 January 2010.

The Prosecutor v. Bahar Idriss Abu Garda, Decision Setting a Time Limit for the Parties' Replies to 20 Applications for Victims' Participation in the Proceedings, Pre-Trial Chamber I, No. ICC-02/05-02/09-240, 29 January 2010.

The Prosecutor v. Bahar Idriss Abu Garda, Decision on the Confirmation of Charges, Pre-Trial Chamber I, No. ICC-02/05-02/09-243-Red, 8 February 2010.

The Prosecutor v. Jean-Pierre Bemba Gombo, Decision Defining the Status of 54 Victims who Participated at the Pre-Trial Stage, and Inviting the Parties' Observations on Applications for Participation by 86 Applicants, Trial Chamber III, No. ICC-01/05-01/08-699, 22 February 2010.

The Prosecutor v. Germain Katanga and Mathieu Ngudjolo Chui, Grounds for the Decision on the 345 Applications for Participation in the Proceedings Submitted by Victims, Trial Chamber II, No. ICC-01/04-01/07-1491-Red-tENG, 10 March 2010.

The Prosecutor v. Thomas Lubanga Dyilo, Decision on the Defense Observations Regarding the Right of the Legal Representatives of Victims to Question Defense Witnesses and on the Notion of Personal Interest -and- Decision on the Defense Application to Exclude Certain Representatives of Victims from the Chamber During the Non-Public Evidence of Various Defense Witnesses, Trial Chamber I, No. ICC-01/04-01/06-2340, 11 March 2010.

The Prosecutor v. Bahar Idriss Abu Garda, Prosecution's Application for Leave to Appeal the "Decision on the Confirmation of Charges," Pre-Trial Chamber I, No. ICC-02/05-02/09-252-Red, 15 March 2010.

The Prosecutor v. Germain Katanga and Mathieu Ngudjolo Chui, Motifs de la troisième décision relative à 8 demandes de participation de victimes à la procedure, Trial Chamber II, No. ICC-01/04-01/07-1967, 16 March 2010 [English translation not available].

The Prosecutor v. Bahar Idriss Abu Garda, Decision on Applications a/0655/09, a/0656/09, a/0736/09 to a/0747/09, and a/0750/09 to a/0755/09 for Participation in the Proceedings at the Pre-Trial Stage of the Case, Pre-Trial Chamber I (Single Judge), No. ICC-02/05-02/09-255, 19 March 2010.

Situation in the Republic of Kenya, Decision Pursuant to Article 15 of the Rome Statute on the Authorization of an Investigation into the Situation in the Republic of Kenya, Pre-Trial Chamber II, No. ICC-01/09-19, 31 March 2010.

The Prosecutor v. Bahar Idriss Abu Garda, Decision on the "Prosecution's Application for Leave to Appeal the 'Decision on the Confirmation of Charges,'" Pre-Trial Chamber I, No. ICC-02/05-02/09-267, 23 April 2010.

The Prosecutor v. Germain Katanga and Mathieu Ngudjolo Chui, Decision on the Participation of Victims in the Appeal of Mr. Katanga against the "Decision on the Modalities of Victim Participation at Trial," Appeals Chamber, No. ICC-01/04-01/07-2124, 24 May 2010.

The Prosecutor v. Thomas Lubanga Dyilo, Redacted Decision on Intermediaries, Trial Chamber I, No. ICC-01/04-01/06-2434-Red2, 31 May 2010.

Situation in Democratic Republic of the Congo, Demande du représentant légal de VPRS 3 et 6 aux fins de mise en cause de Monsieur Jean-Pierre Bemba en sa qualité de chef militaire au sens de l'article 28-a du Statut pour les crimes dont ses troupes sont présumées coupables en Ituri, Pre-Trial Chamber I (Single Judge), No. ICC-01-04-564, 28 June 2010 [English translation not available].

The Prosecutor v. Jean-Pierre Bemba Gombo, Decision on the Participation of Victims in the Trial and on 86 Applications by Victims to Participate in the Proceedings, Trial Chamber III, No. ICC-01/05-01/08-807, 30 June 2010.

The Prosecutor v. Thomas Lubanga Dyilo, Redacted Decision on the Prosecution's Urgent Request for Variation of the Time-Limit to Disclose the Identity of Intermediary 143 or Alternatively to Stay Proceedings Pending Further Consultations with the VWU, Trial Chamber I, No. ICC-01/04-01/06-2517-Red, 8 July 2010.

The Prosecutor v. Omar Hassan Ahmad Al Bashir, Decision on 8 Applications for Victims' Participation in the Proceedings, Pre-Trial Chamber I (Single Judge), No. ICC-02/05-01/09-93, 9 July 2010.

The Prosecutor v. Jean-Pierre Bemba Gombo, Corrigendum to Decision on the Participation of Victims in the Trial and on 86 Applications by Victims to Participate in the Proceedings, Trial Chamber III, No. ICC-01/05-01/08-807-Corr, 12 July 2010.

Situation in Democratic Republic of the Congo, Response of the Office of Public Counsel for the Defense to the "Demande du represéntant légal de VPRS 3 et 6 aux fins de mise en cause de Monsieur Jean-Pierre Bemba en sa qualité de chef militaire au sens de l'article 28-a du Statut pour les crimes dont ses troupes sont présumées coupables en Ituri," Pre-Trial Chamber I (Single Judge), No. ICC-01/04-566, 15 July 2010.

The Prosecutor v. Germain Katanga and Mathieu Ngudjolo Chui, Judgment on the Appeal of Mr. Katanga against the Decision of Trial Chamber II of 22 January 2010 Entitled "Decision on the Modalities of Victim Participation at Trial," Appeals Chamber, No. ICC-01/04-01/07-2288, 16 July 2010.

The Prosecutor v. Callixte Mbarushimana, Decision on the Prosecutor's Application for a Warrant of Arrest against Callixte Mbarushimana, Pre-Trial Chamber I, No. ICC-01/04-01/10-1, 28 September 2010.

Situation in Democratic Republic of the Congo, Prosecution's Observations to the "Demande du représentant légal de VPRS 3 et 6 aux fins de mise en cause de Monsieur Jean-Pierre Bemba en sa qualité de chef militaire au sens de l'article 28-a du Statut pour les crimes dont ses troupes sont présumées coupables en Ituri," Pre-Trial Chamber (Single Judge), No. ICC-01/04-581, 29 September 2010.

The Prosecutor v. Thomas Lubanga Dyilo, Judgment on the Appeal of Prosecutor against the Oral Decision of Trial Chamber I of 15 July 2010 to Release Thomas Lubanga Dyilo, Appeals Chamber, No. ICC-01/04-01/06-2583, 8 October 2010.

The Prosecutor v. Jean-Pierre Bemba Gombo, Defense Response to the Third Transmission of Victims' Applications for Participation in the Proceedings, Trial Chamber III, No. ICC-01/05-01/08-945, 11 October 2010.

The Prosecutor v. Abdallah Banda Abakaer Nourain and Saleh Mohammed Jerbo Jamus, Joint Submission by the Office of the Prosecutor and the Defense as to Agreed Facts and Submissions Regarding Modalities for the Conduct of the Confirmation Hearing, Pre-Trial Chamber I, No. ICC-02/05-03/09-80, 19 October 2010.

The Prosecutor v. Jean-Pierre Bemba Gombo, Defense Observations on the "Fourth Transmission to the Parties and Legal Representatives of Redacted Versions of Applications for Participation in the Proceedings," Trial Chamber III, No. ICC- 01/05-01/08-968, 22 October 2010.

Situation in Democratic Republic of the Congo, Decision on the Request of the Legal Representatives of Victims VPRS 3 and VPRS 6 to Review an Alleged Decision of the Prosecution not to Proceed, Pre-Trial Chamber I, No. ICC-01/04-583, 25 October 2010.

The Prosecutor v. Abdallah Banda Abakaer Nourain and Saleh Mohammed Jerbo Jamus, Decision on Victims' Participation at the Hearing on the Confirmation of the Charges, Pre-Trial Chamber I, No. ICC-02/05-03/09-89, 29 October 2010.

Situation in the Republic of Kenya, Decision on Victims' Participation in Proceedings Related to the Situation in the Republic of Kenya, Pre-Trial Chamber II, No. ICC-01/09-24, 3 November 2010.

The Prosecutor v. Germain Katanga and Mathieu Ngudjolo Chui, Décision aux fins d'autorisation de comparution des victimes a/0381/09, a/0018/09, a/0191/08 et pan/0363/09 agissant au nom de a/0363/09, Trial Chamber II, No. ICC-01/04-01/07-2517, 9 November 2010 [English translation not available].

The Prosecutor v. Jean-Pierre Bemba Gombo, Decision on Common Legal Representation of Victims for the Purpose of Trial, Trial Chamber III, No. ICC-01/05-01/08-1005, 10 November 2010.

The Prosecutor v. Abdallah Banda Abakaer Nourain and Saleh Mohammed Jerbo Jamus, Decision on Issues Related to the Hearing on the Confirmation of Charges, Pre-Trial Chamber I, No. ICC-02/05-03/09-103, 17 November 2010.

The Prosecutor v. Jean-Pierre Bemba Gombo, Decision on Directions for the Conduct of the Proceedings, Trial Chamber III, No. ICC-01/05-01/08-1023, 19 November 2010.

The Prosecutor v. Thomas Lubanga Dyilo, Redacted Decision on the Disclosure of Information from Victims' Applications Forms (a/0225/06, a/0229/06 and a/0270/07), Trial Chamber I, No. ICC-01/04-01/06-2586-Red, 23 November 2010.

The Prosecutor v. Jean-Pierre Bemba Gombo, Defense Observations on the "Seventh Transmission to the Parties and Legal Representatives of Redacted Versions of Applications for Participation in the Proceedings," Trial Chamber III, No. ICC-01/05-01/08-1053, 26 November 2010.

The Prosecutor v. Abdallah Banda Abakaer Nourain and Saleh Mohammed Jerbo Jamus, Prosecution Objection to the Continued Representation of Victims a/1646/10 and a/1647/10 by Messrs Geoffrey Nice and Rodney Dixon, Pre-Trial Chamber I, No. ICC-02/05-03/09-110, 6 December 2010.

The Prosecutor v. Abdallah Banda Abakaer Nourain and Saleh Mohammed Jerbo Jamus, Defense Application to Restrain Legal Representation for the Victims a/1646/10 and a/1647/10 from Acting in Proceedings and for an Order Excluding the Involvement of

Specified Intermediaries, Pre-Trial Chamber I, No. ICC-02/05-03/09-113, 6 December 2010.

The Prosecutor v. Abdallah Banda Abakaer Nourain and Saleh Mohammed Jerbo Jamus, Submission by Legal Representatives for Victims a/1646/10 and 1647/10 in Light of Urgent Prosecution Objection, Trial Chamber I, No. ICC-02/05-03/09-115, 7 December 2010.

Situation in the Republic of Kenya, Decision on Application for Leave to Submit *Amicus Curiae* Observations, Pre-Trial Chamber II, No. ICC-01/09-35, 18 January 2011.

United States Domestic Cases

People ex rel. Luceno v. Cuozzo, 412 N.Y.S.2d 748 (1978).
State of West Virginia v. Calvin O. Atkins, 261 S.E.2d 55 (W. Va. 1979)
State v. Harton, 296 S.E.2d 112 (1982).
State ex rel. Wild v. Otis, 257 N.W.2d 361 (Minn. 1977).
Commonwealth v. Eisemann, 453 A.2d 1045 (1982).
United States ex rel v. Vuitton, 481 U.S. 787 (1987).
New Jersey v Kinder, 701 F. Supp. 486 (D.N.J. 1988).
People v. Blevins, 96 N.E. 214 (1911).
State v. Westbrook, 181 S.E.2d 572 (1972).

United Kingdom Domestic Cases

R v. Sussex Justices ex parte McCarthy, 1 KB 256 (1924).

INDEX

R

S

T

U

W

Curriculum Vitae

Brianne McGonigle Leyh is an attorney specializing in international criminal law and procedure, human rights, victims' rights and transitional justice. In 2002 she received her Bachelors degree (BA) from Boston University, graduating *magna cum laude* with a self-crafted major in the study of international law and human rights. She received her Law degree (JD) in 2006 from American University's Washington College of Law, graduating *cum laude*, and one year later her Masters degree (MA) in International Affairs from American University's School of International Service. In 2006 she began working for Utrecht University's Netherlands Institute of Human Rights as a PhD candidate and lecturer and since April 2011 holds a research position with this same institute. In addition to her academic work she co-Directs the Netherlands Office of the Public International Law & Policy Group, which is a global *pro bono* law firm that provides legal assistance to states and non-state entities on the negotiation and implementation of peace agreements, the drafting of post-conflict constitutions, and the creation and operation of war crimes tribunals. Previously, she has worked as co-Counsel on a legal team representing civil parties before the Extraordinary Chambers in the Courts of Cambodia and has held a Visiting Professional position at the International Criminal Court's Office of Public Counsel for Victims. Brianne is married with one daughter and currently resides in the Netherlands.

School of Human Rights Research Series

The School of Human Rights Research is a joint effort by human rights researchers in the Netherlands. Its central research theme is the nature and meaning of international standards in the field of human rights, their application and promotion in the national legal order, their interplay with national standards, and the international supervision of such application. The School of Human Rights Research Series only includes English titles that contribute to a better understanding of the different aspects of human rights.

Published titles within the Series:

1 Brigit C.A. Toebes, *The Right to Health as a Human Right in International Law*
ISBN 90-5095-057-4

2 Ineke Boerefijn, *The Reporting Procedure under the Covenant on Civil and Political Rights. Practice and Procedures of the Human Rights Committee*
ISBN 90-5095-074-4

3 Kitty Arambulo, *Strengthening the Supervision of the International Covenant on Economic, Social and Cultural Rights. Theoretical and Procedural Aspects*
ISBN 90-5095-058-2

4 Marlies Glasius, *Foreign Policy on Human Rights. Its Influence on Indonesia under Soeharto*
ISBN 90-5095-089-2

5 Cornelis D. de Jong, *The Freedom of Thought, Conscience and Religion or Belief in the United Nations (1946-1992)*
ISBN 90-5095-137-6

6 Heleen Bosma, *Freedom of Expression in England and under the ECHR: in Search of a Common Ground. A Foundation for the Application of the Human Rights Act 1998 in English Law*
ISBN 90-5095-136-8

7 Mielle Bulterman, *Human Rights in the External Relations of the European Union*
ISBN 90-5095-164-3

8 Esther M. van den Berg, *The Influence of Domestic NGOs on Dutch Human Rights Policy. Case Studies on South Africa,Namibia, Indonesia and East Timor*
ISBN 90-5095-159-7

9 Ian Seiderman, *Hierarchy in International Law: the Human Rights Dimension*
ISBN 90-5095-165-1

10 Anna Meijknecht, *Towards International Personality: the Position of Minorities and Indigenous Peoples in International Law*
ISBN 90-5095-166-X

11 Mohamed Eltayeb, *A Human Rights Approach to Combating Religious Persecution. Cases from Pakistan, Saudi Arabia and Sudan*
ISBN 90-5095-170-8

12 Machteld Boot, *Genocide, Crimes Against Humanity, War Crimes: Nullum Crimen Sine Lege and the Subject Matter Jurisdiction of the International Criminal Court*
ISBN 90-5095-216-X

13 Corinne Packer, *Using Human Rights to Change Tradition. Traditional Practices Harmful to Women's Reproductive Health in sub-Saharan Africa*
ISBN 90-5095-226-7

14 Theo R.G. van Banning, *The Human Right to Property*
ISBN 90-5095-203-8

15 Yvonne M. Donders, *Towards a Right to Cultural Identity?*
ISBN 90-5095-238-0

16 Göran K. Sluiter, *International Criminal Adjudication and the Collection of Evidence: Obligations of States*
ISBN 90-5095-227-5

17 Nicola Jägers, *Corporate Human Rights Obligations: in Search of Accountability*
ISBN 90-5095-240-2

18 Magdalena Sepúlveda, *The Nature of the Obligations under the International Covenant on Economic, Social and Cultural Rights*
ISBN 90-5095-260-7

19 Mitsue Inazumi, *Universal Jurisdiction in Modern International Law: Expansion of National Jurisdiction for Prosecuting Serious Crimes under International Law*
ISBN 90-5095-366-2

20 Anne-Marie L.M. de Brouwer, *Supranational Criminal Prosecution of Sexual Violence: The ICC and the Practice of the ICTY and the ICTR*
ISBN 90-5095-533-9

21 Jeroen Gutter, *Thematic Procedures of the United Nations Commission on Human Rights and International Law: in Search of a Sense of Community*
ISBN 90-5095-557-6

22 Hilde Reiding, *The Netherlands and the Development of International Human Rights Instruments*
ISBN 978-90-5095-654-3

23 Ingrid Westendorp, *Women and Housing: Gender Makes a Difference*
ISBN 978-90-5095-669-7

24 Quirine A.M. Eijkman, *We Are Here to Serve You! Public Security, Police Reform and Human Rights Implementation in Costa Rica*
ISBN 978-90-5095-704-5

25 Antoine Ch. Buyse, *Post-conflict Housing Restitution. The European Human Rights Perspective with a case study on Bosnia and Herzegovina*
ISBN 978-90-5095-770-0

26 Gentian Zyberi, *The Humanitarian Face of the International Court of Justice. Its Contribution to Interpreting and Developing International Human Rights and Humanitarian Law Rules and Principles*
ISBN 978-90-5095-792-2

27 Dragoş Cucereanu, *Aspects of Regulating Freedom of Expression on the Internet*
ISBN 978-90-5095-842-4

28 Ton Liefaard, *Deprivation of Liberty of Children in Light of International Human Rights Law and Standards*
ISBN 978-90-5095-838-7

29 Laura van Waas, *Nationality Matters. Statelessness under International Law*
ISBN 978-90-5095-854-7

30 Jeroen Denkers, *The World Trade Organization and Import Bans in Response to Violations of Fundamental Labour Rights*
ISBN 978-90-5095-855-4

31 Irene Hadiprayitno, *Hazard or Right? The Dialectics of Development Practice and the Internationally Declared Right to Development, with Special Reference to Indonesia*
ISBN 978-90-5095-932-2

32 Michał Gondek, *The Reach of Human Rights in a Globalising World: Extraterritorial Application of Human Rights Treaties*
ISBN 978-90-5095-817-2

33 Jeff Handmaker, *Advocating for Accountability: Civic-State Interactions to Protect Refugees in South Africa*
ISBN 978-90-5095-910-0

34 Anna Oehmichen, *Terrorism and Anti-Terror Legislation: The Terrorised Legislator? A Comparison of Counter-Terror Legislation and Its Implications on Human Rights in the Legal Systems of the United Kingdom, Spain, Germany and France*
ISBN 978-90-5095-956-8

35 Simon Walker, *The Future of Human Rights Impact Assessments of Trade Agreements*
ISBN 978-90-5095-986-5

36 Fleur van Leeuwen, *Women's Rights Are Human Rights: The Practice of the United Nations Human Rights Committee and the Committee on Economic, Social and Cultural Rights*
ISBN 978-90-5095-980-3

37 Eva Rieter, *Preventing Irreparable Harm. Provisional Measures in International Human Rights Adjudication*
ISBN 978-90-5095-931-5

38 Desislava Stoitchkova, *Towards Corporate Liability in International Criminal Law*
ISBN 978-94-000-0024-7

39 Paulien Muller, *Scattered Families. Transnational Family Life of Afghan Refugees in the Netherlands in the Light of the Human Rights-Based Protection of the Family*
ISBN 978-94-000-0021-6

40 Bibi van Ginkel, *The Practice of the United Nations in Combating Terrorism from 1946 to 2008. Questions of Legality and Legitimacy*
ISBN 978-94-000-0076-6

41 Christophe Paulussen, *Male captus bene detentus? Surrendering suspects to the International Criminal Court*
ISBN 978-94-000-0100-8